Handbook of Software Fault Localization

About IEEE Computer Society

IEEE Computer Society is the world's leading computing membership organization and the trusted information and career-development source for a global workforce of technology leaders including: professors, researchers, software engineers, IT professionals, employers, and students. The unmatched source for technology information, inspiration, and collaboration, the IEEE Computer Society is the source that computing professionals trust to provide high-quality, state-of-the-art information on an on-demand basis. The Computer Society provides a wide range of forums for top minds to come together, including technical conferences, publications, and a comprehensive digital library, unique training webinars, professional training, and the Tech Leader Training Partner Program to help organizations increase their staff's technical knowledge and expertise, as well as the personalized information tool my Computer. To find out more about the community for technology leaders, visit http://www.computer.org.

IEEE/Wiley Partnership

The IEEE Computer Society and Wiley partnership allows the CS Press authored book program to produce a number of exciting new titles in areas of computer science, computing, and networking with a special focus on software engineering. IEEE Computer Society members receive a 35% discount on Wiley titles by using their member discount code. Please contact IEEE Press for details.

To submit questions about the program or send proposals, please contact Mary Hatcher, Editor, Wiley-IEEE Press: Email: mhatcher@wiley.com, John Wiley & Sons, Inc., 111 River Street, Hoboken, NJ 07030-5774.

Handbook of Software Fault Localization

Foundations and Advances

Edited by

W. Eric Wong
Department of Computer Science, University of Texas at Dallas, Richardson, TX, USA

T.H. Tse
Department of Computer Science, The University of Hong Kong, Pokfulam, Hong Kong

IEEE computer society

IEEE PRESS

WILEY

This edition first published 2023

Published by John Wiley & Sons, Inc., Hoboken, New Jersey.
Published simultaneously in Canada.

Library of Congress Cataloging-in-Publication Data

Names: Wong, W. Eric, editor. | Tse, T.H., editor. | John Wiley & Sons, publisher.
Title: Handbook of software fault localization : foundations and advances / edited by W. Eric Wong, T.H. Tse.
Description: Hoboken, New Jersey : Wiley, [2023] | Includes bibliographical references and index.
Identifiers: LCCN 2022037789 (print) | LCCN 2022037790 (ebook) | ISBN 9781119291800 (paperback) | ISBN 9781119291817 (adobe pdf) | ISBN 9781119291824 (epub)
Subjects: LCSH: Software failures. | Software failures–Data processing. | Debugging in computer science. | Computer software–Quality control.
Classification: LCC QA76.76.F34 H36 2023 (print) | LCC QA76.76.F34 (ebook) | DDC 005.1–dc23/eng/20220920
LC record available at https://lccn.loc.gov/2022037789
LC ebook record available at https://lccn.loc.gov/2022037790

Cover designed by T.H. Tse

Set in 9.5/12.5pt STIXTwoText by Straive, Pondicherry, India

Contents

Editor Biographies

W. Eric Wong, PhD, is a Full Professor, Director of Software Engineering Program, and the Founding Director of Advanced Research Center for Software Testing and Quality Assurance in Computer Science at the University of Texas at Dallas. He also has an appointment as a Guest Researcher with the National Institute of Standards and Technology, an agency of the US Department of Commerce.

Professor Wong's research focuses on helping practitioners improve software quality while reducing production cost. In particular, he is working on software testing, program debugging, risk analysis, safety, and reliability. He was the recipient of the ICST 2020 (The 13th IEEE International Conference on Software Testing, Verification, and Validation) Most Influential Paper award for his paper titled "Using Mutation to Automatically Suggest Fixes for Faulty Programs" published at ICST 2010. He also received a JSS 2020 (*Journal of Systems and Software*) Most Influential Paper award for his paper titled "A Family of Code Coverage-based Heuristics for Effective Fault Localization" published in Volume 83, Issue 2, 2010. The conference version of this paper received the Best Paper Award at the 31st IEEE International Computer Software and Applications Conference.

Professor Wong was the award recipient of the 2014 IEEE Reliability Society Engineer of the Year. In addition, he was the Editor-in-Chief of the *IEEE Transactions on Reliability* for six years ending on 31 May 2022. He has also been an Area Editor of Elsevier's *Journal of Systems and Software* since 2017. Dr. Wong received his MS and PhD in Computer Science from Purdue University, West Lafayette, IN, USA. More details can be found at Professor Wong's homepage https://personal.utdallas.edu/~ewong

T.H. Tse received his PhD in Information Systems from the London School of Economics and was a Visiting Fellow at the University of Oxford. He is an Honorary Professor in Computer Science with The University of Hong Kong after retiring from the full professorship in 2014. His research interest is in program testing and debugging. He has more than 270 publications, including a book in the Cambridge Tracts in Theoretical Computer Science series, Cambridge University Press. He is ranked internationally as no. 2 among experts in metamorphic testing. The 2010 paper titled "Adaptive Random Testing: the ART of Test Case Diversity" by Professor Tse and team has been selected as the Grand Champion of the Most Influential Paper Award by the *Journal of Systems and Software*.

Professor Tse is a Steering Committee Chair of the IEEE International Conference on Software Quality, Reliability, and Security; and an Associate Editor of *IEEE Transactions on Reliability*. He served on the Search Committee for the Editor-in-Chief of *IEEE Transactions on Software Engineering* in 2013. He is a Life Fellow of the British Computer Society and a Life Senior Member of the IEEE. He was awarded an MBE by Queen Elizabeth II of the United Kingdom.

List of Contributors

Rui Abreu
Department of Informatics Engineering, Faculty of Engineering University of Porto, Porto, Portugal

Hira Agrawal
Peraton Labs, Basking Ridge, NJ, USA

Peggy Cellier
INSA, CNRS, IRISA, Universite de Rennes, Rennes, France

Vidroha Debroy
Department of Computer Science
University of Texas at Dallas
Richardson, TX, USA
and
Dottid Inc., Dallas, TX, USA

Mireille Ducassé
INSA, CNRS, IRISA, Universite de Rennes, Rennes, France

Sébastien Ferré
CNRS, IRISA, Universite de Rennes
Rennes, France

Ruizhi Gao
Sonos Inc., Boston, MA, USA

Alex Gorce
School of Informatics, Computing, and Cyber Systems, Northern Arizona University, Flagstaff
AZ, USA

Robert Hirschfeld
Department of Computer Science
Universität Potsdam, Brandenburg
Germany

Birgit Hofer
Institute of Software Technology
Graz University of Technology, Graz
Austria

Linghuan Hu
Google Inc., Mountain View
CA, USA

Hua Jie Lee
School of Computing, Macquarie University, Sydney, NSW
Australia

Dongcheng Li
Department of Computer Science
University of Texas at Dallas
Richardson, TX, USA

Yihao Li
School of Information and Electrical Engineering, Ludong University
Yantai, China

David Lo
School of Computing and Information Systems, Singapore Management University, Singapore

Wolfgang Mayer
Advanced Computing Research Centre, University of South Australia
Adelaide, SA, Australia

Lee Naish
School of Computing and Information Systems, The University of Melbourne
Melbourne, Australia

Michael Perscheid
Department of Computer Science
Universität Potsdam, Brandenburg
Germany

Olivier Ridoux
CNRS, IRISA, Universite de Rennes
Rennes, France

Markus Stumptner
Advanced Computing Research Centre, University of South Australia
Adelaide, SA, Australia

T.H. Tse
Department of Computer Science, The University of Hong Kong, Pokfulam
Hong Kong

W. Eric Wong
Department of Computer Science
University of Texas at Dallas
Richardson, TX, USA

Franz Wotawa
Institute of Software Technology, Graz University of Technology, Graz
Austria

Xin Xia
Software Engineering Application Technology Lab, Huawei, China

Xiaoyuan Xie
School of Computer Science, Wuhan University, Wuhan, China

Xiangyu Zhang
Department of Computer Science
Purdue University, West Lafayette
IN, USA

Zhenyu Zhang
Institute of Software, Chinese Academy of Sciences, Beijing, China

1

Software Fault Localization: an Overview of Research, Techniques, and Tools

W. Eric Wong[1], Ruizhi Gao[2], Yihao Li[3], Rui Abreu[4], Franz Wotawa[5], and Dongcheng Li[1]

[1] *Department of Computer Science, University of Texas at Dallas, Richardson, TX, USA*
[2] *Sonos Inc., Boston, MA, USA*
[3] *School of Information and Electrical Engineering, Ludong University, Yantai, China*
[4] *Department of Informatics Engineering, Faculty of Engineering, University of Porto, Porto, Portugal*
[5] *Institute of Software Technology, Graz University of Technology, Graz, Austria*

1.1 Introduction

Software fault localization, the act of identifying the locations of faults in a program, is widely recognized to be one of the most tedious, time-consuming, and expensive – yet equally critical – activities in program debugging. Due to the increasing scale and complexity of software today, manually locating faults when failures occur is rapidly becoming infeasible, and consequently, there is a strong demand for techniques that can guide software developers to the locations of faults in a program with minimal human intervention. This demand in turn has fueled the proposal and development of a broad spectrum of fault localization techniques, each of which aims to streamline the fault localization process and make it more effective by attacking the problem in a unique way. In this book, we categorize and provide a comprehensive overview of such techniques and discuss key issues and concerns that are pertinent to software fault localization.

Software is fundamental to our lives today, and with its ever-increasing usage and adoption, its influence is practically ubiquitous. At present, software is not just employed in, but is critical to, many security and safety-critical systems in industries such as medicine, aeronautics, and nuclear energy. Not surprisingly,

This chapter is an extension of Wong, W.E., Gao, R., Li, Y., Abreu, R., and Wotawa, F. (2016). A survey on software fault localization. *IEEE Transactions on Software Engineering* 42 (8): 707–740.

Handbook of Software Fault Localization: Foundations and Advances, First Edition.
Edited by W. Eric Wong and T.H. Tse.

Published 2023 by John Wiley & Sons, Inc.

this trend has been accompanied by a drastic increase in the scale and complexity of software. Unfortunately, this has also resulted in more software bugs, which often lead to execution failures with huge losses [1–3]. On 15 January 1990, the AT&T operation center in Bedminster, NJ, USA, had an increase of red warning signals appearing across the 75 screens that indicated the status of parts of the AT&T worldwide network. As a result, only about 50 percent of the calls made through AT&T were connected. It took nine hours for the AT&T technicians to identify and fix the issue caused by a misplaced break statement in the code. AT&T lost $60 to $75 million in this accident [4].

Furthermore, software faults in safety-critical systems have significant ramifications not only limited to financial loss, but also to loss of life, which is alarming [5]. On 20 December 1995, a Boeing 757 departed from Miami, FL, USA. The aircraft was heading to Cali, Colombia. However, it crashed into a 9800 feet mountain. A total of 159 deaths resulted; leaving only five passengers alive. This event marked the highest death toll of any accident in Colombia at the time. This accident was caused by the inconsistencies between the naming conventions of the navigational charts and the flight management system. When the crew looked up the waypoint "Rozo", the chart indicated the letter "R" as its identifier. The flight management system, however, had the city paired with the word "Rozo". As a result, when the pilot entered the letter "R", the system did not know if the desired city was Rozo or Romeo. It automatically picked Romeo, which is a larger city than Rozo, as the next waypoint.

A 2006 report from the National Institute of Standards and Technology (NIST) [6] indicated that software errors are estimated to cost the US economy $59.5 billion annually (0.6 percent of the GDP); the cost has undoubtedly grown since then. Over half the cost of fixing or responding to these bugs is passed on to software users, while software developers and vendors absorb the rest.

Even when faults in software are discovered due to erroneous behavior or some other manifestation of the fault(s),[1] finding and fixing them is an entirely different matter. Fault localization, which focuses on the former, i.e. identifying the locations of faults, has historically been a manual task that has been recognized to be time-consuming and tedious as well as prohibitively expensive [7], given the size and complexity of large-scale software systems today. Furthermore, manual fault localization relies heavily on the software developer's experience, judgment, and intuition to identify and prioritize code that is likely to be faulty. These limitations have led to a surge of interest in developing techniques that can partially or fully automate the localization of faults in software while reducing human input. Though some techniques are similar and some very different (in terms of the type of data consumed, the program components focused on, comparative effectiveness and efficiency, etc.), they each try to attack the problem of fault localization from a unique perspective, and typically offer both advantages and disadvantages relative to one another. With many techniques already in existence and others continually being proposed, as well as with advances being made both from a theoretical and practical perspective, it is important to catalog and overview current state-of-the-art techniques in fault localization in order to offer a comprehensive resource for those already in the area and those interested in making contributions to it.

In order to provide a complete survey covering most of the publications related to software fault localization since the late 1970s, in this chapter, we created a publication repository that includes 587 papers published from 1977 to 2020. We also searched for Masters' and PhD theses closely related to software fault localization, which are listed in Table 1.1.

Table 1.1 A list of recent PhD and Masters' theses on software fault localization.

Author	Title	Degree	University	Year
Ehud Y. Shapiro [8]	Algorithmic Program Debugging	PhD	Yale University	1983
Hiralal Agrawal [9]	Towards Automatic Debugging of Computer Programs	PhD	Purdue University	1991
Hsin Pan [10]	Software debugging with dynamic instrumentation and test-based knowledge	PhD	Purdue University	1993
W. Bond Gregory [11]	Logic Programs for Consistency-based Diagnosis	PhD	Carleton University	1994
Benjamin Robert Liblit [12]	Cooperative Bug Isolation	PhD	The University of California, Berkeley	2004
Bernhard Peischl [13]	Automated Source-Level Debugging of Synthesizeable VHDL Designs	PhD	Graz University of Technology	2004
Haifeng He [14]	Automated Debugging using Path-based Weakest Preconditions	Master	University of Arizona	2004
Alex David Groce [15]	Error Explanation and Fault Localization with Distance Metrics	PhD	Carnegie Mellon University	2005

(Continued)

Table 1.1 (Continued)

Author	Title	Degree	University	Year
Emmanuel Renieris [16]	A Research Framework for Software-Fault Localization Tools	PhD	Brown University	2005
Daniel Köb [17]	Extended Modeling for Automatic Fault Localization in Object-Oriented Software	PhD	Graz University of Technology	2005
David Hovemeyer [18]	Simple and Effective Static Analysis to Find Bugs	PhD	University of Maryland	2005
Peifeng Hu [19]	Automated Fault Localization: a Statistical Predicate Analysis Approach	PhD	The University of Hong Kong	2006
Xiangyu Zhang [20]	Fault Localization via Precise Dynamic Slicing	PhD	The University of Arizona	2006
Rafi Vayani [21]	Improving Automatic Software Fault Localization	Master	Delft University of Technology	2007
Ramana Rao Kompella [22]	Fault Localization in Backbone Networks	PhD	University of California, San Diego	2007
Andreas Griesmayer [23]	Debugging Software: from Verification to Repair	PhD	Graz University of Technology	2007
Tao Wang [24]	Post-Mortem Dynamic Analysis For Software Debugging	PhD	Fudan University	2007
Sriraman Tallam [25]	Fault Location and Avoidance in Long-Running Multithreaded Applications	PhD	The University of Arizona	2007
Ophelia C. Chesley [26]	CRISP-A fault localization Tool for Java Programs	Master	Rutgers, The State University of New Jersey	2007
Shan Lu [27]	Understanding, Detecting and Exposing Concurrency Bugs	PhD	University of Illinois at Urbana-Champaign	2008

Table 1.1 (Continued)

Author	Title	Degree	University	Year
Naveed Riaz [28]	Automated Source-Level Debugging of Synthesizable Verilog Designs	PhD	Graz University of Technology	2008
James Arthur Jones [29]	Semi-Automatic Fault Localization	PhD	Georgia Institute of Technology	2008
Zhenyu Zhang [30]	Software Debugging through Dynamic Analysis of Program Structures	PhD	The University of Hong Kong	2009
Rui Abreu [31]	Spectrum-based Fault Localization in Embedded Software	PhD	Delft University of Technology	2009
Dennis Jefferey [32]	Dynamic State Alteration Techniques for Automatically Locating Software Errors	PhD	University of California Riverside	2009
Xinming Wang [33]	Automatic Localization of Code Omission Faults	PhD	The Hong Kong University of Science and Technology	2010
Fabrizio Pastore [34]	Automatic Diagnosis of Software Functional Faults by Means of Inferred Behavioral Models	PhD	University of Milan Bicocca	2010
Mihai Nica [35]	On the Use of Constraints in Automated Program Debugging – From Foundations to Empirical Results	PhD	Graz University of Technology	2010
Zachary P. Fry [36]	Fault Localization Using Textual Similarities	Master	The University of Virginia	2011
Hua Jie Lee [37]	Software Debugging Using Program Spectra	PhD	The University of Melbourne	2011

(*Continued*)

Table 1.1 (Continued)

Author	Title	Degree	University	Year
Vidroha Debroy [38]	Towards the Automation of Program Debugging	PhD	The University of Texas at Dallas	2011
Alberto Gonzalez Sanchez [39]	Cost Optimizations in Runtime Testing and Diagnosis	PhD	Delft University of Technology	2011
Jared David DeMott [40]	Enhancing Automated Fault Discovery and Analysis	PhD	Michigan State University	2012
Xin Zhang [41]	Secure and Efficient Network Fault Localization	PhD	Carnegie Mellon University	2012
Xiaoyuan Xie [42]	On the Analysis of Spectrum-based Fault Localization	PhD	Swinburne University of Technology	2012
Alexandre Perez [43]	Dynamic Code Coverage with Progressive Detail Levels	Master	University of Porto	2012
Raul Santelices [44]	Change-effects Analysis for Effective Testing and Validation of Evolving Software	PhD	Georgia Institute of Technology	2012
George. K. Baah [45]	Statistical Causal Analysis for Fault Localization	PhD	Georgia Institute of Technology	2012
Swarup K. Sahoo [46]	A Novel Invariants-based Approach for Automated Software Fault Localization	PhD	University of Illinois at Urbana-Champaign	2012
Birgit Hofer [47]	From Fault Localization of Programs written in 3rd level Language to Spreadsheets	PhD	Graz University of Technology	2013
Aritra Bandyopadhyay [48]	Mitigating the Effect of Coincidental Correctness in Spectrum-based Fault Localization	PhD	Colorado State University	2013

Table 1.1 (Continued)

Author	Title	Degree	University	Year
Shounak Roychowdhury [49]	A Mixed Approach to Spectrum-based Fault Localization Using Information Theoretic Foundations	PhD	The University of Texas at Austin	2013
Shaimaa Ali [50]	Localizing State-Dependent Faults Using Associated Sequence Mining	PhD	The University of Western Ontario	2013
Christian Kuhnert [51]	Data-driven Methods for Fault Localization in Process Technology	PhD	Karlsruhe Institute of Technology	2013
Dawei Qi [52]	Semantic Analyses to Detect and Localize Software Regression Errors	PhD	Tsinghua University	2013
William N. Sumner [53]	Automated Failure Explanation Through Execution Comparison	PhD	Purdue University	2013
Mark A. Hays [54]	A Fault-based Model of Fault Localization Techniques	PhD	University of Kentucky	2014
Sang Min Park [55]	Effective Fault Localization Techniques for Concurrent Software	PhD	Georgia Institute of Technology	2014
Gang Shu [56]	Statistical Estimation of Software Reliability and Failure-causing Effect	PhD	Case Western Reserve University	2014
Lucia [57]	Ranking-based Approaches for Localizing Faults	PhD	Singapore Management University	2014
Seok-Hyeon Moon [58]	Effective Software Fault Localization using Dynamic Program Behaviors	Master	Korea Advanced Institute of Science and Technology	2014

(Continued)

Table 1.1 (Continued)

Author	Title	Degree	University	Year
Yepang Liu [59]	Automated Analysis of Energy Efficiency and Performance for Mobile Applications	PhD	The Hong Kong University of Science and Technology	2014
Cuiting Chen [60]	Automated Fault Localization for Service-Oriented Software Systems	PhD	Delft University of Technology	2015
Matthias Rohr [61]	Workload-sensitive Timing Behavior Analysis for Fault Localization in Software Systems	PhD	Kiel University	2015
Ozkan Bayraktar [62]	Ela: an Automated Statistical Fault Localization Technique	PhD	The Middle East Technical University	2015
Azim Tonzirul [63]	Fault Discovery, Localization, and Recovery in Smartphone Apps	PhD	University of California Riverside	2016
Laleh Gholamosseinghandehari [64]	Fault Localization based on Combinatorial Testing	PhD	The University of Texas at Arlington	2016
Ruizhi Gao [65]	Advanced Software Fault Localization for Programs with Multiple Bugs	PhD	The University of Texas at Dallas	2017
Shih-Feng Sun [66]	Statistical Fault Localization and Causal Interactions	PhD	Case Western Reserve University	2017
Rongxin Wu [67]	Automated Techniques for Diagnosing Crashing Bugs	PhD	The Hong Kong University of Science and Technology	2017
Arjun Roy [68]	Simplifying dataleft fault detection and localization	PhD	University of California San Diego	2018

Table 1.1 (Continued)

Author	Title	Degree	University	Year
Yun Guo [69]	Towards Automatically Localizing and Repairing SQL Faults	PhD	George Mason University	2018
Nasir Safdari [70]	Learning to Rank Relevant Files for Bug Reports Using Domain knowledge, Replication and Extension of a Learning-to-Rank Approach	Master	Rochester Institute of Technology	2018
Dai Ting [71]	A Hybrid Approach to Cloud System Performance Bug Detection, Diagnosis and Fix	PhD	North Carolina State University	2019
George Thompson [72]	Towards Automated Fault Localization for Prolog	Master	North Carolina A&T State University	2020
Xia Li [73]	An Integrated Approach for Automated Software Debugging via Machine Learning and Big Code Mining	PhD	The University of Texas at Dallas	2020
Muhammad Ali Gulzar [74]	Automated Testing and Debugging for Big Data Analytics	PhD	University of California, Los Angeles	2020
Mihir Mathur [75]	Leveraging Distributed Tracing and Container Cloning for Replay Debugging of Microservices	Master	University of California, Los Angeles	2020

All papers in our repository[2] are sorted by year, and the result is displayed in Figure 1.1. As shown in the figure, the number of publications grew rapidly after 2001, indicating that more and more researchers began to devote themselves to the area of software fault localization over the last two decades.

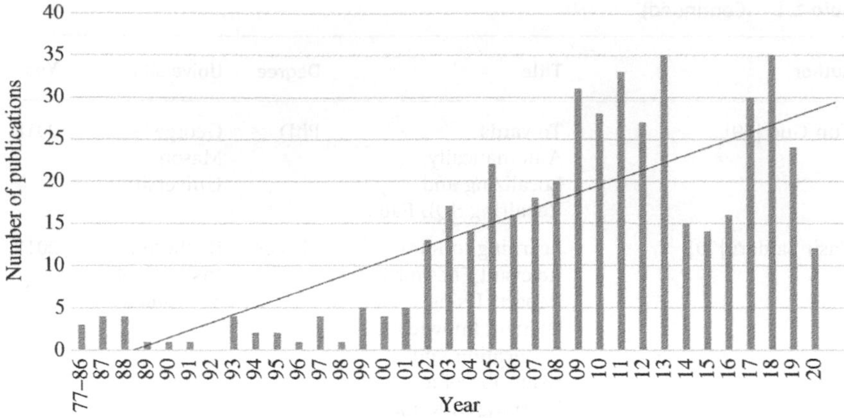

Figure 1.1 Papers on software fault localization from 1977 to 2020.

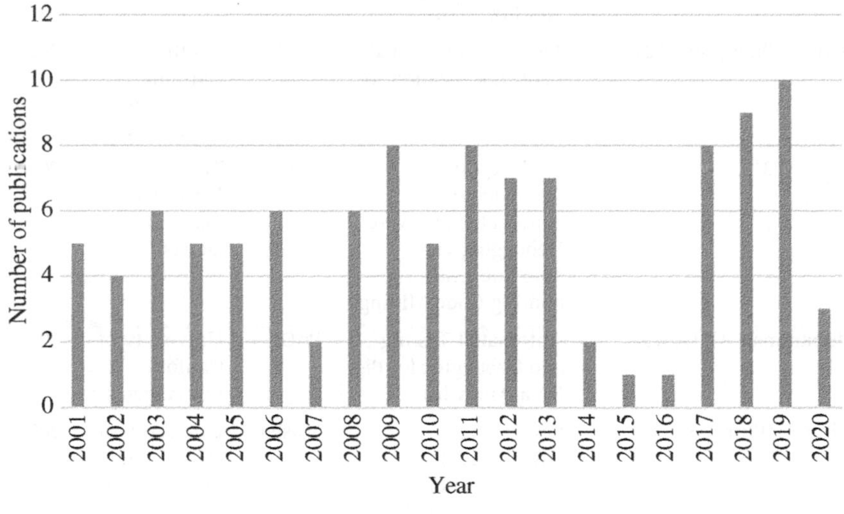

Figure 1.2 Publications on software fault localization in top venues from 2001 to 2020.

Also, as per our repository, Figure 1.2. gives the number of publications related to software fault localization that have appeared in top quality and leading journals and conferences that focus on Software Engineering – *IEEE Transactions on Software Engineering, ACM Transactions on Software Engineering and*

Methodology, International Conference on Software Engineering, ACM International Symposium on Foundations of Software Engineering, and ACM International Conference on Automated Software Engineering – from 2001 to 2019. This trend again supports the claim that software fault localization is not just an important but also a popular research topic and has been discussed very heavily in top quality software engineering journals and conferences over the last two decades.

There is thus a rich collection of literature on various techniques that aim to facilitate fault localization and make it more effective. Despite the fact that these techniques share similar goals, they can be quite different from one another and often stem from ideas that originate from several different disciplines. While we aim to comprehensively cover as many fault localization techniques as possible, no article, regardless of breadth or depth, can cover all of them. In this book, our primary focus is on the techniques for locating Bohrbugs [76]. Those for diagnosing Mandelbugs [76] such as performance bugs, memory leaks, software bloats, and security vulnerabilities are not included in the scope. Also, due to space limitations, we group techniques into appropriate categories for collective discussion with an emphasis on the most important features and leave other details of these techniques to their respectively published papers. This is especially the case for techniques targeting a specific application domain, such as fault localization for concurrency bugs and spreadsheets. For these, we provide a review that helps readers with general understanding.

The following terms appear repeatedly throughout this chapter, and thus for convenience, we provide definitions for them here per the taxonomy provided in [77]:

- A failure is when a service deviates from its correct behavior.
- An error is a condition in a system that may lead to a failure.
- A fault is the underlying cause of an error, also known as a bug.

In this book, we group fault localization techniques into appropriate categories (including traditional, slicing-based, spectrum-based, statistics-based, machine learning-based, data mining-based, information-retrieval-based, model-based, spreadsheet-based, and emerging techniques) for collective discussion with an emphasis on the most important features. We introduce the popular subject programs that have been used in different case studies and discuss how these programs have evolved through the years. Different evaluation metrics to assess the effectiveness of fault localization techniques are also described as well as a discussion of fault localization tools and theoretical studies. Moreover, we explore some critical aspects of software fault localization, including (i) fault localization for programs with multiple bugs, (ii) inputs, outputs, and impact of test cases, (iii) coincidental correctness, (iv) faults introduced by missing code, (v) combination of multiple fault localization techniques, (vi) ties within fault localization rankings, and (vii) fault localization for concurrency bugs. The general information of each chapter is introduced as follows.

This book begins by introducing traditional software fault localization techniques in Chapter 2, including program logging, assertions, and breakpoints. Examples will also be provided to clearly explain these techniques.

Program slicing is a technique to abstract a program into a reduced form by deleting irrelevant parts such that the resulting slice will still behave in the same way as the original program with respect to certain specifications. Chapter 3 introduces slicing-based fault localization techniques, which can be classified into three major categories: static slicing, dynamic slicing, and execution slicing-based techniques. Examples will be given to illustrate the differences among these categories. Techniques based on other slicing such as dual slicing, thin slicing, and relevant slicing are also included.

Program spectrum-based techniques are presented in Chapter 4. A program spectrum details the execution information of a program from certain perspectives, such as execution information for conditional branches or loop-free intra-procedural paths. It can be used to track program behavior. A list of different kinds of program spectra will be provided. Also discussed are issues and concerns related to program spectrum-based techniques.

Software fault localization techniques based on well-defined statistical analyses (e.g. parametric and nonparametric hypothesis testing, causal-inference analysis, and cross tabulation analysis) are described in Chapter 5.

Machine learning is the study of computer algorithms that improve through experience. These techniques are adaptive and robust and can produce models based on data, with limited human interaction. Such properties have led to their employment in many disciplines including bioinformatics, natural language processing, cryptography, computer vision, etc. In the context of software fault localization, the problem at hand can be identified as trying to learn or deduce the location of a fault based on input data such as statement coverage and the execution result (success or failure) of each test case. Chapter 6 covers fault localization techniques based on machine learning techniques.

Along the lines of machine learning, data mining also seeks to produce a model using pertinent information extracted from data. Data mining can uncover hidden patterns in samples of data that may not be discovered by manual analysis alone, especially due to the sheer volume of information. Efficient data mining techniques transcend such problems and do so in reasonable amounts of time with high degrees of accuracy. The software fault localization problem can be abstracted to a data mining problem – for example, we wish to identify the pattern of statement execution that leads to a failure. Data mining-based techniques are reviewed and analyzed in Chapter 7.

Chapter 8 introduces information retrieval (IR)-based fault localization techniques. Fault localization is the problem of identifying buggy source code files given a textual description of a bug. This problem is important since many bugs are reported through bug tracking systems like Bugzilla and Jira, and the number of bug reports is often too many for developers to handle. This necessitates an automated tool that can help developers identify relevant files given a bug report. Due to the textual nature of bug reports, IR techniques are often employed to solve this problem. Many IR-based fault localization techniques have been proposed in the literature.

Program models can be used for software fault localization. The first part of Chapter 9 discusses techniques based on different program models such as dependency-based models, abstraction-based models, and value-based models. The second part emphasizes model checking-based techniques.

Spreadsheets are one of the most popular types of end-user software and have been used in many sectors, especially in business. Chapter 10 discusses how techniques using value-based or dependency-based models can effectively locate bugs in cells with erroneous formulae and avoid incorrect computation.

Instead of being evaluated empirically, the effectiveness of software fault localization techniques can also be analyzed from theoretical perspectives. Chapter 11 discusses theoretical studies on software fault localization.

Many of the software fault localization techniques assume that there is only one bug in the program under study. This assumption may not be realistic in practice. Mixed failed test cases associated with different causative bugs may reduce the fault localization effectiveness. In Chapter 12, we present fault localization techniques for programs with multiple bugs.

Finally, Chapter 13 presents emerging aspects of software fault localization, including how to apply the scientific method to fault localization, how to locate faults when the oracle is not available, how to automatically predict fault localization effectiveness, and how to integrate fault localization into automatic test generation tools.

The remaining part of this Chapter is organized in the following manner: we begin by describing traditional and intuitive fault localization techniques in Section 1.2, moving on to more advanced and complex techniques in Section 1.3. In Section 1.4, we list some of the popular subject programs that have been used in different case studies and discuss how these programs have evolved through the years. Different evaluation metrics to assess the effectiveness of fault localization techniques are described in Section 1.5, followed by a discussion of fault localization tools in Section 1.6. Finally, critical aspects and conclusions are presented in Section 1.7 and Section 1.8, respectively.

1.2 Traditional Fault Localization Techniques

This section describes traditional and intuitive fault localization techniques, including program logging, assertions, breakpoints, and profiling.

1.2.1 Program Logging

Statements (such as `print`) used to produce program logging are commonly inserted into the code in an ad-hoc fashion to monitor variable values and other program state information [78]. When abnormal program behavior is detected, developers examine the program log in terms of saved log files or printed run-time information to diagnose the underlying cause of failure.

1.2.2 Assertions

Assertions are constraints added to a program that have to be true during the correct operation of a program. Developers specify these assertions in the program code as conditional statements that terminate execution if they evaluate to false. Thus, they can be used to detect erroneous program behavior at runtime. More details of using assertions for program debugging can be found in [79, 80].

1.2.3 Breakpoints

Breakpoints are used to pause the program when execution reaches a specified point and allow the user to examine the current state. After a breakpoint is triggered, the user can modify the value of variables or continue the execution to observe the progression of a bug. Data breakpoints can be configured to trigger when the value changes for a specified expression, such as a combination of variable values. Conditional breakpoints pause execution only upon the satisfaction of a predicate specified by the user. Early studies (e.g. [81, 82]) use this approach to help developers locate bugs while a program is executed under the control of a symbolic debugger. The same approach is also adopted by more advanced debugging tools such as GNU GDB [83] and Microsoft Visual Studio Debugger [84].

1.2.4 Profiling

Profiling is the runtime analysis of metrics such as execution speed and memory usage, which is typically aimed at program optimization. However, it can also be leveraged for debugging activities, such as the following:

- Detecting unexpected execution frequencies of different functions (e.g. [85]).
- Identifying memory leaks or code that performs unexpectedly poorly (e.g. [86]).
- Examining the side effects of lazy evaluation (e.g. [87]).

Tools that use profiling for program debugging include GNU's gprof [88] and the Eclipse plugin TPTP [89].

1.3 Advanced Fault Localization Techniques

With the massive size and scale of software systems today, traditional fault localization techniques are not effective in isolating the root causes of failures. As a result, many advanced fault localization techniques have surfaced recently using the idea of *causality* [90, 91], which is related to philosophical theories with an objective to characterize the relationship between events/causes (program bugs in our case) and a phenomenon/effect (execution failures in our case). There are different causality models [91] such as counterfactual-based, probabilistic- or statistical-based, and causal calculus models. Among these, probabilistic causality models are the most widely used in fault localization to identify suspicious code that is responsible for execution failures.

In this chapter, we classify fault localization techniques into nine categories, including slicing-based, spectrum-based, statistics-based, machine learning-based, data mining-based, IR-based, model-based, spreadsheet-based techniques, and additional emerging techniques. Many studies that evaluate the effectiveness of specific fault localization techniques have been reported [92–124]. However, none of them offer a comprehensive discussion on all these techniques.

1.3.1 Slicing-Based Techniques

Program slicing is a technique to abstract a program into a reduced form by deleting irrelevant parts such that the resulting slice will still behave the same as the original program with respect to certain specifications. Hundreds of papers on this topic have been published [125–127] since Weiser first proposed *static slicing* in 1979 [128].

One of the important applications of static slicing [129] is to reduce the search domain while programmers locate bugs in their programs. This is based on the idea that if a test case fails due to an incorrect variable value at a statement, then the defect should be found in the static slice associated with that variable-statement pair, allowing us to confine our search to the slice rather than looking at the entire program. Lyle and Weiser extend the above approach by constructing a program dice (as the set difference of two groups of static slices) to further reduce the search domain for possible locations of a fault [130]. Although static slice-based techniques have been experimentally evaluated and confirmed to be useful in fault localization [109], one problem is that handling pointer variables can make data-flow analysis inefficient because large sets of data facts that are introduced by dereferences of pointer variables need to be stored. Equivalence analysis, which identifies equivalence relationships among the various memory locations accessed by a procedure, is used to improve the efficiency of data-flow analyses in the presence of pointer variables [131]. Two equivalent memory locations share identical sets of data facts in a procedure. As a result, data-flow analysis only needs to compute information for a representative memory location, and data-flow for other equivalent locations can be garnered from the representative location. Static slicing is also applied for fault localization in binary executables [132], and type-checkers [133].

A disadvantage of static slicing is that the slice for a given variable at a given statement contains all the executable statements that could possibly affect the value of this variable at the statement. As a result, it might generate a dice with certain statements that should not be included. This is because we cannot predict some run-time values via a static analysis. To deal with the imprecision of static slicing, Zhang and Santelices [134] propose PRIOSLICE to refine the results reported by static slicing.

A good approach to exclude such extra statements from a dice (as well as a slice) is to use *dynamic slicing* [135, 136] instead of static slicing, as the former can identify the statements that do affect a particular value observed at a particular location, rather than possibly affecting such a value as with the latter. Studies such as [121, 122, 132, 134, 137–159], which use the dynamic slicing concept in program debugging, have been reported. In [156], Wotawa combines dynamic slicing with model-based diagnosis to achieve more effective fault localization. Using a given test suite against a program, dynamic slices for erroneous variables discovered are collected. Hitting-sets are constructed, which contain at least one statement from each dynamic slice. The probability that a statement is faulty is calculated based on the number of hitting-sets that cover that statement [160]. Zhang et al. [157] propose the multiple-points dynamic slicing technique, which intersects slices of three techniques: backward dynamic slice (*BwS*), forward dynamic slice (*FwS*), and bidirectional dynamic slice (*BiS*). The *BwS* captures any executed statements that affect the output value of a faulty variable, while the *FwS* is computed based on the minimal input difference between a failed and a successful test case, isolating the parts of the input that trigger a failure. The *BiS* flips the values of certain predicates in the execution of a failed test case so that the program generates a correct output. Qian and Xu [152] propose a scenario-oriented program slicing technique. A user-specified scenario is identified as the extra slicing parameter, and all program parts related to a special computation are located under the given execution scenario. There are three key steps to implementing the scenario-oriented slicing technique: scenario input, identification of scenario relevant codes, and, finally, gathering of scenario-oriented slices. Ocariza et al. [150] propose an automated technique based on dynamic backward slicing of the web application to localize DOM-related JavaScript faults. The proposed fault localization approach is implemented in a tool called AUTOFLOX. Ishii and Kutsuna [143] propose an effective fault localization method for Simulink model. They use the satisfiability modulo theories (SMT) solver to generate distinct dynamic slicing result for each failed test case. Guo et al. [161] apply dynamic slicing and delta debugging to localize faults in SQL predicates. First, in order to identify any suspicious clause, row-based dynamic slicing execute the query for each row in the provided test data, and record the predicate and the Boolean result for each clause. Second, delta debugging is employed to mutate the column values of the failed rows and replace them with the corresponding values from the successful rows. If the mutated row passes, then the clause containing this column is faulty.

One limitation of dynamic slicing-based techniques is that they cannot capture execution omission errors, which may cause the execution of certain critical statements in a program to be omitted and thus result in failures [162]. Gyimothy et al. [163] propose the use of *relevant slicing* to locate faulty statements responsible for execution omission errors. Given a failed execution, the relevant slicing first constructs a dynamic dependence graph in the same way that classic dynamic slicing does. It then augments the dynamic dependence graph with *potential dependence edges*, and a relevant slice is computed by taking the *transitive closure* of the incorrect output on the augmented dynamic dependence graph. However, incorrect dependencies between program statements may be included to produce oversized relevant slices. To address this problem, Zhang et al. [162] introduce the concept of *implicit dependencies*, in which dependencies can be obtained by predicate switching. A similar idea has been used by Weeratunge et al. [164] to identify root causes of omission errors in concurrent programs, in which *dual slicing*, a combination of dynamic slicing and trace differencing, is used. Wang and Liu [165] propose a hierarchical multiple predicate switching technique (HMPS). It reduces the search scope of critical predicates to highly suspicious functions identified by spectrum-based fault localization (SBFL) techniques, and then assigns the functions into combinations following the call dependency graph.

An alternative approach to static and dynamic slicing is the use of *execution slicing* based on data-flow tests to locate program bugs [166] in which an execution slice with respect to a given test case contains the set of statements executed by this test. The reason for choosing execution slicing over static slicing is that a static slice focuses on finding statements that could possibly have an impact on the variables of interest for *any* inputs, versus statements that are executed by a *specific* input. This implies that a static slice does not make any use of the input values that reveal the fault and violates a very important concept in debugging that suggests programmers analyze the program behavior under the test case that fails and not under a generic test case. Collecting dynamic slices may consume excessive time and file space, even though different algorithms [167–170] have been proposed to address these issues. Conversely, it is relatively easy to construct the execution slice for a given test case if we collect code coverage data from the execution of the test. Different execution slice-based debugging tools have been developed and used in practice such as χSuds at Telcordia (formerly Bellcore) [171, 172] and eXVantage at Avaya [173]. Agrawal et al. [166] apply the execution slice to fault localization by examining the execution dice of one failed and one successful test to locate program bugs. Jones et al. [174, 175] and Wong et al. [176] extend that study by using multiple successful and failed tests based on the following observations:

- The more successful tests that execute a piece of code, the less likely it is for the code to contain a bug.
- The more failed tests with respect to a given bug that execute a piece of code, the more likely that it contains this bug.

We use the following example to demonstrate the differences among static, dynamic, and execution slicing. Use the code in column 2 of Table 1.2 as the reference. Assume it has one bug at s_7. The static slice for the output variable, *product*, contains all statements that could possibly affect the value of *product*, s_1, s_2, s_4, s_5, s_7, s_8, s_{10}, and s_{13}, as shown in the third column. The dynamic slicing for *product* only contains the statements that do affect the value of *product* with respect to a given test case, which includes s_1, s_2, s_5, s_7, and s_{13} (as shown in the fourth column) when $a = 2$. The execution slice with respect to a given test case contains all statements executed by this test. Therefore, the execution slice for a test case, $a = 2$, consists of s_1, s_2, s_3, s_4, s_5, s_6, s_7, s_{12}, s_{13} as shown in the fifth column of Table 1.2.

Table 1.2 An example showing the differences among static, dynamic, and execution slicing.

	Code with a bug at s_7	**Static slice for** ***product***	**Dynamic slice for** ***product*** **with respect to a test case** $a = 2$	**Execution slice for** ***product*** **with respect to a test case** $a = 2$
s_1	input (a)	input (a)	input (a)	input (a)
s_2	i = 1;	i = 1;	i = 1;	i = 1;
s_3	sum = 0;			sum = 0;
s_4	product = 1;	product = 1;		product = 1;
s_5	if (i < a) {	if (i < a) {	if (i < a) {	if (i < a) {
s_6	sum = sum + i;			sum = sum + i;
s_7	product = product * i; // bug: product = product * 2 * i	product = product * i;	product = product * i;	product = product * i;
s_8	} else {	} else {	}	}
s_9	sum = sum - i;			
s_{10}	product = product / i;	product = product / i;		
s_{11}	}	}		
s_{12}	print (sum);			print (sum);
s_{13}	print (product);	print (product);	print (product);	print (product);

Source: Wong et al. [177]/IEEE.

One problem with the aforementioned slice-based techniques is that the bug may not be in the dice. Even if a bug is in the dice, there may still be too much code that needs to be examined. To overcome this problem, an inter-block data dependency-based augmentation and a refining method is proposed in [178]. The former includes additional code in the search domain for inspection based on its inter-block data dependency with the code currently being examined, whereas the latter excludes less suspicious code from the search domain using the execution slices of additional successful tests. Additionally, slices are problematic because they are always lengthy and hard to understand. In [179], the notion of using *barriers* is proposed to provide a filtering approach for smaller program slices and better comprehensibility. Stridharan et al. [180] propose *thin slicing* in order to find only *producer statements* that help compute and copy a value to a particular variable. Statements that explain why producer statements affect the value of a particular variable are excluded from a thin slice.

1.3.2 Program Spectrum-Based Techniques

Following the discussion in the beginning of Section 1.3, we would like to emphasize that many spectrum-based techniques are inspired by the probabilistic- and statistical-based causality models. With this understanding, we now explain the details of these techniques.

A program spectrum details the execution information of a program from certain perspectives, such as execution information for conditional branches or loop-free intra-procedural paths [181]. It can be used to track program behavior [182]. An early study by Collofello and Cousins [183] suggests that such spectra can be used for software fault localization. When the execution fails, such information can be used to identify suspicious code that is responsible for the failure. Code coverage, or executable statement hit spectrum (ESHS), indicates which parts of the program under testing have been covered during an execution. With this information, it is possible to identify which components were involved in a failure, narrowing the search for the faulty component that made the execution fail. Masri [184] presents a comprehensive survey of state-of-the-art SBFL techniques proposed from 2005 to February 2016, describing the most recent advances and challenges.

1.3.2.1 Notation

p a program
a_{ef} Number of failed test cases that cover a statement
a_{nf} Number of failed test cases that do not cover a statement

a_{es}	Number of successful test cases that cover a statement
a_{ns}	Number of successful test cases that do not cover a statement
a_e	Total number of test cases that cover a statement
a_n	Total number of test cases that do not cover a statement
a_S	Total number of successful test cases
a_f	Total number of failed test cases
t_i	The ith test case

1.3.2.2 Techniques

Early studies [145, 185–187] only use failed test cases for SBFL, though this approach has subsequently been deemed ineffective [107, 117, 166]. Later studies achieve better results using both the successful and failed test cases and emphasizing the contrast between them. Set union and set intersection are proposed in [188]. The set union focuses on the source code that is executed by the failed test but not by any of the successful tests. Such code is more suspicious than others. The set intersection excludes the code that is executed by all the successful tests but not by the failed test. Renieris and Reiss [188] propose another ESHS-based technique, nearest neighbor, which contrasts a failed test with a successful test that is most similar to the failed one in terms of the *distance* between them. If a bug is in the difference set, it is located. For a bug that is not contained in the difference set, the process continues by first constructing a program dependence graph (PDG) and then including and checking adjacent unchecked nodes in the graph step by step until all the nodes in the graph are examined. The idea of nearest neighbor is similar to Lewis' counterfactual reasoning [189], which claims that, for two events A and B, A causes B (in world w) if and only if, in all *possible worlds* that are *maximally similar* to w, A does not take place and B also does not happen. The theory of counterfactual reasoning is also found in other studies such as [190–192].

Intuitively, the *closer* the execution pattern of a statement is to the failure pattern of all test cases, the more likely the statement is to be faulty, and consequently the more suspicious the statement seems. By the same token, the *farther* the execution pattern of a statement is to the failure pattern, the less suspicious the statement appears to be. Similarity coefficient-based measures can be used to quantify this *closeness*, and the degree of closeness can be interpreted as the suspiciousness of the statements.

A popular ESHS-based similarity coefficient-based technique is Tarantula [174], which uses the coverage and execution result (success or failure) to compute the suspiciousness of each statement as $\left(a_{ef}/a_f\right)/\left(a_{ef}/a_f + a_{es}/a_s\right)$. A study on the *Siemens* suite [107] shows that Tarantula inspects less code before the first faulty statement is identified, making it a more effective fault localization technique when compared to others such as set union, set intersection, nearest neighbor, and cause transition [193]. Based on the suspiciousness computed by Tarantula, studies like [174, 175] use different colors (from red to yellow to green) to provide a visual mapping of the participation of each program statement in the execution of a test suite. The more failed test cases that execute a statement, the brighter (redder) the color assigned to the statement will be. In [103], Debroy et al. further revise the Tarantula technique. Statements executed by the same number of failed test cases are grouped together, and then groups are ranked in descending order by the number of failed test cases. Using Tarantula, statements are ranked by suspiciousness within each group.

For discussion purposes, let us use the code in Table 1.2 again. Assume that we have two successful test cases ($a = 0$ and $a = 1$) and one failed test case ($a = 2$). The suspiciousness value of each statement can be computed, for example, using the Tarantula technique discussed above. The results are as shown in Table 1.3.

The third to fifth columns in Table 1.3 represent the statement coverage of the three test cases. An entry with a "•" means the statement is covered by the corresponding test case, while an empty entry means the statement is not. The values of a_{ef} and a_{es} for each statement are given in the sixth and seventh columns. Based on the definition of Tarantula, the suspiciousness value of each statement is computed and displayed in the eighth column. The ranking of each statement is given in the rightmost column. As we can observe, the faulty statement s_7 has the highest ranking.

In recent years, other techniques have also been proposed that perform at the same level with, or even surpass, Tarantula in terms of their effectiveness at fault localization. The Ochiai similarity coefficient-based technique [94] is generally considered more effective than Tarantula, and its formula is as follows:

$$\text{Suspiciousness(Ochiai)} = \frac{a_{ef}}{\sqrt{a_f \times (a_{ef} + a_{es})}}$$

There are two major differences between Ochiai and the nearest neighbor model: (i) the nearest neighbor model utilizes a single failed test case, while Ochiai uses multiple failed test cases and (ii) the nearest neighbor model only selects the successful test case that most closely resembles the failed test case, while Ochiai includes all successful test cases. Ochiai2 [113] is an extension of Ochiai, and its formula is as follows:

$$\text{Suspiciousness(Ochiai2)} = \frac{a_{ef} \times a_{ns}}{\sqrt{(a_{ef}+a_{es}) \times (a_{ns}+a_{nf}) \times (a_{ef}+a_{nf}) \times (a_{ep}+a_{ns})}}$$

Table 1.3 An example showing the suspiciousness values computed by Tarantula.

Code with a bug at s_7	$a = 0$	$a = 1$	$a = 2$	a_{ef}	a_{es}	Suspiciousness	Ranking
s_1 `input(a)`	●	●	●	1	2	0.5	3
s_2 `i = 1;`	●	●	●	1	2	0.5	3
s_3 `sum = 0;`	●	●	●	1	2	0.5	3
s_4 `product = 1;`	●	●	●	1	2	0.5	3
s_5 `if (i < a){`	●	●	●	1	2	0.5	3
s_6 `sum = sum + i;`			●	1	0	1	1
s_7 `product = product * i;` `// bug: product = product * 2 * i`			●	1	0	1	1
s_8 `} else {`	●	●		0	2	0	10
s_9 `sum = sum - i;`	●	●		0	2	0	10
s_{10} `product = product / i;`	●	●		0	2	0	10
s_{11} `}`	●	●		0	2	0	10
s_{13} `print (product);`	●	●	●	1	2	0.5	3
Execution result	Successful	Successful	Failed				

Source: Wong et al. [177]/IEEE.

In [113], Naish et al. propose two techniques, O and O^P. The technique O is designed for programs with a single bug, while O^P is better applied to programs with multiple bugs. Data from their experiments suggest that O and O^P are more effective than Tarantula, Ochiai, and Ochiai2 for single-bug programs. On the other hand, Le et al. [194] present a different view by showing that Ochiai can be more effective than O and O^P for programs with single bugs.

$$\text{Suspiciousness}(O) = \begin{cases} -1 \text{ if } a_{nf} > 0 \\ a_{ns} \text{ otherwise} \end{cases}$$

Table 1.4 lists 31 similarity coefficient-based techniques, along with their algebraic forms, which have been used in different studies such as [195–197]. A few additional techniques using similar approaches can be found in [198]. Tools like Zoltar [199] and DEPUTO [200] are available to compute the suspiciousness with respect to selected techniques. Empirical studies have also shown that techniques proposed in [117, 197, 201–203] are, in general, more effective than Tarantula.

Comparisons among different SBFL techniques are frequently discussed in recent studies [95, 113, 194, 197, 204, 205]. However, there is no technique claiming that it can outperform all others under every scenario. In other words, an optimum spectrum-based technique does not exist, which is supported by Yoo et al.'s study [206].

A few additional examples of program SBFL techniques are listed below.

- ***Program Invariants Hit Spectrum (PIHS)-Based:*** This spectrum records the coverage of program invariants [207], which are the program properties that remain unchanged across program executions. PIHS-based techniques try to find violations of program properties in failed program executions to locate bugs. *Potential invariants* [208], also called *likely invariants* [209], are program properties that are observed to hold in some sets of successful executions but, unlike *invariants*, may not necessarily hold for all possible executions. The major obstacle in applying such techniques is how to automatically identify the necessary program properties required for the fault localization. To address this problem, existing PIHS-based techniques often take the invariant spectrum of successful executions as the program properties. In study [210], Alipour and Groce propose *extended invariants* by adding execution features such as the execution count of blocks to the invariants. They claim that extended invariants are helpful in fault localization. Shu et al. [211] propose FLSF technique based on Tarantula. They use statement frequency, instead of coverage information, to evaluate the suspiciousness of each statement. FLSF first counts the statement frequency of each program statement in each test case execution so as to construct a statement frequency matrix. Second, each weighted element of the constructed matrix is normalized to a value between 0 and 1. Finally, the suspiciousness of each statement

Table 1.4 Some similarity coefficients used for fault localization.

	Coefficient	Algebraic form		Coefficient	Algebraic form
1	Braun-Banquet	$\frac{a_{ef}}{\max\left(a_{ef}+a_{es}, a_{ef}+a_{nf}\right)}$	17	Harmonic Mean	$\frac{\left(a_{ef}\times a_{ns}-a_{nf}\times a_{es}\right)\times\left(\left(a_{ef}+a_{es}\right)\times\left(a_{ns}+a_{nf}\right)+\left(a_{ef}+a_{nf}\right)\times\left(a_{es}+a_{ns}\right)\right)}{\left(a_{ef}+a_{es}\right)\times\left(a_{ns}+a_{nf}\right)\times\left(a_{ef}+a_{nf}\right)\times\left(a_{es}+a_{ns}\right)}$
2	Dennis	$\frac{\left(a_{ef}\times a_{ns}\right)-\left(a_{es}\times a_{nf}\right)}{\sqrt{n\times\left(a_{ef}+a_{es}\right)\times\left(a_{ef}+a_{nf}\right)}}$	18	Rogot2	$\frac{1}{4}\left(\frac{a_{ef}}{a_{ef}+a_{es}}+\frac{a_{ef}}{a_{ef}+a_{nf}}+\frac{a_{ns}}{a_{ns}+a_{es}}+\frac{a_{ns}}{a_{ns}+a_{nf}}\right)$
3	Mountford	$\frac{a_{ef}}{0.5\times\left(\left(a_{ef}\times a_{es}\right)+\left(a_{ef}\times a_{nf}\right)\right)+\left(a_{es}\times a_{nf}\right)}$	19	Simple Matching	$\frac{a_{ef}+a_{ns}}{a_{ef}+a_{es}+a_{ns}+a_{nf}}$
4	Fossum	$\frac{n\times\left(a_{ef}-0.5\right)^2}{\left(a_{ef}+a_{es}\right)\times\left(a_{ef}+a_{nf}\right)}$	20	Rogers and Tanimoto	$\frac{a_{ef}+a_{ns}}{a_{ef}+a_{ns}+2\left(a_{nf}+a_{es}\right)}$
5	Pearson	$\frac{n\times\left(\left(a_{ef}\times a_{ns}\right)-\left(a_{es}\times a_{nf}\right)\right)^2}{\Phi_e\times\Phi_n\times\Phi_S\times\Phi_F}$	21	Hamming	$a_{ef}+a_{ns}$
6	Gower	$\frac{a_{ef}\times a_{ns}}{\sqrt{\Phi_F\times\Phi_e\times\Phi_n\times\Phi_S}}$	22	Hamann	$\frac{a_{ef}+a_{ns}-a_{nf}-a_{es}}{a_{ef}+a_{nf}+a_{es}+a_{ns}}$
7	Michael	$\frac{4\times\left(\left(a_{ef}\times a_{ns}\right)-\left(a_{es}\times a_{nf}\right)\right)}{\left(a_{ef}\times a_{ns}\right)^2+\left(a_{es}\times a_{nf}\right)^2}$	23	Sokal	$\frac{2\left(a_{ef}+a_{ns}\right)}{2\left(a_{ef}+a_{ns}\right)+a_{nf}+a_{es}}$
8	Pierce	$\frac{\left(a_{ef}\times a_{nf}\right)+\left(a_{nf}\times a_{es}\right)}{\left(a_{ef}\times a_{nf}\right)+\left(2\times\left(a_{nf}\times a_{ns}\right)\right)+\left(a_{es}\times a_{ns}\right)}$	24	Scott	$\frac{4\left(a_{ef}\times a_{ns}-a_{nf}\times a_{es}\right)-\left(a_{nf}-a_{es}\right)^2}{\left(2a_{ef}+a_{nf}+a_{es}\right)\left(2a_{ns}+a_{nf}+a_{es}\right)}$
9	Baroni-Urbani and Buser	$\frac{\sqrt{\left(a_{ef}\times a_{ns}\right)}+a_{ef}}{\sqrt{\left(a_{ef}\times a_{ns}\right)}+a_{ef}+a_{es}+a_{nf}}$	25	Rogot1	$\frac{1}{2}\left(\frac{a_{ef}}{2a_{ef}+a_{nf}+a_{es}}+\frac{a_{ns}}{2a_{ns}+a_{nf}+a_{es}}\right)$
10	Tarwid	$\frac{\left(n\times a_{ef}\right)-\left(\Phi_F\times\Phi_e\right)}{\left(n\times a_{ef}\right)+\left(\Phi_F\times\Phi_e\right)}$	26	Kulczynski	$\frac{a_{ef}}{a_{nf}+a_{es}}$

(Continued)

Table 1.4 (Continued)

Coefficient		Algebraic form	Coefficient		Algebraic form
11	Ample	$\left\lvert \frac{a_{ef}}{(a_{ef} + a_{nf})} - \frac{a_{es}}{(a_{es} + a_{ns})} \right\rvert$	27	Anderberg	$\frac{a_{ef}}{a_{ef} + 2(a_{nf} + a_{es})}$
12	Phi (Geometric Mean)	$\frac{a_{ef} \times a_{ns} - a_{nf} \times a_{es}}{\sqrt{(a_{ef} + a_{es}) \times (a_{ef} + a_{nf}) \times (a_{es} + a_{ns}) \times (a_{nf} + a_{ns})}}$	28	Dice	$\frac{2a_{ef}}{a_{ef} + a_{nf} + a_{es}}$
13	Arithmetic Mean	$\frac{2(a_{ef} \times a_{ns} - a_{nf} \times a_{es})}{(a_{ef} + a_{ns}) \times (a_{ns} + a_{nf}) + (a_{ef} + a_{nf}) \times (a_{es} + a_{ns})}$	29	Goodman	$\frac{2a_{ef} - a_{nf} - a_{es}}{2a_{ef} + a_{nf} + a_{es}}$
14	Cohen	$\frac{2(a_{ef} \times a_{ns} - a_{nf} \times a_{es})}{(a_{ef} + a_{ns}) \times (a_{ns} + a_{es}) + (a_{ef} + a_{nf}) \times (a_{nf} + a_{ns})}$	30	Jaccard	$\frac{a_{ef}}{a_{ef} + a_{nf} + a_{es}}$
15	Fleiss	$\frac{4(a_{ef} \times a_{ns} - a_{nf} \times a_{es}) - (a_{nf} - a_{es})^2}{(2a_{ef} + a_{nf} + a_{es}) + (2a_{ns} + a_{nf} + a_{es})}$	31	Sorensen-Dice	$\frac{2a_{ef}}{2a_{ef} + a_{nf} + a_{es}}$
16	Zoltar	$\frac{a_{ef}}{a_{ef} + a_{nf} + a_{es} + \frac{10000 \times a_{nf} \times a_{es}}{a_{ef}}}$			

Source: Wong et al. [177]/IEEE.

is computed according to its frequency value. The proposed technique is evaluated using Siemens suite and is reported to be better than Tarantula. Le et al. [212] propose a fault localization technique that employs a learning-to-rank strategy, using likely program invariants and suspiciousness scores as features, to rank program methods based on their likelihood of being a root cause of a failure.

- ***Predicate Count Spectrum (PRCS)-Based:*** PRCS records how predicates are executed and can be used to track program behavior that is likely to be erroneous. These techniques are often labeled as *statistical debugging* techniques because the PRCS information is analyzed using statistical methods. Fault localization techniques in this category include Liblit05 [213], SOBER [214], etc. See Section 1.3.3 for more details. Naish et al. [112] suggest that using PRCS could achieve a better fault localization effectiveness than that using ESHS.
- ***Method Calls Sequence Hit Spectrum (MCSHS)-Based:*** Information regarding the sequences of method calls covered during program execution is collected. In one study, Dallmeier et al. [215] collect execution data from Java programs and demonstrate fault localization through the identification and analysis of method call sequences. Both incoming method calls (how an object is used) and outgoing calls (how it is implemented) are considered. In another study, Liu et al. [216] construct software behavior graphs from collected program execution data, including the calling and transition relationships between functions. They define a framework to mine closed frequent graphs based on behavior graphs and use them to train classifiers that help identify suspicious functions.
- ***Time Spectrum-Based:*** A time spectrum [217–219] records the execution time of every method in successful or failed executions. Observed behavior models are created using time spectra collected from successful executions. Deviations from these models in failed executions are identified and ranked as potential causes of failures.

Other program spectra such as those in Table 1.5 [181] can also be applied to identify suspicious code in a program.

1.3.2.3 Issues and Concerns

A variety of issues and concerns about SBFL has also been identified and studied in depth. One problem is that most spectrum-based techniques do not calibrate the contribution of failed and successful tests. In [220], all statements are divided into suspicious and unsuspicious groups. The suspicious group contains statements that have been executed by at least one failed test case, while the unsuspicious group contains the remaining statements. Risk is only calculated for suspicious statements, and unsuspicious statements are simply assigned the lowest value.

Table 1.5 Additional program spectra relevant to fault localization.

	Name	Description
BHS	Branch Hit Spectrum	Conditional branches that are executed
CPS	Complete Path Spectrum	Complete path that is executed
PHS	Path Hit Spectrum	Intra-procedural, loop-free path that is executed
PCS	Path Count Spectrum	Number of times each intra-procedural, loop-free path is executed
DHS	Data-dependence Hit Spectrum	Definition-use pairs that are executed
DCS	Data-dependence Count Spectrum	Number of times each definition-use pair is executed
OPS	Output Spectrum	Output that is produced
ETS	Execution Trace Spectrum	Execution trace that is produced

It is possible, however, that successful test cases may also contain bugs. In [117], Wong et al. focus on the question of how each additional failed or successful test case can aid in locating program bugs. They describe that with respect to a piece of code, the contribution of the first failed test case that executes it in computing its suspiciousness is larger than or equal to that of the second failed test case that executes it, which in turn is larger than or equal to that of the third failed test case that executes it, and so on. This principle is also applied to the contribution provided by successful test cases. In addition, the total contribution from all the successful test cases that execute a statement should be less than the total contribution from all the failed tests that execute it. Recognizing that fault localization often proceeds by comparing information associated with a failed test case to that with a successful test case, Wong and Qi [178] and Guo et al. [221] attempt to answer the question of which successful test case should be selected for comparison, in the interests of more effective fault localization. Choosing the successful test case whose execution sequence is most similar to that of a failed test case, according to a control flow-based difference metric, can minimize the search domain of the fault.

For most spectrum-based techniques, if statements exhibit the same execution pattern, there is a high likelihood that the suspiciousness score assigned to these statements will be exactly the same. Statements with the same suspiciousness will result in ties in the ranking. To break these ties, the information related to statement execution frequency in addition to statement coverage can also be utilized [222, 223]. In [120], Xu et al. evaluate different tie-breaking strategies, including statement order-based strategy, confidence-based strategy, and data dependency-based strategy. Tie-breaking methods will be further discussed in Section 1.7.6. Another problem is that almost all spectrum-based techniques have assumed that a test oracle exists, which restricts their practical applicability. Thus, Xie et al. [224, 225] propose a fault localization technique based on the integration of metamorphic relations and slices, in which a program execution slice is replaced by a metamorphic slice; an individual test case is replaced by a metamorphic test group; and the success/failure result of a test case is replaced by the violation/non-violation result of a metamorphic test group. Chen et al. [226] use metamorphic relations and symbolic evaluation to integrate program proving, testing, and debugging. See Chapter 11 of the Handbook. Tolksdorf et al. [227] apply metamorphic test cases to interactive debuggers. They transform both the debugged code and the debugging actions in a way that the behavior of the original and the transformed inputs can differ only in specific ways.

Zhao et al. [228, 229] posit that using only individual coverage information may not reveal the execution paths. Therefore, they first use the program control-flow graph to analyze the program execution and then map the distribution of failed executions to different control flows. They use *bug proneness* to qualify how each block contributes to the failure and *bug free confidence* to quantify the likelihood of each block being bug-free by comparing the distributions of blocks on the same failed execution path.

Guo et al. [230] discuss the instability of SBFL techniques. They provide a stochastic technique to measure the instability quantity of SBFL. Then, the necessity of evaluating SBFL instability is proven by experimental studies. Finally, the authors propose several factors such as the test suite size and the risk evaluation formula to measure the instability of SBFL. Keller et al. [231] find that SBFL has limitation in locating bugs on large-size benchmarks. Studies in [232–235] report that combining SBFL with mutation-based fault localization (MBFL) [236, 237] can improve FL effectiveness for real faults compared to using SBFL or MBFL alone. Li et al. [238] assign weights to the traditional binary executions in SBFL using the probabilities of branch executions. Instead of using 0 or 1 to represent the execution information of each statement in a test case, the value is replaced by the ratio of the number of executions of a statement located in a branch of a module to the total number of executions of the module.

Instrumentation overhead is another issue, which introduces a considerable cost in the fault localization process, especially in a resource-constrained environment. In order to mitigate this problem, Perez et al. [239] propose coined dynamic code coverage by using coarser instrumentation to reduce such overhead. This technique starts by analyzing coverage traces for large components of the program (e.g. package or class) and then progressively increases the instrumentation granularity for possible faulty components until the statement level is reached.

1.3.3 Statistics-Based Techniques

A statistical debugging technique (Liblit05) that can isolate bugs in programs with instrumented predicates at particular points is presented in [213]. For each predicate P, Liblit05 first computes the probability that P being true implies failure, *Failure*(P), and the probability that the execution of P implies failure, *Context*(P). Predicates that have *Failure*(P) − *Context*(P) ≤ 0 are discarded. The remaining predicates are prioritized based on their *importance* scores, which give an indication of the relationship between predicates and program bugs. Predicates with a higher score should be examined first. Chilimbi et al. [240] propose that replacing predicates with path profiles may improve the effectiveness of Liblit05. Path profiles are collected during execution and are aggregated across the execution of multiple test cases through feedback reports. The *importance score* is calculated for each path and the top results are selected and presented as potential root causes.

In [214], Liu et al. propose the SOBER technique to rank suspicious predicates. A predicate P can be evaluated as true more than once in the execution of one test case. They compute $\pi(P) = n(t)/(n(t) + n(f))$, the probability that P is evaluated as true in each execution of a test case, where $n(t)$ is the number of times P is evaluated as true and $n(f)$ is the number of times P is evaluated as false. If the distribution of $\pi(P)$ in failed executions is significantly different from that in successful executions, then P is related to a fault. Hu et al. [241] use a similar heuristic to rank all predicates. In addition, they apply nonparametric hypothesis testing to determine the degree of difference between the spectra of predicates for successful and failed test cases. This new enhancement has been empirically evaluated to be effective [123, 242].

The study in [202] presents a cross tabulation (a.k.a. crosstab) analysis-based technique to compute the suspiciousness of statements. A crosstab is constructed for each statement with two vertical categories (covered/not covered) and two horizontal categories (successful execution/failed execution). A hypothesis test is used to provide a reference of dependency/independency between the execution results and the coverage of each statement. The exact suspiciousness of each statement depends on the degree of association between its coverage and the execution results.

The primary difference among crosstab, SOBER, and Liblit05 is that crosstab can be generally applied to rank suspicious program elements (i.e. statement, predicate, and function/method), whereas the last two only rank suspicious predicates for fault localization. For Liblit05 and SOBER, the corresponding statements of the top k predicates are taken as the initial set to be examined for locating the bug. As suggested by Jones and Harrold in [107], Liblit05 provides no way to quantify the ranking for all statements. An ordering of the predicates is defined, but the approach does not detail how to order statements related to any bug that lies outside a predicate. For SOBER, if the bug is not in the initial set of statements, additional statements have to be included by performing a breadth-first search on the corresponding PDG, which can potentially be time-consuming. However, such a search is not required for crosstab, as all the statements of the program are ranked based on their suspiciousness. Results reported in [202] suggest that crosstab is almost always more effective in locating bugs in the Siemens suite than Liblit05 and SOBER. Similar to crosstab [202], Yang et al. [243] use conditional probability to quantify the dependence between program spectra and execution results, and compute the suspiciousness score accordingly. Henderson and Podgurski [244] randomly sample suspicious subgraphs of dynamic control flow graphs of successful and failed executions. Metrics used in coverage-based SBFL are adapted to select the most suspicious subgraphs.

In program execution, *short-circuit evaluation* may occur frequently, which means, for a predicate with more than one condition, if the first condition suffices to determine the results of the predicate, the following conditions will not be evaluated (executed). Zhang et al. [245, 246] identify the short-circuit evaluations of an individual predicate and produce one set of evaluation sequences for each predicate. Using such information, their proposed *Debugging through Evaluation Sequences* (DES) approach is compared to existing predicated-based techniques such as SOBER and Liblit05. You et al. [247] propose a statistical approach employing the behavior of two sequentially connected predicates in the execution. They construct a weighted execution graph for each execution of a test case with predicates as vertices and the transition of two sequential predicates as edges. For each edge, a suspiciousness value is calculated to quantify its fault-relevant likelihood. Baah et al. [248] apply *causal-inference* techniques to the problem of fault localization. A linear model is built on program control-flow graphs to estimate the causal effect of covering a given statement on the occurrence of failures. This model is able to reduce *confounding bias* and thereby help generate better fault localization rankings. In [249], they further enhance the linear model toward better fault localization effectiveness by including information on data-flow dependence. In [250], Modi et al. explore the usage of *execution phase* information such as cache miss rates, CPU, and Memory usages in statistical program debugging. They suggest coupling *execution phases* with predicates results in higher bug localization accuracy as opposed to when phase information is not used. Wang et al. [251] propose a variable type-based predicate designation (VTPD) approach to improve the ability of fault-relevant predicate identification and mitigate the confounding effect. The approach begins with designing two kinds of predicates: the original type for branch statements and indeed type for assignments and return statements. The indeed type is further broken into several variable types based on the programming language, e.g. there are numeric, Boolean, character, and reference types in Java. Then, the authors conduct a dependency analysis technique using the casual graph model to examine the potential confounding effect of control and data dependences. Finally, based on the analysis result, the authors build a linear regression model to estimate the suspiciousness of predicates by calculating the contribution to the failure result, and the control and data dependencies. Sun and Podgurski [205] analyze several coverage-based statistical fault localization metrics to compare their efficiency. They first identify the key elements for these metrics. Their results suggest relative recall and symmetric Klosgen are the most effective metrics. In addition, for multiple-fault programs, symmetric Klosgen, relative Ochiai, relative F1, and enhanced Tarantula all performed similarly well.

Feyzi and Parsa [252] proposed to incorporate fault-proneness analysis into statistical fault localization in order to address the fact that statistical fault localization techniques are biased by data collection from distinct executions of a program under analysis. Their evaluation shows that such combination is beneficial to fault localization.

1.3.4 Program State-Based Techniques

A program state consists of variables and their values at a particular point during program execution, which can be a good indicator for locating program bugs. One way to use program states in software fault localization is by relative debugging [253], in which faults in the development version can be located via a runtime comparison of the internal states to a "reference" version of the program. Another approach is to modify the values of some variables to determine which one causes erroneous program execution. Zeller [192] and Zeller and Hildebrandt [254] propose a technique, delta debugging, by contrasting program states between executions of a successful test and a failed test via their memory graphs described in [255]. Variables are tested for suspiciousness by replacing their values from a successful test with their corresponding values from the same point in a failed test, and repeating the program execution. Unless the identical failure is observed, the variable is no longer considered suspicious. Note that the idea of simplifying failure-inducing inputs discussed in [192, 254] is orthogonal to other techniques, as it significantly reduces the original execution length. The delta tool [256] has been widely used in industry for automated debugging. In [193], Cleve and Zeller extend delta debugging to the cause transition technique to identify the locations and times where the cause of a failure changes from one variable to another. An algorithm named *cts* is proposed to quickly locate cause transitions in a program execution. Similar studies [257–259] based on combinatorial testing are reported, which separate input parameters into *faulty-possible* and *healthy-possible* and identify minimal failure-inducing combinations of parameters.

However, the cause transition technique is a relatively high-cost approach; there may exist thousands of states in a program execution, and delta debugging at each matching point requires additional test executions to narrow down the causes. Another problem is that the identified locations may not be where the bugs reside. Gupta et al. [260] introduce the concept of a failure-inducing chop as an extension to the cause transition technique to overcome this issue. First, delta debugging is used to identify input and output variables that are causes of failure. Dynamic slices are then constructed for these variables. The code at the intersection of the forward slicing of the input variables and the backward slicing of the output variables is considered suspicious.

Sumner et al. further improve the robustness, precision, and efficiency of delta debugging by combining it with more precise *execution alignment* techniques [261–263]. However, there are still three limitations to delta debugging: it fails to handle confounding of partial state replacement, it cannot locate execution omission errors, and it suffers from poor efficiency. To address these limitations, Sumner and Zhang [264] propose a cause inference model, *comparative causality*, to provide a systematic technique explaining the difference between a failed execution and a successful execution. Hashimoto et al. [265] propose a rule-based approach to minimize the set of changes to facilitate delta debugging. It uses tree differencing on ASTs to decompose changes into independent components both syntactically and semantically so that invalid subsets that do not result in testable programs can be avoided.

Predicate switching [266], proposed by Zhang et al., is another program state-based fault localization technique where program states are changed to forcefully alter the executed branches in a failed execution. A predicate that, if switched, can make the program execute successfully is labeled as a critical predicate. The technique starts by finding the first erroneous value in variables. Different searching strategies, such as last-executed-first-switched (LEFS) ordering and prioritization-based (PRIOR) ordering, can help determine the next candidates for critical predicates. Wang and Roychoudhury [267] present a similar technique that analyzes the execution path of a failed test and alters the outcome of branches in that path to produce a successful execution. The branch statements with outcomes that have been changed are recorded as bugs. A deficiency of predicate switching is that the alternation of program states is never guided by program dependence analysis, even though faults are intrinsically propagated through the chain of program dependences. The study in [268] extends the predicate switching technique and reduces the search space of program states by selecting a subset of trace points in a failed execution based on dependence analysis. Li et al. [269] propose minimum debugging frontier set (MDFS) to reduce the state exploration cost. Given an observed and reproducible failure, its execution trace is analyzed and successively narrowed by cutting the dynamic dependence graph into two parts from the corresponding trace points. Based on the result of sparse symbolic exploration, one part is removed from further exploration. This process continues until the fault is reached. The set of statement instances in the chosen cut is called a MDFS.

Jeffrey et al. [270] present a value profile-based technique for fault localization to assist developers in software debugging. The approach involves computing interesting value mapping pairs (IVMPs) that show how values used in particular program statements can be altered so that failed test cases will produce the correct output instead. Alternate sets of values are selected from profiling information taken from the executions of all test cases in an available test suite. Different alternate value sets are used to perform value replacements in each statement instance for every failed test case. Using these IVMPs, each statement can then be ranked according to the number of failed executions in which at least one IVMP is identified for that statement. In [271], Zhang et al. claim that a bug within a statement may propagate a series of *infected program states* before it manifests the failure. Also, even if every failed execution executes a particular statement, this statement is not necessarily the root cause of the failure. Thus, they use edge profiles to represent program executions and assess the suspiciousness of the infected program states propagated through each edge. By associating basic blocks with edges, a suspiciousness ranking is generated to locate program bugs.

1.3.5 Machine Learning-Based Techniques

Machine learning is the study of computer algorithms that improve through experience. Machine learning techniques are adaptive and robust and can produce models based on data, with limited human interaction. This has led to their employment in many disciplines such as bioinformatics, natural language processing, cryptography, computer vision, etc. In the context of fault localization, the problem at hand can be identified as trying to learn or deduce the location of a fault based on input data such as statement coverage and the execution result (success or failure) of each test case (e.g. [272–276]).

Wong and Qi [277] propose a fault localization technique based on a back-propagation (BP) neural network, one of the most popular neural network models in practice [278]. A BP neural network has a simple structure, which makes it easy to implement using computer programs. Also, BP neural networks have the ability to approximate complicated nonlinear functions [279]. The coverage data of each test case and the corresponding execution result are collected, and they are used together to train a BP neural network so that the network can learn the relationship between them. Then, the coverage of a suite of virtual test cases that each covers only one statement in the program is input to the trained BP network, and the outputs can be regarded as the likelihood of each statement containing the bug.

Ascari et al. [98] extend the BP-based technique [277] to Object-Oriented programs. As BP neural networks are known to suffer from issues such as paralysis and local minima, Wong et al. [201] propose another approach based on radial basis function (RBF) networks, which are less susceptible to these problems and have a faster learning rate [280, 281]. The RBF network is trained using an approach similar to the BP network. Once the training is completed, the output with respect to the coverage of each virtual test case is considered to be the suspiciousness of the corresponding statement. There are three novelties of this approach: (i) a method for representing test cases, coverage information, and execution results within a modified RBF neural network formalism, (ii) an innovative algorithm to simultaneously estimate the number of hidden neurons and their receptive field centers, and (iii) a weighted bit-comparison-based distance (instead of the Euclidean distance) to measure the distance between the coverage of two test cases.

In [282], Briand et al. use the C4.5 decision tree algorithm to construct rules that classify test cases into various partitions such that failed test cases in the same partition most likely fail due to the same causative fault. The underlying premise is that distinct failure conditions for test cases can be identified depending on the inputs and outputs of the test case (category partitioning). Each path in the decision tree represents a rule modeling distinct failure conditions, possibly originating from different faults, and leads to a distinct failure probability prediction. The statement coverage of both the failed and successful test cases in each partition is used to rank the statements using a heuristic similar to Tarantula [107] to form a ranking. These individual rankings are then consolidated to form a final statement ranking that can be examined to locate the faults. Jonsson et al. [283] build a supervised linear Bayesian model based on the text information extracted from historical bug reports to predict where bugs are located in a component.

Mariani et al. [284] present LOUD for localizing faults in cloud systems. It first uses machine learning to detect anomalies in KPIs and reveal causal relationships among them. Later, it employs graph centrality algorithms to localize the faulty resources responsible for generating and propagating anomalies. Kim et al. [285] propose PRINCE that uses genetic programming to train a statement suspiciousness ranking model using information extracted from program spectrums of both original and mutated programs, program dependency, and program structural complexity. Zhang et al. [286] propose PRFL, which combines SBFL with the PageRank algorithm. Given the original program spectrum information, PRFL uses PageRank to recompute the spectrum information by considering the contributions of different tests. Then, SBFL techniques can be applied on the recomputed spectrum information. The combination of fault localization and defect prediction techniques can further improve the accuracy of both processes [287]. Sohn and Yoo [288] extend SBFL with code and change metrics such as size, age, and code churn that are used in defect prediction. Using suspiciousness values from existing SBFL formulas and the source code metrics as features, Genetic Programming and linear rank Support Vector Machines are applied to learn these features for fault localization. Li et al. [289] propose DeepFL, which uses TensorFlow to learn the spectrum-, mutation-, complexity-, and textual-based features for fault localization.

1.3.6 Data Mining-Based Techniques

Along the lines of machine learning, data mining also seeks to produce a model using pertinent information extracted from data. Data mining can uncover hidden patterns in samples of data that may not be discovered by manual analysis alone, especially due to the sheer volume of information. Efficient data mining techniques transcend such problems and do so in reasonable amounts of time with high degrees of accuracy [290, 291]. The software fault localization problem can be abstracted to a data mining problem – for example, we wish to identify the pattern of statement execution that leads to a failure. In addition, although the complete execution trace of a program is a valuable resource for fault localization, the huge volume of data makes it unwieldy for usage in practice. Therefore, some studies have creatively applied data mining techniques to execution traces [292].

Nessa et al. [293] generate statement subsequences of length *N*, referred to as *N*-grams, from the trace data. The failed execution traces are then examined to find the *N*-grams with a rate of occurrence that is higher than a certain threshold. A statistical analysis is conducted to determine the conditional probability that a certain *N*-gram appears in a given failed execution trace – this probability is known as the *confidence* for that *N*-gram. *N*-grams are sorted in descending order of confidence and the corresponding statements in the program are displayed based on their first appearance in the list. Case studies on the Siemens suite as well as the *space* and *grep* programs have shown that this technique is more effective at locating faults than Tarantula.

Cellier et al. [294, 295] discuss a combination of association rules and Formal Concept Analysis to assist in fault localization. The proposed technique tries to identify rules regarding the association between statement coverage and corresponding execution failures. The frequency of each rule is measured. A threshold is decided upon to indicate the minimum number of failed executions that should be covered by a selected rule. A large number of rules so generated are partially ranked using a rule lattice. The ranking is then examined to locate the fault.

In [296], the authors propose a technique taking advantage of the recent progress in multi-relational data mining for fault localization. More specifically, this technique is based on Markov logic, combining first-order logic and Markov random fields with weighted satisfiability testing for efficient inference and a voted perceptron algorithm for criminative learning. When applied to fault localization, Markov logic combines different information sources such as statement coverage, static program structure information, and prior bug knowledge into a solution to improve the effectiveness of fault localization. Their technique is empirically shown to be more effective than Tarantula on some programs of the Siemens suite.

Denmat et al. [297] propose a technique that reinterprets Tarantula as a data-mining problem. In this technique, association rules that indicate the relationship between a single statement and a program failure are mined based on the coverage information and execution results of a test suite. The relevance values of these rules are evaluated based on two metrics, *conf* and *lift*, which are commonly used by classical data mining problems. Such values can be interpreted as the suspiciousness of a statement that may contain bugs.

Bian et al. [298] present EAntMiner, which applies a divide-and-conquer approach to exclude irrelevant statements that are irrelevant to certain critical operations and transform representations of the same logic into a canonical form. Later a k-nearest neighbors (kNN)-based method is developed to identify bugs that are difficult to be detected due to the interferences of return statements that are form identical but semantics different.

Hanam et al. [299] propose BugAID, a data mining technique for discovering common unknown bug patterns. BugAID uses unsupervised machine learning to identify language construct-based changes distilled from AST differencing of bug fixes in the code.

1.3.7 Model-Based Techniques

With respect to each model-based technique, a critical concern is the model's expressive capability, which has a significant impact on the effectiveness of that technique.

While using model-based diagnosis [300], it is assumed that a correct model of each program being diagnosed is available. That is, these models can be served as the *oracles* of the corresponding programs. Differences between the behavior of a model and the actual observed behavior of the program are used to help find bugs in the program [301, 302]. On the other hand, for model-based software fault localization [155, 303–315], models are generated directly from the actual programs, which may contain bugs. Differences between the observed program executions and the expected results (provided by programmers or testers) are used to identify model elements that are responsible for such observed misbehavior. As demonstrated by the Java diagnosis experiments (JADE) in [316, 317], model-based software fault localization can be viewed as an application of model-based diagnosis [318].

Dependency-based models are derived from dependencies between statements in a program, by means of either static or dynamic analysis. Mateis et al. [308] present a functional dependency model for Java programs that can handle a subset of features for the Java language, such as classes, methods, conditionals, assignments, and while-loops. In their model, the structure of a program is described with dependency-based models, while logic-based languages, such as first-order logic, are applied to model the behavior of the target program. This dependency-based model is then extended to handle unstructured control flows in Java programs [319, 320], such as exceptions, recursive method calls, and return and jump statements. The notion of a dependence graph has also been extended to model behavior of a program over a test suite. Baah et al. [304] use a probabilistic PDG to model the internal behavior of a program, facilitating probabilistic analysis and reasoning about uncertain program behavior, especially those that are likely associated with faults.

Xu et al. [321] propose to do fault localization based on a single failed execution. They consider debugging as a probabilistic inference problem where the likelihood of each executed statement/variable being correct/faulty is represented by a random variable. Human knowledge, human-like reasoning rules, and program semantics are modeled as probabilistic constraints, which can be solved to identify the most likely faulty statements. Yu et al. propose to reason about observed program failures using a Bayesian Network based on probabilistic PDG s to pinpoint suspicious code entities [322, 323].

Wotawa et al. [313] use first-order logic to construct dependency-based models based on source code analysis of target programs to represent program structures and behavior. Test cases with expected outputs are also transformed into observations in terms of first-order logic. If the execution of a target program on a test case fails, conflicts between the test case and the models (which can be shown as equivalent to either static or dynamic slices [155]) are used to identify suspicious statements responsible for the failure. For each statement, a default assumption is made to suggest whether the statement is correct or incorrect. These assumptions are to be revised during fault localization until the failure can be explained. The limitation is that their study only focuses on loop-free programs. To fix this problem, Mayer and Stumptner [310] propose an abstraction-based model in which abstract interpretation [324, 325] is applied to handle loops, recursive procedures, and heap data structures. Additionally, abstract interpretation is used to improve the effectiveness of slice-based and other model-based fault localization techniques [326].

In addition to dependency-based and abstraction-based models, value-based models [327, 328] that represent data-flow information in programs are also applied to locate components that contain bugs. However, value-based models are more computationally intensive than dependency-based and are only practical for small programs [302].

We now discuss model checking-based fault localization techniques that rely on the use of model checkers to locate bugs [190, 329–336]. If a model does not satisfy the corresponding program specifications (implying that the model contains at least one bug), a model checker can be used to provide counter-examples showing how the specifications will be violated. A counter-example does not directly specify which parts of a model are associated with a given bug; however, it can be viewed as a failed test case to help identify the *causality* of the bug [15].

Ball et al. [329] propose to use a model checker to explore all program paths except that of the counter-example. Successful execution paths (those that do not cause a failure) are recorded. An algorithm is used to identify the *transitions* that appear in the execution path of the counter-example but not in any successful execution paths. Program components related to these *transitions* are those that are likely to contain the causes of bugs. This technique suffers from two weaknesses. First, as suggested by Groce and Visser [333], generating all successful execution paths can be very expensive. Second, only one counter-example is used to locate bugs, even though the same bug may be triggered by multiple counter-examples. If this occurs, using only one example can introducc possible bias. To overcome these problems, for a given counter-example, Groce and Visser use a technique to generate additional execution paths such that they are *close* to the path of the counter-example but different in a small number of actions. A metric [15, 190] based on the theory of *causality* and *counterfactual reasoning* [90, 189] is proposed to measure the distance between two execution paths. A tool, *explain* [334], is implemented to support their technique. Additional execution paths so generated may or may not cause a failure. Model components in the failed paths but not in the successful paths are possible bug locations. Chaki et al. further extend Groce's technique by combining it with *predicate abstraction* [330]. However, these techniques [15, 190, 329, 330, 333, 334] all require at least one successful execution.

Griesmayer et al. [331, 332] argue that a successful execution path can be very different from the path of the counter-example and cannot be easily identified using the above techniques. Instead of searching for successful execution paths with small changes from that of the original counter-example, they make minimal changes to the program model so that the counter-example will not fail in the revised model. Assuming there is only one bug in one model component, Griesmayer et al. propose a technique with two steps: (i) revising the program specification in such a way that if any one component in the original model is changed, then the original specification cannot be satisfied and (ii) creating variants of the original model such that each variant has exactly one component replaced by a different component with an *alternative behavior*. For each model variant, if a model checker can find a counter-example violating the revised specification, then the replaced component is potentially responsible for the failure. Since more than one component may be responsible for the failure, programmers have to manually inspect these components to identify the one containing the bug. Experiments in [331] use the model Checker CBMC, whereas extended studies using an additional model checker SATABS are reported in [332].

Based on a similar idea described in [331, 332], Könighofer and Bloem [335] use symbolic execution to locate bugs for imperative programs. An important point stated by Griesmayer [332] is that the extensive use of a model checker makes their techniques less efficient (in terms of time) than those in [190, 329, 330, 333, 334]; however, fault localization using model checkers can be used to refine results from less precise techniques.

Last but not least, the idea of modifying a model so that test cases that fail on the original model can be executed successfully on the modified model [331, 332, 335] is also used in other studies for automatic bug fixing [337–340].

Additional model-based fault localization techniques also exist. They can be applied to functional programs [341], hardware description languages like VHDL [342, 343], and spreadsheets [47, 344]. Studies such as [345, 346] make use of constraint solving, in which programs are automatically compiled into a set of constraints. Shchekotykhin et al. [312] identify the preferred system diagnosis by determining a subset of minimal conflicts. Then, a set of minimal hitting sets for this subset of conflicts can be derived to find the true causes of unexpected behavior. In [347], an expert-system approach called FLABot was proposed to assist developers in fault-localization tasks by reasoning about faults using software architecture models. Chittimalli and Shah [348] propose an approach that applies the fault localization technique to BPMN models. In the approach, the test scripts are generated per the BPMN model, and then executed by the test automation tool to produce an execution traceability matrix. The process model of test scripts now acts as source entities in the fault localization techniques, namely, Tarantula and statistical bug isolation (SBI). Finally, the analysis of the test scripts can lead the testing team to conclude root for the failure. In [305], DeMillo et al. propose a model for analyzing software failures and faults for debugging purposes. Failure modes and failure types are defined to identify the existence of program failures and to analyze the nature of program failures, respectively. Failure modes are used to answer the question "How do we know the execution of a program fails?" and failure types are used to answer the question "What is the failure?" When abnormal behavior is observed during program execution, the failure is classified by its corresponding failure mode. Referring to some pre-established relationships between failure modes and failure types, certain failure types can be identified as possible causes for the failure. Heuristics based on dynamic instrumentation (such as dynamic slice) and testing information are then used to reduce the search domain for locating the fault by predicting possible faulty statements. A significant drawback of using this model is that it is extremely difficult, if not impossible, to obtain an exhaustive list of failure modes because different programs can have very different abnormal behavior and symptoms when they fail. As a result, we do not have a complete relationship between all possible failure modes and failure types, and we might not be able to identify possible failure types responsible for the failure being analyzed. Lehmann and Pradel [349] propose DBDB to test real-life debuggers. It builds a finite-state model to capture common features of debuggers and compares the behavior of two debuggers with generated sequences of debugging actions. The diverging behavior and other noteworthy differences indicate a potential bug in the debugger. Wang et al. [350] apply topic model to learn and rank bug patterns for bugs located in complex program loops. Troya et al. [351] use model transformations (MTs) and assertions for fault localization. Given a set of MTs (mechanisms that manipulate and transform models), a set of assertions and source models, the violated assertions will be identified. Together with the MT coverage information, the transformation rules that deal with the construction of part of the target model will be ranked according to their suspiciousness of containing a bug.

1.3.8 Additional Techniques

In addition to those discussed above, there are other techniques for software fault localization. Many of them focus on specific program languages or testing scenarios. Listed below are a few examples.

Development of software systems, while enhancing functionality, will inevitably lead to the introduction of new bugs, which may not be detected immediately. Tracing the behavior changes to code changes can be highly time-consuming. Bohnet et al. [352] propose a technique to identify recently introduced changes. Dynamic, static, and code change information is combined to reduce the large number of changes that may have an impact on faulty executions of the system. In this way, root cause changes can be semiautomatically located.

In spite of using garbage collection, Java programs may still suffer from memory leaks due to unwanted references. Chen and Chen [353] develop an aspect-based tool, FindLeak, utilizing an aspect to gather memory consumption statistics and object references created during a program execution. Collected information is then analyzed to help detect memory leaks.

An implicit social network model is presented in [354] to predict possible locations of faults using fault locations cited by similar historical bug reports retrieved from bug report managing systems (BRMS).

In [355], de Souza and Chaim propose a technique using integration coverage data to locate bugs. By ranking the most suspicious pairs of method invocations, *roadmaps*, which are sorted lists of methods to be investigated, are created.

Gong et al. [356] propose an interactive fault localization technique, TALK, which incorporates programmers' feedback into SBFL techniques. Each time a programmer inspects a suspicious program element in the ranking generated by a fault localization technique, they can judge the correctness of the element and provide this information as feedback to reorder the ranking of elements that are not yet inspected. The authors demonstrate that using programmers' feedback can help increase the effectiveness of existing fault localization techniques. Lin et al. [357] propose a feedback-based fault localization technique. Given a faulty program, the execution trace is first recorded and later developers will provide light-weight feedback on trace steps. Based on the feedbacks, suspicious steps on the trace are identified. In addition, the proposed method is able to learn and approximate bug-free paths to reduce the volume of feedbacks for the debugging process. Li et al. [358] propose another interactive, feedback-based fault localization technique. They ask developers contextualized questions in terms of queries regarding the inputs and outputs related to concrete instances of suspicious method invocations.

To better understand a program's behavior, software developers must translate their questions into code-related queries, speculating about the causes of faults. Whyline [359] is a debugging tool that avoids such speculation by enabling developers to select from a set of "why did" and "why didn't" questions derived from source code. Using a combination of static and dynamic slicing, and precise call graphs, the tool can find possible explanations of failures.

Cheng et al. [360] propose a software fault localization technique that mines bug signatures within a program. A bug signature is a set of program elements that are executed by most failed tests but not by successful tests in general. Bug signatures are ranked in descending order by a discriminative significance score indicating how likely it is to be related to the bug. This ranking is used to help identify the location of the bug.

Maruyama et al. [361] indicate that the culprit of an overwritten variable is always the last write-access to the memory location where the bug first appeared. Removing such bugs begins with finding the last write, followed by moving the control point of execution back to the time when the last write was executed. Generally, the statement that makes the last write will be faulty.

Liu et al. [362, 363] propose SimFL, a fault localization approach for Simulink models by combining statistical debugging and dynamic model slicing. For Simulink models, engineers not only identify whether a test case passes or fails but also routinely and explicitly determine which specific outputs are correct and which ones are incorrect for each given test case. Relying on this observation, they use a dynamic slicing technique in conjunction with statistical debugging to generate one spectrum per output and each test case. Hence, a set of spectra that is significantly larger than the size of the test suite is obtained. The authors then use this set of spectra to rank model blocks using statistical ranking formulas (Tarantula, Ochiai, and D*).

Wang et al. [364] investigate the factors that will affect the effectiveness of IR-based fault localization on four open-source programs. They found that the quality of bug reports determines the result of IR-based fault localization. Specifically, quality reports that contain program entity names tend to result in good ranked list of suspiciousness. In addition, the authors report that in practice the ranked lists generated by the IR-based fault localization techniques do not always help users debug; they only help when the techniques can generate perfect lists for bugs without rich, identifiable information in the reports. Moreover, if the generated list is not good enough, it can even harm developers' performance by leading them to focus on the wrong files.

Recently, some studies [365–374] have applied IR techniques to software fault localization. These studies use an initial bug report to rank the source code files in descending order based on their relevance to the bug report. The developers can then examine the ranking and identify the files that contain bugs. Unlike SBFL techniques, IR-based techniques do not require program coverage information, but their generated ranking is based solely on source code files rather than on program elements with finer granularity such as statements, blocks, or predicates. Rahman and Roy [375] combine context-aware query reformulation and IR to localize faulty entities from project source. It first determines whether there are excessive program entities in a bug report, then applies reformations to the query, and finally uses the improved query for fault localization with IR. Amar and Rigby [376] argue that faulty statements should appear only in failed test logs, but not successful test logs. In light of this, they remove from failed test logs all the statements that occur also in successful test logs, and then apply IR and kNN to flag the most suspicious lines for further investigation. Le et al. [377] propose using four types of features (i.e. suspiciousness score features, text features, topic model features, and metadata features) extracted from a bug report and an FL ranking list to build a model to predict the effectiveness of an IR-based FL technique. Hoang et al. [378] propose NetML, which utilizes multimodal information from both bug reports and program spectra for bug localization. Specifically, NetML applies network Lasso regularization to cluster both bug reports and program methods based on the similarity of their suspiciousness features. This clustering enforcement allows similar bug reports or methods to reach a consensus that leads to the same bug.

Algorithmic debugging (also called declarative debugging), first discussed in Shapiro's dissertation [8] with more details in [379, 380], decomposes a complex computation into a series of sub-computations to help locate program bugs. The outcome of each sub-computation is checked for its correctness with respect to given input values. Based on this, an algorithmic debugger is used to identify a portion of code that may contain bugs. One issue of applying this technique in practice is that testing oracles may not available for sub-computations.

Formula-based fault localization techniques [212, 381–386] rely on an encoding of failed execution traces into *error trace formulae*. By proving the unsatisfiability of an error trace formula using certain tools or algorithms, the programmer may capture the relevant statements causing the failure. Jose and Majumdar [383, 384] propose a technique, BugAssist, which uses a MAX-SAT solver to compute the maximal set of statements that may cause the failure from a failed execution trace. In [382], Ermis et al. introduce *error invariants*, which provide a semantic argument as to why certain statements of a failed execution trace are irrelevant to the root cause of the failure. By removing such statements, the bug can be located with less manual effort. A common weakness of these techniques [382–384] is that they only report a set of statements that may be responsible for the failure without providing the exact input values that make the executions go to those statements. Christ et al. [381] address this problem by reporting an extended study based on error invariants [382] that encodes a failed execution trace into a *flow-sensitive error trace formula*. In addition to providing a set of statements that are relevant to the failure, they also specify how these statements can be executed using different input values. Lamraoui and Nakajima [385] propose a formula-based fault localization method for automatic fault localization, which combines the SAT-based formal verification techniques with Reiter's model-based diagnosis theory. They implement their method by following the MaxSAT approach and the using Yices SMT solver. Their method gives a high performance in both single and multiple fault problems according to experiments using their tool SNIPER. Le et al. [212] propose Savant, a new fault localization approach that employs a learning-to-rank strategy, using likely invariant diffs and suspiciousness scores as features, to rank methods based on their likelihood of being a root cause of a failure. Savant has four steps: method clustering and test case selection, invariant mining, feature extraction, and method ranking. Savant then produces a ranked list of potentially buggy methods. However, such learning-to-rank strategy can be greatly influenced by the size of the recommended files with respect to the efficiency in detecting bugs [387]. Roychoudhury and Chandra [386] give a discussion about computer-assisted Debugging techniques. First, the authors present a major challenge in debugging – the lack of specifications capturing the intended behavior of the program. Then, they discuss how the symbolic execution techniques help debugging against this challenge. Finally, they give a forward-looking view of symbolic analysis used for automated program repair.

During program maintenance, source code may be modified to fix bugs or enhanced to support new functionalities. Regression testing is also conducted to prevent invalidation of previously tested functionality. If an execution fails, the programmer needs to find the failure-inducing changes. Crisp [16] is a tool to build a compliant intermediate version of the program by adding a partial edit (i.e. a subset of recent changes) to the code before the maintenance is performed. This tool helps programmers focus on a specific portion of changes in the code during the debugging. Wu et al. [388] conduct an empirical study to characterize the crash inducing changes. Later, a learning model that uses these features and historical crash data is built to locate crashing changes from a given set of crash reports.

Chen et al. [389] apply SFBL to diagnose problems in SDN network. The SDN-based coverage matrix consists of entries of flow rules, test cases constructed by rows and columns of association table, as well as the result vector that represents the state of the last judged network behavior.

Christi et al. [390] apply SFBL to reduce search space in test-based software modification (TBSM) when building resource-adaptive software. The modification is the diff between the original program and the adaptation. The purpose of resource adaptations is to avoid faults in correctness or performance that occur in low-resource settings. In order to map FL to TBSM, the "faulty code" in TBSM is the code that needs to be modified or removed for an adaptation, the "failing tests" are the labeled tests that are marked as pertaining to a feature to be removed from the program, and the "passing tests" are the unlabeled tests or retained tests.

Concurrent programs are becoming more prevalent in applications that affect our everyday lives. However, due to their non-determinism, it is very difficult to debug these programs. It is proposed that injecting random timing noise into many points within a program can assist in eliciting bugs. Once the bug is triggered, the objective is to identify a small set of points that indicate the source of the bug. In [247], the authors propose an algorithm that iteratively samples a lower dimensional projection of the program space and identifies candidate-relevant points. Refer to Section 1.7.7 for more discussions.

1.3.9 Distribution of Papers in Our Repository

Figure 1.3 shows the distribution of papers in our repository across all categories. Spectrum-based is the most dominant category with 34% of all the papers[3] followed by model-based, which contains 17%, and sliced-based, which contains 16%. The number of papers in each of the statistics-based, program state-based, spreadsheet-based, and others categories is between 5 and 9%, followed by machine learning-based, which is 3%. The data mining and IR-based categories have the fewest number of papers, constituting only 2% each.

We present below the distribution using a different classification: static and dynamic slice-based, execution slice and program spectrum-based, and other techniques (see Endnote 3 for the rationale). Figure 1.4 gives the number of papers published each year with respect to this new classification. The first (leftmost) bar gives the total number of papers from 1977 to 1995, the last (rightmost) only

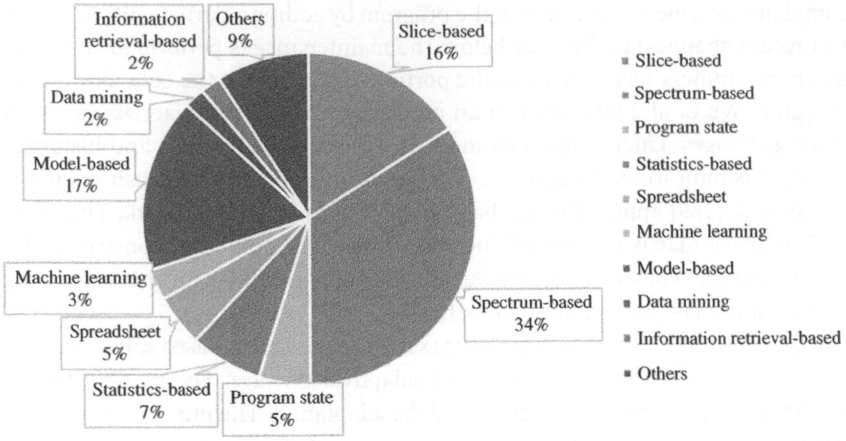

Figure 1.3 Distribution of papers in our repository.

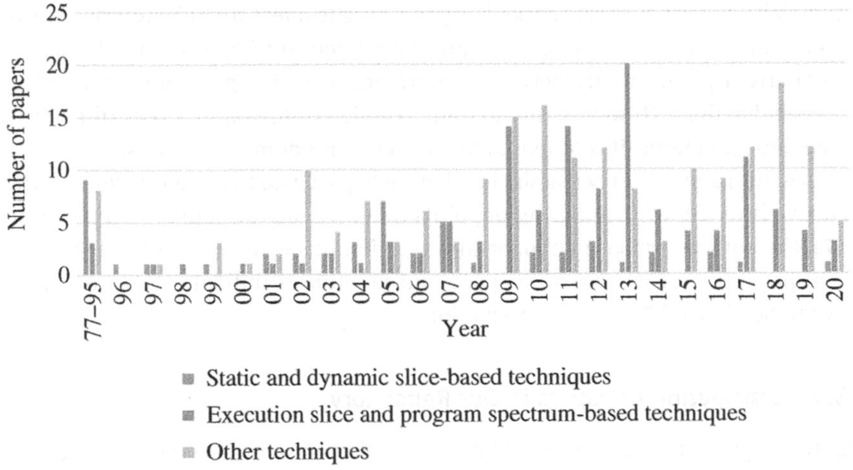

Figure 1.4 Number of papers published each year with respect to three different categories.

counts papers from 2016, and those in between give the number in the corresponding year. Figure 1.5 displays the information from a cumulative point of view. Each data point gives the cumulative number of papers published up to the corresponding year. From these two figures, we make the following observations:

- Static and dynamic slice-based techniques were popular between 2002 and 2007. However, the number of papers each year in this category has decreased since then.

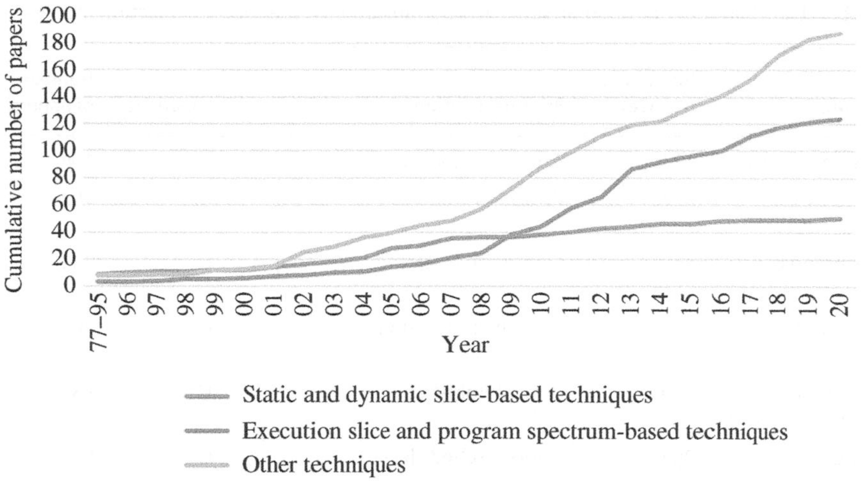

Figure 1.5 Cumulative number of papers with respect to three different categories.

- The number of papers on execution slice and program spectrum-based techniques has increased dramatically since 2008, indicating that more studies are focused on these techniques rather than static or dynamic slice-based techniques in the recent years.

1.4 Subject Programs

Table 1.6 presents a list of popular subject programs used to study the effectiveness of different fault localization techniques. This table gives the name, the size (lines of code), a brief description of the functionality, the programming language, and the number of papers that use this program.

We notice that the Siemens suite is the most frequently used. However, every program in the suite is very small, with less than 600 lines of code (excluding blank lines). Another important point worth noting is that most of the bugs used in the experiments are mutation-based artificially injected bugs. Although mutation has been shown to be an effective approach to simulate realistic faults [214, 391–393], some real-life bugs are very delicate and cannot be modeled by simple first-order mutants.

With the introduction of advanced techniques in software fault localization, more accurate cross comparisons of their effectiveness are in demand. Furthermore, the feasibility of a technique and the benefits of using it should be

Table 1.6 Summary of popular subject programs used in the fault localization studies.

Name	Size (Lines of code)	Brief description	Language	Number of papers
Siemens: tcas	173	Altitude separation	C	106
Siemens: schedule	412	Priority scheduler	C	102
Siemens: print_tokens	565	Lexical analyzer	C	102
Siemens: replace	563	Pattern recognition	C	100
Siemens: print_tokens2	510	Lexical analyzer	C	98
Siemens: schedule2	307	Priority scheduler	C	98
Siemens: tot_info	406	Information measure	C	97
grep	12 653	Command-line utility for searching plain-text data sets	C	38
space	9126	ADL Interpreter	C	36
gzip	6573	Data compression	C	36
sed	12 062	GNU batch stream editor	C	20
flex	13 892	Lexical analyzer generator	C	18
NanoXML	7646	XML parser	Java	17
Unix: Cal	202	Print a calendar for a specified year or month	C	13
Unix: Col	308	Filter reverse line	C	13
Unix: Tr	137	Translate characters	C	13
Unix: Spline	338	Interpolate smooth curves based on given data	C	12
Unix: Uniq	143	Report or remove adjacent duplicate lines	C	12
Unix: Chckeq	102	Report missing or unbalanced delimiters and .EQ/.EN pairs	C	11
make	20 014	Manage building of executable and other products from code	C	10
Ant	75 333	Java applications builder	Java	10
XML-sec	21 613	Library for XML encryption	C	9

Table 1.6 (Continued)

Name	Size (Lines of code)	Brief description	Language	Number of papers
Unix: Look	170	Find words in the system dictionary or lines in a sorted list	C	7
Unix: Comm	167	Select or reject lines common to two sorted files	C	6
tar	25 854	Tool to create file archives	C	6
DC	2700	Reverse-polish desk calculator	Java	5
Unix: Crypt	134	Encrypt and decrypt a file using a user-supplied password	C	5
Unix: Sort	913	Sort and merge files	C	5
gcc	222 196	GNU C compiler	C	5
apache	85 661	HTTP server for hosting web applications	C	5
schoolmate	4263	A PHP/MySQL solution for administering schools	PHP	4
FAQforge	734	A tool for creating and managing documents	PHP	4
webchess	2226	An online chess game	JS and PHP	4
jtopas	5400	Text parser	Java	4
timeclock	13 879	A web-based clock system	C	3
phpsysinfo	7745	Displays system information, e.g. uptime, CPU, and memory	C	3
TCC	1900	A small and fast compiler for the C programming language	C	3
Xerces	52 528	XML parser	C++	3
Mozilla Firefox	21M	Web browser	C and C++	3
tidy	31 132	A text editor for editing web content	C++	3

demonstrated in an industry-like environment, in contrast to an academic laboratory-oriented controlled environment. In response to these challenges, more and more studies use larger and complex programs in their experiments. Another trend is to use bugs actually introduced at the development phase such as those from Bugzilla for the gcc program and the bugs for Mozilla Firefox.

1.5 Evaluation Metrics

Since a program bug may span multiple lines of code, which are not necessarily contiguous or in the same module, the examination of suspicious code stops as long as one faulty location is identified. This is because the focus is to help programmers find a good starting point to initiate the bug-fixing process rather than to provide the complete set of code that must be modified, deleted, or added with respect to each bug. With this in mind, the effectiveness of a software fault localization technique is defined as the percentage of code[4] that needs to be examined before the first faulty location for a given bug is identified.

The T-score [188, 214] estimates the percentage of code a programmer need not examine before the first faulty location is found. A PDG is constructed, and the nodes are marked as *faulty* if they are reported by differencing the correct and the faulty versions of the program, and *blamed* if they are reported by the localizer. For a node n, the corresponding *k-dependency sphere set* (DS_k) is the set of nodes for which there is a directed path of length no more than k that joins n and them. For example, DS_0 contains the node n itself. DS_1 includes not only n but also all the nodes such that there is an edge from them to n, or from n to them. For a report R (i.e. a set of nodes the localizer indicates as possible locations of the bug), let $DS_*(R)$ be the smallest dependency sphere that includes a faulty node. The T-score of a given R is computed using the ratio of the number of nodes in its smallest dependency sphere to the number of nodes in the entire PDG:

$$\text{T-score} = 1 - \frac{| DS_*(R) |}{| PDG |}$$

The use of T-score requires that programmers are able to distinguish defects from non-defects at each location and can do so at the same cost for each location considered [193]. Furthermore, it assumes that programmers can follow the control- and/or data-dependency relations among statements while searching for faults.

The EXAM [117, 144, 201, 202, 277] or *Expense* [107] score is the percentage of statements in a program that has to be examined until the first faulty statement is reached:

$$\text{EXAM score} = \frac{\text{Number of statements examined}}{\text{Total number of statements in the program}} \times 100\%$$

In [107], the authors use the executable statements instead of the total number of statements. For techniques such as [394] that generate a ranking of predicates (instead of statements) sorted in descending order of their fault relevance, the

EXAM score can also be computed in terms of percentage of predicates that need to be examined. The P-score [123] defined as follows uses the same approach:

$$\text{P-score} = \frac{\text{1-based index of } P \text{ in } L}{\text{number of predicates in } L} \times 100\%$$

where L is a list of sorted predicates as described above, P is the most fault-relevant predicate to a fault, and the notation of 1-based index means the first predicate of L is indexed by 1 (rather than 0). Studies in [117, 197, 201, 202, 277] also provide figures that report the percentage of all the faulty versions of a given program in which faults can be located by the examination of an amount of code less than or equal to a given EXAM score. A similar idea is subsequently used by Gong et al. to define the N-score [105]:

$$\text{N-score} = \frac{N_{\text{detected}}}{N_{\text{statistic}}} \times 100\%$$

When compared to T-score, EXAM is easier to understand, as it is directly proportional to the amount of code to be examined rather than to an indirect measurement in terms of the amount of code that does not need to be examined (as what T-score does). In summary, the lower the EXAM score (or *Expense* or P-score), the more effective the technique, whereas it is the opposite for the T-score (i.e. the lower the T-score, the less effective the technique).

The Wilcoxon signed-rank test (an alternative to the paired Student's t-test when a normal distribution of the population cannot be assumed) can also be used as a metric to present an evaluation from a statistical point of view [197, 203]. If we assume a technique α is more effective than another technique β, we examine the one-tailed alternative hypothesis that β requires the examination of an equal or greater number of statements than α. The confidence with which the alternative hypothesis can be accepted helps us determine whether α is statistically more effective than β. Another metric is the total (cumulative) number of statements that need to be examined to locate all bugs of a given scenario [117, 197, 201, 202]. This metric gives a global view in contrast to the Wilcoxon test, which focuses more on individual pairwise comparisons.

An effective fault localization technique should assign a unique suspiciousness value to each statement; in practice, however, the same suspiciousness may be assigned to different statements. If this happens, two different levels of effectiveness result: the *best* and the *worst*. The *best* effectiveness assumes that the faulty statement is the first to be examined among all the statements of the same suspiciousness. The *worst* effectiveness occurs if the faulty statement is the last to be examined. Reporting only the worst case (such as [139, 395]) or only the best case (such as the P-score in [123]) may not give the complete picture because it is very unlikely that programmers will face the worst or the best case scenario in practice.

In most cases, they will see something between the best and the worst. It is straightforward to compute the average effectiveness from the best and worst effectiveness. However, the converse is not true. Providing the average effectiveness offers no insights on where the best and worst effectiveness may lie, and, more seriously, can be ambiguous and misleading. For example, two techniques can have the same average effectiveness, but one has a smaller range between the best and the worse cases while the other has a much wider range. As a result, these two techniques should not be viewed as equally effective as suggested by their average effectiveness. Thus, a better approach is to report the effectiveness for both the best and the worst cases such as [117, 201, 202, 277] and perform the cross-evaluation under each scenario.

All the evaluation metrics discussed above are based on an assumption of perfect bug detection, which is the same as having an *ideal user* [188] to examine suspicious code to determine whether it contains bugs. That is, a bug in a statement will be detected if the statement is examined. However, a recent study [396] indicates that such an assumption does not always hold in practice. If so, the number of statements that need to be examined to find the bug may increase. Xie et al. [397] report that fault localization techniques might even slightly weaken programmers' abilities in identifying the root faults. On the other hand, Xia et al. [398] suggest that the studies [396] and [397] suffer from several drawbacks: (i) only using small-sized programs, (ii) only involving students, and (iii) only using dated fault localization techniques. The discussion by Le et al. [399] is also similar. In response, Xia et al. conduct a study based on four large-sized open-source projects with professional software programmers. They find that fault localization techniques can help professionals reduce their debugging time, and the improvements are statistically significant and substantial. To investigate how fault localization should be improved to better benefit practitioners, Kochhar et al. [204] highlight some directions by conducting a literature review.

There are other factors that may affect the effectiveness of a software fault localization technique. Bo et al. [100] present a metric, *Relative Expense*, to study the impact of test set size on the *Expense* score. More discussion regarding the impact of test cases on fault localization appears in Section 1.7.2. Monperrus [400] suggests that effectiveness should be evaluated with respect to different classes of faults. It is possible that one technique is more effective than another for bugs that can be triggered consistently under some well-defined conditions (namely, Bohrbugs in [76]), but less effective for bugs whose failures cannot be systematically reproduced (namely, Mandelbugs). Instrumentation overhead, interference within multiple bugs, and programming language also have an impact on effectiveness of fault localization [401, 402].

Last but not least, it is important to realize that software fault localization techniques should not be evaluated only in terms of effectiveness as described above

[396]. Other factors such as computational overhead, time and space for data collection, amount of human effort, and tool support need also be considered. In addition, we also need to emphasize user-centered aims such as how programmers actually debug, how they reveal the cause-effect chains of failures, and how they decide upon solutions beyond a suspiciousness ranking of code. Unfortunately, none of the published studies has reported a comprehensive evaluation covering all these aspects.

1.6 Software Fault Localization Tools

One challenge for many empirical studies on software fault localization is that they require appropriate tool support for automatic or semiautomatic data collection and suspiciousness computation. Table 1.7 gives a list of commonly used tools, including name, a brief description, availability, and which papers use the tool. Out of the 82 tools, three are commercial, 20 are open source, 12 are openly accessible but the source code is not available, and the rest may be acquired by contacting their authors.

Table 1.7 Summary of tools used in the fault localization studies.

Name	Brief description	Availability	Papers using the tool
Ample	Eclipse plug-in for identifying faulty classes in Java program	Openly accessible	[95]
Apollo	Automatic tool that efficiently finds and localizes malformed HTML and execution failures in web applications that execute PHP code on the server side	Via author	[403]
Atomizer	A dynamic atomicity checker	Via author	[404]
AUTOFLOX	Automated fault localization tool based on dynamic backward slicing	Via author	[150]
ATAC/χslice	Slicing and dicing tool for ANSI C programs	Via author	[140, 166, 175]
BARINEL	Framework to combine spectrum-based fault localization and model-based diagnosis	Via author	[318]
BigDebug	Interactive debugger for big data analytics in Apache Spark	Via author	[405, 406]

(*Continued*)

Table 1.7 (Continued)

Name	Brief description	Availability	Papers using the tool
BigSift	Debugging tool kit for big data analytics	Via author	[405, 407]
BugAssist	Fault localization tool for ANSI-C programs	Via author	[383, 384]
BugFix	A machine learning-based tool for program debugging	Via author	[408]
C2V	Validation tool for C code coverage tools	Via author	[409]
Chianti	Impact analyzer of program changes for Java programs	Via author	[26]
Chislice	Execution slicing tool	Via author	[166]
Chord	Debugging tool for concurrent program	Via author	[410]
CIL framework	Tool for extracting control flow graph and data flow information from C programs	Via author	[304]
Clover	Tool for collecting execution trace information for Java programs	Commercial	[101]
CnC	Static checking and testing tool	Openly accessible	[411]
CPTEST	A framework for automatic fault detection, localization, and correction of constraint programs	Via author	[412]
CRADLE	Validation tool for deep learning libraries	Via author	[413]
Crisp	Eclipse plug-in for constructing intermediate versions of a Java program that is being edited	Via author	[26]
Daikon	Dynamic invariant detector	Open source	[207, 414]
DBGBENCH	Tool benchmark for debugging in practice	Openly accessible	[415]
DejaVu	Regression test selection tool	Via author	[181]
Delta	Tool for delta debugging	Open source	[256]
Diablo	A link-time optimizer	Open source	[260]
DiffJ	Tool for comparing different versions of programs to find bugs	Open source	[139]

Table 1.7 (Continued)

Name	Brief description	Availability	Papers using the tool
Doxygen	Source code documentation generator and static analysis	Open source	[352]
DrDebug	Debugging tool integrating dynamic slicing and GDB debugger	Open source	[142, 154]
ESC/Java	Compile-time program checker to detect precondition violations	Open source	[411]
FindLeaks	Aspect-based tool to locate memory leaks in Java programs	Via author	[353]
Gcov	Profiling tool to collect program spectra	Open source	[100, 104, 223, 416]
GNU GDB	A debugger developed by GNU	Open source	[83]
gprof	GNU's profiling tool	Open source	[88]
GoalDebug	Constraint-based spreadsheet debugging tool	Via author	[417]
GZoltar	An automated testing and debugging framework	Openly accessible	[418, 419]
HOLMES	Statistical debugging tool	Via author	[240]
HSFal	Hybrid slice spectrum fault locator	Via author	[144]
iFL	A support tool for interactive fault localization in Eclipse IDE	Open source	[420]
JaCoCo	Java code coverage library	Open source	[419]
Jaguar	A spectrum-based fault localization tool	Open source	[421]
JARDIS	Debugging tool for JavaScript/Node.js	Via author	[422]
JavaPDG	A new platform for program dependence analysis	Openly accessible	[423]
JCoverage	A tool for coverage analysis	Open source	[215]
JCrasher	Java test cases generator to exhibit the error	Open source	[411]
Jhawk	Java static analysis tool	Commercial	[97]
JMutator	Mutation tool using seven mutation operators for Java programs	Open source	[424]
JTracor	Tool for collecting execution trace for Java programs	Via author	[424]

(*Continued*)

Table 1.7 (Continued)

Name	Brief description	Availability	Papers using the tool
JUMBLE	Tool for detecting destructive races	Via author	[425]
Phoenix Framework	A framework for developing compilers as well as program analysis, testing, and optimization	Openly accessible (from Microsoft)	[240]
MCFuzz	Debugging tool for software model checkers	Via author	[426]
MDebugger	A model-level debugger for RTE systems in the context of UML-RT	Via author	[427]
Microsoft Visual Studio Debugger	A debugging tool embedded in Microsoft Visual Studio	Commercial	[84]
MZoltar	Automatic debugging tool for android applications	Via author	[419]
N-Prog	Tool for bug detection and test case generation using random mutation and N-variant systems	Via author	[428]
NonDex	Tool for detecting and debugging wrong assumptions on Java API specifications	Via author	[429]
Pinpoint	Fault localization tool using Jaccard coefficient	Via author	[95]
Penelope	Tool for atomicity violations detection	Via author	[430]
RADAR	Debugging tool for regression problems in C/C++ programs	Openly accessible	[431]
RacerX	Debugging tool for concurrent program	Via author	[432]
Reactive Inspector	Debugger for reactive programs integrated with Eclipse Scala IDE	Open source	[433]
RxFiddle	Visualization and debugging tool for reactive extensions	Via author	[434]
Signpost	Tool for matching program behavior against known faults	via author	[435]
SLAM toolkit	Debugging tool using static analysis	Openly accessible	[329]
SLforge	CPS tool chain testing scheme	Via author	[436]

Table 1.7 (Continued)

Name	Brief description	Availability	Papers using the tool
SLOCCount	Tool for counting executable statements	Open source	[214, 241]
SmartDebug	Interactive debug assistant for Java	Via author	[437]
Spyder	Back-tracing debugger based on dynamic slicing	Via author	[140]
SNIPER	A formula-based fault localization tool	Via author	[385]
Tarantula	Fault localization tool using Tarantula	Openly accessible	[95, 175, 214]
TPTP	Eclipse plugin for profiling	Openly accessible	[89]
VART	Eclipse plugin for debugging regression faults	Openly accessible	[438]
VIDA	Visual interactive debugging tool	Via author	[439]
VHDLDIAG	A VHDL fault localization tool based on model-based diagnosis	Via author	[343]
WhoseFault	Debugging assignment tool	Via author	[440]
Whyline	An interactive debugging tool	Openly accessible	[359]
Xlab	X window system events recorder	Open source	[361]
Zoltar	Spectrum-based fault localization tool	Via author	[199]
Zoltar-M	Tool for detecting multiple bugs	Via author	[416]
χProf	Tool using execution trace to locate performance bottlenecks	Via author	[171]
χRegress	Regression test set minimization tool using program coverage and execution cost	Via author	[171]
χSuds	Tool for collecting execution trace information for C programs	Via author	[117, 171, 173, 178, 197, 201–203, 277]
χVue	Heuristics involving the control graph, execution trace, and the maintainer's knowledge to help locate features and identify feature interactions	Via author	[171]

1.7 Critical Aspects

In this section, we explore some critical aspects of software fault localization.

1.7.1 Fault Localization with Multiple Bugs

The majority of published papers in software fault localization focus on programs with a single bug (i.e. each faulty program has exactly one bug) [441]. However, this is not the case for real-life software, which in general contains multiple bugs [442]. Results of a study [443] based on an analysis of fault and failure data from two large, real-world projects show that individual failures are often triggered by multiple bugs spread throughout the system. Another study [444] also reports a similar finding. This observation raises doubts concerning the validity of some heuristics and assumptions based on the single-bug scenario. In response, studies have been conducted using programs with multiple bugs [104, 270, 394, 401, 445–457].

A popular assumption is that multiple bugs in the same program perform independently [458]. Debroy and Wong [401] examine possible interactions that may take place between different bugs, and they find that such interferences may manifest themselves to either trigger or mask some execution failures. Results based on their experiments indicate that destructive interference (when execution fails due to a bug but no longer fails when another bug is added to the same program) is more common than constructive interference (when execution fails in the presence of two bugs in the same program but does not in the presence of either bug alone) because failures are masked more often than triggered by additional bugs. It is also possible that a program with multiple bugs suffers from both destructive and constructive interferences. DiGiuseppe and Jones [104] also report that multiple bugs have an adverse impact on the effectiveness of spectrum-based techniques.

One way to debug a multiple-bug program is to follow the *one-bug-at-a-time* approach. Perez et al. [441] study the prevalence of single-fault fixes in open-source Java projects and suggest that a software application may have many dormant bugs; however, they can be detected and fixed individually, therefore constituting single-faulted events. If a program experiences some failures while it is executed against test cases of a given test suite, this approach helps programmers find and fix a bug. Then, the modified program is tested again using all the test cases in the given test suite. If any of the executions fail, additional debugging is required to find and fix the next bug. This process continues until no failure is observed. At this point, even though the program may still contain other bugs, they cannot be detected by the current suite of test cases. This approach has been adopted in studies using the DStar technique [197] and a reasoning fault localization technique based on a Bayesian reasoning framework [318]. A potential weakness of most techniques based on Bayesian reasoning (e.g. [318, 459, 460]) is that they all assume program components fail independently; in other words, interferences among multiple bugs are ignored, which is not necessarily the case in practice.

In [449], Jones et al. suggest that multiple bugs in a program can be located in parallel. The first step is to group failed test cases into different *fault-focusing* clusters such that those in the same cluster are related to the same bug. Then, the Tarantula fault localization technique [107], failed tests in each cluster, and all the successful tests are used to identify the suspicious code for the corresponding bug.

There are different ways to cluster failed test cases. One approach is to use execution profiles. Podgurski et al. [450] apply *supervised and unsupervised pattern classifications* as well as *multivariate visualization* to execution profiles of failed test cases in order to group them into fault-focusing clusters. Steimann and Frenkel [452] use the *Weil–Kettler algorithm*, a technique widely used in integer linear programming, to cluster failed test cases. It is very critical to choose the right clustering algorithm, as misgrouping can significantly decrease the FL effectiveness for programs with multiple bugs [461].

However, clustering based on the similarity between execution profiles may not reflect an accurate causation relationship between certain faults and the corresponding failed executions. For example, two failed tests, even associated with the same bug, may have very different execution profiles. It is possible for clustering techniques based on execution profiles to separate these two failed tests into different clusters.

To overcome this problem, Liu and Han [462, 463] further investigate the *due-to* relationship between failed tests and underlying bugs. They apply SOBER [443] to each failed test case and all the successful tests to generate a corresponding predicate ranking. The weighted Kendall tau distance is computed between these rankings. The distance between two rankings is small if they identify similar suspicious predicates. It also implies the rank-proximity (R-proximity) between them is high. Failed test cases with high R-proximity are clustered together, as they are likely to have the same *due-to* relationship.

Other variations include the use of more effective fault localization techniques (such as crosstab [202], RBF [201], and DStar [197]) instead of Tarantula or SOBER, or using only a subset, rather than all, of the successful tests (see Section 1.7.2). These variations are yet to be explored.

Gao and Wong [464] propose MSeer for locating multiple bugs in parallel. It first uses a revised Kendall tau distance to measure the distance between two failed tests, and then applies an approach to simultaneously estimate the number of clusters and assign initial medoids to these clusters. Later, an improved K-medoids clustering algorithm is implemented to identify failed tests and their corresponding bugs. Their case studies suggest that MSeer outperforms Jones's technique [449] in terms of both effectiveness and efficiency for parallel debugging.

1.7.2 Inputs, Outputs, and Impact of Test Cases

In addition to failed and successful test cases, many (although not all) techniques discussed in Section 1.3 also need information about how the underlying program/model is executed with respect to each test case. Such details can be provided via different execution profiles (e.g. coverage in terms of statement and predicate).

The output of many spectrum-based (Section 1.3.2) fault localization techniques (such as Tarantula) is a suspiciousness ranking with statements ranked in descending order of their suspiciousness values (such as the rightmost column of Table 1.3). To locate a bug, programmers will examine statements at higher positions of a ranking before statements at lower positions because the former, with higher suspiciousness values, are more likely to contain bugs than the latter. On the other hand, many slice-based techniques (Section 1.3.1) only return a set of statements without specific ranking. Referring to Table 1.2, the static slice for the variable *product* is a set of eight statements, including s_1, s_2, s_4, s_5, s_7, s_8, s_{10}, and s_{13}. However, it does not tell programmers which statements are more likely to contain bugs and should therefore be examined first for possible bug locations.

Techniques discussed in Section 1.3.3 (statistics-based), Section 1.3.5 (machine learning-based), and Section 1.3.6 (data mining-based) are likely[5] to generate outputs in terms of suspiciousness rankings similar to those generated by the spectrum-based techniques, whereas program state-based (Section 1.3.4) and model-based (Section 1.3.7) techniques are more likely to output a set of program/model components that will possibly contain bugs but do not explicitly specify the ranking of each component. Although both types of outputs provide suspicious components (statements, predicates, etc.) to help locate bugs, the former further prioritizes these components based on their suspiciousness values, but the latter does not.

The suite of test cases used in the program debugging is another important factor that may affect the effectiveness of a fault localization technique [93, 465, 466]. Some fault localization techniques (e.g. [166, 188, 192, 193, 221, 331, 332]) focus on locating program bugs using either a single failed test case or a single failed test case with a few successful test cases. Others (e.g. [107, 117, 176, 178, 201, 202, 213, 214, 277]) use multiple failed and successful test cases. These latter techniques take advantage of more test cases than the former, so it is likely that the latter are more effective in locating program bugs. For example, Tarantula [107], which uses multiple failed and multiple successful tests, has been shown to be more effective than nearest neighbor [188], a technique that only uses one failed and one successful test. However, it is important to note that by considering only one successful and one failed test, it may be possible to align the two test cases and arrive at a more detailed root-cause explanation of the failure [193] when compared to the techniques that take into account multiple successful and failed test cases simultaneously.

Although techniques using multiple failed and multiple successful test cases may have better fault localization effectiveness, an underlying assumption is that a large set of such tests is available. This may also lead to the assumption of existence of an oracle that can be used to automatically determine whether an execution is successful or failed. Unfortunately, this may not be true in the real world, as a test oracle can be incomplete, out-of-date, or ambiguous. Studies such as [467, 468] have reported that for many systems and for much of testing as currently practiced in industry, testers do not have formal specifications, assertions, or automated oracles. As a result, they face the potentially daunting task of manually checking the system's behavior for all test cases executed. In response to this challenge, researchers have presented various solutions [469–472]. Nevertheless, how to generate an automated test oracle still remains an issue that needs to be further explored. Hence, we cannot take it for granted that there are multiple tests with all execution results (successes or failures) known.

Using a test suite that does not achieve high coverage of the target program may have an adverse impact on the fault localization results. During test generation, different criteria (e.g. requirements-based boundary value analysis, or white-box-based statement or decision coverage) can be used as guidance. Diaz et al. [473] use a meta-heuristic technique (a so-called Tabu Search approach) to automatically generate a test suite to obtain maximum branch coverage. In [403, 474, 475], Artzi et al. present a tool called Apollo to generate test cases automatically based on combined concrete and symbolic executions. Apollo first executes a program on an empty input and records a path constraint that reflects the program's executed control-flow predicates. New inputs are then generated by changing predicates in the path constraint and solving the resulting constraints. Executing the program on these inputs produces additional control-flow paths. Failures observed during executions are recorded. This process is repeated until a predefined threshold of statements coverage is reached, a sufficient number of faults are detected, or the time budget is exhausted. Xu et al. [476] introduce a bug detection mechanism for Python programs. The mechanism first collects an execution trace, and later encodes this trace and branches that are unexecuted to symbolic constraints. By solving these constraints, potential bugs as well as their triggering inputs can be identified. Jiang et al. [477] suggest that test suites satisfying branch coverage are better than those satisfying statement coverage in effectively supporting fault localization, whereas Jiang et al. [478] claim that test suites satisfying MC/DC coverage are better than those satisfying branch coverage. Furthermore, in [479], Santelices et al. study the fault localization effectiveness of Tarantula using three types of program coverage – statements, branches, and define-use pair. They conclude that Tarantula using define-use pair coverage is more effective and stable than that using branch coverage, which is more effective than that using statement coverage. Based on this, the authors further propose to use a combination of the three types of coverage to achieve better fault localization effectiveness.

Some researchers argue that it is not efficient to use all the test cases in a given test suite to locate program bugs. Instead, they use either *test case reduction* by selecting only a subset of test cases or *test case prioritization* by assigning different priorities to different cases to improve the efficiency of fault localization techniques [100, 477, 480–496]. One approach of test prioritization is to give higher priority to failed test cases that execute fewer statements, as they provide more information and minimize the search domain [497]. In [498, 499], the authors propose an approach to generate balanced test suites in order to improve fault localization effectiveness by cloning failed test cases a suitable number of times to match the number of successful test cases. Rößler et al. [500] propose a technique, BUGEX, which applies dynamic symbolic execution to generate test cases with a minimal difference from the execution path of a single failed test case. Based on the generated test cases, the branches that are executed by more failed test cases but fewer successful test cases are more likely to cause the failure. The study in [191] applies a similar test case generation approach, but the generated test cases are instead used with a SBFL technique to rank basic blocks in descending order according to their suspiciousness values. Hui [489] propose a test case generation technique GIA for fault localization, which combines genetic algorithm and artificial immune algorithm. Kim et al. [491] propose the Sungkyunkwan enhanced method, which is a fault localization method with a test case optimization technique. Zhang et al. [496] propose and evaluate the strategy to remove redundant test cases with repeated spectrum in coverage information. Results show that test cases are reduced by 58–99% on average without losing the performance of fault localization. Li et al. [492] propose a test case selection strategy using the concept of dynamic basic block (DBB) to select test cases that can potentially distinguish non-faulty statements from faulty statements. First, they identify all the DBBs such that the statements in the same DBB are covered by the same test cases in the target program. Then, they identify all the groups in the target program such that any two DBBs in the same group are covered by the same test cases. Finally, they identify one failed test case and use it to initiate the test case selection procedure. Li et al. [501] apply genetic algorithm to generate test cases for software product lines with the integration of FL techniques. Each test case is first converted into a unique binary string. Then, existing test cases are modified via the use of evolutionary operators such as crossover and mutation to create new test cases. This process is repeated until a predefined coverage criterion is satisfied. Then, the test set created to test a product is evaluated by FL techniques and reused to test another product of the same family. Liu et al. [502] propose two test case selection strategies to assist debugging process in real life. The first uses coefficient of variance (CV) to reveal failed test cases. The higher the CV of suspiciousness score of a failed test case, the more complex will be the distribution of suspiciousness scores of the statements covered by this test case, therefore requiring more effort for failure comprehension. The second strategy identifies coincidentally correct test cases and compares them with similar successful and failed test cases for better fault diagnosis. Chen et al. [503] suggest clustering the failed and successful test cases into different groups, each group having the same execution path. They improve FL effectiveness by selecting one failed group and its nearest successful group. Lekivetz and Morgan [504] argue that prior knowledge can help assume potential input combinations and finally identify failure-causing input combinations by analyzing their occurrence frequency in a test suite.

Baudry et al. [424] use a bacteriological approach (which is an adaptation of genetic algorithms) to bridge the gap between testing and diagnosis (fault localization) based on a *test-for-diagnosis* criterion. Test cases are generated to satisfy this criterion so that diagnosis algorithms can be used more efficiently. Their objective is to achieve a better diagnosis (a more efficient fault localization) using a minimal number of test cases. Perez et al. [505] evaluate a test suite's diagnosability for test optimization according to its density (how frequent the components are involved with tests), diversity (to what extent the combinations of components are distributed throughout the input domain), and uniqueness (to what extent the spectra related to the components are distinguishable). Studies such as [111, 486] focus on a cross-evaluation of the impacts of different test reduction and prioritization techniques on the efficiency of software fault localization.

Based on manual analysis of more than 100 bug reports and triggering tests, Just et al. [506] find that developer-provided tests supply more information for fault localization than user-provided tests. On the other hand, developer-provided tests may overestimate a technique's ability to rank a statement by suspiciousness.

Test execution sequence also has an impact on program debugging [507]. For example, it is possible that a program execution fails not because of the current test but because of a previous test that does not set up an appropriate execution environment for the current test. If a failure cannot be observed unless a group of test cases are executed in a specific sequence, then these test cases should be bundled together as one single failed test.

1.7.3 Coincidental Correctness

The concept of *coincidental correctness*, introduced by Budd and Angluin in [508], discusses the circumstances under which a test case produces one or more errors in the program state but the output of the program is still correct. This phenomenon can occur for many reasons. For example, given a faulty statement in which a variable is assigned with an incorrect value, in one test execution, this value may affect the output of the program and result in a failure. However, in another test execution, the value of this variable is later overwritten. Thus, the output of the program is not affected and failure is not triggered. Studies discussing *coincidental correctness* have been reported in recent years [329, 509–517].

Coincidental correctness can negatively impact the effectiveness of fault localization techniques. Ball et al. [329] claim that this is the reason why their technique fails to locate bugs in 3 out of 15 single-bug programs. Wang et al. [514] conclude that the effectiveness of Tarantula decreases when the frequency of *coincidental correctness* is high and increases when the frequency is low.

To overcome this problem, Masri and Assi [512] propose a technique to clean test suites by removing test cases that may introduce possible coincidental correctness for better fault localization effectiveness. Their technique is further enhanced by using fuzzy test suites and clustering analysis [518]. Liu et al. [517] propose to deal with coincidental correctness using a weighted fuzzy classification approach to identify and manipulate coincidentally correct test cases for fault localization. Bandyopadhyay and Ghosh [509] suggest a different approach by first measuring the likelihood of coincidental correctness of a successful test case based on the average proximity of its execution profile with that of all failed test cases. Such likelihood is assigned as the weight of the corresponding successful test case and used for subsequent suspiciousness computation. Zhang et al. [515] present FOnly, a technique that relies only on failed test cases to locate bugs statistically, even though fault localization commonly relies on both successful and failed tests. Zhang et al. [519] propose a fault localization technique, BlockRank, to calculate, contrast, and propagate the *mean edge profiles* between successful and failed executions to alleviate the impact of coincidental correctness. Zhou et al. [520] propose a new fault-localization approach based on the probability of coincidental correctness estimated via data-flow and control-flow analyses. They first estimate the probabilities of wrong temporal values of variables in memory generated by faulty statements that do not affect the final outputs, and then apply the control flows of the statements that have use-definition dependencies on these values to revise the probabilities.

1.7.4 Faults Introduced by Missing Code

One claim that can generally be made against fault localization techniques discussed in this chapter is that they are incapable of locating bugs resulting from missing code. For example, slice-based techniques will never be able to locate such bugs – since the *faulty* code is not even in the program. Therefore, this code will not appear in any of the slices. Based on this, one might conclude that most fault localization techniques are inappropriate for locating such bugs. Although this argument seems to be reasonable, it overlooks some important details. Admittedly, the missing code cannot be found in any of the slices. However, the omission of the code may trigger some adverse effects elsewhere in the program execution, such as the traversal of an incorrect branch in a decision statement. An abnormal program execution path (and, thus, the appearance of unexpected code in the corresponding slice) with respect to a given test case should hint to programmers that some omitted statements may be leading to control-flow anomalies. This implies that we are still able to identify suspicious code related to the omission error, such as the affected decision branch using slice-based techniques. A similar argument can also be made for other techniques, including but not limited to program spectrum-based (Section 1.3.2), statistics-based (Section 1.3.3), and program state-based techniques (Section 1.3.4). Thus, even though software fault localization techniques may not be able to pinpoint the exact locations of missing code, they can still provide a good starting point for the search.

1.7.5 Combination of Multiple Fault Localization Techniques

The effectiveness of a fault localization technique is very much scenario dependent, affected by successful and failed test cases, program structures and semantics, nature of the bugs, etc. There is no single technique superior to all others in every scenario. Thus, it makes sense to combine multiple techniques and retain the good qualities of individual techniques while mitigating the drawbacks of each. In [101, 521], Debroy et al. propose a way to do so by combining the rankings of statements generated by multiple techniques. The advantage of this approach (i.e. combining the rankings) over a design-based integration approach (in which the actual techniques would somehow be incorporated to form a new technique) is that it is more cost-effective to realize and is always extensible. Based on a similar idea, Lucia et al. [522] and Tang et al. [523] independently propose normalization methods to combine results of different fault localization techniques.

In [200], Abreu et al. address the inherent limitations of SBFL techniques, stating that component semantics of the program are not considered. They propose a way to enhance the diagnostic quality of a SBFL technique by combining it with a model-based debugging approach using the abstraction interpretation generated by a framework called DEPUTO. More precisely, a model-based approach is used to refine the ranking via filtering to exclude those components that do not explain the observed failures when the program's semantics are considered.

In [524], Wang et al. use two different search algorithms, simulated annealing and genetic algorithm, to find approximate optimal compositions from 22 existing

SBFL techniques. However, a search-based approach lacks flexibility and efficiency [525]. For flexibility, the search must be re-performed to update the optimal composition whenever a new fault localization technique is included. Also, an optimal composition for one program may not be the optimal for another program, which means the search process needs to be re-performed when the subject program changes. For efficiency, the potential large size of search space makes the search process very time-consuming.

Spectrum-based and slice-based techniques are both widely used. Combinations between techniques from these two categories have been reported [139, 395, 526, 527]. For example, in [139], Alves et al. combine Tarantula and dynamic slicing to improve fault localization effectiveness. First, all the statements in a program are ranked based on their suspiciousness calculated by using the Tarantula technique. Then, a dynamic slice with respect to a failure-indicating variable at the failure point is generated. Statements not in this slice will be removed from the ranking to further reduce the search domain. In [144], Ju et al. propose a hybrid slice-based fault localization technique combining dynamic and execution slices. A prototype tool, hybrid slice spectrum fault locator (HSFal), is implemented to support this technique.

Hofer and Wotawa [395] emphasize that SBFL techniques (e.g. Ochiai [95]) operated at a basic block level do not provide fine-grained results, whereas techniques based on slicing-hitting-set-computation (e.g. the HS-Slice algorithm [156]) sometimes produce an undesirable ranking with statements (such as constructors), which are executed by many test cases, at the top. To eliminate these drawbacks, there have been attempts to combine techniques of these two types [528, 529]. Similar in nature, the work of Christi et al. combine delta debugging with SBFL to focus the localization to the relevant parts of the program [530].

Other combinations have also been explored. Xuan and Monperrus [531] propose Multric, a learning-based approach to combining multiple fault localization techniques. In [403], Artzi et al. combine Tarantula and a technique for output mapping to reduce the number of statements that need to be examined. A similar approach is repeated in which Tarantula is replaced by Ochiai and Jaccard [474]. In [532], Gopinath et al. apply spectrum-based localization in synergy with specification-based analysis to more accurately locate bugs. The key idea is that unsatisfiability analysis of violated specifications, enabled by SAT technology, can be used to compute unsatisfiable cores, including statements that are likely to contain bugs. In [533], Burger and Zeller propose a technique, JINSI, which combines delta debugging and dynamic slicing for effective fault localization. JINSI takes a single failed execution and treats it as a series of object interactions (e.g. method calls and returns) that eventually produce the failure. The number of interactions will be reduced to the minimum number required to reproduce the failure, which will reduce the search space needed to locate the corresponding bug.

1.7.6 Ties Within Fault Localization Rankings

As discussed earlier (in Section 1.3.2), statements with the same suspiciousness are tied for the same position in a ranking. Results of a study by Xu et al. [120], using three fault localization techniques on four sets of programs, show that the symptom of assigning the same suspiciousness to multiple statements (i.e. the existence of ties in a produced ranking) appears everywhere and is not limited to any particular technique or program. Under such a scenario, the total number of statements that a programmer needs to examine in order to find the bugs may vary considerably. In response, two levels of effectiveness, the *best* and the *worst*, are computed (see Section 1.5). In practice, the more the ties, the bigger the difference between the best and the worst effectiveness. Ties also make the exact effectiveness of a fault localization technique more uncertain.

In voting scenarios when voters are unable to select between two or more alternatives, the candidates are ranked based on some key or natural ordering, such as an alphabetical ordering, to break ties. Similarly, when two statements are tied for the same ranking, the line numbers assigned to them in a text editor can serve as the key. Other techniques such as confidence-based strategy and data dependency-based strategy are also used to break ties [117, 120, 202, 224].

1.7.7 Fault Localization for Concurrency Bugs

Concurrent programs suffer most from three kinds of access anomalies: data race [534, 535], atomicity violation [536–538], and atomic-set serializability violations [138, 329].

Among the approaches that have mushroomed in recent years, predictive analysis-based techniques haven drawn significant attention [404, 537–541]. Generally speaking, these techniques record a trace of program execution, statically generate other permutations of these events, and expose unexercised concurrency bugs. One potential problem of these techniques is that they may sometimes report a large number of false positives. For example, only 6 of 97 reported atomicity violations in a study using Atomizer (a dynamic atomicity checker) are real [404]. On the contrary, a study in [430] using a different tool, Penelope, for atomicity violations detection reports no false positive.

Tools such as Chord [410] and RacerX [432] can statically analyze a program to find concurrency bugs. However, since all paths need to be explored, it is impractical to apply these tools to large, complicated programs. A runtime analysis (such as [462, 535, 542]), on the other hand, is less powerful than a static analysis but also produces fewer false alarms. The drawback is that only faults manifested in some specific executions can be detected.

Another approach for bug localization in concurrent programs is to use model checking [543–546]. For instance, Shacham et al. [546] use a model checker to construct the evidence for data race reported by the lockset algorithm. However, due to the possible exponential size of the search space, it is difficult to adopt this approach for large-sized programs without compromising its detection capability.

There are other techniques for detecting concurrency bugs. For example, Flanagan and Freund use a prototype tool JUMBLE to explore the non-determinism of relaxed memory models and to detect destructive races in the program [425]. Park et al. apply a CTrigger testing framework [547] to detect real atomicity violations by controlling the program execution to exercise low-probability thread interleavings. Park also presents a study to debug non-deadlock concurrency bugs [548]. Wang et al. [549] propose a technique to locate buggy shared memory accesses that are responsible for triggering concurrency bugs. Torlak et al. [550] propose a tool, MEMSAT, to help in debugging memory models. Koca et al. [551] locate faults in concurrency programs using an idea similar to SBFL techniques. Xu et al. [552] apply delta debugging to identify the threads and method invocations that are essential for causing the failure, while other threads and method invocations are removed to obtain a smaller stress test for concurrent data structures. The new execution is forced to replay the original failed execution trace, and guided back to the failed trace when the execution diverges.

1.7.8 Spreadsheet Fault Localization

Spreadsheet systems represent a landmark in the history of generic software products. It is estimated that 95% of all US firms use spreadsheets for financial reporting [553], 90% of all analysts in the industry perform calculations in spreadsheets [553], and 50% of all spreadsheets are the basis for decisions [554]. Such wide usage, however, has not been accompanied by effective mechanisms for bug prevention and detection, as shown by studies such as [555, 556]. As a result, bugs in spreadsheets are to be blamed for a long list of real problems compiled and available at the European Spreadsheet Risk Interest Group's (EuSpRIG) website (http://www.eusprig.org). A recent study by Reinhart and Rogoff [557] also gives a similar conclusion. In response to this, many studies regarding spreadsheet fault localization have been reported [344, 558–569].

A model-based spreadsheet fault localization technique is presented in [344], using an extended hitting-set algorithm and user-specified or historical test cases and assertions to identify possible error causes. Hofer et al. [565] apply a constraint-based representation of spreadsheets and a general constraint solver to locate bugs in spreadsheets. Another constraint-based approach for debugging faulty spreadsheets (CONBUG) is presented by Abreu et al. [570, 571], taking a spreadsheet and one test case as input to compute a set of faulty candidates. Getzner et al. [572] propose using dynamic slicing and grouping to reduce search space and using tie-breaking strategies to prioritize cells in order to further improve the effectiveness of spreadsheets debugging. Almasi et al. [573] apply a search-based approach to detect deviation failures in financial applications by generating tests to maximize the discrepancies between the newly implemented Java program and its legacy version in the form of an Excel spreadsheet. Abraham and Erwig [417] describe a tool, GoalDebug, for debugging spreadsheets, using a constraint-based approach similar to that in [565]. Whenever the computed output of a cell is incorrect, users can provide an expected value, which is employed to produce a list of possible changes to the corresponding formulae that, when applied, will generate the user-specified output. This involves mutating the spreadsheet based on a set of predefined change (repair) rules and ascertaining whether user expectations are met. A similar approach also appears in other studies such as [337] and [338]. Debroy and Wong [337] propose a strategy for automatically fixing bugs in both Java and C programs by combining mutation testing and software fault localization. An approach of using path-based weakest preconditions is discussed in [338] to generate program modifications for bug fixing.

Hofer et al. [574] evaluate the effectiveness of 42 spectrum-based techniques in spreadsheets fault localization. 803 spreadsheets of 2 subject corpora are used in the experiment. By evaluating the scores of each spectrum-based technique in best, average, and worst scenarios, the experiment results show that Jaccard, Ochiai, and Sorensen-Dice are the best performing techniques to diagnose spreadsheets with SBFL.

Hofer and Wotawa [575] investigate the impact of erroneous cell classification on the effectiveness of SBFL on spreadsheet debugging. Cases studies on 33 spreadsheets show that SBFL still computes acceptable results in the case of erroneous cell classifications: for more than 60% of the evaluated data sets, the number of cells that must be manually inspected (before the first faulty cell is found) doubles at most when one cell value is misclassified. When there are two misclassified cell values, for more than 40% of the spreadsheets, the effort doubles at most.

Abraham and Erwig also present a system, UCheck, which infers header information in spreadsheets, performs a unit analysis, and notifies users when bugs are detected [559]. Hermans et al. [562] suggest a way to locate spreadsheet smells (possible weak points in the spreadsheet design) and display them to users in data-flow diagrams. An approach to detect and visualize data clones (caused by copying the value computed by a formula in one cell as plain text to a different cell) in spreadsheets is reported in [563].

Other techniques aimed at reducing the occurrence of errors in spreadsheets include code inspection [576], refactoring [577], and adoption of better spreadsheet design practices [578, 579].

1.7.9 Theoretical Studies

Instead of being evaluated empirically, the effectiveness of software fault localization techniques can also be analyzed from theoretical perspectives.

Briand et al. [282] report that the formula used to compute the suspiciousness of a given statement by Tarantula can be re-expressed so that the suspiciousness only depends on the ratio of the number of failed tests (a_{ef}) to the number of successful tests (a_{es}) that execute the statement. Lee et al. [37, 580] prove that Tarantula always produces a ranking identical to that of a technique where the suspiciousness function is formulated as $a_{ef}/(a_{ef} + a_{es})$. A study by Naish et al. [113] examines over 30 formulae and divides them into groups such that those in the same group are equivalent for ranking. Independently, Debroy and Wong [102] also report a similar study showing that some similarity coefficient-based fault localization techniques are equivalent to one another. Studies such as Zhang et al. [520] focus on a cross-evaluation of the impacts of different test reduction and prioritization techniques on the efficiency of software fault localization.

Xie et al. [581] perform a theoretical study on the effectiveness of some SBFL techniques. Based on the *risk values* (which is the same as *suspiciousness* discussed in this book), program statements are assigned to one of the three sets, S_B^R, S_F^R, and S_A^R, based on whether their risk values are higher than, the same as, or lower than the value of the statement containing the bug. The authors make three assumptions: (i) a faulty program has exactly one fault; (ii) for any given single-fault program, there is exactly one faulty statement; and (iii) this faulty statement must be executed by all failed tests. They also assume that the underlying test suite must have 100% statement coverage. Unfortunately, some of these assumptions are oversimplified and do not hold for real-life programs. With respect to some selected techniques (many of which are similarity coefficient-based), they examine the *subset* relation between S_B^R and S_A^R generated by the corresponding ranking formulae and conclude that for two techniques, R_1 and R_2, if $S_B^{R_1} \subseteq S_B^{R_2}$ and $S_A^{R_2} \subseteq S_A^{R_1}$, then R_1 is *better* (more *effective*) than R_2 such that the number of statements examined by R_1 is less than that examined by R_2 to find the first faulty statement. One problem of this proof as reported in [197] is that it does not consider statements in S_F^R. As a result, for some special cases, even though the proof indicates that one technique is more effective than another, the former has to examine more statements than or the same number of statements as the latter – contradicting the result of the proof. Another controversy is that some advanced and effective techniques (e.g. [197, 201, 214, 318]) are excluded, even though they use exactly the same input data as those included in [581]. Le et al. [194] also question the validity of [581]. They compare the effectiveness of the five *best* fault localization techniques based on the theoretical study in [581] with the effectiveness of Tarantula and

Ochiai, and they find that the latter are significantly more effective than the former. This directly contradicts the conclusion of [581]. Xie et al. [582, 583] also apply their theoretical analysis framework to genetic programming-evolved formulae and show that these formulae can be used for effective fault localization. However, they make the same oversimplified assumptions as those in [581]. In addition, Ju et al. [584] provide a theoretical analysis on the efficiency of some FL formulas in debugging programs with multiple bugs based on the number of faults that are located from certain top statements of the ranking list. However, this analysis is not applicable to one-bug-at-a-time and parallel debugging, which are mainstream strategies for multi-fault localization.

There are other theoretical studies for single-bug programs. For example, Lee et al. [585] identify a class of *strictly rational* fault localization techniques in which the suspicious value of a statement strictly increases if this statement is executed by more failed test cases and strictly decreases if this statement is executed by more successful test cases. The authors claim that strictly rational techniques do not necessarily outperform those that are not. Therefore, limited attention should be given to these strictly rational techniques. In [586], Lee et al. further identify a class of *optimal* fault localization techniques for locating *deterministic* bugs (similar to Bohrbugs defined in [76]) that will always cause test cases to fail whenever they are executed. In [587], the authors revisit their previously published framework for theoretically analyzing the performance of risk evaluation formulas that are used for SBFL. Specifically, they provide justification to the assumptions/concerns of their framework such as coverage criteria, omission fault, multiple faults, and inconsistence between empirical and theoretical analyses.

1.8 Conclusion

As today's software has become larger and more complex than ever before, software fault localization accordingly requires a greater investment of time and resources. Consequently, locating program bugs is no longer an easily automated mechanical process. In practice, locations based on intelligent guesses of experienced programmers with expert knowledge of the software being debugged should be examined first. However, if this fails, an appropriate fallback would be to use a systematic technique (such as those discussed in this survey) based on solid reasoning and supported by case studies, rather than to use an unsubstantiated ad hoc approach. This is why techniques that can help programmers effectively locate bugs are highly in demand, which also stimulates the proposal of many fault localization techniques from a widespread perspective. It is imperative that software engineers involved with developing reliable and dependable systems have a good understanding of existing techniques, as well as an awareness of emerging trends and developments in the area. To facilitate this, we conduct a detailed survey and present the results so that software engineers at all program debugging experience levels can quickly gain necessary background knowledge and the ability to apply cost-effective software fault localization techniques tailored to their specific environments.

A publication repository has been created, including 587 papers and 68 PhD and Masters' theses on software fault localization from 1977 to 2020. These techniques are classified into nine categories: slicing-based, spectrum-based, statistics-based, machine learning-based, data mining-based, IR-based, model-based, spreadsheet-based, and additional emerging techniques. The figures and tables presented in the previous sections strongly indicate that software fault localization has become an important research topic on the front burner and suggest the trend of ongoing research directions.

Our analysis shows that the numbers of published papers in each category differ from each other and that the research interest shifts from one category to another as time moves on. For example, static and dynamic slice-based techniques were popular between 2004 and 2007, whereas execution slice and program spectrum-based techniques have dominated since 2008.

Different metrics to evaluate the effectiveness of software fault localization techniques (in terms of how much code needs to be examined before the first faulty location is identified) are reviewed, including T-score, EXAM score/*Expense*, P-score, N-score, and Wilcoxon signed-rank test. Subject programs and debugging tools used in various empirical evaluations are summarized. Results of different empirical studies using these metrics, programs, and tools suggest that no one category is completely superior to another. In fact, techniques in each category have their own advantages and disadvantages.

Additionally, effectiveness of these techniques can also be analyzed from theoretical perspectives. However, such analyses very often make oversimplified and nonrealistic assumptions that do not hold for real-life programs. Hence, their conclusions in general are only applicable within limited scopes. This implies that a theoretical analysis alone is not enough. It is advisable to apply both empirical evaluations and theoretical analyses to provide a more complete assessment.

We emphasize that effectiveness is not the only attribute of a software fault localization technique that should be considered. Other factors, including overhead for computing the suspiciousness of each program component, time and space for data collection, human effort, and tool support, should be included as well. We also discuss aspects that are critical to software fault localization, such as fault localization on programs with multiple bugs, concurrent programs, and spreadsheets, as well as impacts of test cases, coincidental correctness, and faults introduced by missing code.

To conclude, our objective is to use this book to provide the software engineering community with a better understanding of state-of-the-art research in software fault localization, and identify potential drawbacks and deficiencies of existing techniques, so that additional studies can be conducted to improve their practicality and robustness.

Notes

1 In this chapter, the terms "software" and "program" are used interchangeably. Also, "fault" and "bug" are used interchangeably.
2 In the rest of paper, "all papers" is used to represent "all papers in our repository."
3 Papers that only use execution slice-based techniques (e.g., [166, 178]) are included in the spectrum-based category because a statement-based execution slice is the same as ESHS (see Section 1.3.2). The slice-based category contains papers only using static slicing and/or dynamic slicing.
4 The code can be represented by statements, predicates, functions, and so on
5 Since there are many techniques in each category, it is possible that a particular technique may behave differently from others in the same category in terms of the types of outputs generated.

References

1 Munson, J.C. and Khoshgoftaar, T.M. (1992). The detection of fault-prone programs. *IEEE Transactions on Software Engineering* 18 (5): 423–433.
2 Pai, G.J. and Dugan, J.B. (2007). Empirical analysis of software fault content and fault proneness using bayesian methods. *IEEE Transactions on Software Engineering* 33 (10): 675–686.
3 Wright, C.S. and Zia, T.A. (2011). A quantitative analysis into the economics of correcting software bugs. *Proceedings of the International Conference on Computational Intelligence in Security for Information Systems*, Torremolinos, Spain (8–10 June 2011), 198–205.
4 Burke, D. All circuits are busy now: the 1990 AT&T long distance network collapse. http://users.csc.calpoly.edu/~jdalbey/SWE/Papers/att_collapse.html (accessed January 2022).
5 Wong, W.E., Debroy, V., Surampudi, A. et al. (2010). Recent catastrophic accidents: investigating how software was responsible. *Proceedings of the 4th International Conference on Secure Software Integration and Reliability*

Improvement, Singapore, Singapore (9–11 June 2010), 14–22. IEEE. https://doi.org/10.1109/SSIRI.2010.38.

6 NIST. Software errors cost U.S. economy $59.5 billion annually. http://www.abeacha.com/NIST_press_release_bugs_cost.htm (accessed January 2022).

7 Vessy, I. (1985). Expertise in debugging computer programs: a process analysis. *International Journal of Man-Machine Studies* 23 (5): 459–494.

8 Shapiro, E. (1982). Algorithmic program debugging. PhD dissertation. Yale University.

9 Agrawal, H. (1991). Towards automatic debugging of computer program. PhD dissertation. Purdue University.

10 Pan, H. (1993). Software debugging with dynamic instrumentation and test-based knowledge. PhD dissertation. Purdue University.

11 Gregory, W.B. (1994). Logic programs for consistency-based diagnosis. PhD dissertation. Carleton University.

12 Liblit, B. (2004). Cooperative bug isolation. PhD dissertation. University of California, Berkeley.

13 Peischl, B. (2004). Automated source-level debugging of synthesizable VHDL designs. PhD dissertation. Graz University of Technology.

14 He, H. and Gupta, N. (2004). Automated debugging using path-based weakest preconditions. *International Conference on Fundamental Approaches to Software Engineering*, Barcelona, Spain (29 March to 2 April 2004), 267–280. Springer.

15 Groce, A. (2005). Error explanation and fault localization with distance metrics. PhD dissertation. Carnegie Mellon University.

16 Renieris, E. (2005). A research framework for software-fault localization tools. PhD dissertation. Brown University.

17 Kob, D. (2005). Extended modeling for automated fault localization in object-oriented software. PhD dissertation. Graz University of Technology.

18 Hovemeyer, D. (2005). Simple and effective static analysis to find bugs. PhD dissertation. University of Maryland.

19 Hu, P. (2006). Automated fault localization: a statistical predicate analysis approach. PhD dissertation. The University of Hong Kong.

20 Zhang, X. (2007). Fault localization via precise dynamic slicing. PhD dissertation. University of Arizona.

21 Vayani, R. (2007). Improving automatic software fault localization. Master thesis. Delft University of Technology.

22 Kompella, R.R. (2007). Fault localization in backbone networks. PhD dissertation. University of California.

23 Griesmayer, A. (2007). Debugging software: from verification to repair. PhD dissertation. Graz University of Technology.

24 Wang, T. (2007). Post-mortem dynamic analysis for software debugging. PhD dissertation. National University of Singapore.

25 Tallam, S. (2007). Fault location and avoidance in long-running multithreaded applications. PhD dissertation. University of Arizona.

26 Chesley, O.C., Ren, X., Ryder, B.G., and Tip, F. (2007). Crisp – a fault localization tool for java programs. *29th International Conference on Software Engineering (ICSE '07)*, Minneapolis, MN, USA (20–26 May 2007), 775–779. IEEE.

27 Lu, S. (2008). Understanding, detecting, and exposing concurrency bugs. PhD dissertation. University of Illinois at Urbana-Champaign.

28 Peischl, B., Riaz, N., and Wotawa, F. (2008). Advances in automated source-level debugging of verilog designs. In: *New Challenges in Applied Intelligence Technologies* (ed. N.T. Nguyen and R. Katarzyniak), 363–372. Berlin, Heidelberg: Springer.

29 Jones, J.A. (2008). Semi-Automatic Fault Localization. PhD dissertation, Georgia Institute of Technology.

30 Zhang, Z. (2009). Software debugging through dynamic analysis of program structures. PhD dissertation. The University of Hong Kong.

31 Abreu, R. (2009). Spectrum-based fault localization in embedded software. PhD dissertation. University of Minho geboren te Fão.

32 Jeffrey, D. (2009). Dynamic state alteration techniques for automatically locating software errors. PhD dissertation. University of California Riverside.

33 Wang, X. (2010). Automatic localization of code omission faults. PhD dissertation. The Hong Kong University of Science and Technology.

34 Pastore, F. (2010). Automatic diagnosis of software functional faults by means of inferred behavioral models. PhD dissertation. Università degli Studi di Milano Bicocca.

35 Nica, M. (2010). On the use of constraints in automated program debugging – from foundations to empirical results. PhD dissertation. Graz University of Technology.

36 Fry, Z.P. (2011). Fault localization using textual similarities. Master thesis. University of Virginia.

37 Lee, H. (2011). Spectral debugging. PhD dissertation. The University of Melbourne.

38 Debroy, V. (2011). Towards the automation of program debugging. PhD dissertation. The University of Texas at Dallas.

39 Sanchez, A. (2011). Cost optimizations in runtime testing and diagnosis. PhD dissertation. Delft University of Technology.

40 DeMott, J.D. (2012). Enhancing automated fault discovery and analysis. PhD dissertation. Michigan State University.

41 Zhang, X. (2012). Secure and efficient network fault localization. PhD dissertation. Carnegie Mellon University.

42 Xie, X. (2012). On the analysis of spectrum-based fault localization. PhD dissertation. Swinburne University of Technology.

43 Perez, A. (2012). Dynamic code coverage with progressive detail levels. PhD dissertation. University of Porto.

44 Santelices, R. (2012). Change-effects analysis for effective testing and validation of evolving software. PhD dissertation. Georgia Institute of Technology.
45 Baah, G.K. (2012). Statistical causal analysis for fault localization. PhD dissertation. Georgia Institute of Technology.
46 Sahoo, S.K. (2013). A novel invariants-based approach for automated software fault localization. PhD dissertation. University of Illinois at Urbana-Champaign.
47 Hofer, B. (2013). From fault localization of programs written in third level language to spreadsheets. PhD dissertation. Graz University of Technology.
48 Bandyopadhyay, A. (2013). Mitigating the effect of coincidental correctness in spectrum based fault localization. PhD dissertation. Colorado State University.
49 Roychowdhry, S. (2013). A mixed approach to spectrum-based fault localization using information theoretic foundations. PhD dissertation. University of Texas at Austin.
50 Ali, S. (2013). Localizing state-dependent faults using associated sequence mining. Ph.D. dissertation. The University of Western Ontario.
51 Kühnert, C. (2013). *Data-Driven Methods for Fault Localization in Process Technology 15*. KIT Scientific Publishing.
52 Qi, D. (2013). Semantic analyses to detect and localize software regression errors. PhD dissertation. National University of Singapore.
53 Sumner, W.N. (2013). Automated failure explanation through execution comparison. PhD dissertation. Purdue University.
54 Hays, M. (2014). A fault-based model of fault localization techniques. PhD dissertation. University of Kentucky.
55 Park, S. (2014). Effective fault localization techniques for concurrent software. PhD dissertation. Georgia Institute of Technology.
56 Shu, G. (2014). Statistical estimation of software reliability and failure-causing effect. PhD dissertation. Case Western Reserve University.
57 Lucia, L. (2014). Ranking-based approaches for localizing faults. PhD dissertation. Singapore Management University.
58 Moon, S. (2014). Effective software fault localization using dynamic program behaviors. Master thesis. Korea Advanced Institute of Science and Technology.
59 Liu, Y. (2015). Automated analysis of energy efficiency and performance for mobile application. PhD dissertation. The Hong Kong University of Science and Technology.
60 Chen, C. (2015). Automated fault localization for service-oriented software systems. PhD dissertation. Delft University of Technology.
61 Rohr, M. (2015). Workload-sensitive timing behavior analysis for fault localization in software systems. PhD dissertation. Kiel University.
62 Bayraktar, O. (2015). Ela: an automated statistical fault localization technique. PhD dissertation. The Middle East Technical University.

63 Tonzirul, A. (2016). Fault discovery, localization, and recovery in smartphone apps. PhD dissertation. University of California Riverside.

64 Gholamosseinghandehari, L. (2016). Fault localization based on combinatorial testing. PhD dissertation. The University of Texas at Arlington.

65 Gao, R. (2017). Advanced Fault Localization for Programs with Multiple Bugs. PhD dissertation. University of Texas at Dallas.

66 Sun, S. (2017). Statistical fault localization and causal interactions. PhD dissertation. Case Western Reserve University.

67 Wu, R. (2017). Automated techniques for diagnosing crashing bugs. PhD dissertation. The Hong Kong University of Science and Technology.

68 Roy, A. (2018). Simplifying datacenter fault detection and localization. PhD dissertation. University of California San Diego.

69 Guo, Y. (2018). Towards automatically localizing and repairing SQL faults. PhD dissertation. George Mason University.

70 Safdari, N. (2018). Learning to rank relevant files for bug reports using domain knowledge, replication and extension of a learning-to-rank approach. Master thesis. Rochester Institute of Technology.

71 Ting, D. (2019). A hybrid approach to cloud system performance bug detection, diagnosis and fix. PhD dissertation. North Carolina State University.

72 Thompson, G. (2020). Towards automated fault localization for prolog. Master thesis. North Carolina A&T State University.

73 Li, X. (2020). An integrated approach for automated software debugging via machine learning and big code mining. PhD dissertation. The University of Texas at Dallas.

74 Gulzar, M.A. (2020). Automated testing and debugging for big data analytics. PhD dissertation. University of California, Los Angeles.

75 Mathur, M. (2020). Leveraging Distributed Tracing and Container Cloning for Replay Debugging of Microservices. Master thesis. University of California, Los Angeles.

76 Grottke, M. and Trivedi, K.S. (2005). A classification of software faults. *Journal of Reliability Engineering Association of Japan* 27 (7): 425–438.

77 Avizienis, A., Laprie, J.C., Randell, B., and Landwehr, C.E. (2004). Basic concepts and taxonomy of dependable and secure computing. *IEEE Transactions on Dependable and Secure Computing* 1 (1): 11–33.

78 Edwards, J.C. (2003). Method, system, and program for logging statements to monitor execution of a program. US Patent 6,539,501 B1, filed 16 December 1999 and issued 25 March 2003.

79 Rosenblum, D.S. (1995). A practical approach to programming with assertions. *IEEE Transactions on Software Engineering* 21 (1): 19–31.

80 Rosenblum, D.S. (1992). Towards a method of programming with assertions. *Proceedings of the 14th international Conference on Software Engineering*

(ICSE '92), Melbourne, Australia (11–15 May 1992), 92–104. ACM. https://dl.acm.org/doi/pdf/10.1145/143062.143098.

81 Coutant, D.S., Meloy, S., and Ruscetta, M. (1988). DOC: a practical approach to source-level debugging of globally optimized code. *Proceedings of the ACM SIGPLAN Conference on Program Language Design and Implementation*, Atlanta, GA, USA (June 1988), 125–134.

82 Hennessy, J. (1982). Symbolic debugging of optimized code. *ACM Transactions on Programming Languages and Systems* 4 (3): 323–344.

83 GNU. GDB: the GNU Project Debugger. http://www.gnu.org/software/gdb/ (accessed January 2022).

84 MSDN. Debugging in Visual Studio. https://msdn.microsoft.com/en-us/library/sc65sadd.aspx (accessed January 2022).

85 Ball, T. and Larus, J.R. (1994). Optimally profiling and tracing programs. *ACM Transactions on Programming Languages and Systems* 16 (4): 1319–1360.

86 Hauswirth, M. and Cillmbi, T.M. (2004). Low-overhead memory leak detection using adaptive statistical profiling. *Proceedings of the International Conference on Architectural Support for Programming Languages and Operating Systems*, Boston, MA, USA (October 2004), 156–164.

87 Runciman, C. and Wakeling, D. (1993). Heap profiling of lazy functional programs. *Journal of Functional Programming* 3 (02): 217–245.

88 GNU gprof. http://sourceware.org/binutils/docs/gprof/ (accessed January 2022).

89 Eclipse. Archived Eclipse Projects. http://www.eclipse.org/tptp (accessed January 2022).

90 Lewis, D. (1973). Causation. *Journal of Philosophy* 70 (17): 556–567.

91 Pearl, J. (2000). *Causality: Models, Reasoning, and Inference*. Cambridge University Press.

92 Abreu, R., González, A., Zoeteweij, P., and van Gemund, A.J. (2008). Automatic software fault localization using generic program invariants. *Proceedings of the ACM Symposium on Applied Computing,* Ceara, Brazil (March 2008), 712–717.

93 Abreu, R., Zoeteweij, P., Golsteijn, R., and van Gemund, A.J. (2009). A practical evaluation of spectrum-based fault localization. *Journal of Systems and Software* 82 (11): 1780–1792.

94 Abreu, R., Zoeteweij, P., and van Gemund, A.J. (2006). An evaluation of similarity coefficients for software fault localization. *Proceedings of the Pacific Rim International Symposium on Dependable Computing*, Riverside, CA, USA (December 2006), 39–46.

95 Abreu, R., Zoeteweij, P., and van Gemund, A.J. (2007). On the accuracy of spectrum-based fault localization. *Proceedings of Testing: Academic and Industrial Conference Practice and Research Techniques – MUTATION*, Windsor, CT, USA (September 2007), 89–98.

96 Ali, S., Andrews, J.H., Dhandapani, T., and Wang, W. (2009). Evaluating the accuracy of fault localization techniques. *Proceedings of the 2009 IEEE/ACM*

International Conference on Automated Software Engineering, Auckland, New Zealand (November 2009), 76–87.

97 Arisholm, E., Briand, L.C., and Johannessen, E.B. (2010). A systematic and comprehensive investigation of methods to build and evaluate fault prediction models. *Journal of Systems and Software* 83 (1): 2–17.

98 Ascari, L.C., Araki, L.Y., Pozo, A.R.T., and Vergilio, S.R. (2009). Exploring machine learning techniques for fault localization. *Proceedings of the 10th Latin American Test Workshop,* Buzios, Brazil (March 2009), 1–6.

99 Bandyopadhyay, A. and Ghosh, S. (2011). On the effectiveness of the tarantula fault localization technique for different fault classes. *Proceedings of the IEEE International Symposium on High-Assurance Systems Engineering*, Boca Raton, FL, USA (November 2011), 317–324.

100 Bo, J., Zhang, Z., Tse, T.H., and Chen, T.Y. (2009). How well do test case prioritization techniques support statistical fault localization. *Proceedings of the Annual IEEE Computer Software and Applications Conference (COMPSAC '09),* Seattle, WA, USA (20–24 July 2009), 99–106.

101 Debroy, V. and Wong, W.E. (2013). A consensus-based strategy to improve the quality of fault localization. *Software: Practice and Experience* 43 (8): 989–1011.

102 Debroy, V. and Wong, W.E. (2011). On the equivalence of certain fault localization techniques. *Proceedings of the ACM Symposium on Applied Computing*, TaiChung, Taiwan (March 2011), 1457–1463.

103 Debroy, V., Wong, W.E., Xu, X. and Choi, B. (2010). A grouping-based strategy to improve the effectiveness of fault localization techniques. *Proceedings of the International Conference on Quality Software*, Zhangjiajie, China (July 2010), 13–22.

104 DiGiuseppe, N. and Jones, J.A. (2011). On the influence of multiple faults on coverage-based fault localization. *Proceedings of the International Symposium on Software Testing and Analysis*, Toronto, BC, Canada (July 2011), 210–220.

105 Gong, C., Zheng, Z., Li, W., and Hao, P. (2012). Effects of class imbalance in test suites: an empirical study of spectrum-based fault localization. *Proceedings of the IEEE Annual Computer Software and Applications Conference Workshops (COMPSAC Workshops '12)*, Izmir, Turkey (July 2012), 470–475.

106 Jiang, B., Zhang, Z., Chan, W.K. et al. (2012). How well does test case prioritization integrate with statistical fault localization? *Journal of Information and Software Technology* 54 (7): 739–758.

107 Jones, J.A. and Harrold, M.J. (2005). Empirical evaluation of the tarantula automatic fault-localization technique. *Proceedings of the International Conference Automated Software Engineering*, Long Beach, CA, USA (November 2005), 273–282.

108 Kim, J. and Lee, E. (2014). Empirical evaluation of existing algorithms of spectrum based fault localization. *Proceedings of the International Conference on Information*

Networking 2014 (ICOIN '14), Phuket, Thailand (10–12 February 2014), 346–351. IEEE. https://doi.org/10.1109/ICOIN.2014.6799702.

109 Kusumoto, S., Nishimatsu, A., Nishie, K., and Inoue, K. (2002). Experimental evaluation of program slicing for fault localization. *Empirical Software Engineering* 7 (1): 49–76.

110 Le, T.B. and Lo, D. (2013). Will fault localization work for these failures? An automated approach to predict effectiveness of fault localization tools. *Proceedings of the 29th IEEE International Conference on Software Maintenance*, Eindhoven, Netherland (September 2013), 310–319.

111 McMaster, S. and Memon, A. (2007). Fault detection probability analysis for coverage-based test suite reduction. *Proceedings of the International Conference on Software Maintenance*, Paris, France (October 2007), 335–344.

112 Naish, L., Lee, H.J., and Ramamohanarao, K. (2010). Statements versus predicate in spectral bug localization. *Proceedings of the Asia-Pacific Software Engineering Conference*, Sydney, Australia (November 2010), 375–384.

113 Naish, L., Lee, H.J., and Ramamohanarao, K. (2011). A model for spectra-based software diagnosis. *Journal of the ACM Transactions on Software Engineering and Methodology* 20 (3): 1–32.

114 Qi, Y., Mao, X., Lei, Y., and Wang, C. (2013). Using automated program repair for evaluating the effectiveness of fault localization techniques. *Proceedings of the 2013 International Symposium on Software Testing and Analysis*, Lugano, Switzerland (July 2013), 191–201.

115 Rao, P., Zheng, Z., Chen, T.Y. et al. (2013). Impacts of test suite's class imbalance on spectrum-based fault localization techniques. *Proceedings of the 13th International Conference on Quality Software*, Nanjing, China (July 2013), 260–267.

116 Stumptner, M. and Wotawa, F. (1998). A survey of intelligent debugging. *AI Communications* 11 (1): 35–51.

117 Wong, W.E., Debroy, V., and Choi, B. (2010). A family of code coverage-based heuristics for effective fault localization. *Journal of Systems and Software* 83 (2): 188–208.

118 Xu, J., Chan, W.K., Zhang, Z. et al. (2011). A dynamic fault localization technique with noise reduction for java programs. *Proceedings of the International Conference on Quality Software*, Madrid, Spain (July 2011), 11–20.

119 Xu, J., Zhang, Z., Chan, W.K. et al. (2013). A general noise-reduction framework for fault localization of java program. *Information and Software Technology* 55 (5): 880–896.

120 Xu, X., Debroy, V., Wong, W.E., and Guo, D. (2011). Ties within fault localization rankings: exposing and addressing the problem. *International Journal of Software Engineering and Knowledge Engineering* 21 (6): 803–827.

121 Zhang, X., Gupta, N., and Gupta, R. (2007). A study of effectiveness of dynamic slicing in locating real faults. *Empirical Software Engineering* 12 (2): 143–160.

122 Zhang, X., He, H., Gupta, N., and Gupta, R. (2005). Experimental evaluation of using deynamic slices for fault location. *Proceedings of the International Workshop on Automated Debugging*, Monterey, CA, USA (September 2005), 33–42.

123 Zhang, Z., Chan, W.K., Tse, T.H. et al. (2009). Is non-parametric hypothesis testing model robust for statistical fault localization? *Information and Software Technology* 51 (11): 1573–1585.

124 Zheng, J., Williams, L., Nagappan, N. et al. (2006). On the value of static analysis for fault detection in software. *IEEE Transactions on Software Engineering* 32 (4): 240–253.

125 Binkley, D. and Harman, M. (2004). A survey of empirical results on program slicing. *Advances in Computers* 62: 105–178.

126 Tip, F. (1995). A survey of program slicing techniques. *Journal of Programming Languages* 3 (3): 121–189.

127 Xu, B., Qian, J., Zhang, X. et al. (2005). A brief survey of program slicing. *ACM SIGSOFT Software Engineering Notes* 30 (2): 1–36.

128 Weiser, M. (1979). Program slicing: formal, psychological, and practical investigations of an automatic program abstraction method. PhD dissertation. University of Michigan.

129 Weiser, M. (1984). Program slicing. *IEEE Transactions on Software Engineering* 10 (4): 352–357.

130 Lyle, J.R. and Weiser, M. (1987). Automatic program bug location by program slicing. *Proceedings of the International Conference on Computer and Applications*, Beijing, China (23–27 June 1987), 877–883. IEEE. ISBN: 0-8186-0780-7.

131 Liang, D. and Harrold, M.J. (2002). Equivalence analysis and its application in improving the efficiency of program slicing. *ACM Transactions on Software Engineering and Methodology* 11 (3): 347–383.

132 Kiss, Á., Jász, J., and Gyimóthy, T. (2005). Using dynamic information in the interprocedural static slicing of binary executables. *Software Quality Control* 13 (3): 227–245.

133 Tip, F. and Dinesh, T.B. (2001). A slicing-based approach for locating type errors. *ACM Transactions on Software Engineering and Methodology* 10 (1): 5–55.

134 Zhang, Y. and Santelices, R.A. (2016). Prioritized static slicing and its application to fault localization. *Journal of Systems and Software* 114: 38–53.

135 Agrawal, H. and Horgan, J.R. (1990). Dynamic program slicing. *Proceedings of the ACM SIGPLAN Conference on Programming Language Design and Implementation*, White Plains, NY, USA (June 1990), 246–256.

136 Korel, B. and Laski, J. (1988). Dynamic program slicing. *Information Processing Letters* 29 (3): 155–163.

137 Agrawal, H., DeMillo, R.A., and Spafford, E.H. (1993). Debugging with dynamic slicing and backtracking. *Software–Practice & Experience* 23 (6): 589–616.

138 Al-Khanjari, Z.A., Woodward, M.R., Ramadhan, H.A., and Kutti, N.S. (2005). The efficiency of critical slicing in fault localization. *Journal of Software Quality Control* 13 (2): 129–153.

139 Alves, E., Gligoric, M., Jagannath, V. and d'Amorim, M. (2011). Fault-localization using dynamic slicing and change impact analysis. *Proceedings of the IEEE International Symposium on Automated Software Engineering*, Lawrence, KS, USA (November 2011), 520–523.

140 DeMillo, R.A., Pan, H., and Spafford, E.H. (1996). Critical slicing for software fault localization. *Proceedings of the International Symposium on Software Testing and Analysis*, San Diego, CA, USA (January 1996), 121–134.

141 DiGiuseppe, N. and Jones, J.A. (2015). Fault density, fault types, and spectra-based fault localization. *Empirical Software Engineering* 20 (4): 928–967.

142 DrDebug. Deterministic replay based debugging with pin. www.drdebug.org (accessed January 2022).

143 Ishii, Y. and Kutsuna, T. (2016). Effective fault localization using dynamic slicing and an SMT solver. *Proceedings of the 9th IEEE International Conference on Software Testing, Verification and Validation Workshops*, Chicago, IL, USA (April 2016), 180–188.

144 Ju, X., Jiang, S., Chen, X. et al. (2014). HSFal: effective fault localization using hybrid spectrum of full slices and execution slices. *Journal of Systems and Software* 90: 3–17.

145 Korel, B. (1988). PELAS – program error-locating assistant system. *IEEE Transactions on Software Engineering* 14 (9): 1253–1260.

146 Lian, L., Kusumoto, S., Kikuno, T. et al. (1997). A new fault localizing method for the program debugging process. *Information and Software Technology* 39 (4): 271–284.

147 Liu, C., Zhang, X., Han, J. et al. (2007). Indexing noncrashing failures: a dynamic program slicing-based approach. *Proceedings of the International Conference on Software Maintenance*, Paris, France (October 2007), 455–464.

148 Mao, X., Lei, Y., Dai, Z. et al. (2014). Slice-based statistical fault localization. *Journal of Systems and Software* 89: 51–62.

149 Mohapatra, D.P., Mall, R., and Kumar, R. (2004). An edge marking technique for dynamic slicing of object-oriented programs. *Proceedings of the International Computer Software and Applications Conference (COMPSAC '04)*, Hong Kong (September 2004), 60–65.

150 Ocariza, F.S. Jr., Li, G., Pattabiraman, K., and Mesbah, A. (2016). Automatic fault localization for client-side javascript. *Software Testing, Verification and Reliability* 26 (1): 69–88.

151 Pan, H. and Spafford, E. (1992). Heuristics for Automatic Localization of Software Faults. Technical Report, SERC-TR-116-P. Purdue University.

152 Qian, J. and Xu, B. (2008). Scenario oriented program slicing. *Proceedings of the ACM Symposium on Applied Computing*, Fortaleza, Brazil (March 2008), 748–752.

153 Sterling, C.D. and Olsson, R.A. (2005). Automated bug isolation via program chipping. *Proceedings of the International Symposium on Automated and Analysis-Driven Debugging*, Monterey, CA, USA (September 2005), 23–32.

154 Wang, Y., Patil, H., Pereira, C. et al. (2014). DrDebug: deterministic replay based cyclic debugging with dynamic slicing. *IEEE International Symposium on Code Generation and Optimization*, Orlando, FL, USA (February 2014), 98–108.

155 Wotawa, F. (2002). On the relationship between model-based debugging and program slicing. *Artificial Intelligence* 135 (1–2): 125–143.

156 Wotawa, F. (2010). Fault localization based on dynamic slicing and hitting-Set computation. *Proceedings of the International Conference on Quality Software*, Zhangjiajie, China (July 2010), 161–170.

157 Zhang, X., Gupta, N., and Gupta, R. (2007). Locating faulty code by multiple points slicing. *Software Practice and Experience* 37 (9): 935–961.

158 Treffer, A. and Uflacker, M. (2016). The slice navigator: focused debugging with interactive dynamic slicing. *Proceedings of the 2016 IEEE 27th IEEE International Symposium on Software Reliability Engineering Workshops (ISSREW '16)*, Ottawa, ON, Canada (23–27 October 2016), 175–180. IEEE. https://doi.org/10.1109/ISSREW.2016.17.

159 Sun, C.A., Ran, Y., Zheng, C. et al. (2018). Fault localisation for WS-BPEL programs based on predicate switching and program slicing. *Journal of Systems and Software* 135: 191–204.

160 Tu, J., Xie, X., Chen, T.Y., and Xu, B. (2019). On the analysis of spectrum based fault localization using hitting sets. *Journal of Systems and Software* 147: 106–123.

161 Guo, Y., Motro, A., and Li, N. (2017). Localizing faults in SQL predicates. *Proceedings of the 2017 IEEE International Conference on Software Testing, Verification and Validation*, Tokyo, Japan (March 2017), 1–11.

162 Zhang, X., Tallam, S., Gupta, N., and Gupta, R. (2007). Towards locating execution omission errors. *Proceedings of the ACM SIGPLAN Conference on Programming Language Design and Implementation*, San Diego, CA, USA (June 2007), 415–424.

163 Gyimothy, T., Beszedes, A., and Forgacs, I. (1999). An efficient relevant slicing method for debugging. *Proceedings of the European Software Engineering Conference, held jointly with the ACM SIGSOFT Symposium on the Foundation of Software Engineering*, Toulouse, France (September 1999), 303–321.

164 Weeratunge, D., Zhang, X., Sumner, W.N., and Jagannathan, S. (2010). Analyzing concurrency bugs using dual Slicing. *Proceedings of the International Symposium on Software Testing and Analysis*, Trento, Italy (July 2010), 253–264.

165 Wang, X. and Liu, Y. (2015). Automated fault localization via hierarchical multiple predicate switching. *Journal of Systems and Software* 104: 69–81.

166 Agrawal, H., Horgan, J.R., London, S., and Wong, W.E. (1995). Fault localization using execution slices and dataflow tests. *Proceedings of the Sixth International Symposium on Software Reliability Engineering (ISSRE '95)*, Toulouse, France (October 1995), 143–151.

167 Beszedes, A., Gergely, T., Szabo, Z. et al. (2001). Dynamic slicing method for maintenance of large C programs. *Proceedings of the European Conference on Software Maintenance and Reengineering*, Lisbon, Portugal (March 2001), 105–113.

168 Korel, B. and Yalamanchili, S. (1994). Forward Computation of Dynamic Program Slices. *Proceedings of the International Symposium on Software Testing and Analysis*, Seattle, WA, USA (August 1994), 66–79.

169 Zhang, X., Gupta, R., and Zhang, Y. (2003). Precise dynamic slicing algorithms. *Proceedings of the International Conference on Software Engineering (ICSE '03)*, Portland, OR, USA (May 2003), 319–329.

170 Zhang, X., Gupta, R., and Zhang, Y. (2004). Efficient forward computation of dynamic slices using reduced ordered binary decision diagrams. *Proceedings of the International Conference on Software Engineering (ICSE '04)*, Edinburgh, UK (May 2004), 502–511.

171 Agrawal, H., Horgan, J.R., Li, J.J. et al. (1998). Mining system tests to aid software maintenance. *Computer* 31 (7): 64–73.

172 Bellcore (1998). *χSuds User's Manual*. Bridgewater, NJ, USA: Telcordia Technologies (formerly Bellcore). https://www.cs.purdue.edu/homes/apm/foundationsBook/Labs/coverage/xsuds.pdf.

173 Wong, W.E. and Li, J.J. (2005). An integrated solution for testing and analyzing java applications in an industrial setting. *Proceedings of the Asia-Pacific Software Engineering Conference*, Taipei, Taiwan (December 2005), 576–583.

174 Jones, J.A., Harrold, M.J., and Stasko, J. (2001). Visualization for fault localization. *Proceedings of the Workshop on Software Visualization, 23rd International Conference on Software Engineering (ICSE '01)*, Toronto, ON, Canada (May 2001), 71–75.

175 Jones, J.A., Harrold, M.J., and Stasko, J. (2002). Visualization of test information to assist fault localization. *Proceedings of the International Conference on Software Engineering (ICSE '02)*, Orlando, FL, USA (May 2002), 467–477.

176 Wong, W.E., Sugeta, T., Qi, Y., and Maldonado, J.C. (2005). Smart debugging software architectural design in SDL. *Journal of Systems and Software* 76 (1): 15–28.

177 Eric Wong, W., Gao, R., Li, Y. et al. (2016). A survey on software fault localization. *IEEE Transactions on Software Engineering* 42 (8): 707–740.

178 Wong, W.E. and Qi, Y. (2006). Effective program debugging based on execution slices and inter-block data dependency. *Journal of Systems and Software* 79 (7): 891–903.

179 Krinke, J. (2004). Slicing, chopping, and path conditions with barriers. *Software Quality Control* 12 (4): 339–360.

180 Stridharan, M., Fink, S.J., and Bodik, R. (2007). Thin Slicing. *Proceedings of the ACM SIGPLAN Conference on Programming Language Design and Implementation*, San Diego, CA, USA (June 2007), 112–122.

181 Harrold, M.J., Rothermel, G., Sayre, K. et al. (2000). An empirical investigation of the relationship between spectra differences and regression faults. *Journal of Software Testing, Verification and Reliability* 10 (3): 171–194.

182 Reps, T., Ball, T., Das, M., and Larus, J. (1997). The use of program profiling for software maintenance with applications to the Year 2000 problem. *Proceedings of the ACM SIGSOFT Symposium on Foundations of Software Engineering*, Zurich (September 1997), 432–449.

183 Collofello, J.S. and Cousins, L. (1987). Towards automatic software fault location through decision-to-decision path analysis. *Proceedings of the International Workshop on Managing Requirements Knowledge*, Chicago, IL, USA (June 1987), 539–544.

184 Masri, W. (2015). Automated fault localization: advances and challenges. *Advances in Computers* 99: 103–156.

185 Agrawal, H., DeMillo, R.A., and Spafford, E.H. (1991). An execution backtracking approach to program debugging. *IEEE Software* 8 (3): 21–26.

186 Korel, B. and Laski, J. (1988). STAD: a system for testing and debugging: user perspective. *Proceedings of the Workshop on Software Testing, Verification, and Analysis*, Banff, AB, Canada (19–21 July 1988), 13–14. IEEE.

187 Taha, A.B., Thebaut, S.M., and Liu, S.S. (1989). An approach to software fault localization and revalidation based on incremental data flow analysis. *Proceedings of the International Conference Computer Software and Applications*, Orlando, FL, USA (20–22 September 1989), 527–534. IEEE. https://doi.org/10.1109/CMPSAC.1989.65142.

188 Renieris, M. and Reiss, S.P. (2003). Fault localization with nearest neighbor queries. *Proceedings of the International Conference on Automated Software Engineering*, Montreal, QC, Canada (October 2003), 30–39.

189 Lewis, D. (2013). *Counterfactuals*. Wiley.

190 Groce, A., Chaki, S., Kroening, D., and Strichman, O. (2006). Error explanation with distance metrics. *International Journal on Software Tools for Technology Transfer* 8 (3): 229–247.

191 Jin, W. and Orso, A. (2013). F3: fault localization for field failures. *Proceedings of the International Symposium on Software Testing and Analysis*, Lugano, Switzerland (July 2013), 213–223.

192 Zeller, A. (2002). Isolating cause-effect chains from computer programs. *Proceedings of the ACM SIGSOFT Symposium on Foundations of Software Engineering*, Charleston, SC, USA (November 2002), 1–10.

193 Cleve, H. and Zeller, A. (2005). Locating causes of program failures. *Proceedings of the IEEE International Conference on Software Engineering (ICSE '05)*, Louis, MO, USA (May 2005), 342–351.

194 Le, T.B., Thung, F., and Lo, D. (2013). Theory and practice, do they match? A case with spectrum-based fault localization. *Proceedings of the IEEE International Conference on Software Maintenance*, Eindhoven, Netherland (September 2013), 380–383.

195 Choi, S., Cha, S., and Tappert, C.C. (2010). A survey of binary similarity and distance measures. *Journal of Systemics, Cybernetics and Informatics* 8 (1): 43–48.

196 Willett, P. (2003). Similarity-based approaches to virtual screening. *Biochemical Society Transactions* 31 (3): 603–606.

197 Wong, W.E., Debroy, V., Gao, R., and Li, Y. (2014). The DStar method for effective software fault localization. *IEEE Transactions on Reliability* 63 (1): 290–308.

198 Lucia, L., Lo, D., Jiang, L. et al. (2014). Extended comprehensive study of association measures for fault localization. *Journal of Software: Evaluation and Process* 26 (2): 172–219.

199 Janssen, T., Abreu, R., and van Germund, A.J.C. (2009). Zoltar: a spectrum-based fault localization tool. *Proceedings of the ESEC/FSE Workshop on Software Integration and Evaluation*, Amsterdam, Netherlands (August 2009), 23–30.

200 Abreu, R., Mayer, W., Stumptner, M., and van Gemund, A.J. (2009). Refining spectrum-based fault localization rankings. *Proceedings of the ACM Symposium on Applied Computing*, Honolulu, HI, USA (March 2009), 409–414.

201 Wong, W.E., Debroy, V., Golden, R. et al. (2012). Effective software fault localization using an RBF neural network. *IEEE Transactions on Reliability* 61 (1): 149–169.

202 Wong, W.E., Debroy, V., and Xu, D. (2012). Towards better fault localization: a crosstab-based statistical approach. *IEEE Transactions on Systems, Man and Cybernetics, Part C: Applications and Reviews* 42 (3): 378–396.

203 Wong, W.E., Debroy, V., Li, Y., and Gao, R. (2012). Software fault localization using DStar (D*). *Proceedings of the Sixth International Conference on Software Security and Reliability*, Gaithersburg, MD, USA (June 2012), 21–30.

204 Kochhar, P.S., Xia, X., Lo, D., and Li, S. (2016). Practitioners' expectations on automated fault localization. *Proceedings of the 25th International Symposium on Software Testing and Analysis*, Saarbrücken, Germany (July 2016), 165–176.

205 Sun, S. and Podgurski, A. (2016). Properties of effective metrics for coverage-based statistical fault localization. *Proceedings of the 9th IEEE International Conference on Software Testing, Verification and Validation*, Chicago, IL, USA (April 2016), 124–134.

206 Yoo, S., Xie, X., Kuo, F. et al. (2014). No Pot of Gold at the End of Program Spectrum Rainbow: Greatest Risk Evaluation Formula Does Not Exist. *Research Note RN/14/14*. University College London.

207 Ernst, M.D., Cockrell, J., Griswold, W.G., and Notkin, D. (2001). Dynamically discovering likely program invariants to support program evolution. *IEEE Transactions on Software Engineering* 27 (2): 99–123.

208 Pytlik, B., Renieris, M., Krishnamurthi, S., and Reiss, S.P. (2003). Automated fault localization using potential invariants. arXiv preprint cs/0310040.

209 Sahoo, S.K., Criswell, J., Geigle, C., and Adve, V. (2013). Using likely invariants for automated software fault localization. *Proceedings of the International Conference on Architectural Support for Programming Languages and Operating Systems*, Houston, TX, USA (March 2013), 139–152.

210 Alipour, M.A. and Groce, A. (2012). Extended program invariants: applications in testing and fault localization. *Proceedings of the Ninth International Workshop on Dynamic Analysis*, Minneapolis, MN, USA (July 2012), 7–11.

211 Shu, T., Ye, T., Ding, Z., and Xia, J. (2016). Fault localization based on statement frequency. *The Information of the Science* 360: 43–56.

212 Le, T.B., Lo, D., Le Goues, C., and Grunske, L. (2016). A learning-to-rank based fault localization approach using likely invariants. *Proceedings of the 25th International Symposium on Software Testing and Analysis*, Saarbrücken, Germany (July 2016), 177–188.

213 Liblit, B., Naik, M., Zheng, A.X. et al. (2005). Scalable statistical bug isolation. *Proceedings of the ACM SIGPLAN Conference on Programming Language Design and Implementations*, Chicago, IL, USA (June 2005), 15–26.

214 Liu, C., Fei, L., Yan, X. et al. (2006). Statistical debugging: a hypothesis testing-based approach. *IEEE Transactions on Software Engineering* 32 (10): 831–848.

215 Dallmeier, V., Lindig, C., and Zeller, A. (2005). Lightweight defect localization for java. *Proceedings of the European Conference on Object-Oriented Programming*, Glasgow, UK (July 2005), 528–550.

216 Liu, C., Yan, X., Yu, H. et al. (2005). Mining behavior graphs for "Backtrace" of noncrashing bugs. *Proceedings of the SIAM International Conference on Data Mining*, Newport Beach, CA, USA (April 2005), 286–297.

217 Yilmaz, C., Paradkar, A., and Williams, C. (2008). Time will tell: fault localization using time spectra. *Proceedings of the International Conference on Software Engineering (ICSE '08)*, Leipzig, Germany (May 2008), 81–90.

218 Miraglia, A., Vogt, D., Bos, H. et al. (2016). Peeking into the past: efficient checkpoint-assisted time-traveling debugging. *Proceedings of the 2016 IEEE 27th International Symposium on Software Reliability Engineering (ISSRE '16)*, Ottawa, ON, Canada (23–27 October 2016), 455–466. IEEE. https://doi.org/10.1109/ISSRE.2016.9.

219 Treffer, A. and Uflacker, M. (2017). Back-in-time debugging in heterogeneous software stacks. *Proceedings of the 2017 IEEE International Symposium on Software Reliability Engineering Workshops (ISSREW '17)*, Toulouse, France (October 2017), 183–190. IEEE.

220 Xie, X., Chen, T.Y., and Xu, B. (2010). Isolating suspiciousness from spectrum-based fault localization techniques. *Proceedings of the International Conference on Quality Software*, Zhangjiajie, China (July 2010), 385–392.

221 Guo, L., Roychoudhury, A., and Wang, T. (2006). Accurately choosing execution runs for software fault localization. *Proceedings of the International Conference on Compiler Construction*, Vienna, Austria (March 2006), 80–95.

222 Abreu, R., González, A., and Gemund, A.J. (2010). Exploiting count spectra for bayesian fault localization. *Proceedings of the 6th International Conference on Predictive Models in Software Engineering*, Article No. 12, Timisoara, Romania (September 2010).

223 Lee, H.J., Naish, L., and Ramamohanarao, K. (2010). Effective software bug localization using spectral frequency weighting function. *Proceedings of the Annual IEEE International Computer Software and Applications Conference (COMPSAC '10)*, Seoul, Korea (July 2010), 218–227.

224 Xie, X., Wong, W.E., Chen, T.Y., and Xu, B. (2011). Spectrum-based fault localization: testing oracles are no longer mandatory. *Proceedings of the International Conference on Quality Software*, Madrid, Spain (July 2011), 1–10.

225 Xie, X., Wong, W.E., Chen, T.Y., and Xu, B. (2013). Metamorphic slice: an application in spectrum-based fault localization. *Information and Software Technology* 55 (5): 866–879.

226 Chen, T.Y., Tse, T.H., and Zhou, Z.Q. (2011). Semi-proving: an integrated method for program proving, testing, and debugging. *IEEE Transactions on Software Engineering* 37 (1): 109–125.

227 Tolksdorf, S., Lehmann, D., and Pradel, M. (2019). Interactive metamorphic testing of debuggers. *Proceedings of the 2019 ACM International Symposium on Software Testing and Analysis*, Beijing, China (July 2019), 273–283.

228 Zhao, L., Wang, L., Xiong, Z., and Gao, D. (2010). Execution-aware fault localization based on the control flow analysis. *Proceedings of the International Conference on Information Computing and Applications*, Tangshan, China (October 2010), 158–165.

229 Zhao, L., Wang, L., and Yin, X. (2011). Context-aware fault localization via control flow analysis. *Journal of Software* 6 (10): 1977–1984.

230 Guo, Y., Zhang, X., and Zheng, Z. (2016). Exploring the instability of spectra based fault localization performance. *Proceedings of the IEEE 40th Annual Computer Software and Applications Conference (COMPSAC '16)*, Atlanta, GA, USA (June 2016), 191–196.

231 Keller, F., Grunske, L., Heiden, S. et al. (2017). A critical evaluation of spectrum-based fault localization techniques on a large-scale software system. *Proceedings of the IEEE International Conference on Software Quality, Reliability, and Security (QRS '17)*, Prague, Czech Republic (July 2017), 114–125.

232 Li, Z., Yan, L., Liu, Y. et al. (2018). MURE: making use of mutations to refine spectrum-based fault localization. *Proceedings of the IEEE International Conference on Software Quality, Reliability, and Security Companion (QRS-C '18)*, Lisbon, Portugal (July 2018), 56–63.

233 Pearson, S. (2016). Evaluation of fault localization techniques. *Proceedings of the ACM SIGSOFT International Symposium on the Foundations of Software Engineering*, Seattle, WA, USA (November 2016), 1115–1117.

234 Pearson, S., Campos, J., Just, R. et al. (2017). Evaluating and improving fault localization. *Proceedings of the IEEE/ACM International Conference on Software Engineering (ICSE '17)*, Buenos Aires, Argentina (May 2017), 609–620.

235 de Oliveira, A.A.L., Camilo-Junior, C.G., de Andrade Freitas, E.N., and Vincenzi, A.M.R. (2018). FTMES: a failed-test-oriented mutant execution strategy for mutation-based fault localization. *Proceedings of the 2018 IEEE 29th International Symposium on Software Reliability Engineering (ISSRE '18)*, Memphis, TN, USA (15–18 October 2018), 155–165. IEEE. https://doi.org/10.1109/ISSRE.2018.00026.

236 Liu, Y., Li, Z., Wang, L. et al. (2017). Statement-oriented mutant reduction strategy for mutation based fault localization. *Proceedings of the IEEE International Conference on Software Quality, Reliability, and Security (QRS '17)*, Prague, Czech Republic (July 2017), 126–137.

237 Jeon, J. and Hong, S. (2020). Threats to validity in experimenting mutation-based fault localization. *Proceedings of the ACM/IEEE 42nd International Conference on Software Engineering (ICSE '20): New Ideas and Emerging Results*, Seoul, South Korea (27 June to 19 July 2020), 1–4. ACM. https://dl.acm.org/doi/10.1145/3377816.3381746.

238 Li, A., Lei, Y., and Mao, X. (2016). Towards more accurate fault localization: an approach based on feature selection using branching execution probability. *Proceedings of the IEEE International Conference on Software Quality, Reliability, and Security (QRS '16)*, Vienna, Austria (August 2016), 431–438.

239 Perez, A., Abreu, R., and Riboira, A. (2014). A dynamic code coverage approach to maximize fault localization efficiency. *Journal of Systems and Software* 90: 18–28.

240 Chilimbi, T.M., Liblit, B., Mehra, K. et al. (2009). HOLMES: effective statistical debugging via efficient path profiling. *Proceedings of the IEEE International Conference on Software Engineering (ICSE '09)*, Vancouver, ON, Canada (May 2009), 34–44.

241 Hu, P., Zhang, Z., Chan, W.K., and Tse, T.H. (2008). Fault localization with non-parametric program behavior model. *Proceedings of the International Conference on Quality Software*, Oxford, UK (12–13 August 2008), 385–395.

242 Zhang, Z., Chan, W.K., Tse, T.H. et al. (2011). Non-parametric statistical fault localization. *Journal of Systems and Software* 84 (6): 885–905.

243 Yang, Y., Deng, F., Yan, Y., and Gao, F. (2019). A fault localization method based on conditional probability. *Proceedings of the IEEE International Conference on Software Quality, Reliability, and Security Companion (QRS-C '19)*, Sofia, Bulgaria (July 2019), 213–218

244 Henderson, T.A.D. and Podgurski, A. (2018). Behavioral fault localization by sampling suspicious dynamic control flow subgraphs. *Proceedings of the 2018 IEEE*

International Conference on Software Testing, Verification and Validation, Vasteras, Sweden (April 2018), 93–104.

245 Zhang, Z., Jiang, B., Chan, W.K., and Tse, T.H. (2008). Debugging through evaluation sequences: a controlled experimental study. *Proceedings of the International Computer Software and Applications Conference (COMPSAC '08)*, Turku, Finland (28 July to 1 August 2008), 128–135.

246 Zhang, Z., Jiang, B., Chan, W.K. et al. (2010). Fault localization through evaluation sequences. *Journal of Systems and Software* 83 (2): 174–187.

247 You, Z., Qin, Z., and Zheng, Z. (2012). Statistical fault localization using execution sequence. *Proceedings of the International Conference on Machine Learning and Cybernetics*, Xi'an, China (July 2012), 899–905.

248 Baah, G.K., Podgurski, A., and Harrold, M.J. (2010). Causal inference for statistical fault localization. *Proceedings of the International Symposium on Software Testing and Analysis*, Trento, Italy (July 2010), 73–83.

249 Baah, G.K., Podgurski, A., and Harrold, M.J. (2011). Mitigating the confounding effects of program dependences for effective fault localization. *Proceedings of the European Software Engineering Conference and ACM SIGSOFT Symposium on the Foundations of Software Engineering*, Szeged, Hungary (September 2011), 146–156.

250 Modi, V., Roy, S., and Aggarwal, S.K. (2013). Exploring program phases for statistical bug localization. *Proceedings of the ACM SIGPLAN-SIGSOFT Workshop on Program Analysis for Software Tools and Engineering*, Seattle, WA, USA (June 2013), 33–40.

251 Wang, X., Jiang, S., Ju, X. et al. (2015). Mitigating the dependence confounding effect for effective predicate-based statistical fault localization. *Proceedings of the IEEE 39th Annual Computer Software and Applications Conference (COMPSAC '15)*, Taichung, Taiwan (July 2015), 105–114.

252 Feyzi, F. and Parsa, S. (2018). FPA-FL: incorporating static fault-proneness analysis into statistical fault localization. *Journal of Systems and Software* 136: 39–58.

253 Abramson, D., Foster, I., Michalakes, J., and Sosic, R. (1995). Relative debugging and its application to the development of large numerical models. *Proceedings of the 8th International Conference for High Performance Computing, Networking, Storage, and Analysis*, no. 51, San Diego, CA, USA (December 1995).

254 Zeller, A. and Hildebrandt, R. (2002). Simplifying and isolating failure-inducing input. *IEEE Transactions on Software Engineering* 28 (2): 183–200.

255 Zimmermann, T. and Zeller, A. (2001). Visualizing memory graphs. In: *Software Visualization* (ed. Diehl, S.), 191–204. Berlin, Heidelberg: Springer.

256 Wikipedia. Delta debugging. https://en.wikipedia.org/wiki/Delta_debugging (accessed January 2022).

257 Nie, C. and Leung, H. (2011). The minimal failure-causing schema of combinatorial testing. *ACM Transactions on Software Engineering and Methodology* 20 (4): 1–38.

258 Niu, X., Nie, C., Lei, Y., and Chan, A.T., Identifying failure-inducing combinations using tuple relationship. *Proceedings of the International Conference on Software Testing, Verification, and Validation Workshops*, Luxembourg (March 2013), 271–280.

259 Ghandehari, L.S., Lei, Y., Kacker, R. et al. (2018). A combinatorial testing-based approach to fault localization. *IEEE Transactions on Software Engineering* 46 (6): 616–645.

260 Gupta, N., He, H., Zhang, X., and Gupta, R. (2005). Locating faulty code using failure inducing chops. *Proceedings of the International Conference on Automated Software Engineering*, Long Beach, CA, USA (November 2005), 263–272.

261 Sumner, W.N and Zhang, X. (2010). Memory indexing: canonicalizing addresses across executions. *Proceedings of the International Symposium on Foundations of Software Engineering*, Santa Fe, NM, USA (November 2010), 217–226.

262 Sumner, W.N. and Zhang, X. (2009). Algorithms for automatically computing the causal paths of failure. *Proceedings of the International Conference on Fundamental Approaches to Software Engineering*, York, UK (March 2009), 335–369.

263 Xin, B., Sumner, W.N., and Zhang, X. (2008). Efficient program execution indexing. *ACM SIGPLAN Notices* 43 (6): 238–248.

264 Sumner, W.N. and Zhang, X. (2013). Comparative causality: explaining the differences between executions. *Proceedings of the International Conference on Software Engineering (ICSE '13)*, San Francisco, CA, USA (May 2013), 272–281.

265 Hashimoto, M., Mori, A., and Izumida, T. (2018). Automated patch extraction via syntax-and semantics-aware delta debugging on source code changes. *Proceedings of the 2018 26th ACM Joint Meeting on European Software Engineering Conference and Symposium on the Foundations of Software Engineering*, Lake Buena Vista, FL, USA (November 2018), 598–609.

266 Zhang, X., Gupta, N., and Gupta, R. (2006). Locating faults through automated predicate switching. *Proceedings of the International Conference on Software Engineering (ICSE '06)*, Shanghai, China (May 2006), 272–281.

267 Wang, T. and Roychoudhury, A. (2005). Automated path generation for software fault localization. *Proceedings of the International Conference on Automated Software Engineering*, Long Beach, CA, USA (November 2005), 347–351.

268 Li, F., Huo, W., Chen, C. et al. (2013). Effective fault localization based on minimum debugging frontier set. *Proceedings of the International Symposium on Code Generation and Optimization*, Shenzhen, China (February 2013), 1–10.

269 Li, F., Li, Z., Huo, W., and Feng, X. (2017). Locating software faults based on minimum debugging frontier set. *IEEE Transactions on Software Engineering* 43 (8): 760–776.

270 Jeffrey, D., Gupta, N. and Gupta, R. (2008). Fault localization using value replacement. *Proceedings of the International Symposium on Software Testing and Analysis*, Seattle, WA, USA (July 2008), 167–178.

271 Zhang, Z., Chan, W.K., Tse, T.H. et al. (2009). Capturing propagation of infected program states. *Proceedings of the 7th Joint Meeting of the European Software Engineering Conference and the ACM SIGSOFT International Symposium on Foundation of Software Engineering*, Amsterdam, The Netherlands (24–28 August 2009), 43–52.

272 Yang, B., He, Y., Liu, H. et al. (2020). A lightweight fault localization approach based on XGBoost. *Proceedings of the 2020 IEEE 20th International Conference on Software Quality, Reliability and Security (QRS '20)*, Macau, China (11–14 December 2020), 168–179. IEEE. https://doi.org/10.1109/QRS51102.2020.00033.

273 Zhong, H. and Mei, H. (2020). Learning a graph-based classifier for fault localization. *Science China Information Sciences* 63 (6): 1–22.

274 Nishiura, K., Choi, E., and Mizuno, O. (2017). Improving faulty interaction localization using logistic regression. *Proceedings of the 2017 IEEE International Conference on Software Quality, Reliability and Security (QRS '17)*, Prague, Czech Republic (25–29 July 2017), 138–149. IEEE. https://doi.org/10.1109/QRS.2017.24.

275 Xiao, Y., Keung, J., Bennin, K.E., and Mi, Q. (2019). Improving bug localization with word embedding and enhanced convolutional neural networks. *Information and Software Technology* 105: 17–29.

276 Xiao, Y., Keung, J., Bennin, K.E., and Mi, Q. (2018). Machine translation-based bug localization technique for bridging lexical gap. *Information and Software Technology* 99: 58–61.

277 Wong, W.E. and Qi, Y. (2009). BP neural network-based effective fault localization. *International Journal of Software Engineering and Knowledge Engineering* 19 (4): 573–597.

278 Fausett, L. (1994). *Fundamentals of Neural Networks: Architectures, Algorithms, and Applications*. Prentice Hall.

279 Hecht-Nielsen, R. (1989). Theory of the backpropagation neural network. *Proceedings of the International Joint Conference on Neural Networks*, Washington DC, USA (June 1989), 593–605. IEEE.

280 Lee, C.C., Chung, P.C., Tsai, J.R., and Chang, C.I. (1999). Robust radial basis function neural networks. *IEEE Transactions on Systems, Man, and Cybernetics: Part B Cybernetics* 29 (6): 674–685.

281 Wasserman, P.D. (1993). *Advanced Methods in Neural Computing*. Van Nostrand Reinhold.

282 Briand, L.C., Labiche, Y., and Liu, X. (2007). Using machine learning to support debugging with tarantula. *Proceedings of the IEEE International Symposium on Software Reliability*, Trolhattan, Sweden (November 2007), 137–146.

283 Jonsson, L., Broman, D., Magnusson, M. et al. (2016). Automatic localization of bugs to faulty components in large scale software systems using bayesian classification. *Proceedings of the IEEE International Conference on Software Quality, Reliability, and Security (QRS '16)*, Vienna, Austria (August 2016), 423–430.

284 Mariani, L., Monni, C., Pezzé, M. et al. (2018). Localizing faults in cloud systems. *Proceedings of the 2018 IEEE International Conference on Software Testing, Verification and Validation*, Vasteras, Sweden (April 2018), 262–273.

285 Kim, Y., Mun, S., Yoo, S., and Kim, M. (2019). Precise learn-to-rank fault localization using dynamic and static features of target programs. *ACM Transactions on Software Engineering and Methodology* 28 (4) Article 23.

286 Zhang, M., Li, X., Zhang, L., and Khurshid, S. (2017). Boosting spectrum-based fault localization using pagerank. *Proceedings of the 2017 ACM International Symposium on Software Testing and Analysis*, Santa Barbara, CA, USA (July 2017), 261–272.

287 Sohn, J. (2020). Bridging fault localisation and defect prediction. *Proceedings of the 2020 IEEE/ACM 42nd International Conference on Software Engineering: Companion Proceedings (ICSE-Companion '20)*, Seoul, South Korea (27 June to 19 July 2020), 214–217. ACM. https://dl.acm.org/doi/10.1145/3377812.3381403.

288 Sohn, J. and Yoo, S. (2017). FLUCCS: using code and change metrics to improve fault localization. *Proceedings of the 2017 ACM International Symposium on Software Testing and Analysis*, Santa Barbara, CA, USA (July 2017), 273–283.

289 Li, X., Li, W., Zhang, Y., and Zhang, L. (2019). DeepFL: integrating multiple fault diagnosis dimensions for deep fault localization. *Proceedings of the 2019 ACM International Symposium on Software Testing and Analysis*, Beijing, China (July 2019), 169–180.

290 Near, J.P. and Jackson, D. (2016). Finding security bugs in web applications using a catalog of access control patterns. *Proceedings of the 2016 IEEE/ACM 38th IEEE International Conference on Software Engineering (ICSE '16)*, Austin, TX, USA (14–22 May 2016), 947–958. ACM. https://dl.acm.org/doi/10.1145/2884781.2884836.

291 Santos, D., Rodrigues, C.A., and Matias, R. Jr. (2018). Failure patterns in operating systems: an exploratory and observational study. *Journal of Systems and Software* 137: 512–530.

292 Zhou, X., Peng, X., Xie, T. et al. (2019). Latent error prediction and fault localization for microservice applications by learning from system trace logs. *Proceedings of the 2019 27th ACM Joint Meeting on European Software Engineering Conference and Symposium on the Foundations of Software Engineering*, Tallinn, Estonia (26–30 August 2019), 683–694. ACM. https://dl.acm.org/doi/10.1145/3338906.3338961.

293 Nessa, S., Abedin, M., Wong, W.E. et al. (2009). Fault localization using N-gram analysis. *Proceedings of the Third International Conference on Wireless Algorithms, Systems, and Applications*, Dallas, TX (26–28 October 2008), 548–559. ACM. https://doi.org/10.1007/978-3-540-88582-5_51.

294 Cellier, P., Ducasse, M., Ferre, S., and Ridoux, O. (2008). Formal concept analysis enhances fault localization in software. *Proceedings of the International Conference on Formal Concept Analysis*, Montreal, QC, Canada (February 2008), 273–288.

295 Cellier, P., Ducasse, M., Ferre, S., and Ridoux, O. (2011). Multiple fault localization with data mining. *Proceedings of the International Conference on Software Engineering and Knowledge Engineering*, Miami, FL, USA (July 2011), 238–243.

296 Zhang, S. and Zhang, C. (2014). Software bug localization with Markov logic. *Companion Proceedings of the 36th International Conference on Software Engineering (ICSE Companion '14)*, Hyderabad, India (31 May to 7 June 2014), 424–427.

297 Denmat, T., Ducassé, M., and Ridoux, O. (2005). Data mining and cross-checking of execution traces. *Proceedings of the International Conference on Automated Software Engineering*, Long Beach, CA, USA (November 2005), 396–399.

298 Bian, P., Liang, B., Zhang, Y. et al. (2019). Detecting bugs by discovering expectations and their violations. *IEEE Transactions on Software Engineering* 45 (10): 984–1001.

299 Hanam, Q., de Brito, F.S.M., and Mesbah, A. (2016). Discovering bug patterns in JavaScript. *Proceedings of the 2016 24th ACM SIGSOFT International Symposium on Foundations of Software Engineering*, Seattle, WA, USA (13–18 November 2016), 144–156. ACM. https://dl.acm.org/doi/10.1145/2950290.2950308.

300 Reiter, R. (1987). A theory of diagnosis from first principles. *Artificial Intelligence* 32 (1): 57–95.

301 Mayer, W. and Stumptner, M. (2007). Model-based debugging: state of the art and future challenges. *Electronic Notes in Theoretical Computer Science* 174 (4): 61–82.

302 Mayer, W. and Stumptner, M. (2008). Evaluating models for model-based debugging. *Proceedings of the ACM International Conference on Automated Software Engineering*, L'Aquila, Italy (September 2008), 128–137.

303 Abreu, R. and van Gemund, A.J.C. (2009). A low-cost approximate minimal hitting set algorithm and its application to model-based diagnosis. *Proceedings of the Eight Symposium on Abstraction, Reformulation, and Approximation*, Lake Arrowhead, CA, USA (August 2009).

304 Baah, G.K., Podgurski, A., and Harrold, M.J. (2010). The probabilistic program dependence graph and its application to fault diagnosis. *IEEE Transactions on Software Engineering* 36 (4): 528–545.

305 DeMillo, R.A., Pan, H., and Spafford, E.H. (1997). Failure and fault analysis for software debugging. *Proceedings of the Twenty-First Annual International Computer Software and Applications Conference (COMPSAC '97)*, Washington, DC, USA (11–15 August 1997), 515–521. IEEE. https://doi.org/10.1109/CMPSAC.1997.625061.

306 Friedrich, G., Stumptner, M., and Wotawa, F. (1999). Model-based diagnosis of hardware designs. *Artificial Intelligence* 1–2: 3–39.

307 de Kleer, J. and Williams, B.C. (1987). Diagnosing multiple faults. *Artificial Intelligence* 32 (1): 97–130.

308 Mateis, C., Stumptner, M., and Wotawa, F. (2000). Modeling java programs for diagnosis. *Proceedings of the 14th European Conference on Artificial Intelligence*, Berlin, Germany (20–25 August 2000), 171–175. IOS Press.

309 Mayer, W., Abreu, R., Stumptner, M., and van Gemund, A.J.C. (2008). Prioritizing model-based debugging diagnostic reports. *Proceedings of the International Workshop on Principles of Diagnosis*, Blue Mountains, Australia (September 2008), 127–134.

310 Mayer, W. and Stumptner, M. (2004). Approximate modeling for debugging of program loops.

311 Mayer, W. and Stumptner, M. (2003). Model-based debugging using multiple abstract models. arXiv preprint cs/0309030.

312 Shchekotykhin, K.M., Schmitz, T., and Jannach, D. (2016). Efficient sequential model-based fault-localization with partial diagnose. *Proceedings of the 25th International Joint Conference on Artificial Intelligence*, New York City, NY, USA (July 2016), 1251–1257.

313 Wotawa, F., Stumptner, M., and Mayer, W. (2002). Model-based debugging or how to diagnose programs automatically. *Proceedings of the International Conference on Industrial and Engineering, Applications of Artificial Intelligence and Expert Systems*, Cairns, Australia (June 2002), 746–757.

314 Wotawa, F., Weber, J., Nica, M., and Ceballos, R. (2009). On the complexity of program debugging using constraints for modeling the program's syntax and semantics. *Proceedings of the Conference of the Spanish Association for Artificial Intelligence*, Seville, Spain (November 2009), 22–31.

315 Wu, J., Jia, X., Liu, C. et al. (2004). A statistical model to locate faults at input levels. *Proceedings of the International Conference on Automated Software Engineering*, Linz, Austria (September 2004), 274–277.

316 Mateis, C., Stumptner, M., Wieland, D., and Wotawa, F. (2002). JADE – AI support for debugging java programs. *Proceedings of the IEEE International Conference on Tools with Artificial Intelligence*, Vancouver, BC, Canada (November 2002), 62.

317 Mayer, W., Stumptner, M., Wieland, D., and Wotawa, F. (2002). Towards an integrated debugging environment. *Proceedings of the European Conference on Artificial Intelligence*, Lyon, France (July 2002), 422–426.

318 Abreu, R., Zoeteweij, P., and van Gemund, A.J. (2009). Spectrum-based multiple fault localization. *Proceedings of the 24th IEEE/ACM International Conference on Automated Software Engineering*, Auckland, New Zealand (November 2009), 88–99.

319 Mayer, W. and Stumptner, M. (2002). Modeling programs with unstructured control flow for debugging. *Australian Joint Conference on Artificial Intelligence*, Canberra, Australia (December 2002), 107–118.

320 Mayer, W. and Stumptner, M. (2003). Extending diagnosis to debug programs with exceptions. *Proceedings of the 18th IEEE International Conference on Automated Software Engineering*, Montreal, QC, Canada (6–10 October 2003), 240–244. IEEE. https://doi.org/10.1109/ASE.2003.1240312.

321 Xu, Z., Ma, S., Zhang, X. et al. (2018). Debugging with the intelligence via probabilistic inference. *Proceedings of the IEEE/ACM International Conference on Software Engineering (ICSE '18)*, Gothenburg, Sweden (May 2018), 1171–1181.

322 Yu, X., Liu, J., Yang, Z.J. et al. (2016). Bayesian network based program dependence graph for fault localization. *Proceedings of the 2016 IEEE International Symposium on Software Reliability Engineering Workshops (ISSREW '16)*, Ottawa, ON, Canada (23–27 October 2016), 181–188. IEEE. https://doi.org/10.1109/ISSREW.2016.35.

323 Yu, X., Liu, J., Yang, Z., and Liu, X. (2017). The Bayesian network based program dependence graph and its application to fault localization. *Journal of Systems and Software* 134: 44–53.

324 Bourdoncle, F. (1993). Abstract debugging of higher-order imperative languages. *Proceedings of the ACM SIGPLAN Conference on Programming Language Design and Implementation,* Albuquerque, NM, USA (June 1993), 46–55.

325 Cousot, P. and Cousot, R. (1977). Abstract interpretation: a unified lattice model for static analysis of programs by construction or approximation of fixpoints. *Proceedings of the IEEE International Symposium on Principles of Programming Languages*, Los Angeles, CA, USA (January 1977), 238–252.

326 Mayer, W. and Stumptner, M. (2007). Abstract interpretation of programs for model-based debugging. *Proceedings of the International Joint Conference on Artificial Intelligence*, Hyderabad, India (January 2007), 471–476.

327 Kob, D. and Wotawa, F. (2004). Introducing alias information into model-based debugging. *Proceedings of the European Conference on Artificial Intelligence*, Valencia Spain (August 2004), 833–837

328 Mayer, W., Stumptner, M., Wieland, D., and Wotawa, F. (2002). Can AI help to improve debugging substantially? Debugging experiences with value-based models. *Proceedings of the European Conference on Artificial Intelligence*, Lyon, France (July 2002), 417–421

329 Ball, T., Naik, M., and Rajamani, S.K. (2003). From symptom to cause: localizing errors in counterexample traces. *Proceedings of the ACM SIGPLAN-SIGACT Symposium on Principles of Programming Languages*, New Orleans, LA, USA (January 2003), 97–105.

330 Chaki, S., Groce, A., and Strichman, O. (2004). Explaining abstract counterexamples. *Proceedings of the 12th ACM SIGSOFT Twelfth International Symposium on Foundations of Software Engineering*, Newport Beach, CA, USA (31 October to 6 November 2004), 73–82. ACM.

331 Griesmayer, A., Staber, S., and Bloem, R. (2007). Automated fault localization for C programs. *Electronic Notes in Theoretical Computer Science* 174 (4): 95–111.

332 Griesmayer, A., Staber, S., and Bloem, R. (2010). Fault localization using a model checker. *Software Testing, Verification and Reliability* 20 (2): 149–173.

333 Groce, A. and Visser, W. (2003). What went wrong: explaining counterexamples. *Proceedings of the International Conference on Model Checking Software*, Portland, OR, USA (May 2003), 121–136.

334 Groce, A., Kroening, D., and Lerda, F. (2004). Understanding counterexample with explain. *International Conference on Computer Aided Verification*, Boston, MA, USA (July 2004), 453–456.

335 Könighofer, R. and Bloem, R. (2011). Automated error localization and correction for imperative programs. *Proceedings of the International Conference on Formal Methods in Computer-Aided Design*, Austin, TX, USA (October 2011), 91–100.

336 da Alves, E.H.S., Cordeiro, L.C., and Eddiefilho, B.d.L. (2017). A method to localize faults in concurrent C programs. *Journal of Systems and Software* 132: 336–352.

337 Debroy, V. and Wong, W.E. (2014). Combining mutation and fault localization for automated program debugging. *Journal of Systems and Software* 90: 45–60.

338 He, H. and Gupta, N. (2004). Automated debugging using path-based weakest preconditions. *Proceedings of the Fundamental Approaches to Software Engineering*, Barcelona, Spain (March 2004), 267–280.

339 Kaleeswaran, S., Tulsian, V., Kanade, A., and Orso, A. (2014). MintHint: automated synthesis of repair hints. *Proceedings of the 36th International Conference on Software Engineering (ICSE '14)*, Hyderabad, India (31 May to 7 June 2014), 266–276. ACM. https://dl.acm.org/doi/10.1145/2568225.2568258.

340 Nguyen, H., Qi, D., Roychoudhury, A., and Chandra, S. (2013). SemFix: program repair via semantic analysis. *Proceedings of the International Conference on Software Engineering (ICSE '13)*, San Francisco, CA, USA (May 2013), 772–781.

341 Stumptner, M. and Wotawa, F. (1999). Debugging functional program. *Proceedings of the International Joint Conference on Artificial Intelligence*, Stockholm, Sweden (31 July to 6 August 1999), 1074–1079.

342 Peischl, B. and Wotawa, F. (2006). Automated source-level error localization in hardware designs. *IEEE Design and Test of Computers* 23 (1): 8–19.

343 Wotawa, F. (2002). Debugging hardware designs using a value-based model. *Applied Intelligence* 16 (1): 71–92.

344 Jannach, D. and Engler, U. (2010). Toward model-based debugging of spreadsheet programs. *Proceedings of the Joint Conference on Knowledge-Based Software Engineering*, Kaunas, Lithuania (August 2010), 252–264.

345 Nica, M., Nica, S., and Wotawa, F. (2013). On the use of mutations and testing for debugging. *Software, Practice and Experience* 43 (9): 1121–1142.

346 Wotawa, F., Nica, M., and Moraru, I. (2012). Automated debugging based on a constraint model of the program and a test case. *The Journal of Logic and Algebraic Programming* 81 (4): 390–407.

347 Soria, A., Pace, J.A.D., and Campo, M.R. (2015). Architecture-driven assistance for fault-localization tasks. *Expert Systems* 32 (1): 1–22.

348 Chittimalli, P.K. and Shah, V. (2015). Fault localization during system testing. *Proceedings of the IEEE 23rd International Conference on Program Comprehension*, Florence, Italy (May 2015), 285–286.

349 Lehmann, D. and Pradel, M. (2018). Feedback-directed differential testing of interactive debuggers. *Proceedings of the ACM SIGSOFT International Symposium on the Foundations of Software Engineering*, Lake Buena Vista, FL, USA (November 2018), 610–620.

350 Wang, Y., Li, J., Yan, N. et al. (2018). Bug patterns localization based on topic model for bugs in program loop. *Proceedings of the IEEE International Conference on Software Quality, Reliability, and Security Companion (QRS-C '18)*, Lisbon, Portugal (July 2018), 366–370.

351 Troya, J., Segura, S., Parejo, J.A., and Ruiz-Cortés, A. (2018). Spectrum-based fault localization in model transformations. *ACM Transactions on Software Engineering and Methodology* 27 (3): 1–50, Article 13.

352 Bohnet, J., Voigt, S., and Döllner, J. (2009). Projecting code changes onto execution traces to support localization of recently introduced bugs. *Proceedings of the ACM Symposium on Applied Computing*, Honolulu, HI, USA (March 2009), 438–442.

353 Chen, K. and Chen, J. (2007). Aspect-based instrumentation for locating memory leaks in java programs. *Proceedings of the Annual International Computer Software and Applications Conference (COMPSAC '07)*, Beijing, China (July 2007), 23–28.

354 Chen, I., Yang, C., Lu, T., and Jaygarl, H. (2008). Implicit social network model for predicting and tracking the location of faults. *Proceedings of the Annual International Computer Software and Applications Conference (COMPSAC '08)*, Turku, Finland (August 2008), 136–143.

355 de Souza, H.A. and Chaim, M.L. (2013). Adding context to fault localization with integration coverage. *Proceedings of the International Conference on Automated Software Engineering*, Silicon Valley, CA, USA (November 2013), 628–633.

356 Gong, L., Lo, D., Jiang, L., and Zhang, H. (2012). Interactive fault localization leveraging simple user feedback. *Proceedings of the International Conference on Software Maintenance*, Trento, Italy (September 2012), 67–76.

357 Lin, Y., Sun, J., Xue, Y. et al. (2017). Feedback-based debugging. *Proceedings of the IEEE/ACM International Conference on Software Engineering (ICSE '17)*, Buenos Aires, Argentina (May 2017), 393–403.

358 Li, X., Zhu, S., d'Amorim, M., and Orso, A. (2018). Enlightened debugging. *Proceedings of the IEEE/ACM International Conference on Software Engineering (ICSE '18)*, Gothenburg, Sweden (May 2018), 82–92.

359 Ko, A.J. and Myers, B.A. (2008). Debugging reinvented: asking and answering why and why not questions about program behavior. *Proceedings of the International Conference on Software Engineering (ICSE '08)*, Leipzig, Germany (May 2008), 301–310.

360 Cheng, H., Lo, D., Zhou, Y. et al. (2009). Identifying bug signatures using discriminative graph mining. *Proceedings of the International Symposium on Software Testing and Analysis*, Chicago, IL, USA (July 2009), 141–152.

361 Maruyama, K. and Terada, M. (2003). Debugging with reverse watchpoint. *Proceedings of the International Conference on Quality Software*, Dallas, TX, USA (November 2003), 116–116.

362 Liu, B., Nejati, L.S., Briand, L.C., and Bruckmann, T. (2016). Simulink fault localization: an iterative statistical debugging approach. *Software Testing, Verification and Reliability* 26 (6): 431–459.

363 Liu, B., Nejati, S., and Briand, L.C. (2019). Effective fault localization of automotive Simulink models: achieving the trade-off between test oracle effort and fault localization accuracy. *Empirical Software Engineering* 24 (1): 444–490.

364 Wang, Q., Parnin, C., and Orso, A. (2015). Evaluating the usefulness of IR-based fault localization techniques. *Proceedings of the 24th International Symposium on Software Testing and Analysis*, Baltimore, MD, USA (July 2015), 1–11.

365 Dallmeier, V. and Zimmermann, T. (2007). Extraction of bug localization benchmarks from history. *Proceedings of the International Conference on Automated Software Engineering*, Atlanta, GA, USA (November 2007), 433–436.

366 Lee, J., Kim, D., and Bissyandé, T.F. (2018). Bench4BL: reproducibility study on the performance of IR-based bug localization. *Proceedings of the 2018 ACM International Symposium on Software Testing and Analysis*, Amsterdam, Netherlands (July 2018), 61–72.

367 Lukins, S.K., Kraft, N.A., and Etzkorn, L.H. (2008). Source code retrieval for bug localization using latent dirichlet allocation. *Proceedings of the Working Conference on Reverse Engineering*, Antwerp, Belgium (October 2008), 155–164.

368 Rao, S. and Kak, A. (2011). Retrieval from software libraries for bug localization: a comparative study of generic and composite text models. *Proceedings of the Working Conference on Mining Software Repositories*, Honolulu, HI, USA (May 2011), 43–52.

369 Saha, R.K., Lease, M., Kunshid, S., and Perry, D.E. (2013). Improving bug localization using structured information retrieval. *Proceedings of the International Conference on Automated Software Engineering*, Silicon Valley, CA, USA (November 2013), 345–355.

370 Zhou, J., Zhang, H., and Lo, D. (2012). Where should the bugs be fixed? – More accurate information retrieval-based bug localization based on bug reports. *Proceedings of the International Conference on Software Engineering (ICSE '12)*, Zurich, Switzerland (June 2012), 14–24.

371 Chaparro, O., Florez, J.M., and Marcus, A. (2019). Using bug descriptions to reformulate queries during text-retrieval-based bug localization. *Empirical Software Engineering* 24 (5): 2947–3007.

372 Tantithamthavorn, C., Abebe, S.L., Hassan, A.E. et al. (2018). The impact of IR-based classifier configuration on the performance and the effort of method-level bug localization. *Information and Software Technology* 102: 160–174.

373 Khatiwada, S., Tushev, M., and Mahmoud, A. (2018). Just enough semantics: an information theoretic approach for IR-based software bug localization. *Information and Software Technology* 93: 45–57.

374 Zhang, L. and Zhang, Z. (2018). SeTCHi: selecting test cases to improve history-guided fault localization. *Proceedings of the 2018 IEEE 29th International Symposium on Software Reliability Engineering Workshops (ISSREW '18)*, Memphis, TN, USA (15–18 October 2018), 200–207. IEEE. https://doi.org/10.1109/ISSREW.2018.00007.

375 Rahman, M.M. and Roy, C.K. (2018). Improving IR-based bug localization with context-aware query reformulation. *Proceedings of the ACM SIGSOFT International Symposium on the Foundations of Software Engineering*, Lake Buena Vista, FL, USA (November 2018), 621–632.

376 Amar, A. and Rigby, P.C. (2019). Mining historical test logs to predict bugs and localize faults in the test logs. *Proceedings of the IEEE/ACM International Conference on Software Engineering (ICSE '19)*, Montréal, QC, Canada (May 2019), 140–151.

377 Le, T.B., Thung, F., and Lo, D. (2017). Will this localization tool be effective for this bug? Mitigating the impact of unreliability of information retrieval based bug localization tools. *Empirical Software Engineering* 22: 2237–2279.

378 Hoang, T., Oentary, R.J., Le, T.B., and Lo, D. (2019). Network-clustered multimodal bug localization. *IEEE Transactions on Software Engineering* 45 (10): 1002–1023.

379 Silva, J. (2011). A survey on algorithmic debugging strategies. *Advances in Engineering Software* 42 (11): 976–991.

380 Zeller, A. (2006). *Why Programs Fail – A Guide to Systematic Debugging*. Elsevier.

381 Christ, J., Ermis, E., Schaf, M. and Wies, T. (2013). Flow-sensitive fault localization. *Proceedings of the International Conference on Verification, Model Checking, and Abstract Interpretation*, Rome, Italy (January 2013), 189–208.

382 Ermis, E., Schaf, M., and Wies, T. (2012). Error invariants. *Proceedings of the International Symposium on Formal Methods*, Paris, France (August 2012), 187–201.

383 Jose, M. and Majumdar, R. (2011). Bug-assist: assisting fault localization in ANSI-C programs. *Proceedings of the International Conference on Computer Aided Verification*, Snowbird, UT, USA (July 2011), 504–509.

384 Jose, M. and Majumdar, R. (2011). Cause clue clauses: error localization using maximum satisfiability. *Proceedings of the ACM SIGPLAN Conference on Programming Language Design and Implementation*, San Jose, CA, USA (June 2011), 437–446.

385 Lamraoui, S. and Nakajima, S. (2016). A formula-based approach for automatic fault localization of multi-fault programs. *Journal of Information Processing* 24 (1): 88–98.

386 Roychoudhury, A. and Chandra, S. (2016). Formula-based software debugging. *Communications of the ACM* 59 (7): 68–77.

387 Zhao, F., Tang, Y., Yang, Y. et al. (2015). Is learning-to-rank cost-effective in recommending relevant files for bug localization? *Proceedings of the 2015 IEEE International Conference on Software Quality, Reliability and Security (QRS '15)*, Vancouver, BC, Canada (August 2015), 293–303.

388 Wu, R., Wen, M., Cheung, S., and Zhang, H. (2018). ChangeLocator: locate crash-inducing changes based on crash reports. *Empirical Software Engineering* 23: 2866–2900.

389 Chen, H., Lv, H., Huang, S. et al. (2015). Diagnosing SDN network problems by using spectrum-based fault localization techniques. *Proceedings of the IEEE International Conference on Software Quality, Reliability, and Security Companion (QRS-C '15)*, Vancouver, BC, Canada (August 2015), 121–127.

390 Christi, A., Groce, A., and Gopinath, R. (2019). Evaluating fault localization for resource adaptation via test-based software modification. *Proceedings of the IEEE International Conference on Software Quality, Reliability, and Security (QRS '19)*, Sofia, Bulgaria (July 2019), 26–33.

391 Andrews, J.H., Briand, L.C., and Labiche, Y. (2005). Is mutation an appropriate tool for testing experiments? *Proceedings of the 27th International Conference on Software Engineering (ICSE '05)*, St. Louis, MO, USA (May 2005), 402–411.

392 Do, H. and Rothermel, G. (2006). On the use of mutation faults in empirical assessments of test case prioritization techniques. *IEEE Transactions on Software Engineering* 32 (9): 733–752.

393 Namin, A.S., Andrews, J.H., and Labiche, Y. (2006). Using mutation analysis for assessing and comparing testing coverage criteria. *IEEE Transactions on Software Engineering* 32 (8): 608–624.

394 Liu, C. and Han, J. (2006). Failure proximity: a fault localization-based approach. *Proceedings of the ACM SIGSOFT International Symposium on Foundations of Software Engineering*, Portland, OR, USA (November 2006), 46–56.

395 Hofer, B. and Wotawa, F. (2012). Spectrum enhanced dynamic slicing for better fault localization. *Proceedings of the European Conference on Artificial Intelligence*, Montpellier, France (August 2012), 420–425.

396 Parnin, C. and Orso, A. (2011). Are automated debugging techniques actually helping programmers? *Proceedings of the International Symposium on Software Testing and Analysis*, Toronto, ON, Canada (July 2011), 199–209.

397 Xie, X., Liu, Z., Song, S. et al. (2016). Revisit of automatic debugging via human focus-tracking analysis. *Proceedings of the International Conference on Software Engineering (ICSE '16)*, Austin, TX, USA (May 2016), 808–819.

398 Xia, X., Bao, L., Lo, D., and Li, S. (2017). "Automated debugging considered harmful" considered harmful: a user study revisiting the usefulness of spectra-based fault localization techniques with professionals using real bugs from large systems. *Proceedings of the International Conference on Software Maintenance and Evolution*, Raleigh, NC, USA (January 2017), 267–278.

399 Le, T.B., Lo, D., and Thung, F. (2015). Should I follow this fault localization tool's output? – Automated prediction of fault localization effectiveness. *Empirical Software Engineering* 20 (5): 1237–1274.

400 Monperrus, M. (2014). A critical review of "automated patch generation learned from human-written patches" essay on the problem statement and the evaluation of automatic software repair. *Proceedings of the International Conference on Software Engineering (ICSE '14)*, Hyderabad, India (June 2014), 234–242.

401 Debroy, V. and Wong, W.E. (2009). Insights on fault interference for programs with multiple bugs. *Proceedings of the International Symposium on Software Reliability Engineering (ISSRE '09)*, Karnataka, India (November 2009), 165–174.

402 Steimann, F., Frenkel, M., and Abreu, R. (2013). Threats to the validity and value of empirical assessments of the accuracy of coverage-based fault locators. *Proceedings of the International Symposium on Software Testing and Analysis*, Lugano, Switzerland (July 2013), 314–324.

403 Artzi, S., Dolby, J., Tip, F., and Pistoia, M. (2010). Practical fault localization for dynamic web applications. *Proceedings of the IEEE International Conference on Software Engineering (ICSE '10)*, Cape Town, South Africa (May 2010), 265–274.

404 Flanagan, C, Freund, S. N., and Yi, J. (2008). Velodrome: a sound and complete dynamic atomicity checker for multithreaded programs. *Proceedings of the ACM SIGPLAN Conference on Programming Language Design and Implementation*, Tucson, AZ, USA (June 2008), 293–303.

405 Gulzar, M.A., Interlandi, M., Condie, T., and Kim, M. (2016). BigDebug: debugging primitives for interactive big data processing in spark. *Proceedings of the IEEE/ACM International Conference on Software Engineering (ICSE '16)*, Austin, TX, USA (May 2016), 784–795.

406 Gulzar, M.A., Interlandi, M., Yoo, S. et al. (2016). BigDebug: interactive debugger for big data analytics in apache spark. *Proceedings of the 2016 24th ACM SIGSOFT International Symposium on Foundations of Software Engineering*, Seattle, WA, USA (13–18 November 2016), 1033–1037. ACM. https://dl.acm.org/doi/10.1145/2950290.2983930.

407 Gulzar, M.A., Wang, S., and Kim, M. (2018). BigSift: automated debugging of big data analytics in data-intensive scalable computing. *Proceedings of the ACM SIGSOFT International Symposium on the Foundations of Software Engineering*, Lake Buena Vista, FL, USA (November 2018), 863–866.

408 Jeffrey, D., Feng, M., Gupta, N., and Gupta, R. (2009). BugFix: a learning-based tool to assist developers in fixing bugs. *Proceedings of the International Conference on Program Comprehension*, Vancouver, BC, Canada (May 2009), 70–79.

409 Yang, Y., Zhou, Y., Sun, H. et al. (2019). Hunting for bugs in code coverage tools via randomized differential testing. *Proceedings of the IEEE/ACM International Conference on Software Engineering (ICSE '19)*, Montréal, QC, Canada (May 2019), 488–498.

410 Naik, M., Aiken, A., and Whaley, J. (2006). Effective static race detection for java. *Proceedings of the ACM SIGPLAN Conference on Programming Language Design and Implementation*, Ottawa, ON, Canada (June 2006), 308–319.

411 Csallner, C. and Smaragdakis, Y. (2005). Check 'n' crash: combining static checking and testing. *Proceedings of the IEEE International Conference on Software Engineering (ICSE '05)*, Louis, MO, USA (May 2005), 422–431.

412 Lazaar, N. (2011). CPTEST: a framework for the automatic fault detection, localization and correction of constraint programs. *Proceedings of the Fourth International Conference on Software Testing, Verification, and Validation Workshops*, Berlin, Germany (March 2011), 320–321.

413 Pham, H.V., Lutellier, T., Qi, W., and Tan, L. (2019). CRADLE: cross-backend validation to detect and localize bugs in deep learning libraries. *Proceedings of the IEEE/ACM International Conference on Software Engineering (ICSE '19)*, Montréal, QC, Canada (May 2019), 1027–1038.

414 Brun, Y. and Ernst, M.D. (2004). Finding latent code errors via machine learning over program executions. *Proceedings of the IEEE International Conference on Software Engineering (ICSE '04)*, Edinburgh, UK (May 2004) 480–490.

415 Böhme, M., Soremekun, E.O., Chattopadhyay, S. et al. (2017). Where is the bug and how is it fixed? An experiment with practioners. *Proceedings of the ACM SIGSOFT International Symposium on the Foundations of Software Engineering*, Paderborn, Germany (September 2017), 117–128.

416 Abreu, R., Zoeteweij, P., and Gemund, A.J. (2009). Localizing software faults simultaneously. *Proceedings of the Ninth International Conference on Quality Software*, Jeju, Korea (August 2009), 367–376.

417 Abraham, R. and Erwig, M. (2007). Goaldebug: a spreadsheet debugger for end users. *Proceedings of the IEEE International Conference on Software Engineering (ICSE '07)*, Minneapolis, MN, USA (May 2007), 251–260.

418 Gouveia, C., Campos, J., and Abreu, R. (2013). Using HTML5 visualizations in software fault localization. *Proceedings of the first IEEE Working Conference on Software Visualization*, Eindhoven, Netherland (September 2013), 1–10.

419 Machado, P., Campos, J., and Abreu, R. (2013). MZoltar: automatic debugging of android applications. *Proceedings of the International Workshop on Software Development Lifecycle for Mobile*, Saint Petersburg, Russia (August 2013), 9–16.

420 Balogh, G., Horváth, F., and Beszédes, Á. (2019). Poster: aiding java developers with interactive fault localization in eclipse IDE. *Proceedings of the 2019 IEEE International Conference on Software Testing, Verification and Validation*, Xi'an, China (April 2019), 371–374.

421 Ribeiro, H.L., de Araujo, R.P.A., Chaim, M.L. (2018). Jaguar: a spectrum-based fault localization tool for real-world software. *Proceedings of the 2018 IEEE International Conference on Software Testing, Verification and Validation*, Vasteras, Sweden (April 2018), 404–409.

422 Barr, E.T., Marron, M., Maurer, E. et al. (2016). Time-travel debugging for JavaScript/Node.js. *Proceedings of the ACM SIGSOFT International Symposium on the Foundations of Software Engineering*, Seattle, WA, USA (November 2016), 1003–1007.

423 Shu, G., Sun, B., Henderson, T.A.D., and Podgurski, A. (2013). JavaPDG: a new platform for program dependence analysis. *Proceedings of the International Conference on Software Testing, Verification and Validation*, Luxembourg (March 2013), 408–415.

424 Baudry, B., Fleurey, F., and Le Traon, Y. (2006). Improving test suites for efficient fault localization. *Proceedings of the IEEE International Conference on Software Engineering (ICSE '06)*, Shanghai, China (May 2006), 82–91.

425 Flanagan, C. and Freund, S.N. (2010). Adversarial memory for detecting destructive races. *Proceedings of the ACM SIGPLAN Conference on Programming Language Design and Implementation*, Toronto, ON, Canada (June 2010), 244–254.

426 Zhang, C., Su, T., Yan, Y. et al. (2019). Finding and understanding bugs in software model checkers. *Proceedings of the ACM SIGSOFT International Symposium on the Foundations of Software Engineering*, Tallinn, Estonia (August 2019), 763–773.

427 Bagherzadeh, M., Hili, N., and Dingel, J. (2017). Model-level, platform-independent debugging in the context of the model-driven development of real-time systems. *Proceedings of the ACM SIGSOFT International Symposium on the Foundations of Software Engineering*, Paderborn, Germany (September 2017), 419–430.

428 Kellogg, M. (2016). Combining bug detection and teset case generation. *Proceedings of the ACM SIGSOFT International Symposium on the Foundations of Software Engineering*, Seattle, WA, USA (November 2016), 1124–1126.

429 Gyori, A., Lambeth, B., Shi, A. et al. (2016). NonDex: a tool for detecting and debugging wrong assumptions on java API specifications. *Proceedings of the ACM SIGSOFT International Symposium on the Foundations of Software Engineering*, Seattle, WA, USA (November 2016), 993–997.

430 Sorrentino, F., Farzan, A., and Parthasarathy, M. (2010). Penelope: weaving threads to expose atomicity violations. *Proceedings of the ACM SIGSOFT Symposium on Foundations of Software Engineering*, Santa Fe, NM, USA (November 2010), 37–46.

431 Pastore, F., Mariani, L., and Goffi, A. (2013). RADAR: a tool for debugging regression problems in C/C++ software. *Proceedings of the International Conference on Software Engineering (ICSE '13)*, San Francisco, CA, USA (May 2013), 1335–1338.

432 Engler, D. and Ashcraft, K. (2003). Racerx: effective, static detection of race conditions and deadlocks. *Proceedings of the ACM Symposium on Operating Systems Principles*, Bolton Landing, NY, USA (October 2003), 237–252.

433 Salvaneschi, G. and Mezini, M. (2016). Debugging for reactive programming. *Proceedings of the IEEE/ACM International Conference on Software Engineering (ICSE '16)*, Austin, TX, USA (May 2016), 796–807.

434 Banken, H., Meijer, E., and Gousios, G. (2018). Debugging data flows in reactive programs. *Proceedings of the IEEE/ACM International Conference on Software Engineering (ICSE '18)*, Gothenburg, Sweden (May 2018), 752–763.

435 Andrews, M. (2003). Signpost: matching program behavior against known faults. *IEEE Software* 20 (6): 84–89.

436 Chowdhury, S.A. (2018). Automatically finding bugs in commercial cyber-physical system development tool chains. *Proceedings of the IEEE/ACM International Conference on Software Engineering: Companion Proceedings (ICSE Companion '18)*, Gothenburg, Sweden (May 2018), 506–508.

437 Guo, X. (2016). SmartDebug: an interactive debug assistant for java. *Proceedings of the ACM SIGSOFT International Symposium on the Foundations of Software Engineering*, Seattle, WA, USA (November 2016), 1127–1129.

438 Pastore, F. and Mariani, L. (2017). VART: a tool for the automatic detection of regression faults. *Proceedings of the ACM SIGSOFT International Symposium on the Foundations of Software Engineering*, Paderborn, Germany (September 2017), 964–968.

439 Hao, D., Zhang, L., Zhang, L. et al. (2009). VIDA: visual interactive debugging. *Proceedings of the International Conference on Software Engineering (ICSE '09)*, Vancouver, BC, Canada (May 2009), 583–586.

440 Servant, F. and Jones, J.A. (2012). WhoseFault: automatic developer-to-fault assignment through fault localization. *Proceedings of the International Conference on Software Engineering (ICSE '12)*, Zurich, Switzerland (June 2012), 36–46.

441 Perez, A., Abreu, R., and d'Amorim, M. (2017). Prevalence of single-fault fixes and its impact on fault localization. *Proceedings of the 2017 IEEE International Conference on Software Testing, Verification and Validation*, Tokyo, Japan (March 2017), 12–22.

442 Ang, A., Perez, A., Deursen, A.V., and Abreu, R. (2017). Revisiting the practical use of automated software fault localization techniques. *Proceedings of the 2017 IEEE 28th International Symposium on Software Reliability Engineering Workshops (ISSREW '17)*, Toulouse, France (23–26 October 2017), 175–182. IEEE. https://doi.org/10.1109/ISSREW.2017.68.

443 Hamill, M. and Goseva-Popstojanova, K. (2009). Common trends in software fault and failure data. *IEEE Transactions on Software Engineering* 35 (4): 484–496.

444 Lucia, L., Thung, F., Lo, D., and Jiang, L. (2012). Are faults localizable? *Proceedings of the IEEE Working Conference on Mining Software Repositories*, Zurich, Switzerland (June 2012), 74–77.

445 Dean, B.C., Pressly, W.B., Malloy, B.A., and Whitley, A.A. (2009). A linear programming approach for automated localization of multiple faults. *Proceedings of the International Conference on Automated Software Engineering*, Auckland, New Zealand (November 2009), 640–644.

446 Dickinson, W., Leon, D., and Fodgurski, A. (2001). Finding failures by cluster analysis of execution profiles. *Proceedings of the International Conference on Software Engineering (ICSE '01)*, Toronto, ON, Canada (May 2001), 339–348.

447 Gong, C., Zheng, Z., Zhang, Y. et al. (2012). Factorising the multiple fault localization problem: adapting single-fault localizer to multi-fault programs. *Proceedings of the Asia-Pacific Software Engineering Conference*, Hong Kong (December 2012), 729–732.

448 Jeffrey, D., Gupta, N., and Gupta, R. (2009). Effective and efficient localization of multiple faults using value replacement. *Proceedings of the International Conference on Software Maintenance*, Edmonton, AB, Canada (September 2009), 221–230.

449 Jones, J.A., Bowring, J., and Harrold, M.J. (2007). Debugging in parallel. *Proceedings of the ACM SIGSOFT International Symposium on Software Testing and Analysis*, London, UK (July 2007), 16–26.

450 Podgurski, A., Leon, D., Francis, P. et al. (2003). Automated support for classifying software failure reports. *Proceedings of the International Conference on Software Engineering (ICSE '03)*, Portland, OR, USA (May 2003), 465–477.

451 Steimann, F. and Bertschler, M. (2009). A simple coverage-based locator for multiple faults. *Proceedings of the International Conference on Software Testing, Verification and Validation*, Denver, CO, USA (April 2009), 366–375.

452 Steimann, F. and Frenkel, M. (2012). Improving coverage-based localization of multiple faults using algorithms from integer linear programming. *Proceedings of the International Symposium on Software Reliability Engineering (ISSRE '12)*, Dallas, TX, USA (November 2012), 121–130.

453 Wei, Z. and Han, B. (2013). Multiple-bug oriented fault localization: a parameter-based combination approach. *Proceedings of the Seventh International Conference on Software Security and Reliability Companion*, Gaithersburg, MD, USA (June 2013), 125–130.

454 Xue, X. and Namin, A.S. (2013). How significant is the effect of fault interactions on coverage-based fault localizations? *Proceedings of the 2013 ACM/IEEE International Symposium on Empirical Software Engineering and Measurement*, Baltimore, MD, USA (October 2013), 113–122.

455 Zheng, A.X., Jordan, M.I., Liblit, B. et al. (2006). Statistical debugging: simultaneous isolation of multiple bugs. *Proceedings of the International Conference on Machine Learning*, Pittsburgh, PA, USA (June 2006), 26–29.

456 Zakari, A., Lee, S.P., Abreu, R. et al. (2020). Multiple fault localization of software programs: a systematic literature review. *Information and Software Technology* 124: 106312.

457 Zheng, Y., Wang, Z., Fan, X. et al. (2018). Localizing multiple software faults based on evolution algorithm. *Journal of Systems and Software* 139: 107–123.

458 Yan, X., Liu, B., and Li, J. (2017). The failure behaviors of multi-faults programs: an empirical study. *Proceedings of the IEEE International Conference on Software*

Quality, Reliability, and Security Companion, Prague, Czech Republic (July 2017), 1–7.

459 Cardoso, N. and Abreu, R. (2013). A kernel density estimate-based approach to component goodness modeling. *Proceedings of the Twenty-Seventh AAAI Conference on Artificial Intelligence,* Bellevue, WA, USA (14–18 July 2013), 152–158.

460 de Kleer, J. (2009). Diagnosing multiple persistent and intermittent faults. *Proceedings of the International Joint Conference on Artificial Intelligence*, Pasadena, CA, USA (July 2009), 733–738.

461 Li, Z., Wu, Y., and Liu, Y. (2019). An empirical study of bug isolation on the effectiveness of multiple fault localization. *Proceedings of the IEEE International Conference on Software Quality, Reliability, and Security (QRS '19)*, Sofia, Bulgaria (July 2019), 18–25.

462 Hammer, C., Dolby, J., Vaziri, M., and Tip, F. (2008). Dynamic detection of atomic-set-serializability violations. *Proceedings of the International Conference on Software Engineering (ICSE '08)*, Leipzig, Germany (May 2008), 231–240.

463 Liu, C., Zhang, X., and Han, J. (2008). A systematic study of failure proximity. *IEEE Transactions on Software Engineering* 34 (6): 826–843.

464 Gao, R. and Wong, W.E. (2019). MSeer-an advanced technique for locating multiple bugs in parallel. *IEEE Transactions on Software Engineering* 45 (3): 301–318.

465 Zhang, X., Zheng, Z., and Cai, K. (2018). Exploring the usefulness of unlabelled test cases in software fault localization. *Journal of Systems and Software* 136: 278–290.

466 Xu, Y., Yin, B., Zheng, Z. et al. (2019). Robustness of spectrum-based fault localisation in environments with labelling perturbations. *Journal of Systems and Software* 147: 172–214.

467 Hierons, R.M. (2012). Oracles for distributed testing. *IEEE Transactions on Software Engineering* 38 (3): 629–641.

468 Hierons, R.M. (2009). Verdict functions in testing with a fault domain or test hypotheses. *ACM Transactions on Software Engineering and Methodology* 18 (4): 1–19.

469 Afshan, S., McMinn, P., and Stevenson, M. (2013). Evolving readable string test inputs using a natural language model to reduce human oracle cost. *Proceedings of the IEEE Sixth International Conference on Software Testing, Verification and Validation*, Luxembourg (March 2013), 352–361.

470 Harman, M., Kim, S.G., Lakhotia, K. et al. (2010). Optimizing for the number of tests generated in search based test data generation with an application to the oracle cost problem. *Proceedings of the International Conference on Software Testing, Verification, and Validation Workshops*, Paris, France (April 2010), 182–191.

471 McMinn, P., Stevenson, M., and Harman, M. (2010). Reducing qualitative human oracle costs associated with automatically generated test data. *Proceedings of the*

International Workshop on Software Test Output Validation, Trento, Italy (July 2010), 1–4.

472 He, Z., Chen, Y., Huang, E. et al. (2019). A system identification based oracle for control-CPS software fault localization. *Proceedings of the IEEE/ACM International Conference on Software Engineering (ICSE '19)*, Montréal, QC, Canada (May 2019), 116–127.

473 Diaz, E., Tuya, J., and Blanco, R. (2003). Automated software testing using a metaheuristic technique based on tabu search. *Proceedings of the Conference on Automated Software Engineering*, Montreal, QC, Canada (October 2003), 310–313.

474 Artzi, S., Kiezun, A., Dolby, J. et al. (2010). Finding bugs in web applications using dynamic test generation and explicit-state model checking. *IEEE Transactions on Software Engineering* 36 (4): 474–494.

475 Artzi, S., Dolby, J., Tip, F., and Pistoia, M. (2010). Directed test generation for effective fault localization. *Proceedings of the IEEE International Symposium on Software Testing and Analysis,* Trento, Italy (July 2010), 49–60.

476 Xu, Z., Liu, P., Zhang, X., and Xu, B. (2016). Python predictive analysis for bug detection. *Proceedings of the ACM SIGSOFT International Symposium on the Foundations of Software Engineering*, Seattle, WA, USA (November 2016), 121–132.

477 Jiang, B., Chan, W.K., and Tse, T.H. (2011). On practical adequate test suites for integrated test case prioritization and fault localization. *Proceedings of the International Conference on Quality Software*, Madrid, Spain (13–14 July 2011), 21–30.

478 Jiang, B., Zhai, K., Chan, W.K. et al. (2013). On the adoption of MC/DC and control-flow adequacy for a tight integration of program testing and statistical fault localization. *Information and Software Technology* 55 (5): 897–917.

479 Santelices, R., Jones, J.A., Yu, Y., and Harrold, M.J. (2009). Lightweight fault-localization using multiple coverage types. *Proceedings of the 2009 IEEE 31st International Conference on Software Engineering (ICSE '09)*, Vancouver, BC, Canada (16–24 May 2009), 56–66. IEEE. https://doi.org/10.1109/ICSE.2009.5070508.

480 Bandyopadhyay, A. (2011). Improving spectrum-based fault localization using proximity-based weighting of test cases. *Proceedings of the IEEE International Symposium on Automated Software Engineering*, Lawrence, KS, USA (November 2011), 660–664.

481 Bandyopadhyay, A. and Ghosh, S. (2011). Proximity based weighting of test cases to improve spectrum based fault localization. *Proceedings of the IEEE International Symposium on Automated Software Engineering*, Lawrence, KS, USA (November 2011), 420–423.

482 Cai, K., Jing, T., and Bai, C. (2005). Partition testing with dynamic partitioning. *Proceedings of the Annual International Computer Software and Applications Conference (COMPSAC '05)*, Edinburgh, UK (July 2005), 113–116.

483 Campos, J., Abreu, R., Fraser, G., and Amorim, M. (2013). Entropy-based test generation for improved fault localization. *Proceedings of the 28th International*

Conference on Automated Software Engineering, Silicon Valley, CA, USA (November 2013), 257–267.

484 Gong, L., Lo, D., Jiang, L., and Zhang,H. (2012). Diversity maximization speedup for fault. *Proceedings of the International Conference on Automated Software Engineering*, Essen, Germany (September 2012), 30–39.

485 Gonzalez-Sanchez, A., Piel, E., Gross, H., and van Gemund, A.J. (2010). Prioritizing tests for software fault localization. *Proceedings of the International Conference on Quality Software*, Zhangjiajie, China (July 2010), 42–51.

486 Gonzalez-Sanchez, A., Abreu, R., Gross, H., and van Gemund, A.J.C. (2011). An empirical study on the usage of testability information to fault localization in software. *Proceedings of the ACM Symposium on Applied Computing*, TaiChung, Taiwan (March 2011), 1398–1403.

487 Gonzalez-Sanchez, A., Abreu, R., Gross, H., and van Gemund, A.J.C. (2011). Prioritizing tests for fault localization through ambiguity group reduction. *Proceedings of the International Conference on Automated Software Engineering*, Lawrence, KS, USA (November 2011), 83–92.

488 Hao, D., Zhang, L., Zhong, H. et al. (2005). Eliminating harmful redundancy for testing-based fault localization using test suite reduction: an experimental study. *Proceedings of the International Conference on Software Maintenance*, Budapest, Hungary (September 2005), 683–686.

489 Hui, Z. (2016). Fault localization method generated by regression test cases on the basis of genetic immune algorithm. *Proceedings of the IEEE 40th Annual Computer Software and Applications Conference Workshops (COMPSAC Workshops '16)*, Atlanta, GA, USA (June 2016), 46–51.

490 Jiang, B. and Chan, W.K. (2010). On the integration of test adequacy, test case prioritization, and statistical fault localization. *Proceedings of the International Conference on Quality Software*, Zhangjiajie, China (July 2010), 377–384.

491 Kim, J., Park, J., and Lee, E. (2016). A new spectrum-based fault localization with the technique of test case optimization. *Journal of Information Science and Engineering* 32 (1): 177–196.

492 Li, Y., Chen, J., Ni, F. et al. (2015). Selecting test cases for result inspection to support effective fault localization. *Journal of Computer Science and Engineering* 9 (3): 142–154.

493 Vidacs, L., Bezedes, A., Tengeri, D. et al. (2014). Test suite reduction for fault detection and localization: a combined approach. *Proceedings of the IEEE Conference on Software Maintenance, Reengineering and Reverse Engineering*, Antwerp, Belgium (February 2014), 204–213.

494 Weiglhofer, M., Fraser, G., and Wotawa, F. (2009). Using spectrum-based fault localization for test case grouping. *Proceedings of the International Conference on Automated Software Engineering*, Auckland, New Zealand (November 2009), 630–634.

495 Yu, Y., Jones, J., and Harrold, M.J. (2008). An empirical study of the effects of test-suite reduction on fault localization. *Proceedings of the International Conference on Software Engineering (ICSE '08)*, Leipzig, Germany (May 2008), 201–210.

496 Zhang, X., Wang, Z., Zhang, W. et al. (2015). Spectrum-based fault localization method with test case reduction. *Proceedings of the IEEE 39th Annual Computer Software and Applications Conference Workshops (COMPSAC Workshops '15)*, Taichung, Taiwan (July 2015), 548–549.

497 Naish, L., Lee, H.J., and Ramamohanarao, K. (2009). Spectral debugging with weights and incremental ranking. *Proceedings of the Asia-Pacific Software Engineering Conference*, Batu Ferringhi, Malaysia (December 2009), 168–175.

498 Gao, Y., Zhang, Z., Zhang, L. et al. (2013). A theoretical study: the impact of cloning failed test cases on the effectiveness of fault localization. *Proceedings of the International Conference on Quality Software*, Nanjing, China (July 2013), 288–291.

499 Zhang, L., Yan, L., Zhang, Z. et al. (2017). A theoretical analysis on cloning the failed test cases to improve spectrum-based fault localization. *Journal of Systems and Software* 129: 35–57.

500 Rößler, J., Fraser, G., Zeller, A., and Orso, A. (2012). Isolating failure causes through test case generation. *Proceedings of the International Symposium on Software Testing and Analysis*, Minneapolis, MN, USA (July 2012), 309–319.

501 Li, X., Wong, W.E., Gao, R. et al. (2018). Genetic algorithm-based test generation for software product line with the integration of fault localization techniques. *Empirical Software Engineering* 23: 1–51.

502 Liu, M., Liu, P., Yang, X., and Zhao, L. (2016). Fault localization guided execution comparison for failure comprehension. *Proceedings of the IEEE International Conference on Software Quality, Reliability, and Security Companion (QRS-C '16)*, Vienna, Austria (August 2016), 163–166.

503 Chen, R., Chen, S., and Zhang, N. (2016). Iterative path clustering for software fault localization. *Proceedings of the IEEE International Conference on Software Quality, Reliability, and Security Companion (QRS-C '16)*, Vienna, Austria (August 2016), 292–297.

504 Lekivetz, R. and Morgan, J. (2018). Fault localization: analyzing covering arrays given prior information. *Proceedings of the IEEE International Conference on Software Quality, Reliability, and Security Companion*, Lisbon, Portugal (July 2018), 116–121.

505 Perez, A., Abreu, R., and van Deursen, A. (2017). A test-suite diagnosability metric for spectrum-based fault localization approaches. *Proceedings of the IEEE/ACM International Conference on Software Engineering (ICSE '17)*, Buenos Aires, Argentina (May 2017), 654–664.

506 Just, R., Parnin, C., Drosos, I., and Ernst, M.D. (2018). Comparing developer-provided to user-provided tests for fault localization and automated program

repair. *Proceedings of the 2018 ACM International Symposium on Software Testing and Analysis*, Amsterdam, Netherlands (July 2018), 287–297.

507 Gambi, A., Bell, J., and Zeller, A. (2018). Practical test dependency detection. *Proceedings of the 2018 IEEE International Conference on Software Testing, Verification and Validation*, Vasteras, Sweden (April 2018), 1–11.

508 Budd, T.A. and Angluin, D. (1982). Two notions of correctness and their relation to testing. *Acta Infomatica* 18 (1): 31–45.

509 Bandyopadhyay, A. (2012). Mitigating the effect of coincidental correctness in spectrum based fault localization. *Proceedings of the International Conference on Software Testing, Verification, and Validation*, Montreal, QC, Canada (April 2012), 479–482.

510 Hierons, R.M. (2006). Avoiding coincidental correctness in boundary value analysis. *ACM Transactions on Software Engineering and Methodology* 15 (3): 227–241.

511 Li, Y. and Liu, C. (2012). Using cluster analysis to identify coincidental correctness in fault localization. *Proceedings of the International Conference on Computational and Information Sciences*, Chongqing, China (August 2012), 357–360.

512 Masri, W. and Assi, R.A. (2010). Cleansing test suites from coincidental correctness to enhance fault-localization. *Proceedings of the International Conference on Software Testing, Verification, and Validation*, Paris, France (April 2010), 165–174.

513 Miao, Y., Chen, Z., Li, S. et al. (2012). Identifying coincidental correctness for fault localization clustering test cases. *Proceedings of the 24th International Conference on Software Engineering and Knowledge Engineering*, Redwood City, CA, USA (1–3 July 2012), 267–272. KSI Research Inc.

514 Wang, X., Cheung, S.C., Chan, W.K., and Zhang, Z. (2009). Taming coincidental correctness: refine code coverage with context pattern to improve fault localization. *Proceedings of the 31st International Conference on Software Engineering (ICSE '09)*, Vancouver, BC, Canada (16–24 May 2009), 45–55. IEEE. https://doi.org/10.1109/ICSE.2009.5070507.

515 Zhang, Z., Chan, W.K., and Tse, T.H. (2012). Fault localization based only on failed runs. *Computer* 45 (6): 64–71.

516 Zhou, X., Wang, H., and Zhao, J. (2015). A fault-localization approach based on the coincidental correctness probability. *Proceedings of the 2015 IEEE International Conference on Software Quality, Reliability and Security*, Vancouver, BC, Canada (August 2015), 292–297.

517 Liu, Y., Li, M., Wu, Y., and Li, Z. (2019). A weighted fuzzy classification approach to identify and manipulate coincidental correct test cases for fault localization. *Journal of Systems and Software* 151: 20–37.

518 Masri, W. and Assi, R.A. (2014). Prevalence of coincidental correctness and mitigation of its impact on fault localization. *ACM Transactions on Software Engineering and Methodology* 23 (1): 1–28.

519 Zhang, Z., Jiang, B., Chan, W.K., and Tse, T.H. (2011). Precise propagation of fault-failure correlations in program flow graphs. *Proceedings of the 35th Annual International Computer Software and Applications Conference (COMPSAC '11)*, Munich, Germany (18–22 July 2011), 58–67.

520 Hofer, B. (2017). Removing coincidental correctness in spectrum-based fault localization for circuit and spreadsheet debugging. *Proceedings of the 2017 IEEE 28th International Symposium on Software Reliability Engineering Workshops (ISSREW '17)*, Toulouse, France (23–26 October 2017), 199–206. IEEE. https://doi.org/10.1109/ISSREW.2017.18.

521 Debroy, V. and Wong, W.E. (2011). On the consensus-based application of fault localization techniques. *Proceedings of the IEEE Annual Computer Software and Applications Conference Workshops (COMPSAC Workshops '11)*, Munich, Germany (July 2011), 506–511.

522 Lucia, L., Lo, D., and Xia, X. (2014). Fusion fault localizers. *Proceedings of the IEEE International Conference on Automated Software Engineering*, Vasteras, Sweden (September 2014), 127–138.

523 Tang, C.M., Keung, J., Yu, Y.T., and Chan, W.K. (2016). DFL: dual-service fault localization. *Proceedings of the IEEE International Conference on Software Quality, Reliability, and Security*, Vienna, Austria (August 2016), 412–422.

524 Wang, S., David, L., Jiang, L. (2011). Search-based fault localization. *Proceedings of the 2011 IEEE/ACM International Conference on Automated Software Engineering*, Lawrence, KS, USA (November 2011), 556–559.

525 Leitao-Junior, P.S., Freitas, D.M., Vergilio, S.R. et al. (2020). Search-based fault localisation: a systematic mapping study. *Information and Software Technology* 123: 106295.

526 Lei, Y., Mao, X., Dai, Z., and Wang, C. (2012). Effective statistical fault localization using program slices. *Proceedings of the Annual IEEE International Computer Software and Applications Conference (COMPSAC '12)*, Izmir, Turkey (July 2012), 1–10.

527 Wen, W. (2012). Software fault localization based on program slicing Spectrum. *Proceedings of the International Conference on Software Engineering (ICSE '12)*, Zurich, Switzerland (June 2012), 1511–1514.

528 Reis, S., Abreu, R., and d'Amorim, M. (2019). Demystifying the combination of dynamic slicing and spectrum-based fault localization. *Proceedings of the Twenty-Eighth International Joint Conference on Artificial Intelligence*, Macao, China (10–16 August 2019), 4760–4766. https://doi.org/10.24963/ijcai.2019/661.

529 Li, X. and Orso, A. (2020). More accurate dynamic slicing for better supporting software debugging. *2020 IEEE 13th International Conference on Software Testing, Validation and Verification (ICST)*, Porto, Portugal (October 2020). IEEE.

530 Christi, A., Olson, M.L., Alipour, M.A., and Groce, A. (2018). Reduce before you localize: delta-debugging and spectrum-based fault localization. *Proceedings of the 2018 IEEE 29th International Symposium on Software Reliability Engineering*

Workshops (ISSREW '18), Memphis, TN, USA (15–18 October 2018), 184–191. IEEE. https://doi.org/10.1109/ISSREW.2018.00005.

531 Xuan, J. and Morperrus, M. (2014). Learning to combine multiple ranking metrics for fault localization. *Proceedings of the IEEE International Conference on Software Maintenance and Evolution*, Victoria, BC, Canada (September 2014), 191–200.

532 Gopinath, D., Zaeem, R.N., and Khurshid, S. (2012). Improving the effectiveness of spectra-based fault localization using specifications. *Proceedings of the International Conference on Automated Software Engineering*, Essen, Germany (September 2012), 40–49.

533 Burger, M. and Zeller, A. (2011). Minimizing reproduction of software failures. *Proceedings of the International Symposium on Software Testing and Analysis*, Toronto, BC, Canada (July 2011), 221–231.

534 Artho, C., Havelund, K., and Biere, A. (2003). High-level data races. *Journal on Software Testing, Verification and Reliability* 13 (4): 207–227.

535 Savage, S., Burrows, M., Nelson, G. et al. (1997). Eraser: a dynamic data race detector for multi-threaded programs. *ACM Transactions on Computer Systems* 15 (4): 391–411.

536 Farzan, A. and Madhusudan, P. (2006). Causal atomicity. *Proceedings of the International Conference Computer Aided Verification*, Seattle, WA, USA (August 2006), 315–328.

537 Flanagan, C. and Freund, S.N. (2004). Atomizer: a dynamic atomicity checker for multithreaded programs. *Proceedings of the ACM SIGPLAN-SIGACT Symposium on Principles of Programming Languages*, Venice, Italy (January 2004), 256–267.

538 Flanagan, C., Freund, S.N., and Qadeer, S. (2005). Exploiting purity for atomicity. *IEEE Transactions on Software Engineering* 31 (4): 275–291.

539 Farzan, A., Madhusudan, P., and Sorrentino, F. (2009). Meta-analysis for atomicity violations under nested locking. *Proceedings of the International Conference Computer Aided Verification*, Grenoble, France (July 2009), 248–262

540 Sen, K., Rosu, G., and Agha, G. (2003). Runtime safety analysis of multithreaded programs. *Proceedings of the ACM SIGSOFT Symposium on Foundations of Software Engineering*, Helsinki, Finland (September 2003), 337–346.

541 Wang, L. and Stoller, S.D. (2006). Accurate and efficient runtime detection of atomicity errors in concurrent programs. *Proceedings of the ACM SIGPLAN Symposium on Principles and Practice of Parallel Programming*, New York, NY, USA (29–31 March 2006), 137–146. ACM. https://doi.org/10.1145/1122971.1122993.

542 Xu, M., Bodik, R., and Hill, M.D. (2005). A serializability violation detector for shared-memory server programs. *Proceedings of the ACM SIGPLAN Conference on Programming Language Design and Implementation*, Chicago, IL, USA (12–15 June 2005), 1–14.

543 Burckhardt, S., Alur, R., and Martin, M.M.K. (2007). Checkfence: checking consistency of concurrent data types on relaxed memory models. *Proceedings of* *the ACM SIGPLAN Conference on Programming Language Design and Implementation*, San Diego, CA, USA (10–13 June 2007), 12–21.

544 Kidd, N., Reps, T., Dolby, J., and Vaziri, M. (2009). Finding concurrency-related bugs using random isolation. *Proceedings of the International Conference on Verification, Model Checking, and Abstract Interpretation*, Savannah, GA, USA (18–20 January 2009), 198–213.

545 Musuvathi, M., Qadeer, S., Ball, T. et al. (2008). Finding and reproducing heisenbugs in concurrent programs. *Proceedings of the USENIX Symposium on Operating Systems Design and Implementation*, San Diego, CA, USA (December 2008), 267–280.

546 Shacham, O., Sagiv, M., and Schuster A. (2005). Scaling model checking of dataraces using dynamic information. *Proceedings of the ACM SIGPLAN Symposium on Principles and Practice of Parallel Programming*, Chicago, IL, USA (June 2005), 107–118.

547 Park, S., Lu, S., and Zhou, Y. (2009). Ctrigger: exposing atomicity violation bugs from their hiding places. *Proceedings of the International Conference on Architectural Support for Programming Language*, Washington, DC, USA (7–11 March 2009), 25–36.

548 Park, S. (2013). Debugging non-deadlock concurrency bugs. *Proceedings of the 2013 International Symposium on Software Testing and Analysis*, Lugano, Switzerland (July 2013), 358–361.

549 Wang, W., Wu, C., Yew, P. (2014). Concurrency bug localization using shared memory access pairs. *Proceedings of the 19th ACM SIGPLAN symposium on Principles and Practices of Parallel Programming*, Orlando, FL, USA (February 2014), 375–376.

550 Torlak, E., Vaziri, M., and Dolby, J. (2010). MemSAT: checking axiomatic specifications of memory models. *Proceedings of the ACM SIGPLAN Conference on Programming Language Design and Implementation*, Toronto, BC, Canada (June 2010), 341–350.

551 Koca, F., Sozer, H., and Abreu, R. (2013). Spectrum-based fault localization for diagnosing concurrency faults. *Proceedings of the International Conference on Testing Software and Systems*, Istanbul, Turkey (November 2013), 239–254.

552 Xu, J., Lei, Y., and Carver, R. (2017). Using delta debugging to minimize stress tests for concurrent data structures. *Proceedings of the 2017 IEEE International Conference on Software Testing, Verification and Validation*, Tokyo, Japan (March 2017), 35–46.

553 Panko, R.R. and Ordway, N. (2008). Sarbanes-oxley: what about all the spreadsheets? arXiv preprint arXiv:0804.0797. https://arxiv.org/ftp/arxiv/papers/0804/0804.0797.pdf.

554 Hermans, F., Pinzger, M., and van Deursen, A. (2011). Supporting professional spreadsheet users by generating leveled dataflow diagrams. *Proceedings of* *the International Conference on Software Engineering (ICSE '11)*, Waikiki, HI, USA (May 2011), 451–460.

555 Panko, R. (2006). Facing the problem of spreadsheet errors. *Decision Line* 37 (5): 8–10.

556 Panko, R.R. (2000). Spreadsheet errors: what we know. What we think we can do. arXiv preprint arXiv:0802.3457.

557 Reinhart, C.M. and Rogoff, K.S. (2010). Growth in a time of debt. *American Economic Review* 100 (2): 573–578.

558 Abraham, R. and Erwig, M. (2004). Header and unit inference for spreadsheets through spatial analyses. *Proceedings of the IEEE Symposium on Visual Languages and Human Centric Computing*, Roma, Italy (September 2004), 165–172.

559 Abraham, R. and Erwig, M. (2007). UCheck: a spreadsheet type checker for end users. *Journal of Visual Languages and Computing* 18 (1): 71–95.

560 Ahmad, Y., Antoniu, T., Goldwater, S., and Krishnamurthi, S. (2003). A type system for statically detecting spreadsheet errors. *Proceedings of the IEEE International Symposium on Automated Software Engineering*, Montreal, QC, Canada (October 2003), 174–183.

561 Bregar, A. (2004). Complexity metrics for spreadsheet models. arXiv preprint arXiv:0802.3895.

562 Hermans, F., Pinzger, M., and van Deursen, A. (2012). Detecting and visualizing inter-worksheet smells in spreadsheets. *Proceedings of the International Conference on Software Engineering (ICSE '12)*, Zurich, Switzerland (June 2012), 441–451.

563 Hermans, F., Sedee, B., Pinzger, M., and van Deursen, A. (2013). Data clone detection and visualization in spreadsheets. *Proceedings of the 2013 35th International Conference on Software Engineering (ICSE '13)*, San Francisco, CA, USA (18–26 May 2013), 292–301. IEEE. https://doi.org/10.1109/ICSE.2013.6606575.

564 Hodnigg, K. and Mittermeir, R.T. (2008). Metrics-based spreadsheet visualization: support for focused maintenance. arXiv preprint arXiv:0809.3009.

565 Hofer, B., Riboira, A., Wotawa, F. et al. (2013). On the empirical evaluation of fault localization techniques for spreadsheets. *International Conference on Fundamental Approaches to Software Engineering*, Rome, Italy (March 2013), 68–82.

566 Rothermel, K.J., Li, L., DuParis, C., and Burnett, M. (1998). What you see is what you test: a methodology for testing form-based visual programs. *Proceedings of the 1998 International Conference on Software Engineering (ICSE '98)*, Kyoto, Japan (April 1998), 198–207.

567 Ruthruff, J., Creswick, E., Burnett, M. et al. (2003). End-user software visualizations for fault localization. *Proceedings of the ACM Symposium on Software Visualization*, San Diego, CA, USA (June 2003), 123–132.

568 Abreu, R., Cunha, J., Fernandes, J.P. et al. (2014). Faultysheet detective: when smells meet fault localization. *Proceedings of the 2014 IEEE International*

Conference on Software Maintenance and Evolution, Victoria, BC, Canada (28 September to 3 October 2014), 625–628. IEEE.

569 Abreu, R., Cunha, J., Fernandes, J.P. et al. (2014). Smelling faults in spreadsheets. *Proceedings of the 2014 IEEE International Conference on Software Maintenance and Evolution*, Victoria, BC, Canada (28 September to 3 October 2014), 111–120. IEEE.

570 Abreu, R., Hofer, B., Perez, A., and Wotawa, F. (2014). Using constraints to diagnose faulty spreadsheets. *Software Quality Journal* 23 (2): 297–322.

571 Abreu, R., Riboira, A., and Wotawa, F. (2012). Constraint-based debugging of spreadsheets. *Proceedings of the 15th Iberoamerican Conference on Software Engineering (CIbSE 2012)*, Buenos Aires, Argentina (24–27 April 2012), 1–14.

572 Getzner, E., Hofer, B., and Wotawa, F. (2017). Improving spectrum-based fault localization for spreadsheet debugging. *Proceedings of the IEEE International Conference on Software Quality, Reliability, and Security*, Prague, Czech Republic (July 2017), 102–113.

573 Almasi, M.M., Hemmati, H., and Fraser, G. (2018). Search-based detection of deviation failures in the migration of legacy spreadsheet applications. *Proceedings of the 2018 ACM International Symposium on Software Testing and Analysis*, Amsterdam, Netherlands (July 2018), 266–275.

574 Hofer, B., Perez, A., Abreu, R., and Wotawa, F. (2015). On the empirical evaluation of similarity coefficients for spreadsheets fault localization. *Automated Software Engineering* 22 (1): 47–74.

575 Hofer, B. and Wotawa, F. (2015). Fault localization in the light of faulty user input. *Proceedings of the 2015 IEEE International Conference on Software Quality, Reliability and Security*, Vancouver, BC, Canada (August 2015), 282–291.

576 Panko, R.R. (1999). Applying code inspection to spreadsheet testing. *Journal of Management Information Systems* 16 (2): 159–176.

577 Badame, S., Dig, D. (2012). Refactoring meets spreadsheet formulas. *Proceedings of the International Conference on Software Maintenance*, Trento, Italy (September 2012), 399–409.

578 Cunha, J., Erwig, M., Saraiva, J. (2010). Automatically inferring classsheet models from spreadsheets. *Proceedings of the IEEE Symposium on Visual Language and Human-Centric Computing*, Leganes-Madrid, Spain (September 2010), 93–100.

579 Cunha, J., Fernandes, J.P., Mendes, J., and Saraiva, J. (2012). MDSheet: a framework for model-driven Spreadsheet Engineering. *Proceedings of the IEEE International Conference on Software Engineering (ICSE '12)*, Zurich, Switzerland (June 2012), 1395–1398.

580 Lee, H.J., Naish, L., and Ramamohanarao, K. (2009). Study of the relationship of bug consistency with respect to performance of spectra metrics. *Proceedings of the 2009 2nd IEEE International Conference on Computer Science and Information*

Technology, Beijing, China (8–11 August 2009), 501–508. IEEE. https://doi.org/10.1109/ICCSIT.2009.5234512.

581 Xie, X., Chen, T.Y., Kuo, F.-C., and Xu, B.W. (2013). A theoretical analysis of the risk evaluation formulas for spectrum-based fault localization. *ACM Transactions on Software Engineering and Methodology* 22 (4): 1–40.

582 Xie, X., Kuo, F., Chen, T.Y. et al. (2013). Provably optimal and human-competitive results in SBSE for spectrum based fault localization. *Proceedings of the International Symposium on Search Based Software Engineering*, Saint Petersburg, Russia (August 2013), 224–238.

583 Yoo, S., Xie, X., Kuo, F. et al. Human competitiveness of genetic programming in spectrum-based fault localisation: theoretical and empirical analysis. *ACM Transactions on Software Engineering and Methodology* 26 (1): 1–30, Article 4.

584 Ju, X., Chen, X., Yang, Y. et al. (2017). An in-depth study of the efficiency of risk evaluation formulas for multi-fault localization. *Proceedings of the IEEE International Conference on Software Quality, Reliability, and Security Companion*, Prague, Czech Republic (July 2017), 304–310.

585 Naish, L., Lee, H.J., and Ramamohanarao, K. (2012). Spectral debugging: how much better can we do. *Proceedings of the Australian Software Engineering Conference*, Melbourne, Australia (January 2012), 96–106.

586 Naish, L. and Lee, H.J. (2013). Duals in spectral fault localization. *Proceedings of the Australian Software Engineering Conference*, Melbourne, Australia (June 2013), 51–59.

587 Chen, T.Y., Xie, X., Kuo, F., and Xu, B. (2015). A revisit of a theoretical analysis on spectrum-based fault localization. *Proceedings of the IEEE 39th Annual Computer Software and Applications Conference (COMPSAC '15)*, Taichung, Taiwan (July 2015), 17–22.

2

Traditional Techniques for Software Fault Localization

Yihao Li[1], Linghuan Hu[2], W. Eric Wong[3], Vidroha Debroy[3,4], and Dongcheng Li[3]

[1] *School of Information and Electrical Engineering, Ludong University, Yantai, China*
[2] *Google Inc., Mountain View, CA, USA*
[3] *Department of Computer Science, University of Texas at Dallas, Richardson, TX, USA*
[4] *Dottid Inc., Dallas, TX, USA*

As mentioned in Chapter 1, software fault localization is one of the most expensive activities in program debugging. The high demand for automatic fault localization techniques that can guide programmers to the locations of faults, with minimal human intervention, has fueled the proposal and development of various techniques over recent decades. Slice-based, program spectrum-based, statistics-based, machine learning-based, model-based, and other such techniques have greatly advanced the effectiveness of fault localization. While a thorough discussion of these advanced techniques is quite essential (starting from Chapter 3), it is necessary to review some traditional and intuitive fault localization techniques that have been commonly adopted in debugging research and applications. In this way, we can obtain a comprehensive understanding of progress, issues, and concerns in software fault localization. Therefore, this chapter will focus on the traditional and intuitive fault localization techniques, including program logging, assertions, breakpoints, and profiling.

2.1 Program Logging

Program logging is both a common and an essential software development practice that is used to record vital information regarding a program's execution [1]. This saved information is later used by developers to determine and analyze the

Handbook of Software Fault Localization: Foundations and Advances, First Edition.
Edited by W. Eric Wong and T.H. Tse.

Published 2023 by John Wiley & Sons, Inc.

Table 2.1 Additional program spectra relevant to fault localization.

Level	Description
TRACE	Very detailed information
DEBUG	Detailed information on the flow through the system
INFO	Interesting runtime events (such as startups and shutdowns)
WARNING	Runtime oddities and recoverable errors
ERROR	Other runtime errors or unexpected conditions
FATAL	Severe errors causing premature termination

Source: Adapted from log4j [2].

elements of the source code that were present in successful or failed executions. When abnormal program behavior is detected, developers examine the program log in terms of saved log files or printed run-time information to diagnose the underlying cause of failure. Messages can be logged at various levels, which often indicate different levels of severity of the cause and/or verbosity of the logging. For example, Table 2.1 provides a list of common levels from Apache Commons Logging [3]. The sample code in Table 2.2 illustrates a typical usage pattern of Simple Logging Facade for Java (SLF4J) [4], a simple facade or abstraction for various logging frameworks (such as log4j [5], Logback [6], and Java Logging API [7]), which allows the end user to plug in the desired logging framework at deployment time. In addition, Table 2.3 shows a list of popular logging frameworks with their corresponding log levels and supported programming languages. As shown in the table, C logging framework sclog4c has the most (12) log levels, while frameworks

Table 2.2 SLF4J – a logging façade.

```
import org.slf4j.Logger;
import org.slf4j.LoggerFactory;

public class HelloWorld {
  final Logger logger = LoggerFactory.getLogger(HelloWorld.class);
  public void doSomething() {
    // some other code
    logger.debug("This is a DEBUG level message");
    logger.info("This is an INFO level message");
    logger.warning("This is a WARNING level message");
    logger.error ("This is an ERROR level message");
    logger.fatal("This is a FATAL level message");
  }
}
```

Source: Adapted from log4j [2].

Table 2.3 Summary of tools used in the fault localization studies.

Framework	Log levels	Language
log4j [5]	FATAL; ERROR; WARN; INFO; DEBUG; TRACE	Java
Java Logging API [7]	SEVERE; WARNING; INFO; CONFIG; FINE; FINER; FINEST	Java
Apache Common Logging [3]	FATAL; ERROR; WARN; INFO; DEBUG; TRACE	Java
SLF4J [4]	ERROR; WARN; INFO; DEBUG; TRACE	Java
tinylog [8]	ERROR; WARNING; INFO; DEBUG; TRACE	Java
Logback [6]	ERROR; WARN; INFO; DEBUG; TRACE;	Java
Object Guy [9]	DEBUG; INFO STATUS; WARNING; ERROR; CRITICAL; FATAL	Java; .Net
Smart Inspect [10]	DEBUG; VERBOSE; MESSAGE; WARNING; ERROR; FATAL	Java; .Net
NLog [11]	DEBUG; TRACE; INFO; WARN; ERROR; FATA	.Net
log4net [12]	DEBUG; INFO; WARN; ERROR; FATA	.Net
Enterprise Library [13]	VERBOSE; INFORMATION; WARNING; ERROR; CRITICAL	.Net
log4c [14]	VERBOSE; INFORMATION; WARNING; ERROR; CRITICAL	C
sclog4c [15]	ALL; FINEST; FINER; FINE; DEBUG; CONFIG; INFO; WARNING; ERROR; SEVERE; FATAL; OFF	C
Syslog [16]	EMERGENCY; ALERT; CRITICAL; ERROR; WARNING; NOTICE; INFORMATION; DEBUG	C
zlog [17]	NOTICE; INFO; WARNING; ERROR; CRITICAL; FATAL; UNKNOWN	C
Pantheios [18]	EMERGENCY; ALERT; CRITICAL; ERROR; WARNING; NOTICE; INFO; DEBUG	C; C++

SLF4J, tinylog, Logback, Enterprise Library, log4c, Syslog, and zlog have the least (5) log levels. The three most commonly used levels are WARN/WARNING (17), INFO/INFORMATION/INFOSTATUS (16), and ERROR (16).

2.2 Assertions

Assertions [19] are constraints added to a program that are required to be true during the correct operation of a program. Developers specify these assertions in the program code as conditional statements that will terminate execution if

```
static void Main (string[] args)
{
  string inputString;
  int minutes;
  do
  {
   Console.WriteLine("Enter the number of minutes to add.");
   inputString = Console.ReadLine();
  } while (!int.TryParse(inputString, out minutes));

  ShowTimePlusMinutes(minutes);
  Console.ReadLine();
}

static void ShowTimePlusMinutes(int minutes)
{
  Debug.Assert(minutes >= 0);
  DateTime time = DateTime.Now.AddMinutes(minutes);
  Console.WriteLine("In {0} minutes it will be {1}", minutes, time);
}
```

Figure 2.1 Debugging using assertion in a C# program. *Source:* Carr [20]/BlackWasp.

they evaluate to false. Thus, they can be used to detect erroneous program behavior at runtime. For example, Figure 2.1 shows how to create an assertion in C# using the static Assert method of the Debug class [21]. This class is found within the System.Diagnostics namespace. To demonstrate the use of this method, create a new console application and add the following statement to the top of the class containing the Main method: using System.Diagnostics. The simplest syntax for the Debug.Assert method requires only a single Boolean parameter. This parameter contains the predicate that evaluates to true under normal conditions. As shown in the table, the program requests the additional number of minutes from the user. Once a valid number has been entered, the program outputs the resulting time after that number of minutes. In the ShowTimePlusMinutes method, the first line asserts the precondition that the number of minutes is zero or more.

The program in Figure 2.1 contains a bug. The ShowTimePlusMinutes method assumes that the number of minutes has been pre-validated and will be a non-negative integer. However, the Main method has not correctly validated the user input and will allow the number of minutes to be negative. This means that the assertion can be triggered by entering a negative number. Suppose a user executes the program and enters a negative value. As shown in Figure 2.2, the assertion is triggered and a dialog box is displayed. Specifically, the dialog box shows the stack trace at the point where the assertion fails. It provides the user with three options. If the user selects Abort, the program will be immediately halted and closed. If Retry is selected, the program will enter the debug mode to allow the user to

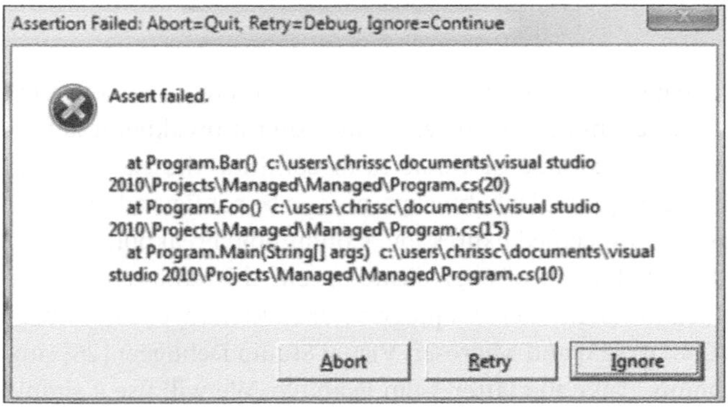

Figure 2.2 A dialog box is displayed when the assertion is triggered. *Source:* Schmich [22].

investigate and go through the code as required. Otherwise, the Ignore option will ignore the assertion and instruct the program to continue execution.

Murillo et al. [6] proposed system-wide assertions, which enable the observation and correlation of Hardware/Software interactions among several cores, devices, and software tasks. A language, SWAT, was developed to create such assertions to facilitate debugging at the system level. Al-Sharif et al. [3] introduced Dynamic Temporal Assertions (DTA) into the conventional source-level debugging session. Each assertion is capable of: (1) validating a sequence of execution states, named the temporal interval, and (2) referencing outof-scope variables, which may not be live in the execution state at evaluation time. Boos et al. [23] proposed BRACE, a framework that enables developers to correlate cyber and physical properties of the system via assertions. First, BRACE introduces new forms of assertions catering to the unique demands of cyber-physical systems (CPS). For example, CPS assertions can span logical and physical variables and nodes, and specify both spatial and temporal properties. They are checked by an external, omniscient process that can independently observe the physical states. Second, BRACE supports asynchronous checking of CPS assertions to avoid critical timing failures caused by processing latencies. Third, BRACE supports explicit actuation of error handling code. For example, when an assert ion is violated, the system can be configured to either halt or execute a user-provided callback function. Fourth, BRACE can be configured to tolerate spatial and temporal discrepancies. Schwartz-Narbonne et al. [15] proposed parallel assertions, a mechanism for expressing correctness criteria in parallel code. These parallel assertions allow users to use intuitive syntax and semantics to express the assumptions in a multi-threaded program involving both the current state and any actions that other parallel executing threads may take (such as accesses to shared memory).

2.3 Breakpoints

Breakpoints are used to pause the program when the execution reaches a specified point, to allow the user to examine the current state. After a breakpoint is triggered, the user can modify the value of variables or continue the execution to observe the progress of the program. Data breakpoints can be configured to trigger when the value changes for a specified expression. Conditional breakpoints pause the execution upon the satisfaction of a predicate specified by the user. These breakpoints can be added to statements in a program or class library [24]. Debugging tools such as GNU GDB [25] and Microsoft Visual Studio Debugger [26] support the use of breakpoints. Take the latter as an example. We will use a simple console application (Figure 2.3) that computes and displays multiplication tables.

A breakpoint can be added by positioning the cursor on the desired line before selecting "Toggle Breakpoint" from the Debug menu. To test this, position the cursor in the first line of code containing a Console.WriteLine statement. The line should change color, and you will see a circular icon appear in the gray margin area to the left of the code as shown in Figure 2.4. This icon is called a breakpoint glyph. The filled circle glyph indicates an active, normal breakpoint. When the

```
for (int i = 1; i <= 10; i++)
{
  Console.WriteLine("Multiplication table {0}.\n", i);
  for (int j = 1; j <= 10; j++)
  {
    Console.WriteLine("{0} x {1} = {2}", j, i, i * j);
  }
  Console.WriteLine("\n");
}
```

Figure 2.3 A console application.

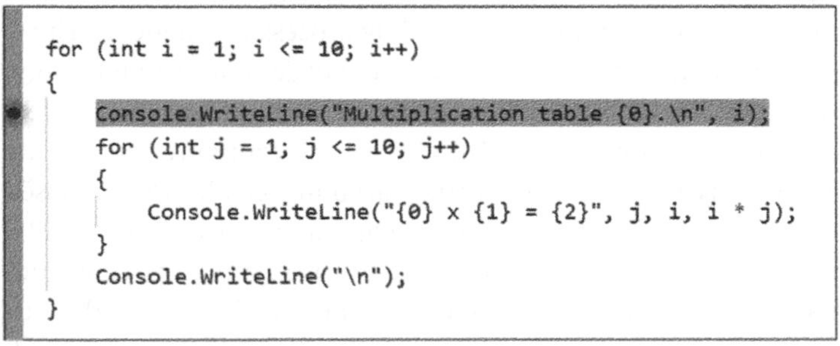
for (int i = 1; i <= 10; i++)
{
Console.WriteLine("Multiplication table {0}.\n", i);
for (int j = 1; j <= 10; j++)
{
Console.WriteLine("{0} x {1} = {2}", j, i, i * j);
}
Console.WriteLine("\n");
}

Figure 2.4 Add a breakpoint under Visual Studio.

```
for (int i = 1; i <= 10; i++)
{
    Console.WriteLine("Multiplication table {0}.\n", i);
    for (int j = 1; j <= 10; j++)
    {
        Console.WriteLine("{0} x {1} = {2}", j, i, i * j);
    }
    Console.WriteLine("\n");
}
```

Figure 2.5 Disable a breakpoint under Visual Studio.

above code is executed, the breakpoint location will be hit. The program will enter break mode, allowing users to go through the code using the debugging tools.

If a breakpoint is no longer required, it can be removed using the same actions used to create it. Users can select the marked line of code and choose the "Toggle Breakpoint" command. Alternatively, simply click the breakpoint glyph. When a breakpoint is successfully removed, the glyph disappears as shown in Figure 2.5. When debugging large programs, it is common to set many breakpoints, possibly in several different files. Once the debugging operation is complete, users can remove all of the breakpoints in a project by selecting the "Delete All Breakpoints" option from the Debug menu. If users still want to prevent a breakpoint from halting execution without deleting it completely, they can disable all of the breakpoints in the project by selecting the "Disable All Breakpoints" command from the Debug menu. To disable a single breakpoint, right-click its glyph and choose "Disable Breakpoint" from the context-sensitive menu that appears.

2.4 Profiling

Profiling in software engineering refers to the runtime analysis that measures the performance of a program from different perspectives, such as execution time, CPU/GPU usage, and memory usage, which helps practitioners inspect and optimize the program implementation. Table 2.4 shows a list of profiling tools, such as Eclipse Test & Performance Tools Platform (TPTP) [28], gprof [29], and JVM Monitor [30], which provide comprehensive profiling solutions.

Typically, profiling is used for performance optimization rather than fault localization. However, many fault localization techniques use profiling to collect data for analysis. To reduce the overhead, some advanced profiling techniques are proposed so that the analysis can be conducted in a cost-effective way. One of the most

Table 2.4 A list of profiling tools (some also appear in [27]).

Name	Vendor	Language/Technology
AppDynamics	AppDynamics	Java/.NET/PHP/Node.js/C++/ Python/ Apache Web Server/GoLang
Dynatrace	Dynatrace	Java/.NET/Node.js/AWS/Azure/ Cloud Foundry/OpenShift/Docker/OpenStack/ VMware/OracleDB/MySQL
JProfiler	EJ Technologies	Java
Visual Studio Build-in Profile	Microsoft	C/C++
VisualVM	Oracle	Java
NetBeans Profiler	Oracle	Java
JBoss Profiler	Red Hat	Java
AQTime Pro	SmartBear	Java/.NET/C/C++/Delphi/JScript/JavaScript/ VBScript/Silverlight/ Native 64-bit Application
Prefix	Stackify	Java/.NET
Retrace	Stackify	Java/.NET
YourKit	YourKit	Java/.NET
XRebel	Perforce	Java
GCC	GNU	C
Valgrind	Valgrind	C
Callgrind	Valgrind	C++
KCachegrind	N/A	C
gprof	GNU	C/C++
Shark	Apple	C
gperftools	Google	C
OProfile	N/A	Linux Kernel
VTune	Intel	C/C++/ C#/ Fortran/Java/Python/Go/ASM assembly
TAU	Advanced Computing Laboratory	Fortran/C/C++/UPC/Java/Python
CodeAnalyst	AMD	Java/CLR/Native Code
perf	N/A	Linux System
ANTS	Red Gate	.NET/ASP.NET
Arm Map	Arm Holdings	C/C++/Fortran

Table 2.4 (Continued)

Name	Vendor	Language/Technology
DevPartner Studio	Micro Focus	C/C++/.NET
DTrace	Sun Microsystems	Assembly language /C /C++ /Java/Erlang/ JavaScript/Perl/PHP /Python/Ruby/Shell Script/Tcl
FusionReactor	FusionReactor	Java/ColdFusion/MongoDB
GlowCode	Electric Software	C++/ C#/.NET
Intel Advisor	Intel	C/C++/Fortran/C#
LTTng	N/A	C/ C+ +/Java/Python
Oracle Solaris Studio	Oracle	C/C++/Java/Scala/Fortran
Oracle Developer Studio	Oracle	C/C++/Java/Scala/Fortran
PAPI	Innovative Computing Laboratory	C/C++/Fortran/Java/MATLAB
Chrome DevTools	Google	JavaScript
Firefox Developer Tools	Firefox	JavaScript
Xcode	Apple	Objective-C/Swift
TPTP	IBM	Java
JVM Monitor	N/A	Java

Source: Adapted from List of Performance Analysis Tools [27].

common uses of profiling in fault localization is to provide the program spectrum, which details the execution information of a program from certain perspectives, such as execution information for conditional branches or loop-free intra-procedural paths. For example, Hauswirth and Chilimbi [31] proposed SWAT to identify memory leaks or code that performs unexpectedly poorly. SWAT monitors the subject program's memory allocations for objects and their loads to construct a heap model that can report potential leaks. Based on the assumption that many hidden or longstanding bugs often lurk in some rarely executed locations, an adaptive profiling that samples executions of code segments at a rate inversely proportional to their execution frequency was used to collect the data to improve detection strength with low overhead. Results indicated that SWAT can identify potential memory leaks as well as their locations in the code. Chilimbi et al. [32] developed a debugging tool, HOLMES, to identify the causes of program failures from failing executions and successful executions. The path profiling was used to collect the execution histories of program paths. To achieve low overhead, an adaptive scheme that only starts profiling after observing a failure was adopted. The data collected were then analyzed to identify the locations that are highly likely to contain bugs. Runciman and Wakeling [33] designed and implemented a tool to profile the content of heap memory such as the memory usage of lazy functional programs. By doing so, it helped users optimize the implementation by reducing the memory consumption as well as identify potential space faults of the lazy functions.

2.5 Discussion

Logging is an important aspect of software development and promotes traceability of actions and operations. Well-written logging code offers quick debugging, easy maintenance, and structured storage of an application's runtime information. However, it can slow down an application if too verbose, which can cause scrolling blindness [5].

The role of assertions is to identify bugs in a program. In practice, the major benefit of assertions is to make testing more effective. An assertion that is never executed does not provide any value. An assertion is only useful if the path containing it is executed [34]. Assuming the code is being properly tested, assertions can aid from the following aspects [34]:

- Detecting subtle errors that might otherwise go undetected.
- Detecting errors soon after they occur.
- Declaratively stating conditions of the code that are guaranteed to be true.

However, there are downsides to assertions. One of the biggest is that, like other code, assertions may themselves contain errors. A bug in an assertion will likely cause one of the following problems [34]:

- Reporting an error where none exists. This kind of bug can lead an unwary programmer down a blind alley. Most programmers will learn to approach assertion failures with the proper skepticism after making such mistakes a few times.
- Failing to report a bug that does exist. This problem is less severe than the first one. If the program uses assertions heavily, it is likely that the error will be caught sooner or later by another assertion. Since an assertion that actually

detects errors is more valuable than one that does not, it is a good idea to simulate failed test cases to identify relevant assertions that actually do fail.

- Not being side-effect free. This problem can be very dangerous. Assertions are not supposed to affect the logic of a program, i.e. the program should run in the same way with or without them. Assertions are usually stripped out of a program before the final program binaries are delivered to customers. However, side effects do sometimes slip in when the assertions are not properly stripped out, or when the assertions are not stripped out because they were thought to be benign but actually change the program behavior. In the worst cases, these will introduce severe bugs to the build released to the customer. One way to avoid these kinds of bugs is to test the release build (with assertions stripped out) before releasing to the customer.

Moreover, assertions can and often do impact the program from nonfunctional perspectives. They can take time to execute and consume extra memory. For example, simple assertions such as the common check for null are relatively inexpensive, but more stringent checks, especially in assertion-heavy code, can measurably slow down the execution, sometimes severely so. Assertions also take up space, and not necessarily just for the code itself. For example, C/C++ assert macros often embed the string representation of the assertion's Boolean expression as well as the filename and line number of the assertion in the source code. This can add up if assertions make up a substantial percentage of the code. Normally, assertions are turned off for builds that are released to actual customers for performance reasons. Sometimes, organizations would rather have a program crash in an unexplained fashion than display a message that an end user will find disturbing (especially if they then have to choose between terminating the application, throwing an exception, or continuing as if nothing happened). When programmers identify an assertion failure, they can either fix the bug or, in extreme cases, disable the assertion. When assertions allow execution to continue (either by default or by user choice), one often runs into exactly the opposite problem, where testing should have been blocked but was not. In this scenario, a tester reports many different symptoms of the original bug as separate bugs. When an exception is thrown to attempt recovery, the situation can be even worse. Sometimes, the throwing of the exception causes more harm than good, resulting in many bugs that would never occur if execution had simply been allowed to continue.

Breakpoints provide a powerful tool that enables users to suspend execution where and when they need to. Rather than stepping through the code line by line or instruction by instruction, the program will run until it hits a breakpoint, and then it starts to debug. This speeds up the debugging process, especially for the case of large programs. Breakpoints can be deleted or changed without having to change the program's source code. Because breakpoints are not statements, they never produce any extra code when a release version of a program is built [35]. Implementing data breakpoints in software, however, can reduce the performance of the application being debugged, since it is using additional resources on the same processor.

Profilers are great for finding hot paths in code, such as figuring out what uses a large percent of the total CPU usage and determining how to improve that. They help people look for methods that can lead to improvements. They are also useful for finding memory leaks and understanding the performance of dependency calls and transactions. Profilers usually have two different levels: high and low. A high-level profiler tracks performance of key methods in the code. These profilers will perform transaction timing, such as tracking how long a web request takes, while also providing visibility to errors and logs. Low-level profiling can be very slow and has a large amount of overhead. A low-level profiler usually tracks the performance of every single method in the code and potentially every single line of code within each method [36].

2.6 Conclusion

In this chapter, we have reviewed traditional techniques that are commonly used for fault localization, including program logging, assertions, breakpoints, and profiling. Program logging is used to record diagnostic information regarding a program's execution. However, it slows down an application if it is too verbose, which can cause scrolling blindness. Assertions are constraints added to a program that have to be true during the correct operation of a program. They can help detect subtle errors that might otherwise go undetected and speed up error detection after they have occurred. The major challenge for assertions is that they may themselves contain errors, which will cause unexpected problems not in the original code. Using breakpoints allow developers to suspend execution where and when they need to. Using breakpoints may reduce the performance of the application being debugged as they take up additional resources on the same processor. Profiling analyzes the performance of a program from different perspectives and helps practitioners inspect and optimize the program implementation. This process can be very slow and can have a large amount of overhead when using a low-level profiler, which usually tracks the performance of every single method and potentially every single line of code within each method. In general, these techniques focus on manual inspections based on hints and deductions from pre-defined rules or pre-conducted analyses. This leads to the study of a more advanced and automatic process to locate software faults both effectively and efficiently.

References

1 Saini, S., Sardana, N., and Lal, S. (2016). Logger4u: predicting debugging statements in the source code. *Proceedings of the 2016 Ninth International Conference on Contemporary Computing (IC3 '16)*, Noida, India (11–13 August 2016), 1–7. IEEE. https://doi.org/10.1109/IC3.2016. 7880255.

2 log4j (2022). Logging levels. https://www.tutorialspoint.com/log4j/log4j_logging_levels (accessed 1 January 2022).

3 Al-Sharif, Z.A., Jeffery, C.L., and Said, M.H. (2014). Debugging with dynamic temporal assertions. *Proceedings of the 2014 IEEE International Symposium on Software Reliability Engineering Workshops*, Naples, Italy (3–6 November 2014), 257–262. IEEE. https://doi.org/10.1109/ISSREW.2014.60.

4 SLF4J (2022). Simple logging facade for Java (SLF4J). https://www.slf4j.org (accessed 1 January 2022).

5 log4j (2022). Apache log4j 2. https://logging.apache.org/log4j/2.x (accessed 1 January 2022).

6 Murillo, L.G., Bücs, R.L., Hincapie, D. et al. (2015). SWAT: assertion-based debugging of concurrency issues at system level. *Proceedings of the 20th Asia and South Pacific Design Automation Conference*, Chiba, Japan (19–22 January 2015), 600–605. IEEE. https://doi.org/10.1109/ASPDAC.2015.7059074.

7 Java Platform (2022). Package java.util.logging. https://docs.oracle.com/javase/7/docs/api/java/util/logging/package-summary.html (accessed 1 January 2022).

8 Winandy, M. (2022). tinylog. https://tinylog.org (accessed 1 January 2022).

9 The Object Guy (2022). Java logging framework. http://windowsbulletin.com/files/dll/bit-factory-inc/the-object-guy-s-logging-framework (accessed 1 July 2022).

10 Gurock Software (2022). SmartInspect. https://www.gurock.com/testrail/about (accessed 1 July 2022).

11 NLog (2022). NLog. https://nlog-project.org (accessed 1 July 2022).

12 log4net (2022). Apache log4net. http://logging.apache.org/log4net (accessed 1 January 2022).

13 Microsoft (2022). Enterprise library. https://en.wikipedia.org/wiki/Microsoft_Enterprise_Library (accessed 1 July 2022).

14 log4c (2022). Log4c: logging for C library. http://log4c.sourceforge.net (accessed 1 January 2022).

15 Schwartz-Narbonne, D., Liu, F., Pondicherry, T. et al. (2011). Parallel assertions for debugging parallel programs. *Proceedings of the 9th ACM/IEEE International Conference on Formal Methods and Models for Codesign (MEMPCODE '11)*, Cambridge, UK (11–13 July 2011), 181–190. IEEE. https://doi.org/10.1109/MEMCOD.2011.5970525.

16 Stackify (2022). Syslog tutorial: how it works, examples, best practices, and more. https://stackify.com/syslog-101 (accessed 1 January 2022).

17 Simpson, H. (2022). zlog: a reliable pure C logging library. http://hardysimpson.github.io/zlog (accessed 1 January 2022).

18 Pantheios (2022). Pantheios. http://www.pantheios.org/index.html (accessed 1 January 2022).

19 Rosenblum, D.S. (1995). A practical approach to programming with assertions. *IEEE Transactions on Software Engineering* 21 (1): 19–31. ISSN 0098-5589. https://doi.org/10.1109/32.341844.

20 Carr, R. (2008). Debugging using assertions. http://www.blackwasp.co.uk/DebugAssert.aspx (accessed 1 January 2022).

21 Coutant, D.S., Meloy, S., and Ruscetta, M. (1988). DOC: a practical approach to source-level debugging of globally optimized code. *Proceedings of the ACM SIGPLAN 1988 Conference on Programming Language Design and Implementation (PLDI '88),* Atlanta, GA, USA (22–24 June 1988), 125–134. ACM. http://doi.acm.org/10.1145/53990.54003. ISBN 0-89791-269-1.

22 Schmich, C. (2010). Insert line number in Debug.Assert statement. https://stackoverflow.com/questions/3868644/insert-line-number-in-debug-assert-statement (accessed 1 January 2022).

23 Boos, K., Fok, C., Julien, C., and Kim, M. (2012). BRACE: an assertion framework for debugging cyber-physical systems. *Proceedings of the 2012 34th International Conference on Software Engineering (ICSE '12),* Zurich, Switzerland (2–9 June 2012), 1341–1344. IEEE. https://doi.org/10.1109/ICSE.2012.6227084.

24 BlackWasp (2022). Breakpoints and tracepoints in visual studio. http://www.blackwasp.co.uk/VSBreakpoints.aspx (accessed 1 January 2022).

25 GNU (2022). GDB: the GNU project debugger. http://www.gnu.org/software/gdb (accessed 1 January 2022).

26 Microsoft (2022). Debugging in visual studio. https://msdn.microsoft.com/en-us/library/sc65sadd.aspx (accessed 1 January 2022).

27 List of Performance Analysis Tools (2022). https://en.wikipedia.org/wiki/List_of_performance_analysis_tools (accessed 1 July 2022).

28 Eclipse-Foundation (2022). Test and performance tools platform. https://projects.eclipse.org/projects/tptp.platform/developer (accessed 1 January 2022).

29 GNU (2022). GNU gprof. http://sourceware.org/binutils/docs/gprof (accessed 1 January 2022).

30 JVMMonitor project (2022). JVMMonitor: Java profiler integrated with Eclipse. http://jvmmonitor.org (accessed 1 January 2022).

31 Hauswirth, M. and Chilimbi, T.M. (2004), Low-overhead memory leak detection using adaptive statistical profiling. *Proceedings of the 11th International Conference on Architectural Support for Programming Languages and Operating Systems (ASPLOS '04),* Boston, MA, USA (7–13 October 2004), 156–164. ACM. http://doi.acm.org/10.1145/1024393.1024412. ISBN 1-58113-804-0.

32 Chilimbi, T.M., Liblit, B., Mehra, K. et al. (2009). HOLMES: effective statistical debugging via efficient path profiling. *Proceedings of the 2009 IEEE 31st International Conference on Software Engineering (ICSE '09)*, Vancouver, BC, Canada (16–24 May 2009), 34–44. IEEE. https://doi.org/10.1109/ICSE.2009.5070506.

33 Runciman, C. and Wakeling, D. (1993). Heap profiling of lazy functional programs. *Journal of Functional Programming* 3 (2): 217–245. https://doi.org/10.1017/S0956796800000708.

34 Cary, D. (2022). What are assertions. http://wiki.c2.com/?WhatAreAssertions (accessed 1 January 2022).

35 Microsoft (2022). Debugging basics: breakpoints. https://docs.microsoft.com/en-us/visualstudio/debugger/using-breakpoints?view=vs-2022 (accessed 1 July 2022).

36 Stackify (2022). What is code profiling? Learn the 3 types of code profilers. https://stackify.com/what-is-code-profiling (accessed 1 January 2022).

3

Slicing-Based Techniques for Software Fault Localization

W. Eric Wong[1], Hira Agrawal[2], and Xiangyu Zhang[3]

[1] *Department of Computer Science, University of Texas at Dallas, Richardson, TX, USA*
[2] *Peraton Labs, Basking Ridge, NJ, USA*
[3] *Department of Computer Science, Purdue University, West Lafayette, IN, USA*

3.1 Introduction

Software is now becoming increasingly large and complex, which makes it difficult to maintain, test, and debug. Therefore, it is common that programmers raise questions such as:

- If I change this statement, what parts of the program will be affected?
- Where are the values that flow into this statement coming from?
- How can I limit the functionality to only what I need?

How can we answer these questions? In this chapter, we will introduce the concepts and application of program slicing and dicing in the area of software fault localization, which aims to tackle these issues. Program slicing is a technique to abstract a program into a reduced form by deleting irrelevant parts such that the resulting slice will still behave the same as the original program with respect to certain specifications [1, 2]. In other words, by deleting specific parts of the program, programmers can focus only on the relevant parts and gain a better understanding of the program under analysis.

The main applications of program slicing include various software engineering activities such as program understanding, debugging, testing, program maintenance, complexity measurement, and so on. The notion of program slicing was first pioneered by Weiser in 1979 [3] as a useful software engineering technique aimed at expediting many software development tasks such as program component extraction, program comprehension, debugging, and maintenance.

Handbook of Software Fault Localization: Foundations and Advances, First Edition.
Edited by W. Eric Wong and T.H. Tse.

Published 2023 by John Wiley & Sons, Inc.

Over the last few decades, hundreds of papers have been published with special focus on fault localization. While they focus on similar fundamental principles, the projects can be further divided into four distinctive categories: static slicing-based, dynamic slicing-based, execution slicing-based, and other slicing-based fault localization.

3.2 Static Slicing-Based Fault Localization[1]

One of the important applications of static slicing [5] is to reduce the search domain while programmers locate bugs[2] in their programs. This is based on the idea that if a test case fails due to an incorrect variable value at a statement, then the defect should be found in the static slice associated with that variable–statement pair, allowing us to confine our search to the slice rather than looking at the entire program.

3.2.1 Introduction

A *static program slice* (*SPS*), as originally defined by Weiser [5], consists of all statements in program *P* that may affect the value of variable *v*. Weiser introduced a set theoretic algebraic approach to extract static program slices. Ottenstein and Ottenstein [6] later devised a more efficient graph-theoretic approach to extract SPS of individual program functions/procedures using their data- and control-dependence graphs.

One of the most important applications of static slicing is to reduce the search domain that programmers need to go through when trying to locate specific bugs in their programs. Intuitively, if a program fails due to an incorrect variable *v* at a specific statement *s*, the bug should reside in the static slice associated with *v* and *s*. Therefore, instead of examining the entire program, programmers can focus on the static slice of a variable-statement set denoted as $\langle v, s \rangle$ to locate the bug more efficiently and effectively.

As displayed in Table 3.1, we include a sample program to illustrate the basic idea of static slicing. The original program contains two independent variables, `sum` and `product`. Without loss of generality, we now focus on the variable `sum`. Therefore, as illustrated in the slice for variable `sum`, those statements not related to `sum` are ignored in the slice. In fact, most static slicing techniques, including Weiser's own technique [5], will also remove the `write(sum)` statement because the value of `sum` is not dependent on the statement itself.

Another endeavor was made by Lyle and Weiser, who extended the above approach by constructing a program dice (as the set difference of two

Table 3.1 Static slicing with valid slice for variable `sum` at statement 8.

	Original program	Valid slice for `sum`
1	`int i;`	`int i;`
2	`int sum = 0;`	`int sum = 0;`
3	`int product = 1;`	
4	`for (i = 1; i < N; ++i) {`	`for (i = 1; i < N; ++i) {`
5	`sum=sum + i;`	`sum=sum + i;`
6	`product=product * i;`	
7	`}`	`}`
8	`write(sum);`	`write(sum);`
9	`write(product);.`	

Source: Adapted from Kaya and Fawcett [7]/IEEE.

groups of static slices) to further reduce the search domain for possible locations of a fault [8].

3.2.2 Program Slicing Combined with Equivalence Analysis[3]

Although static slicing-based techniques have been experimentally evaluated and confirmed to be useful in fault localization [10], one problem is that handling pointer variables can make data-flow analysis inefficient because large sets of data introduced by dereferencing of pointer variables need to be stored. Equivalence analysis, which identifies equivalence relations among the various memory locations accessed by a procedure, is used to improve the efficiency of dataflow analyses in the presence of pointer variables [4]. Stated differently, Liang et al. [4] proposed a technique that uses equivalence classes computed to improve the efficiency of Harrold and Ci's [11] reuse-driven slicing algorithm when slicing programs that use pointers. Before introducing the technique itself, we first provide a high-level introduction of the reuse-driven slicing algorithm.

We use s to represent a specific statement in a procedure/program and l to represent a location with specific value. To compute the slice for a slicing criterion $\langle s, l \rangle$, the reuse-driven slicing algorithm first invokes the partial slicer on $[s, l]$ in $\mathcal{P}_s$, the procedure that contains s. If $\mathcal{P}_S$ is not procedure *main* in the program, then the statements in procedures that call P_S may also affect the value of l at s by affecting the values of the relevant inputs with respect to $[s, l]$. If this is the case, the algorithm maps each relevant input back to the variable at each callsite that calls $\mathcal{P}_s$. The process continues until it reaches procedure *main*. Therefore, the slice for $\langle s, l \rangle$ contains all the statements included in all partial slices computed by the algorithm.

For example, for the program in Figure 3.1 to compute the slice for ⟨18, `sum`⟩, the slicer first invokes the partial slicer on [18, `sum`]. The partial slicer returns

```
1   int j, sum, t;
2   main() {
3       int sum1, i1, i2;
4       reset(&sum);
5       reset(&i1)
6       read(&j);
7       while (i1 < 10)
8         f(&i1);
9       sum1 = sum;
10      reset(&i2);
11      while (i2 < 20)
12        f(&i2);
13      t = i1 + i2;
14  }
15  f(int *p) {
16      if (j< 0) {
17        j = -j
18      sum = sum + j;
19      incr(p);
20      read(&j);
21  }
22  incr(int *q) {
23    *q = *q + 1;
24  }
25  reset(int *s) {
26    *s = 0;
27  } }
```

Procedure	Equivalence classes for non-local
main()	{sum}, {j}
f()	{i1,i2}, {sum}, {j}
incr()	{i1,i2}
reset()	{i1,i2,sum}

Figure 3.1 An example program (top) and its equivalence classes (bottom).

Statements 16, 17, and 18 as the partial slice, and returns `sum` and `j` as the relevant inputs. Since `f()` is not the main procedure, the slicer binds these memory locations back to the callsites at Statements 8 and 12. The slicer then invokes the partial slicer on [8, `sum`], [8, `j`], [12, `sum`], and [12, `j`] to continue the computation of the slice.

By using equivalence analysis, the proposed technique can increase the reuse of the partial slices and relevant inputs computed by the partial slicer. Given a partial slicing criterion [s, l], where s is a statement in procedure P, the partial slicer first looks for the representative memory location r in the equivalence class that contains l in P. The partial slicer then looks up the information for [s, r] in the cache. If such information is not available, then the partial slicer computes the partial slice and the relevant inputs for [s, r] and stores the results in the cache. If the information is available, then the partial slicer reuses the information.

3.2.3 Further Application

Tip et al. [12] also applied static slicing to the fault localization for type errors. The location associated with an error message e is denoted as a slice $\mathcal{P}_e$ of the program P being type-checked. The approach can precisely locate the program entities in P that caused error e.

3.3 Dynamic Slicing-Based Fault Localization[4]

Before moving any further, we first introduce the basic concepts related to program dependence graphs and the notation used to explain the approaches. Korel and Laski extended Weiser's static slicing algorithms based on data-flow equations for the dynamic case [14]. However, their definition of a dynamic slice may yield unnecessarily large dynamic slices.

The dynamic slicing introduced in this section is based on the work by Agrawal and Horgan [13]. As illustrated in Figure 3.2, the program dependence graph of a program has one node for each simple statement (such as assignment, read, and write, as opposed to compound statements like `if-then-else` and `while-do`) and one node for each control predicate expression (such as the condition expression in `if-then-else` or `while-do`). Two types of directed edges[5] are denoted in Figure 3.2b to represent the data- and control-dependences, respectively.

(a)

```
1   read(X)
2   if(X<0){
3     Y=f1(X);
4     Z=g1(X);
    }
5   else if (X=0){
6     Y=f2(X);
7     Z=g2(X);
    }
    else {
8     Y=f3(X);
9     Z=g3(X);
    }
10  write(Y);
11  write(Z);
```

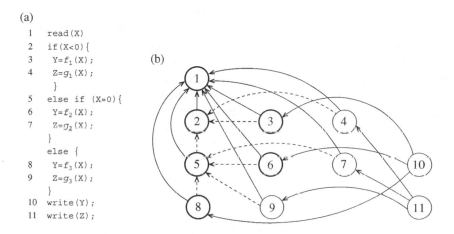

(b)

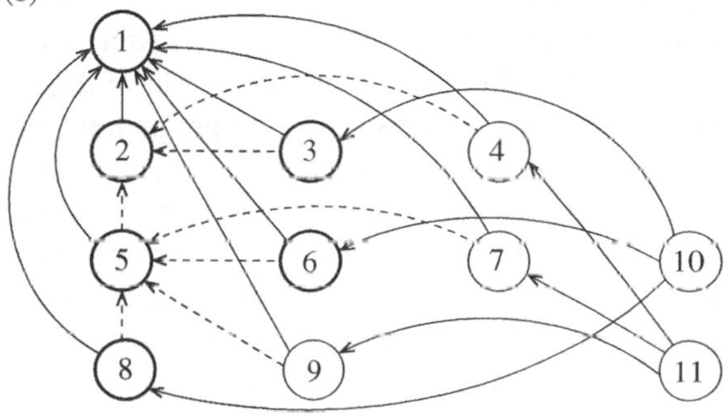

(c)

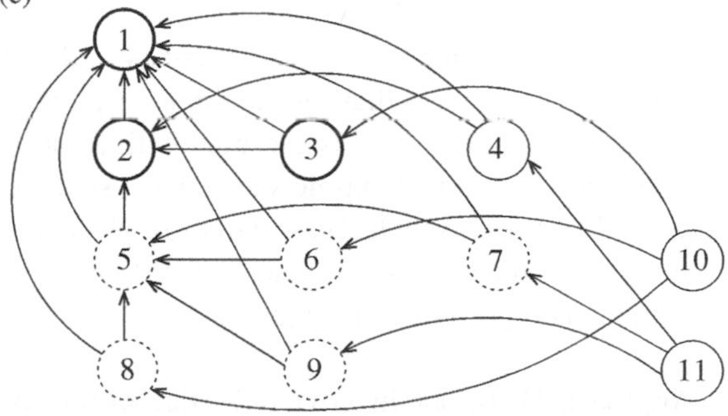

Figure 3.2 Program dependence graph: (a) Original program; (b) Program dependence graph with data- and control-dependences; and (c) Dynamic slice for X = −1. A node is solid if it is executed; a node is bold if it is traversed when determining the dynamic slice using Approach 1. *Source:* Agrawal and Horgan [13]/ACM.

```
1 read(N);
2 Z = 0;
3 Y = 0;
4 I = 1;
5 while (I <= N) do {
6      Z = f1(Z, Y);
7      Y = f2(Y);
8      I = I + 1;
  }
9 write(Z);
```

Figure 3.3 Sample program for execution history. *Source:* Agrawal and Horgan [13]/ACM.

A data-dependence edge (solid edge as denoted in Figure 3.2b) from vertex v_i to v_j indicates that the computation performed at vertex v_i directly depends on the value achieved at vertex v_j. For example, the edge from vertex 2 to vertex 1 indicates that the value of X at statement 2 is dependent on statement 1. A control-dependence edge (dashed edge as denoted in Figure 3.2b) from v_i to v_j means that the Boolean outcome at v_j has a direct impact on whether v_i is executed or not. With respect to the dashed edge from vertex 3 to vertex 2, the Boolean outcome at statement 2 determines if statement 3 should be executed.

In addition, we denote the execution history of the program under a given test case by the sequence $\langle v_1, v_2, ..., v_n \rangle$ of vertices in the program dependence graph appended in the order in which they are visited during execution. Also, superscripts 1, 2, etc., are utilized to indicate multiple visits of the same node in the execution history. For example, with respect to the program in Figure 3.3, the execution history of a test case with N = 2 is $\langle 1, 2, 3, 4, 5^1, 6^1, 7^1, 8^1, 5^2, 6^2, 7^2, 8^2, 5^3, 9 \rangle$.

Given an execution history *hist* of a program *P* for a test case *t*, and a variable *var*, the dynamic slice of *P* with respect to *hist* and *var* is the set of all statements in *hist* whose execution had some effects on the value of *var* as observed at the end of the execution. Note that unlike static slicing, where a slice is defined with respect to a given location in the program, we define dynamic slicing with respect to the end of execution history. If a dynamic slice with respect to some intermediate point in the execution is desired, then we simply need to consider the partial execution history up to that point.

As demonstrated in Figure 3.2a, the static slice with respect to ⟨Y, statement 10⟩ contains statements 1, 2, 3, 5, 6, and 8, which have been marked as bold vertices in Figure 3.2b. One thing we need to consider is that for the three assignment statements (statements 3, 6, and 8), only one of them is executed with respect to any given test case. Therefore, to determine the dynamic slice for ⟨Y, statement 10⟩, we only take the nodes executed for the current test case. For example, with respect to a test case X = −1, the dynamic slice using Approach 1 for ⟨Y, statement 10⟩ contains statements 1, 2, and 3, as represented in Figure 3.2c.

> Dynamic slicing (Approach 1): To obtain a dynamic slice with respect to a variable for a given execution history, first take a "projection" of the program dependence graph with respect to the nodes that occur in the execution history, and then use the static slicing algorithm on the projected dependence graph to find the desired dynamic slice [13].

However, Approach 1 does not always guarantee dynamic slices: extra statements may be included in the slice that do not have effects on *var* for the given *hist*. This is because a statement may have multiple reaching definitions with respect to the same variable in the program flow graph. Selection of a node with multiple outgoing data dependence edges implies that all nodes to which it has outgoing edges are also selected, even though the corresponding data definitions may not have affected the current node. Therefore, the following should be applied:

A revised Approach 2 described below is proposed.

> Dynamic slicing (Approach 2): Mark the edges of a program dependence graph as the corresponding dependencies arise during the program execution; then, traverse the graph only along the marked edges to find the slice [13].

For example, with N = 1, the execution history of the program in Figure 3.3 using Approach 2 is $\langle 1, 2, 3, 4, 5^1, 6, 7, 8, 5^2, 9\rangle$. Imagine that all the edges in Figure 3.4 are drawn as dotted lines initially. As statements are executed, edges corresponding to the new dependences that occur are changed to solid lines. Then, the graph is traversed only along solid edges, and the nodes reached are made bold. The set of all bold nodes at the end gives the dynamic slice for the variable Z in statement 9, which is shown in Figure 3.4. It is obvious that statement 7 assigns a value to Y that is never used later, since none of the statements that appear after statement 7 (namely, statements 8, 5, and 9) uses the variable Y. Hence, statement 7, which was included in the slice of Approach 1, is not included if Approach 2 is used.

Approach 2 performs accurately if a program has no loop. In the presence of loops, the slice generated may include more statements than necessary. Consider the program in Figure 3.5 with N = 2 and two values of X as −4 and 3. For the first

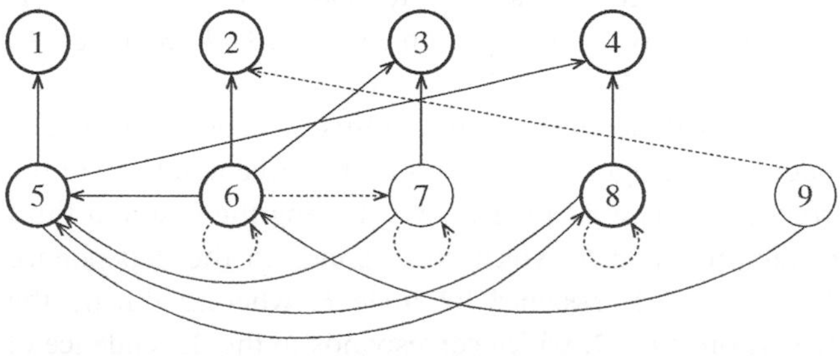

Figure 3.4 Dynamic slice using Approach 2 for N = 1 with respect to program in Figure 3.3. *Source:* Agrawal and Horgan [13]/ACM.

```
1   read(N);
2   I = 1;
3   while (I <= N) do {
4       read(X);
5       if (X < 0)
6          Y = f1(X);
7       else
           Y = f2(X);
8       Z = f3(X);
    }
9       write(Z);
10      I = I + 1;
    }
```

Figure 3.5 An example. *Source:* Agrawal and Horgan [13]/ACM.

time through the loop, statement 6 (the *then* part of the *if* statement) is executed. For the second time through the loop, statement 7 (the *else* part) is executed. Now, suppose the execution has reached just past statement 9 the second time through the loop, and the second value of Z printed is found to be wrong. The execution history thus far is $\langle 1, 2, 3^1, 4^1, 5^1, 6, 8^1, 9^1, 10^1, 3^2, 4^2, 5^2, 7, 8^2, 9^2\rangle$. By using Approach 2 to determine the slice for variable Z for this execution history, we would have both statements 6 and 7 included in the slice, even though the value of Z in this case is only dependent on statement 7.

The problem is caused by the fact that a statement may have multiple occurrences in an execution history, and different occurrences of the statement may have different reaching definitions of the same variable used by the statement. In other words, different occurrences of the same statement may have different dependences, and it is possible that one occurrence contributes to the slice and another does not. To overcome this issue, a third approach (Approach 3) is proposed:

> Dynamic slicing (Approach 3): Create a separate node for each occurrence of a statement in the execution history, with outgoing dependence edges to only those statements (their specific occurrences) on which this statement occurrence is dependent [13].

In this case, every node in the new dependence graph will have at most one outgoing edge for each variable used at the statement. The revised graph is called the dynamic dependence graph. A program will have different dynamic dependence graphs for different execution histories.

Consider again the program in Figure 3.5 with the test case N = 3, X = −4, 3, −2. The corresponding execution history using Approach 3 is $\langle 1, 2, 3^1, 4^1, 5^1, 6^1, 8^1, 9^1, 10^1, 3^2, 4^2, 5^2, 7^1, 8^2, 9^2, 10^2, 3^3, 4^3, 5^3, 6^2, 8^3, 9^3, 10^3, 3^4\rangle$.

Figure 3.6 shows the dynamic dependence graph for this execution history. The middle three rows of nodes in the figure correspond to the three iterations of the loop. Notice the occurrences of node 8 in these rows. During the first and third iterations, node 8 depends on node 6, which corresponds to the dependence of statement 8 for the value of Y assigned by node 6, whereas during the second iteration, it depends on node 7, which corresponds to the dependence of statement 8 for the value of Y assigned by node 7. Note that using Approach 3, statement 6 belongs to the slice, whereas statement 7 does not. On the other hand, Approach 2 would have included statement 7 as well.

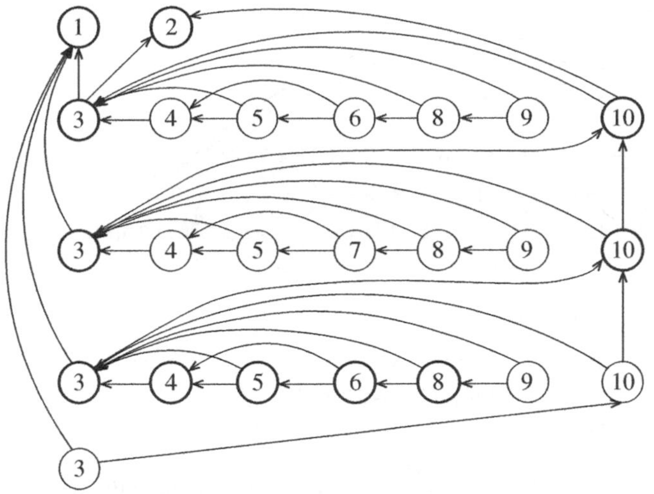

Figure 3.6 Dynamic dependence graph using Approach 3 for the program in Figure 3.5 for the test case (N = 3, X = −4, 3, −2). Nodes in bold give the dynamic slice for this test case with respect to variable Z at the end of execution. *Source:* Agrawal and Horgan [13]/ACM.

The size of a dynamic dependence graph (total number of nodes and edges) is, in general, *unbounded*. This is because the number of nodes in the graph is equal to the number of statements in the execution history, which, in general, may depend on values of run-time inputs. For example, for the program in Figure 3.3, the number of statements in its execution history, and hence the size of its dynamic dependence graph, depends on the value read by variable N at statement 1.

On the other hand, we know that every program can have only a finite number of possible dynamic slices—each slice being a subset of the (finite) program. This suggests that we ought to be able to restrict the number of nodes in a dynamic dependence graph so its size is not a function of the length of the corresponding execution history. Approach 4 exploits this observation.

> Dynamic slicing (Approach 4): Instead of creating a new node for every occurrence of a statement in the execution history, create a new node only if another node with the same transitive dependencies does not already exist [13].

We call this new graph the reduced dynamic dependence graph.

Consider again the program in Figure 3.5 with the test case N = 3, X = −4, 3, −2. The corresponding execution history using Approach 4 is $\langle 1, 2, 3^1, 4^1, 5^1, 6^1, 8^1, 9^1, 10^1, 3^2, 4^2, 5^2, 7^1, 8^2, 9^2, 10^2, 3^3, 4^3, 5^3, 6^2, 8^3, 9^3, 10^3, 3^4 \rangle$.

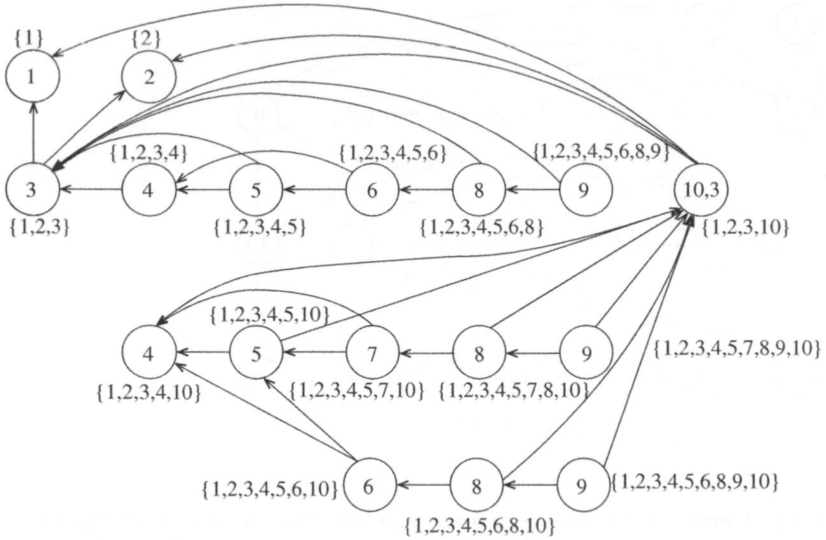

Figure 3.7 Reduced dynamic dependence graph using Approach 4. *Source:* Agrawal and Horgan [13]/ACM.

Figure 3.7 shows the reduced dynamic dependence graph for this execution history. Every node in the graph is annotated with the set of all reachable statements from that node. To obtain the dynamic slice for any variable *var*, we first find the entry for *var* in the *DefnNode* table. The *ReachableStmts* set associated with that entry gives the desired dynamic slice. For example, the dynamic slice for variable z is given by the *ReachableStmts* set {1, 2, 3, 4, 5, 6, 8, 10} associated with node 8 in the last row, as that was the last node to define the value of z.

3.3.1 Dynamic Slicing and Backtracking Techniques[6]

In [1, 15], Agrawal et al. applied dynamic slicing and backtracking to fault localization. The approach repeatedly performs the following steps:

Step 1: Determine which statements in the code had an influence on the value of a given variable observed at a given location.
Step 2: Select one of these statements to examine the program state.
Step 3: Recreate the program state at the selected statement to examine specific variables.

With respect to the first two steps, it is acceptable for the engineers to perform the tasks by themselves. For the third task, if we were debugging using a conventional debugger, we would need to set a breakpoint at a specific selected statement and re-execute the program from the beginning. The state can be recreated once the program stops at the statement. We may then analyze the variables at this particular state and see if we can locate the error. If the error cannot be located, a breakpoint needs to be set up in an earlier location and the program must be re-executed again from the beginning. This can be cumbersome and time-consuming.

The approach proposed in [1] provides an execution backtracking facility with which the program state can be restored to an earlier location without having to re-execute the entire program. Similar to forward program execution, in which the run is suspended whenever a breakpoint is encountered, the approach can "execute" the program in the reverse order and continue executing backward until a breakpoint is reached.

For example, consider again the program in Figure 3.8. If the program execution is stopped at line 46, and we discover that the value of `sum` is incorrect there, we may set a breakpoint on line 43 and start the backward execution. As the loop was iterated twice for this test case, the second iteration will be reached first during the backward execution. When this execution stops at line 43, the program state will be exactly the same as if the execution had stopped there during the forward execution. If we examine the value of `sum` there, we will obtain its value just before the last assignment was executed as shown in Figure 3.8. Notice the value of `sum` before and after the "backup" command, as displayed in the bottom (output) window. If we find this previous value of `sum` to be correct, we may conclude that it is the current value of *area* that is incorrect. If we wanted to back up to the same location during the previous iteration, we simply need to continue our backward execution from there on. As no other breakpoint is encountered during the same iteration, the backward execution is again suspended when it reaches the breakpoint at line 43 during the previous iteration.

3.3.2 Dynamic Slicing and Model-Based Techniques

Wotawa [16] provided an in-depth discussion of the relationship between debugging using a dependence-based model and dynamic program slicing. The paper first demonstrated that model-based diagnosis can be used for debugging with similar capabilities provided by program slicing. Then, the author showed that program slices and conflict sets are equivalent, which helps improve debugging using a model-based system. Instead of computing the logical model and then computing conflict sets, only the slices for incorrect variables need to be considered.

In a more recently published paper [17], Wotawa provided a fault localization technique based on the combination of dynamic slicing and model-based diagnosis. The basic idea of the approach is to combine slices for faulty variables in a way that minimizes the resulting diagnoses, i.e. statements that potentially lead to the detected misbehavior.

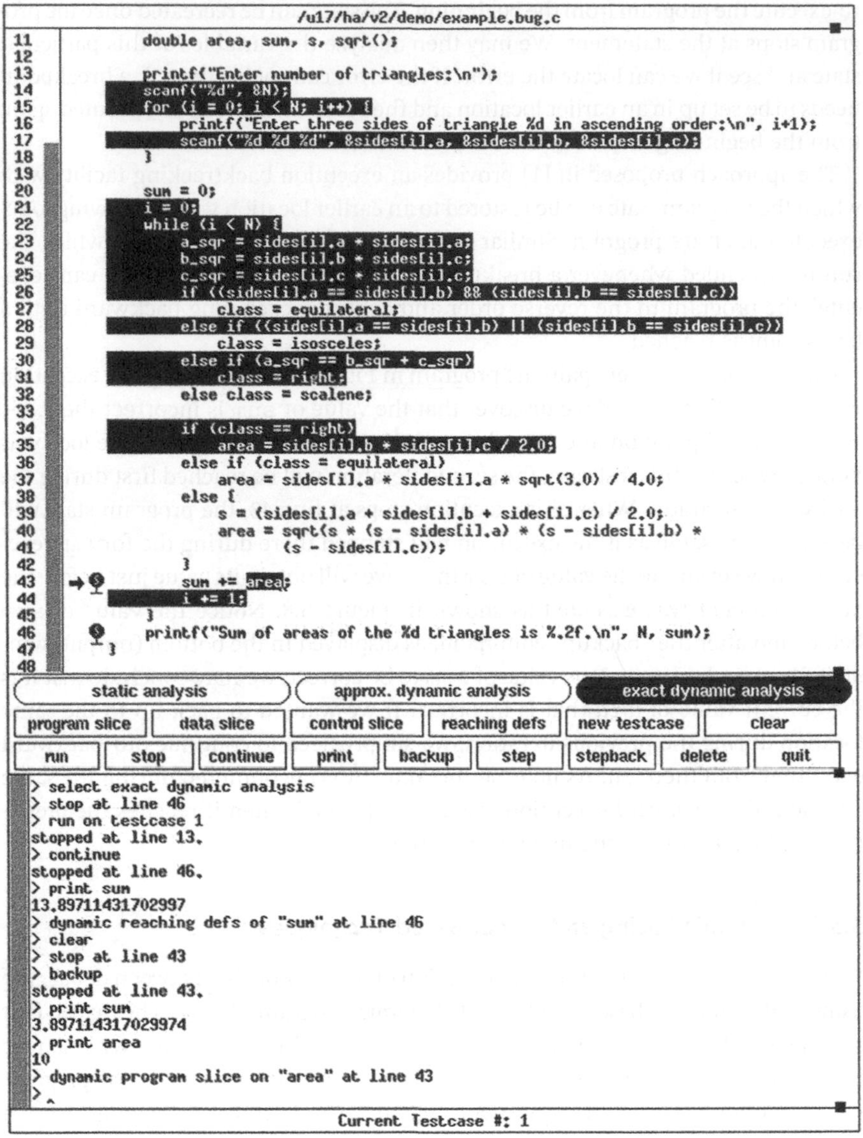

Figure 3.8 An example showing the backtracking. *Source:* Agrawal et al. [15]/Wiley.

Figure 3.9 is a sample program demonstrating dynamic slicing and model-based technique. It is assumed that the balance of the account is never less than or equal to the specified limit. The transferTo() method requires that the balance of the account to be transferred is larger than zero, which is not the case for our example program. Such kind of fault is not very unlikely. They usually occur after extending a program as part of maintenance activities. For example, it may be the case that

```
public class BankAccount extends Object {
  public String owner;
  public long balance;
  public long limit;
  public void withdraw(long amount) {
     if ((balance - amount) > limit) {
       balance = balance - amount;
     }
  }
   public void deposit(long amount) {
     balance = balance + amount;
  }
   public void transferTo(Bank Account acc){
     long money = this.balance;
     if (money != 0) { // BUG: Should be >
       this.withdraw(money);
       acc.deposit(money);
    }
  }
}
```

Figure 3.9 A sample program demonstrating dynamic slicing and model-based technique. *Source:* Wotawa [17]/IEEE.

the transfer function was implemented before introducing a certain limit for the account's balance.

Such a fault would be easily detected through unit tests. Figure 3.10 shows a unit test that can reveal the fault:

Let *t* be a unit test case that reveals the fault. The test case is passed if a transfer of an account having a negative balance does not change the balances of both accounts. Otherwise, either the assertions at line t_9 or t_{10} cause an exception. Note that in this case, both of the instance variables al.balance and a2.balance have wrong values. Hence, *t* is a failure-revealing test case.

To identify the root cause of the misbehavior, one way would be to compute the dynamic slices for both variables and check which line of code is incorrect. The

```
t1  BankAccount al = new BankAccount();
t2  al.setOwner("romeo");
t3  al.setLimit(new Long(-1000));
t4  al.withdraw(new Long(100));
t5  BankAccount a2 = new BankAccount();
t6  a2.set Owner ("julia");
t7  a2.deposit(new Long(200));
t8  al.transferTo(a2);
t9  Assert.assertEquals(-100, al.balance);
t10 Assert.assertEquals(200, a2.balance);
```

Figure 3.10 A JUnit test suite that reveals the fault. *Source:* Wotawa [17]/IEEE.

slice for al.balance includes statements 7, 8, 17, 18, and 19. The slice for variable a2. balance contains the statements 13, 17, 18, and 20. Hence, it is more likely that statements 17 and 18 are faulty because both of them are an element of both slices. On the other hand, any combination of elements from both slices may be an explanation of the misbehavior when considering multiple faults or double faults in this case.

In addition, the notion of probability slices is also introduced to support focusing on potentially faulty statement and to increase the accuracy of the proposed technique.

3.3.3 Critical Slicing[7]

In [18], the authors explored a new approach to enhance the process of fault localization based on dynamic program slicing and mutation-based testing. The approach can be referred to as critical slicing, which is based on the "statement deletion" mutation operator (`ssdl`).

Suppose that a sequence of statements $S = \langle S_1, S_2, ..., S_i, ..., S_F \rangle$ is an execution path when a faulty program P is executed against a given failure-revealing test case t with a failure type F, and S_F is the statement where F occurs. For example, S_F could be the last statement being executed, and the output variables are wrong; or S_F is the statement where an exception failure (such as division by zero) occurs. For the failure types with incorrectly valued output variables, the incorrect values are considered as features of the related failure type.

Definition 3.1 *A statement S_i in S of P is critical to a selected variable v in the failure F_i at statement S_F for test case t if and only if the execution of P without S_i (i.e. a statement-deletion mutant M of P by deleting S_i from P) against the test case t reaches S_F with a different value of v from the one in F_i.*

An example program is provided in Figure 3.11. Statements 1, 2, 3, 4, 5, 7, 8, and 9 are executed. The static slice with respect to the output variable x at statement 9 contains $\langle 1, 2, 3, 4, 5, 8, 9 \rangle$. In addition, the dynamic slice contains $\langle 2, 3, 8, 9 \rangle$. Statements 3, 4, 5, 8, and 9 are in the critical slice with respect to the failure, with wrong output value 5 for input data 7 at statement 9.

This means that not only is M killed because the execution against t has a different result from the original one in F_i, but also the execution reaches the same failure point S_F. For failure types with wrong output variables, the incorrect values of the erroneous output variables are used to decide whether M has the same result (values) as the original of the failure type. The requirement of reaching S_F guarantees that the effect of executing S propagates to the same failure point. Meanwhile, killing M indicates that the effect of executing S_i makes a difference in the result. S_i is therefore critical to the failure. A set of statements with the same feature of S_i forms a critical slice with the following formal definition:

```
1  Input a; /* input for a is 7 */
2  x = 0;
3  j = 5;
4  a = a - 10; /* correct version a = a + 10; */
5  if (a > j) {
6      x = x + 1;
       }
       else {
7      z = 0;
       }
8  x = x + j;
9  print x; /* x is 5, but should be 6 */
```

Figure 3.11 An example for critical slice. *Source:* DeMillo et al. [18]/ACM.

Definition 3.2 *A Critical Slice is based on a 5-tuple* $\langle P, F_i, v, S_F, t\rangle$ *with definition* $CS(P, F_i, v, S_F, t) = \{S_i \mid S_i$ *is critical to the variable v of the program P in the failure* F_i *at location* S_F *for test case t*$\}$.

The properties of critical slicing, which include the relationships among critical slicing and other dynamic slicing techniques, the cost to obtain it, and its effectiveness, have also been discussed in [18] as follows.

3.3.3.1 Relationships Between Critical Slices (CS) and Exact Dynamic Program Slices (DPS)

A dynamic program slice *DPS*(*P*, *v*, *l*, *t*) consists of all the statements in a program *P* that actually affect the current value of a variable *v* at location *l* when *P* is executed against a given test case *t*. We will refer to such a slice as an *exact dynamic program slice* (a.k.a. "*exact DPS*", or simply "*DPS*").

The following two examples demonstrate that there is no superset or subset relationship between CS and DPS.

Example 3.1 If an assignment statement has no effect on the defined variable (i.e. the value of the defined variable on the left-hand side of the statement is the same before and after the statement is executed), then the value of the defined variable will be propagated and have the same effect on the result regardless of whether the statement is executed. The result is thus unchanged if the statement is removed. Therefore, the statement is not in a corresponding critical slice. At the same time, it is possible that the defined variable actually affects the result and is thus in a corresponding exact DPS. In this case, the statement is not in the critical slice but in the corresponding exact DPS.

For instance, the defined variable x (on the left-hand side) of statement 2 in Figure 3.11 is assigned zero, which is the same as the value of x before statement 2 is executed, if the memory initialization is zero for all variables. However, statement 2 has data dependence on statement 8 that assigns the output variable x at statement 9. Thus, statement 2 is not in the critical slice but in the corresponding exact DPS.

Example 3.2 For a given program *P*, variable *v*, location *l*, and test case *t*, if a block of statements enclosed by an executed predicate statement contains assignment statements in the corresponding static slice (with respect to *v* and *l*) but not in the corresponding exact dynamic program slice *DPS*(*P*, *v*, *l*, *t*), then the predicate statement potentially affects *v* at *l* for *t*. In other words, the predicate statement keeps the value of *v* at *l* for *t* "intact."

Although the predicate statement is not in the corresponding exact DPS, the predicate statement still contributes to the result by keeping the value of the corresponding variable intact within its scope. Therefore, the predicate statement is critical to the result if it is not executed and is thus in the corresponding critical slice. In this case, the statement is in the critical slice but not in the corresponding exact DPS. For instance, statement 5 in Figure 3.11 is in the critical slice but not in the exact DPS.

3.3.3.2 Relationship Between Critical Slices and Executed Static Program Slices

The relationship between CS and ESPS is described in the following theorem.

Theorem 3.1 *The set of statements in a critical slice are a subset of the set of statements in the corresponding executed static program slice, i.e.* $CS \subseteq ESPS$.

Proof. By definition, all statements in a critical slice make a difference in the results at the selected point. These statements in the critical slice either actually or potentially affect the results.

For the first case, actually affecting the results, statements are included in the corresponding exact DPS and executed static slice according to the definition of DPS and ESPS, respectively. For the second case, potentially affecting the results, statements are included in the corresponding executed static slice according to the definition of ESPS. Therefore, *CS* is a subset of *ESPS*.

On the whole, the subset relationships among *CS*, *DPS*, *ESPS*, and *SPS* are depicted in Figure 3.12.

3.3.3.3 Construction Cost

To construct a critical slice, if we verify each statement by executing a new program in the same way as the original one, except for removing the selected statement, then the total number of executions will be the number of all executable statements in the original program for each given test case. In other words, for a given program *P* and a test case set *T*, the cost of constructing a critical slice will

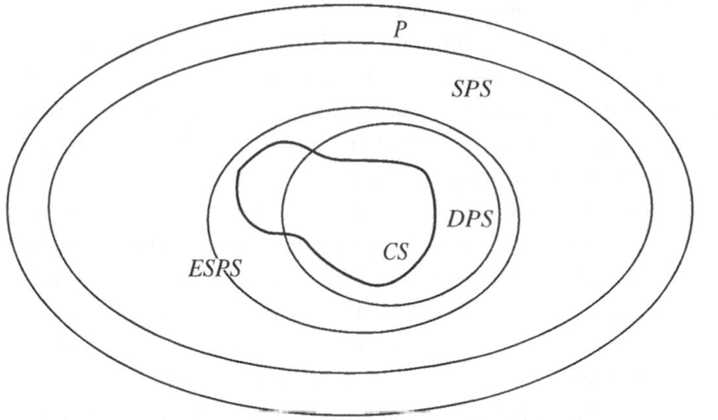

Figure 3.12 Subset relationships among *CS*, *DPS*, *ESPS*, and *SPS*. *Source:* DeMillo et al. [18]/ACM.

be $O(|P| \times |T|)$, i.e. program size (the number of executable statements) times the test set size (the number of test cases in the given set). The cost is obviously high. As suggested above, we can construct a critical slice by selecting statements in the corresponding executed SPS instead of all executable statements. This is one step to reduce the cost and corresponds to the computation of simple statement coverage for particular test cases.

Furthermore, if the debugging process is integrated with a mutation-based testing tool, we can obtain critical slices for debugging purpose during the testing phase without additional cost because the concept of building critical slices is derived from killing `ssdl` mutants. Eliminating `ssdl` mutants is usually one of the criteria first satisfied. Thus, we can obtain critical slices automatically while killing `ssdl` mutants in the testing phase with minor instrumentation.

For instance, the mutation-based testing tool will ask users to identify the failure type *F*, variable *v*, failure location S_F, and test case *t*, after *t* has manifested the failure. While executing *t* to kill `ssdl`, an enhanced testing tool would compare the execution results to decide whether the original statement of the `ssdl` mutation statement is in the corresponding critical slice. In this case, the cost of constructing critical slices is not a concern.

Al-Khanjari et al. [19] also performed an empirical study on the efficiency of critical slicing in fault localization with the help of the Mothra Mutation Testing System. Their paper showed similar positive results as those reported in [18].

3.3.4 Multiple-Points Dynamic Slicing[8]

In [21], Zhang et al. proposed the multiple-points dynamic slicing approach to compute the dynamic slices. The technique intersects slices of three techniques: backward dynamic slice (*BwS*), forward dynamic slice (*FwS*), and bidirectional dynamic slice (*BiS*).

3.3.4.1 *BwS* of an Erroneous Computed Value

The *BwS* of a value at a point in the execution includes all the executed statements that affect the computation of that value. In other words, statements that directly or indirectly influence the computation of faulty values through chains of dynamic data and/or control dependences are included in the *BwSs*. The method utilized in [21] to compute *BwS* is similar to the approach proposed in [15].

The following example in Figure 3.13 illustrates the benefit of backward slicing by using a program with a bug that causes a heap overflow error. In this program, a sufficiently large heap buffer is not allocated, which causes overflow. The code corresponding to the error is shown in Figure 3.13. The heap array `arrays` allocated at line number 167 overflows at line 177, causing the program to crash. Therefore, the dynamic slice is computed starting at the address of `arrays[indx]` that causes the segmentation fault. Since the computation of the address involves `arrays[]` and `indx`, both statements at lines 167 and 176 are included in the dynamic slice. By examining statements at lines 167 and 176, the cause of the failure becomes evident to the programmer. It is easy to see that although a count entries have been allocated at line 167, `v_count` entries are accessed according to the loop bounds of the for statement at line 176. This is the cause of the heap overflow at line 177.

3.3.4.2 *FwS* of Failure-Inducing Input Difference

FwS was proposed based on the delta debugging introduced by Zeller. In [22], the notion was used to determine the causes of program behavior by looking at the differences (the deltas) between the old and new configurations of the programs. Zeller and Hildebrandt [23] then applied the delta debugging approach to simplify and isolate the failure-inducing input difference. The basic idea of delta debugging is as follows: given two program runs r_s and r_f corresponding to inputs I_s and I_f, respectively, such that the program fails in run r_f and completes execution successfully in

```
File : storage.c
void
more_arrays() {
        . . .

167   arrays = (bc_var_array **) bc_malloc(
                 a_count * sizeof(bc_var_array*);
      . . .
176   for(; indx < v_count; indx++)
177     arrays[indx] = NULL;
      . . .
}
```

Figure 3.13 A heap overflow bug. *Source:* Zhang et al. [21]/Wiley.

run r_S, the delta debugging algorithm can be used to systematically produce a pair of inputs I'_s and I'_f with minimal difference such that the program fails for I'_f and executes successfully for I'_s. The difference between these two inputs isolates the failure-inducing difference part of the input. These inputs are such that their values play a critical role in distinguishing a successful run from a failed run.

Since the minimal failure-inducing input difference leads to the execution of faulty code and hence causes the program to fail, we can identify an *FCS* by computing an *FwS* starting at this input as shown in Figure 3.14. In other words, all statements that are influenced by the input value directly or indirectly through a chain of data and/or control dependences are included in the *FCS*. Thus, now we have a means of producing a new type of dynamic slice that also represents an *FCS*.

The following example in Figure 3.15 illustrates how to apply the above approach to a well-known buffer overflow bug in gzip-1.0.7. On the left-hand side of Figure 3.15, we show the relevant code segment for the problem. The problem occurs in the `strcpy` statement at line 844. Variable *ifname* is a global array defined at line 198. The size of the array is defined as 1024. Before the `strcpy` statement at line 844, there is no check on the length of string *iname*. If the length of string *iname* is longer than 1024, the buffer overflows and the program crashes. The memory layout of the gzip program is shown on the right-hand side of Figure 3.15. We can see from the figure that there is a global pointer *env* located in an address space above array *ifname*. The difference between *env* and *ifname* is 3604 bytes. If the length of string *iname* is larger than 3604, the value of *env* will be changed as a result of buffer overflow. When we look at the function `do_exit` at line 1341, before the program quits, it tries to free the memory pointed to by *env*. If the value of *env* is an illegal memory address owing to buffer overflow, it causes a segmentation fault at line 1344.

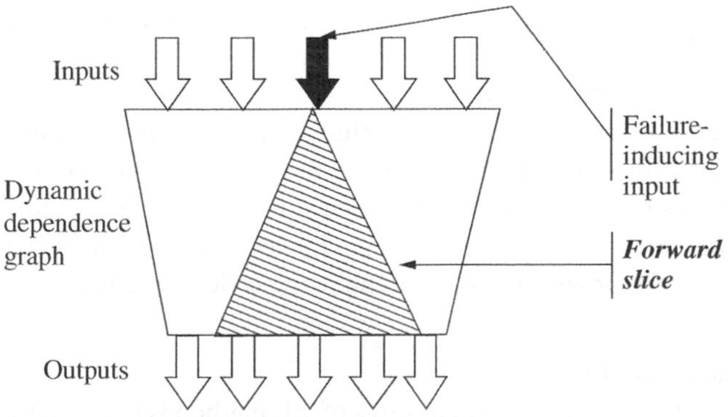

Figure 3.14 *FwS. Source:* Zhang et al. [21]/Wiley.

```
strcpy.c
   36 strcpy(char* _restrict to, const char* _restrict from)
   ...
   40       for (; (*to = *from) != 0; ++from, ++to);
   41       return (save);
   ...

gzip.c:
   152 #define MAX_PATH_LEN 1024
   ...
   193 char* env;
   198 CHAR ifname[MAX_PATH_LEN];


   836 locat int get_istat(iname, sbuf)
   ...
   844         strcpy(ifname, iname);
   845         errno = 0;


   1341 local void do_exit(exitcode)
   ...
   1344        if (env != NULL) free (env), env = NULL;
```

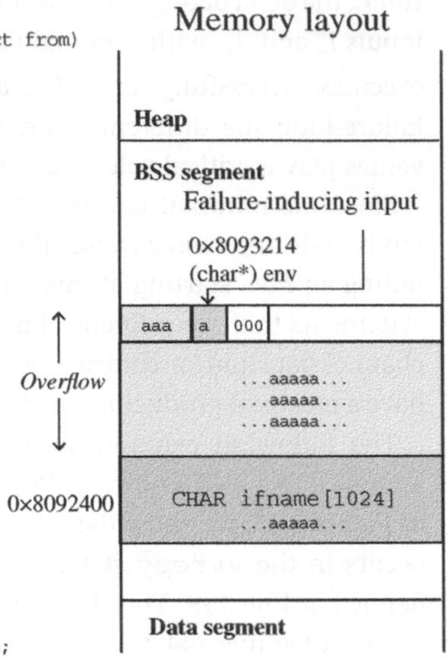

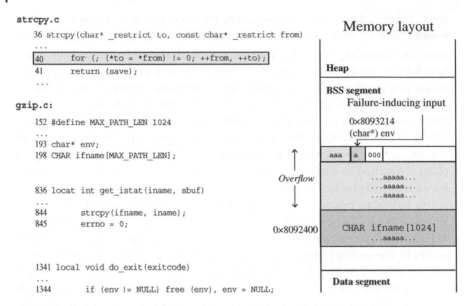

Figure 3.15 Buffer overflow bug in gzip. *Source:* Zhang et al. [21]/Wiley.

To test the gzip program, we picked two inputs: the first input is a filename "aaaaa", which is a successful input, and the second input is a filename $\underbrace{\text{``aaa...aaa''}}_{3610}$, which is a failure input because the length is larger than 3604. After applying the sddmin algorithm [23] on them, we have two new inputs: the new successful input is a filename $\underbrace{\text{``aaa...aaa''}}_{3604}$ and the new failed input is a filename $\underbrace{\text{``aaa...aaa''}}_{3605}$. The failure-inducing input difference between them is the last character "a" in the new failed input.

We used slicing to compute the forward slice of the failure-inducing input difference in the failed input. The size of the forward slice is three, which includes the for statement at line 40 in `strcpy.c`. This is the place where the buffer overflow occurred. Our slicing implementations run on the binary code level and thus can check the memory space of a program and even check the code in the library.

3.3.4.3 *BiS* of a Critical Predicate

Given an erroneous run of the program, the objective of this method is to explicitly force the control flow of the program along an alternate path at a critical branch predicate such that the program produces the correct output. The basic idea of this approach is inspired by the following observation: given an input on which the execution of a program fails, a common approach to debugging is to run the program on this input again, interrupt the execution at certain points to make changes to the program state, and then see the impact of changes on continued execution. If we can discover the changes to the program state that cause the program to terminate correctly, we obtain a good idea of the error that otherwise was causing the program to fail. However, automating the search of state changes is prohibitively expensive and difficult to realize because the search space of potential state changes is extremely large (e.g. even possible changes for the value of a single variable are enormous if the type of the variable is an integer or floating point number). On the other hand, changing the outcomes of predicate instances greatly reduces the state search space as a branch predicate has only two possible outcomes, true or false. Therefore, through forced switching of the outcomes of some predicate instances at runtime, it may be possible to cause the program to produce correct results.

Having identified a critical predicate instance, an *FCS* can be computed as the *BiS* of the critical predicate instance, as shown in Figure 3.16. This bidirectional slice is essentially the union of the *BwS* and the *FwS* of the critical predicate instance. Intuitively, the reason why the slice must include both the *BwS* and *FwS* is as follows: consider the situation in which the effect of executing faulty code is to cause the predicate to evaluate incorrectly. In this case, the *BwS* of the critical predicate instance will capture the faulty code. On the other hand, it is possible that by changing the outcome of the critical predicate instance, we avoid the execution of faulty code and hence the program terminates normally. In this case, the forward slice of the critical predicate instance will capture the faulty code. Therefore, the faulty code will either be in the backward slice or the forward slice.

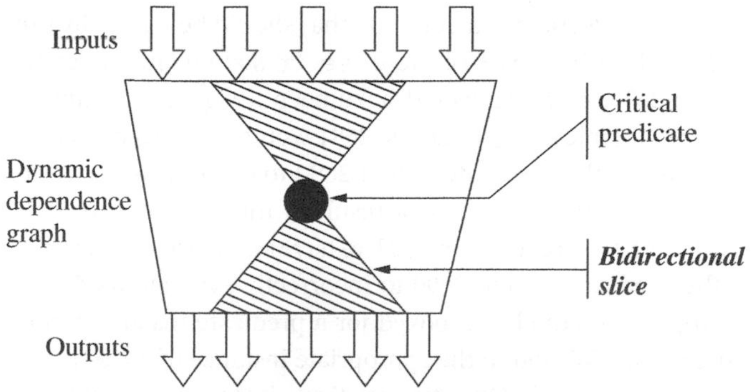

Figure 3.16 *BiS. Source:* Zhang et al. [21]/Wiley.

Next, we briefly describe how a critical predicate instance is found. To search for such an instance, the program is repeatedly re-executed, and during each re-execution, the outcome of a single predicate instance is forcibly changed by our dynamic-instrumentation-based slicing tool. During the program run, a large number of predicate instances is present, so a strategy is needed to order predicate instances such that they are tested for being a critical predicate instance in that order. We have identified a simple ordering heuristic that, in practice, rapidly locates a critical predicate instance. This heuristic orders the predicate instances that belong to the *BwS* of the erroneous output using their dependence distance from the erroneous output. In other words, it first examines the predicate instances (in the *BwS* of the erroneous output) that are linked by a shorter chain of dynamic dependence edges to the erroneous output before the predicate instances that are linked by a longer chain of dynamic dependences to the erroneous output. In general, there may be many critical predicate instances that suffice for computing a bidirectional slice. The algorithm, however, finds the first critical predicate instance and then uses it to compute the *BiS*. While multiple critical predicate instances can be found in some cases, the search for these additional critical predicates will incur additional execution time cost.

It should be noted that, as stated earlier, dynamic slices are not guaranteed to capture the faulty code. In addition, this technique has the limitation that a critical predicate may not exist. For example, if the fault is sufficiently complex, changing the outcome of a single predicate instance may not be able to produce the correct output.

We illustrate the notion of critical predicate with the faulty version of the *flex* program shown in Figure 3.17, which is taken from the Siemens suite. This program is derived from flex-2.4.7 and augmented by the provider of the program with a bug, which is circled in the figure: `base[i + 1]` should actually be `base[i]`. We took the first provided input that produced an erroneous output. We observed that the output is different from the expected output for the 538th character. A "`1`" is produced as output owing to the execution of *printf* in the *else* part (line 2696) of the `else if` statement at line 2690, instead of a "`0`" that should be output by execution of the `printf` in the `then` part of the `else if` statement. Under the correct execution at line 2673, `offset` would have been assigned the value of `base[0]`, which is `1`. The variable `chk[0]` at line 2681 would have been assigned `ACTION_POSITION`, causing the predicate at line 2690 to evaluate to `true` for the loop iteration corresponding to `i = 0`. As a result of the error at line 2673, an incorrect value of `offset` (= `3`) causes `chk[0]` to have an incorrect stale value (= `1`), which causes the predicate at line 2690 to incorrectly evaluate its `false` outcome. Using our proposed method, we looked for a predicate instance whose switching corrected the output. We found the appropriate instance of the `else if` predicate instance through this search. Once this predicate instance was found, we could easily determine by following the data dependences backward that the

```
970     base = ...
        . . .
2565    base[...] = ...
        . . .
2667    for (i = 0; i <= lastdfa; ++i)
2668        {
            . . .
2673        int offset = base[i+1];
            . . .
2677        chk[offset] = EOB_POSITION;
            . . .
2681        chk[offset - 1] = ACTION_POSITION;
            . . .
2683        }
2684
2685    for (i = 0; i <= tblend; ++i)
2686        {
            . . .
2690        else if (chk[i] == ACTION_POSITION)
                printf("%7d, %5d,", 0, ...);
            . . .
2696        else    /* verify transition */
                printf("%7d, %5d,", chk[i], ...);
            . . .
2699        }
```

Figure 3.17 Incorrect output bug in *flex*. *Source:* Zhang et al. [21]/Wiley.

incorrect `chk[0]` was due to a stale value and that it did not come from the most recent execution of the `for` loop at line 2667. Thus, it was clear that the error was in the statement at line 2673, which sets the `offset` value.

In the above example, we demonstrated that by enforcing the outcome of a predicate, we avoided searching for potential modifications of values for `chk[]`, `offset`, or `base[]`, which are integer variables and thus have a wide possible range of values. The above example also illustrates that it is important to alter the outcome of selected predicate instances as opposed to all execution instances of a given predicate. This is because the fault need not be in the predicate but elsewhere, and thus all evaluations of the predicate need not be incorrect.

3.3.4.4 *MPSs:* Dynamic Chops

We have described three different ways of computing *FCSs* in the preceding section. Each *FCS* captures the faulty code. Therefore, it follows that if more than one kind of dynamic slice is available, we can further reduce the size of the *FCS* by intersecting the single-point dynamic slices. In fact, the idea of intersecting dynamic slices to obtain smaller slices has been explored by researchers in the development of dynamic chopping. In essence, a dynamic chop is a dynamic slice specific to a given definition and a given use. First, Figure 3.18a shows that by

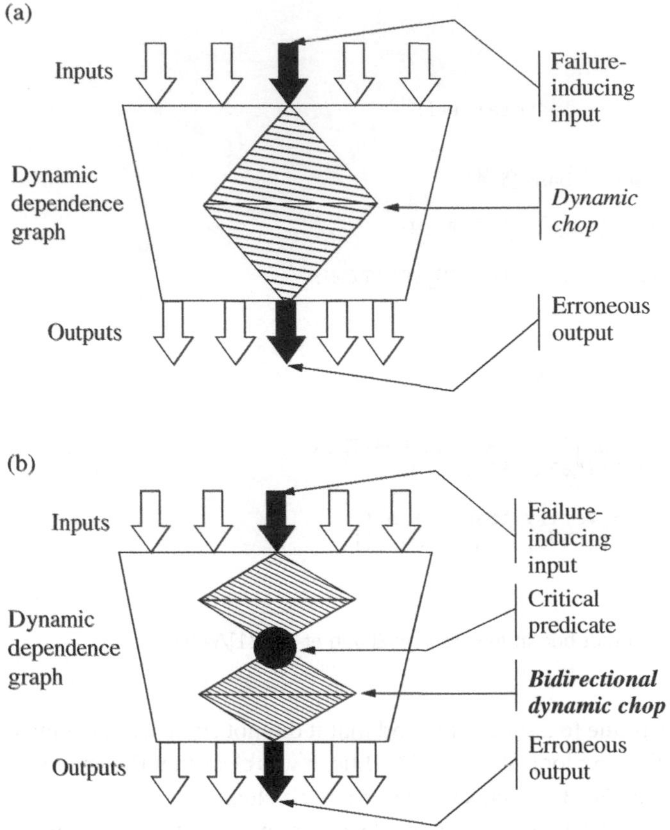

Figure 3.18 *MPSs*: (a) dynamic chop and (b) bidirectional dynamic chop. *Source:* Zhang et al. [21]/Wiley.

intersecting the *FwS* and *BwS*, we can obtain a dynamic chop. The dynamic chop captures the faulty code and is smaller than both the *FwS* and *BwS*. Next, if the *BiS* is available, it can be intersected with the dynamic chop to further reduce the size of the *FCS*. As shown in Figure 3.18b, the result of this operation is a pair of dynamic chops, which we refer to as a bidirectional dynamic chop, one between the failure-inducing input difference and a critical predicate and the other between a critical predicate and the erroneous output value.

3.3.5 Execution Indexing[9]

During program execution, a static program statement could be executed multiple times, resulting in different execution points. A fundamental challenge in dynamic program analysis is to uniquely identify individual execution points so that the correlation between points in one execution can be inferred and the correspondence between execution points across multiple executions can be established. Solving this problem is significant for a wide range of applications, such as profiling, debugging, dynamic instrumentation, and execution comparison.

In [22], Xin et al. proposed a general execution indexing scheme based on execution structure and program state. The basic idea is to parse program executions according to their nesting structure, which is expressed as a set of grammar rules. The set of rules constructed from the parsing of a given execution point reveals its structure and thus constitutes its index. To improve the flexibility and expressiveness of the indexing scheme, the grammar rules can be augmented with semantic information such as values at particular execution points.

3.3.5.1 Concepts

Before introducing the *structural indexing scheme*, we first formally define the concept of *execution index*, which is the foundation of the proposed technique.

Definition 3.3 (Execution Index)
Given a program P, the index of an execution $P(\vec{i})$, *denoted as* $EI^{P(\vec{i})}$ *with* $\vec{i}$ *being the input vector, is a function of execution points in* $P(\vec{i})$ *that satisfies the following property:*

For any two execution points $x \neq y$, $EI^{P(\vec{i})}(x) \neq EI^{P(\vec{i})}(y)$

From the definition, any function that uniquely identifies an execution point can serve as an index. A very important property of an index function is that it establishes a correspondence relation between points in multiple executions.

Definition 3.4 (Execution Correspondence)
Two execution points, x in execution ε and y in ε′, correspond to each other iff $EI^{\varepsilon}(x) \equiv EI^{\varepsilon'}(y)$, *where ε and ε′ may correspond to different inputs, or even though they have the same input, ε′ is a perturbation of ε, caused by nondeterministic scheduling, and so on.*

Simple indexing schemes are not sufficient in providing meaningful correspondence. Consider the example in Figure 3.19. The program reads input from a file within a loop and then reads another piece of input outside the loop. Suppose that in the original execution, `p1` takes the value sequence of true, true, and false. As a result, function `get_input()` is called three times, twice from inside the loop. The logged events are highlighted by boxes and labeled with *E1*, *E2*, and *E3*. Assume a failure happens and the programmer tries to identify the correlation between `p1` and the failure by changing the branch outcome of the first instance of `p1`, i.e. from true to false, and observes whether the failure disappears.

The programmer replays the execution using the event log and perturbs the replayed execution by switching `p1` at its first evaluation. As the perturbed replay relies on the event log collected in the original run, the challenge lies in correctly supplying events during replay. In this case, it is to associate event *E3* with statement 9 in the perturbed run. Note that we assume *E3* is independent of *E1* and *E2*. This often occurs when the program parses *E1* and *E2* for one structure and then parses *E3* for another structure. The simplest indexing scheme that uses the time order fails because the first event in the original run is *E1*, whereas the first event expected in the perturbed execution is *E3*. A smarter indexing that represents an execution point is s_i, meaning the *i*th instance of statement *s*. Although such an approach has been widely used in existing dynamic analyses [24, 25], it is not sufficient either. *E1* has the index of 91, which is the same as *Ex*'s. In other words, *E1* is the correspondence of *Ex*, and thus *E1* is supplied to statement 9 during replay, which is wrong.

In the approach proposed in [22], an indexing technique based on execution structure serves as the fundamental concepts. In Figure 3.19, event *E1* is processed at statement 9, which is nested in the method call made at 3, which in turn is nested in the true branch of predicate `p1` at 2. Other executed statements such as the second and third calls at 3 are not related to the nesting structure of *E1* and should not be part of the index. Therefore, *E1* has the index of ⟨2, 3, 9⟩. *E2* has the index of ⟨2, 2, 3, 9⟩. The two consecutive 2s in the index indicate that the event is nested in the second iteration of the loop. Both *E3* and *Ex* have the same index ⟨5, 9⟩, meaning that the structures of these two events occur within the calls made at 5 and are not related to other statements such as 2 or 3. Based on the structural indices, *E3* is provided as the expected event. Note that using call stacks does not work because *El* and *E2* have the same call stack. In other words,

Code:

```
1      . . .
2      while (p1) {
3        get_input(buf);
         ...
4      }
5      get_input(buf);
6      ...
7      void get_input(char* buf)
8      {
9        read(buf, 512);
10     }
```

Original Execution (p1=TTF)

```
2   while (p1)
3   get_input(buf);
9   read(buf, 512);        E1
2   while (p1)
3   get_input (buf);
9   read(buf, 512);        E2
2   while (p1)
5   get_input(buf);
9   read(buf, ...);        E3
```

Perturbed Execution (p1=F)

```
2   while (p1)
5   get_input(buf);
9   read(buf, ...);        Ex
```

Figure 3.19 Log-based replay with perturbation. *Source:* Xin et al. [22]/ACM.

call stacks are not a valid execution index function. This is because call stacks only record a partial image of the nesting structure. The proposed indexing scheme not only succeeds in establishing desired correspondence for points across different executions in many cases, but also facilitates highly efficient online computation.

3.3.5.2 Structural Indexing

Another key observation of [22] is that *all possible executions of a program can be described by a language called execution description language (EDL) based on the structure*. An execution is a string of the language.

Table 3.2 presents the EDLs for a list of basic programming language constructs. The first column shows sequential code without nesting, whose execution is described by a grammar rule that lists all the statements. Note that a terminal symbol s is denoted as $\tilde{s}$ here. In the second column, the `if-else` construct introduces a level of nesting, and thus the EDL has two rules, one expressing the top-level structure that contains statement 1 and the intermediate symbol $R1$ representing the substructure led by 1. The two alternative rules of $R1$ denote the substructure of the construct. The self-recursion in the grammar rule for the `while` loop in the third column expresses the indefinite iterations of the loop. From these examples, we can see that EDLs are different from programming languages. The strings of EDLs are executions, whereas the strings of programming languages are program instructions. The alphabet of an EDL contains all the statement ids in the program, whereas that of a programming language contains program constructs, variable identifiers, and so on. The second observation is that program control dependence perfectly reflects the execution structure. A statement x is control dependent on another statement y, usually a predicate or a method call statement, if y directly decides the execution of x. The formal definition can be found in the seminal paper [26]. For example, in the second column of Table 3.2, statement 2 is control dependent on statement 1. The statements that share the same control dependence

Table 3.2 EDLs for simple constructs.

Code	1 `s1;` 2 `s2;` 3 `s3;` 4 `s4;`	1 `if (...)` 2 `s1;` 3 `else` 4 `s2;`	1 `while (...) {` 2 `s1;` 3 `}` 4 `s2;`	1 `void A() {` 2 `B();` 3 `}` 4 `void B() {` 5 `s1;` 6 `}`
EDL	$S \rightarrow \tilde{1}\ \tilde{2}\ \tilde{3}\ \tilde{4}$	$S \rightarrow \tilde{1}\ R1$ $\mathrm{R1} \rightarrow \tilde{2} \mid \tilde{4}$	$S \rightarrow \tilde{1}\ R1\ \tilde{4}$ $\mathrm{R1} \rightarrow \tilde{2}\ \tilde{1}\ \mathrm{R1} \mid \tilde{4}$	$S \rightarrow \tilde{2}\ RB$ $RB \rightarrow \tilde{5}$
Str.	1 2 3 4	1 2 1 4	1 2 1 4 1 2 1 2 1 4	2 5

Source: Xin et al. [22]/ACM.

are present on the right-hand side of the same rule, representing the same level of nesting. Consider the rules for the `while` construct. Statements 1 and 4 have the same dependence. And they are listed on the right-hand side of the first rule; the body of rule $R1$ lists the statements that are dependent on statement 1. Note that statement 1 is control dependent on itself as the execution of a loop iteration is decided by its previous iteration.

We define the EDL of a program as follows:

Definition 3.5 (Execution Description Language)
Given a program P, its execution description language, denoted as EDL(P), is the language described by the grammar rules generated by Algorithm 3.1.

```
Input: a program P
Output: a set of grammar rules that describe the executions of P
function ConstructGrammar(P)
    rules = ∅;
    foreach method M do
        /* CD denotes control dependence */
        T = statements in M in flow order satisfying CD = START_M;
        rules ∪= RM → T;
        foreach statement s in M do
            if s is a predicate then
                T = statements in flow order s.t. CD = s^true;
                F = statements in flow order s.t. CD = s^false;
                rules ∪= Rs → T | F;
            end
        end
    end
    /* post processing to complete the rules */
    foreach rule r → X do
        foreach symbol s ∈ X do
            if s is a predicate then
                replace s with "s Rs" in X;
            end
            if s is a call to M then
                replace s with "s RM" in X;
            end
        end
    end
end
```

Algorithm 3.1 Grammar construction. *Source:* Xin et al. [22]/ACM.

While there exist different grammar rules that describe the same language, we rely on the rules generated by Algorithm 3.1 as they lead to a clear and concise definition of execution index, which will be discussed later in this subsection. Algorithm 3.1 is based on program control dependence: a grammar rule is created for statements that share the same control dependence. It consists of two major steps. Lines 3–14 describe the first step, in which statements in individual methods are clustered based on their control dependences. Here, we consider all statements in a method that have empty control dependence to be control dependent on the method. In the second step (lines 16–22), the rules generated in the first step are scanned, and symbols that have control dependents are appended with the grammar rules that describe the substructures of their control dependents.

To illustrate Algorithm 3.1, we use a more complete example in Figure 3.20. The code contains a recursive call (line 9) and nonstructural control flow (line 5). The first rule in represents the top-level structure of method A. Due to the return statement at line 5, as shown by the CFG, only statements 2 and 3 are control dependent on the start node of A, namely, $START_A$. The second step of the algorithm inserts $R3$ right behind symbol 3 in the rule, denoting the lower level composition that are control dependent on 3. Note that the top-level rule RA does not reflect the syntactic structure of method A as a rule derived from the syntactic structure, i.e. $RA \rightarrow \tilde{2},\tilde{3},R3,\tilde{7},R7,\tilde{12}$ fails to describe executions such as $\langle 2, 3, 4, 16, 5 \rangle$. Statements 4 and 5 are control dependent on the true branch of 3, and statements 7 and 12 are dependent on the false branch. Adding the intermediate symbols denoting the substructures led by 4, 7, and 12 results in the second rule in Figure 3.21. The remaining rules are similarly derived.

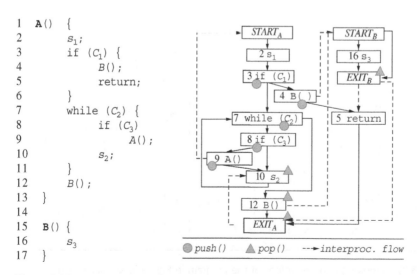

```
1   A()  {
2          s1;
3          if (C1) {
4                B();
5                return;
6          }
7          while (C2) {
8                if (C3)
9                      A();
10               s2;
11         }
12         B();
13  }
14
15  B() {
16         s3
17  }
```

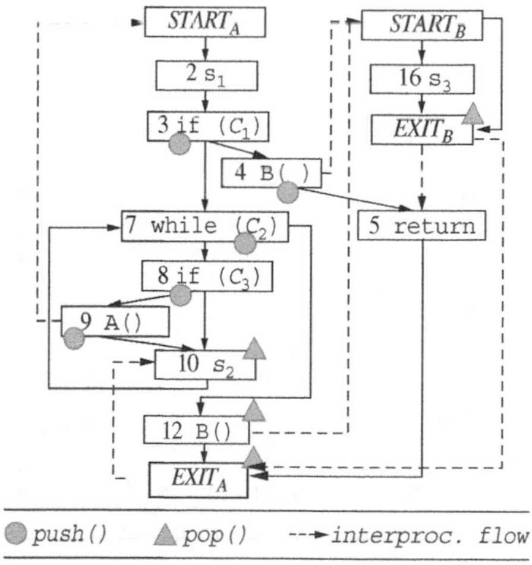

Figure 3.20 Example for structural indexing. *Source:* Xin et al. [22]/ACM.

$$
\begin{array}{lll}
RA & \longrightarrow & \tilde{2}\ \tilde{3}\ R3 \\
R3 & \longrightarrow & \tilde{4}\ RB\ \tilde{5} \mid \tilde{7}\ R7\ \tilde{12}\ RB \\
R7 & \longrightarrow & \tilde{8}\ R8\ \tilde{10}\ \tilde{7}\ R7 \mid \epsilon \\
RB & \longrightarrow & \tilde{16} \\
R8 & \longrightarrow & \tilde{9}\ RA \mid \epsilon
\end{array}
$$

Figure 3.21 The grammar generated by Algorithm 3.1 for Figure 3.20. *Source:* Xin et al. [22]/ACM.

Recall that our goal is to design an execution indexing technique. Based on EDLs, we are ready to introduce our indexing scheme. As illustrated earlier, any execution of a program *P* is a string of EDL(*P*). The index of an execution point can be defined according to the derivation tree of the string.

Definition 3.6 (Structural Indexing)

Given a program P and its EDL(P), the structural index of a point x in execution $P(\vec{i})$*, denoted as* $SEI^{P(\vec{i})}(x)$*, is the path from the root of the derivation tree to the leaf node representing x.*

According to the definition of EDL, each grammar rule captures the statements at the same nesting level. Therefore, the path in the derivation tree, which leads from the root to a terminal symbol and contains all the intermediate symbols, denotes the top-down nesting structure and serves as a perfect structural index. Figure 3.22 shows the indices for two executions of the code in Figure 3.20.

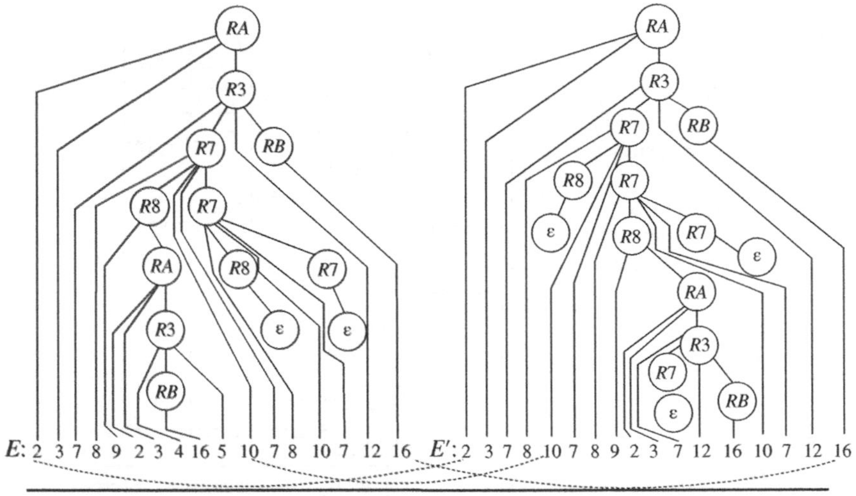

Figure 3.22 Indexing two executions of the program in Figure 3.20. *Source:* Xin et al. [22]/ACM.

Execution E recursively calls $A()$ in the first iteration of the `while` loop, whereas the recursive call happens in the second iteration in E'. We can see $SEI^{E}(2_1) = SEI^{E'}(2_1) = [RA]$, in which 2_1 denotes the first instance of statement 2 in the traces. Thus, the two executions of the first exercised statement 2 correspond to each other, as linked by the dotted line. $SEI^{E}(16_1) = [RA, R3, R7, RS, ...]$, which clearly expresses the nesting structure of the first executed statement 16. In contrast, the index of 16_1 in the second execution is $SEI^{E'}(16_1) = [RA, R3, R7, R7, ...]$, which is different from $SEI^{E}(16_1)$. The indices imply that the 161 in E' is nested in the second iteration of the `while` loop whereas the 16_1 in E is nested in the first iteration. Therefore, the two 16_1s do not structurally correspond.

3.3.6 Dual Slicing to Locate Concurrency Bugs[10]

Weeratunge et al. [27] proposed a dynamic analysis technique that identifies the root cause of different kinds of concurrency bugs based on a new technique, dual slicing. Informally, the technique works as follows: two runs (one successful and the other failed as controlled by two deterministic schedules), produces a sequence of execution points in both runs that are causally related and lead from the program point representing the root cause of the failure to the program point at which the failure is detected. By computing the trace differences, the technique exploits the assumption that the two runs only differ after the first diversity in schedule. It then uses dual slicing that works on both runs alternatively and iteratively to causally connect these trace differences to construct the causal path.

The technique consists of two phases, trace comparison and dual slicing, which will be introduced in Section 3.3.6.

3.3.6.1 Trace Comparison

Execution comparison can be carried out on traces. In general, traces may either be lossy or lossless. Lossless traces [28] record dynamic information for each execution step and thus require space proportional to the execution length. In contrast, lossy traces are acquired by accumulation. For example, a lossy trace captures control flow using program counters, or sometimes more elaborately, as a set of tuples such as *instruction: frequency* and *path: frequency*. The main benefit of lossy traces is that their space requirement can be made linear in static program size. Comparison based on lossy traces is simply comparison of tuples with the same key.

Despite its simplicity and space efficiency, lossy trace comparison is insufficient for our purposes. For example, consider a case in which one run executes a statement s i times, denoted as a frequency pair $s{:}i$, while the other run executes $s(i+1)$ times. Although lossy trace comparison can reveal that s is different in the two runs, it fails to identify which instance of s is correlated with the failure. This degree of precision is essential for the technique proposed in [27].

Furthermore, in a concurrent setting, it may occur that a statement *s* has exactly the same value and execution frequency in both runs and hence is not a trace difference, but it is still strongly correlated to the failure if it is involved in a data race.

The technique therefore relies on comparing lossless traces. In the context of comparing traces induced by different schedules, the space requirement of lossless tracing is significantly alleviated because we do not need to record any dynamic information before the first schedule difference, since the two executions are identical before that point. Hence, the main challenge lies in solving the problem of trace alignment. Due to schedule variance, the perturbed execution often makes different function invocations, has different predicate outcomes leading to different control flows, and computes different values for the same variables. If the two traces are not precisely aligned, the computed differences may be due to misalignment, i.e. a trace difference may not be a real difference but instead may be caused by the comparison being carried out at inappropriate points. For example, due to non-determinism, if the same request is served by thread t in one run E but by $t+1$ in the other run E', and trace alignment lines up in E with t in E', the resulting trace differences are meaningless. Therefore, correctly aligning the two traces before they are compared is critical. To retain the high degree of precision required, execution comparison is therefore performed on lossless traces [28] in which dynamic information is recorded at each execution step. In addition, the proposed approach aligns two traces of concurrent executions based on their execution structure, leveraging execution indexing as discussed previously.

The challenge of trace comparison in the presence of schedule perturbations is that the order of statement execution may change, leading to different values produced for the same execution point in the two runs. Intuitively, trace alignment provides a canonical order of statement execution so that comparison can be performed between corresponding (i.e. aligned) execution points, even though they may occur at completely different points in the overall execution order. For instance, with respect to the program in Figure 3.23, statement 22 in the two runs are aligned even though they occur at different places in the traces. Then, the comparison of the aligned instances of statement 22 determines that it does not have a faulty state in the failed run. In contrast, the second instances of the `while` statement 34 in the two runs are aligned according to the index tree. The loop predicate takes a false value in the successful run and a true value in the failed run. Note that the canonicalization induced by the execution index tree does not mean that we discard schedule differences. Instead, schedule differences will be faithfully reflected as state differences at aligned points. For instance, it might appear that aligning the instances of statement 22 incorrectly masks a schedule difference. In fact, the effect of the different schedules is captured by the different values of the aligned instances of statement 33, one of which acquires its value from statement 22 (in the successful run) while the other (in the failed run) does not.

```
1   int cnt = 2;
2   void main() {
3    Queue reqs;
4    spawn(t_configure());
5    while (!reqs.isEmpty()) {
6     spawn(t_request(reqs.pop()));
7    }
8   }

20  void t_configure() {
21    if (command == "change count")
22       cnt = readInt();
23       ...
24  }
```

data race

```
30  void t_request() {
31    int A[100], B[100];
32    int sum = 0, j = 0, t_cnt;
33    t_cnt = cnt;
34    while (j < t_cnt) {
35       A[j] = readInt();
36       sum = sum + A[j];
37       B[j] = integrate(B, j);
38       j++;
39    }
40    if (t_cnt % 2 == 0)
41       sum = sum + A[0];
42    else
43       sum = sum - A[0];
44    output (sum);
45  }
```

Figure 3.23 A program with a data race. The race lies in lines 22 and 33. If, by chance, line 33 is executed before line 22, t_cnt receives the old value of cnt and leads to an unexpected output. *Source:* Weeratunge et al. [27]/ACM.

Next, the trace differences can be defined based on execution indexing. We assume that the value of each execution instance is also recorded as part of the trace entry. We use *val(s)* to represent the value of an execution point *s*. The value of a statement is the value stored in the destination variable. The value of a predicate is its Boolean outcome. The value of a method invocation is the return value.

Definition 3.7 *Given an execution E and a reference execution E′, an execution point s ∈ E is a trace difference if one of the following three conditions is satisfied:*

1) *idx(s) is not a valid index in E′.*
2) *There is an execution point s′ in E′ such that idx(s) = idx(s′), but val(s)≠val(s′).*
3) *There is an execution point s′ in E′ such that idx(s) = idx(s′), but s and s′ have at least, on two definitions d and d′, where idx(d) ≠ idx(d′).*

If condition (1) is satisfied, s is called a flow difference. If (2) is satisfied, s is called a value difference. If (3) is satisfied, it is called a defuse difference. Observe that conditions (2) and (3) may be satisfied simultaneously.

According to the definition, an execution point *s* is a flow difference if it is not aligned with any point in the reference execution. If it does have an alignment but its alignment has a different value, it is a *value difference.* Thus, if *s* is a value difference, it implies that s has an alignment. Finally, if an execution point has an alignment, but some of the subterms of the aligned statement are themselves not aligned, the point is a *defuse difference.*

In Figure 3.24, the bullets represent value differences and the triangles represent flow differences. Statement 33 in the successful run is a value difference because although `t_cnt` has a value of 1 at this point, it has a value of 2 at its alignment in the failed run. For the same reason, statement 33 in the failed run is also a value difference. Also note that statement 33 in the successful run is data dependent on statement 22, whereas it is data dependent on statement 1 in the failed run (see Figure 3.23). This is a defuse difference. Statement 43 in the successful run is a flow difference as it is not aligned with any statement in the failed run. Similarly, statement 41 in the failed run is a flow difference. The second instances of statements 35, 36, 37, and 38 in the failed run are also flow differences.

Observe that our trace differences are defined over statement instances, meaning that we can identify the specific instance of a statement as a trace difference even though the statement might be executed multiple times in a run. We will discuss how to make use of these trace differences in the next subsection.

3.3.6.2 Dual Slicing

Trace differences alone cannot localize the root cause of concurrency failures. To clearly understand a failure, it is necessary to observe a minimum sequence of statement executions that are causally connected, leading from the root cause to the failure. Trace differences often contain excessive redundant information not related to the failure. For example, the second instance of statement 37 in Figure 3.24 assigned to `B[j]` in the failed run is a trace difference. But it has nothing to do with the observed wrong output at statement instance 44. In experimental settings, trace differences for realistic concurrent program executions often subsume 100K or more statements, even though the portion relevant to the failure can be localized to a few tens of statements.

In [27], the authors proposed to combine dynamic slicing with trace differencing to identify the root cause of a concurrency failure, and enable the construction of the salient execution path from this root to the failure point. The advantage of dynamic slicing is that it can overcome the aforementioned limitations of trace comparison. More specifically, trace differences can be connected through dependence edges, which essentially represent causality. Redundant information can be pruned by slicing if the failure is not (transitively) dependent on the information. On the other hand, trace differencing substantially improves the effectiveness of dynamic slicing. For example, the slice of statement instance 44 in the failed run includes the first instance of statement 36 because 44 is data dependent on 41, which in turn is data dependent on the second instance of 36 and then the first instance of 36. Similarly, the first instances of 34, 35, and 38 are also in the

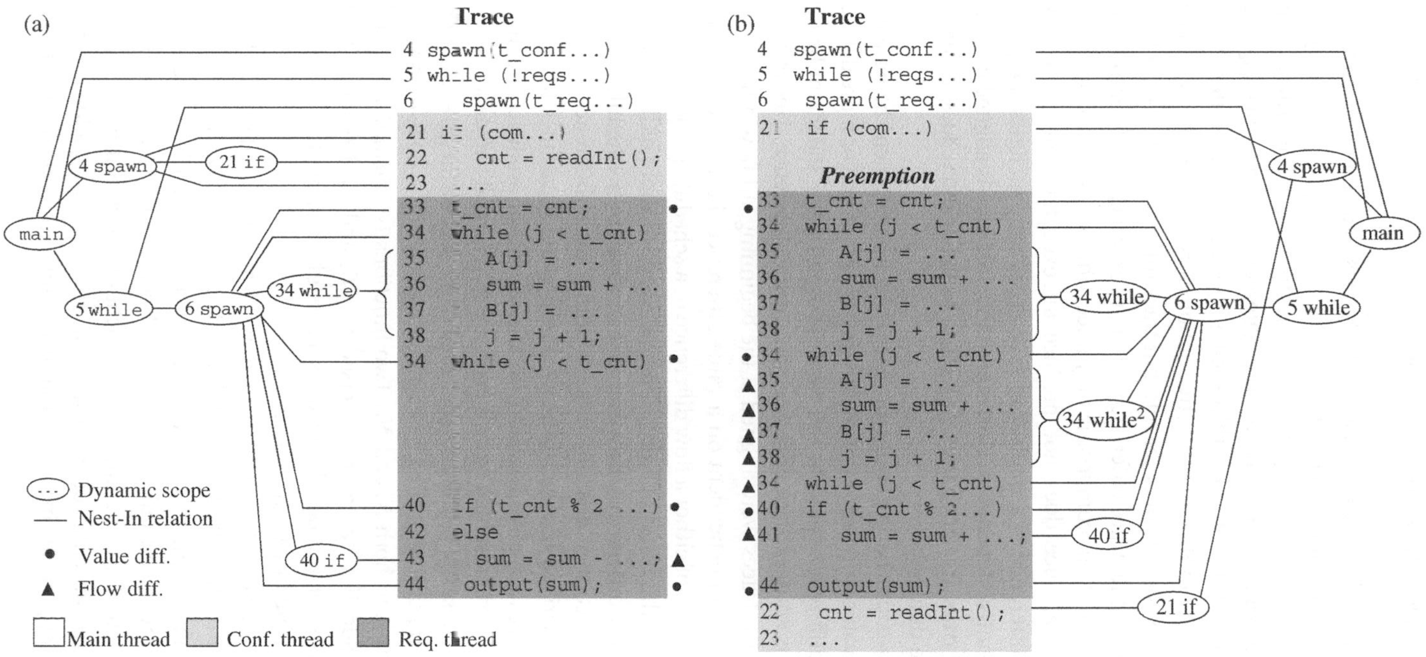

Figure 3.24 Trace comparison: (a) Successful run and (b) Failed run. *Source:* Weeratunge et al. [27]/ACM.

slice. Using trace differencing, we can easily identify these statement instances as having benign effect, and do not need to include them in the output of the analysis.

Slicing determines the parts of a program "relevant" to some slicing criterion. In traditional slicing, relevance is defined as any statement possibly affecting the values computed by the criterion. Like thin slicing [29], dual slicing differs from classical slicing primarily in its more selective notion of relevance. Given a trace difference, its dual slice consists of other relevant trace differences. A trace difference *d*1 is relevant to another trace difference d_2 if there exist a chain of control and data dependences from d_1 to d_2 comprising only trace differences. Hence, unlike a traditional slice, a dual slice does not produce an executable program. For instance, the value difference of a traditional slice necessarily includes the predicate on which it is control dependent. However, if the predicate is aligned in both successful and failed runs, it is not a trace difference by itself, and it does not need to be included in the dual slice.

A value difference could be the result of the particular statement being data dependent on other value differences, or its uses being part of one or more defuse differences. A flow difference could be the result of a particular statement being control dependent on another flow difference or a value difference. However, if we assume that the two traces were aligned at the beginning, all flow differences must eventually be control dependent on a value difference. Lastly, a defuse difference could be the result of either a flow difference or a schedule perturbation. If the defuse difference is the result of a flow difference, one or more of its defining statements must be flow differences. However, if it is caused by a schedule perturbation, it is not data or control dependent on any other trace difference.

The algorithm is described in Algorithm 3.2. For brevity, it assumes that data and control dependences are already available. The algorithm produces the dual slice of the failure point, represented by two node sets $N_f(N_p)$ and two dependence edge sets $E_f(E_p)$. The subscript represents the failed (f) or successful (p) execution. A node is an execution point identified by its index, e.g. d and t. A node representing a value difference is in both N_f and N_p. Two functions *isVisitedInPass*(s) and *isVisitedInFail*(s) decide if s has been traversed in $-T_p$ and T_f. Notations *f_wl* and *p_wl* are worklists for the failed and the successful runs, while t and d are execution points identified by their indexes.

In the algorithm, the slice node set in the failed run N_f and the failed run worklist *f_wl* are initialized with the failure point at line 1. The `while` loop in lines 3–29 describes the main dual slicing process. It alternatively and iteratively slices the failed run and then the successful run. Lines 4–25 correspond to the slicing of the failed run. At line 6, if a value difference is encountered and it has not been encountered in the construction of the successful run slice, it is added to the successful run worklist *p_wl* at line 7 and the successful slice node set N_p at line

```
Inputs:   • T_f and T_p: the traces of the failing run and the passing run.
          • DTYPE_f/p(s): decides if s is a value difference (VAL_D) or
            a flow difference (FLOW_D); the subscripts denote the run.
          • DEP_f/p(s): the set of execution instances that s depends on,
            including data and control dependences.
Outputs:  N_f/p, E_f/p: slice node sets and edge sets.
1  N_f ← f_wl ← {the failure point in T_f};
2  N_p ← p_wl ← ∅;
3  while f_wl ≠ ∅ and p_wl ≠ ∅ do
4     while f_wl ≠ ∅ do
5        t ← f_wl.pop();
6        if DTYPE_f(t) ≡ VAL_D and !isVisitedInPass(t) then
7           p_wl ← p_wl ∪ {t};
8           N_p ← N_p ∪ {t};
9        end
10       foreach d ∈ DEP_f(t) do
11          if DTYPE_f(d) = VAL_D or DTYPE_f(d) = FLOW_D then
12             N_f ← N_f ∪ {d};
13             E_f ← E_f ∪ {t → d};
14             if !isVisitedInFail(d) then
15                f_wl ← f_wl ∪ {d};
16             end
17          else
18             d' ← The dependence in DEP_p(t) that corresponds to d
19             if d ≠ d' then
20                N_f ← N_f ∪ {d};
21                E_f ← E_f ∪ {t → d};
22             end
23          end
24       end
25    end
26    while p_wl ≠ ∅ do
27       Slicing T_p. adding nodes into f_wl. It is symmetric to failure run slicing.
28    end
29 end
```

Algorithm 3.2 Algorithm for dual slicing. *Source:* Weeratunge et al. [27]/ACM.

8. The `for-loop` in lines 10–24 examines *t*'s dependences. In lines 11–17, the algorithm adds a dependence *d* to the slice and the work list, if *d* is a value difference or a flow difference. Otherwise, the algorithm handles `def-use` differences by adding the dependence *d* to the slice if the dependence d' corresponding to *d* in the successful run does not align with *d* (lines 18–23). Observe that although *d* is added to the slice, it is not placed in the work list. Slicing the successful run is symmetric to slicing the failed run and omitted for brevity.

The dual slice of the example in Figure 3.24 is presented in Figure 3.25. During the analysis, the algorithm first adds the index of 44_1, denoting the first instance of statement 44 in the failed trace, to *f_wl*. The index is then popped from the worklist at line 5 of the algorithm. Since it is a value difference, it is added to *p_wl* and N_p in lines 7 and 8. Next, the algorithm adds the dependence of 44_1, namely, 41_1 to the dual slice and *f_wl*. Since 41_1 is not a value difference, the algorithm simply adds its control dependence 40_1 and the data dependence 36_2 to N_f and *f_wl*. The index of 40_1 is added to *p_wl* as well since it is a value difference. The failure slicing loop terminates when 33_1 is reached because 33_1 is not dependent on any trace differences. At this point, all the shaded nodes and their edges as shown in Figure 3.25 have been added to the dual slice, and the successful run worklist contains the indices 44_1, 40_1, 34_2, and 33_1. The algorithm switches to slicing the successful run with these criteria. After the successful slicing loop has terminated, all the executions represented by plain nodes and their edges are added. This time, no new value differences are added to *f_wl*, and the main computation loop terminates. The rectangular nodes represent either value differences or flow differences. The rounded nodes are non-trace differences added to the slice since they define values used by defuse differences. For example, 22_1 and 1_1 are added to the slice since the values they define are used by the defuse difference at 33_1.

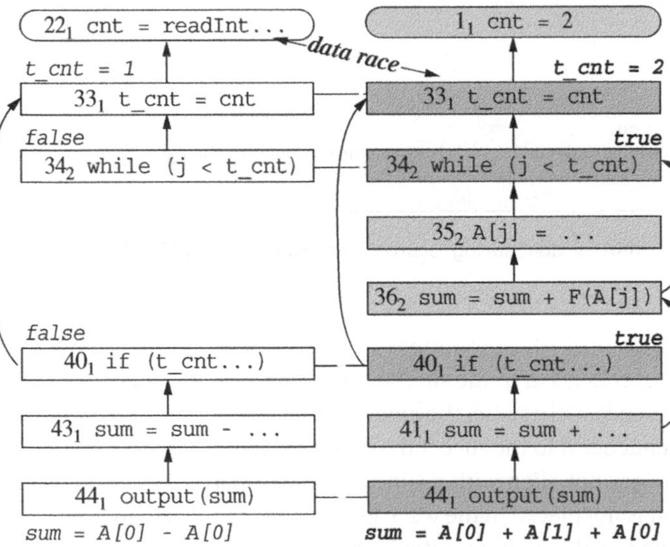

Figure 3.25 The dual slice of the failure in Figure 3.24. *Source:* Weeratunge et al. [27]/ACM.

3.3.7 Comparative Causality: a Causal Inference Model Based on Dual Slicing[11]

Delta debugging is a classic debugging technique that can minimize failure-inducing inputs or faulty internal program states essential to reproducing a failure [23, 31]. Delta debugging and its recent improvements all use *causal state minimization* (CSM). However, the following limitations of CSM discussed in [30] often lead to low-quality failure summaries.

- **Confounding caused by partial state replacement.** The first problem with CSM is that *replacing only a subset of the states in an execution can induce new behavior that was not present in either of the original executions.* We call this problem the *confounding of partial state replacement.* The introduced new behavior can affect the validity of a causality test. Particularly, a causal chain may terminate prematurely because the key faulty state is excluded due to confounding, or it may contain additional states that do not pertain to the failure. In the worst case, the entire chain may not even be relevant for explaining the failure.
- **Execution omission.** The second problem is that CSM *may miss important causal states in the presence of execution omission errors,* where the faulty target states are identified because statements were *not executed* due to the bug. In such cases, the computed failure summaries are usually incomplete. The root cause of the problem is that CSM is *asymmetric,* meaning the faulty and correct executions have asymmetric roles in the process: CSM reasoning is based on modifying states only in the correct execution; its final results only include information from the faulty execution.
- **Efficiency**. CSM may require a large number of re-executions. The number of state differences can be as large as the size of the allocated memory. The number of possible subsets that need to be tested for causality is potentially combinatorial in terms of the full set. To combat this, existing approaches use *delta debugging* to perform a generalized binary search over the subsets. However, the number of re-executions can still be quadratic on the size of all used memory. Even the most recent implementation of CSM may take a few hours to reason about a failure while the original execution time is just a few milliseconds.

To overcome these limitations, a more effective and precise causal inference model called *comparative causality* (CC) was proposed [30]. This model focuses on *symmetrically* reasoning about two executions, one faulty and the other one correct, in order to explain why they differ from each other. It also enables efficient and practical implementation. In the following, we first define the notation and concepts. Then, we study the intended properties of the new model.

- **Execution point**: We use a superscripted label l^e to denote a point in execution e. The symbol $l^{(e1,\, e2)}$ denotes a point that appears in both executions e_1 and e_2, determined by the given control flow alignment [22]. It is also called an *aligned point*.

- **State difference**: We use $\{x \mapsto (v_1, v_2)\}$ to denote that a variable x has value v_1 in e_1 and value v_2 in e_2, with $v_1 \neq v_2$.
- **Problem statement**: Given a set of state differences Δ at an aligned execution point $l_{\blacklozenge}^{(e_1,\, e_2)}$ and a preceding aligned point $l_{\lozenge}^{(e_1,\, e_2)}$, we want to find a set of state differences at $l_{\lozenge}^{(e_1,\, e_2)}$ that is relevant, sufficient, and minimal for inducing Δ.

The preceding execution point is the *cause* point and the latter one the *effect* point. We need to consider aligned points because state comparison is not meaningful at nonaligned points. An inducing state difference in the cause point is called a *cause*; a state difference in$\Delta$is called an *effect*.

3.3.7.1 Property One: Relevance

The causes identified by CC must be *relevant* to the target effects. Intuitively, a difference d is relevant to a later difference d_s if d_s is (transitively) produced from d through a sequence of differences. It represents the notion that "a faulty state must be derived from some preceding faulty state (except the root cause)".

Consider the example presented in Figure 3.26. The state difference {z ↦ (3, 6)} on line 3 is not relevant to {y ↦ (2, 3)} on line 7 even though there is a dynamic dependence path from line 3 to line 7, because the difference of z is neutralized on line 4, which yields `false` in both runs. In contrast, the difference {y ↦ (1, 2)} on line 2 is relevant to {y ↦ (2, 3)} on line 7.

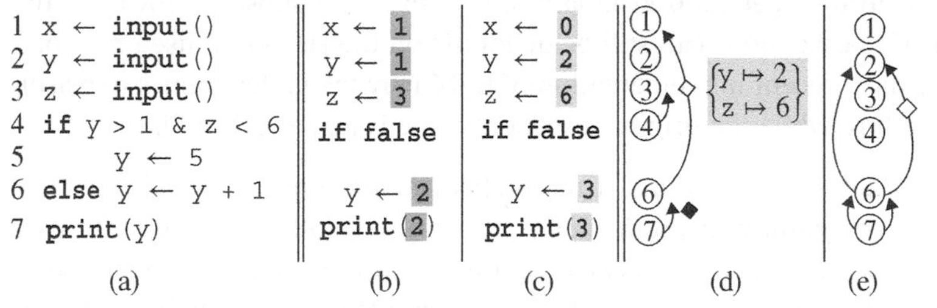

Figure 3.26 (a) An example program; (b)–(c) executions with different inputs; (d) CSM result; and (e) dual slice. Symbols ◇ and ◆ denote the *cause* point and *effect* point, respectively. The set in (d) represents the causal state set. *Source:* Sumner and Zhang [30]/IEEE.

A formal definition for *relevance* is as follows:

Definition 3.8 (Relevance)

A state difference $\delta_\diamond$ at $l_\diamond^{(e_1,\, e_2)}$ is relevant to a target state difference $\delta_\blacklozenge$ at a later effect point $l_\blacklozenge^{(e_1,\, e_2)}$ if either of the following conditions is satisfied:

1) *There exists a dynamic program dependence path from $\delta_\blacklozenge$ to $\delta_\diamond$ in e_1 (e_2, respectively), where all the statement computations along the path yield different results from the other execution e_2 (e_1, respectively).*
2) *There exists a state difference δ_x in an aligned point in between $l_\diamond^{(e_1,\, e_2)}$ and $l_\blacklozenge^{(e_1,\, e_2)}$ such that $\delta_\diamond$ is relevant to δ_x and δ_x is relevant to $\delta_\blacklozenge$.*

3.3.7.2 Property Two: Sufficiency

The identified set of causes must sufficiently induce the target effect of *each* of the two executions within its opposing execution. This inducement acts as a new causality test and witnesses the causal relationship between the identified causes and the target state.

The property is *symmetric* as it requires the set of effects in either execution to be induced by the causes. It means that if for all the variables in the cause set, we copy their values from execution e_1 to e_2, we can induce the target effect of e_1 at the effect point in e_2, and vice versa.

Consider the example in Figure 3.27. State differences {y ↦ (3,6), x ↦ (5,1)} on line 5 form a sufficient set regarding the effect {x ↦ (3,1)} on line 7. In contrast, the difference {x ↦ (5,1)} itself is insufficient because although replacing x's value of 5 with 1 in (b) can induce the effect {x ↦ 1} on line 7, replacing x's value of 1 with 5 in (c) cannot induce the effect {x ↦ 3}. This symmetry ensures that we capture relevance due to execution omission.

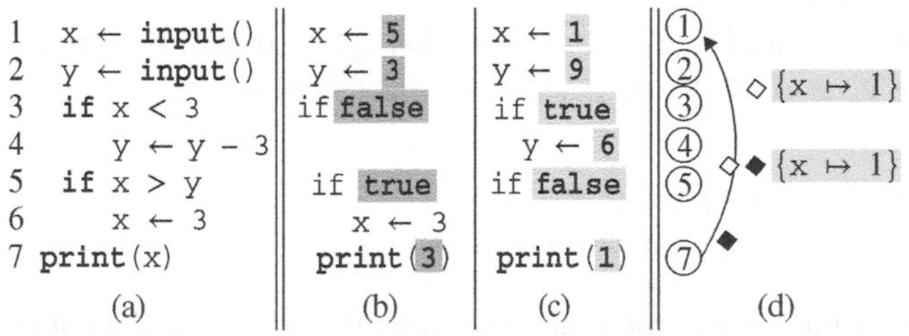

Figure 3.27 Missing causes by execution omission: (a) an example program; (b)–(c) executions with different inputs; and (d) CSM result. *Source:* Sumner and Zhang [30]/IEEE.

A formal definition for *sufficiency* is as follows:

Definition 3.9 (Sufficiency)
A cause set $\Delta_{\diamond}$ at $l_{\diamond}^{(e_1,\, e_2)}$ is sufficient for a given target effect set $\Delta_{\blacklozenge}$ at a later effect point $l_{\blacklozenge}^{(e_1,\, e_2)}$ if and only if, in the absence of confounding, copying the state of e_2 in $\Delta_{\diamond}$ to e_1 at the cause point induces the effect of e_2 in $\Delta_{\blacklozenge}$ in execution e_1 at the effect point, and vice versa.

One key condition is that re-execution should be confounding-free. Unfortunately, normal program execution cannot guarantee this. The remainder of this subsection focuses on discussing confounding.

What is confounding? Determining sufficiency involves replacing part of the state in one execution with values from the opposing execution. However, the continuation of the modified execution entangles the state due to both original executions, affecting each other's results and inducing undesirable and unexpected results in causal inference.

Consider Figure 3.26 again. We saw that partially changing the state of execution (b) with the single desired cause variable y yielded output different than those from either execution (b) or (c). In addition, we found that including z as a cause along with y would yield the target state, although z is not relevant to the output. Both of these are unexpected results that we call confounding from partial state replacement. These confounding effects do not just have the capability to include an arbitrary state within the set of identified causes. They can exclude an arbitrary state as well.

At a high level, these unexpected results occur because partial state replacement *created new behavior that did not exist in either of the original executions.*

A formal definition for *confounding* is as follows:

Definition 3.10 (Confounding)
Given executions e_1 and e_2 as well as a patched execution e_p constructed from them, a causality test using e_p is confounded if either of the following conditions are satisfied:

1) *An execution point in e_p is not present in e_1 or e_2.*
2) *A data dependence in e_p is not exercised in e_1 or e_2.*

Condition (1) corresponds to control flow confounding and (2) to data flow confounding, which means that confounding can occur without exhibiting any new control flow.

Consider the example in Figure 3.28. This time, the target state is $\{x\,[y] \mapsto (1, 2)\}$ with cause and effect points at lines 4 and 5, respectively. Observe that in each execution, the read from and written to elements of x are different. Thus, the only

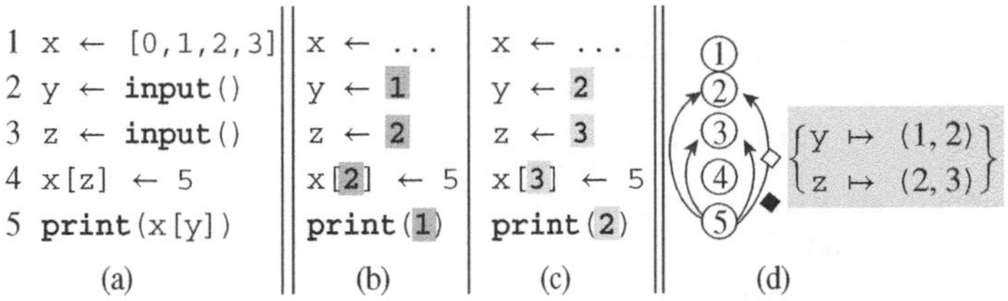

Figure 3.28 Data flow confounding example: (a) an example program; (b)–(c) executions with different inputs; and (d) confounded explanation. *Source:* Sumner and Zhang [30]/IEEE.

identified cause for the difference in outputs should be the different values of `y`, which provides the index read from the list. However, when only the value of `y` is replaced on line 4 in (b), the patched execution reads the new value written to the list on line 4. Thus, the target state is not induced. Observe that in this case, a new data dependence from line 5 to line 4 is exercised.

3.3.8 Implicit Dependences to Locate Execution Omission Errors[12]

Execution omission errors are known to be difficult to locate using dynamic analysis. These errors lead to a failure at runtime because of the omission of execution of some statements that would have been executed if the program had no errors. Since dynamic analysis is typically designed to focus on dynamic information arising from executed statements, and statements whose execution is omitted do not produce dynamic information, detection of execution omission errors becomes a challenging task. For example, while dynamic slices are very effective in capturing faulty code for other types of errors, they fail to capture faulty code in the presence of execution omission errors.

An example of execution omission error is depicted in Figure 3.29. The code is taken from version *v*3 run r1 of `gzip`. The shaded statements are the ones that are executed. As shown by this figure, the error resides in the assignment to `save_orig_name`. Since `save_orig_name` contains the wrong value `false`, branch S_4 is not taken, and thus `flags` has the wrong value 0 while it should have been defined as `ORIG_NAME` at S_5. This wrong `flags` value is eventually observed at S_{10}. Let us assume that we try to locate the error by computing the dynamic slice of the wrong value, i.e. find the set of executed statements that affect the wrong value through data and/or control dependence. The resulting dynamic slice contains S_2, S_3, S_6, and S_{10}, from which the root cause, S_1, is missing. This happens because dynamic slicing is able to capture the fact that the definition at S_2 reaches S_6 but fails to discover that the branch outcome of S_4 also affects the value of `flags` at S_6. The difficulty of analyzing an execution omission error is an inherent

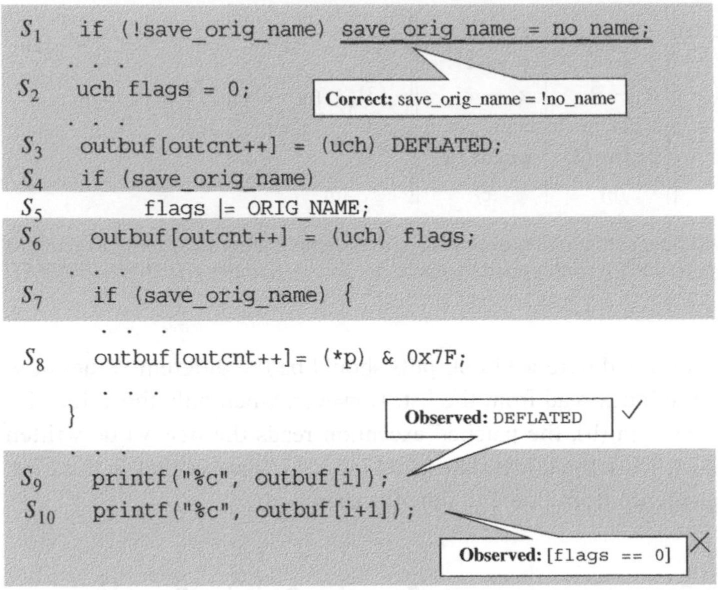
S1 if (!save_orig_name) save_orig_name = no_name;
. . .
S2 uch flags = 0;
Correct: save_orig_name = !no_name
. . .
S3 outbuf[outcnt++] = (uch) DEFLATED;
S4 if (save_orig_name)
S5 flags |= ORIG_NAME;
S6 outbuf[outcnt++] = (uch) flags;
. . .
S7 if (save_orig_name) {
. . .
S8 outbuf[outcnt++]= (*p) & 0x7F;
. . .
}
Observed: DEFLATED
. . .
S9 printf("%c", outbuf[i]);
S10 printf("%c", outbuf[i+1]);
Observed: [flags == 0]

Figure 3.29 Execution omission error: an example. *Source:* Zhang et al. [33]/ACM.

limitation of dynamic analysis as the analysis is based on information collected from executed statements, not the ones whose execution was incorrectly omitted.

To address this issue, Gyimothy et al. [32] proposed the use of *relevant slicing*. Given a failed execution, the relevant slicing first constructs a dynamic dependence graph in the same way that classic dynamic slicing does. It then augments the dynamic dependence graph with potential dependence edges, and a relevant slice is computed by taking the transitive closure of the incorrect output on the augmented dynamic dependence graph. The basic idea of relevant slicing is to introduce a potential dependence between predicate S_4 and assignment S_6. Now, the root cause becomes reachable from the wrong output through dependence edges such that it is included in the dynamic slice. Potential dependence is essentially a static concept in the sense that an edge is conservatively added if there is potentially a dependence. For example, S_{10} potentially depends on S_7 as well because the definition at S8 could reach S_{10}, even though in fact S_7 does not affect the value at S_{10}. Furthermore, potential dependence edges are uniformly introduced for all the nodes in a dynamic dependence graph before any relevant slices can be computed. Therefore, the conservative effects accumulate, resulting in much larger slices being computed.

To overcome the shortcoming of relevant slicing, a fully dynamic solution for handling execution omission errors is proposed in our work in [33]. The essence of this solution lies in adding a dependence edge between the *predicate* and the *use* only if the dependence *can be made observable* rather than just being *potential*. A dependence is observable only if changing the value at the predicate affects the use. Therefore, the basic idea of our approach is as follows: given a predicate *p* and a use *u* such that *p* precedes *u*, and *u* is not directly or indirectly data/control dependent on *p*, we re-execute the program with the same input and then *switch* the branch outcome of the predicate. If the point that corresponds to *u* is affected, we conclude that there is a dependence between *p* and *u* in the original execution. We also refer to such dependence as an *implicit dependence* because even though this dependence exists, it is not established via a chain of explicit data and/or control dependences. Let us consider the example in Figure 3.29. To verify whether there is a dependence between S_4 and S_6, we re-execute *gzip* with the same input and then switch the execution to take the *true* branch at S_4. We observe that the value at S_6 is altered by switching the predicate. Thus, it can be concluded that there is a dependence between S_4 and S_6. Likewise, we find that there is no dependence between S_7 and S_{10}.

3.3.9 Other Dynamic Slicing-Based Techniques

Alves et al. [2] used dynamic slicing to help improve the performance of spectrum-based fault localization. Korel [34] proposed an assistant system that guides a programmer in debugging Pascal programs. It was developed based on dependence network and backtracking reasoning. In [35], Mao et al. combined dynamic slicing and statistical analysis to measure the suspiciousness of each program entity being faulty. Sterling et al. [36] proposed a more efficient approach based on program chipping to help programmers locate bugs in software systems. Similar to slicing, program chipping uses very simple techniques based on the syntactic structure of the program. Qian and Xu [37] proposed a scenario-oriented program slicing technique. A user-specified scenario was identified as the extra slicing parameter, and all program parts related to a special computation were located under the given execution scenario. There are three key steps to implementing the scenario-oriented slicing technique: scenario input, identification of scenario relevant codes, and, finally, gathering of scenario-oriented slices.

3.4 Execution Slicing-Based Fault Localization

3.4.1 Fault Localization Using Execution Dice[13]

Agrawal et al. [38] recommend an alternative approach for fault localization by integrating static and dynamic slicing. They proposed the notion of execution slicing based on dataflow testing, in which an execution slice with respect to a given test case comprises the set of statements executed by this test case. The reason for choosing execution slicing over static slicing is that the latter focuses on finding statements that may possibly have an impact on the variables of interest for any inputs, rather than statements executed by a specific input. This implies that a static slice does not make any use of the input values that reveal the fault and violates a very important concept in debugging that suggests analyzing the program behavior under the test case that fails and not under a generic test case. Collecting dynamic slices may consume excessive time and file space, even though different algorithms [39–42] have been proposed to address these issues. Conversely, it is relatively easy to construct the execution slice for a given test case if we collect code coverage data from the execution of the test.

An execution dice is the set of statements in one execution slice which do not appear in the other execution slice. A strategy for fault localization using execution dices proceeds as follows. The fault resides in the slice of a test case that fails on execution. Attention is focused on that slice and the rest of the program is ignored in searching for the fault. To narrow the search further, we assume that the fault does not lie in the slice of a test case that succeeds. We then limit our attention to the statements in the failed slice that do not appear in the successful slice, i.e. the dice. By way of illustration, consider Figure 3.30. Here, the left-most oval represents slice B, a successful slice, while the right-most oval represents slice A, a failed slice. A fault α is in slice A and not in slice B and so will be in the dice of A–B. The area of the dice is smaller than the area of the slice A and the programmer is saved the effort of searching the shaded area for fault α. The approach has also been implemented in a tool suite called χSuds [43].

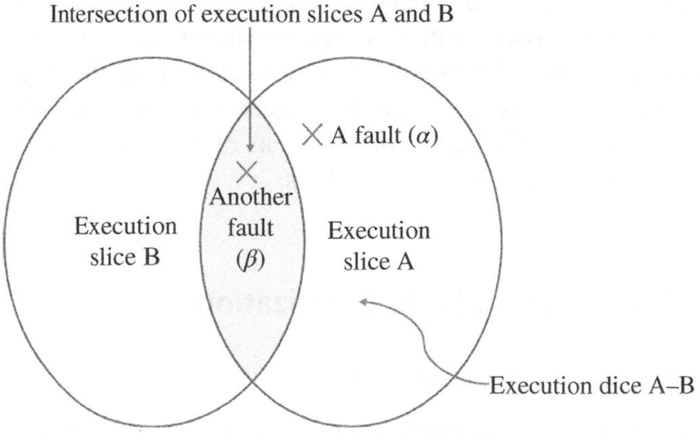

Figure 3.30 Executions slides, dice, and program bugs. *Source:* Agrawal et al. [38]/IEEE.

However, a fault β may reside in the shaded intersection of the two slices. As a result, it is not in the dice of A and B, the right-most crescent. To locate such faults, Jones et al. [44] and Wong et al. [45] proposed to use multiple successful and failed tests based on the following observations:

- The more successful test cases that execute a piece of code, the less likely it is for the code to contain a fault.
- The more failed test cases with respect to a given fault that execute a piece of code, the more likely that it contains this fault.

3.4.2 A Family of Fault Localization Heuristics Based on Execution Slicing[14]

Though various fault localization techniques have been proposed to help engineers locate bugs, few existing studies distinguish the contribution of one failed test case from another or one successful test case from another. Ref. [46] addresses how the contribution of each additional test case (successful or failed) should be taken into account when computing the suspiciousness of code based on execution slices.

Given a piece of code, we first identify how many successful and failed test cases execute it. We then explore whether all the failed test executions provide the same contribution toward program debugging and whether all the successful test case executions provide the same contribution. Our intuition tells us that the answer should be "no." Our proposal is that if a piece of code has already been executed successfully by 994 test cases, then the contribution of the 995th successful execution is likely to be less than that of the second successful execution when the code is only executed successfully once. In fact, for a given piece of code, the contribution of the first successful test case is larger than or equal to that of the second successful test case, which in turn is larger than or equal to that of the third successful test case, and so on. The same also applies to failed test cases. Stated differently, for successful and failed test cases alike, we propose that the contribution of the kth successful (or failed) test case is always greater than or equal to that of the $(k + 1)$th successful (or failed) test case.

Given a piece of code (a statement, say S) and a specific bug (say $\mathcal{B}$), suppose we want to determine how likely it is that S contains the bug $\mathcal{B}$. To facilitate discussion, the notation with respect to S and $\mathcal{B}$ is defined in Table 3.3. From the table, we have $N_F \leq \Phi_F$, $N_S \leq \Phi_S$, $\mathcal{N}_F = \sum_{i=1}^{\mathcal{G}_F} n_{F,i}$, and $\mathcal{N}_S = \sum_{i=1}^{\mathcal{G}_S} n_{S,i}$. Note that N_F, N_S, $n_{F,i}$, and $n_{S,i}$ depend on S (which statement is considered), whereas $\mathcal{X}_{F/S}$ does not, as its value is fixed for a given bug. We present below three heuristics to show how the above information can be used to prioritize statements in terms of their likelihood of containing a program bug.

Table 3.3 Notation used in this section.

t_i	The ith test case
S_j	The jth statement
Φ_F	Total number of failed test cases for $\mathcal{B}$
Φ_S	Total number of successful test cases for $\mathcal{B}$
$\mathcal{N}_F$	Total number of failed test cases with respect to $\mathcal{B}$ that execute S
$\mathcal{N}_S$	Total number of successful test cases that execute S
$c_{F,i}$	Contribution from the ith failed test case that executes S
$c_{S,i}$	Contribution from the ith successful test case that executes S
$\mathcal{G}_F$	Number of groups for the failed test cases that execute S
$\mathcal{G}_S$	Number of groups for the successful test cases that execute S
$n_{F,i}$	Maximal number of failed test cases in the ith failed group
$n_{S,i}$	Maximal number of successful test cases in the ith successful group
$w_{F,i}$	Contribution from each test in the ith failed group
$w_{S,i}$	Contribution from each test in the ith successful group
$\chi_{F/S}$	Φ_F/Φ_S

Source: Wong et al. [46]/Elsevier.

3.4.2.1 Heuristic I

If the program execution fails on a test case, it is natural to assume that the corresponding bug resides in the set of statements executed by the failed test case. In addition, if a statement is executed by two failed test cases, our intuition suggests that this statement is more likely to contain the bug than a statement that is executed only by one failed test case. If we also assume that every failed test case that executes S provides the same contribution in program debugging (i.e. $c_{F,i} = c_{F,j}$, for $1 \leq i, j, \leq N_F$), then we have the likelihood that S contains the bug is proportional to the number of failed test cases that execute it. In this way, we define the suspiciousness of the jth statement as

$$\text{Suspiciousness}(j) = \sum_{i=1}^{N_F+N_s} C_{i,j} \times r_i \tag{3.1}$$

$$\text{where } C_{i,j} = \begin{cases} 1, & \text{if } t_i \text{ executes } S_j \\ 0, & \text{if } t_i \text{ does not execute } S_j \end{cases}$$

$$\text{and } r_i = \begin{cases} 1, & \text{if the program fails on } t_i \\ 0, & \text{if the program suceeds on } t_i \end{cases}$$

Let us use the example in Figure 3.31 to demonstrate how Heuristic I computes the suspiciousness of each statement. The left matrix shows how every statement is executed by each test case. An entry of 1 indicates that the statement is executed by the corresponding test case, and an entry of 0 means it is not executed. For example, the entry at the intersection of t_2 and S_3 is 0, which implies that S_3 is not executed by t_2. The right matrix shows the execution result with an entry of 1 for a

	s_1	s_2	s_3	s_4	s_5	s_6	s_7	s_8	s_9	s_{10}	r	
t_1	1	0	0	0	1	1	0	1	1	1	1	Failed test
t_2	1	1	0	1	0	0	0	0	1	0	0	
t_3	1	0	1	0	0	1	1	1	1	1	1	Failed test
t_4	1	1	1	1	0	0	1	1	1	0	0	
t_5	1	1	1	1	0	1	1	1	1	0	0	
t_6	1	0	0	0	0	0	1	1	1	1	0	
t_7	1	1	0	0	0	1	1	0	1	1	0	
t_8	1	1	1	1	0	0	1	1	1	0	0	
t_9	0	1	0	0	0	1	0	0	1	1	0	
t_{10}	1	0	0	0	1	0	1	1	1	1	1	Failed test
t_{11}	0	1	1	0	0	0	0	1	1	0	0	
t_{12}	1	1	0	1	1	0	1	0	1	1	0	
t_{13}	1	0	1	0	0	0	1	1	1	0	0	
t_{14}	0	1	0	1	1	0	1	0	1	1	0	
t_{15}	1	0	1	0	1	0	1	1	1	1	1	Failed test
t_{16}	0	1	0	1	0	0	0	1	1	0	0	
t_{17}	1	1	1	1	0	0	1	1	1	0	0	
t_{18}	1	0	1	0	1	1	0	1	1	1	1	Failed test
t_{19}	1	1	1	1	0	0	1	0	1	0	0	
t_{20}	0	0	1	1	1	1	1	0	1	1	0	
Suspiciousness of each statement	5	0	3	0	4	3	3	5	5	5		

S_3 is not executed by t_2

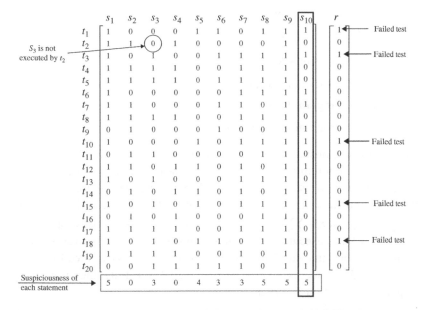

Figure 3.31 An example of Heuristic I. *Source:* Wong et al. [46]/Elsevier.

failed execution and an entry of 0 for a successful execution. Referring to Figure 3.31, program execution fails on test cases t_1, t_3, t_{10}, t_{15}, and t_{18}. To compute the suspiciousness of S_{10}, we find that it is executed by all five failed test cases. From (3.1), the suspiciousness of S_{10} equals $\sum_{i=1}^{20}(C_{i,10} \times r_i) = 5$. Similarly, S_1, S_8, and S_9 also have the same suspiciousness of 5 because each of them is executed by five failed test cases, whereas S_5 has a suspiciousness of 4 as it is executed by four failed test cases, and S_3, S_6, and S_7 have a suspiciousness of 3 for three failed executions. As for S_2 and S_4, their suspiciousness is zero because they are not executed by any failed test case.

3.4.2.2 Heuristic II

In Heuristic I, we only take advantage of failed test cases to compute the suspiciousness of a statement. However, we also observe that if a statement is executed by a successful test case, its likelihood of containing a bug is reduced. Moreover, the more successful test cases that execute a statement, the less likely that it will contain a bug. If we also assume that every successful test case that executes S provides the same contribution in program debugging (i.e. $c_{S,i} = c_{S,j}$ for $1 \le i, j \le N_S$), then we have the likelihood that S contains the bug is inversely proportional to the number of successful test cases that execute it. Combined with our observation on the failed test cases, we define the suspiciousness of the jth statement as:

$$\text{Suspiciousness}(j) = \sum_{i=1}^{N_F+N_s} C_{i,j} \times r_i - \sum_{i=1}^{N_F+N_s} C_{i,j} \times (1 - r_i) \tag{3.2}$$

$$\text{where } C_{i,j} = \begin{cases} 1, & \text{if } t_i \text{ executes } S_j \\ 0, & \text{if } t_i \text{ does not execute } S_j \end{cases}$$

$$\text{and } r_i = \begin{cases} 1, & \text{if the program fails on } t_i \\ 0, & \text{if the program suceeds on } t_i \end{cases}$$

This gives the suspiciousness of each statement as equal to the number of failed test cases that execute it minus the number of successful test cases that execute it. Let us use the same matrices in Figure 3.31 to demonstrate how Heuristic II computes the suspiciousness of each statement. From (3.2), the suspiciousness of S_{10} equals $\sum_{i=1}^{20} C_{i,10} \times r_i - \sum_{i=1}^{20} C_{i,10} \times (1 - r_i) = 5 - 6 = -1$. This is consistent with the fact that S_{10} is executed by five failed and six successful test cases. Similarly, S_6 also has the same suspiciousness of −1 because it is executed by three failed test cases and four successful test cases. Figure 3.32 illustrates the suspiciousness computation based on Heuristic II.

	s_1	s_2	s_3	s_4	s_5	s_6	s_7	s_8	s_9	s_{10}	r	
t_1	1	0	0	0	1	1	0	1	1	1	1	← Failed test
t_2	1	1	0	1	0	0	0	0	1	0	0	
t_3	1	0	1	0	0	1	1	1	1	1	1	← Failed test
t_4	1	1	1	1	0	0	1	1	1	0	0	
t_5	1	1	1	1	0	1	1	1	1	0	0	
t_6	1	0	0	0	0	0	1	1	1	1	0	
t_7	1	1	0	0	0	1	1	0	1	1	0	
t_8	1	1	1	1	0	0	1	1	1	0	0	
t_9	0	1	0	0	0	1	0	0	1	1	0	
t_{10}	1	0	0	0	1	0	1	1	1	1	1	← Failed test
t_{11}	0	1	1	0	0	0	0	1	1	0	0	
t_{12}	1	1	0	1	1	0	1	0	1	1	0	
t_{13}	1	0	1	0	0	0	1	1	1	0	0	
t_{14}	0	1	0	1	1	0	1	0	1	1	0	
t_{15}	1	0	1	0	1	0	1	1	1	1	1	← Failed test
t_{16}	0	1	0	1	0	0	0	1	1	0	0	
t_{17}	1	1	1	1	0	0	1	1	1	0	0	
t_{18}	1	0	1	0	1	1	0	1	1	1	1	← Failed test
t_{19}	1	1	1	1	0	0	1	0	1	0	0	
t_{20}	0	0	1	1	1	1	1	0	1	1	0	
	5	0	3	0	4	3	3	5	5	5		← Number of failed tests that execute each statement
	10	12	8	10	3	4	11	8	15	6		← Number of successful tests that execute each statement
	-5	-12	-5	-10	1	-1	-8	-3	-10	-1		← Suspiciousness of each statement

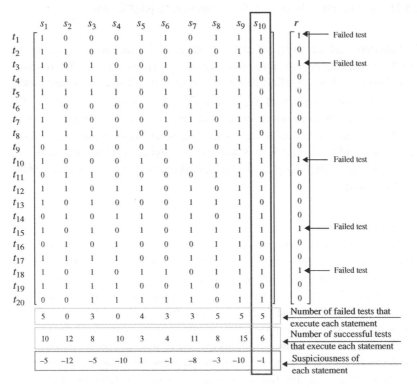

Figure 3.32 An example of Heuristic II. *Source:* Wong et al. [46]/Elsevier.

3.4.2.3 Heuristic III[15]

In the first two heuristics, we make no distinction between the contributions from different successful or failed test cases. The contribution provided by one failed test case is identical to that of each of the other failed test cases; similarly, a successful test case makes the same contribution as each of the other successful test cases. However, if S has been executed by many successful test cases, then the contribution of each additional successful execution to the suspiciousness of S is likely to be less than that of the first few successful test cases. Similarly, if S has already been executed by many failed test cases, the contribution of each additional failed execution to the suspiciousness of S is likely to be less than the contribution of the first few failed test cases. Hence, we propose that for a given statement S, the contribution introduced by the first successful test case that executes it in computing its likelihood of containing a bug is larger than or equal to that of the second successful test case that executes it, which is larger than or equal to that of the third successful test case that executes it, and so on. This implies that $c_{S,1} \geq c_{S,2} \geq c_{S,3} \geq ... \geq c_{S,N_S}$. The same also applies to failed tests, i.e. $c_{F,1} \geq c_{F,2} \geq c_{F,3} \geq ... \geq c_{F,N_F}$.

One significant drawback of Heuristic II is that it cannot distinguish a statement (say S_α) executed by one successful and one failed test case from another statement (say S_β) executed by 10 successful and 10 failed test cases. The suspiciousness of both S_α and S_β computed by using Heuristic II is zero as the first one is $1 - 1 = 0$ and the second one is $10 - 10$, which is also zero. This is counterintuitive because S_β should be more suspicious than S_α, as the former is executed by more failed test cases than the latter.

To overcome this problem, Heuristic III is proposed, such that if the statement S is executed by at least one failed test case, then the total contribution from all the successful test cases that execute s should be less than the total contribution from all the failed test cases that execute s (namely, $\sum_{i=1}^{N_S} c_{S,i} < \sum_{k=1}^{N_F} c_{F,k}$). We assume that failed test cases that execute S are divided into G_F groups such that the first failed group has at most $n_{F,1}$ test cases (the first $n_{F,1}$ test cases), the second failed group has at most $n_{F,2}$ test cases from the remaining, the third has at most $n_{F,3}$ test cases from the rest, and so on. These groups are filled in order such that the test cases are assigned to each group starting from the first to the last group. We propose that all the test cases in the same failed group have the same contribution toward program debugging, but test cases from different groups have different contributions. For example, every test case in the ith failed group has a contribution of $w_{F,i}$ and every test in the jth failed group ($i \neq j$) has a contribution of $w_{F,i}$ which is different from $w_{F,i}$. The same also applies to the successful test cases that execute S. With this in mind, the suspiciousness of S can then be defined as:

$$\text{Suspiciousness}(s) = \sum_{i=1}^{G_F} w_{F,i} \times n_{F,i} - \sum_{i=1}^{G_S} w_{S,i} \times n_{S,i} \tag{3.3}$$

where $\sum_{i=1}^{N_S} c_{S,i} < \sum_{k=1}^{N_F} c_{F,k}$

Let us use the same matrices in Figure 3.31 to demonstrate how Heuristic III computes the suspiciousness of each statement. For illustrative proposes, we set $\mathcal{G}_F = \mathcal{G}_S = 3$, $n_{F,1} = n_{S,1} = 2$, and $n_{F,2} = n_{S,2} = 4$. That is, the first failed (or successful) group has at most two test cases, the second group has at most four from the remaining, and the third has everything else, if any. We also assume that each test case in the first, second, and third failed groups gives a contribution of 1, 0.1, and 0.01, respectively ($w_{F,1} = 1$, $w_{F,2} = 0.1$, and $w_{F,3} = 0.01$). Similarly, we set $w_{S,1} = 1$, $w_{S,2} = 0.1$, and $w_{S,3}$ is a small value defined as $\alpha \times \mathrm{X}_{F/S}$, where α is a scaling factor. Eq. (3.3) can be rewritten as:

$$\begin{aligned}\text{Suspiciousness}(s) = {} & [(1.0) \times n_{F,1} + (0.1) \times n_{F,2} + (0.01) \times n_{F,3}] \\ & - \left[(1.0) \times n_{S,1} + (0.1) \times n_{S,2} + \alpha \times \chi_{F/S} \times n_{S,3}\right] \end{aligned} \tag{3.4}$$

where

$$n_{F,1} = \begin{cases} 0, & \text{if } N_F = 0 \\ 1, & \text{if } N_F = 1 \\ 2, & \text{if } N_F \geq 2 \end{cases}$$

$$n_{F,2} = \begin{cases} 0, & \text{if } N_F \leq 2 \\ N_F - 2, & \text{if } 3 \leq N_F \leq 6 \\ 4, & \text{if } N_F > 6 \end{cases}$$

$$n_{F,3} = \begin{cases} 0, \text{ if } N_F \leq 6 \\ N_F - 6, \text{ if } N_F > 6 \end{cases}$$

$$n_{S,1} = \begin{cases} 0, \text{ if } n_{F,1} = 0, 1 \\ 1, \text{ if } n_{F,1} = 2 \text{ and } N_S \geq 1 \end{cases}$$

$$n_{S,2} = \begin{cases} 0, \text{ if } N_S \leq n_{S,1} \\ N_S - n_{S,1}, \text{ if } n_{S,1} < N_S < n_{F,2} + n_{S,1} \\ n_{F,2}, \text{ if } N_S \geq n_{F,2} + n_{S,1} \end{cases}$$

$$n_{S,3} = \begin{cases} 0, \text{ if } N_S < n_{S,1} + n_{S,2} \\ N_S - n_{S,1} - n_{S,2}, \text{ if } N_F \geq n_{S,1} + n_{S,2} \end{cases}$$

From (3.4), when $\alpha = 0.01$, the suspiciousness of S_{10} equals

$$[(1.0) \times 2 + (0.1) \times 3 + (0.01) \times 0] - [(1.0) \times 1 + (0.1) \times 3 + 0.01 \times 5/15 \times 2] = 0.993$$

and the suspiciousness of S_2 equals

$$[(1.0) \times 0 + (0.1) \times 0 + (0.01) \times 0] - [(1.0) \times 0 + (0.1) \times 0 + 0.01 \times 5/15 \times 12] = 0.040.$$

Figure 3.33 gives the suspiciousness computation based on Heuristic III with $\alpha = 0.01$.

	s_1	s_2	s_3	s_4	s_5	s_6	s_7	s_8	s_9	s_{10}	r	
t_1	1	0	0	0	1	1	0	1	1	1	1	← Failed test
t_2	1	1	0	1	0	0	0	0	1	0	0	
t_3	1	0	1	0	0	1	1	1	1	1	1	← Failed test
t_4	1	1	1	1	0	0	1	1	1	0	0	
t_5	1	1	1	1	0	1	1	1	1	0	0	
t_6	1	0	0	0	0	0	1	1	1	1	0	
t_7	1	1	0	0	0	1	1	0	1	1	0	
t_8	1	1	1	1	0	0	1	1	1	0	0	
t_9	0	1	0	0	0	1	0	0	1	1	0	
t_{10}	1	0	0	0	1	0	1	1	1	1	1	← Failed test
t_{11}	0	1	1	0	0	0	0	1	1	0	0	
t_{12}	1	1	0	1	1	0	1	0	1	1	0	
t_{13}	1	0	1	0	0	0	1	1	1	0	0	
t_{14}	0	1	0	1	1	0	1	0	1	1	0	
t_{15}	1	0	1	0	1	0	1	1	1	1	1	← Failed test
t_{16}	0	1	0	1	0	0	0	1	1	0	0	
t_{17}	1	1	1	1	0	0	1	1	1	0	0	
t_{18}	1	0	1	0	1	1	0	1	1	1	1	← Failed test
t_{19}	1	1	1	1	0	0	1	0	1	0	0	
t_{20}	0	0	1	1	1	1	1	0	1	1	0	
Number of failed tests that execute each statement	5	0	3	0	4	3	3	5	5	5		
Number of successful tests that execute each statement	10	12	8	10	3	4	11	8	15	6		
Suspiciousness of each statement	0.980	–0.04	0.980	0.033	1.000	0.993	0.970	0.987	0.963	0.993		

	$n_{F,1}$	$n_{F,2}$	$n_{F,3}$	$\sum_{i=1}^{N_F} C_{F,i}$	$n_{S,1}$	$n_{S,2}$	$n_{S,3}$	$\sum_{i=1}^{N_F} C_{S,i}$
S_1	2	3	0	2.3	1	3	6	1.320
S_2	0	0	0	0	0	0	12	0.040
S_3	2	1	0	2.1	1	1	6	1.120
S_4	0	0	0	0	0	0	10	0.033
S_5	2	2	0	2.2	1	2	0	1.200
S_6	2	1	0	2.1	1	1	2	1.107
S_7	2	1	0	2.1	1	1	9	1.130
S_8	2	3	0	2.3	1	3	4	1.313
S_9	2	3	0	2.3	1	3	11	1.337
S_{10}	2	3	0	2.3	1	3	2	1.307

Computation based on the number of test cases in the first, second, and third failed and successful groups

Figure 3.33 An example of Heuristic III with $\alpha = 0.01$. *Source:* Wong et al. [46]/Elsevier.

The following can also be observed:

- Neither S_2 nor S_4 is executed by any failed test case, but S_2 is executed by 12 successful test cases and S_4 is only executed by 10 successful test cases. The suspiciousness of S_2 computed by Eq. (3.4) is −0.040, which is less than −0.033, the suspiciousness of S_4. Similarly, S_{10}, S_8, S_1, and S_9 are all executed by five failed test cases but by different numbers of successful test cases (namely, 6, 8, 10, and 15, respectively). Their suspiciousness computed by Eq. (3.4) is 0.993, 0.987, 0.980, and 0.963. Both cases are consistent with our claim that "more successful executions imply a lower likelihood to contain the bug."
- All the statements, except S_2 and S_4, have at least one failed test case and their suspiciousness computed satisfies $\sum_{i=1}^{N_S} c_{S,i} < \sum_{k=1}^{N_F} c_{F,k}$. This is also consistent with the requirement set by Heuristic III.

3.4.3 Effective Fault Localization Based on Execution Slices and Inter-block Data Dependence[16]

As discussed in Section 3.4.1, the execution slice for a given test case is the set of code (e.g. statements) executed by this test case. An execution slicing-based technique as reported in [38] can be effective in locating some program bugs, but not for others, especially those in the code that is executed by both the failed and the successful tests. Another problem with this technique is that even if a bug is in the dice obtained by subtracting the execution slice of a successful test case from that of a failed test case, there may still be too much code that needs to be examined.

Wong and Qi [51] proposed an augmentation method and a refining method to overcome these problems. The former includes additional code in the search domain for inspection based on its inter-block data dependence with the code currently being examined, whereas the latter excludes less suspicious code from the search domain using the execution slices of additional successful test cases. Stated differently, the augmentation and refining methods are used to help programmers better prioritize code based on its likelihood of containing program bug(s) for an effective fault localization.

Suppose that for a given program bug, we have identified one failed test case (say *F*) and one successful test case (say *S*). Suppose also that their execution slices are denoted by E_F and E_S, respectively. We can construct a dice $\mathcal{D}^{(1)} = E_F - E_S$. We present two methods to help programmers effectively locate this bug: an augmentation method to include additional code for inspection if the bug is not in $\mathcal{D}^{(1)}$, and a refining method to exclude code from being examined if $\mathcal{D}^{(1)}$ contains too much code.

3.4.3.1 Augmenting a Bad $\mathcal{D}^{(1)}$

If the bug is not in $\mathcal{D}^{(1)}$, we need to examine additional code from the rest of the failed execution slice, i.e. code from E_F–$\mathcal{D}^{(1)}$. Let us use Φ to represent the set of code that is in E_F–$\mathcal{D}^{(1)}$. For a block β, the notation $\beta \in \Phi$ implies that β is in the failed execution slice E_F but not in $\mathcal{D}^{(1)}$. We also define a "direct data dependence" relation Δ such that $\beta \,\Delta\, \mathcal{D}^{(1)}$ if and only if β defines a variable x that is used in $\mathcal{D}^{(1)}$, or β uses a variable y defined in $\mathcal{D}^{(1)}$. We say that β is directly data dependent on $\mathcal{D}^{(1)}$. Instead of examining all the code in Φ at the same time (i.e. having code in Φ with the same priority), a better approach is to prioritize such code based on its likelihood of containing the bug. To do so, the augmentation procedures outlined as follows is used:

A₁: Construct $\mathcal{A}^{(1)}$, the augmented code segment from the first iteration, such that $\mathcal{A}^{(1)} = \{\beta \in \phi \,|\, \beta \,\Delta\, \mathcal{D}^{(1)}\}$

A₂: Set $k = 1$

A₃: Examine the code in $\mathcal{A}^{(k)}$ to see whether it contains the bug.

A₄: If **YES,** then **STOP** because we have located the bug.

A₅: Set $k = k + 1$.

A₆: Construct $\mathcal{A}^{(k)}$, the augmented code segment from the kth iteration such that

$$\mathcal{A}^{(k)} = \mathcal{A}^{(k-1)} \cup \left\{\beta \in \phi \,|\, \beta \,\Delta\, \mathcal{A}^{(k-1)}\right\}.$$

A₇: If $\mathcal{A}^{(k-1)} = \mathcal{A}^{(k-1)}$ (i.e. no new code can be included from the (k–1)th iteration to the kth iteration), then STOP. At this point we have $\mathcal{A}^{(*)}$, the final augmented code segment, equals $\mathcal{A}^{(k)}$ (and $\mathcal{A}^{(k-1)}$ as well).

A₈: Go back to step A₃.

Stated differently, $\mathcal{A}^{(1)}$ contains the code that is directly data dependent on $\mathcal{D}^{(1)}$, and $\mathcal{A}^{(2)}$ is the union of $\mathcal{A}^{(1)}$ and additional code that is directly data dependent on $\mathcal{A}^{(1)}$. It is clear that $\mathcal{A}^{(1)} \subset \mathcal{A}^{(2)} \subset \mathcal{A}^{(3)} \subset \ldots \subset \mathcal{A}^{(*)}$.

Our incremental approach is that if a program bug is not in $\mathcal{D}^{(1)}$, we will then try to locate it starting from $\mathcal{A}^{(1)}$ followed by $\mathcal{A}^{(2)}$ and so on until $\mathcal{A}^{(*)}$. For each iteration, we include additional code that is data dependent on the previous augmented code segment. One exception is the first iteration where $\mathcal{A}^{(1)}$ is data dependent on $\mathcal{D}^{(1)}$. The rationale behind this augmentation method is that even though a program bug is not in the suspicious area (such as $\mathcal{D}^{(1)}$), it is very likely that it has something to do with the code that is directly data dependent on the code in $\mathcal{D}^{(1)}$ or some $\mathcal{A}^{(k)}$ constructed at step **A₆**.

One important point worth noting is that if the procedure stops at step **A₄**, we have successfully located the bug. However, if the procedure stops at **A₇**, we have constructed $\mathcal{A}^{(*)}$ which still does not contain the bug. In this case, we need to examine the code that is in the failed execution slice (E_F) but not in $\mathcal{D}^{(1)}$ nor in $\mathcal{D}^{(1)}$ (i.e. code in $E_F - \mathcal{D}^{(1)} - \mathcal{A}^{(*)}$). Although in theory this is possible, our conjecture is that in practice it does not seem to occur often. Moreover, even if the bug is in $E_F - \mathcal{D}^{(1)} - \mathcal{A}^{(*)}$, we at most examine the entire failed execution slice (i.e. every piece of code in E_F). This implies that even in the worst case the above augmentation method does not require a programmer to examine any extra code that is not in E_F.

3.4.3.2 Refining a Good $\mathcal{D}^{(1)}$

Suppose that a program bug is in $\mathcal{D}^{(1)}$; we may still end up with too much code that needs to be examined. In other words, $\mathcal{D}^{(1)}$ still contains too much code. If that is the case, we can further prioritize code in this good $\mathcal{D}^{(1)}$ by using additional successful test cases. More specifically, we can use the refining procedure outlined in the following:

R$_1$: Randomly select additional k distinct successful test cases (say, $t_1, t_2, ..., t_k$).
R$_2$: Construct the corresponding execution slices (denoted by $\theta_1, \theta_2, ..., \theta_k$).
R$_3$: Set $m = k$.
R$_4$: Construct $\mathcal{D}^{(m+1)}$ such that $\mathcal{D}^{(m+1)} = \{\beta \in \mathcal{D}^{(1)} \mid \beta \notin \theta_n \text{ for } n = 1, 2, ..., m\}$,
that is, $\mathcal{D}^{(m+1)} = \mathcal{D}^{(1)} - \cup\{\theta_n \text{ for } n = 1, 2, ..., m\}$
R$_5$: Examine code in $\mathcal{D}^{(m+1)}$ to see whether it contains the bug.
R$_6$: If YES, then STOP because we have located the bug.
R$_7$: Set $m = m - 1$.
R$_8$: If $m = 0$, then STOP and examine code in $\mathcal{D}^{(1)}$.
R$_9$: Go back to step **R$_4$**.

Stated differently, $\mathcal{D}^{(2)} = \mathcal{D}^{(1)} - \theta_1 = E_F - E_S - \theta_1$, $\mathcal{D}^{(3)} = \mathcal{D}^{(1)} - \theta_1 - \theta_2 = E_F - E_S - \theta_1 - \theta_2$, etc. This implies $\mathcal{D}^{(2)}$ is constructed by subtracting the union of the execution slices of two successful tests (E_S and θ_1 in our case) from the execution slice of the failed test (E_F in our case), whereas $\mathcal{D}^{(3)}$ is obtained by subtracting the union of the execution slices of three successful tests (namely, E_S, θ_1, and θ_2) from E_F. Based on this definition, we have $\mathcal{D}^{(1)} \supseteq \mathcal{D}^{(2)} \supseteq \mathcal{D}^{(3)}$, etc.

For explanatory purposes, assume $k = 2$. Our refining method suggests that we can reduce the code to be examined by first inspecting code in $\mathcal{D}^{(3)}$ followed by $\mathcal{D}^{(2)}$ and then $\mathcal{D}^{(1)}$. The rationale behind this is that if a piece of code is executed by some successful tests, then it is less likely to contain any fault. In this example, if $\mathcal{D}^{(3)}$ or $\mathcal{D}^{(2)}$ contains the bug, the refining procedure stops at step **R$_6$**. Otherwise, we have the bug in $\mathcal{D}^{(1)}$, but not in $\mathcal{D}^{(2)}$ nor in $\mathcal{D}^{(3)}$. If so, the refining procedure stops at step **R$_8$** where all the code in $\mathcal{D}^{(1)}$ will be examined.

An important point worth noting is that at the beginning of our discussion on the proposed refining method, we assume $\mathcal{D}^{(1)}$ contains the bug and then put our focus on how to prioritize code in $\mathcal{D}^{(1)}$ so that the bug can be located before all the code in $\mathcal{D}^{(1)}$ is examined. However, knowing the location of a program bug in advance is not possible except for a controlled experiment. In response to this challenge, Wong and Qi [51] suggested an incremental strategy described below.

3.4.3.3 An Incremental Debugging Strategy

Effectively locating a bug in a program requires good expert knowledge of the program being debugged. If a programmer has a strong instinct regarding where a bug might be, they should definitely examine that part of the program. However, if this does not reveal the bug, it is better to use a systematic approach by adopting some heuristics supported by good reasoning and proven to be effective in case studies, rather than taking an ad hoc approach without any intuitive support, to find the location of the bug.

For explanatory purposes, let us assume we have one failed test case and three successful test cases. We suggest an incremental debugging strategy by first examining the code in $\mathcal{D}^{(3)}$, followed by $\mathcal{D}^{(2)}$, and then $\mathcal{D}^{(1)}$. This is based on the assumption that the bug is in the code that is executed by the failed test case but not the successful test case(s). If this assumption does not hold (i.e. the bug is not in $\mathcal{D}^{(1)}$), then we need to inspect additional code in E_F (the failed execution slice) but not in $\mathcal{D}^{(1)}$. We can follow the augmentation procedure discussed earlier to start with the code in $\mathcal{A}^{(1)}$, followed $\mathcal{A}^{(2)}$, ..., up to $\mathcal{A}^{(*)}$. If $\mathcal{A}^{(*)}$ does not contain the bug, then we need to examine the last piece of code, namely, $E_F - \mathcal{D}^{(1)} - \mathcal{A}^{(*)}$. In short, we prioritize the code in a failed execution slice based on its likelihood of containing the bug. The prioritization is done by first using the refining method and then the augmentation method. In the worst case, we have to examine all the code in the failed execution slice.

We provide below an example to explain in detail how the approach can be used to prioritize suspicious code in a program for effectively locating a bug. Without resorting to complex semantics, we use a program P that takes two inputs `a` and `b` and computes two outputs `x` and `y` as shown in Figure 3.34. Suppose that P has a bug at S_8, and the correct statement should be "`y = 2 * c + d`" instead of "`y = c + d`". The execution of P on a test case t_1 where `a` = 1 and `b` = 2 fails because `y` should be 16 instead of 13. However, the execution of P on another test case t_2 where `a` = −0.5 and `b` = 3 does not cause any problems. This is because when `c` is zero (computed at S_2), the bug is masked (i.e. there is no difference between "`2 * c + d`" and "`c + d`" when `c` is zero). As a result, we have found one failed test case t_1 and one successful test case t_2.

The execution slices for t_1 (E_1) and t_2 (E_2) are displayed in Figure 3.34a and b. Figure 3.34c gives $\mathcal{D}^{(1)}$ obtained by subtracting E_2 from E_1. It contains only one statement S_3. The first step is to examine the code in $\mathcal{D}^{(1)}$, which, unfortunately, does not contain the bug. Next, rather than trying to locate the bug from the code E_1 (the failed execution slice) but not in $\mathcal{D}^{(1)}$ (S_3 in our case), a better approach is to

(a)

```
     #include <stdio.h>

     int main() {
     float a, b, c, d, x, y;

S0   scanf("%f%f", &a, &b);
S1   if (a <= 0)
S2       c = 2 * a + 1;
     else
S3       c = 3 * a;
S4   if (b <= 0)
S5       d = b * b - 4 * a * c;
     else
S6       d = 5 * b;
S7   x = b + d;
S8   y = c + d;
S9   printf("x = %f & y = %f\n", x, y);
     }
```

(b)

```
     #include <stdio.h>

     int main() {
     float a, b, c, d, x, y;

S0   scanf("%f%f", &a, &b);
S1   if (a <= 0)
S2       c = 2 * a + 1;
     else
S3       c = 3 * a;
S4   if (b <= 0)
S5       d = b * b - 4 * a * c;
     else
S6       d = 5 * b;
S7   x = b + d;
S8   y = c + d;
S9   printf("x = %f & y = %f\n", x, y);
     }
```

(c)

```
     #include <stdio.h>

     int main() {
     float a, b, c, d, x, y;

S0   scanf("%f%f", &a, &b);
S1   if (a <= 0)
S2       c = 2 * a + 1;
     else
S3       c = 3 * a;
S4   if (b <= 0)
S5       d = b * b - 4 * a * c
     else
S6       d = 5 * b;
S7   x = b + d;
S8   y = c + d;
S9   printf("x = %f & y = %f\n", x, y);
     }
```

(d)

```
     #include <stdio.h>

     int main() {
     float a, b, c, d, x, y;

S0   scanf("%f%f", &a, &b);
S1   if (a <= 0)
S2       c = 2 * a + 1;
     else
S3       c = 3 * a;
S4   if (b <= 0)
S5       d = b * b - 4 * a * c
     else
S6       d = 5 * b;          Bug! Should be 2 * c
S7   x = b + d;
S8   y = c + d;
S9   printf("x = %f & y = %f\n", x, y);
     }
```

Figure 3.34 An example of the proposed approach: (a) the failed execution slice with respect to test case t_1; (b) the successful execution slice with respect to test case t_2; (c) $\mathcal{D}^{(1)}$ obtained by subtracting the successful execution slice in (b) from the failed execution slice in (a); and (d) Code that has direct data dependency with S_3 (i.e. code in $A^{(1)}$). *Source:* Wong and Qi [51]/Elsevier.

prioritize such code based on its likelihood of containing the bug. Stated differently, instead of having S_0, S_1, S_4, S_6, S_7, S_8, and S_9 with the same priority, we give a higher priority to the code that has data dependence with S_3. As shown in Figure 3.34d, $\mathcal{A}^{(1)}$ (the augmented code after the first iteration) contains additional code at S_0 and S_8. This is because the variable a used at S_3 is defined at S_0 through a *scanf* statement, and the variable c defined at S_3 is used at S_8. This also implies S_0 and S_8 should have a higher priority and should be examined next. Since S_8 is part of the code to be examined next, we conclude that we have successfully located the bug.

Note that $\mathcal{A}^{(2)}$ (the augmented code after the second iteration) contains additional code at S_1, S_4, S_6, S_7, and S_9 because (1) S_1 uses the variable *a* defined at S_0, (2) S_4, S_6, and S_7 use the variable b defined at S_0, and (3) S_9 uses the variable y defined at S_8. Hence, although S_1, S_4, S_6, S_7, and S_9 are not included in $\mathcal{A}^{(1)}$, they will eventually be in $\mathcal{A}^{(*)}$ (or more precisely, $\mathcal{A}^{(2)}$ in this case). However, there is no need to go through more than one iteration in this example, i.e. no need to examine S_1, S_4, S_6, S_7, and S_9.

3.4.4 Other Execution Slicing-Based Techniques in Software Fault Localization

In addition to the techniques discussed above, execution slicing has also been applied to help developers locate real bugs in industrial settings. For example, Wong and Li [52] developed a tool suite, *eXVantage,* that was applied to a large and complex software system from Avaya during its implementation and testing phases. The results suggested that programmers and testers can benefit from using *eXVantage* to monitor the testing process, gain confidence about the quality of their software, detect bugs that are otherwise difficult to reveal, and identify performance bottlenecks in terms of the part of code most frequently executed.

3.5 Discussions

The concept of slicing has been widely used in the area of fault localization. Although there exist various types of slicing-based techniques, the core idea of slicing remains unchanged: to delete the parts of the program that can be determined to have no effect on the semantics of interests. In this way, developers can only focus on the statements with high suspiciousness. This is also the reason why the original motivation for program slicing was to aid fault localization during debugging activities. With respect to the techniques introduced in this chapter, each category of techniques has its unique advantage and disadvantages. First of all, the computational complexity of static slicing is the most insignificant among all slicing-based techniques and can therefore be attributed as a relatively efficient way for fault localization. Inevitably, a disadvantage of static slicing is that the slice for a given variable at a given statement contains all the executable statements that could possibly affect the value of this variable at the statement. As a result, it may generate a dice with certain statements that should not be included. This is because we cannot predict some run-time values via static analysis. To exclude such extra statements from a dice (as well as a slice), we need to use dynamic slicing instead of static slicing.

However, we cannot conclude that static slicing is rendered obsolete by dynamic slicing. We still require static slicing for some applications where the slice must be sound for every possible execution. For example, suppose we are interested in reusing the part of a program that implements a particularly efficient and well-tested approach to some problem. Often, in such situations (particularly with legacy code), the code we want to reuse will be intermingled with all sorts of other unrelated code that we do not want. In this situation, static slicing is ideal as a technique for extracting the part of the program we require, while leaving behind the part of the program we are not interested in.

This observation highlights the trade-off between the static and dynamic paradigms. Static slices will typically be larger but will cater to every possible execution of the original program. Dynamic slices will typically be much smaller, but they will only cater to a single input.

Another limitation of dynamic slicing is that they cannot capture execution omission errors, which may cause the execution of certain critical statements in a program to be omitted and thus result in failures [33]. To handle this shortcoming, execution slicing, relevant slicing, dual slicing, and other methods have been introduced and proven to be effective in these situations.

Another problem with the aforementioned slicing-based techniques is that the bug may not be in the dice. Even if a bug is in the dice, there may still be too much code that needs to be examined. To overcome this problem, an interblock data dependence-based augmentation and a refining method were proposed in [51]. The former includes additional code in the search domain for inspection based on its inter-block data dependence on the code currently being examined, whereas the latter excludes less suspicious code from the search domain using the execution slices of additional successful test cases. Additionally, slices are problematic because they are always lengthy and hard to understand. In [53], the notion of using barriers was proposed to provide a filtering approach for smaller program slices and better comprehensibility. Sridharan et al. [29] proposed thin slicing in order to find only producer statements that help compute and copy a value to a particular variable. Other statements that explained why producer statements affect the value of a particular variable were excluded from a thin slice.

3.6 Conclusion

In this chapter, we discuss state-of-the-art slicing-based techniques in the area of software fault localization. Three major types of slicing have been utilized in the techniques, namely, static slicing, dynamic slicing, and execution slicing. Different types of techniques have unique advantages and can be applied to different settings. For example, while static slicing-based techniques are easy to use and may not include additional computational overhead, dynamic slicing-based techniques are more accurate, but more time and endeavors are needed to generate these slices. Therefore, how to effectively and efficiently apply these techniques in real-life software projects still remains a challenge.

Notes

1 Part of Section 3.2 is from Ref. [4].
2 In this chapter, we use "bug" and "fault" interchangeably. We also use "programs" and "software" interchangeably.
3 Part of Section 3.2.2 is from Refs. [4, 9].
4 Part of Section 3.3 is from Ref. [13].
5 Other types of edges also exist in other applications like vectorizing compilers program dependence graphs, including anti-dependence and output-dependence, but for the purposes of program slicing, the data- and control-dependence suffice.
6 Part of Section 3.3.1 is from Refs. [1, 15].
7 Part of Section 3.3.3 is from Ref. [18].
8 Part of Section 3.3.4 is from Refs. [20, 21].
9 Part of Section 3.3.5 is from Ref. [22].
10 Part of Section 3.3.6 is from Ref. [27].
11 Part of Section 3.3.7 is from Ref. [30].
12 Part of Section 3.3.8 is from Refs. [32, 33].
13 Part of Section 3.4.1 is from Ref. [38].
14 Part of Section 3.4.2 is from Ref. [46].
15 Heuristic III was initially proposed by Wong et al. [47] and referenced as Wong3 by Naish et al. [48, 49]. This Heuristic was later revised by Wong et al. [46] with an improved fault localization effectiveness. Eq. (3.3) in this chapter is the revised Heuristic III. In particular, Heuristic III(c) with $\alpha = 0.0001$ is referenced as Wong4 by Naish et al. [48, 50].
16 Part of Section 3.4.3 is from Ref. [51].

References

1 Agrawal, H., DeMillo, R.A., and Spafford, E.H. (1991). An execution-backtracking approach to debugging. *IEEE Software* 8 (3): 21–26. ISSN 0740-7459. http://dx.doi.org/10.1109/52.88940.

2 Alves, E., Gligoric, M., Jagannath, V., and d'Amorim, M. (2011). Fault-localization using dynamic slicing and change impact analysis. *Proceedings of the 2011 26th IEEE/ACM International Conference on Automated Software Engineering (ASE '11)*, Lawrence, KS, USA (6–10 November 2011), 520–523. IEEE. https://doi.org/10.1109/ASE.2011.6100114.

3 Weiser, M.D. (1979). Program slices: formal, psychological, and practical investigations of an automatic program abstraction method. PhD thesis. Ann Arbor, MI, USA: University of Michigan. Order no. AAI8007856.

4 Liang, D. and Harrold, M.J. (2002). Equivalence analysis and its application in improving the efficiency of program slicing. *ACM Transactions on Software Engineering Methodology* 11 (3): 347–383. ISSN 1049-331X. http://doi.acm.org/10.1145/567793.567796.

5 Weiser, M. (1984). Program slicing. *IEEE Transactions on Software Engineering* SE-10 (4): 352–357. ISSN 0098-5589. https://doi.org/10.1109/TSE.1984.5010248.

6 Ottenstein, K.J. and Ottenstein, L.M. (1984). The program dependence graph in a software development environment. *ACM SIGSOFT Software Engineering Notes* 19 (5): 177–184. ISSN 0362-1340. http://doi.acm.org/10.1145/390011.808263.

7 Kaya, M. and Fawcett, J.W. (2012). A new cohesion metric and restructuring technique for object oriented paradigm. *2012 IEEE 36th Annual Computer Software and Applications Conference Workshops*, Izmir, Turkey (16–20 July 2012), 296–301. IEEE.

8 Lyle, J.R. and Weiser, M. (1987). Automatic program bug location by program slicing. *Proceedings of the 2nd International Conference on Computers and Applications*, Beijing, China (23–27 June 1987), 877–883. IEEE. ISBN 0-8186-0780-7.

9 Wong, W.E., Gao, R., Li, Y. et al. (2016). A survey on software fault localization. *IEEE Transactions on Software Engineering* 42 (8): 707–740. ISSN 0098-5589. https://doi.org/10.1109/TSE.2016.2521368.

10 Kusumoto, S., Nishimatsu, A., Nishie, K., and Inoue, K. (2002). Experimental evaluation of program slicing for fault localization. *Empirical Software Engineering* 7 (1): 49–76. ISSN 1573-7616. https://doi.org/10.1023/A:1014823126938.

11 Harrold, M.J. and Ci, N. (1998). Reuse-driven interprocedural slicing. *Proceedings of the 20th International Conference on Software Engineering*, Kyoto, Japan (19–25 April 1998), 74–83. IEEE. https://doi.org/10.1109/ICSE.1998.671104.

12 Tip, F. and Dinesh, T.B. (2001). A slicing-based approach for locating type errors. *ACM Transactions on Software Engineering and Methodology* 10 (1): 5–55. ISSN 1049-331X. http://doi.acm.org/10.1145/366378.366379.

13 Agrawal, H. and Horgan, J.R. (1990). Dynamic program slicing. *ACM SIGPLAN Notices* 25 (6): 246–256. ACM. ISSN 0362-1340. https://doi.org/10.1145/93548.93576.

14 Korel, B. and Laski, J. (1988). Dynamic program slicing. *Information Processing Letters* 29 (3): 155–163. ISSN 0020-0190. https://doi.org/10.1016/0020-0190(88)90054-3.

15 Agrawal, H., DeMillo, R.A., and Spafford, E.H. (1993). Debugging with dynamic slicing and backtracking. *Software: Practice and Experience* 23 (6): 589–616. https://doi.org/10.1002/spe.4380230603.

16 Wotawa, F. (2002). On the relationship between model-based debugging and program slicing. *Artificial Intelligence* 135 (1): 125–143. ISSN 0004-3702. https://doi.org/10.1016/S0004-3702(01)00161-8.

17 Wotawa, F. (2010). Fault localization based on dynamic slicing and hitting-set computation. *Proceedings of the 2010 10th International Conference on Quality Software (QSIC '10)*, Zhangjiajie, China (14–15 July 2010), 161–170. IEEE. ISSN 1550-6002. https://doi.org/10.1109/QSIC.2010.51.

18 DeMillo, R.A., Pan, H., and Spafford, E.H. (1996). Critical slicing for software fault localization. *Proceedings of the 1996 ACM SIGSOFT International Symposium on Software Testing and Analysis (ISSTA '96)*, San Diego, CA, USA (8–10 January 1996), 121–134. ACM. ISBN 0-89791-787-1. https://doi.org/10.1145/229000.226310.

19 Al-Khanjari, Z.A., Woodward, M.R., Ramadhan, H.A., and Kutti, N.S. (2005). The efficiency of critical slicing in fault localization. *Software Quality Journal* 13 (2): 129–153. ISSN 1573-1367. https://doi.org/10.1007/s11219-005-6214-x.

20 Zhang, X. (2006). *Fault Location via Precise Dynamic Slicing*. The University of Arizona.

21 Zhang, X., Gupta, N., and Gupta, R. (2007). Locating faulty code by multiple points slicing. *Software: Practice and Experience* 37 (9): 935–961. ISSN 0038-0644. http://dx.doi.org/10.1002/spe.v37:9.

22 Xin, B., Sumner, W.N., and Zhang, X. (2008). Efficient program execution indexing. *Proceedings of the ACM SIGPLAN 2008 Conference on Programming Language Design and Implementation*, Tucson, AZ, USA (7–13 June 2008), 238–248. ACM. ISBN 978-1-59593-860-2. https://doi.org/10.1145/1379022.1375611.

23 Zeller, A. and Hildebrandt, R. (2002). Simplifying and isolating failure-inducing input. *IEEE Transactions on Software Engineering* 28 (2): 183–200. ISSN 0098-5589. http://dx.doi.org/10.1109/32.988498.

24 Masri, W., Podgurski, A., and Leon, D. (2004). Detecting and debugging insecure information flows. *Proceedings of the 15th International Symposium on Software Reliability Engineering*, Saint-Malo, France (2–5 November 2004), 198–209. IEEE. ISSN 1071-9458. https://doi.org/10.1109/ISSRE.2004.17.

25 Zhang, Y. and Gupta, R. (2001). Timestamped whole program path representation and its applications. *Proceedings of the ACM SIGPLAN 2001 Conference on Programming Language Design and Implementation*, Snowbird, UT, USA (20–22 June 2001), 180–190. ACM. ISBN 1-58113-414-2. https://doi.org/10.1145/378795.378835.

26 Ferrante, J., Ottenstein, K.J., and Warren, J.D. (1987). The program dependence graph and its use in optimization. *ACM Transactions on Programming Languages and Systems* 9 (3): 319–349. ISSN 016-0925.

27 Weeratunge, D., Zhang, X., Sumner, W.N., and Jagannathan, S. (2010). Analyzing concurrency bugs using dual slicing. *Proceedings of the 19th International Symposium on Software Testing and Analysis*, Trento, Italy (12–16 July 2010), 253–264. ACM. ISBN 978-1-60558-823-0. https://doi.org/10.1145/1831708.1831740.

28 Larus, J.R. (1999). Whole program paths. *Proceedings of the 1999 ACM SIGPLAN Conference on Programming Language Design and Implementation (PLDI)*, Atlanta, GA, USA (1–4 May 1999), 259–269. ACM. ISBN 1-58113-094-5. https://doi.org/10.1145/301618.301678.

29 Sridharan, M., Fink, S.J., and Bodik, R. (2007). Thin slicing. *Proceedings of the ACM SIGPLAN 2007 Conference on Programming Language Design and Implementation*, San Diego, CA, USA (10–13 June 2007), 112–122. ACM. ISBN 978-1-59593-633-2. https://doi.org/10.1145/1250734.1250748.

30 Sumner, W.N. and Zhang, X. (2013). Comparative causality: explaining the differences between executions. *Proceedings of the 35th International Conference on Software Engineering (ICSE '13)*, San Francisco, CA, USA (18–26 May 2013), 272–281. IEEE. ISSN 0270-5257. https://doi.org/10.1109/ICSE.2013.6606573.

31 Zeller, A. (2002). Isolating cause-effect chains from computer programs. *Proceedings of the 10th ACM SIGSOFT Symposium on Foundations of Software Engineering (SIGSOFT '02/FSE-10)*, Charleston, SC, USA (18–22 November 2002), 1–10. ACM. ISBN 1-58113-514-9. https://doi.org/10.1145/587051.587053.

32 Gyimóthy, T., Beszédes, A., and Forgács, I. (1999). An efficient relevant slicing method for debugging. *Proceedings of the 7th European Software Engineering Conference Held Jointly with the 7th ACM SIGSOFT International Symposium on Foundations of Software Engineering (ESEC/FSE-7)*, Toulouse, France (6–10 September 1999), 303–321. Springer. ISBN 3-540-66538-2. https://doi.org/10.1007/3-540-48166-4_19.

33 Zhang, X., Tallam, S., Gupta, N., and Gupta, R. (2007). Towards locating execution omission errors. *Proceedings of the 28th ACM SIGPLAN Conference on Programming Language Design and Implementation (PLDI '07)*, San Diego, CA, USA (10–13 June 2007), 415–424. ACM. ISBN 978-1-59593-633-2. https://doi.org/10.1145/1250734.1250782.

34 Korel, B. (1988). PELAS - program error-locating assistant system. *IEEE Transactions on Software Engineering* 14 (9): 1253–1260. ISSN 0098-5589. https://doi.org/10.1109/32.6169.

35 Mao, X., Lei, Y., Dai, Z. et al. (2014). Slice-based statistical fault localization. *Journal of Systems and Software* 89: 51–62. ISSN 0164-1212. http://www.sciencedirect.com/science/article/pii/S0164121213002185.

36 Sterling, C.D. and Olsson, R.A. (2005). Automated bug isolation via program chipping. *Proceedings of the Sixth International Symposium on Automated Analysis-*

Driven Debugging, Monterey, CA, USA (19–21 September 2005), 748–752. ACM. https://dl.acm.org/doi/pdf/10.1145/1085130.1085134.

37 Qian, J. and Xu, B. (2008). Scenario oriented program slicing. *Proceedings of the 2008 ACM Symposium on Applied Computing*, Fortaleza, Ceara, Brazil (16–20 March 2008), 748–752. ACM. http://doi.acm.org/10.1145/1363686.1363861.

38 Agrawal, H., Horgan, J.R., London, S., and Wong, W.E. (1995). Fault localization using execution slices and dataflow tests. *Proceedings of the Sixth International Symposium on Software Reliability Engineering*, Toulouse, France (24–27 October 1995), 143–151. IEEE. https://doi.org/10.1109/ISSRE.1995.497652.

39 Beszedes, A., Gergely, T., Mihaly Szabo, Z. et al. (2001). Dynamic slicing method for maintenance of large C programs. *Proceedings of the Fifth European Conference on Software Maintenance and Reengineering*, Lisbon, Portugal (14–16 March 2001), 105–113. IEEE. https://doi.org/10.1109/CSMR.2001.914974.

40 Korel, B. and Yalamanchili, S. (1994). Forward computation of dynamic program slices. *Proceedings of the 1994 ACM SIGSOFT International Symposium on Software Testing and Analysis*, Seattle, WA, USA (17–19 August 1994), 66–79. ACM. ISBN 0-89791-683-2. http://doi.acm.org/10.1145/186258.186514.

41 Zhang, X., Gupta, R., and Zhang, Y. (2003). Precise dynamic slicing algorithms. *Proceedings of the 25th International Conference on Software Engineering (ICSE '03)*, Portland, OR, USA (3–10 May 2003), 319–329. IEEE. https://doi.org/10.1109/ICSE.2003.1201211.

42 Zhang, X., Gupta, R., and Zhang, Y. (2004). Efficient forward computation of dynamic slices using reduced ordered binary decision diagrams. *Proceedings of the 26th International Conference on Software Engineering*, Edinburgh, UK (28–28 May 2004), 502–511. IEEE. https://doi.org/10.1109/ICSE.2004.1317472.

43 Bellcore (1998). *χSuds Software Understanding System User's Manual.* Bridgewater, NJ, USA: Telcordia Technologies (formerly Bellcore). https://www.cs.purdue.edu/homes/apm/foundationsBook/Labs/coverage/xsuds.pdf.

44 Jones, J.A., Harrold, M.J., and Stasko, J. (2002). Visualization of test information to assist fault localization. *Proceedings of the 24th International Conference on Software Engineering*, Orlando, FL, USA (19–25 May 2002), 467–477. IEEE. https://doi.org/10.1145/581396.581397.

45 Wong, W.E., Sugeta, T., Qi, Y., and Maldonado, J.C. (2005). Smart debugging software architectural design in SDL. *Journal of Systems and Software* 76 (1): 15–28.

46 Wong, W.E., Debroy, V., and Choi, B. (2010). A family of code coverage-based heuristics for effective fault localization. *Journal of Systems and Software* 83 (2): 188–208. ISSN 0164-1212. https://doi.org/10.1016/j.jss.2009.09.037.

47 Wong, W.E., Qi, Y., Zhao, L., and Cai, K. (2007). Effective fault localization using code coverage. *Proceedings of the 31st Annual International Computer Software and Applications Conference* 1, Beijing, China (24–27 July 2007), 449–456. IEEE. https://doi.org/10.1109/COMPSAC.2007.109.

48 Lee, H.J. (2011). Software debugging using program spectra. PhD thesis. The University of Melbourne.

49 Naish, L., Lee, H.J., and Ramamohanarao, K. (2011). A model for spectra-based software diagnosis. *ACM Transactions on Software Engineering and Methodology* 20 (3): 11:1–11:32. ISSN 1049-331X. http://doi.acm.org/10.1145/2000791.2000795.

50 Lee, H.J., Naish, L., and Ramamohanarao, K. (2010). Effective software bug localization using spectral frequency weighting function. *Proceedings of the 2010 IEEE 34th Annual Computer Software and Applications Conference*, Seoul, South Korea (19–23 July 2010), 218–227. IEEE. https://doi.org/10.1109/COMPSAC.2010.26.

51 Wong, W.E. and Qi, Y. (2006). Effective program debugging based on execution slices and inter-block data dependency. *Journal of Systems and Software* 79 (7): 891–903. ISSN 0164-1212. http://dx.doi.org/10.1016/j.jss.2005.06.045.

52 Wong, W.E. and Li, J. (2005). An integrated solution for testing and analyzing Java applications in an industrial setting. *Proceedings of the 12th Asia-Pacific Software Engineering Conference*, Taipei, Taiwan (15–17 December 2005), 8. IEEE. https://doi.org/10.1109/APSEC.2005.39.

53 Krinke, J. (2004). Slicing, chopping, and path conditions with barriers. *Software Quality Journal* 12 (4): 339–360. ISSN 1573-1367. https://doi.org/10.1023/B:SQJO.0000039792.93414.a5.

4

Spectrum-Based Techniques for Software Fault Localization

W. Eric Wong[1], Hua Jie Lee[2], Ruizhi Gao[3], and Lee Naish[4]

[1] *Department of Computer Science, University of Texas at Dallas, Richardson, TX, USA*
[2] *School of Computing, Macquarie University, Sydney, NSW, Australia*
[3] *Sonos Inc., Boston, MA, USA*
[4] *School of Computing and Information Systems, The University of Melbourne, Melbourne, Australia*

4.1 Introduction

In software fault[1] localization, there are two types of analysis: static analysis and dynamic analysis. Static analysis [1] is always performed through examining program code and reasons over all possible behaviors that might arise at run time. This technique has been successful due to its use being unintrusive and not requiring running the program [2]. Dynamic analysis [1] is always performed through program execution. In practice, numerous test cases are written to ensure program requirements have been met. Test case failure leads to the discovery of bugs in the program code. Code coverage information can be captured using dynamic analysis. The analysis indicates the extent of the program code that has been executed by the test cases. Different types of code coverage can be used in dynamic analysis to locate potential faults in the program code. These types are statements, blocks, functions, predicates, and paths of programs.

Spectrum-based fault localization (SBFL) is a typical approach in dynamic analysis. It consists of information on the parts of a program that are executed during the test case executions. These parts can be statements, basic blocks, branches, or larger regions such as functions. In the context of this chapter, we use statements. Using statements is equivalent to considering basic blocks, assuming normal termination, where a statement within a basic block is executed if and only if the whole block is executed. De Souza et al. [3] proposed a concept map, which is shown in Figure 4.1, to better organize and represent knowledge in the field of SBFL. Through this map, we can identify the contribution of a paper to the area,

Handbook of Software Fault Localization: Foundations and Advances, First Edition.
Edited by W. Eric Wong and T.H. Tse.

Published 2023 by John Wiley & Sons, Inc.

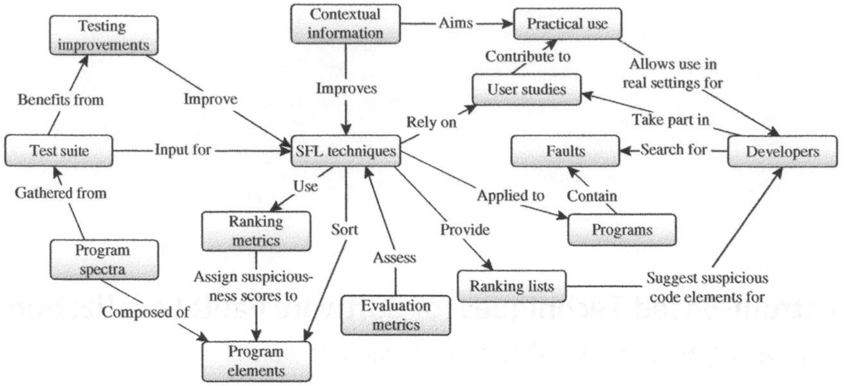

Figure 4.1 A concept map of SBFL. *Source:* de Souza et al. [3]/arXiv.

the issues that a study address, how studies relate to each other, and future research topics. Attention should be paid to the following observations:

- Different SBFL techniques have proposed different ranking metrics, and it seems that there is not a best ranking metric for all scenarios.
- Empirical studies have shown that some metrics produce equivalent results.
- Regarding evaluation metrics, many studies have focused on the number or percentage of program elements (e.g. lines of code (LOC)) that needs to be examined. Although this can be a criterion to compare different SBFL techniques, it may not be useful to evaluate how techniques will be used in practice as developers do not seem to be willing to examine a large chuck of code.
- There is a need for studies in real development settings, with professional developers, which can bring new findings to understand the practical use of SBFL.
- SBFL is a process that involves: (i) selecting test cases and spectra; (ii) calculating the suspiciousness of program elements; (iii) understanding the strengths and weaknesses of an SBFL technique through different characteristics of programs and their faults; (iv) measuring SBFL effectiveness; (v) proposing useful SBFL outputs; and (vi) assessing their practical use. By understanding and relating all these issues, we can propose ways to improve SBFL.

In this chapter, we focus on the following:

- introduce the concepts of program spectra and SBFL,
- describe spectra metrics, their characteristics, and equivalences of some spectra metrics,
- discuss strictly rational metrics, single bug optimal metrics, and deterministic bugs,

- present several empirical studies related to program spectra,
- explain different refinements studies of SBFL, and
- report empirical evaluations.

4.2 Background and Notation[2]

Let us assume that we have a program that consists of n executable statements. We consider program components to be executable statements with the understanding that, without loss of generality, they could just as easily have been other components such as functions, (basic) blocks, predicates, etc. Also consider that we have a test set that comprises of m different test cases. The program is executed against each of these test cases and execution traces are collected, each of which records which statements in the program are covered (executed)[3] by the corresponding test case. The information on which test cases lead to successful executions (successful test cases), and which ones to failed executions (failed test cases), is also recorded. A successful execution is one where the observed output of a program matches the expected output, and conversely, a failed execution is one where the observed output of the program is different from that which is expected. This is consistent with the taxonomy defined in [6] where a failure is defined as an event that occurs when a delivered service deviates from correct (i.e. expected) service.

The collected data can be represented as shown in Figure 4.2 which depicts a *coverage matrix* and a *result vector*. The former reports on if a statement has been

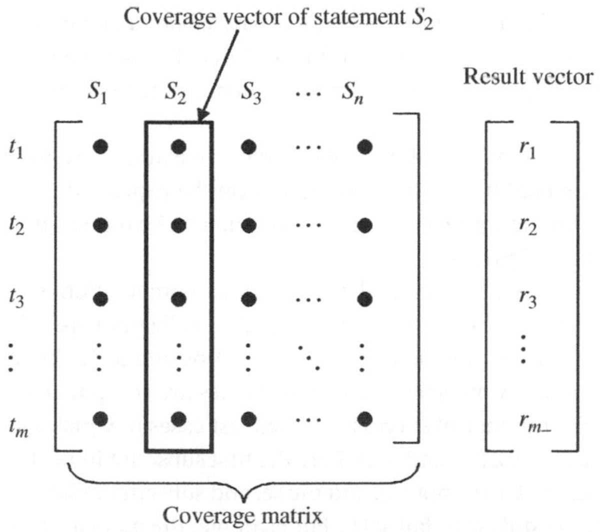

Figure 4.2 Data used in the fault localization process. *Source:* Debroy and Wong [4]/ACM.

covered by a test case, and the latter reports the outcome of the corresponding test case. The coverage matrix and the result vector are binary such that each entry (i, j) in the matrix is "1" if test case i covers statement j, and "0" if it does not; and each entry i in the result vector is "1" if test case i results in failure, and "0" if it is successful. Thus, each row of the coverage matrix reveals which statements have been covered by the corresponding test case, and each column provides the coverage vector of the corresponding statement.

4.2.1 Similarity Coefficient-Based Fault Localization

Intuitively, the *closer* (i.e. *more similar*) the execution pattern (i.e. the coverage vector) of a particular statement is to the failure pattern (result vector) of the test cases, the more likely the statement is to be faulty, and consequently the more suspicious the statement seems. By the same token, the *farther* (i.e. *less similar* or more *dissimilar*) the execution pattern of a statement is to the failure pattern, the less suspicious the statement appears to be. Similarity measures or coefficients[4] can therefore be used to measure this closeness/similarity, and the degree of similarity can be interpreted as the suspiciousness of the statements.

Binary similarity measures are typically expressed by Operational Taxonomic Units [7, 8], where each unit corresponds to a combination of matches and mismatches between the two vectors being evaluated for their similarity. Assuming two hypothetical vectors $\boldsymbol{u}$ and $\boldsymbol{v}$, by way of notation, a is the number of features for which values of $\boldsymbol{u}$ and $\boldsymbol{v}$ are both 1; b is the number of features for which $\boldsymbol{u}$ has a value of 0 and $\boldsymbol{v}$ has a value of 1; c is the number of features for which $\boldsymbol{u}$ has a value of 1 and $\boldsymbol{v}$ has a value of 0; and d is the number of features where both $\boldsymbol{u}$ and $\boldsymbol{v}$ have a value of 0. The sum $a + d$ represents the total number of matches between the two vectors, and the sum $b + c$ represents the total number of mismatches between the two vectors.

The aggregate sum $a + b + c + d$ represents the total number of features in either vector,[5] which is typically denoted by n. This information can be expressed via a 2×2 contingency table, and in the context of fault localization can be represented for any statement as shown in Figure 4.3.

Note that the quantities a, b, c, and d (and their various combinations) in Figure 4.3 have been annotated with their equivalent fault localization-specific terms. These annotations have been done to enhance readability, and to facilitate the discussions that are to follow. More specifically, four values are computed for each statement to indicate the number of successful/failed test cases in which the statement is/is not executed, a_{ns}, a_{nf}, a_{es}, and a_{ef}, where the first subscript indicates whether the statement is executed (e) or not (n), and the second subscript indicates whether the execution is successful (s) or failed (f). For example, the a_{es} of a statement refers to the number of successful test cases that have executed the

Figure 4.3 Contingency table in the context of fault localization. *Source:* Debroy and Wong [4]/ACM.

		Is the statement covered? Yes (1)	No (0)	SUM
Execution result	Failed (0)	a (a_{ef})	b (a_{nf})	$a+b$ (Φ_F)
	Successful (0)	c (a_{es})	d (a_{ns})	$c+d$ (Φ_S)
SUM		$a+c$ (Φ_E)	$b+d$ (Φ_N)	n (Φ)

statement. In addition, with respect to each statement, we use Φ_S, Φ_F, and Φ to represent the total number of successful test cases, the total number of failed test cases, and the total number of test cases, respectively; and Φ_E and Φ_N are the total number of test cases that have executed/not executed the statement. We have $\Phi_S + \Phi_F = \Phi$ and $\Phi_E + \Phi_N = \Phi$.

Each fault localization technique discussed herein consists of a suspiciousness function (or a ranking mechanism) that makes use of (some or all of) these quantities to assign a suspiciousness value to a statement. This approach is illustrated via an example Section 4.2.2.

4.2.2 An Example of Using Similarity Coefficient to Compute Suspiciousness

Consider the case where we have a program with five statements and six test cases as shown in Table 4.1. Different similarity measures may produce very different results, and to illustrate this, let us make use of the *s* similarity measure and the *Simple-Matching* similarity measure. Note that the former is also referred to as the Ochiai coefficient [7, 9] and has been shown to be effective at fault localization in [10]; and the latter, while not so effective at fault localization [10], is also referred to as the *Sokal and Michener* coefficient [7].

As per the taxonomical units shown in Figure 4.3, the cosine similarity (Ochiai coefficient) can be computed as:

$$\frac{a}{\sqrt{(a+b)(a+c))}} \quad \text{or} \quad \frac{a_{ef}}{\sqrt{\left(a_{ef}+a_{nf}\right)\times\left(a_{ef}+a_{es}\right)}} \tag{4.1}$$

Table 4.1 An example.

Test cases	Statements					Execution result
	S_1	S_2	S_3	S_4	S_5	
t_1	1	1	0	0	1	1
t_2	1	0	1	1	0	1
t_3	1	1	1	0	1	1
t_4	1	1	1	0	0	1
t_5	0	1	0	0	1	0
t_6	1	1	0	1	0	1

Source: Debroy and Wong [4]/ACM.

for any statement S. By the same convention, the Simple-Matching measure (Sokal and Michener coefficient) is computed as:

$$\frac{a+d}{a+b+c+d} \text{ or } \frac{a_{ef}+a_{ns}}{a_{ef}+a_{nf}+a_{es}+a_{ns}} \tag{4.2}$$

for any statement S. The respective suspiciousness values (along with the corresponding rankings), based on the application of the similarity coefficients to the example in Table 4.1, is presented in Table 4.2.

Table 4.2 shows statements ranked in decreasing order of their suspiciousness. Note that the Simple-Matching measure cannot distinguish between statements S_2 and S_3, and S_4 and S_5, assigning the same suspiciousness (and therefore, the same rank) to the respective pairs. In contrast, the cosine measure is able to distinguish each statement from the other, as it assigns each statement a different suspiciousness value (though this may not always be the case). This helps illustrate how the rankings produced using different similarity measures may vary considerably, and consequently, so might the resultant fault localization effectiveness.[6]

Table 4.3 gives some similarity coefficients that can be used to compute the suspiciousness of program statements. Hereafter, we treat each similarity coefficient

Table 4.2 Suspiciousness and rankings for the example in Table 4.1.

Statement	Simple-Matching		Cosine	
	Suspiciousness	Rank	Suspiciousness	Rank
S_1	1	1	1	1
S_2	0.667	2, 3	0.8	2
S_3	0.667	2, 3	0.775	3
S_4	0.334	4, 5	0.632	4
S_5	0.334	4, 5	0.516	5

Source: Debroy and Wong [4]/ACM.

Table 4.3 Some similarity coefficients used for fault localization.

Coefficient		Algebraic form	Coefficient		Algebraic form
1	Braun-Banquet	$\frac{a_{ef}}{\max\left(a_{ef}+a_{es},\ a_{ef}+a_{nf}\right)}$	17	Harmonic Mean	$\frac{\left(a_{ef}\times a_{ns}-a_{nf}\times a_{es}\right)\times\left(\left(a_{ef}+a_{es}\right)\times\left(a_{ns}+a_{nf}\right)+\left(a_{ef}+a_{nf}\right)\times\left(a_{es}+a_{ns}\right)\right)}{\left(a_{ef}+a_{es}\right)\times\left(a_{ns}+a_{nf}\right)\times\left(a_{ef}+a_{nf}\right)\times\left(a_{es}+a_{ns}\right)}$
2	Dennis	$\frac{\left(a_{ef}\times a_{ns}\right)-\left(a_{es}\times a_{nf}\right)}{\sqrt{n\times\left(a_{ef}+a_{es}\right)\times\left(a_{ef}+a_{nf}\right)}}$	18	Rogot2	$\frac{1}{4}\left(\frac{a_{ef}}{a_{ef}+a_{es}}+\frac{a_{ef}}{a_{ef}+a_{nf}}+\frac{a_{ns}}{a_{ns}+a_{es}}+\frac{a_{ns}}{a_{ns}+a_{nf}}\right)$
3	Mountford	$\frac{a_{ef}}{0.5\times\left(\left(a_{ef}\times a_{es}\right)+\left(a_{ef}\times a_{nf}\right)\right)+\left(a_{es}\times a_{nf}\right)}$	19	Simple-Matching	$\frac{a_{ef}+a_{ns}}{a_{ef}+a_{es}+a_{ns}+a_{nf}}$
4	Fossum	$\frac{n\times\left(a_{ef}-0.5\right)^2}{\left(a_{ef}+a_{es}\right)\times\left(a_{ef}+a_{nf}\right)}$	20	Rogers and Tanimoto	$\frac{a_{ef}+a_{ns}}{a_{ef}+a_{ns}+2\left(a_{nf}+a_{es}\right)}$
5	Pearson	$\frac{n\times\left(\left(a_{ef}\times a_{ns}\right)-\left(a_{es}\times a_{nf}\right)\right)^2}{\Phi_e\times\Phi_n\times\Phi_S\times\Phi_F}$	21	Hamming	$a_{ef}+a_{ns}$
6	Gower	$\frac{a_{ef}\times a_{ns}}{\sqrt{\Phi_F\times\Phi_e\times\Phi_n\times\Phi_S}}$	22	Hamann	$\frac{a_{ef}+a_{ns}-a_{nf}-a_{es}}{a_{ef}+a_{nf}+a_{es}+a_{ns}}$
7	Michael	$\frac{4\times\left(\left(a_{ef}\times a_{ns}\right)-\left(a_{es}\times a_{nf}\right)\right)}{\left(a_{ef}\times a_{ns}\right)^2+\left(a_{es}\times a_{nf}\right)^2}$	23	Sokal	$\frac{2\left(a_{ef}+a_{ns}\right)}{2\left(a_{ef}+a_{ns}\right)+a_{nf}+a_{es}}$
8	Pierce	$\frac{\left(a_{ef}\times a_{nf}\right)+\left(a_{rf}\times a_{es}\right)}{\left(a_{ef}\times a_{nf}\right)+\left(2\times\left(a_{nf}\times c_{ns}\right)\right)+\left(a_{es}\times a_{ns}\right)}$	24	Scott	$\frac{4\left(a_{ef}\times a_{ns}-a_{nf}\times a_{es}\right)-\left(a_{nf}-a_{es}\right)^2}{\left(2a_{ef}+a_{nf}+a_{es}\right)\left(2a_{ns}+a_{nf}+a_{es}\right)}$
9	Baroni-Urbani and Buser	$\frac{\sqrt{\left(a_{ef}\times a_{ns}\right)}+a_{ef}}{\sqrt{\left(a_{ef}\times a_{ns}\right)}+a_{ef}+a_{es}-a_{nf}}$	25	Rogot1	$\frac{1}{2}\left(\frac{a_{ef}}{2a_{ef}+a_{nf}+a_{es}}+\frac{a_{ns}}{2a_{ns}+a_{nf}+a_{es}}\right)$
10	Tarwid	$\frac{\left(n\times a_{ef}\right)-\left(\Phi_F\times\Phi_e\right)}{\left(n\times a_{ef}\right)+\left(\Phi_F\times\Phi_e\right)}$	26	Kulczynski	$\frac{a_{ef}}{a_{nf}+a_{es}}$
11	Ample	$\left\lvert\frac{a_{ef}}{\left(a_{ef}+a_{nf}\right)}-\frac{a_{es}}{\left(a_{es}+a_{ns}\right)}\right\rvert$	27	Anderberg	$\frac{a_{ef}}{a_{ef}+2\left(a_{nf}+a_{es}\right)}$

(Continued)

Table 4.3 (Continued)

Coefficient		Algebraic form	Coefficient		Algebraic form
12	Phi (Geometric Mean)	$\frac{a_{ef} \times a_{ns} - a_{nf} \times a_{es}}{\sqrt{(a_{ef} + a_{es}) \times (a_{ef} + a_{nf}) \times (a_{es} + a_{ns}) \times (a_{nf} + a_{ns})}}$	28	Dice	$\frac{2a_{ef}}{a_{ef} + a_{nf} + a_{es}}$
13	Arithmetic Mean	$\frac{2(a_{ef} \times a_{ns} - a_{nf} \times a_{es})}{(a_{ef} + a_{ns}) \times (a_{ns} + a_{nf}) + (a_{ef} + a_{nf}) \times (a_{es} + a_{ns})}$	29	Goodman	$\frac{2a_{ef} - a_{nf} - a_{es}}{2a_{ef} + a_{nf} + a_{es}}$
14	Cohen	$\frac{2(a_{ef} \times a_{ns} - a_{nf} \times a_{es})}{(a_{ef} + a_{ns}) \times (a_{ns} + a_{es}) + (a_{ef} + a_{nf}) \times (a_{nf} + a_{ns})}$	30	Jaccard	$\frac{a_{ef}}{a_{ef} + a_{nf} + a_{es}}$
15	Fleiss	$\frac{4(a_{ef} \times a_{ns} - a_{nf} \times a_{es}) - (a_{nf} - a_{es})^2}{(2a_{ef} + a_{nf} + a_{es}) + (2a_{ns} + a_{nf} + a_{es})}$	31	Sorensen-Dice	$\frac{2a_{ef}}{2a_{ef} + a_{nf} + a_{es}}$
16	Zoltar	$\frac{a_{ef}}{a_{ef} + a_{nf} + a_{es} + \frac{10000 \times a_{nf} \times a_{es}}{a_{ef}}}$			

Source: Wong et al. [5]/IEEE.

(a.k.a. a spectrum-based metric) as its own fault localization technique, and refer to the coefficient and the technique interchangeably. For example, unless otherwise specified, when we refer to the Ochiai fault localization technique (or just "Ochiai" for short) we mean a fault localization technique that makes use of the Ochiai coefficient, in the manner described in this section.

In addition to those in Table 4.3, there are other coefficient-based metrics. For example, Cosine, a more general version of the metric Ochiai, has been used in the field of information retrieval [12]. Kulczynski1 and Kulczynski2 have been introduced and evaluated in the field of clustering using the Self-Organizing Maps (SOM) algorithm [13, 14]. These metrics have since been used in the studies of software fault localization [10, 15, 16].

Naish et al. also evaluated the performance of a simplified version of O, called Binary, which ignores a_{ns} and allows programmers to see the relative importance of the two components of O [16]. Tarantula is another popular metric for fault localization. Table 4.4 gives a list of additional similarity coefficient-based metrics for fault localization that are not included in Table 4.3.

Table 4.4 Additional similarity coefficients used for fault localization.

Name	Formula	Name	Formula
Naish1 [16]	$\begin{cases} -1 & \text{if } a_{ef} < \Phi_F \\ a_{es} & \text{if } a_{ef} = \Phi_F \end{cases}$	Wong3 [17][a]	$a_{ef} - k$ where $k = \begin{cases} a_{es} & \text{if } a_{es} \le 2 \\ 2 + 0.1(a_{es} - 2) & \text{if } 3 \le a_{es} \le 10 \\ 2.8 + 0.001(a_{es} - 10) & \text{if } a_{es} \ge 11 \end{cases}$
Naish2 [16]	$a_{ef} - \frac{a_{es}}{\Phi_S + 1}$	O [16]	-1 if $a_{nf} > 0$; otherwise a_{ns}
CBI Inc. [18]	$\frac{a_{ef}}{a_{ef} + a_{es}} - \frac{\Phi_F}{\Phi_F + \Phi_S}$	O^p [16]	$a_{ef} - \frac{a_{es}}{a_{es} + a_{ns} + 1}$
q_e [19]	$\frac{a_{ef}}{a_{ef} + a_{es}}$	Binary [16]	$\begin{cases} 0 & \text{if } a_{ef} < \Phi_F \\ 1 & \text{if } a_{ef} = \Phi_F \end{cases}$
Tarantula [20]	$\frac{a_{ef}/\Phi_F}{a_{ef}/\Phi_F + a_{es}/\Phi_S}$	Russel and Rao [21]	$\frac{a_{ef}}{\Phi_F + \Phi_S}$
Euclid [13]	$\sqrt{a_{ef} + a_{ns}}$	Kulcznski2 [22]	$\frac{a_{ef}}{2\Phi_F} + \frac{a_{ef}}{2a_{ef} + 2a_{es}}$
Wong1 [17][a]	a_{ef}	Ochiai [23]	$\frac{a_{ef}}{\sqrt{\Phi_F(a_{ef} + a_{es})}}$
Wong2 [17][a]	$a_{ef} - a_{es}$		

[a] Wong1 (Heuristic I), Wong2 (Heuristic II), Wong3 (Heuristic III(a), III(b), III(c)) [17, 24]. See also Section 4.6.1. More details of these heuristics can be found in Section 3.4.2.

4.3 Insights of Some Spectra-Based Metrics[7]

We provide more insights on some metrics including O^p [16], Wong4 [25] (a.k.a. Heuristic III(c) with $\alpha = 0.0001$ [17]), Tarantula [26], and Ochiai [10, 23]. Referring to Figures 4.4–4.7, z-axis is the suspiciousness computed using these metrics, where the x- and y-axes are a_{es} and a_{ef}, respectively, for a range from 0 to 100.

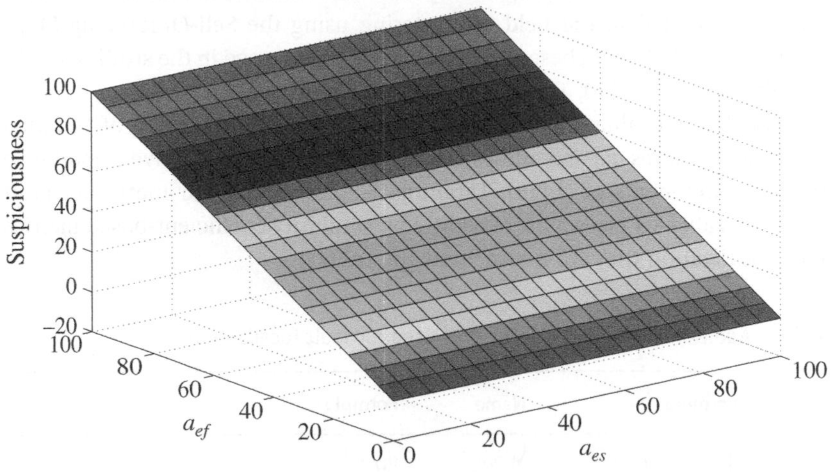

Figure 4.4 Surface for O^p metric. *Source:* Lee [25]/The University of Melbourne.

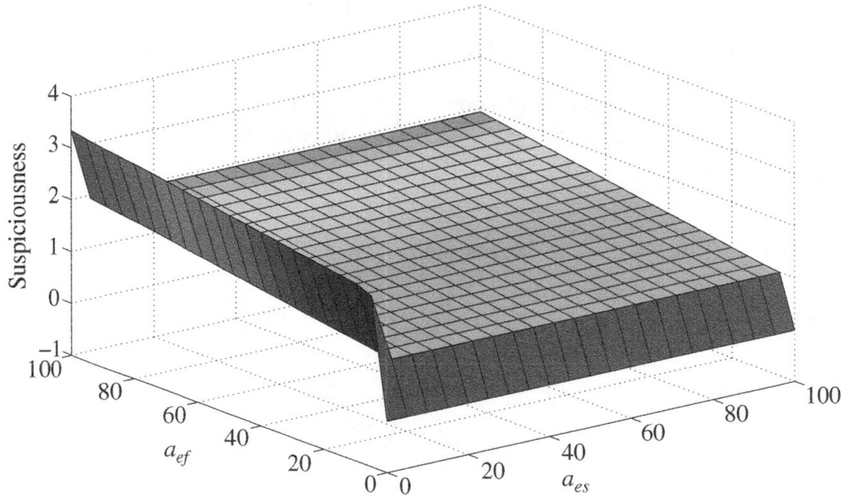

Figure 4.5 Surface for Wong4 metric. *Source:* Lee [25]/ The University of Melbourne.

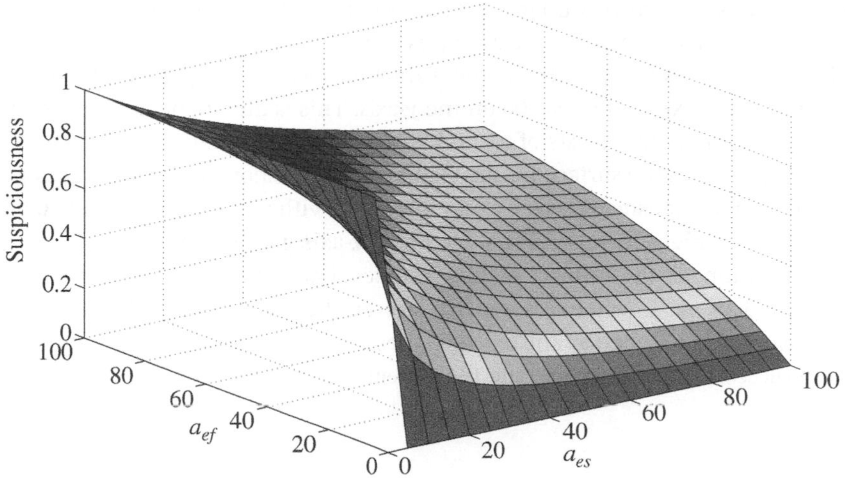

Figure 4.6 Surface for Tarantula metric. *Source:* Lee [25]/The University of Melbourne.

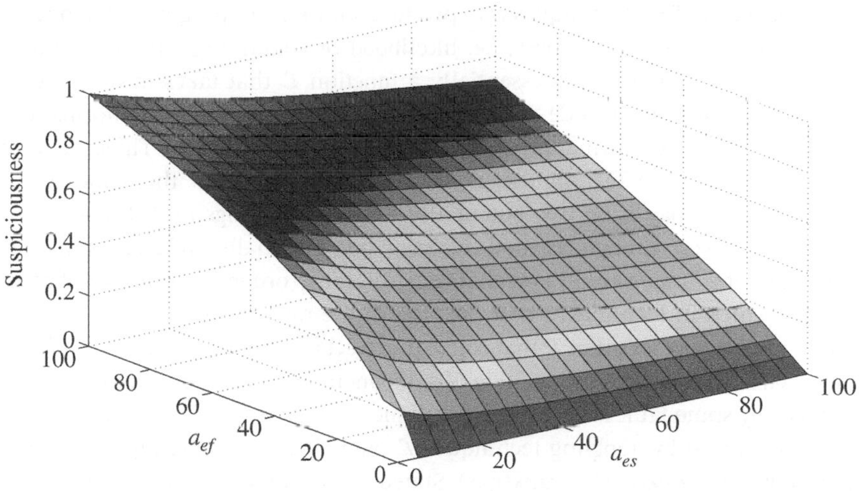

Figure 4.7 Surface for Ochiai metric. *Source:* Lee [25]/The University of Melbourne.

Figure 4.4 shows the surface of the O^p metric. It peaks on the suspiciousness value (z-axis) when the a_{ef} value (y-axis) is high. While the a_{ef} value is at the maximum and the a_{es} value increases, the surface of the O^p metric slants lower (the suspiciousness slightly drops). However, it is still higher than any other points on the surface.

Figure 4.5 shows the surface of the Wong4 metric. It shows an interesting surface that peaks along the y-axis, a_{ef}, when the x-axis, a_{es}, is at 0. When the y-axis, a_{ef}, is at

0, the surface skews downward to create a steep slope. It starts to create an upward slope in the surface when the y-axis, a_{ef}, is at 5.

Figure 4.6 shows the surface for the Tarantula metric. The peak is at 1 when $a_{es} = 0$ on the x-axis and $a_{ef} = 100$ on the y-axis. This is due to the metric design, where the numerator consists of a_{ef} and part of the denominator consists of a_{es}.

Figure 4.7 shows the surface for the Ochiai metric. It shows an increasing slope toward the suspiciousness (z-axis) as a_{ef} increases, with a minimum value of 0 on a_{es}. As the a_{es} values increase, the slope of the z-axis goes down.

In conclusion, all the surfaces of these metrics share an identical characteristic. These surfaces peak when a_{ef} and a_{es} are at the maximum and minimum, respectively, that is, when all the failed test cases execute that particular statement but no successful test cases execute the statement.

4.4 Equivalence Metrics[8]

The objective of SBFL techniques is to produce a ranking of program components (in order of their suspiciousness, i.e. likelihood of containing faults). An SBFL technique for this purpose is essentially a function $\mathcal{L}$ that takes in our case as input (x), consisting of code coverage and test execution result information, and transforms that information into a ranking of components (r). Thus, we have $\mathcal{L}(x) \rightarrow r$. Given two techniques, $\mathcal{L}_\alpha$ and $\mathcal{L}_\beta$ (operating on the same set of input data), we may have two potentially different rankings as $\mathcal{L}_\alpha(x) \rightarrow r_\alpha$ and $\mathcal{L}_\beta(x) \rightarrow r_\beta$. Even though r_α and r_β may be potentially different rankings (orderings), it is important to note that they still rank (order) the same set of components, which in turn means that the sizes of the rankings shall be the same.

With respect to a program $\mathcal{P}$ that consists of a set of components Ω, let $rank(r,s)$ be a function that returns the position of component $s \in \Omega$ with respect to ranking r produced by some fault localization technique. Two fault localization rankings r_α and r_β (produced by applying techniques $\mathcal{L}_\alpha$ and $\mathcal{L}_\beta$ to the same input data) are equal if, $\forall s \in \Omega$, $rank(r_\alpha,s) = rank(r_\beta,s)$. Stated simply, two fault localization rankings are equal if for every component, the position of the component is the same in either ranking. Note that this definition is independent of the suspiciousness values in components, and for the two rankings to be equal, it is not necessary that the suspiciousness value assigned to a component in one ranking be the same as the suspiciousness value assigned to the same component in the other ranking.

Furthermore, if two fault localization techniques $\mathcal{L}_\alpha$ and $\mathcal{L}_\beta$ always produce rankings that are equal to each other (regardless of the subject program considered), then the techniques are said to be *equivalent*, i.e. $\mathcal{L}_\alpha \equiv \mathcal{L}_b$. Clearly this is reflexive ($\mathcal{L}_\alpha \equiv \mathcal{L}_\alpha$), symmetric ($\mathcal{L}_\alpha \equiv \mathcal{L}_\beta \Leftrightarrow \mathcal{L}_\beta \equiv \mathcal{L}_\alpha$), and transitive (if $\mathcal{L}_\alpha \equiv \mathcal{L}_\beta$ and $\mathcal{L}_\beta \equiv \mathcal{L}_\theta$, then $\mathcal{L}_\alpha \equiv \mathcal{L}_\theta$), and hence represents an *equivalence* relation.

Though the equivalence relation defined above is equally applicable to any and all fault localization techniques, for the purposes of this chapter, we focus on SBFL techniques. Its applicability to other types of techniques is further discussed in detail in Section 4.4.1.

Lee et al. [19] prove that Tarantula always produces a ranking identical to that of a technique where the suspiciousness function is formulated as $a_{ef}/(a_{ef} + a_{es})$. Below, we prove the equivalence between other metrics.

The suspiciousness equations are statistical estimates rather than mathematical identities. Hence, they may not be valid when extrapolated to extremes. In the remainder of Section 4.4, we assume that the denominator of each equation is not zero.

Theorem 4.1 Sorensen-Dice ≡ Anderberg

The Sorensen-Dice metric [10] computes the suspiciousness for a statement S as

$$\frac{2a_{ef}}{2a_{ef} + a_{nf} + a_{es}}$$

which means

$$\frac{2 \times \mathit{failedExecuted}(S)}{2 \times \mathit{failedExecuted}(S) + \mathit{failedNotExecuted}(S) + \mathit{successfulExecuted}(S)} \tag{4.3}$$

The Anderberg metric [10] computes the suspiciousness as

$$\frac{a_{ef}}{a_{ef} + 2(a_{nf} + a_{es})}$$

which means

$$\frac{\mathit{failedExecuted}(S)}{\mathit{failedExecuted}(S) + 2 \times (\mathit{failedNotExecuted}(S) + \mathit{successfulExecuted}(S))} \tag{4.4}$$

Beginning with Eq. (4.3), i.e. Sorensen-Dice, dividing both the numerator and the denominator by $2 \times \mathit{failedExecuted}(S)$ has no effect on either the suspiciousness or the ranking. Hence, we have

$$\mathit{susp}(S) = \frac{1}{1 + \dfrac{\mathit{failedNotExecuted}(S) + \mathit{successfulExecuted}(S)}{2 \times \mathit{failedExecuted}(S)}} \tag{4.5}$$

Adding 1 to the denominator for the suspiciousness computation of every statement does not affect the ranking. Thus, it may be safely reduced to

$$susp(S) = \frac{\frac{1}{failedNotExecuted(S) + successfulExecuted(S)}}{2 \times failedExecuted(S)} \tag{4.6}$$
$$= \frac{2 \times failedExecuted(S)}{failedNotExecuted(S) + successfulExecuted(S)}$$

Finally, scaling the suspiciousness by a factor of 2 for each statement has no effect on the ranking, and therefore this is equivalent to

$$susp(S) = \frac{failedExecuted(S)}{failedNotExecuted(S) + successfulExecuted(S)} \tag{4.7}$$

Now, referring to Eq. (4.4), i.e. Anderberg, dividing both the numerator and the denominator by *failedExecuuted(S)* has no effect on either the suspiciousness or the final ranking. Hence, we have

$$susp(S) = \frac{1}{1 + \frac{2 \times (failedNotExecuted(S) + successfulExecuted(S))}{failedExecuted(S)}} \tag{4.8}$$

As before, adding 1 to the denominator in the case of every suspiciousness computation has no effect on the final ranking, and neither does dividing each suspiciousness value by 2. Thus, this may be reduced to

$$susp(S) = \frac{failedExecuted(S)}{failedNotExecuted(S) + successfulExecuted(S)} \tag{4.9}$$

Equation (4.9) is the same as Eq. (4.7), and since these transformations did not alter the rankings (they were order preserving), and therefore did not alter the effectiveness of either fault localization technique, we have successfully shown that Sorensen-Dice ≡ Anderberg.

By showing this equivalence, it is clear that if a fault localization technique performs better (or worse) than any one of these techniques (either Sorensen-Dice or Anderberg), then it also performs better (or worse) than the other. In [10], the Ochiai technique is compared to both Sorensen-Dice and Anderberg using case studies, which is somewhat redundant as shown above, i.e. only one comparison would have been sufficient. Thus, the notion of fault localization equivalence can help theoretically evaluate fault localization techniques with respect to one another, and as in this case, can eliminate the need for potentially time-consuming and costly empirical case studies.

The authors of [10] also compare the Ochiai technique to the Jaccard technique. However, we posit that such a comparison is also somewhat redundant because of the following claim.

Theorem 4.2 Jaccard ≡ Sorensen-Dice ≡ Anderberg

The Jaccard [10] metric computes the suspiciousness for a statement S as $\frac{a_{ef}}{a_{ef} + a_{nf} + a_{es}}$, which means

$$\frac{failedExecuted(S)}{failedExecuted(S) + failedNotExecuted(S) + successfulExecuted(S)} \tag{4.10}$$

Dividing both the numerator and the denominator by *failedExecuted*(S) has no effect on either the suspiciousness or the ranking. Hence, we have

$$susp(S) = \frac{1}{1 + \dfrac{failedNotExecuted(S) + successfulExecuted(S)}{failedExecuted(S)}} \tag{4.11}$$

Again, adding 1 to the denominator for the suspiciousness computation of every statement does not affect the ranking. Thus, it may be safely reduced to

$$\begin{aligned} susp(S) &= \frac{1}{\dfrac{failedNotExecuted(S) + successfulExecuted(S)}{failedExecuted(S)}} \\ &= \frac{failedExecuted(S)}{failedNotExecuted(S) + successfulExecuted(S)} \end{aligned} \tag{4.12}$$

The resultant equation (i.e. Eq. (4.12)) is the same as Eqs. (4.7) and (4.9), and therefore we can conclude that the Jaccard technique is equivalent to the Sorensen-Dice and Anderberg techniques, i.e. Jaccard ≡ Sorensen-Dice ≡ Anderberg.

Theorem 4.3 Simple-Matching ≡ Rogers and Tanimoto

Also evaluated for their fault localization effectiveness in [10] are the Simple-Matching and the Rogers and Tanimoto metrics. The former computes the suspiciousness for a statement as

$$\frac{failedExecuted(S) + successfulNotExecuted(S)}{failedExecuted(S) + failedNotExecuted(S) + successfulExecuted(S) + successfulNotExecuted(S)} \tag{4.13}$$

The latter can be expressed as $\frac{a_{ef} + a_{ns}}{a_{ef} + a_{ns} + 2(a_{es} + a_{ns})}$, which implies that the suspiciousness for a statement S would be computed as:

$$\frac{failedExecuted(S) + successfulNotExecuted(S)}{failedExecuted(S) + successfulNotExecuted(S) + 2 \times (successfulNotExecuted(S) + successfulExecuted(S))} \tag{4.14}$$

Starting from Eq. (4.13) (Simple-Matching), dividing both the numerator and the denominator by *failedExecuted(S)* + *successfulNotExecuted(S)* has no effect on either the suspiciousness or the ranking. This yields

$$susp(S) = \frac{1}{1 + \dfrac{failedNotExecuted(S) + successfulExecuted(S)}{failedExecuted(S) + successfulNotExecuted(S)}} \tag{4.15}$$

Following the same logic as discussed in the previous reductions, Eq. (4.15) can be converted to the equivalent form

$$susp(S) = \frac{failedExecuted(S) + successfulNotExecuted(S)}{failedNotExecuted(S) + successfulExecuted(S)} \tag{4.16}$$

Now, if we also divide the numerator and denominator of Eq. (4.14) by *failedExecuted(S)* + *successfulNotExecuted(S)*, we get

$$susp(S) = \frac{1}{1 + \dfrac{2 \times (failedNotExecuted(S) + successfulExecuted(S))}{failedExecuted(S) + successfulNotExecuted(S)}} \tag{4.17}$$

which, following the same steps as before, is reducible to

$$susp(S) = \frac{failedExecuted(S) + successfulNotExecuted(S)}{failedNotExecuted(S) + successfulExecuted(S)} \tag{4.18}$$

Equations (4.16) and (4.18) are the same, and therefore we can conclude that Simple-Matching ≡ Rogers and Tanimoto. This implies that another comparison conducted in [10] is unnecessary (in the sense that the extra comparison is redundant), and comparing against either Simple-Matching or Rogers and Tanimoto alone, would have been equivalent to comparing against the other.

The Simple-Matching coefficient can also be represented as:

$$susp(S) = \frac{failedExecuted(S) + successfulNotExecuted(S)}{TotalNumberofTestCases} \tag{4.19}$$

where the denominator corresponds to the total number of test cases, and is therefore a constant with respect to each statement. Since this is a nonzero constant, dividing the suspiciousness assigned to each statement by it results in no change to the relative order of the statements, i.e. the ranking. Thus, Eq. (4.19) can be equivalently written as:

$$susp(S) = failedExecuted(S) + successfulNotExecuted(S) \tag{4.20}$$

Since in the context of fault localization, Rogers and Tanimoto has been shown equivalent to Simple-Matching, and since Simple-Matching can be equivalently represented by Eq. (4.20), it follows that Rogers and Tanimoto can also be represented by Eq. (4.20).

Even though not explicitly proved in [4, 16, 27], interested readers will find that

- Simple-Matching, Rogers and Tanimoto, Hamming, Hamann, and Sokal are equivalent to each other as they can all be simplified to $(a_{ef} + a_{ns})/(a_{nf} + a_{es})$.
- Kulczynski, Anderberg, Dice, Goodman, Jaccard, and Sorensen-Dice are equivalent to $a_{ef}/(a_{nf} + a_{es})$.
- Scott and Rogot1 are equivalent because Scott equals $4 \times$ Rogot1 $-$ 1.
- Harmonic Mean and Rogot2 are equivalent as Rogot2 equals (Harmonic Mean + 2)/4.

The above results will be used in Section 4.7.3.2 to avoid redundant cross-comparisons between D* and other similarity coefficient-based fault localization techniques.

4.4.1 Applicability of the Equivalence Relation to Other Fault Localization Techniques

We have restricted the use of the proposed equivalence relation to only prove the equivalence of various similarity coefficient-based metrics. However, we posit that the equivalence relation can also be easily applicable to other types of fault localization techniques. To better illustrate this, we select one of the fault localization techniques (Russell and Rao) evaluated in [10] and show that it is equivalent to a heuristic-based technique proposed in [17].

A common intuition in fault localization is that the suspiciousness of a statement is directly proportional to the number of failed test cases that cover/execute that statement [17, 26]. Based on this intuition alone, a heuristic-based technique, named Wong1 (as it is the first of several heuristics proposed in [17]), is evaluated by Wong et al. [17], that assigns a suspiciousness value to a statement *S* based on the metric:

$$susp(S) = a_{ef} = failedexecuted(S) \tag{4.21}$$

The Russell and Rao coefficient is defined as $\frac{a_{ef}}{a_{ef} + a_{nf} + a_{es} + a_{ns}}$, which, in the context of fault localization, is equivalent to:

$$susp(S) = \frac{failedExecuted(S)}{failedExecuted(S) + failedNotExecuted(S) + successfulExecuted(S) + successfulNotExecuted(S)} \tag{4.22}$$

Let us take a closer look at the suspiciousness functions for Wong1 (Eq. (4.21)) and Russell and Rao (Eq. (4.22)). Wong1 only makes use of the information provided by the failed test cases and ignores the successful test cases. Indeed, the suspiciousness function in Wong1 is also independent of the total number of failed test cases. In contrast, the Russell and Rao technique makes use of the information from successful test cases (using the variables *successfulExecuted(S)* and *successfulNotExecuted(S)*) and is also aware of the total number of failed test cases (because this is simply the quantity *failedExecuted(S)* + *failedNotExecuted(S)*).

On the other hand, the sum *failedExecuted(S)* + *failedNotExecuted(S)* + *successfulExecuted(S)* + *successfulNotExecuted(S)* is equal to the total number of test cases (the variable *TotalNumberofTestCases*), and so Eq. (4.22) may safely be rewritten as:

$$\frac{failedExecuted(S)}{TotalNumberofTestCases} \tag{4.23}$$

Note that *TotalNumberofTestCases* is a nonzero constant with respect to all of the statements, and so dividing each suspiciousness value by it will not alter the ranking of the statements in any way. Thus, Eq. (4.23) really just amounts to:

$$successfulExecuted(S) \tag{4.24}$$

But Eq. (4.24), which is an equivalent form of Russell and Rao, is in fact identical to Eq. (4.21), which corresponds to Wong1. Thus, we have Russell and Rao ≡ Wong1. In this manner, a *similarity coefficient*-based technique (which seemingly uses more information) is shown to be equivalent to a heuristic-based technique (which uses less information). Thus, the use of the equivalence relation is not just limited to similarity coefficient-based techniques but can equally be applied to other fault localization techniques as well.

4.4.2 Applicability Beyond Fault Localization

Given that certain similarity coefficients can be proven equivalent to one another when rankings (based on similarity) of objects are concerned, it follows that fault localization is just one domain of application where the equivalence relation applies. Indeed, in any area of research or practice, where some objects are to be ranked based on similarity, the proofs of equivalency among the similarity coefficients discussed here, shall still apply. The contributions of this section, therefore, are not necessarily limited to fault localization.

However, it is equally relevant to recognize that the equivalency of the similarity coefficients may not apply when absolute values of similarity are concerned, as opposed to the relative values that are used in the formation of rankings. Consider the case where two objects are clustered together if their similarity is greater than

0.7 (just an example threshold value). In this case, the results based on using the Jaccard, Sorensen-Dice, and/or Anderberg coefficients clearly may not be the same, even though in terms of similarity-based rankings they were shown to be equivalent. Thus, it is very important that the equivalency relation not be incorrectly applied outside of its appropriate context.

4.5 Selecting a Good Suspiciousness Function (Metric)[9]

Choosing a good metric to compute the suspiciousness is important. Unfortunately, no single metric is good for all scenarios. To solve this problem, we address the following three issues:

- cost of using a metric (Section 4.5.1),
- optimality for programs with a single bug (Section 4.5.2), and
- optimality for programs with deterministic bugs (Section 4.5.3).

4.5.1 Cost of Using a Metric

One way to measure the cost of a fault localization technique is to use the rank of the highest ranked faulty statement as a percentage of the total number statements. In general, only statements that are executed by at least one test case are counted [5, 10, 16, 17]. If a faulty statement is ranked the highest, which is the best case, the rank is 1. That is, we only need to examine one statement and will be able to locate the bug. This gives the minimum cost.

For most programs and sets of test cases, we cannot expect a faulty statement to be ranked strictly higher than all correct statements, whatever metric is used to produce the ranking. For example, statements in the same basic block as the faulty statement(*s*) (namely, the bug) will be tied with this bug in the ranking, since they have the same a_{ef} and a_{es}. Furthermore, if there are statements with higher a_{ef} and lower a_{es}, they will be ranked higher than the bug. By explicitly considering such statements, we can determine how much of the cost of fault localization could potentially be avoided by choosing a different suspiciousness function (metric) and how much is unavoidable.

The cost of fault localization using a metric is defined by Definition 4.1.

Definition 4.1 (Rank Cost)
Given a ranking of S statements, the rank cost is $(GT + EQ/2)/S$*, where GT is the number of correct statements ranked strictly higher than all bugs, and EQ is the number of correct statements ranked the same as the highest ranked bug.*

A partial order of statements with respect to a metric is defined by Definition 4.2.

Definition 4.2 ($=^{\mathbf{M}}, \leq^{\mathbf{M}}, <^{\mathbf{M}}$)

*Given two statements x and y with respect to a metric **M**:*

$$x =^{\mathbf{M}} y \ \text{if } a_{ef}^{x} = a_{ef}^{y} \wedge a_{es}^{x} = a_{es}^{y}$$

$$x \leq^{\mathbf{M}} y \ \text{if } a_{ef}^{x} \leq a_{ef}^{y} \wedge a_{es}^{x} \geq a_{es}^{y}$$

$$x <^{\mathbf{M}} y \ \text{if } x \leq^{\mathbf{M}} y \wedge \neg\left(a_{ef}^{x} =^{\mathbf{M}} a_{ef}^{y}\right)$$

The unavoidable cost of fault localization is defined by Definition 4.3. This cost is independent of the choice of metric.

Definition 4.3 (Unavoidable Cost)

*Given a set of S statements and a metric **M**, the unavoidable cost is the minimum of UC_b for all bugs b, where*

$$UC_b = \frac{GT_b' + EQ_b'/2}{S}.$$

GT_b' is the number of correct statements c such that $b <^{\mathbf{M}} c$.
EQ_b' is the number of correct statements c such that $b =^{\mathbf{M}} c$.

The unavoidable cost gives a lower bound of using a metric for fault localization. In practice, it is unrealistic to expect that we can achieve a cost as low as the unavoidable cost. However, if the rank cost in Definition 4.1 of using a metric is very close to the unavoidable cost for all scenarios, this metric is good enough and there is no need in searching for other metrics. On the other hand, if there is a wide gap between the rank cost and the unavoidable cost for some faulty programs and sets of test cases, we may be able to reduce the gap with different metrics. A risk of doing so is that it may increase the gap for other programs. If this happens, we cannot determine whether the *new* metric is better or worse than the *original* metric. Hence, the rule of thumb is that reducing the gap on one program should not increase the gap on another program. As a result, there is no single metric that achieves the unavoidable cost for all programs and test sets. Also, if more data than what presents in Figure 4.2 is available for fault localization, the unavoidable cost defined here may no longer be valid.

4.5.2 Optimality for Programs with a Single Bug

The optimality of metrics for programs with a single bug discussed in [16] is presented in Definition 4.4.

Definition 4.4 (Single Bug Optimality)
A metric $\boldsymbol{M}$ *is single bug optimal if the following conditions are satisfied:*

- *When* $a_{ef} < \Phi_F$, *the value returned is always less than any value returned when* $a_{ef} = \Phi_F$.
- *When* $a_{ef} = \Phi_F$, $\boldsymbol{M}$ *is strictly decreasing in* a_{es}.

There are two conditions for a metric to be optimal within the context of our discussion. The first condition is motivated by the fact that for a single bug program, the bug must be executed by all failed test cases. Since $a_{ef} = \Phi_F$ for the bug, statements for which $a_{ef} < \Phi_F$ will be ranked strictly lower. The second condition is motivated by the fact that the bug tends to have a lower a_{es} value than correct statements. Naish et al. [16] proposed a metric O^p defined below to be single bug optimal.

$$a_{ef} - \frac{a_{es}}{a_{es} + a_{ns} + 1} \tag{4.25}$$

4.5.3 Optimality for Programs with Deterministic Bugs

Deterministic bugs are those that cause test case failure whenever they are executed [18] (note that the term "deterministic" here only relates to this definition; it is not about whether the behavior of a program is completely determined by the test case). The relationship between the performance of similarity coefficient-based fault localization and how consistently bugs lead to execution failure has been studied [15, 25]. The term "error detection accuracy," q_e, was used to describe bug consistency in [15] and defined by

$$q_e = a_{ef} / \left(a_{ef} + a_{es}\right) \tag{4.26}$$

Although deterministic bugs (where $q_e = 1$) have been noted in literature, this class of bugs has attracted relatively little attention in fault localization research. In part, this is due to the fact that they are often eliminated early in software development. The vast majority of fault localization efforts is devoted to finding bugs that are not deterministic, so the execution of them results in failure only in some cases (and quite often a very small proportion). For example, the average q_e for bugs in the Siemens Test Suite is only 0.12 [25]. There are no established benchmark sets of deterministic bug programs. In contrast, single bug programs have attracted far more interest, and most of the larger sets of benchmark programs have a strong bias toward single bugs.

Here, we show an interesting relationship between programs with a single bug and programs with only deterministic bugs. This leads to an optimality result for deterministic bug programs analogous to that for single bug programs.

For the bug in a single bug program, $a_{ef} = \Phi_F$ and (equivalently) $a_{nf} = 0$. For deterministic bugs, $a_{es} = 0$ and $a_{ns} = \Phi_S$. With this observation, we can define the class of deterministic bug optimal metrics based on the dual of the class of single bug optimal metrics.

Definition 4.5 (Deterministic Bug Optimality)
A metric $\boldsymbol{M}$ *is deterministic bug optimal if the following conditions are satisfied:*

- *When* $a_{es} > 0$*, the value returned is always less than any value returned when* $a_{es} = 0$.
- *When* $a_{es} = 0$*,* $\boldsymbol{M}$ *is strictly increasing in* a_{ef}.

This class of metrics is indeed optimal for programs with only deterministic bugs, in that no other monotone metric can result in a smaller rank cost.

In summary, Naish et al. [30] identify a class of strictly rational fault localization techniques in which the suspicious value of a statement strictly increases if this statement is executed by more failed test cases and strictly decreases if this statement is executed by more successful test cases. They claim that strictly rational techniques do not necessarily outperform those that are not. Therefore, limited attention should be given to these strictly rational techniques. In [28], Naish et al. further identify a class of optimal fault localization techniques for locating deterministic bugs (similar to Bohrbugs defined in [31]) that will always cause test cases to fail whenever they are executed.

4.6 Using Spectrum-Based Metrics for Fault Localization[10]

In this subsection, we will describe how spectra-based metrics can be used for fault localization, and how to improve their effectiveness by reducing the code that needs to be examined to locate program bugs.

4.6.1 Spectrum-Based Metrics for Fault Localization

Program spectra were introduced by Reps et al. [33] to be used in resolving the problem of the Y2K (year 2000) bug [34]. Reps et al. [33] proposed using the path-based spectra coverage approach, where the path spectrum for each test case execution is compared. They compared the test case executions on the program code before and after the year 2000. The differences could be used to identify the path(s) that caused the Y2K problem. In their study, they suggested several approaches to instrument the paths of the program, listed below:

1) at the source-code (program code) level,
2) as part of compilation by using intermediate representations,
3) as object-code-level transformation by modifying the object-code files, and
4) as post-loader transformation by modifying the executable files.

Jones et al. pioneered the development of a software visualization debugging tool, Tarantula, to distinguish bugs in the program, particularly for imperative language [35]. They instrumented the program code at the statement level. In order to gather statement-based spectra coverage for the program code, they used test suites to execute the program code.

Jones et al. [20] proposed two approaches to distinguish the statements that are likely to be faulty. The first, the discrete approach, uses a three-color system (red, green, and yellow) to visualize statements. Statements that are only executed by successful test case(s) are visualized as green. Statements are visualized as red if they are only executed by failed test case(s). Statements executed by both successful and failed test cases are visualized as yellow. They found that this approach is not useful, as bugs could not be distinguished if the particular statement is executed by both successful and failed test cases.

The second approach, the *continuous approach*, is used to map the color of respective program statements using Definition 4.6. It defines the *low color,* which is red, as one end of the color spectrum, and the *color range* as the other higher end of the color spectrum. The color for a particular statement S is a single number representing a color in the color spectrum. In this definition, the proportion of the number of successful test cases that executed each statement was calculated as a fraction of the total number of successful and failed test cases executing that statement. This proportion forms the complement of one of the spectra metrics, Tarantula (see the metric in Eq. (4.27)). Any other spectra metrics in Table 4.3 can be applied in the visualization debugging tool.

Definition 4.6 *Color visualization using the continuous approach for a statement S can be expressed as follows:*

$$color = low\ color(red) + \left(\frac{\frac{a_{es}}{\Phi_S} \times 100\%}{\frac{a_{es}}{\Phi_S} \times 100\% + \frac{a_{ef}}{\Phi_F} \times 100\%} \right) \times color\ range$$

If most successful test cases execute a program statement, the mapping color shifts toward green. If most failed test cases execute a statement, the mapping color shifts toward red. If a program statement has been executed by a similar number of successful and failed test cases, the color is mapped toward yellow. The intuition of the proposed mapping color is to provide clear color mixtures representing how often the program statement is executed by successful and failed test cases. This helps indicate the likelihood that each statement of the program is faulty.

Jones et al. [20] used the *space* program [36] as their benchmark. This benchmark contains 20 single bug versions of 1000 test suites. The test suites consist of randomly selected test cases from the existing *space* test suite. They also created multiple-bug versions of *space*. In order to do so, they randomly selected two or more single bug versions of *space* and combined them as a multiple-bug program. The selected single bug program versions had to contain different bugs in order to form the multiple-bug versions of *space*. They observed that the Tarantula tool cannot distinguish multiple bugs in the program by using the color spectrum. Therefore, this approach is only useful for locating single bug programs.

Jones et al. [26] extended the previous study of Jones et al. [20] by proposing Tarantula as a metric Eq. (4.27) to locate faults. They used a similar statement-based spectra coverage as that in Jones et al. [20]. Instead of using color to visualize bugs, they used the Tarantula metric to rank program statements likely to be faulty. The empirical data suggests that Tarantula inspects less code before the first faulty statement is identified, making it a more effective fault localization technique when compared to others such as set union, set intersection, nearest neighbor, and cause transition [37].

In another work, Wong et al. proposed several spectra metrics based on successful and failed test cases [17, 24]. They emphasized that less weight should be given to successful (or failed) test cases if a particular statement has already been executed by many successful (or failed) test cases. A tool χSuds [38] was used to instrument and perform test executions on the program. Different metrics were proposed, including Heuristic I (a.k.a. Wong1 in [16, 25]), Heuristic II (Wong2), Heuristic III(a), III(b), and III(c) (Wong3 and Wong4).

For Heuristic I (Wong1), the suspiciousness value of a statement depends on the number of failed test cases. For Heuristic II (Wong2), the suspiciousness value of a statement depends on both the number of successful and failed test cases. In these two heuristics, they make no distinction between the contributions from different successful or failed test cases. The contribution provided by one failed test case is identical to that of each of the other failed test cases; similarly, a successful test case makes the same contribution as each of the other successful test cases. However, if a statement S has been executed by many successful test cases, then the contribution of each additional successful execution to the suspiciousness of S is likely to be less than that of the first few successful test cases. Similarly, if S has already been executed by many failed test cases, the contribution of each additional failed execution to the suspiciousness of *S* is likely to be less than the contribution of the first few failed test cases. Hence, they propose that for a given statement *S*, the contribution introduced by the first successful test case that executes it in computing its likelihood of containing a bug is higher than or equal to that of the second successful test case that executes it, which is higher than or equal to that of the third successful test case that executes it, and so on. Based on this, Heuristic III was initially proposed by Wong et al. [24] and referenced as Wong3 by Naish et al. [16, 25]. This Heuristic was later revised by Wong et al. [17] with an improved fault localization effectiveness. Heuristics III(a), III(b), and III(c) in this chapter are the revised Heuristic III. In particular, III(c) is referenced as Wong4 by Naish et al. [25, 32]. More details of these heuristics can be found in Section 3.4.2.

Abreu et al. proposed to use block-based[11] spectra in order to locate faults in programs [15]. Their study was mainly motivated by [33], and they were particularly interested in capturing the block-based spectra coverage (referred to as block hit spectra). In their study, if a particular block of the program was executed, it referred to the block hit spectra count. A comparison of the similarity of the blocks was made by applying metrics such as Ochiai and Jaccard in their empirical evaluation.

Dallmeier et al. proposed a development plugin known as Analyzing Method Patterns to Locate Errors (AMPLE) for Java IDE Eclipse [39]. They used Byte Code Engineering Library (BCEL) [40] for byte-code instrumentation of the program. In this study, program functions or methods belonging to the respective class of the program were referred to as method sequences. The input of this algorithm is instrumented functions (methods) of program code and test cases (one successful test case and all other test cases fail). Initially, a pair of successful and failed test case is executed to gather coverage of the sequences of methods (method sequence) invoked by the object of the respective classes of the program. This is followed by identifying the originating class of the method sequences. A comparison is made between the method sequence(*s*) of successful and failed test cases for each class in the program. Originating classes of the method sequence that only occur in failed test cases but not successful test cases are assigned more weight. This step is repeated for all the pairs of successful and failed test cases, and the weights of originating classes of the respective method sequences are aggregated. Finally, each class of the program is ranked based on the aggregated weights of the method sequences. The class of program ranked with the highest aggregated weights of method sequences is the most likely bug in the program code. They also proposed using flexibility to adjust the number of methods in a method sequence if the programmer cannot locate a bug. This study was later generalized by Abreu et al. and is better known as the Ample metric [15, 41].

Pinpoint was proposed as a framework to determine and locate faulty components in large Internet services on the J2EE platform [42]. Dynamic analysis was used to gather the web client request traces. Information about components that caused any failures (caught exceptions) in the client requests was gathered. This information took into account of components often used and not often used in client requests. The Jaccard metric was used in the framework to relate the similarity of these components with failures.

The Zoltar metric was developed in the Embedded Software Lab of the Delft University of Technology [43] as a modification of the Jaccard metric. A new term that includes a constant of 10 000 was introduced as the denominator of this metric, which distinguishes between non-faulty and faulty blocks of program. It has been used to compare fault localization performance with other metrics such as the Tarantula, Ochiai, and Jaccard metrics.

Le et al. proposed a technique that evaluates the suspiciousness ranking produced by a fault localization technique to indicate when this output should be used by developers [44]. They used SVM to build an oracle that suggests whether the rankings are reliable for inspection. They identified several features of programs to build the oracle, such as the number of failed test cases and number of program elements with the same suspiciousness. Ma et al. [45] proposed the vector table model to evaluate the fault localization performance of a ranking metric. Keller et al. found that only 88 of 350 bugs from the AspectJ program may be identifiable using SBFL [46]. Pearson et al. [47] showed that O^p performs better for seeded faults, while DStar and Ochiai perform better for real faults. Yu et al. presented a technique for distinguishing test cases that fail due to single faults from those that fail due to multiple bugs [48]. The technique creates test sets composed of one failed test case and all other test cases are successful. Then, they calculated the distance between a failed test case and its most similar successful test case. With the presence of multiple bugs, test cases with large distances were more likely to be related. Xia et al. [49] performed a user study with a total of 16 real bugs from four large open-source projects, with 36 professionals. The study found that both the accurate and mediocre of spectra-based fault localization can help professionals save their debugging time, and the improvements are statistically significant and substantial.

DiGiuseppe and Jones [50] conducted an experiment on six programs consisting of more than 72 000 multiple-bug versions. The results suggested that the impact of multiple bugs exerts a significant but slight influence on fault localization effectiveness. In addition, bugs were categorized according to four existing taxonomies, and they found no correlation between bug type and fault localization interference. In general, even in the presence of many bugs, at least one bug was found by fault localization with similar effectiveness. Additionally, fault localization interference is prevalent and exerts a meaningful influence that may cause a fault's localizability to vary greatly. Debroy and Wong showed that simultaneous faults can cause interferences in which some faults hide the incorrect behavior of other faults [51]. Conversely, some faults can help to manifest failures related to other faults. Lucia et al. [52] leveraged the diversity of existing techniques to better localize bugs using data fusion methods. Their approach consisted of three steps: score normalization, technique selection, and data fusion. The approach was bug specific, where the set of techniques to be fused was adaptively selected for each faulty program based on its spectra.

More discussions of other SBFL techniques can be found in Section 1.3.2 and [25].

4.6.2 Refinement of Spectra-Based Metrics

In recent years, there have been several studies that proposed refinements to the suspiciousness functions (metrics) discussed in the previous sections, including using more information of test coverage, enhancing the ranking approaches, and employing machine learning techniques.

After a suspiciousness ranking is produced, the top-ranked statement will be examined first and the second-ranked statement is only considered after the programmer determines that the top-ranked statement does not contain the bug. Stated differently, the statement with the highest probability of being faulty would be ranked highest. The next highest ranking would be the statement with the highest probability of being faulty given that the top-ranked statement is *correct*, and so on. This approach assumes a *perfect bug detection* as discussed in Section 4.7.3.9.3. Note that under this scenario the suspiciousness of a statement does not depend on the suspiciousness of other statements.

In contrast, Naish et al. proposed a weighted incremental approach [53] that depends on the set of top-ranked (suspect) statements. By no longer considering the top-ranked statement to be a suspect, the number of suspect statements executed by a test case decreases and the weights change potentially changing the ranking. Pseudo-random numbers are used to break the ties of weighted statements, and the highest ranked statement is selected in each iteration.

Lee et al. [32] proposed to use frequency execution counts (see Table 4.5) instead of the binary execution counts (see Table 4.6) with a value of "1" for being executed and "0" for not being executed. For a statement, the frequency information in Table 4.6 indicates how often it is executed by a test case, whereas the corresponding entry in Table 4.6 only shows whether the statement is executed by a test case.

These frequencies are incorporated into suspiciousness computation by using a frequency weighting function, which is a typical sigmoid function to map each frequency to a range of [0, 1]. A sigmoid function is also known as a sigmoid curve or a logistic curve and has been used in different fields including neural networks, biology, and economics [54]. Definition 4.7 defines a sigmoid function in the context of fault localization.

Table 4.5 Test coverage information (frequency counts) and program spectra for each test case.

	t_1	t_2	t_3	t_4	t_5	a_{ns}	a_{nf}	a_{es}	a_{ef}
S_1	60	2	100	0	38	1.00	0.12	1.00	2.88
S_2	70	65	90	0	45	1.00	0.00	1.00	3.00
S_3	25	35	0	4	0	1.02	1.00	0.98	2.00
S_4	80	30	0	42	0	1.00	1.00	1.00	2.00
S_5	42	0	37	48	81	0.00	1.00	2.00	2.00
S_6	0	59	0	0	17	1.01	2.00	0.99	1.00
Test result	Failed	Failed	Failed	Successful	Successful	—	—	—	—

Source: Adapted from Lee et al. [32]/IEEE.

Table 4.6 Test coverage information (binary) and program spectra for each test cases.

	t_1	t_2	t_3	t_4	t_5	a_{ns}	a_{nf}	a_{es}	a_{ef}
S_1	1	1	1	0	1	1	0	1	3
S_2	1	1	1	0	1	1	0	1	3
S_3	1	1	0	1	0	1	1	1	2
S_4	1	1	0	1	0	1	1	1	2
S_5	1	0	1	1	1	0	1	2	2
S_6	0	1	0	0	1	1	2	1	1
Test result	Failed	Failed	Failed	Successful	Successful	—	—	—	—

Source: Adapted from Lee et al. [32]/IEEE.

Definition 4.7 (Adapted Sigmoid Function, SIG)

$$\mathbf{SIG}(k_{St}) = \begin{cases} \dfrac{1}{e^{-\alpha k_{St}} + 1} & \text{if } k_{St} > 0 \\ 0 & \text{otherwise} \end{cases}$$

where k is the frequency count of statement S with respect to test case t, and α is a constant.

In this definition, α is a constant that can be chosen and applied easily. Lee et al. [32] used the adapted sigmoid function **SIG** to map nonzero frequency counts. When there is no execution (the frequency count is zero), the function

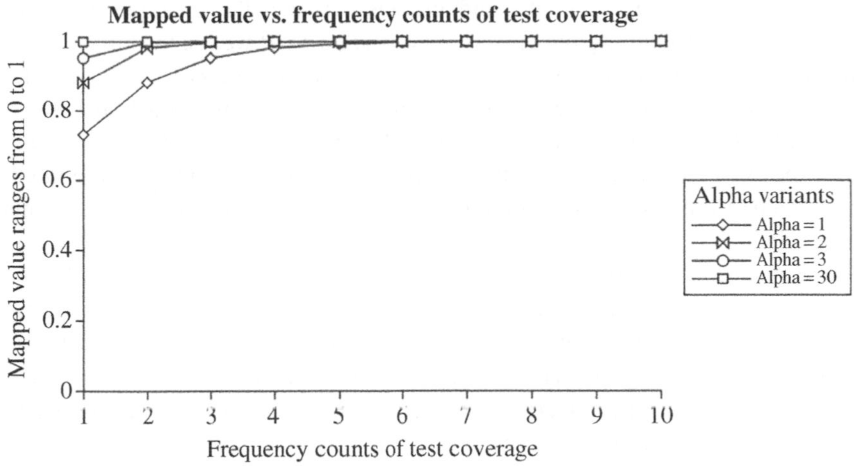

Figure 4.8 Mapped value vs. frequency counts. *Source:* Lee et al. [32]/IEEE.

SIG returns as 0. Different α values representing different frequency weighting functions have been proposed. For illustrative purposes, Figure 4.8 shows a simple mapping of the frequency counts (ranging from 1 to 10) using Definition 4.7 for different α variants (the α value being 1, 2, 3, and 30, respectively). When the frequency count is 0, the value mapped using the function for all the α values will be 0. Hence, this point is not shown in Figure 4.8. As the α value increases, the frequency weighting function curve is steeper. As the α values gets very large (in this example, the α value is 30), the mapping is equivalent to a step function of 0 and 1 similarly to using the binary information of execution count.

An example is shown on the differences of using the proposed frequency execution counts approach and the traditional binary weighting approach (binary information of execution count). Table 4.5 is the matrix of test execution information represented in the form of frequency execution counts. The total number of failed test cases is 3 ($\Phi_F = 3$) and the total number of successful test cases is 2 ($\Phi_S = 2$). Statements S_1 and S_2 have been executed by test case t_1 for 60 and 70 times, respectively. They have also been executed by test case t_2 for 2 and 65 times, respectively. Using the sigmoid function **SIG** defined in Definition 4.7 (assuming the α value is 1), the value mapped to (S_1 and t_2) is 0.88, and the value for (S_2 and t_2) is 1.00. Similarly, statement S_1 has been executed by test case t_1 and t_3 for 60 and 100 times, respectively. The value mapped to both (S_1 and t_1) and (S_1 and t_3) is 1. Statement S_2 has been executed by test case t_1 and t_3 for 70 and 90 times, respectively. The value mapped to both (S_2 and t_1) and (S_2 and t_3) is 1. Therefore, the a_{ef} values for S_1 and S_2 are 2.88 and 3.00, respectively. The a_{nf} and a_{ns} for the respective statements is by subtracting a_{ef} and a_{es} from Φ_F and Φ_S, respectively. For example, we have $a_{nf} = 3 - 2.88 = 0.12$ for S_1 and $a_{nf} = 3 - 3 = 0.00$ for S_2. If we use the binary information in Table 4.6, statements S_1 and S_2 have the same values of a_{ns}, a_{nf}, a_{es}, and a_{ef}. Note that from Table 4.5, S_2 is more likely to be faulty compared with S_1 because the former has a larger a_{ef} (3.00) than the latter (2.88). This shows that using the extra frequency counts information can further differentiate the likelihood of a particular statement being faulty, whereas the binary execution counts cannot do it.

In summary, different suspiciousness rankings will be produced even by the same fault localization technique when different values of α are applied to the sigmoid function **SIG** defined in Definition 4.7. As a result, different statements will be examined at different orders for their likelihood of containing program bugs. This has an impact on the effectiveness (the amount of code that needs to be examined) of fault localization techniques.

Debroy et al. [55] presented a grouping-based strategy (see Figure 4.9) to improve fault localization effectiveness. Given a faulty program to be examined and a set of test cases for the program, the strategy aims to group program components based on the number of failed executions (failed tests) that cover (execute) that component. A fault localization technique is used (without modifying the technique in any way) to assign a suspiciousness value to each program component. However, instead of producing a ranking based on the suspiciousness alone, the groups are first ranked such that a group that contains components that have

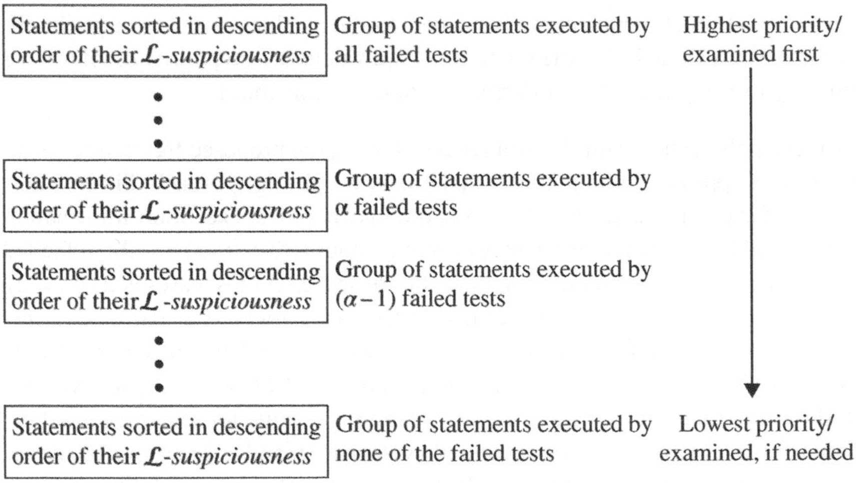

Figure 4.9 Ranking statements using the grouping-based strategy, where $\mathcal{L}$-suspiciousness refers to the suspiciousness computed using fault localizer $\mathcal{L}$. *Source:* Debroy et al. [55]/IEEE.

been covered by more failed tests is placed higher in the ranking. Then, within each group, the components are ranked in order of their suspiciousness (computed by using the chosen fault localizer) to produce the final ranking of components. Their empirical data suggest that this grouping-based strategy can indeed be used in conjunction with existing fault localization techniques to improve their effectiveness.

Xie et al. [56] used similar input of statement-based spectra coverage as [17, 24, 26] and spectra metrics to generate the ranking of the program statements likely to be faulty. From the ranked program statements, they proposed grouping statements into two groups and applying different heuristics to evaluate these groups of statements. More precisely, statements are grouped into a suspicious group, G_S, and a non-suspicious group, G_U. If a statement is executed by any failed test case ($a_{ef} > 0$), it is grouped as the former group. Otherwise, it is grouped as the latter group. An additional suspiciousness of 1 is added to statements in G_S. The suspiciousness of statements in group G_U is penalized by assigning small values, which is the minimum suspiciousness found in the group G_S.

Jones et al. proposed a parallel debugging technique that clusters failed test cases responsible for the respective bugs [57]. Gao and Wong [58] proposed MSeer, an extension of traditional fault localization technique used for programs with a single bug, for locating multiple bugs in parallel.

Högerle et al. investigated factors that impact debugging in parallel for multiple bugs [59]. They highlighted the infeasibility of obtaining pure failure clusters. Such clusters should contain entities and failed test cases entirely related to each fault. A trade-off is to obtain clusters that share program entities, causing what they called a *bug race*. Bug race means that faults can be present in more than one cluster. Another trade-off is obtaining clusters that share test cases instead of program entities. Bug races are avoided in this case, but some clusters may have no faulty program entities.

More discussion of fault localization on programs with multiple bugs appear in Chapter 12: Software Fault Localization for Programs with Multiple Bugs.

In addition, Cai and Xu proposed a technique that uses suspiciousness lists from previous ranking metrics [60]. A k-means algorithm is used to cluster statements of a program, using the suspiciousness rankings obtained from 28 metrics as the features of these statements.

Le et al. combined Tarantula (a SBFL technique) and IRFL (an information retrieval-based fault localization) [61] considering both bug reports and program spectra to map a particular bug to its possible location and identify suspicious words that are highly associated with a bug.

PRFL [62] uses PageRank to recompute the spectrum information by considering the contributions of different test cases.

Perez [63] proposed a topology-based analysis to estimate the program under a test coverage matrix when executed, based on the source code structure. The analysis chose which fault localization technique to use by creating a hierarchical model of the system.

Wang and Liu [64] proposed a hierarchical multiple predicate switching technique, called HMPS, to locate faults. HMPS restricts the search for critical predicates to the scope of highly suspect functions identified by employing SBFL techniques.

Jiang and Su [65] combined feature selection, clustering, and control flow graph traversal to generate faulty control flow paths that help reveal bug locations.

Xuan and Monperrus [66] proposed Multric, a learning-based approach that combines multiple ranking metrics for effective fault localization. In Multric, a suspiciousness score of a program entity is a combination of existing ranking metrics. Multric consists of two major phases: learning and ranking. Based on training faults, Multric builds a ranking model by learning from pairs of faulty and non-faulty source code elements. When a new fault appears, Multric computes the final ranking with the learned model.

Yoo [67, 68] reported that using genetic programming to develop ranking metrics can consistently outperform many human-designed ranking metrics such as Tarantula, Ochiai, Jaccard, and Ample.

4.7 Empirical Evaluation Studies of SBFL Metrics[12]

In this section, we present how to conduct empirical studies to cross-compare the effectiveness of different spectra-based fault localization techniques in terms of the amount code that needs to be examined in order to find a program bug.

There are many published studies on this subject. Below is an empirical evaluation using a technique named DStar (D*) [5, 69] to suggest suspicious locations for fault localization automatically without requiring any prior information on program structure or semantics. D* is evaluated across 24 different subject programs (see Table 4.7), including 7 programs in the Siemens suite, 10 programs in the Unix suite, and gzip, grep, make, Ant, space, flex, and sed. Each program consists of multiple different faulty versions.

D* is also compared to 38 different fault localization techniques, including 31 similarity coefficient-based techniques (Section 4.7.3.2), and 7 other contemporary techniques (Section 4.7.3.7). Both single-bug and multi-bug programs are used.

Table 4.7 Summary of subject programs.

Program		Lines of code	Number of faulty versions used	Number of test cases
Siemens suite	print_tokens	565	5	4 130
	print_tokens2	510	10	4 115
	schedule	412	9	2 650
	schedule2	307	9	2 710
	replace	563	32	5 542
	tcas	173	41	1 608
	tot_info	406	23	1 052
Unix suite	cal	202	20	162
	checkeq	102	20	166
	col	308	30	156
	comm	167	12	186
	crypt	134	14	156
	look	170	14	193
	sort	913	21	997
	spline	338	13	700
	tr	137	11	870
	uniq	143	17	431
	gzip	6 573	23	211
	grep	12 653	18	470
	make	20 014	29	793
	Ant	75 333	23	871
	space	9 126	34	13 585
	flex	13 892	22	525
	sed	12 062	20	360

Source: Adapted from Wong et al. [5]/IEEE.

An empirical evaluation is also included to illustrate how the effectiveness of D* increases as the exponent * grows, and then levels off when the exponent * exceeds a critical value. Discussions are presented to support such observations.

4.7.1 The Construction of D*

Let us first list our various intuitions regarding how the suspiciousness of a statement should be computed. Then, we construct a suspiciousness function such that it realizes each of these intuitions appropriately.

Intuition 4.1 The suspiciousness assigned to a statement should be *directly proportional* to the number of failed tests that cover it. The more frequently a statement is executed by failed tests, the more suspicious it should be.

Intuition 4.2 The suspiciousness assigned to a statement should be *inversely proportional* to the number of successful tests that cover it. The more frequently a statement is executed by successful tests, the less suspicious it should be.

Intuition 4.3 The suspiciousness assigned to a statement should be *inversely proportional* to the number of failed tests that do not cover it. If test cases fail without covering a particular statement, then that statement should be considered less suspicious.

Intuition 4.4 Intuition 4.1 is the most sound and should carry a higher weight. We should assign greater importance to the information obtained from observing which statements are covered by failed tests than that obtained from observing which statements are covered by successful tests or which are not covered by failed tests.

Such intuitions are also followed by other fault localization techniques proposed in studies such as [17, 26]. The first three intuitions are readily embodied by the Kulczynski coefficient which is expressed as $a_{ef}/(a_{nf} + a_{es})$. This approach, however, does not really lead to the realization of the fourth intuition, and so is not suitable by itself.

In such a situation, one might be tempted to multiply the numerator by some constant factor such as 2 to increase the weight given to a_{ef} as compared to a_{nf} and a_{es}. But such a modification is of no real benefit in the context of fault localization, as we only care about using the relative suspiciousness of one statement compared with another to produce a ranking of statements arranged in decreasing order of suspiciousness. Scaling the suspiciousness assigned to each statement by a constant factor (excluding zero and infinity) will result in no change to the internal order of the statements.

One solution is to make use of a coefficient such as $(a_{ef})^*/(a_{nf} + a_{es})$, where the value of * is greater than or equal to 1, to compute the suspiciousness of each statement. This coefficient corresponding to D* is thus a modification of the original Kulczynski coefficient, and is able to realize each of the four intuitions as prescribed. The value of * may vary. For discussion purposes, we set * to either 2 or 3 in Section 4.7.2. However, in the following case studies, * has a value in the range from 2 to 50 with an increment of 0.5 (namely, 2.0, 2.5, 3.0, etc.). Note that this approach is not the only way to realize said intuitions, and indeed many other suitable modifications may also be made. Additionally, there is no claim that the intuitions listed herein are the only intuitions that need to be followed in the context of fault localization. Instead, the usefulness of the proposed fault localization technique D*, and its underlying intuitions, is demonstrated via case studies, as presented in Section 4.7.3. Because it is not possible to theoretically prove if one fault localization technique shall always be more effective than another, such empirical validation is typically the norm for fault localization studies [10, 17, 26, 37, 70–74].

4.7.2 An Illustrative Example

Let us now walk through how D* can be applied to generate a ranking of statements for fault localization. Consider the program in Figure 4.10, which computes the sum of two integers. It has an error with regard to the sum computation in statement S_3, i.e. instead of adding the two integers, we accidentally subtract one from the other.

We also have a set of twelve test cases out of which eight execute successfully (t_5, t_6, t_7, t_8, t_9, t_{10}, t_{11}, and t_{12}), while the other four (t_1, t_2, t_3, and t_4) result in failures. The coverage information for each test case is also shown where a dot indicates that the corresponding statement is covered, and the absence of a dot indicates that the statement is not covered by that test case.

We begin by first collecting the required statistics (i.e. $a_{ef,}$ a_{es}, and a_{nf}) with respect to each statement. These statistics are shown in Table 4.8. The suspiciousness of each statement in Columns 5, 7, and 9 of Table 4.8 are computed using $a_{ef}/(a_{nf} + a_{es})$, which is Kulczynski (a.k.a. D^1), $(a_{ef})^2/(a_{nf} + a_{es})$ denoted as D^2, and $(a_{ef})^3/(a_{nf} + a_{es})$ denoted as D^3, respectively.

For Kulczynski, the suspiciousness of S_3 (the faulty statement) is 0.57, tied with S_4, but less than S_6 (1.00) and S_8 (0.67). As a result, three statements (S_6, S_8, and S_3) in the best case, and four (S_6, S_8, S_4, and S_3) in the worst case, have to be examined

Statement	Program (*P*)	t_1	t_2	t_3	t_4	t_5	t_6	t_7	t_8	t_9	t_{10}	t_{11}	t_{12}
		Coverage											
S_1	`read(a,b);`	•	•	•	•	•	•	•	•	•	•	•	•
S_2	`if (a < 10 && b < 10)`	•	•	•	•	•	•	•	•	•	•	•	•
S_3	`result = a - b; // Correct: a + b`	•	•	•	•		•	•	•	•	•	•	•
S_4	`if (result > 0)`	•	•	•	•		•	•	•	•	•	•	•
S_5	`print("positive");`	•					•	•			•	•	•
S_6	`else if (result == 0)`		•	•	•				•	•			
S_7	`print("zero");`		•							•			
S_8	`else print("negative");`			•	•				•				
S_9	`else print("invalid input");`					•							
Execution Results (0 = successful / 1 = failed)		1	1	1	1	0	0	0	0	0	0	0	0

Figure 4.10 A sample program with coverage and execution results for each test case. *Source:* Wong et al. [5]/IEEE.

Table 4.8 Computations of suspicious using Kulczynski, D^2, and D^3.

				Kulczynski (D^1)		D^2		D^3	
Statement	a_{ef}	a_{nf}	a_{es}	**Suspiciousness**	**Rank**	**Suspiciousness**	**Rank**	**Suspiciousness**	**Rank**
S_1	4	0	8	0.50	5	2.00	4	8.00	4
S_2	4	0	8	0.50	5	2.00	4	8.00	4
S_3	4	0	7	0.57	3	2.29	2	9.14	1
S_4	4	0	7	0.57	3	2.29	2	9.14	1
S_5	1	3	5	0.13	8	0.13	8	0.13	8
S_6	3	1	2	1.00	1	3.00	1	9.00	3
S_7	1	3	1	0.25	7	0.25	7	0.25	7
S_8	2	2	1	0.67	2	1.33	6	2.67	6
S_9	0	4	1	0.00	9	0.00	9	0.00	9

Source: Wong et al. [5]/IEEE.

to locate the fault. If D^2 is used, S_3 is tied with S_4 in suspiciousness, but only less than S_6. Hence, two statements (S_6 and S_3) need to be examined in the best case, and three statements (S_6, S_4, and S_3) in the worst case. When the value of * is increased to 3 (namely, using D^3), the suspiciousness of is S_3 still the same as S_4, but higher than the other statements. Hence, only one statement (S_3) needs to be examined in the best case, and two (S_4 and S_3) in the worst case. This example clearly demonstrates how D^* can be used to produce a ranking of program statements, and lead programmers to faults effectively. It also suggests that the effectiveness of D^* increases if a larger value of * is used.

Next, we will present a case study to evaluate D^* against a large set of subject programs, while comparing its effectiveness against other fault localization techniques.

4.7.3 A Case Study Using D*

We first describe the experimental design in detail (Sections 4.7.3.1–4.7.3.4), and then move on to presenting the results of the case studies (Section 4.7.3.5).

4.7.3.1 Subject Programs

In this study, we use nine different sets of programs: the Siemens suite, the Unix suite, gzip, grep, make, Ant, space, flex, and sed. These sets result in 24 different subject programs. An individual description of each set is as follows, with a comprehensive summary in Table 4.7.

The seven programs of the Siemens suite have been employed by many fault localization studies [17, 26, 70, 72–74]. All the correct and faulty versions of the programs and test cases were downloaded from [75]. The Unix suite consists of 10 Unix utility programs [76], and because these programs have been so thoroughly used in industry and research alike, they can be a reliable, credible basis for our evaluations. The Unix suite has also been used in other studies such as [77]. The space program[13] developed at the European Space Agency provides an interface that allows the user to describe the configuration of an array of antennas by using a high-level language. The correct version, its faulty versions, and a test suite were obtained from [75].

Version 1.1.2 of the gzip program (which reduces the size of named files) was downloaded from [75]. Also found at [75] were versions 2.2 of the grep program (which searches for a pattern in a file), 3.76.1 of the make program (which manages building of executables and other products from source code), 1.1 of the flex program (which generates scanners that perform lexical pattern-matching on text), and 2.0 of the sed program (which parses textual input and applies user-specified transformation to it). Because the above programs are all written in the C language, we also decided to use the Java-based Ant program (version 1.6

beta) from the same website. Also packaged with each of these programs was a set of test cases and faulty versions.

For the gzip, grep, make, flex, sed, and Ant programs, further faulty versions were created using mutation-based fault injection, in addition to the ones that were downloaded. This creation was done to enlarge our data sets, and because mutation-based faults have been shown to simulate realistic faults well and provide reliable, trustworthy results [73, 78–80]. For grep, additional faults from [73] were also used. For all of our subject programs, any faulty versions that did not lead to at least one failed test case in our execution environment were excluded. In this way, we assure that each fault examined would be revealed by at least one test case.

The subject programs vary dramatically, both in terms of their size based on the LOC, and their functionality. The programs of the *Siemens* and *Unix* suites are small-sized (less than 1000 LOC); the gzip and space programs are medium-sized (between 1000 and 10 000 LOC); the grep, make, flex, and sed programs are large (between 10 000 and 20 000 LOC); and the Ant program is of a very large size (more than 75 000 LOC). This variation allows us to evaluate across a very broad spectrum of programs, and have more confidence in the ability to generalize our results.

4.7.3.2 Fault Localization Techniques Used in Comparisons

Because the proposed D* technique has its origins in similarity coefficient-based analysis, we first compare it to other similarity coefficient-based techniques.

In addition to the Kulczynski coefficient, we compare D* with 30 other coefficients [16, 81]. They are listed in Table 4.3 along with their algebraic forms based on the notation described in Section 4.2. These coefficients have also been used in different studies such as [7, 9].

Note that we treat each similarity coefficient as its own fault localization technique. For example, unless otherwise specified, when we refer to the Kulczynski technique (or just "Kulczynski" for short), we mean a fault localization technique that uses the Kulczynski coefficient for computing suspiciousness.

Refer to Section 4.4, some coefficients are proved to be equivalent from the fault localization point of view because they always produce the same suspiciousness rankings [4, 16, 27]. However, this result only implies the same statement has the same position in different rankings, but not necessarily the same suspiciousness values. For example, Simple-Matching, Rogers and Tanimoto, Hamming, Hamann, and Sokal are equivalent to each other as they can all be simplified to $(a_{ef} + a_{ns})/(a_{nf} + a_{es})$, and Kulczynski, Anderberg, Dice, Goodman, Jaccard, and Sorensen-Dice are equivalent to $a_{ef}/(a_{nf} + a_{es})$. Coefficients Scott and Rogot1 are also equivalent because Scott equals $4 \times$ Rogot1 $- 1$. Moreover, we prove that Harmonic Mean and Rogot2 are equivalent as Rogot2 equals

(Harmonic Mean + 2)/4 even though this has not been previously shown in [4, 16, 27]. Such equivalence can avoid redundant cross-comparisons between D* and other similarity coefficient-based fault localization techniques.

In addition to the 31 similarity coefficient-based fault localization techniques in Table 4.3, D* is also compared with to other contemporary fault localization techniques (such as crosstab [74], radial basis function (RBF) [70], Heuristics III(b) and III(c) [17],[14] Tarantula [26], Ochiai [10, 23], as well as Ochiai2 [16, 23]), and present the corresponding results in Section 4.7.3.7.

4.7.3.3 Evaluation Metrics and Criteria

For one fault localization technique to be considered more effective (better) than another, we must have suitable metrics of evaluation. Three metrics are used in this paper.

4.7.3.3.1 The EXAM *Score*

Renieres et al. [37] assign a score to every faulty version of each subject program, which is defined as the percentage of the program that need not be examined to find a faulty statement in the program or a faulty node in the corresponding program dependence graph. This score or effectiveness measure is later adopted by Cleve and Zeller in [72] and is defined as 1-|N|/|PDG|, where |N| is the number of all nodes examined, and |PDG| is the number of all nodes in the program dependence graph. Instead of using such a graph, the Tarantula fault localization technique [26] directly uses the program's source code. To make their effectiveness computation comparable to those of the program dependence graph, Jones et al. [26] consider only executable statements to compute their score.

However, while the authors of [26] define their score to be the percentage of code that need not be examined to find a fault, we feel it is more straightforward to present the percentage of code that has to be examined to find the fault. This modified score is hereafter referred to as *EXAM*, and is defined as the percentage of statements that need to be examined until the first faulty statement is reached. Note that our main objective is to provide a good starting point for programmers to begin fixing a bug, rather than identifying all the code that would need to be corrected. From this perspective, even though a fault may span multiple, noncontiguous statements, the fault localization process is halted once the first statement corresponding to the bug is found. Many other fault localization studies observe the same philosophy.

A similar modification is made by the authors of [73]. They define their effectiveness (*T*-score) as $T = (|V_{\text{examined}}|/|V|) \times 100\%$, where $|V|$ is the size of the program dependence graph and $|V_{\text{examined}}|$ is the number of statements examined in a breadth-first search before a faulty node is reached.

In short, the effectiveness of various fault localization techniques can be compared based on the *EXAM* score, and for any faulty program, if the *EXAM* score assigned by technique **A** is less than that of technique **B**, then **A** is considered to be more effective (better) than **B**, as relatively less code needs to be examined to locate faults.

4.7.3.3.2 Cumulative Number of Statements Examined

In addition to using the *EXAM* score, we also consider the total (cumulative) number of statements that need to be examined with respect to all faulty versions of a subject program to find faults. Formally, for any of the given subject programs, supposing we have n faulty versions, and **A**(i) and **B**(i) are the number of statements that must be examined to locate the fault in the ith faulty version by techniques **A** and **B**, respectively, we can say that **A** is more effective than **B** if $\sum_{i=1}^{n} A(i) < \sum_{i=1}^{n} B(i)$.

4.7.3.3.3 Wilcoxon Signed-Rank Test

Additionally, to evaluate D* based on sound statistics, we make use of the Wilcoxon signed-rank test (an alternative to the paired Student's *t*-test when a normal distribution of the population cannot be assumed) [82]. Because we aim to show that D* is more effective than other fault localization techniques, we evaluate the one-tailed alternative hypothesis that the other techniques require the examination of an equal or larger number of statements than D*. The null hypothesis in this case specifies that the other techniques require the examination of a number of statements that is less than required by D*. Stated differently,

> H_0: Number of statements examined by other techniques < Number of statements examined by D*.

Thus, the alternative hypothesis is that D* will require the examination of fewer statements than the other techniques to locate faults, implying that D* is more effective.

4.7.3.4 Statement with Same Suspiciousness Values

The suspiciousness value assigned to a statement may not always be unique. This condition means that two or more statements might be assigned the same suspiciousness, and therefore be tied for the same position in the ranking. Assume that a faulty statement and some correct statements share the same suspiciousness. Then, in the best case, we examine the faulty statement first, and in the worst case, we examine it last and have to examine many correct statements before we discover the fault. We can assume that for the best effectiveness, the faulty statement is at the top of the list of statements with the same suspiciousness, and for the worst effectiveness, it is at the end of the list. In the following, data is presented for these two levels of effectiveness, across all the evaluation metrics (criteria).

Different techniques (such as [83]) can be used to break the ties. Refer to Chapter 11 for more discussion on this topic.

4.7.3.5 Results

With respect to the first evaluation criterion, Figure 4.11 gives a flavor of the results without burdening the readers with too much data. The subject program is Ant. The x-axis represents the percentage of code (statements) examined while the y-axis represents the number of faulty versions where faults are located by the examination of an amount of code less than or equal to the corresponding value on the x-axis. They clearly indicate the superiority of D^2 over the other techniques when evaluated using the *EXAM* score. The same conclusion also applies when D^2 is compared with other techniques in Table 4.3 using other subject programs in Table 4.7.

The reason why only three curves are displayed is purely in the interests of clarity and readability.

With respect to the second evaluation criterion, Table 4.9 gives the cumulative number of statements that need to be examined by each fault localization technique across each of the subject program under study, for both best and worst cases. These values correspond to the aggregate number of statements that each technique requires the examination to locate faults in all of the faulty versions per subject program, as opposed to per faulty version. It shows that D^2 is more effective than other techniques on most of the subject programs under study.

With respect to the third metric of evaluation, Table 4.10 presents data comparing D^2 to the other techniques using the Wilcoxon signed-rank test. Each entry in the table gives the confidence with which the alternative hypothesis (that D^2 requires the examination of fewer statements than a given technique to find faults, thereby making it more effective) can be accepted with respect to a selected program and the corresponding best or worst case.

To take an example, it can be said with 99.99% confidence that D^2 is more effective than Braun-Banquet on the Siemens suite for both the best and the worst cases. Similar observations can also be made for most of the scenarios in Table 4.10 with 99% confidence except for a few. Of the 558 scenarios (31 techniques each with best and worst cases for 9 sets of programs), only 9 have confidence less than 90%.

In summary, the above data suggest that D^2 is more effective than the similarity coefficient-based techniques in Table 4.3 at fault localization.

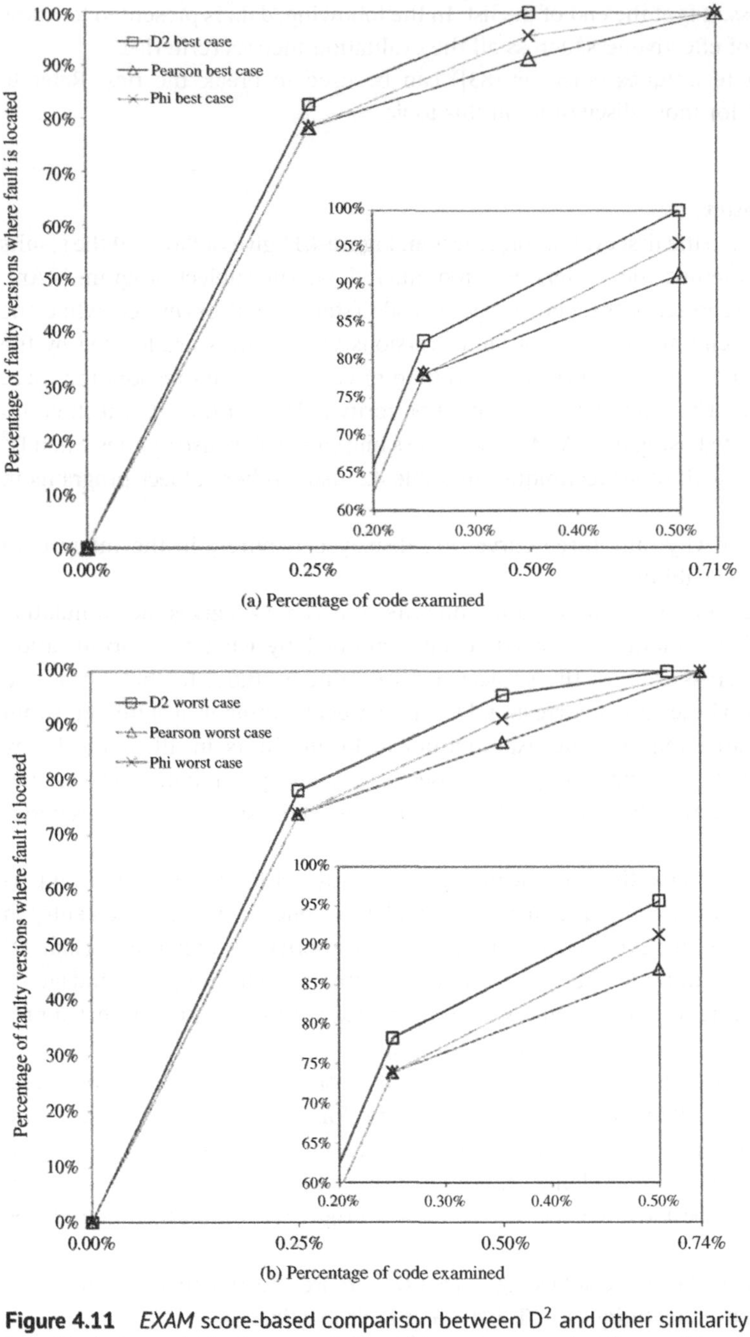

Figure 4.11 *EXAM* score-based comparison between D^2 and other similarity coefficient-based techniques: (a) best case on Ant and (b) worst case on Ant. *Source:* Wong et al. [5]/IEEE.

Table 4.9 Number of statements examined to locate faults for each of the subject programs.

	Best case									Worst case								
	Unix	Siemens	grep	gzip	make	Ant	space	flex	sed	Unix	Siemens	grep	gzip	make	Ant	space	flex	sed
D^2	1805	1754	2596	1215	7689	672	1300	810	1787	5226	2650	4053	2681	13130	1184	2375	1493	3937
Braun-Banquet	2767	2438	3507	1353	8667	2196	2630	1121	2259	6187	3296	4963	2804	14393	2698	3705	1850	4391
Dennis	2934	2206	4869	1955	11544	1974	2253	1651	2315	6504	3074	8030	3406	16757	2476	3328	3499	4448
Mountford	2183	1974	2991	1297	8471	3298	1801	1146	2092	5644	2832	4453	2762	23828	3818	2876	1864	4224
Fossum	2468	2230	13817	4542	16966	150415	4489	1816	5353	5843	3126	18781	6633	22179	150917	5564	2530	7490
Pearson	3581	3279	6003	1445	14515	1188	5766	5172	2837	7221	4247	9601	2896	19855	1690	6942	7068	4969
Gower	8630	6586	40877	22754	122073	967307	59315	48982	36375	12027	7434	42434	24205	127286	967809	63494	49696	38507
Michael	3713	1993	4400	2312	11694	4502	5425	1806	2451	7283	2864	7597	3763	16907	5004	6557	3654	4583
Pierce	11782	8072	15828	19222	28221	322033	57492	39485	24903	23387	15299	57131	38404	154221	1018725	106168	75918	63458
Baroni-Urbani and Buser	3189	3547	4080	1423	9027	4593	5037	985	3356	5605	4404	5536	2874	14240	5195	6112	1700	5488
Tarwid	3399	2453	5164	3105	13415	5964	3608	6527	4061	7883	3321	8611	4605	19467	9935	4826	8817	6655
Ample	3757	3336	7061	2032	16895	1801	6226	5315	3757	7378	4232	10582	3483	22141	3367	7303	7163	5889
Phi (Geometric Mean)	2524	2005	3486	1309	9409	1076	1790	1336	2068	6094	2873	6647	2760	14622	1578	2865	3184	4200
Arithmetic Mean	2615	2049	3683	1316	9621	1399	2031	1347	2014	6185	2917	6844	2767	14834	1901	3106	3195	4146
Cohen	2916	2419	3960	1338	9730	1837	2553	1383	2249	6486	3287	7121	2789	14943	2339	3628	3231	4381
Fleiss	4710	5631	17829	7377	33852	89263	14639	3741	8441	8083	6487	19285	8828	39065	89765	15714	4455	10573

(Continued)

Table 4.9 (Continued)

	Best case									Worst case								
	Unix	Siemens	grep	gzip	make	Ant	space	flex	sed	Unix	Siemens	grep	gzip	make	Ant	space	flex	sed
Zoltar	3449	1737	33634	12766	93284	709633	23497	20669	25633	6881	2635	35090	14217	98497	710135	27658	21383	27765
Harmonic Mean(1)	2675	2274	4021	1297	7745	1283	1770	2888	2053	6324	3142	7182	2748	12958	1785	2845	4736	4185
Rogot(2)	2675	2274	4021	1297	7745	1283	1770	2888	2053	6324	3142	7182	2748	12958	1785	2845	4736	4185
Simple Matching(2)	5545	6335	20952	9082	35461	250414	24352	6721	9895	8977	7187	22475	10637	41493	253631	25450	7466	13164
Rogers and Tanimoto(2)	5545	6335	20952	9082	35461	250414	24352	6721	9895	8977	7187	22475	10637	41493	253631	25450	7466	13164
Hamming(2)	5545	6335	20952	9082	35461	250414	24352	6721	9895	8977	7187	22475	10637	41493	253631	25450	7466	13164
Hammnn(2)	5545	6335	20952	9082	35461	250414	24352	6721	9895	8977	7187	22475	10637	41493	253631	25450	7466	13164
Sokal(2)	5545	6335	20952	9082	35461	250414	24352	6721	9895	8977	7187	22475	10637	41493	253631	25450	7466	13164
Scott(3)	4727	5564	17812	6964	24992	90160	14568	3805	8429	8100	6420	19268	8415	30205	90662	15643	4519	10561
Rogot1(3)	4727	5564	17812	6964	24992	90160	14568	3805	8429	8100	6420	19268	8415	30205	90662	15643	4519	10561
Kulczynski(4)	2361	2327	2971	1268	7909	1565	2107	856	2083	5777	3186	4427	2719	13283	2067	3182	1570	4215
Anderberg(4)	2361	2327	2971	1268	7909	1565	2107	856	2083	5777	3186	4427	2719	13283	2067	3182	1570	4215
Dice(4)	2361	2327	2971	1268	7909	1565	2107	856	2083	5777	3186	4427	2719	13283	2067	3182	1570	4215
Goodman(4)	2361	2327	2971	1268	7909	1565	2107	856	2083	5777	3186	4427	2719	13283	2067	3182	1570	4215
Jaccard(4)	2361	2327	2971	1268	7909	1565	2107	856	2083	5777	3186	4427	2719	13283	2067	3182	1570	4215
Sorensen-Dice(4)	2361	2327	2971	1268	7909	1565	2107	856	2083	5777	3186	4427	2719	13283	2067	3182	1570	4215

Coefficients with the same superscript enclosed in parentheses are equivalent with each other.

Source: Wong et al. [5]/IEEE.

Table 4.10 Confidence with which it can be claimed that D* is more effective than other techniques (best and worst cases).

	Unix		Siemens		grep		gzip		make		Ant		space		flex		sed	
	Best	Worst	Best	Worst	Best	Worst	Best	Worst	Best	Worst	Best	Worst	Best	Worst	Best	Worst	Best	Worst
Braun-Banquet	99.99%	99.99%	99.99%	99.99%	99.90%	99.85%	99.81%	98.05%	99.99%	99.55%	99.81%	99.22%	99.98%	99.99%	99.02%	99.93%	99.95%	99.27%
Dennis	99.99%	99.99%	99.99%	99.99%	99.61%	99.61%	99.99%	99.90%	99.99%	99.99%	99.81%	99.22%	98.44%	98.44%	99.90%	99.99%	99.90%	98.54%
Mountford	99.99%	99.99%	99.99%	99.99%	99.22%	99.81%	93.75%	87.50%	99.81%	97.63%	99.90%	99.81%	96.88%	96.88%	96.88%	99.81%	99.90%	98.93%
Fossum	99.99%	99.99%	99.99%	99.99%	99.81%	99.95%	99.22%	98.83%	99.61%	91.99%	99.22%	96.88%	99.61%	99.61%	93.75%	99.22%	98.44%	92.19%
Pearson	99.99%	99.99%	99.99%	99.99%	99.90%	99.99%	99.22%	94.53%	99.99%	99.99%	99.22%	96.88%	99.81%	99.90%	99.22%	99.90%	99.61%	98.05%
Gower	99.99%	99.99%	99.99%	99.99%	99.99%	99.99%	99.99%	99.99%	99.99%	99.99%	99.99%	99.99%	99.99%	99.99%	99.99%	99.99%	99.99%	99.99%
Michael	99.99%	99.99%	99.69%	99.54%	99.98%	99.98%	99.99%	99.99%	99.99%	99.99%	99.97%	99.97%	99.99%	99.99%	99.02%	99.02%	99.97%	99.96%
Pierce	99.99%	99.99%	99.99%	99.99%	99.99%	99.99%	99.99%	99.99%	99.99%	99.99%	99.99%	99.99%	99.99%	99.99%	99.99%	99.99%	99.99%	99.99%
Baroni-Urbani and Buser	99.99%	99.99%	99.99%	99.99%	99.90%	99.85%	99.81%	98.63%	99.99%	99.63%	99.81%	98.83%	99.81%	99.81%	96.88%	99.61%	99.81%	98.44%
Tarwid	99.99%	99.99%	99.99%	99.99%	99.98%	99.99%	99.99%	99.99%	99.99%	99.99%	99.99%	99.99%	99.99%	99.99%	99.99%	99.99%	99.99%	99.99%
Ample	99.99%	99.99%	99.99%	99.99%	99.90%	99.99%	99.98%	99.54%	99.99%	99.99%	95.70%	98.44%	99.51%	99.46%	99.81%	99.98%	99.41%	97.46%
Phi (Geometric mean)	99.99%	99.99%	99.99%	99.99%	99.61%	99.61%	96.88%	90.63%	99.99%	99.93%	99.22%	96.88%	87.50%	87.50%	96.88%	99.61%	99.22%	96.09%
Arithmetic mean	99.99%	99.99%	99.99%	99.99%	99.61%	99.61%	98.44%	92.19%	99.99%	99.93%	99.22%	96.88%	96.88%	96.88%	96.88%	99.61%	99.61%	97.27%
Cohen	99.99%	99.99%	99.99%	99.99%	99.81%	99.81%	99.81%	97.27%	99.99%	99.93%	99.61%	98.44%	99.22%	99.22%	99.22%	99.90%	99.81%	97.85%
Fleiss	99.99%	99.99%	99.99%	99.99%	99.90%	99.90%	99.98%	99.98%	99.99%	99.99%	99.99%	99.99%	99.51%	99.51%	99.61%	99.95%	99.41%	96.48%
Zoltar	99.99%	99.99%	93.14%	93.19%	99.99%	99.99%	99.99%	99.99%	99.99%	99.99%	99.99%	99.99%	99.99%	99.99%	99.99%	99.99%	99.99%	99.99%

(Continued)

Table 4.10 (Continued)

	Unix		Siemens		grep		gzip		make		Ant		space		flex		sed	
	Best	Worst	Best	Worst	Best	Worst	Best	Worst	Best	Worst	Best	Worst	Best	Worst	Best	Worst	Best	Worst
Harmonic mean(1)	99.99%	99.99%	99.99%	99.99%	99.02%	98.93%	93.75%	87.50%	82.45%	80.12%	94.92%	89.06%	98.13%	98.13%	96.88%	99.61%	98.44%	92.19%
Rogot2(1)	99.99%	99.99%	99.99%	99.99%	99.02%	98.83%	93.75%	87.50%	82.45%	80.12%	94.92%	89.06%	98.13%	98.13%	96.88%	99.61%	98.44%	92.19%
Simple Matching(2)	99.99%	99.99%	99.99%	99.99%	99.98%	99.99%	99.81%	99.71%	99.98%	99.99%	99.90%	99.81%	99.99%	99.99%	98.44%	99.95%	99.90%	99.22%
Rogers and Tanimoto(2)	99.99%	99.99%	99.99%	99.99%	99.98%	99.99%	99.81%	99.71%	99.98%	99.99%	99.90%	99.81%	99.99%	99.99%	98.44%	99.95%	99.90%	99.22%
Hamming(2)	99.99%	99.99%	99.99%	99.99%	99.98%	99.99%	99.81%	99.71%	99.98%	99.99%	99.90%	99.81%	99.99%	99.99%	98.44%	99.95%	99.90%	99.22%
Hamann(2)	99.99%	99.99%	99.99%	99.99%	99.98%	99.99%	99.81%	99.71%	99.98%	99.99%	99.90%	99.81%	99.99%	99.99%	98.44%	99.95%	99.90%	99.22%
Sokal(2)	99.99%	99.99%	99.99%	99.99%	99.98%	99.99%	99.81%	99.71%	99.98%	99.99%	99.90%	99.81%	99.99%	99.99%	98.44%	99.95%	99.90%	99.22%
Scott(3)	99.99%	99.99%	99.99%	99.99%	99.90%	99.90%	99.81%	99.41%	99.99%	99.99%	99.61%	98.44%	99.90%	99.90%	99.22%	99.90%	99.90%	98.54%
Rogot1(3)	99.99%	99.99%	99.99%	99.99%	99.90%	99.90%	99.81%	99.41%	99.99%	99.99%	99.61%	98.44%	99.90%	99.90%	99.22%	99.90%	99.90%	98.54%
Kulczynski(4)	99.99%	99.99%	99.99%	99.99%	99.22%	99.22%	96.88%	94.38%	96.88%	91.25%	99.61%	97.66%	99.22%	99.22%	96.88%	99.61%	99.61%	96.09%
Anderberg(4)	99.99%	99.99%	99.99%	99.99%	99.22%	99.22%	96.88%	94.38%	96.88%	91.25%	99.61%	97.66%	99.22%	99.22%	96.88%	99.61%	99.61%	96.09%
Dice(4)	99.99%	99.99%	99.99%	99.99%	99.22%	99.22%	96.88%	94.38%	96.88%	91.25%	99.61%	97.66%	99.22%	99.22%	96.88%	99.61%	99.61%	96.09%
Goodman(4)	99.99%	99.99%	99.99%	99.99%	99.22%	99.22%	96.88%	94.38%	96.88%	91.25%	99.61%	97.66%	99.22%	99.22%	96.88%	99.61%	99.61%	96.09%
Jaccard(4)	99.99%	99.99%	99.99%	99.99%	99.22%	99.22%	96.88%	94.38%	96.88%	91.25%	99.61%	97.66%	99.22%	99.22%	96.88%	99.61%	99.61%	96.09%
Sorensen-Dice(4)	99.99%	99.99%	99.99%	99.99%	99.22%	99.22%	96.88%	94.38%	96.88%	91.25%	99.61%	97.66%	99.22%	99.22%	96.88%	99.61%	99.61%	96.09%

Coefficients with the same superscript enclosed in parentheses are equivalent with each other.
Source: Wong et al. [5]/IEEE.

4.7.3.6 Effectiveness of D* with Different Values of *

In this section, we investigate the fault localization effectiveness (in terms of the total number of statements examined) of D* with respect to different values of * followed by a detailed discussion of our observations.

An empirical study was conducted to evaluate the impact different values of * have on the effectiveness of D*. The range used was from 2 to 50 with an increment of 0.5 (namely, * = 2.0, 2.5. 3.0, 3.5, ..., 50.0). From Figure 4.12, we observe that the total number of statements examined to locate all the bugs in each set of the Ant program declines (more precisely, the number of statements examined decreases in most cases while occasionally staying unchanged) as the value of * increases, and after that the number remains the same. For example, with respect to the Ant program, 672 statements need to be examined for D^2 in the best case, while the number decreases to 368 for D^3, and further down to 209 for D^6. That is, the effectiveness of D* increases as the value of * increases until it levels off. A similar observation was also made for other subject programs.

A more detailed discussion of how the effectiveness of D* varies along with * can be found in [5]. In particular, the following two questions are addressed:

- Why does the effectiveness of D* increase or remain the same as the value of * increases until it reaches a critical value?
- Why does the effectiveness of D* eventually level off?

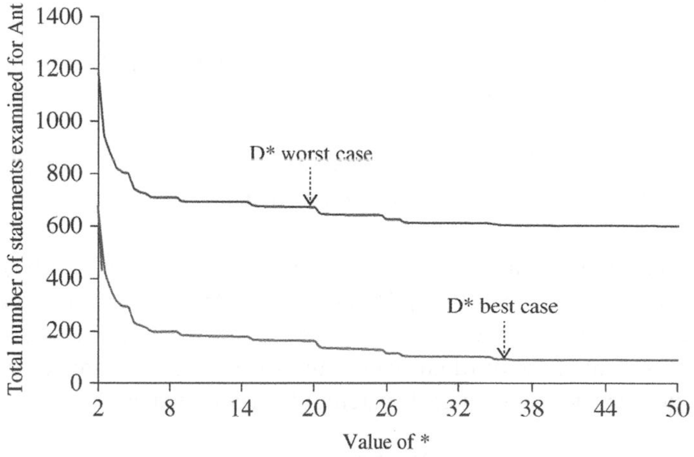

Figure 4.12 Fault localization effectiveness of D* with respect to different values of *. The subject program is Ant. *Source:* Wong et al. [5]/IEEE.

4.7.3.7 D* Versus Other Fault Localization Techniques

In Section 4.7.3.5, D* is cross-compared with other well-known similarity coefficients (Table 4.3) in the context of fault localization, and results suggest that D^2 (where * has a value of 2) is more effective than other competing techniques. However, additional techniques have been reported in other studies that also claim to be effective at fault localization, and so it is important to compare D* to such techniques as well. Since it is impossible to compare D* to all the techniques, a representative set is selected, each of which has been demonstrated to be effective, and compare D* to each of them: Tarantula [26], Ochiai [10, 23], Ochiai2 [16, 23], Heuristics III(b) and III(c) [17], crosstab [74], and RBF [70].

The Tarantula fault localization technique [26] assigns a suspiciousness value to each statement using Eq. (4.27).

$$\frac{\frac{a_{ef}}{\Phi_F}}{\frac{a_{ef}}{\Phi_F}+\frac{a_{es}}{\Phi_S}} \tag{4.27}$$

Tarantula has been shown to be more effective than several other fault localization techniques such as set union, set intersection, nearest neighbor, and cause transitions on the *Siemens* suite [26].

In [10], Abreu et al. evaluate the use of the Ochiai coefficient [23] in the context of software fault localization, which assigns a suspiciousness value to each statement using Eq. (4.28).

$$\frac{a_{ef}}{\sqrt{\Phi_F \times (a_{ef}+a_{es})}} \tag{4.28}$$

The Ochiai2 coefficient, proposed in [23] and used as a fault localization technique in [16], is defined in Eq. (4.29).

$$\frac{a_{ef} \times a_{ns}}{\sqrt{(a_{ef}+a_{es}) \times (a_{ns}+a_{nf}) \times (a_{ef}+a_{nf}) \times (a_{es}+a_{ns})}} \tag{4.29}$$

Furthermore, Wong et al. examined how each additional failed (or successful) test case can help locate program faults [17]. They concluded that the contribution of the first failed test is larger than or equal to that of the second failed test, which is larger than or equal to that of the third failed test, and so on. The same applies to successful tests. The suspiciousness of each statement is computed as

$$\begin{aligned}&\left[(1.0) \times n_{F,1} + (0.1) \times n_{F,2} + (0.01) \times n_{F,3}\right]\\&-\left[(1.0) \times n_{S,1} + (0.1) \times n_{S,2} + \alpha \times \chi_{F/S} \times n_{S,3}\right]\end{aligned} \tag{4.30}$$

where $n_{F,\,i}$ and $n_{S,\,i}$ are the number of failed and successful tests in the ith group, and $\chi_{F/S}$ is the ratio of the total number of failed to the total number of successful tests with respect to a given bug. The technique is named Heuristic III(b) when $\alpha = 0.001$, and Heuristic III(c) with $\alpha = 0.001$, which are different from the less-effective heuristics with the same names in their earlier study [24]. The improvement of [17] over [24] is due to an additional stipulation such that, if a statement has been executed by at least one failed test case, then the total contribution from all the successful tests that execute the statement should be less than the total contribution from all the failed tests that execute it.

Wong et al. presented a cross tabulation (crosstab)-based statistical technique for fault localization [74]. A unique aspect of this technique is that it is based on a well-defined statistical analysis, which has been used to study the relationship between two or more categorical variables [84–86]. In this case, the two variables are the *test execution result* (*success* or *failure*) and the *coverage of a given statement*. The null hypothesis is that they are statistically independent. However, instead of the so-called statistical dependence–independence relationship, we are more interested in the degree of association between the execution result and the coverage of each statement. More precisely, a crosstab is constructed for each statement with two column-wise categorical variables (*executed/covered* and *not executed/not covered*) and two row-wise categorical variables (*successful* and *failed*) to help analyze whether there exists a high (or low) degree of association between the coverage of a statement and the failed (or successful) execution result. In addition, a statistic is computed based on each table to determine the suspiciousness of the corresponding statement. More discussion of the crosstab fault localization technique appears in Chapter 5.

Wong et al. also proposed a fault localization technique using a modified RBF neural network [70]. Such a network consists of a three-layer feed-forward structure: one input layer, one output layer, and one hidden layer, where each neuron uses a Gaussian basis function [54] as the activation function with the distance computed using weighted bit comparison-based dissimilarity. The network is trained to learn the relationship between the statement coverage of a test case and its corresponding success or failure. Once the training is complete, a set of virtual test cases (each covering a single statement) is provided as input, and the output for each virtual test case is considered to be the suspiciousness of the covered statement. More discussion of the RBF fault localization technique appears in Chapter 6.

Table 4.11 presents data on the total number of statements to be examined by using D*, crosstab, RBF, Heuristics III(b) and III(c), Tarantula, Ochiai, and Ochiai2, to locate faults in all the faulty versions of each subject program for both the best and worst cases. As seen from the data, these seven techniques can be further divided into two groups based on their performance. Group I includes

Table 4.11 D^* versus crosstab, RBF, Heuristics III(b), Heuristics III(c), Tarantula, Ochiai, Ochiai2: Total number of statements examined to locate all the faults.

	Best case									Worst case								
	Unix	Siemens	grep	gzip	make	Ant	space	flex	sed	Unix	Siemens	grep	gzip	Make	Ant	space	flex	sed
D^2	1805	1754	2596	1215	7689	672	1300	810	1787	5226	2650	4053	2681	13130	1184	2375	1493	3937
D^3	1667	1526	2528	1084	7676	368	1241	800	1714	5088	2422	3985	2535	13117	880	2316	1490	3864
D^4	1594	1460	2462	1083	7442	293	1200	790	1694	5015	2356	3919	2534	12883	805	2275	1489	3844
D^5	1507	1435	2391	1081	7442	228	1193	769	1675	4928	2331	3848	2532	12883	740	2270	1483	3825
D^6	1455	1400	2358	1081	7442	209	1190	768	1652	4876	2298	3815	2532	12883	721	2265	1482	3802
D^7	1423	1386	2336	1081	7394	196	1185	763	1635	4844	2284	3793	2532	12835	708	2260	1477	3785
D^8	1421	1362	2323	1081	7315	196	1178	762	1629	4840	2260	3780	2532	12756	708	2253	1476	3779
D^9	1418	1328	2285	1081	7315	181	1176	762	1626	4838	2226	3742	2532	12756	693	2251	1476	3776
D^{10}	1415	1327	2279	1081	7315	181	1147	762	1626	4835	2225	3736	2532	12756	693	2222	1476	3776
D^*	1299 (* = 70)		1704 (* = 130)		6560 (* = 30)			674 (* = 115)		4757 (* = 35)				12001 (* = 30)			1393 (* = 115)	
crosstab	2524	2005	3486	1309	9409	1076	1790	1336	2068	6094	2873	6647	2760	14622	1578	2865	3184	4200
RBF	1302	2114	2015	2961	8908	233	1295	695	2977	4758	2980	3796	4412	13947	759	2375	1395	5074
H3b	1763	1439	2662	1530	8524	1358	2224	818	2905	5136	2335	4118	2982	13737	1860	3299	1532	5037
H3c	1717	1396	2345	1530	6911	1320	2199	692	2842	5090	2292	3801	2981	12124	1822	3274	1406	4974
Tarantula	3394	2453	5164	3105	13415	5964	3608	6527	4061	7704	3311	6906	4605	19467	9935	4826	7683	6655
Ochiai	1906	1796	2665	1265	7704	887	1369	840	1829	5322	2692	4121	2716	12917	1389	2444	1554	3961
Ochiai2	3345	2733	5075	1359	11701	1131	3392	2709	3271	7172	3726	8449	2810	16914	1633	4467	4776	5403

Note: The cell with a black background gives the smallest value of * such that D^* outperforms all the competing techniques.
Source: Table VI of Wong et al. [5]/IEEE.

Tarantula, Ochiai, and Ochiai2, which are in general less effective than the other four techniques (crosstab, RBF, III(b), and III(c)) in Group II).

With respect to the *EXAM* score, D* (with an appropriate value for *) performs better than other techniques. This result is consistent with our observations from Table 4.11.

The Wilcoxon signed-rank test was also conducted. The confidence to accept the alternative hypothesis (D* is more effective than the other techniques) in many cases is more than 90%, regardless of the subject programs, or the best or worst case.

Considering all the data, it suggests the superiority of D* (with an appropriate value for *) over the other techniques in locating program bugs.

4.7.3.8 Programs with Multiple Bugs

Thus far, the evaluation of D* has been with respect to programs that have exactly one bug. In this section, we discuss and demonstrate how D* may be applied to programs with multiple bugs. More discussion of fault localization on programs with multiple bugs appear in Chapter 12.

4.7.3.8.1 The Expense *Score-Based Approach*

For programs with multiple faults, the authors of [87] define an evaluation metric, *Expense*, corresponding to the percentage of code that must be examined to locate the first fault as they argue that this is the fault that programmers will begin to fix. We note that the *Expense* score, though defined in a multi-fault setting, is the *same* as the *EXAM* score (see Section 4.7.3.3). Thus, D* can also be applied to and evaluated on programs with multiple bugs in such a manner, and in accordance we conduct a comparison between D* (for * equal to 2 and 3 in this case) and other fault localization techniques using this strategy.

As per [87], all the techniques are evaluated on the basis of the expense required to find only the first fault in the ranking. Note that because the rankings based on D* and the other techniques may vary considerably, it is not necessary that the first fault located by one technique be the same as the first fault located by another technique.

Multi-bug versions of the subject programs are created via a combination of single-fault versions. The programs of the *Siemens* suite have been used for the purposes of this comparison as there are many single-fault versions available which can be combined in a variety of ways to produce many different multi-fault versions. A total of 75 such programs are created based on combinations of the single-fault programs of the *Siemens* suite, and they range from faulty versions with two faults to those with five faults. To evaluate the effectiveness, we compare and against all the similarity coefficient-based techniques in Table 4.3 and also all the contemporary fault localization techniques discussed in Section 4.7.3.7.

Data in Table 4.12 gives the total number of statements that need to be examined to find the first fault across all 75 faulty versions. We observe that, regardless of best

Table 4.12 Number of statements examined for the 75 multi-bug versions of the Siemens suite by D* and other fault localization techniques.

Technique	Best case	Worst case	Technique	Best case	Worst case
D^3	884	1327	Simple-Matching	1870	2231
D^2	932	1374	Rogers & Tanimoto	1870	2231
Braun Banquet	1149	1864	Hamming	1870	2231
Dennis	1334	1736	Hamann	1870	2231
Mountford	1135	1546	Sokal	1870	2231
Fossum	1022	1427	Scott	1786	2154
Pearson	1648	2037	Rogot1	1786	2154
Gower	2619	2926	Kulczynski	1314	1717
Michael	1439	1858	Anderberg	1314	1717
Pierce	2037	3099	Dice	1314	1717
Baroni-Urbani & Buser	1635	1991	Goodman	1314	1717
Tarwid	1451	1853	Jaccard	1314	1717
Ample	1782	2153	Sorensen-Dice	1314	1717
Phi (Geometric Mean)	1191	1601	Crosstab	1191	1601
Arithmetic Mean	1140	1553	RBF	888	1334
Cohen	1388	1782	H3b	2888	3390
Fleiss	1898	2283	H3c	2183	2665
Zoltar	2088	2555	Tarantula	1451	1851
Harmonic Mean	1225	1620	Ochiai	976	1385
Rogot2	1225	1620	Ochiai2	1933	2352

Source: Wong et al. [5]/IEEE.

or worst case, D^3 is the most effective, and D^2 is the third (behind D^3 and RBF) among all the competing techniques.

Part (a) of Figure 4.13 presents the best case comparison using the *Expense* or *EXAM* score, while Part (b) shows the worst. We see that D^3 generally performs better than other techniques. The reason why only three curves are displayed is purely in the interests of clarity and readability. The same conclusion applies to other techniques.

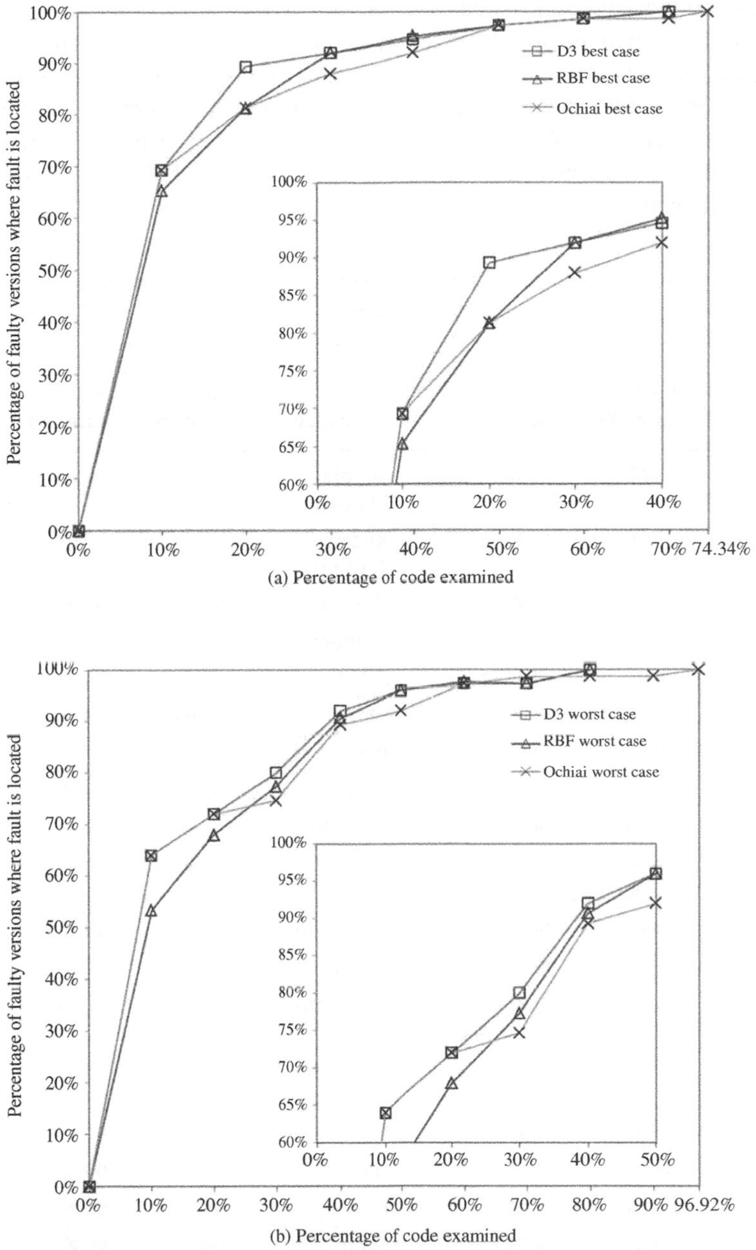

Figure 4.13 Effectiveness comparison for the 75 multi-fault versions of the Siemens suite using the Expense/EXAM score: (a) best case and (b) worst case. *Source:* Wong et al. [5]/IEEE.

With respect to the Wilcoxon signed-rank test, due to the nature of the *Expense* score, the alternative hypothesis in this case would be that D^3 is more effective at *finding the first bug* in a multi-bug program than the technique under comparison. The corresponding confidence levels at which the alternative hypothesis can be accepted is presented in Table 4.13. The data suggests that even for multi-bug programs it can be confidently claimed that D^3 is more effective than the other techniques, irrespective of best or worst case.

Table 4.13 Confidence with which it can be claimed that D^3 is more effective than other techniques (best and worst cases) based on the Expense/Exam score.

Technique	Best case (%)	Worst case (%)	Technique	Best case (%)	Worst case (%)
D^2	98.67	98.66	Simple-Matching	99.99	99.93
Braun Banquet	99.99	99.99	Rogers & Tanimoto	99.99	99.93
Dennis	99.99	99.97	Hamming	99.99	99.93
Mountford	99.70	99.09	Hamann	99.99	99.93
Fossum	99.99	99.87	Sokal	99.99	99.93
Pearson	99.99	99.99	Scott	99.98	99.58
Gower	99.99	99.99	Rogot1	99.98	99.58
Michael	99.99	99.99	Kulczynski	99.99	99.98
Pierce	99.99	99.91	Anderberg	99.99	99.98
Baroni-Urbani & Buser	99.90	98.86	Dice	99.99	99.98
Tarwid	99.99	99.98	Goodman	99.99	99.98
Ample	99.99	99.98	Jaccard	99.99	99.98
Phi (Geometric Mean)	99.90	99.81	Sorensen-Dice	99.99	99.98
Arithmetic Mean	96.00	96.16	Crosstab	99.90	99.27
Cohen	99.99	99.89	RBF	91.11	96.62
Fleiss	99.99	99.97	H3b	97.92	99.82
Zoltar	94.33	98.31	H3c	95.28	98.79
Harmonic Mean	99.89	99.74	Tarantula	99.98	99.92
Rogot2	99.89	99.74	Ochiai	98.41	96.31
			Ochiai2	99.99	99.99

Source: Wong et al. [5]/IEEE.

Together with the data in Table 4.12, Table 4.13, and the curves in Figure 4.13, there is strong evidence for the superiority of D* (with an appropriate value for *) over all the techniques compared in this section.

4.7.3.8.2 The One-Bug-at-a-Time Approach

The *Expense* score, defined in [87] as the percentage of code that needs to be examined to find only the first bug in a multi-bug program, is really part of a bigger process that involves locating and fixing all bugs (that result in at least one failed test case) that reside in the subject program. After the first bug has successfully been located and fixed, the next step is to rerun test cases to detect subsequent failures, whereupon the next bug is located and fixed. The process continues until failures are no longer observed, and we conclude (but not guarantee) that there are no more bugs present in the program.

This process is referred to as the *one-bug-at-a-time* approach, and thus the *Expense* score only assesses the fault localization effectiveness with respect to the first iteration of the process. Because each iteration involves locating a particular bug, there is an *Expense* score associated with every iteration, and the number of iterations would equal the number of bugs. Essentially, the total number of statements examined to find k bugs (i.e. the cumulative *Expense* score) can be quantified as $\sum_{i=1}^{k} a_i$, where a_i is the number of statements examined in the ith iteration. Thus, two fault localization techniques may be compared with one another by virtue of the total number of statements examined (i.e. the cumulative *Expense* score) if the one-bug-at-a-time approach is followed.

To further illustrate this result via example, we randomly select a 5-bug version (a program with five bugs) from among the 75 multi-bug versions generated for the *Siemens* suite (based on the experiments in Section 4.7.3.8.1), and show how D^3, D^2, and other techniques discussed in Sections 4.7.3.2 and 4.7.3.7 might be applied to locate all the bugs sequentially.

Table 4.14 reports the number of statements examined by each technique for both the best and worst effectiveness across each iteration, and its cumulative total. We observe that the total number of statements examined by D^3 is less than D^2, which is less than the other techniques for both the best and the worst cases. Also, except for a few exceptions, D^3 is more effective than or as effective as D^2 for each iteration, which is more effective than or as effective as the other fault localization techniques regardless of whether the best or worst case is considered.

4.7.3.9 Discussion

In this section, we discuss issues related to the intuitions that are used for fault localization and outline the potential threats to validity.

Table 4.14 Number of statements that need to be examined following the one-bug-at-a-time approach.

		Number of statements examined in each iteration					Cumulative total
		1	2	3	4	5	
D^2	Best	1	8	10	32	2	53
	Worst	3	11	10	41	2	67
D^2	Best	1	2	20	77	2	102
	Worst	3	5	20	86	2	116
Braun Banquest	Best	1	32	86	103	5	227
	Worst	3	35	86	112	5	241
Dennis	Best	1	2	79	104	5	191
	Worst	3	5	79	113	5	205
Mountford	Best	1	3	61	99	5	169
	Worst	3	6	61	108	5	183
Fossum	Best	1	6	52	82	2	143
	Worst	3	9	52	91	2	157
Pearson	Best	1	2	61	99	2	165
	Worst	3	5	61	108	2	179
Gower	Best	1	24	73	193	164	455
	Worst	4	26	76	193	172	471
Michael	Best	2	1	25	103	2	133
	Worst	4	4	25	112	2	147
Pierce	Best	1	33	105	108	89	336
	Worst	1	36	223	227	178	667
Baroni-Urbani and Buser	Best	1	3	96	116	27	243
	Worst	3	6	96	125	27	257

Table 4.14 (Continued)

		Number of statements examined in each iteration					Cumulative total
		1	2	3	4	5	
Tarwid	Best	2	33	87	104	5	231
	Worst	4	36	87	113	5	245
Ample	Best	1	2	65	115	2	185
	Worst	3	5	65	124	2	199
Phi (Geometric mean)	Best	1	2	61	99	2	165
	Worst	3	5	61	108	2	179
Arithmetic mean	Best	1	2	61	99	5	168
	Worst	3	5	61	108	5	182
Cohen	Best	1	2	85	104	5	197
	Worst	3	5	85	113	5	211
Fleiss	Best	1	2	104	124	5	236
	Worst	3	5	104	133	5	250
Zoltar	Best	6	112	1	112	2	233
	Worst	15	114	223	114	5	471
Harmonic mean	Best	1	2	61	99	2	165
	Worst	3	5	61	108	2	179
Rogot2	Best	1	2	61	99	2	165
	Worst	3	5	61	108	2	179

(Continued)

Table 4.14 (Continued)

		Number of statements examined in each iteration					Cumulative total
		1	2	3	4	5	
Simple-Matching	Best	1	59	104	124	63	351
	Worst	3	62	104	133	63	365
Rogers and Tanimoto	Best	1	59	104	124	63	351
	Worst	3	62	104	133	63	365
Hamming	Best	1	59	104	124	63	351
	Worst	3	62	104	133	63	365
Hamann	Best	1	59	104	124	63	351
	Worst	3	62	104	133	63	365
Sokal	Best	1	59	104	124	63	351
	Worst	3	62	104	133	63	365
Scott	Best	1	3	104	124	27	259
	Worst	3	6	104	133	27	273
Rogot1	Best	1	3	104	124	27	259
	Worst	3	6	104	133	27	273
Kulczynski	Best	1	2	76	103	5	187
	Worst	3	5	76	112	5	201
Anderberg	Best	1	2	76	103	5	187
	Worst	3	5	76	112	5	201
Dice	Best	1	2	76	103	5	187
	Worst	3	5	76	112	5	201

Table 4.14 (Continued)

		Number of statements examined in each iteration					Cumulative total
		1	2	3	4	5	
Goodman	Best	1	2	76	103	5	187
	Worst	3	5	76	112	5	201
Jaccard	Best	1	2	76	103	5	187
	Worst	3	5	76	112	5	201
Sorensen-Dice	Best	1	2	76	103	5	187
	Worst	3	5	76	112	5	201
crosstab	Best	1	2	61	99	2	165
	Worst	3	5	61	108	2	179
RBF	Best	1	2	61	79	5	148
	Worst	3	5	61	88	5	162
H3b	Best	8	112	121	167	2	410
	Worst	17	112	123	167	5	424
H3c	Best	7	116	122	167	2	414
	Worst	16	116	124	167	5	428
Tarantula	Best	2	33	87	104	5	231
	Worst	4	36	87	113	2	245
Ochiai	Best	1	2	49	79	2	133
	Worst	3	5	49	88	2	147
Ochiai2	Best	1	2	83	116	5	207
	Worst	3	5	83	125	5	221

Source: Wong et al. [5]/IEEE.

4.7.3.9.1 Intuition 4.3

Recall Intuition 4.3 behind the construction of D*, as stated in Section 4.7.1, that asserts the suspiciousness assigned to a statement should be inversely proportional to the number of failed test cases that do not execute it.

Thus, we penalize a statement (viewing it as less suspicious) for every test case that fails without executing it. This intuition in general can be applied to programs with only one fault. However, what if there is more than one fault in the program? In such a situation, one might wonder if it makes sense to penalize a faulty statement by reducing its suspiciousness because of the existence of a test case that fails due to another faulty statement related to a different fault. There are three important factors to keep in mind.

First, the objective of penalizing such statements is to bring down the suspiciousness of non-faulty statements.

Second, the dominant factor in computing the statement suspiciousness using a metric such as D* is still a_{ef}, not a_{nf} (as per the suspiciousness function $(a_{ef})^{*}/(a_{nf}+a_{es})$ because a_{ef} is the term with exponent, not a_{nf}. Thus, the suspiciousness assigned to a statement has much more to do with a_{ef} than a_{nf}.

Third and finally is the fact that the intuition holds empirically because of the superior performance D* compared to the other fault localization techniques, regardless of whether the programs have just one bug (Section 4.7.3.5) or multiple bugs (Section 4.7.3.8). This fact allows us to be confident in the validity and usefulness of Intuition 4.3, and the suspiciousness computation of D* as a whole.

4.7.3.9.2 Best and Worst Effectiveness Versus Other Alternatives

Per the discussion toward the beginning of Section 4.7.3.4, in the event of ties in the statement ranking, there may be two different levels of effectiveness: the best and the worst. Consequently the approach in this chapter has been to provide data with respect to both levels of effectiveness. In contrast, some other fault localization studies follow a different approach. For example, in [26], the convention has been to report only the worst case effectiveness. This is a reasonable approach in that it is conservative. However, the problem lies with the fact that leaving out information on the best case effectiveness does not allow any estimate on where the actual effectiveness is expected to be (somewhere between the best and worst effectiveness; quite possibly the average of these two effectiveness levels).

That being said, one might be tempted to just present data on the average effectiveness (computed by simply taking the arithmetic mean of the best and worst effectiveness). However, this approach is also not flawless because it results in a complete loss of information with respect to the variability of the observed effectiveness. To better understand this approach, consider a scenario where a fault can be located using some technique by examining 6 statements in the best case and 8 statements in the worst, meaning that on average the fault can be located by examining 7 statements. In this case, the variability is small, as both in the best and worst cases, we are only one statement away from the average. But what would happen if another technique allows the fault to be located by examining only 1 statement in the best case and 13 in the worst? On average, the fault can still be located by examining 7 statements. Thus, the two techniques are equal with respect to their average effectiveness, even though they are drastically different in terms of their variability.

To avoid such loss of information, we opted against presenting data on just the worst case or average effectiveness alone, and instead present data corresponding to both the best and the worst case effectiveness.

Different techniques (such as [83]) can be used to break the ties. Refer to Chapter 11 for more discussion on this topic.

4.7.3.9.3 Threats to Validity

The three evaluation metrics or criteria discussed in Section 4.7.3.3 represent a threat to construct validity. While such metrics are suitable measures of fault localization effectiveness, by themselves they do not provide a complete picture of the effort spent in locating faults as developers may not examine statements one at a time, and may not spend the same amount of time examining different statements. We also assume that, if a developer examines a faulty statement, they will identify the corresponding fault(s). By the same token, a developer will not identify a non-faulty statement as faulty. If such perfect bug detection does not hold in practice, then the examination effort may increase. Such concerns apply to all fault localization techniques.

Given that the evaluation of the effectiveness of any fault localization technique discussed in this chapter has been empirical, arguably the results may not be generalized to other programs. One possible solution is to use different subject programs that vary greatly in terms of size (LOC), functionality, number of test cases, etc.

4.8 Conclusion

This chapter explains the basic concept and the background of using program spectra for fault localization, which has emerged as one of the most active fault localization research areas in the software engineering field. It gives a non-exhaustive list of spectra-based metrics and their respective characteristics. Some of these metrics are described in detail. Empirical evaluation of the effectiveness in terms of code that needs to be examined to find a program bug among different fault localization techniques is also presented. Possible refinements of the suspiciousness rankings generated by these techniques are explored. Finally, threats of validity related to the data reported from studies published in the literature are discussed. Overall, this chapter provides readers a comprehensive view of using spectra-based metrics to produce a suspiciousness ranking of all the components (statements in most cases) of a faulty program. Based on these rankings, programmers can effectively identify possible locations that contain bugs.

Notes

1 In this chapter, we use "bug" and "fault" interchangeably. We also use "programs" and "software" interchangeably.
2 Part of Section 4.2 is from Refs. [4, 5].
3 The phrase "a statement is *covered* by a test case" is used interchangeably with "a statement is *executed* by a test case."
4 Since the coverage matrix and result vector are binary, we are essentially only concerned with binary similarity measures/coefficients.
5 For the purposes of this paper, it is assumed that the vectors being evaluated for their mutual similarity are of equal size.
6 There are several measures of fault localization effectiveness in the literature. However, they all essentially gauge the fraction of the code that must/must not be examined in order to locate bugs, albeit from different perspectives. A fault localization technique may be considered better than another if it is able to locate bugs by requiring the examination of a relatively smaller fraction of code than the other [11].
7 Part of Section 4.3 is from Ref. [25].
8 Part of Section 4.4 is from Refs. [4, 16].
9 Part of Section 4.5 is from Refs. [28, 29].
10 Part of Section 4.6 is from Refs. [20, 25, 32].
11 A basic block (a.k.a. a block) is a sequence of consecutive statements or expressions, containing no branches except at the end, such that if one element of the sequence is executed, all are.
12 Part of Section 4.7 is from Ref. [5].
13 Also refer to Section 4.6.1 for a description of the space program.
14 Heuristic III was initially proposed by Wong et al. [24] and referenced as Wong3 by Naish et al. [16, 25]. This Heuristic was later revised by Wong et al. [17] with an improved fault localization effectiveness. Heuristics III (b) and III(c) in this chapter (referenced as Wong4 by Naish et al. [25, 32]) are the revised Heuristic III.

References

1 Ernst, M.D. (2003). Static and dynamic analysis: synergy and duality. *Proceedings of WODA 2003: ICSE Workshop on Dynamic Analysis*, Portland, OR, USA (3–10 May 2003), 24–27. IEEE. https://homes.cs.washington.edu/~mernst/pubs/staticdynamic-woda2003.pdf.

2 Mock, M. (2003). Dynamic analysis from the bottom up. *Proceedings of WODA 2003: ICSE Workshop on Dynamic Analysis*, Portland, OR, USA (3–10 May 2003), 13. IEEE. https://citeseerx.ist.psu.edu/viewdoc/download?doi=10.1.1.12.5686&rep=rep1&type=pdf.

3 de Souza, H.A., Chaim, M.L., and Kon, F. (2016). Spectrum-based software fault localization: a survey of techniques, advances, and challenges. arXiv preprint arXiv:1607.04347, 2016.

4 Debroy, V. and Wong, W.E. (2011). On the equivalence of certain fault localization techniques. *Proceedings of the ACM Symposium on Applied Computing*, TaiChung, Taiwan (21–24 March 2011), 1457–1463. ACM. https://dl.acm.org/doi/pdf/10.1145/1982185.1982498.

5 Wong, W.E., Debroy, V., Gao, R., and Li, Y. (2014). The DStar method for effective software fault localization. *IEEE Transactions on Reliability* 63 (1): 290–308.

6 Avizienis, A., Laprie, J.C., Randell, B., and Landwehr, C. (2004). Basic concepts and taxonomy of dependable and secure computing. *IEEE Transactions on Dependable and Secure Computing* 1 (1): 11–33.

7 Choi, S., Cha, S., and Tappert, C.C. (2010). A survey of binary similarity and distance measures. *The Journal on Systemics, Cybernetics and Informatics* 8 (1): 43–48.

8 Dunn, G. and Everitt, B.S. (1982). *An Introduction to Mathematical Taxonomy*. Cambridge, UK: Cambridge University Press.

9 Willett, P. (2003). Similarity-based approaches to virtual screening. *Biochemical Society Transactions* 31 (3): 603–606.

10 Abreu, R., Zoeteweij, P., Golsteijn, R., and van Gemund, A.J.C. (2009). A practical evaluation of spectrum-based fault localization. *Journal of Systems and Software* 82 (11): 1780–1792.

11 Wong, W.E., Gao, R., Li, Y. et al. (2016). A survey on software fault localization. *IEEE Transactions on Software Engineering* 42 (8): 707–740. ISSN 0098-5589. https://doi.org/10.1109/TSE.2016.2521368.

12 Dunham, M. (2002). *Data Mining: Introductory and Advanced Topics*. PTR Upper Saddle River, NJ, USA: Prentice Hall.

13 Krause, E.F. (1973). Taxicab geometry. *Mathematics Teacher* 66: 695–706.

14 Lourenço, F., Lobo, V., Bacao, F., and de Informação, G. Binary-based similarity measures for categorical data and their application in self-organizing maps. *Proceedings of JOCLAD 2004-XI Jornadas de Classificacao e Anlise de Dados*, Lisbon,

Portugal (1–3 April 2004), 1–8. Academia. https://www.academia.edu/48845879/Binary_based_similarity_measures_for_categorical_data_and_their_application_in_Self_Organizing_Maps (accessed 1 October 2022).

15 Abreu, R., Zoeteweij, P., and Van Gemund, A.J.C. (2006). An evaluation of similarity coefficients for software fault localization. *Proceedings of the 2006 12th Pacific Rim International Symposium on Dependable Computing (PRDC '06)*, Riverside, CA, USA (18–20 December 2006), 39–46. IEEE. https://doi.org/10.1109/PRDC.2006.18.

16 Naish, L., Lee, H.J., and Ramamohanarao, K. (2011). A model for spectra-based software diagnosis. *ACM Transactions on Software Engineering and Methodology* 20 (3): 11:1–11:32.

17 Wong, W.E., Debroy, V., and Choi, B. (2010). A family of code coverage-based heuristics for effective fault localization. *Journal of Systems and Software* 83 (2): 188–208. ISSN 0164-1212. https://doi.org/10.1016/j.jss.2009.09.037.

18 Liblit, B., Naik, M., Zheng, A.X. et al. (2005). Scalable statistical bug isolation. *Proceedings of the 2005 ACM SIGPLAN Conference on Programming Language Design and Implementation (PLDI '05)*, Chicago, IL, USA (12–15 June 2005), 15–26. ACM. https://doi.org/10.1145/1065010.1065014.

19 Lee, H.J., Naish, L., and Ramamohanarao, K. (2009). Study of the relationship of bug consistency with respect to performance of spectra metrics. *Proceedings of the 2009 2nd IEEE International Conference on Computer Science and Information Technology*, Beijing, China (8–11 August 2009), 501–508. IEEE. https://doi.org/10.1109/ICCSIT.2009.5234512.

20 Jones, J.A., Harrold, M.J., and Stasko, J. (2002). Visualization of test information to assist fault localization. *Proceedings of the 24th International Conference on Software Engineering (ICSE '02)*, Orlando, FL, USA (19–25 May 2002), 467–477. ACM. https://doi.org/10.1145/581396.581397.

21 Russell, P.F. and Ramachandra Rao, T. (1940). On habitat and association of species of anopheline larvae in south-eastern Madras. *Journal of the Malaria Institute of India* 3 (1): 153–178.

22 Zhang, Z., Chan, W.K., and Tse, T.H. (2012). Fault localization based only on failed runs. *Computer* 45 (6): 64–71. ISSN 0018-9162. https://doi.org/10.1109/MC.2012.185.

23 Ochiai, A. (1957). Zoogeographic studies on the soleoid fishes found in Japan and its neighboring regions. *Bulletin of the Japanese Society of Scientific Fisheries* 22: 526–530.

24 Wong, W.E., Qi, Y., Zhao, L., and Cai, K. (2007). Effective fault localization using code coverage. *Proceedings of the 31st Annual International Computer Software and Applications Conference (COMPSAC '07)*, Beijing, China (24–27 July 2007), 1: 449–456. IEEE. https://doi.org/10.1109/COMPSAC.2007.109.

25 Lee, H.J. (2011). Software debugging using program spectra. PhD thesis. The University of Melbourne.

26 Jones, J.A. and Harrold, M.J. (2005). Empirical evaluation of the tarantula automatic fault-localization technique. *Proceedings of the 20th IEEE/ACM International Conference on Automated Software Engineering (ASE '05)*, Long Beach, CA, USA, 273–282. ACM. ISBN 1-58113-993-4. https://doi.org/10.1145/1101908.1101949.

27 Meyer, A., Garcia, A., Souza, A., and Souza, C. (2004). Comparison of similarity coefficients used for cluster analysis with dominant markers in maize (*Zea mays* L). *Genetics and Molecular Biology* 27 (1): 83–91.

28 Naish, L. and Lee, H.J. (2013). Duals in spectral fault localization. *Proceedings of the 2013 22nd Australian Software Engineering Conference*, Melbourne, Victoria, Australia (4–7 January 2013), 51–59. IEEE. https://doi.org/10.1109/ASWEC.2013.16.

29 Naish, L., Lee, H.J., and Ramamohanarao, K. (2012). Spectral debugging: how much better can we do. *Proceedings of the Australian Software Engineering Conference*, Melbourne, Australia (30 January to 3 February 2012), 99–106. Australian Computer Society. https://crpit.scem.westernsydney.edu.au/confpapers/CRPITV122Naish%20.pdf.

30 Naish, L., Lee, H.J., and Ramamohanarao, K. (2010). Statements versus predicate in spectral bug localization. *Proceedings of the Asia Pacific Software Engineering Conference*, Sydney, Australia (30 November to 3 December 2010), 375–384. IEEE. https://doi.org/10.1109/APSEC.2010.50.

31 Grottke, M. and Trivedi, K.S. (2005). A classification of software faults. *Proceedings of the Sixteenth International Symposium on Software Reliability Engineering (ISSRE '05)*, Chicago, IL, USA (8–11 November 2005), 4.19–4.20. IEEE. https://www.researchgate.net/profile/Michael-Grottke/publication/228894619_A_classification_of_software_faults/links/5ede5a4592851cf13869833e/A-classification-of-software-faults.pdf.

32 Lee, H.J., Naish, L., and Ramamohanarao, K. (2010). Effective software bug localization using spectral frequency weighting function. *Proceedings of the 2010 IEEE 34th Annual Computer Software and Applications Conference (COMPSAC '10)*, Seoul, Korea (19–23 July 2010), 218–227. IEEE. https://doi.org/10.1109/COMPSAC.2010.26.

33 Reps, T., Ball, T., Das, M., and Larus, J. (1997). The use of program profiling for software maintenance with applications to the year 2000 problem. *Proceedings of the 6th European Software Engineering Conference Held Jointly with the 5th ACM SIGSOFT Symposium on Foundations of Software Engineering (ESEC/FSE '97)*. Zurich, Switzerland (22–25 September 1997), 432–449. Springer Berlin Heidelberg.

34 Thomsett, R. (1998). The year 2000 bug: a forgotten lesson. *IEEE Software* 15 (4): 91–93.

35 Jones, J.A., Harrold, M.J., and Stasko, J.T. Visualization for fault localization. *Proceedings of the ICSE 2001 Workshop on Software Visualization*, Toronto, ON, Canada (12–19 May 2001). 71–75. IEEE. https://citeseerx.ist.psu.edu/viewdoc/download?doi=10.1.1.28.8885.

36 Do, H., Elbaum, S., and Rothermel, G. (October 2005). Supporting controlled experimentation with testing techniques: an infrastructure and its potential impact. *Empirical Software Engineering* 10 (4): 405–435. ISSN 1382-3256. https://doi.org/10.1007/s10664-005-3861-2.

37 Renieres, M. and Reiss, S.P. (2003). Fault localization with nearest neighbor queries. *Proceedings of the 18th IEEE International Conference on Automated Software Engineering (ASE '03)*, Montreal, QC, Canada (6–10 October 2003), 30–39. IEEE. https://doi.org/10.1109/ASE.2003.1240292.

38 Bellcore (1998). *χSuds Software Understanding System User's Manual*. Bridgewater, NJ, USA: Telcordia Technologies (formerly Bellcore). https://www.cs.purdue.edu/homes/apm/foundationsBook/Labs/coverage/xsuds.pdf.

39 Dallmeier, V., Lindig, C., and Zeller, A. (2005). Lightweight bug localization with AMPLE. *Proceedings of the Sixth International Symposium on Automated Analysis-driven Debugging (AADEBUG '05)*, Monterey, CA, USA (19–21 September 2005), 99–104. ACM. ISBN 1-59593-050-7. https://doi.org/10.1145/1085130.1085143.

40 Apache Commons. Commons BCEL. http://commons.apache.org/proper/commons-bcel (accessed January 2022).

41 Abreu, R., Zoeteweij, P., and van Gemund, A.J.C. (2007). On the accuracy of spectrum-based fault localization. *Proceedings of Testing: Academic and Industrial Conference Practice and Research Techniques – MUTATION (TAICPART-MUTATION '07)* Windsor, UK (10–14 September 2007), 89–98. IEEE. https://doi.org/10.1109/TAIC.PART.2007.13.

42 Chen, M.Y., Kiciman, E., Fratkin, E. et al. (2002). Pinpoint: problem determination in large, dynamic internet services. *Proceedings of the International Conference on Dependable Systems and Networks (DSN 2002)*, Bethesda, MD, USA (23–26 June 2002), 595–604. IEEE. https://doi.org/10.1109/DSN.2002.1029005.

43 Sanchez, A. (2007). Automatic error detection techniques based on dynamic invariants. Master's thesis. Delft University of Technology.

44 Le, T.B., Lo, D., and Thung, F. (2015). Should I follow this fault localization tool's output? *Empirical Software Engineering* 20 (5): 1237–1274. ISSN 1573-7616. https://doi.org/10.1007/s10664-014-9349-1.

45 Ma, C., Zhang, Y., Zhang, T. et al. (2014). Uniformly evaluating and comparing ranking metrics for spectral fault localization. *Proceedings of the 2014 14th International Conference on Quality Software (QSIC '14)*, Allen, TX, USA (2–3 October 2014), 315–320. IEEE. https://doi.org/10.1109/QSIC.2014.24.

46 Keller, F., Grunske, L., Heiden, S. et al. (2017). A critical evaluation of spectrum-based fault localization techniques on a large-scale software system. *Proceedings of the 2017 IEEE International Conference on Software Quality, Reliability and Security (QRS '17)*, Prague, Czech Republic (25–29 July 2017), 114–125. IEEE. https://doi.org/10.1109/QRS.2017.22.

47 Pearson, S., Campos, J., Just, R. et al. (2017). Evaluating and improving fault localization. *Proceedings of the 2017 IEEE/ACM 39th International Conference on*

Software Engineering (ICSE '17), Buenos Aires, Argentina (20–28 May 2017), 609–620. IEEE. https://doi.org/10.1109/ICSE.2017.62.

48 Yu, Z., Bai, C., and Cai, K.-Y. (2015). Does the failing test execute a single or multiple faults? An approach to classifying failing tests. *Proceedings of the 37th International Conference on Software Engineering (ICSE '15)*, Florence, Italy (16–24 May 2015), 1: 924–935. IEEE. https://doi.org/10.1109/ICSE.2015.102.

49 Xia, X., Bao, L., Lo, D., and Li, S. (2016). "Automated debugging considered harmful" considered harmful: a user study revisiting the usefulness of spectra-based fault localization techniques with professionals using real bugs from large systems. *Proceedings of the 2016 IEEE International Conference on Software Maintenance and Evolution (ICSME '16)*, Raleign, NC, USA (2–10 October 2016), 267–278. IEEE. https://doi.org/10.1109/ICSME.2016.67.

50 Di Giuseppe, N. and Jones, J.A. (2015). Fault density, fault types, and spectra-based fault localization. *Empirical Software Engineering* 20 (4): 928–967. ISSN 1573-7616. https://doi.org/10.1007/s10664-014-9304-1.

51 Debroy, V. and Wong, W.E. (2009). Insights on fault interference for programs with multiple bugs. *Proceedings of the 20th IEEE International Symposium on Software Reliability Engineering (ISSRE '09)*, Mysuru, Karnataka, India (16–19 November 2009), 165–174. IEEE. https://doi.org/10.1109/ISSRE.2009.14.

52 Lucia Lo, D., and Xia, X. (2014). Fusion fault localizers. *Proceedings of the 29th ACM/IEEE International Conference on Automated Software Engineering (ASE '14)*, Vasteras, Sweden (15–19 September 2014), 127–138. ACM. https://doi.org/10.1145/2642937.2642983.

53 Naish, L., Lee, H.J., and Ramamohanarao, K. (2009). Spectral debugging with weights and incremental ranking. *Proceedings of the 2009 16th Asia-Pacific Software Engineering Conference*, Batu Ferringhi, Penang, Malaysia (1–3 December 2009), 168–175. IEEE. https://doi.org/10.1109/APSEC.2009.32.

54 Hassoun, M.H. (1995). *Fundamentals of Artificial Neural Networks*. Cambridge, Massachusetts: MIT Press.

55 Debroy, V., Wong, W.E., Xu, X., and Choi, B. (2010). A grouping-based strategy to improve the effectiveness of fault localization techniques. *Proceedings of the 2010 10th International Conference on Quality Software (QSIC '10)*, Zhangjiajie, China (14–15 July 2010), 13–22. IEEE. https://doi.org/10.1109/QSIC.2010.80.

56 Xie, X., Chen, T.Y., and Xu, B. (2010). Isolating suspiciousness from spectrum-based fault localization techniques. *Proceedings of the 2010 10th International Conference on Quality Software (QSIC '10)*, Zhangjiajie, China (14–15 July 2010), 385–392. IEEE. https://doi.org/10.1109/QSIC.2010.45.

57 Jones, J.A., Bowring, J.F., and Harrold, M.J. (2007). Debugging in parallel. *Proceedings of the 2007 International Symposium on Software Testing and Analysis (ISSTA '07)*, London, UK (9–12 July 2007), 16–26. ACM. https://doi.org/10.1145/1273463.1273468.

58 Gao, R. and Wong, W.E. (2019). MSeer-an advanced technique for locating multiple bugs in parallel. *IEEE Transactions on Software Engineering* 45 (3): 301–318.

59 Högerle, W., Steimann, F., and Frenkel, M. (2014). More debugging in parallel. *Proceedings of the 2014 IEEE 25th International Symposium on Software Reliability Engineering (ISSRE '14)*, Naples, Italy (3–6 November 2014), 133–143. IEEE. https://doi.org/10.1109/ISSRE.2014.29.

60 Cai, H. and Xu, X. (2012). A new spectrum-based fault localization method by using clustering algorithm. *International Journal of Advancements in Computing Technology* 4 (22): 848–856.

61 Le, T.B., Oentaryo, R.J., and Lo, D. (2015). Information retrieval and spectrum based bug localization: better together. *Proceedings of the 2015 10th Joint Meeting on Foundations of Software Engineering (ESEC/FSE '15)*, Bergamo, Italy (30 August to 4 September 2015), 579–590. ACM. https://doi.org/10.1145/2786805.2786880.

62 Zhang, M., Li, X., Zhang, L., and Khurshid, S. (2017). Boosting spectrum-based fault localization using PageRank. *Proceedings of the 26th ACM SIGSOFT International Symposium on Software Testing and Analysis (ISSTA '17)*, Santa Barbara, CA, USA (10–14 July 2017), 261–272. ACM. https://doi.org/10.1145/3092703.3092731.

63 Perez, A., Riboira, A., and Abreu, R. (2012). A topology-based model for estimating the diagnostic efficiency of statistics-based approaches. *Proceedings of the 2012 IEEE 23rd International Symposium on Software Reliability Engineering Workshops (ISSREW '12)*, Dallas, TX, USA (27–30 November 2012), 171–176. IEEE. https://doi.org/10.1109/ISSREW.2012.15.

64 Wang, X. and Liu, Y. (2015). Automated fault localization via hierarchical multiple predicate switching. *Journal of Systems and Software* 104: 69–81. ISSN 0164-1212. https://doi.org/10.1016/j.jss.2015.02.038.

65 Jiang, L. and Su, Z. (2007). Context-aware statistical debugging: from bug predictors to faulty control flow paths. *Proceedings of the 22nd IEEE/ACM International Conference on Automated Software Engineering (ASE '07)*, Atlanta, GA, USA (5–9 Novermber 2007), 184–193. ACM. ISBN 978-1-59593-882-4. https://doi.org/10.1145/1321631.1321660.

66 Xuan, J. and Monperrus, M. (2014). Learning to combine multiple ranking metrics for fault localization. *Proceedings of the 2014 IEEE International Conference on Software Maintenance and Evolution*, Victoria, BC, Canada (29 September to 3 October 2014), 191–200. IEEE. https://doi.org/10.1109/ICSME.2014.41.

67 Yoo, S. (2012). Evolving human competitive spectra-based fault localisation techniques. In: *Search Based Software Engineering* (ed. G. Fraser and J.T. de Souza), 244–258. Berlin, Germany: Springer. ISBN 978-3-642-33119-0.

68 Yoo, S., Xie, X., Kuo, F. et al. (2017). Human competitiveness of genetic programming in spectrum-based fault localisation: theoretical and empirical analysis. *ACM Transactions on Software Engineering and Methodology* 26 (1): 4:1–4:30. ISSN 1049-331X. https://doi.org/10.1145/3078840.

69 Wong, W.E., Debroy, V., Li, Y., and Gao, R. (2012). Software fault localization using DStar (D*). *Proceedings of the Sixth International Conference on Software Security and Reliability*, Gaithersburg, MD, USA (20–22 June 2012), 21–30. IEEE. https://doi.org/10.1109/SERE.2012.12.

70 Wong, W.E., Debroy, V., Golden, R. et al. (2012). Effective software fault localization using an RBF neural network. *IEEE Transactions on Reliability* 61 (1): 149–169. ISSN 0018-9529. doi: https://doi.org/10.1109/TR.2011.2172031.

71 Agrawal, H., Horgan, J.R., London, S., and Wong, W.E. (1995). Fault localization using execution slices and dataflow tests. *Proceedings of the Sixth International Symposium on Software Reliability Engineering (ISSRE '95)*, Toulouse, France (24–27 October 1995), 143–151. IEEE. https://doi.org/10.1109/ISSRE.1995.497652.

72 Cleve, H. and Zeller, A. (2005). Locating causes of program failures. *Proceedings of the 27th International Conference on Software Engineering (ICSE '05)*, St. Louis, MO, USA (15–21 May 2005), 342–351. ACM. https://dl.acm.org/doi/pdf/10.1145/1062455.1062522.

73 Liu, C., Yan, X., Fei, L. et al. (2005). SOBER: statistical model-based bug localization. *Proceedings of the 10th European Software Engineering Conference Held Jointly with 13th ACM SIGSOFT International Symposium on Foundations of Software Engineering (ESEC/FSE '05)*, Lisbon, Portugal (5–9 September 2005), 286–295. ACM. https://doi.org/10.1145/1081706.1081753.

74 Wong, W.E., Debroy, V., and Xu, D. (2012). Towards better fault localization: a crosstab-based statistical approach. *IEEE Transactions on Systems, Man, and Cybernetics* 42 (3) Part C: 378–396.

75 Software-artifact Infrastructure Repository. https://sir.csc.ncsu.edu/portal/index.php (accessed January 2022).

76 Wong, W.E., Horgan, J.R., London, S., and Mathur, A.P. (1995). Effect of test set minimization on fault detection effectiveness. *Proceedings of the 1995 17th International Conference on Software Engineering (ICSE '95)*, Seattle, WA, USA (24–28 April 1995), 41–50. ACM. https://doi.org/10.1145/225014.225018.

77 Wong, W.E., Horgan, J.R., London, S., and Mathur, A.P. (1998). Effect of test set minimization on fault detection effectiveness. *Software: Practice and Experience* 28 (4): 347–369.

78 Andrews, J.H., Briand, L.C., and Labiche, Y. (2005). Is mutation an appropriate tool for testing experiments? *Proceedings of the 27th International Conference on Software Engineering (ICSE '05)*, St. Louis, MO, USA (15–21 May 2005), 402–411. ACM. https://dl.acm.org/doi/pdf/10.1145/1062455.1062530.

79 Do, H. and Rothermel, G. (2006). On the use of mutation faults in empirical assessments of test case prioritization techniques. *IEEE Transactions on Software Engineering* 32 (9): 733–752.

80 Namin, A.S., Andrews, J.H., and Labiche, Y. (2006). Using mutation analysis for assessing and comparing testing coverage criteria. *IEEE Transactions on Software Engineering* 32 (8): 608–624.

81 Jackson, D.A., Somers, K.M., and Harvey, H.H. (1989). Similarity coefficients: measures of co-occurrence and association or simply measures of occurrence? *The American Naturalist* 133 (3): 436–453.

82 Lyman Ott, R. (1993). *An Introduction to Statistical Methods and Data Analysis*, 4e. Independence, KY, USA: Duxbury Press, Wadsworth Inc.

83 Xu, X., Debroy, V., Wong, W.E., and Guo, D. (2011). Ties within fault localization rankings: exposing and addressing the problem. *International Journal of Software Engineering and Knowledge Engineering* 21 (6): 803–827.

84 Everitt, B.S. (1977). *The Analysis of Contingency Tables*. Boca Raton, FL, USA: Chapman & Hall.

85 Freeman, D. (1987). *Applied Categorical Data Analysis*. New York, NY, USA: Marcel Dekker.

86 Goodman, L.A. (1984). *The Analysis of Cross-Classification Data Having Ordered Categories*. Boston, MA, USA: Harvard University Press.

87 Yu, Y., Jones, J.A., and Harrold, M.J. (2008). An empirical study on the effects of test-suite reduction on fault localization. *Proceedings of the 30th International Conference on Software Engineering (ICSE '08)*, Leipzig, Germany (10–18 May 2008), 201–210. IEEE. https://doi.org/10.1145/1368088.1368116.

5

Statistics-Based Techniques for Software Fault Localization

Zhenyu Zhang[1] and W. Eric Wong[2]

[1] *Institute of Software, Chinese Academy of Sciences, Beijing, China*
[2] *Department of Computer Science, University of Texas at Dallas, Richardson, TX, USA*

5.1 Introduction[1]

Program testing and debugging generally consume half or more of the costs of typical software development projects. Software engineers spend about one-third of their time debugging programs and deploy software knowing that it still contains faults. When an execution of a faulty program passes through a fault, it may result in an error in the internal program states. The program run generally executes other program statements as well, which may propagate the error to other internal program states. If such program statements produce observable effects, the run will cause a visible failure. Once they observe failures, software engineers schedule program debugging to locate the faults, fix them, and confirm their removal. Software debugging involves fault localization, fault repair, and retesting to confirm the fixing of the faults. Fault localization is time-consuming, cannot be done effectively, and is often deemed the major bottleneck in the debugging process.

Chapter 4 introduced the concept of program spectrum-based fault localization (SBFL) techniques, also known as coverage-based fault-localization techniques. It is natural for researchers to consider making further use of the statistics of the test data to identify program faults. This leads to the art of statistics-based fault localization.

In order to allow the present chapter to be as self-contained as possible, we will briefly revisit *Tarantula* [2] and other SBFL techniques in Sections 5.1.1 and 5.2.1.

Handbook of Software Fault Localization: Foundations and Advances, First Edition.
Edited by W. Eric Wong and T.H. Tse.

Published 2023 by John Wiley & Sons, Inc.

A typical fault localization technique based on the statistics of program spectrums involves a number of phases. It first selects a set of program features, and then collects their execution statistics for both passed and failed executions. By comparing the similarities between two such sets of statistics for each feature, it estimates the extents of the program features correlating to a fault and ranks the program features accordingly.

5.1.1 Tarantula

Jones et al. [2] proposed the *Tarantula* technique, which was used initially for the visualization of testing information. To rank program statements, *Tarantula* computes two metrics, suspiciousness and confidence, according to the coverage information on passed and failed test cases. The suspiciousness of a statement *s* is given by the following formula:

$$suspiciousness(s) = \frac{\%failed(s)}{\%failed(s) + \%passed(s)} \tag{5.1}$$

The term *%failed(s)* tallies the percentage of failed test cases that execute statement *s* (among all the failed test cases in the test suite). The term *%passed(s)* is similarly defined. The confidence metric, computed as follows, indicates the degree of confidence on a suspiciousness value:

$$confidence(s) = \max(\%failed(s), \%passed(s)) \tag{5.2}$$

Tarantula ranks all the statements in a program in descending order of suspiciousness and uses the confidence values to resolve ties.

5.1.2 How It Works

Table 5.1 shows a program that finds the middle number among the given three, in which a statement is buggy. With the example, six test cases are also given. With each test case, whether a statement is exercised or not is marked by a dot symbol in Table 5.1. At the same time, each test case is marked "passed" (P) or "failed" (F) according to its real output.

This example demonstrates how *Tarantula* works. Taking the first test case as an example, the program run over the first test input "3, 3, 5" exercises statements $s_1, s_2, s_3, s_4, s_6, s_7$, and s_{13} and finally outputs "3." As a result, it is marked as a passed test case. Taking statement s_4 as an example, it is exercised in three out of five passed test cases and one out of one failed test case. As a result, *%passed* $(s_4) = 3/5$, $\%failed(s_4) = 1$, and $suspiciousness(s_4) = 5/8 \cong 0.63$. Finally, *Tarantula* ranks statement s_7 as the most suspicious statement.

This example demonstrates the *suspiciousness* function and the *confidence* function of *Tarantula*. Statements having higher *suspiciousness* values are deemed

Table 5.1 Illustration of the *Tarantula* technique.

	Test cases							Suspiciousness	Confidence	Ranking
	`mid() {int x,y,z,m;`	t_1	t_2	t_3	t_4	t_5	t_6	—	—	—
s_1	`read("Enter 3 numbers:", x,y,z);`	•	•	•	•	•	•	0.5	1.0	7
s_2	`m = z;`	•	•	•	•	•	•	0.5	1.0	7
s_3	`if (y < z)`	•	•	•	•	•	•	0.5	1.0	7
s_4	`if (x < y)`		•					0.63	1.0	3
s_5	`m = y;`		•					0	0.2	12
s_6	`else if (x < z)`	•				•	•	0.71	1.0	2
s_7	`m = y; //*** bug ***`	•					•	0.83	1.0	1
s_8	`else`	•		•	•			0	0.4	9
s_9	`if (x > y)`			•				0	0.4	9
s_{10}	`m = y;`			•				0	0.2	12
s_{11}	`else if (x > z)`							0	0.2	12
s_{12}	`m = x;`							0	0	13
s_{13}	`print("Middle number is: ", m);}`	•	•	•	•	•	•	0.5	1.0	7
Pass/Fail		P	P	P	P	P	F	—	—	—

Source: Adapted from Jones et al. [2]/IEEE.

more suspicious to contain or be related to faults. However, when statements share identical suspiciousness and identical ranks accordingly, *Tarantula* uses the confidence values to resolve ties. For example, *suspiciousness*(s_9) = 0 and *suspiciousness*(s_{10}) = 0, while *confidence*(s_9) = 0.4 and *confidence*(s_{10}) = 0.2 in the example. The method for computing them for each statement is listed in Table 5.2.

Table 5.2 Computation of suspiciousness and confidence for each statement.

	Suspiciousness(s)	***Confidence(s)***
s_1, s_2, s_3, s_{13}	$1/(1+1) = 0.5$	$\max(1, 1) = 1$
s_4	$1/(1+3/5) = 0.63$	$\max(1, 3/5) = 1$
s_5, s_{10}, s_{11}	$0/(0+1/5) = 0$	$\max(0, 1/5) = 0.2$
s_6	$1/(1+2/5) = 0.71$	$\max(1, 2/5) = 1$
s_7	$1/(1+1/5) = 0.83$	$\max(0, 1/5) = 1$
s_8, s_9	$0/(0+2/5) = 0$	$\max(0, 2/5) = 0.4$
s_{12}	Assign 0 to it, since never exercised.	$\max(0, 0) = 0$

Source: Adapted from Jones et al. [2]/IEEE.

5.2 Working with Statements[2]

Many kinds of statistics-based fault-localization techniques have been proposed. A key insight is based on the assumption that certain dynamic features of program entities are more sensitive to the differences between the set of failed runs and the set of all (or successful) runs. Thus, there are two key elements underlying the successful application of such a class of dynamic analysis techniques. First, a technique should use a feature (or a set of features) to measure sensitivity. For example, the technique *Tarantula* uses program statements as the unit of assessment. Second, the technique should have a function to compare sensitivity values. The function essentially ranks the sensitivity values in a total order. For example, techniques such as *CBI* [4] and *SOBER* [5] produce a real number value to represent sensitivity and sort these values in ascending or descending order. The relative magnitudes of sensitivity values (rather than their absolute values, since the value ranges can be unbounded in general) are popularly used when ranking the program entities. By mapping the relative order of the sensitivity values back to the associated program entities, the techniques can produce a ranked list of program entities accordingly.

Researchers have proposed numerous techniques to help developers locate faults. The statistical fault localization approach [6–8] conducts statistical analysis on program execution traces and pass/fail information of executed test cases to generate a ranked list of suspicious program entities (such as statements) for developers to inspect in turn in the code. Various researchers have proposed techniques, such as Ochiai [9] and χ*Debug* [10]. Abreu et al. [11] used the Jaccard similarity coefficient for binary data as a suspiciousness formula. They also proposed using the Ochiai similarity coefficient as another suspiciousness formula. The technique ranks the statements similarly to *Tarantula* and the Jaccard coefficient. Most of these techniques are similar to *Tarantula*, except that they use different formulas to compute failure-correlation.

5.2.1 Techniques Under the Same Problem Settings

Table 5.3 shows some similarity coefficients that can be used to compute suspiciousness of program statements. Hereafter, we treat each similarity coefficient (a.k.a. a spectrum-based metric) as its own fault localization technique, and refer to the coefficient and the technique inter-changeably. For example, unless otherwise specified, when we refer to the Ochiai fault localization technique (just "Ochiai" for short), we mean a fault localization technique that makes use of the Ochiai coefficient, in the manner described in this section. With respect to variables a_{es}, a_{ns}, a_{ef}, and a_{nf}, the first subscript indicates whether the statement is executed (e) or not (n), and the second subscript indicates whether the execution is successful (s) or failed (f). For example, the a_{es} of a statement refers to the number of successful test cases that have executed the statement. In addition, with respect to each statement, we use Φ_S, Φ_F, and Φ to represent the total number of successful test cases, the total number of failed test cases, and the total number of test cases, respectively; Φ_E and Φ_N are the total number of test cases that executed/not executed the statement. We have $\Phi_S + \Phi_F = \Phi$ and $\Phi_E + \Phi_N = \Phi$.

In addition to those in Table 5.3, there are other coefficient-based metrics. For example, Cosine, a more general version of the Ochiai metric, has been used in the field of information retrieval [13]. Kulczynski1 and Kulczynski2 have been introduced and evaluated in the field of clustering using the self-organizing maps (SOM) algorithm [14, 15]. These metrics have since been used in the studies of software fault localization [11, 16, 17].

Naish et al. also evaluated the performance of a simplified version of O, called *Binary*, which ignores a_{ns} and allows programmers to see the relative importance of the two components of O [16]. *Tarantula* is another popular metric for fault localization. Table 5.4 gives a list of additional similarity coefficient-based metrics for fault localization that are not included in Table 5.3.

Researchers have conducted both empirical evaluations and theoretical proofs to understand the accuracies of these techniques. These were discussed in Chapter 4 and will not be repeated in the present chapter.

5.2.2 Statistical Variances[3]

Researchers have developed many novel fault localization techniques throughout the past two decades. To compare these techniques' applicability, we categorize them according to whether they were originally designed to use passed runs and/or failed runs to locate faults, and, if they were, we identify the respective

Table 5.3 Some similarity coefficients used for fault localization [12].

	Coefficient	Algebraic form		Coefficient	Algebraic form
1	Braun–Banquet	$\frac{a_{ef}}{\max(a_{ef} + a_{es}, a_{ef} + a_{nf})}$	10	Tarwid	$\frac{(n \times a_{ef}) - (\Phi_F \times \Phi_e)}{(n \times a_{ef}) + (\Phi_F \times \Phi_e)}$
2	Dennis	$\frac{(a_{ef} \times a_{ns}) - (a_{es} \times a_{nf})}{\sqrt{n \times (a_{ef} + a_{es}) \times (a_{ef} + a_{nf})}}$	11	Ample	$\left\lvert \frac{a_{ef}}{(a_{ef} + a_{nf})} - \frac{a_{es}}{(a_{es} + a_{ns})} \right\rvert$
3	Mountford	$\frac{a_{ef}}{0.5 \times ((a_{ef} \times a_{es}) + (a_{ef} \times a_{nf})) + (a_{es} \times a_{nf})}$	12	Phi (geometric mean)	$\frac{a_{ef} \times a_{ns} - a_{nf} \times a_{es}}{\sqrt{(a_{ef} + a_{es}) \times (a_{ef} + a_{nf}) \times (a_{es} + a_{ns}) \times (a_{nf} + a_{ns})}}$
4	Fossum	$\frac{n \times (a_{ef} - 0.5)^2}{(a_{ef} + a_{es}) \times (a_{ef} + a_{nf})}$	13	Arithmetic mean	$\frac{2(a_{ef} \times a_{ns} - a_{nf} \times a_{es})}{(a_{ef} + a_{es}) \times (a_{ns} + a_{nf}) + (a_{ef} + a_{nf}) \times (a_{es} + a_{ns})}$
5	Pearson	$\frac{n \times ((a_{ef} \times a_{ns}) - (a_{es} \times a_{nf}))^2}{\Phi_e \times \Phi_n \times \Phi_S \times \Phi_F}$	14	Cohen	$\frac{2(a_{ef} \times a_{ns} - a_{nf} \times a_{es})}{(a_{ef} + a_{es}) \times (a_{ns} + a_{es}) + (a_{ef} + a_{nf}) \times (a_{nf} + a_{ns})}$
6	Gower	$\frac{a_{ef} \times a_{ns}}{\sqrt{\Phi_F \times \Phi_e \times \Phi_n \times \Phi_S}}$	15	Fleiss	$\frac{4(a_{ef} \times a_{ns} - a_{nf} \times a_{es}) - (a_{nf} - a_{es})^2}{(2a_{ef} + a_{nf} + a_{es}) + (2a_{ns} + a_{nf} + a_{es})}$
7	Michael	$\frac{4 \times ((a_{ef} \times a_{ns}) - (a_{es} \times a_{nf}))}{(a_{ef} \times a_{ns})^2 + (a_{es} \times a_{nf})^2}$	16	Zoltar	$\frac{a_{ef}}{a_{ef} + a_{nf} + a_{es} + \frac{10000 \times a_{nf} \times a_{es}}{a_{ef}}}$
8	Pierce	$\frac{(a_{ef} \times a_{nf}) + (a_{nf} \times a_{es})}{(a_{ef} \times a_{nf}) + (2 \times (a_{nf} \times a_{ns})) + (a_{es} \times a_{ns})}$	17	Harmonic mean	$\frac{(a_{ef} \times a_{ns} - a_{nf} \times a_{es}) \times ((a_{ef} + a_{es}) \times (a_{ns} + a_{nf}) + (a_{ef} + a_{nf}) \times (a_{es} + a_{ns}))}{(a_{ef} + a_{es}) \times (a_{ns} + a_{nf}) \times (a_{ef} + a_{nf}) \times (a_{es} + a_{ns})}$
9	Baroni-Urbani and Buser	$\frac{\sqrt{(a_{ef} \times a_{ns})} + a_{ef}}{\sqrt{(a_{ef} \times a_{ns})} + a_{ef} + a_{es} + a_{nf}}$	18	Rogot2	$\frac{1}{4}\left(\frac{a_{ef}}{a_{ef} + a_{es}} + \frac{a_{ef}}{a_{ef} + a_{nf}} + \frac{a_{ns}}{a_{ns} + a_{es}} + \frac{a_{ns}}{a_{ns} + a_{nf}}\right)$

19	Simple matching	$\frac{a_{ef}+a_{ns}}{a_{ef}+a_{es}+a_{ns}+a_{nf}}$	26	Kulczynski1	$\frac{a_{ef}}{a_{nf}+a_{es}}$
20	Rogers and Tanimoto	$\frac{a_{ef}+a_{ns}}{a_{ef}+a_{ns}+2(a_{nf}+a_{es})}$	27	Anderberg	$\frac{a_{ef}}{a_{ef}+2(a_{nf}+a_{es})}$
21	Hamming	$a_{ef}+a_{ns}$	28	Dice	$\frac{2a_{ef}}{a_{ef}+a_{nf}+a_{es}}$
22	*Hamann*	$\frac{a_{ef}+a_{ns}-a_{nf}-a_{es}}{a_{ef}+a_{nf}+a_{es}+a_{ns}}$	29	Goodman	$\frac{2a_{ef}-a_{nf}-a_{es}}{2a_{ef}+a_{nf}+a_{es}}$
23	Sokal	$\frac{2(a_{ef}+a_{ns})}{2(a_{ef}+a_{ns})+a_{nf}+a_{es}}$	30	Jaccard	$\frac{a_{ef}}{a_{ef}+a_{nf}+a_{es}}$
24	Scott	$\frac{4(a_{ef}\times a_{ns}-a_{nf}\times a_{es})-(a_{nf}-a_{es})^2}{(2a_{ef}+a_{nf}+a_{es})(2a_{ns}+a_{nf}+a_{es})}$	31	Sorensen–Dice	$\frac{2a_{ef}}{2a_{ef}+a_{nf}+a_{es}}$
25	Rogot1	$\frac{1}{2}\left(\frac{a_{ef}}{2a_{ef}+a_{nf}+a_{es}}+\frac{a_{ns}}{2a_{ns}+a_{nf}+a_{es}}\right)$			

Table 5.4 Additional similarity coefficients used for fault localization.

Name	Formula	Name	Formula
Naish1 [16]	$\begin{cases} -1 & \text{if } a_{ef} < \Phi_F \\ a_{es} & \text{if } a_{ef} = \Phi_F \end{cases}$	Wong3 [10][a]	$a_{ef} - k$ where $k = \begin{cases} a_{es} & \text{if } a_{es} \leq 2 \\ 2 + 0.1(a_{es} - 2) & \text{if } 3 \leq a_{es} \leq 10 \\ 2.8 + 0.001(a_{es} - 10) & \text{if } a_{es} \geq 11 \end{cases}$
Naish2 [16]	$a_{ef} - \dfrac{a_{es}}{\Phi_S + 1}$	*O* [16]	-1 if $a_{nf} > 0$, otherwise a_{ns}
CBI Inc. [4]	$\dfrac{a_{ef}}{a_{ef} + a_{es}} - \dfrac{\Phi_F}{\Phi_F + \Phi_S}$	O^p [16]	$a_{ef} - \dfrac{a_{es}}{a_{es} + a_{ns} + 1}$
q_e [18]	$\dfrac{a_{ef}}{a_{ef} + a_{es}}$	Binary [16]	$\begin{cases} 0 & \text{if } a_{ef} < \Phi_F \\ 1 & \text{if } a_{ef} = \Phi_F \end{cases}$
Tarantula [2]	$\dfrac{a_{ef}/\Phi_F}{a_{ef}/\Phi_F + a_{es}/\Phi_S}$	Russel and Rao [19]	$\dfrac{a_{ef}}{\Phi_F + \Phi_S}$
Euclid [14]	$\sqrt{a_{ef} + a_{ns}}$	Kulczynski2 [20]	$\dfrac{a_{ef}}{2\Phi_F} + \dfrac{a_{ef}}{2a_{ef} + 2a_{es}}$
Wong1 [10][a]	a_{ef}	Ochiai [9]	$\dfrac{a_{ef}}{\sqrt{\Phi_F(a_{ef} + a_{es})}}$
Wong2 [10][a]	$a_{ef} - a_{es}$		

[a] Wong1 (Heuristic I), Wong2 (Heuristic II), Wong3 (Heuristic III(a), III(b), III(c)) [10, 21]. Also see Section 4.6.1 in Chapter 4. More details of these heuristics can be found in Section 3.4.2 of Chapter 3.

numbers of such runs. The classification is limited to approaches that locate faults in the source code. Table 5.5 summarizes the categorization. The two leftmost columns indicate the numbers of passed and failed runs. The third column lists a representative project for each category.

The use of passed runs, irrespective of the number of instances, is generally susceptible to coincidental correctness, in which a run activates a fault but does not result in a failure. Approaches such as set differencing, similarity correlation, and sequence similarity do not eliminate variations among sets of program statements that are common to passed and failed runs. Consequently, early algorithms like *chislice* [27], nearest neighbor [28], and *Tarantula* [2] cannot reliably locate faults if the passed runs suffer from coincidental correctness. Recent research has attempted to address this problem. *CP* [20] is a technique that locates faulty blocks in Unix utilities in C by computing the transition frequency among basic blocks in a run and backwardly propagating the fault-failure correlations measured by similarity coefficients along the edges of the program's control-flow graph so that the code delivering a fault receives a higher rank. Saha et al. [25] identified faulty program slices in SAP systems in the ABAP language by taking program loops in a failed run that constructs database queries as starting points of individual slices

Table 5.5 Statistical group of statement-level techniques.

No. of passed runs	No. of failed runs	Representative example
0	0	*FindBugs* (Hovemeyer and Pugh [24]) Approach: pattern matching with static analysis. Application: locates bug patterns in Java lib/desktop/server programs.
0	1	Saha et al. [25] Approach: key-based slicing and semantic differencing among traces. Application: locates faulty slices in SAP systems in the ABAP language.
0	Many	*FOnly* (Zhang et al. [26]) Approach: trend estimation Application: locates faulty statements in C utility programs.
1	0	None
1	1	*chislice* (Agrawal et al. [27]) Approach: set differencing. Application: locates faulty slices in C algorithms.
1	Many	None
Many	0	None
Many	1	*Nearest neighbor* (Renieres and Reiss [28]) Approach: sequence similarity. Application: locates faulty statements in C utility programs.
Many	Many	*Tarantula* (Jones et al. [2]) Approach: similarity correlation. Application: locates faulty statements in language interpreter programs in C.

Source: Zhang et al. [20]/IEEE.

and splitting the single failed run into several such slices, some of which are associated with correct database records and deemed as "passed." However, the passed runs generated may still be coincidentally correct. Additional discussions about the coincidental correctness issue can be found in Section 5.4.1.

Wong et al. presented a crosstab (cross tabulation)-based statistical technique for fault localization [22]. A unique aspect of this technique is that it is based on a well-defined statistical analysis, which can be used to study the relationship between two or more categorical variables. In this case, the two variables are the "test execution result (success or failure)" and the "coverage of a given statement." The null hypothesis is that they are independent. However, instead of the so-called "dependence" and "independence" relationships, the degree of association between the execution result and the coverage of each statement are of more interest. More precisely, a crosstab is constructed for each statement with two

Table 5.6 Notation used in this section.

N	Total number of test cases
N_F	Total number of failed test cases
N_S	Total number of successful test cases
$N_C(\omega)$	Number of test cases covering ω
$N_{CF}(\omega)$	Number of failed test cases covering ω
$N_{CS}(\omega)$	Number of successful test cases covering ω
$N_U(\omega)$	Number of test cases not covering ω
$N_{UF}(\omega)$	Number of failed test cases not covering ω
$N_{US}(\omega)$	Number of successful test cases not covering ω

Source: Wong et al. [22]/IEEE.

column-wise categorical variables (covered and not covered) and two row-wise categorical variables (successful and failed) to help analyze whether there exists a high (or low) degree of association between the coverage of a statement and the failed (or successful) execution result. In addition, a statistic is computed based on each table to determine the suspiciousness of the corresponding statement. Consider a statement ω in the program that is being debugged. The notation is provided in Table 5.6 in order to facilitate further discussion regarding the crosstab-based technique.

Crosstab analysis is used to study the relationship between two or more categorical variables. A crosstab, as shown in Table 5.7, is constructed for each statement such that the crosstab has two column-wise categorical variables, *covered* and *not covered*, and two row-wise categorical variables, successful and failed. For each crosstab, a hypothesis test is conducted to check for a dependence relationship. The null hypothesis is that the "program execution result is independent of the coverage of statement ω."

Table 5.7 Crosstab example.

	ω **is covered**	ω **is not covered**	Σ
Successful executions	$N_{CS}(\omega)$	$N_{US}(\omega)$	N_S
Failed executions	$N_{CF}(\omega)$	$N_{UF}(\omega)$	N_F
Σ	$N_C(\omega)$	$N_U(\omega)$	N

Source: Wong et al. [22]/IEEE.

A chi-square test can determine whether this hypothesis should be rejected. The chi-square statistic is given by:

$$\chi^2(\omega) = \frac{(N_{CF}(\omega) - E_{CF}(\omega))^2}{E_{CF}(\omega)} + \frac{(N_{CS}(\omega) - E_{CS}(\omega))^2}{E_{CS}(\omega)} + \frac{(N_{UF}(\omega) - E_{UF}(\omega))^2}{E_{UF}(\omega)} + \frac{(N_{US}(\omega) - E_{US}(\omega))^2}{E_{US}(\omega)} \tag{5.3}$$

where $E_{CF} = \frac{N_C(\omega) \times N_F}{N}$, $E_{CS} = \frac{N_C(\omega) \times N_S}{N}$, $E_{UF} = \frac{N_U(\omega) \times N_F}{N}$, and $E_{US} = \frac{N_U(\omega) \times N_S}{N}$. Under the null hypothesis, the statistic $\chi^2(\omega)$ has an approximately chi-square distribution. Given a level of significance σ, the corresponding chi-square critical value χ^2_σ from the chi-square distribution table can be found. If $\chi^2(\omega) > \chi^2_\sigma$, the null hypothesis is rejected, i.e. the execution result depends on the coverage of ω. Otherwise, the null hypothesis is accepted, i.e. the execution result and the coverage of ω are "independent." Note that the "dependence" relationship indicates a high association between the variables, whereas the "independence" relationship implies a low association. The degree of association between the execution result and the coverage of each statement can be measured based on the standard chi-square statistic. However, such a measure increases with the sample size. As a result, the measure by itself may not give the "true" degree of association. One way to address this is to use the *coefficient of contingency*, which is computed as:

$$M(\omega) = \frac{\chi^2(\omega)/N}{\sqrt{(row - 1)(col - 1)}} \tag{5.4}$$

where *row* and *col* are the numbers of categorical variables in all rows and columns, respectively, of the crosstab. This coefficient lies between 0 and 1. When $\chi^2(\omega) = 0$, $M(\omega)$ has the lower limit 0 for complete independence. In the case of a complete association, the coefficient $M(\omega)$ can reach the upper limit 1 when $row = col$. Also, a larger coefficient implies a higher association between the execution result and the coverage of ω. From Eq. (5.4), if N, *row*, and *col* are fixed (which is true in our example in Table 5.7, as $row = col = 2$), then $M(\omega)$ increases with $\chi^2(\omega)$. Under this condition, the chi-square statistic $\chi^2(\omega)$ for statement ω gives a good indication of the degree of the association between the execution result and the coverage of ω.

The next step is to decide whether the failed or successful execution result is more associated with the coverage of the statement. For each statement ω, $P_F(\omega)$ and $P_S(\omega)$ are computed as $\frac{N_{CF}(\omega)}{N_F}$ and $\frac{N_{CS}(\omega)}{N_S}$, which are the fractions of all failed and successful tests that execute ω. From Table 5.7, if $N_{CF}(\omega) \times N_{US}(\omega)$

$> N_{CS}(\omega) \times N_{UF}(\omega)$, then the coverage of ω is positively associated with the failed execution. This implies that if $P_F(\omega)$ is larger than $P_S(\omega)$, then the association between the failed execution and the coverage of ω is higher than that between the successful execution and the coverage of ω. A statistic is defined as:

$$\varphi(\omega) = \frac{P_F(\omega)}{P_S(\omega)} = \frac{N_{CF}(\omega)/N_F}{N_{CS}(\omega)/N_S} \tag{5.5}$$

If $\varphi(\omega) = 1$, we have $\chi^2(\omega) = 0$, which implies the execution result is completely independent of the coverage of ω. In this case, the coverage of ω makes the same contribution to both the failed and the successful execution result. If $\varphi(\omega) > 1$, the coverage of ω is more associated with the failed execution. Otherwise, the coverage of ω is more associated with the successful execution. Depending on the values of $\chi^2(\omega)$ and $\varphi(\omega)$, statements of the program being debugged can be categorized into one of the following classes:

1) Statements with $\varphi > 1$ and $\chi^2 > \chi^2_\sigma$ that have a high degree of association between their coverage and the failed execution result.
2) Statements with $\varphi > 1$ and $\chi^2 \leq \chi^2_\sigma$ that have a low degree of association between their coverage and the failed execution result.
3) Statements with $\varphi < 1$ and $\chi^2 > \chi^2_\sigma$ that have a high degree of association between their coverage and the successful execution result.
4) Statements with $\varphi < 1$ and $\chi^2 \leq \chi^2_\sigma$ that have a low degree of association between their coverage and the successful execution result.
5) Statements with $\varphi = 1$ (under this situation, $0 = \chi^2 < \chi^2_\sigma$) whose coverage is independent of the execution result.

Statements in the first class are most likely to contain program bugs (i.e. have the highest suspiciousness), followed by those in the second, the fifth, and the fourth classes. Statements in the third class are least likely to contain bugs (i.e. have the lowest suspiciousness). As discussed before, the larger the coefficient $M(\omega)$, the higher the association between the execution result and the coverage of ω. Hence, for statements in the first and the second classes, those with a larger M are more suspicious. On the other hand, for statements in the third and the fourth classes, those with a smaller M are more suspicious. Formally, the suspiciousness of a statement ω can now be defined by a statistic ζ:

$$\zeta(\omega) = \begin{cases} M(\omega) & \text{if } \varphi(\omega) > 1 \\ 0 & \text{if } \varphi(\omega) = 1 \\ -M(\omega) & \text{if } \varphi(\omega) < 1 \end{cases} \tag{5.6}$$

5.3 Working with Non-statements[4]

Ideally, the source code of a program can be statically and completely partitioned into a set of equivalent classes of these features. For instance, basic blocks can be used as an equivalence criterion, in which case every statement in any basic block can be assigned to exactly one partition. Such a partitioning process may also be applied when statements, edges, and predicates, to name a few, are used as a feature. Existing work has proposed many similarity coefficients [4, 5, 10, 28] or derived coefficients [29, 30]. Such a technique abstractly models a program as a set of features, such as nodes [11, 31], edges [20, 29], predicates [4, 5], sequences of edges [32], sequences of conditionals in predicates [33, 34], and data values [35], and it estimates the likelihood (such as fault suspiciousness) that each feature is related to the observed failures or anomalies. From the above list of proposals, finding a good set of features is obviously important.

5.3.1 Predicate: a Popular Trend[5]

One popular strategy is to use predicates as program entities, and use execution counts and execution results as dynamic features [4, 5, 32]. It estimates the difference between the probability of failed runs and the probability of successful runs and then sort the program entities accordingly. Related studies on statistical fault localization [4, 5, 32] have found the fault-relevant predicates in a program by counting the number of times a predicate is evaluated to be true in an execution as well as the number of times it is evaluated to be false, and then comparing these counts in various ways.

Figure 5.1 shows a code excerpt. In this code fragment [30], seven predicates are included, labeled as `P1–P7`. The statement "`goto ret1;`" (labeled as `E1`) is intentionally commented out by the Siemens researchers to simulate a statement omission fault. Locating this kind of fault is often difficult, even if the execution of a failed test case is traced step-by-step.

Here, a program predicate (or simply predicate) about some property of execution at a program location may be evaluated to a certain truth value. For example, the condition "`rdf <= 0 || cdf <= 0`" of the branch statement "`P1: if (rdf <= 0 || cdf <= 0)`" in Figure 5.1 is regarded as a predicate. If this branch statement is exercised in the program execution and the condition is evaluated to be true (e.g. the value of variable "`rdf`" is less than zero), the corresponding predicate is said evaluated to be true with respect to that execution. If this branch statement is exercised in the program execution and the condition is evaluated to be false, the corresponding predicate is said evaluated to be false with respect to that execution. If this branch statement is not exercised and the condition is not evaluated, the predicate is said to be not evaluated with respect to that execution.

```
P1:   if (rdf <= 0 || cdf <= 0) {
        info = -3.0;
        goto ret3;
      }
      ...
P2:   for (i = 0; i < r; ++i) {
        double sum = 0.0;
P3:     for (j = 0; j< c; ++j) {
          long k = x(i, j);
          if (k < 0L) {
            info = -2.0;
E1:         /* goto ret1; */
          sum += (double) k;
        }
        N += xi[i] = sum;
      }
P5:   if (N <= 0.0) {
        info = -1.0;
        goto ret1;
      }
P6:   for (j = 0; j < c; ++j) {
        double sum = 0.0;
P7:     for (i = 0; i < r; ++i) {
          sum += (double) x(i, j);
        xj[j]= sum;
      }
      ...
      ret1:
```

Figure 5.1 Sample program to illustrate predicate-based fault localization. *Source:* Zhang et al. [30]/Elsevier.

The evaluation bias of a predicate [5] is the percentage that it is evaluated to be true among all evaluations in a run. The *SOBER* approach [5] proposes to contrast the differences between a set of evaluation biases due to passed test cases and failure-causing ones for every predicate in the program. It hypothesizes that the greater the difference between such a pair of sets of evaluation biases, the higher the chance that the corresponding predicate is fault-relevant. The *CBI* approach [4] proposes a heuristic that measures the increase in probability that a predicate is evaluated to be true in a set of failure-causing test cases, compared to the whole set of (passed and failure-causing) test cases. These proposals are particularly interested in the evaluation results of predicates. They use the resultant values of the predicates to determine the ranks. A predicate can be semantically modeled as a Boolean expression. The resultant values of a Boolean expression may be calculated from different evaluation sequences [34] or from the whole predicate as one unit. If the information on evaluation sequences is ignored, useful statistics for effective fault localization may be masked out. *DES* [34] investigates whether the effect of a lower-tier concept – evaluation sequences – of predicates can be a significant factor affecting the effectiveness of predicate-based statistical fault localization.

By sampling selected predicates, rather than all predicates or statements, this strategy reduces the overhead in collecting debugging information. It also avoids disclosing a particular aspect of every execution, such as which statements have been executed. Hence, it lowers the risk of information leakage, which is a security concern.

5.3.2 BPEL: a Sample Application[6]

BPEL programs are represented as a set of hierarchical statement blocks. A statement block corresponds to a set of elements enclosed by the matched XML tags and describes the interaction by specifying the activity type, operation name, input variables, output variables, partner link, port type, target link names, and source link names. To simplify the fault localization of BPEL programs, a statement block may be classified as an atomic statement block or a nonatomic statement block [36]. The former refers to an atomic execution step, including assign, invoke, receive, reply, throw, wait, and empty. The latter is a composite of atomic statement blocks and/or nonatomic statement blocks, including sequence, switch, while, flow, and pick. For ease of discussion, statement blocks with similar semantics are abstracted as the same type. In this context, nonatomic statement blocks can be classified into the following four types: sequential statement blocks are those whose child statement blocks are executed in a sequential order, such as sequence activity; optional statement blocks are those where only one child statement block can be executed, such as switch, if/else/elseif, and pick activity; parallel statement blocks are those whose child statement blocks are executed simultaneously, such as flow activity; and loop statement blocks are those whose child statement blocks are executed all the time until some conditions are satisfied, such as *while*, *until While*, and *forEach* activity.

Based on the BPEL programming model and debugging concerns discussed above, a statement block-oriented fault localization framework for BPEL programs was proposed by Sun et al. [36]. Consider a BPEL program $bp\langle s_1, s_{2,\ldots}, s_n\rangle$, where $s_{1,\ldots}, s_n$ denote a set of statement blocks. Let $ts\langle t_1, t_{2,\ldots}, t_m\rangle$ be a set of test cases. The aim is to find the most suspicious statement block that causes the observed failures. The fault location process with our fault localization framework consists of the following four phases [36]:

Phase 1: When a failure *f* is reported during the execution of a BPEL program *bp*, it first manages to restore the test suite *ts* that reveals *f*.

Phase 2: Each test case *t* in *ts* runs *bp* to capture the coverage status *cs* of each statement block with respect to the execution of *t*, which is accordingly identified as "pass" or "fail."

Phase 3: It uses *cs* as input of an existing fault localization formula *r* to calculate the suspiciousness scores for each statement block. The most suspicious statement block is termed *mssb*.

Phase 4: According to the type of *mssb*, the possible position set *pps* is recommended by following the fault localization guidelines [36].

The framework does not limit the use of different fault localization formulas. However, the effectiveness of our fault localization framework is related to the choice of fault localization formulas. To differentiate between the use of various fault localization formulas, it refers to an instantiating of the framework based on a given formula as a synthesized fault localization technique. The proposed framework is very generic and can incorporate a variety of fault localization techniques (algorithms) that have been already developed for typical programs. When these techniques were developed, testing history information was usually expected to be available, such as what test cases were used and what statements were covered. When these fault localization strategies are employed to debug BPEL programs, they must be adapted to the context of statement blocks.

5.4 Purifying the Input

Besides choosing a meaningful feature for the desired application domain and developing more accurate coefficient formulas, purifying input is also a research focus.

5.4.1 Coincidental Correctness Issue

Many techniques use a pair of a passed test case and a failed test case to debug programs. For instance, Renieres and Reiss [28] found the difference in execution traces between a failed execution and its "nearest neighbor" successful execution. However, coincidental correctness may occur in a successful execution [37]. A poorly chosen successful run may adversely affect the effectiveness of the above technique and the like.

A way to address the issue of coincidental correctness is to completely abandon the use of passed runs. Static analyzers like *FindBugs* [24] require neither passed nor failed runs. They may, however, produce warnings even if the programs are correct, necessitating additional runs to confirm such warnings. When only one single failed run is available, early techniques like dynamic program slicing [27] could produce a set of statements per run. Debuggers similar to *Tarantula* [2], such as Ochiai [9], can also be used without any passed runs. The problem is that such brute-force applications are mostly ineffective in fault localization.

On the other hand, modern software often has the built-in facility to detect failures and report them to the original vendor through the Web. Software debuggers are thus faced with a huge number of automatic bug reports. It would be time-consuming for debuggers to generate a similar number of passed runs to compare with the given failed runs. This creates a strong incentive for fault-localization techniques that make good use of failure information only. *FOnly* [26] was proposed to locate faults solely from failed test executions. It is based on the following fault hypothesis: considering a particular run of a faulty program, the more times that the run goes through a faulty program entity such as a statement, the more likely it will consistently lead to failure. If such a trend cannot be observed among the failed runs with respect to another program entity, the latter entity is less likely to be at fault.

Trend estimation, a popular statistical technique, is the basis of *FOnly*. A simple but effective means of trend estimation is to find a regression line using the least-squares fitting process. Such a line reveals the tendencies in the samples. Based on samples of the numbers of times that different failed runs go through the same program entity, *FOnly* finds a regression line that minimizes the fitting error. It then uses the slope of the regression line and the value of the fitting error to compute a signal-to-noise ratio, which represents an estimate of that program entity's fault relevance. Program entities with higher signal-to-noise ratios are deemed to be more fault-relevant.

5.4.2 Class Balance Consideration

When conducting a typical software test, after the execution, each test case in a given test suite of a program can be classified into one of two subsets, the set P of passed test cases and the set F of failed test cases, according to whether or not the execution of the program over the test case produces an expected output. The ratio $P : F$ is referred to as the class balance ratio [38]. If the class balance ratio of a test suite is not close to 1, the test suite is said to be class-imbalanced. It is well known that the class balance ratios of practical test suites of real-world programs are not close to 1. In fact, in most cases, the number of failed test cases is much smaller than the number of passed test cases in the same test suite. On the other hand, Gong et al. [38] reported that if the class balance ratio is much larger than 1, many techniques such as Jaccard [2], *Hamann* [7], Wong2 [10], *Euclid* [14], Ochiai [9], and Wong3 [10] have been shown to result in a low fault-localization accuracy. There is a need to overcome this problem incurred by a given typical test suite so that research results, which have been developed for more than 10 years, can be more readily transferred to the industry.

The general direction to mitigate the class-imbalance problem stated in the last subsection is to construct a class-balanced test suite from a given class-imbalanced suite. An addition-based strategy adds test cases to the given test suite. Adding arbitrary test cases to produce a class-balanced test suite is not feasible. Gao et al. [39] proposed to clone these failed test cases in the given test suite and add them to the above failed subset to make the class balance ratio close to 1. Until sufficient empirical findings accumulate, the particular failed test cases that are to be cloned (or cloned more) cannot be determined. Pursuing the understanding of the influence of the addition-based strategy, Gao et al. proposed to clone the entire given set of failed test cases for a certain number of times until the size of the enlarged set caught up with the size of the set of the passed test cases. They studied the above cloning strategy on the risk evaluation formulas of two techniques, Jaccard [11] and Wong2 [10], in the single-fault scenario through a postmortem analysis. It was empirically shown that both Jaccard and Wong2 became more accurate with more balanced test suites [38].

5.5 Reinterpreting the Output

A conventional statistic-based fault localization technique outputs a list of suspicious program elements, the order of which is based on the degree that each is deemed related to a fault. On one hand, such a format of output may not be what a programmer expects or feels is easy to use. On the other hand, reinterpreting the output can attract the attention of researchers.

5.5.1 Revealing Fault Number[7]

Table 5.8 (from [38]) shows a program excerpt to find the middle number among three inputs. In this program, the main procedure (lines 1–4) reads three inputs *x*, *y*, and *z*, invokes the function *mid* to find the median among them, and creates a buffer string *msg* to receive the answer. In the function mid (lines 6–33), the values of *x*, *y*, and *z* are compared, and an answer is written into the buffer string. When all three inputs are zero, it is deemed uninitialized, and a warning will be given. There exist at least two faults (line 11 and line 25) in the program. Ten test cases are chosen to run the program, and it is found that four of them (t_4, t_6, t_7, and t_9) fail to output correct results. An "F" is used in the "test result" row to indicate a failed run.

The failed test cases confirm the existence of fault(s) in the program. The coverage status for each statement is captured in the program run with respect to each test case. In Table 5.8, we use a dot "•" to indicate that a statement is exercised in a program run; otherwise, the cell is left blank. Suppose a programmer uses *Tarantula* [2] to locate faults. As shown, statements at lines 18, 21, 23, 26, and 29 are assigned the highest suspiciousness value and are given the highest ranking. They

Table 5.8 Adapting single-fault localizer to locate multiple faults in one round of checking.

			Test cases											
			t_1	t_2	t_3	t_4	t_5	t_6	t_7	t_8	t_9	t_{10}	*Score*	*Rank*
The	1:	`string buf[0xf]`	•	•	•	•	•	•	•	•	•	•	0.50	14
first	2:	`read("Input 3 numbers: ", x, y, z);`	•	•	•	•	•	•	•	•	•	•	0.50	14
round:	3:	`invoke mid(x, y, z, buf);`	•	•	•	•	•	•	•	•	•	•	0.50	14
	4:	`write(buf) ;`	•	•	•	•	•	•	•	•	•	•	0.50	14
	5:													
	6:	`function`												
	7:	`mid(int x, int y, int z, string msg)`												
	8:	`{`												
	9:	`msg = "mid: z";`	•	•	•	•	•	•	•	•	•	•	0.50	14
	10:	`if (y < z)`	•	•	•	•	•	•	•	•	•	•	0.50	14
	11:	`if (x >= y) //` **`x < y`**		•	•	•	•	•		•	•	•	0.47	16
	12:	`msg = "mid: y";`		•	•	•	•	•		•	•	•	0.47	16
	13:	`else if (x < z)`												32
	14:	`msg = "mid: x";`												32
	15:	`else if (x > y)`	•						•				0.60	7
	16:	`msg = "mid: y";`												32
	17:	`else if (x > z)`	•						•				0.60	7
	18:	`msg = "mid: x";`							•				1.00	5
	19:													32
	20:	`if (x != y)`	•	•	•	•	•	•	•	•	•	•	0.50	14
	21:	`if (y == z)`				•		•			•		1.00	5

(*Continued*)

Table 5.8 (Continued)

			Test cases											
			t_1	t_2	t_3	t_4	t_5	t_6	t_7	t_8	t_9	t_{10}	*Score*	*Rank*
	22:	`msg = "mid: y or z";`												32
	23:	`else if (x == z)`				•		•			•		1.00	5
	24:	`msg = "mid: x or z";`												32
	25:	`else if (y += z) //` **`y == z`**	•	•	•		•		•	•		•	0.20	17
	26:	`if (x == 0)`							•				1.00	5
	27:	`msg = "warning: uninitialized";`												32
	28:	`else`												32
	29:	`msg = "mid: x, y, or z";`							•				1.00	5
	30:	`else`												32
	31:	`msg = "mid: x or y";`	•	•	•		•			•		•	0.00	18
	32:	`}`												32
		Test result:				F		F	F		F		*the 1st fault*	
The second round	25:	`else if (y += z) //` **`y == z`**	•	•	•		•		•	•		•	0.20	17
		Test result:							F				*the 2nd fault*	
The third round	1:	`char msg[0xf];`	•	•	•	•	•	•	•	•	•	•		
	27:	`msg = "warning: uninitialized";`	•											
		Test result:	F											

Source: Gong et al. [38]/IEEE.

are examined first, but no fault exists in them. Statements 15 and 17 are examined next, and statements 1, 2, 3, 4, 9, 10, and 20 are examined after that. When statements 11 and 12 are examined, a fault is found at statement 11. Now, 16 statements have been examined to locate the first fault, and the effort is 16/32 = 50%. The programmer stops checking the remaining statements, fixes the fault in statement 11, conducts a regression test on all the test cases, and finds a failed run (t_7) in the second round. This time, a 53% effort (17 of the 32 statements are examined) is needed to locate the second fault (in statement 25).

By using *Tarantula* to locate the two faults (at statements 11 and 25), 33 statements are examined in total, and many of them have been checked twice. An interesting phenomenon is that the ranking order of statements in the ranked list of the second round resembles that in the first round to a great extent. Can one simply skip the statements examined in the first round when locating the second fault (in the second round)? The answer is no, and in fact, such a heuristic is very risky. For example, after fixing the second fault, the regression testing is conducted on all the test cases, and one run (t_1) fails in the third round. The third fault is found on statement 1, which unsuitably allocates space for a buffer string used in statement 27. However, since statement 27 is never exercised in the former two rounds, there is no clue to point out the faultiness of statement 1, even if it has been checked in the former two rounds. Blindly skipping the statements examined in previous rounds will result in a high chance of missing a fault.

Let us revisit the checking round to find clues. When the first fault (at statement 11) is located, it is found exercised in the program runs of test cases t_2, t_3, t_4, t_5, t_6, t_8, t_9, and t_{10}. The failure observed with test case t_7 is not explained [38] because the located fault (statement 11) is not exercised in the program run of t_7. As a result, one has evidence that there remains at least one fault in the program, and the most promising action is to continue checking the rest candidates. The next suspicious candidate is statement 25, which is found to be faulty. As a result, a 53% effort (17 of the 32 statements are examined) is used to locate two faults with one checking round. The improved efficiency is satisfactory. It can be seen that statement 25 is exercised in the program run of t_7. Since the found faults (at statements 11 and 25) can explain all the observed failures, one can stop checking, fix the two faults, and conduct regression testing as usual.

5.5.2 Noise Reduction[8]

Surprisingly, when a typical technique focuses on one partition A during the fault suspiciousness assessment process, it (or its coefficient similarity formula) consistently ignores other partitions in the same execution, and yet the failure verdict for partition A is in fact related to all the partitions along the same execution. For a long-lived execution, the noise introduced by such deliberately ignored partitions may exhibit a significant impact on the accuracy of the measured correlation value.

Xu et al. [40] introduced the notion of noise reduction and proposed a technique to reduce noise incurred in *Tarantula*. They showed that reducing the noise from unwanted features improves the effectiveness of *Tarantula*. They also proposed a feature known as key chain for fault localization, which intuitively means a chain of basic blocks, and showed that it can synthesize a more promising novel technique *MKBC*. Their experiment showed that *MKBC* was more effective than *Tarantula*, Jaccard, and Ochiai in locating faults in three medium-scaled program subjects.

Xu et al. also showed that reducing the noise means subtracting the possibility of not executing a feature causing a failure, and they proposed to exchange the executed and non-executed parts to estimate the noise. In the same manner, a_{nf} was used instead of a_{ef}, a_{ns} instead of a_{es}, a_{ef} instead of a_{nf}, and a_{es} instead of a_{ns}, to estimate the noise in *Tarantula* as follows:

$$Tarantula' = Tarantula - Noise = \frac{\dfrac{a_{ef}}{a_{ef}+a_{nf}}}{\dfrac{a_{ef}}{a_{ef}+a_{nf}} + \dfrac{a_{es}}{a_{es}+a_{ns}}} - \frac{\dfrac{a_{nf}}{a_{ef}+a_{nf}}}{\dfrac{a_{nf}}{a_{ef}+a_{nf}} + \dfrac{a_{ns}}{a_{es}+a_{ns}}} \tag{5.7}$$

Their work thus generalized the concept of noise-reduction in *MKBC* to propose a general fault-localization framework that can be used to synthesize various fault-localization techniques based on the inputted existing technique. Empirical studies showed that a majority of existing techniques can benefit from such a noise-reduction strategy.

Notes

1 Part of Section 5.1 is from Ref. [1].
2 Part of Section 5.2 is from Ref. [3].
3 Part of Section 5.2.2 is from Refs. [20, 22, 23].
4 Part of Section 5.3 is from Ref. [1].
5 Part of Section 5.3.1 is from Ref. [3].
6 Part of Section 5.3.2 is from Ref. [36].
7 Part of Section 5.5.1 is from Ref. [38].
8 Part of Section 5.5.2 is from Ref. [3].

References

1 Xu, J., Zhang, Z., Chan, W.K., and Tse, T.H. (2013). A general noise-reduction framework for fault localization of Java programs. *Information and Software Technology* 55 (5): 880–896. ISSN 0950-5849. https://doi.org/10.1016/j.infsof.2012.08.006.

2 Jones, J.A., Harrold, M.J., and Stasko, J. (2002). Visualization of test information to assist fault localization. *Proceedings of the 24th International Conference on Software Engineering (ICSE '02)*, Orlando, FL, USA (19–25 May 2002), 467–477. IEEE. https://doi.org/10.1145/581396.581397.

3 Zhang, Z., Jiang, B., Chan, W.K. et al. (2010). Fault localization through evaluation sequences. *Journal of Systems and Software* 83 (2): 174–187. ISSN 0164-1212. https://doi.org/10.1016/j.jss.2009.09.041.

4 Liblit, B., Naik, M., Zheng, A.X. et al. (2005). Scalable statistical bug isolation. *Proceedings of* the *2005 ACM SIGPLAN Conference on Programming Language Design and Implementation (PLDI '05)*, Chicago, IL, USA (12–15 June 2005), 15–26. ACM. https://doi.org/10.1145/1065010.1065014. ISBN 1-59593-056-6.

5 Liu, C., Fei, L., Yan, X. et al. (2006). Statistical debugging: a hypothesis testing based approach. *IEEE Transactions on Software Engineering* 32 (10): 831–848. ISSN 0098-5589. https://doi.org/10.1109/TSE.2006.105.

6 Cohen, J. (1960). A coefficient of agreement for nominal scales. *Educational and Psychological Measurement* 20 (1): 37–46.

7 Hamming, R.W. (1950). Error detecting and error correcting codes. *The Bell System Technical Journal* 29 (2): 147–160. ISSN 0005-8580. https://doi.org/10.1002/j.1538-7305.1950.tb00463.x.

8 Jaccard, P. (1901). Etude de la distribution florale dans une portion des Alpes et du Jura. *Bulletin de la Societe Vaudoise des Sciences Naturelles* 37: 547–579. https://doi.org/10.5169/seals-266450.

9 Ochiai, A. (1957). Zoogeographical studies on the soleoid fishes found Japan and its neighboring regions. *Bulletin of the Japanese Society of Scientific Fischeries* 22 (9): 526–530.

10 Wong, W.E., Debroy, V., and Choi, B. (2010). A family of code coverage-based heuristics for effective fault localization. *Journal of Systems and Software* 83 (2): 188–208. ISSN 0164-1212. https://doi.org/10.1016/j.jss.2009.09.037.

11 Abreu, R., Zoeteweij, P., Golsteijn, R., and van Gemund, A.J.C. (2009). A practical evaluation of spectrum-based fault localization. *Journal of Systems and Software* 82 (11): 1780–1792.

12 Wong, W.E., Debroy, V., Gao, R., and Li, Y. (2014). The DStar method for effective software fault localization. *IEEE Transactions on Reliability* 63 (1): 290–308. https://doi.org/10.1109/TR.2013.2285319.

13 Dunham, M. (2002). *Data Mining: Introductory and Advanced Topics. Pearson Education India.*

14 Krause, E.F. (1973). Taxicab geometry. *Mathematics Teacher* 66 (8): 695–706.

15 Lourenço, F., Lobo, V., and Bacao, F. (2004). Binary-based similarity measures for categorical data and their application in self-organizing maps. In *JOCLAD 2004-XI Jornadas de Classificacao e Anlise de Dados*, Lisbon (1–3 April 2004), 1–18.

16 Naish, L., Lee, H.J., and Ramamohanarao, K. (2011). A model for spectra-based software diagnosis. *ACM Transactions on Software Engineering and Methodology* 20 (3): 11:1–11:32. ISSN 1049-331X. https://doi.org/10.1145/2000791.2000795.

17 Abreu, R., Zoeteweij, P., and Van Gemund, A.J.C. (2006). An evaluation of similarity coefficients for software fault localization. *Proceedings of the 2006 12th Pacific Rim International Symposium on Dependable Computing (PRDC '06)* (18–20 December 2006), 39–46. IEEE. https://doi.org/10.1109/PRDC.2006.18.

18 Lee, H.J., Naish, L., and Ramamohanarao, K. (2009). Study of the relationship of bug consistency with respect to performance of spectra metrics. *Proceedings of the 2009 2nd IEEE International Conference on Computer Science and Information Technology*, Beijing, China (8–11 August 2009), 501–508. IEEE. https://doi.org/10.1109/ICCSIT.2009.5234512.

19 Russell, P.F. and Rao., T.R. (1940). On habitat and association of species of Anopheline Larvae in south-eastern Madras. *Journal of the Malaria Institute of India* 3 (1): 153–178.

20 Zhang, Z., Chan, W.K., and Tse, T.H. (2012). Fault localization based only on failed runs. *Computer* 45 (6): 64–71. ISSN 0018-9162. https://doi.org/10.1109/MC.2012.185.

21 Wong, W.E., Qi, Y., Zhao, L., and Cai, K. (2007). Effective fault localization using code coverage. *Proceedings of the 31st Annual International Computer Software and Applications Conference (COMPSAC '07)*, Beijing, China (24–27 July 2007), 1: 449–456. IEEE. https://doi.org/10.1109/COMPSAC.2007.109.

22 Wong, W.E., Debroy, V., and Xu, D. (2012). Towards better fault localization: a crosstab-based statistical approach. *IEEE Transactions on Systems, Man, and Cybernetics, Part C (Applications and Reviews)* 42 (3): 378–396. ISSN 1094-6977. https://doi.org/10.1109/TSMCC.2011.2118751.

23 Wong, W.E., Wei, T., Qi, Y., and Zhao, L. (2008). A crosstab-based statistical method for effective fault localization. *Proceedings of the 2008 International Conference on Software Testing, Verification, and Validation*, Lillehammer, Norway (9–11 April 2008), 42–51. IEEE. ISSN 2159-4848. https://doi.org/10.1109/ICST.2008.65.

24 Hovemeyer, D. and Pugh, W. (2004). Finding bugs is easy. *ACM SIGPLAN Notices* 39 (12): 92–106. ISSN 0362-1340. https://doi.org/10.1145/1052883.1052895.

25 Saha, D., Nanda, M.G., Dhoolia, P. et al. (2011). Fault localization for data-centric programs. *Proceedings of the 19th ACM SIGSOFT Symposium and the 13th European Conference on Foundations of Software Engineering (ESEC/FSE '11)*, Szeged, Hungary

(5–9 September 2011), 157–167. ACM. https://doi.org/10.1145/2025113.2025137. ISBN 978-1-4503-0443-6.

26 Zhang, X., Gupta, N., and Gupta, R. (2006). Locating faults through automated predicate switching. *Proceedings of the 28th International Conference on Software Engineering (ICSE '06)*, Shanghai, China (20–28 May 2006), 272–281. ACM. https://doi.org/10.1145/1134285.1134324. ISBN 1-59593-375-1.

27 Agrawal, H., Horgan, J.R., London, S., and Wong, W.E. (1995). Fault localization using execution slices and dataflow tests. *Proceedings of the Sixth International Symposium on Software Reliability Engineering (ISSRE '95)*, Toulouse, France (24–27 October 1995), 143–151. IEEE. https://doi.org/10.1109/ISSRE.1995.497652.

28 Renieres, M. and Reiss, S.P. (2003). Fault localization with nearest neighbor queries. *Proceedings of the 18th IEEE International Conference on Automated Software Engineering, 2003*, Montreal, QC, Canada (6–10 October 2003), 30–39. IEEE. https://doi.org/10.1109/ASE.2003.1240292.

29 Santelices, R., Jones, J.A., and Harrold, M.J. (2009). Lightweight fault-localization using multiple coverage types. *Proceedings of the 2009 IEEE 31st International Conference on Software Engineering*, Vancouver, BC, Canada (16–24 May 2009), 56–66. IEEE. https://doi.org/10.1109/ICSE.2009.5070508.

30 Zhang, Z., Chan, W.K., Tse, T.H. et al. (2009). Is non-parametric hypothesis testing model robust for statistical fault localization? *Information and Software Technology* 51 (11): 1573–1585. ISSN 0950-5849. https://doi.org/10.1016/j.infsof.2009.06.013.

31 Jones, J.A. and Harrold, M.J. (2005). Empirical evaluation of the Tarantula automatic fault-localization technique. *Proceedings of the 20th IEEE/ACM International Conference on Automated Software Engineering (ASE '05)*, Long Beach, CA, USA (7–11 November 2005), 273–282. ACM. https://doi.org/10.1145/1101908.1101949. ISBN 1-58113-993-4.

32 Chilimbi, T.M., Liblit, B., Mehra, K. et al. (2009). HOLMES: effective statistical debugging via efficient path profiling. *Proceedings of the 2009 IEEE 31st International Conference on Software Engineering*, Vancouver, BC, Canada (16–24 May 2009), 34–44. IEEE. https://doi.org/10.1109/ICSE.2009.5070506.

33 Nainar, P.A., Chen, T., Rosin, J., and Liblit, B. (2007). Statistical debugging using compound boolean predicates. *Proceedings of the ACM/SIGSOFT International Symposium on Software Testing and Analysis (ISSTA '07),* London, UK (9–12 July 2007), 5–15. ACM. https://doi.org/10.1145/1273463.1273467.

34 Zhang, Z., Chan, W.K., Tse, T.H. et al. (2011). Fault localization. *Journal of Systems and Software* 84 (6): 885–905. ISSN 0164-1212. https://doi.org/10.1016/j.jss.2010.12.048.

35 Jeffrey, D., Gupta, N., and Gupta, R. (2008). Fault localization using value replacement. *Proceedings of the 2008 International Symposium on Software Testing and Analysis (ISSTA '08)*, Seattle, WA, USA (20–24 July 2008), 167–178. ACM. https://doi.org/10.1145/1390630.1390652. ISBN 978-1-60558-050-0.

36 Sun, C., Zhai, Y., Shang, Y., and Zhang, Z. (2013). BPELDebugger: an effective BPEL-specific fault localization framework. *Information and Software Technology* 55 (12): 2140–2153. ISSN 0950-5849. https://doi.org/10.1016/j.infsof.2013.07.009.

37 Wang, X., Cheung, S.C., Chan, W.K., and Zhang, Z. (2009). Taming coincidental correctness: coverage refinement with context patterns to improve fault localization. *Proceedings of the 2009 IEEE 31st International Conference on Software Engineering*, Vancouver, BC, Canada (16–24 May 2009), 45–55. IEEE. https://doi.org/10.1109/ICSE.2009.5070507.

38 Gong, C., Zheng, Z., Zhang, Y. et al. (2012). Factorising the multiple fault localization problem: adapting single-fault localizer to multi-fault programs. *Proceedings of the 2012 19th Asia-Pacific Software Engineering Conference (APSEC '12)*, Hong Kong (4–7 December 2012), 1: 729–732. https://doi.org/10.1109/APSEC.2012.22.

39 Gao, Y., Zhang, Z., Zhang, L. et al. (2013). A theoretical study: the impact of cloning failed test cases on the effectiveness of fault localization. *Proceedings of the 2013 13th International Conference on Quality Software*, Nanjing, China (29–30 July 2013), 288–291. IEEE. https://doi.org/10.1109/QSIC.2013.23.

40 Xie, X., Chen, T.Y., Kuo, F., and Xu, B. (2013). A theoretical analysis of the risk evaluation formulas for spectrum-based fault localization. *ACM Transactions on Software Engineering and Methodology* 22 (4): 31:1–31:40. ISSN 1049-331X. https://doi.org/10.1145/2522920.2522924.

6

Machine Learning-Based Techniques for Software Fault Localization

W. Eric Wong

Department of Computer Science, University of Texas at Dallas, Richardson, TX, USA

6.1 Introduction

Arthur Samuel, an American pioneer in the field of computer gaming and artificial intelligence, coined the term "machine learning" in 1959 [1] while working at IBM. Machine learning is the study of computer algorithms that improve through experience. Machine learning techniques are adaptive and robust and can produce models based on data, with limited human interaction. This has led to their employment in many disciplines such as bioinformatics, natural language processing, cryptography, and computer vision.

With the increase in the computational abilities of modern computer systems, machine learning is becoming the most popular area in the current decade. This trend will, with little doubt, last for the next couple of decades. Due to the fact that one of the most time-consuming activities during software testing is debugging, it is of significant interest to researchers and engineers from both academia and industry to apply machine learning algorithms and other techniques to this area. In the context of fault localization, the problem at hand can be identified as trying to learn or deduce the location of a fault based on input data, such as the statement coverage and the execution result (success or failure) of each test case.

In the existing literature, three unique approaches have been proposed. In Section 6.2, a back-propagation (BP) neural network-based approach is introduced. It aims to build a model to discover the underlying relationships between test inputs and the results of these test cases (failed or successful). In Section 6.3, an improved approach is introduced based on radial basis function (RBF) neural

Handbook of Software Fault Localization: Foundations and Advances, First Edition.
Edited by W. Eric Wong and T.H. Tse.

Published 2023 by John Wiley & Sons, Inc.

networks, which is not only more efficient but also reduces several disadvantages of BP neural networks. In Section 6.4, a machine learning approach based on decision trees is briefly described. Finally, Section 6.5 presents simulated annealing with statement pruning to tailor a spectrum-based fault localization (SBFL) formula for a specific data set.

6.2 BP Neural Network-Based Fault Localization[1]

In [2], a fault localization approach based on a BP neural network was proposed. The approach aims to utilize the computational ability of advanced computers by applying one of the most popular neural network models, the BP neural network, in practice [3].

A BP neural network has a simple structure, which makes it easy to implement using computer programs or circuits. At the same time, BP neural networks have the ability to approximate complicated nonlinear functions [4]. They have been successfully applied in software engineering. For example, Neumann [5] proposed a technique that combines principal component analysis and BP neural networks for software risk analysis. Tadayon [6] presented a BP neural network approach for software cost estimation. Su and Huang [7] reported a BP neural network-based study for software reliability estimation. Anderson, Mayrhauser, and Mraz [8] applied BP neural networks to predict the severity levels of program faults that are likely to be uncovered, if any, by each test case.

Before we can use a BP network to identify suspicious code for possible locations of program bugs, we need to run the program on a set of test cases and collect the coverage data with respect to each test execution. This is done by using a coverage measurement tool such as χSuds [9]. In the proposed approach, the coverage data of each test case is focused on the statement coverage in terms of which statements are executed by which test case. The execution result (success or failure) of each test case is also collected. Together, the coverage data and the execution result are used to train a BP neural network so that the network can learn the relationship between them. A set of virtual test cases is also used, and each of these test cases covers only one statement in the program. When these coverage data are input into a trained BP network, the outputs can be regarded as the likelihood (i.e. suspiciousness) that each statement contains the bug. Programmers can examine these statements from the top of the rank one by one until they find the bug(s).

6.2.1 Fault Localization with a BP Neural Network

Suppose we have a program P with m executable statements and exactly one fault. Suppose also that P is executed on n test cases, of which k tests are successful and

Table 6.1 Notation.

m	Number of executable statements
n	Number of test cases
t	A test case executed on P
$\mathbf{c}_t$	The coverage vector of t
$S(t)$	The set of executable statements covered by the running of t
r_t	The execution result of t ("successful" or "failed")

Source: Wong and Qi [2]/World Scientific Publishing.

$n - k$ failed. Table 6.1 lists the notation that is used in Section 6.2. Figure 6.1 gives an example of coverage data (statement coverage, in this case) and execution results that we need for the proposed fault localization method. Each row contains the statement coverage (1 means the statement is covered and 0 means not covered) and the execution result (0 means the execution is successful and 1 means failed) of a test case. For example, statement s_6 is covered by a successful test t_1, and statement s_5 is not covered by a failed test t_6.

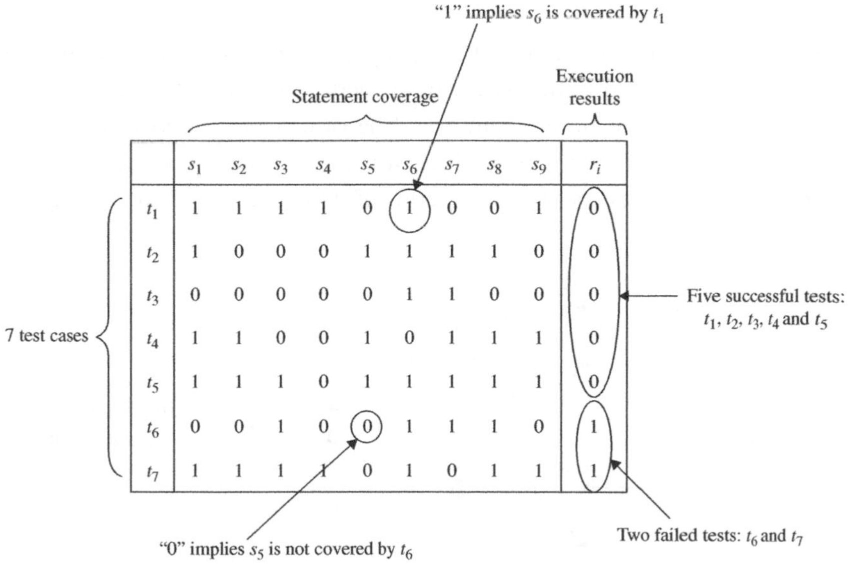

Figure 6.1 Sample coverage data and execution results. *Source:* Wong and Qi [2]/World Scientific Publishing.

Vector $\mathbf{c}_{t_i}$ denotes the coverage data obtained from the execution of test case t_i. For example, $\mathbf{c}_{t_1} = (1, 1, 1, 1, 0, 1, 0, 0, 1)$ extracted from the first row in Figure 6.1 gives the statement coverage of the execution of t_1. We refer to $\mathbf{c}_{t_i}$ as the coverage vector of t_i. Assume there is a set of virtual test cases $v_1, v_2, \ldots, v_m$, whose coverage vectors are $\mathbf{c}_{v_1}, \mathbf{c}_{v_2}, \ldots, \mathbf{c}_{v_m}$, where

$$\begin{bmatrix} \mathbf{c}_{v_1} \\ \mathbf{c}_{v_2} \\ \vdots \\ \mathbf{c}_{v_m} \end{bmatrix} = \begin{bmatrix} 1 & 0 & \cdots & 0 \\ 0 & 1 & \cdots & \vdots \\ \vdots & \vdots & \ddots & \vdots \\ 0 & 0 & \cdots & 1 \end{bmatrix} \tag{6.1}$$

The execution of virtual test case v_i ($i = 1, 2, \ldots, m$) covers only one statement s_i. If the execution of v_i fails, the probability that the fault is contained in s_i is high. This implies that during the fault localization, we should first examine the statements whose corresponding virtual test case fails. However, we cannot find $v_1, v_2, \ldots, v_m$ in the real world. In order to estimate the execution results of these virtual test cases, we build a three-layer BP neural network with m input-layer neurons, three hidden-layer neurons, and one output-layer neuron, and train it using $\mathbf{c}_{t_i}$ and r_{t_i} ($i = 1, 2, \ldots, n$) as the input data and corresponding expected output, respectively. The structure of such a BP neural network is shown in Figure 6.2. The transfer functions of the neurons are set to the sigmoid function $y = 1/(1 + e^{-x})$.

When the coverage vector $\mathbf{c}_{v_i}$ ($i = 1, 2, \ldots, m$) of a virtual test case v_i is input to the trained neural network, the output of the neural network (denoted by r'_{v_i}) is an estimation of the execution result of v_i. The value of r'_{v_i} is between 0 and 1. The larger the value of r'_{v_i}, the more likely it is that s_i contains the bug. We can treat r'_{v_i} as the suspiciousness of s_i in terms of its likelihood of containing the

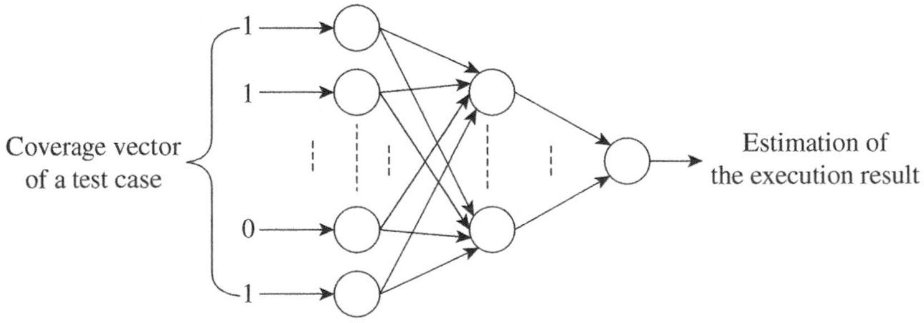

Figure 6.2 The BP neural network used in the approach. *Source:* Wong and Qi [2]/World Scientific Publishing.

bug. Figure 6.3 shows the process of computing the suspiciousness of each executable statement using a BP neural network. We summarize this part as follows:

A_1: Build up a BP neural network with m input-layer neurons, three hidden-layer neurons, and one output-layer neuron. The transfer function of each neuron is set to the sigmoid function $y = 1/(1 + e^{-x})$.

A_2: Train the neural network using $\mathbf{c}_{t_i}$ and $r_{t_i}(i = 1, 2, ..., n)$ as the input data and the corresponding expected output data, respectively. The overfitting problem is handled by the Bayesian regularization.

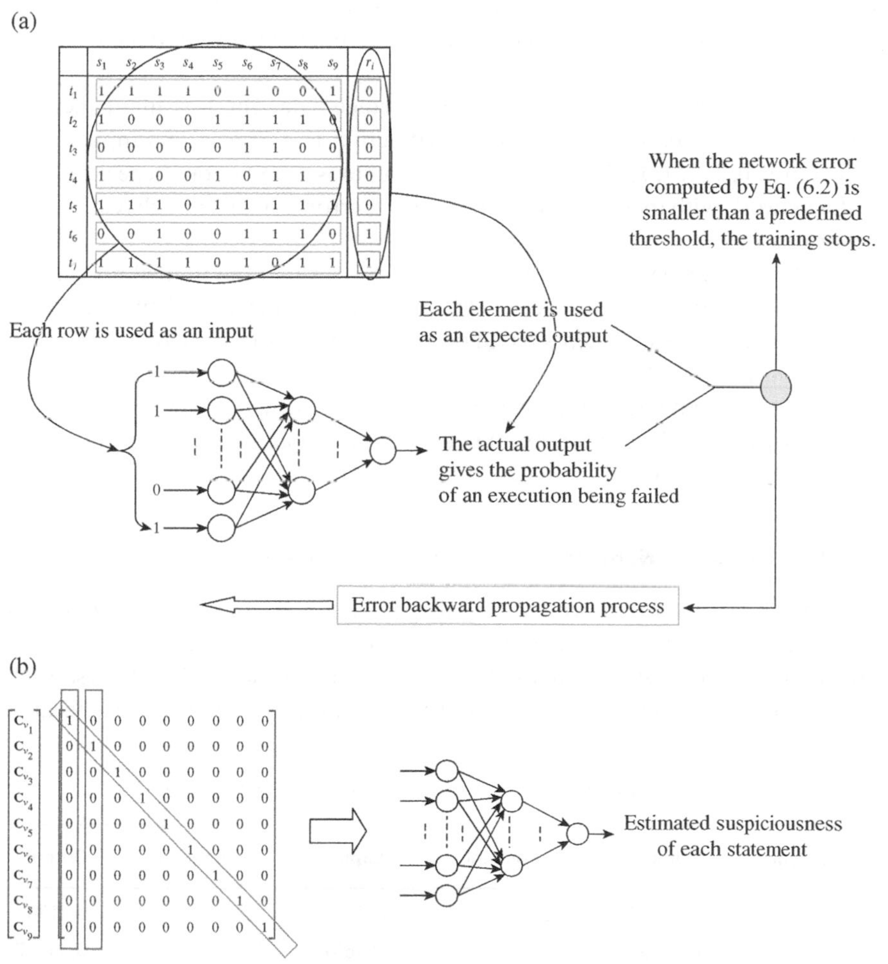

Figure 6.3 (a) Train a BP neural network and (b) estimate the suspiciousness of each statement using a trained BP neural network. *Source:* Wong and Qi [2]/World Scientific Publishing.

A3: Input $\mathbf{c}_{v_1}, \mathbf{c}_{v_2}, \ldots, \mathbf{c}_{v_m}$ in Eq. (6.1) into the trained neural network and obtain the outputs $r'_{v_1}, r'_{v_2}, \ldots, r'_{v_m}$.

A4: Rank $s_1, s_2, \ldots, s_m$ based on $r'_{v_1}, r'_{v_2}, \ldots, r'_{v_m}$ in descending order and examine the statements one by one from the top until the fault is located.

Let us demonstrate our method through an example. Suppose we have a program with nine statements ($m = 9$) and one fault in statement s_8. We executed seven test cases ($n = 7$) on it, two of which failed. Figure 6.1 shows the coverage data and execution result of each test case. We perform the following:

- Construct a BP neural network with nine input neurons, one output neuron, and three middle-layer neurons. The *transfer* functions of neurons are set to the sigmoid function.
- Train the BP neural network with the coverage data. The first input vector is (1, 1, 1, 1, 0, 1, 0, 0, 1) and the expected output is 0. The second input vector is (1, 0, 0, 0, 1, 1, 1, 1, 0) and the expected output is 0, and so on. Repeat training the network with these data until the network error is small enough (e.g. 10^{-3} in our case).
- Input the coverage vectors of the virtual test cases into the trained neural network. The output with respect to each statement is shown in Table 6.2.
- After ranking the statements based on their suspiciousness, we obtain s_4, s_3, s_9, s_8, s_6, s_1, s_5, s_7, s_2. That is, s_4 is most likely to contain the fault.
- Examine the statements one by one in order of s_4, s_3, s_9, s_8, s_6, s_1, s_5, s_7, s_2. The fault will be found when s_8 is examined. In this example, we examined four statements before we found the location of the fault.

6.2.2 Reduce the Number of Candidate Suspicious Statements

The BP neural network-based fault localization method can be further improved by considering execution slices of failed tests. An execution slice with respect to a given test case in our study contains the set of statements executed by the test. Such a slice can be constructed very easily if we know the coverage of the test, because

Table 6.2 Actual output with respect to each statement of the example.

Statement	Output	Statement	Output	Statement	Output
s_1	0.11187	s_4	0.72339	s_7	0.01806
s_2	0.01254	s_5	0.03651	s_8	0.20847
s_3	0.49732	s_6	0.18736	s_9	0.21079

Source: Wong and Qi [2]/World Scientific Publishing.

the corresponding execution slice of the test can be obtained simply by converting the coverage data collected during the testing into another format. More specifically, instead of reporting the coverage percentage, it reports which statements are executed. Since many of the statements are unrelated to the faults, we can develop additional heuristics to reduce the number of candidate suspicious statements. By doing so, we also reduce the number of statements whose suspiciousness have to be computed using our neural network. This makes our method more efficient.

In general, the fault should be covered by failed tests, or at least related to the statements covered by failed tests. This implies that the most suspicious statements are the statements covered by all the failed executions. Let S_I denote the set of the statements covered by all failed executions. We have

$$S_I = S(t_{f_1}) \cap S(t_{f_2}) \cap \ldots \cap S(t_{f_{n-k}}) \quad (6.2)$$

where $t_{f_1}, t_{f_2}, \ldots, t_{f_{n-k}}$ are the failed test cases and $S(t_{f_i})$ is the set of statements covered by t_{f_i}, i.e. the set of statements covered by t_{f_i}. In special cases, S_I may not contain the faulty statement(s). A good solution to this problem is to find a failed test t_{f_M} that covers the fewest statements and examine the unchecked statements covered by t_{fM} (that is, those in the execution slice of t_{f_M} but not in S_I). For simplicity, let us use S_M as the set of the statements covered by t_{f_M} (i.e. $S_M = S(tf_{n-k})$). Based on the above discussion, when we are looking for a fault, the statements in S_I should first be examined; if the faulty statement is not there, the statements in $S_M - S_I$ should be examined next. For example, with respect to the sample in Figure 6.1, $S_I = S(t_6) \cap S(t_7) = \{s_3, s_6, s_8\}$, $S_M = S(t_6) = \{s_3, s_6, s_7, s_8\}$, and $S_M - S_I = \{s_7\}$. This implies that we should first search for the fault ins_3, s_6,and s_8. The order of these three statements to be examined is decided by their suspiciousness. If the fault is not in these three statements, s_7 is the next statement that should be examined. In the example, we only had to examine three statements before we found the location of the fault. In other words, with the additional heuristic discussed above, the number of statements that had to be examined is reduced from four to three.

Integrating this execution slice-based heuristic with the neural network-based approach discussed in Section 6.2.1, we summarize our fault localization approach as follows:

Step 1: Obtain the intersection of all failed execution slices (S_I) and the smallest failed execution slice (S_M).

Step 2: Apply Procedure I (in Section 6.2.1) to the statements in S_I to examine whether the fault is in these statements. If the fault location is found, go to Step 4.

Step 3: Apply Procedure I to the statements in $S_M - S_I$. That is, compute the suspiciousness of these statements, rank them in descending order based on their suspiciousness, and examine them one by one from the top until the fault is found.

Step 4: STOP.

6.3 RBF Neural Network-Based Fault Localization[2]

In Section 6.2, we introduced the use of BP neural networks in the area of software fault localization. Although BP networks are widely used networks, RBF neural networks, whose output layer weights are trained in a supervised way, are even better in our case as they can learn faster than BP networks and do not suffer from pathologies like paralysis and local minima problems as BP networks do [12, 13]. In this section, we will briefly introduce an RBF neural network-based fault localization approach [10].

6.3.1 RBF Neural Networks

An RBF is a real-valued function whose value depends only on the distance from its receptive field center $\boldsymbol{\mu}$ to the input $\mathbf{x}$. It is a strictly positive radially symmetric function, where the center has a unique maximum, and the value drops off rapidly to zero away from the center. When the distance between $\mathbf{x}$ and $\boldsymbol{\mu}$ (denoted as $\|\mathbf{x}-\boldsymbol{\mu}\|$) is smaller than the receptive field width σ, the function has an appreciable value.

A typical RBF neural network has a three-layer feed-forward structure. The first layer is the input layer, which passes inputs to the (second) hidden layer without changing their values. The hidden layer is where all neurons simultaneously receive the n-dimensional real-valued input vector $\mathbf{x}$. Each neuron in this layer uses an RBF as the activation function. In [10], the authors made use of the Gaussian basis function [14], as it is one of the most popular choices for employment in RBF networks [15].

$$R_j(\mathbf{x}) = \exp\left(-\frac{\|\mathbf{x}-\boldsymbol{\mu}_j\|^2}{2\sigma_j^2}\right) \tag{6.3}$$

Usually, the distance in Eq. (6.3) is the Euclidean distance between $\mathbf{x}$ and $\boldsymbol{\mu}$, but in [10], a weighted bit-comparison-based dissimilarity is employed. To make a distinction, hereafter, we use $\|\mathbf{x}-\boldsymbol{\mu}\|$ to represent a *generic* distance, and $\|\mathbf{x}-\boldsymbol{\mu}\|_{\mathrm{WBC}}$ for the weighted bit-comparison-based dissimilarity. The third layer is the output

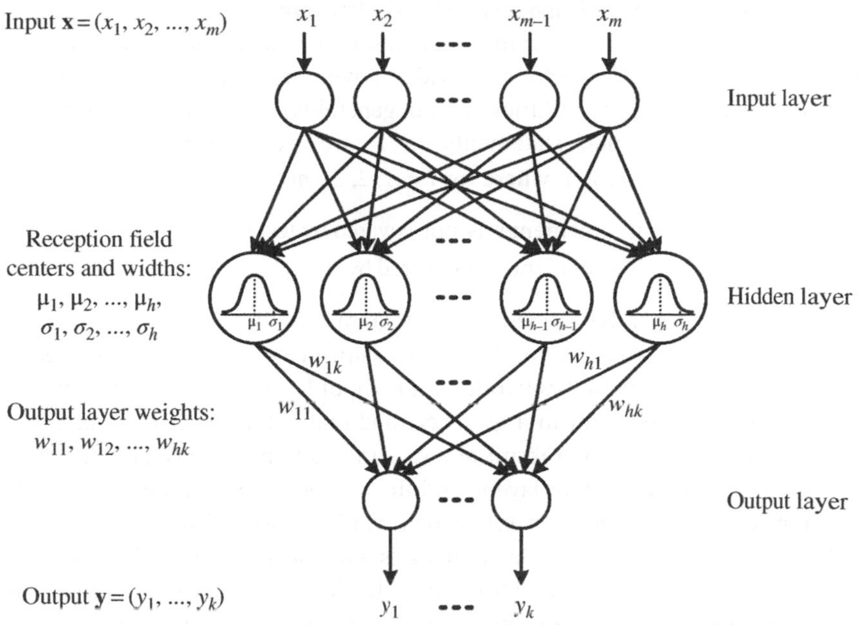

Figure 6.4 A sample three layer RBF neural network. *Source:* Wong et al. [10]/IEEE.

layer. The output can be expressed as $\mathbf{y} = \langle y_1, y_2, ..., y_k \rangle$ with y_i as the output of the ith neuron given by:

$$y_i = \sum_{j=1}^{h} w_{ji} R_j(\mathbf{x}), \quad \text{for } i = 1, 2, ..., k \tag{6.4}$$

An RBF network implements a mapping from the m dimensional real-valued input space to the k dimensional real-valued output space with a hidden layer space in between. The transformation from the input space to the hidden-layer space is nonlinear, whereas the transformation from the hidden-layer space to the output space is linear. Figure 6.4 shows an RBF network with m neurons in the input layer, h neurons in the hidden layer, and k neurons in the output layer. The parameters to be trained are the centers ($\mu_1, \mu_2, ..., \mu_h$) and widths ($\sigma_1, \sigma_2, ..., \sigma_h$) of the receptive fields of hidden-layer neurons and the output layer weights.

6.3.2 Methodology

With the basic knowledge provided in Section 6.3.1, we will now describe the RBF neural network-based fault localization approach.

6.3.2.1 Fault Localization Using an RBF Neural Network

Suppose we have a program P with statements, executed on n test cases. Let s_j be the jth statement of P. The vector $\mathbf{c}_{t_i}$ provides us with information on how the program P is covered by test t_i. Without loss of generality, such coverage is reported here in terms of which statements in P are executed by t_i. We have $\mathbf{c}_{t_i} = \langle(\mathbf{c}_{t_i})_1, (\mathbf{c}_{t_i})_2, \ldots, (\mathbf{c}_{t_i})_m\rangle$, where for $j = 1, 2, \ldots, m$,

$$(\mathbf{c}_{t_i})_j = \begin{cases} 0, & \text{if statement } s_j \text{ is not covered by test } t_i \\ 1, & \text{if statement } s_j \text{ is covered by test } t_i \end{cases} \tag{6.5}$$

The value of r_{t_i} depends on whether the program execution of t_i succeeds or fails. It has a value of 1 if the execution fails and a value of 0 if the execution succeeds. We construct an RBF neural network with m input layer neurons, each of which corresponds to one element in a given $\mathbf{c}_{t_i}$, and one output layer neuron, corresponding to r_{t_i}, the execution result of test t_i. In addition, there is a hidden layer between the input and output layers, and the number of hidden neurons can be determined by using Algorithm 6.1, which will be explained in Section 6.3.2.2. Each of these neurons uses the Gaussian basis function as the activation function. The receptive field center and width of each hidden-layer neuron, as well as the output layer weights, are established by training the underlying network.

The procedure for using the RBF technique for fault localization is described as follows:

Step 1: Build a modified RBF neural network with m input neurons and one output neuron. Each neuron in the hidden layer uses the Gaussian basis function as its activation function.

```
Inputs  : C = {c_t1, c_t2, ..., c_tn} and β
Output  : O

O ← Ø
foreach c ∈ C do
    Temp ← false foreach μ ∈ O do
        if (|c − μ|_WBC < β) then
            Temp ← true break
        end
    end
    if Temp == false then
        O ← {c} ∪ O
    end
end
output O
```

Algorithm 6.1 The algorithm to determine the number of hidden neurons and their receptive field centers. *Source:* Wong et al. [10]/IEEE.

Step 2: Determine the number of hidden neurons h and the receptive field center and width of each hidden neuron.

Step 3: Use the generalized inverse (Moore–Penrose pseudo-inverse) to compute the optimal linear mapping from the hidden neurons to the output neuron.

Step 4: Use the virtual coverage vectors $\mathbf{c}_{v_1}, \mathbf{c}_{v_2}, \ldots, \mathbf{c}_{v_m}$ as inputs to the trained network, to produce the outputs $\hat{r}_{v_1}, \hat{r}_{v_2}, \ldots, \hat{r}_{v_m}$.

Step 5: Assign $\hat{r}_{v_1}, \hat{r}_{v_2}, \ldots, \hat{r}_{v_m}$ as the suspiciousness of the 1st, 2nd, ..., mth statement.

6.3.2.2 Training of the RBF Neural Network

The training of an RBF neural network can be divided into two stages [13]. First, the number of neurons in the hidden layer, the receptive field center, and width of each hidden-layer neuron should be assigned values. Second, the output layer weights have to be trained. Many methods have been proposed to determine the receptive field centers. Using standard k-means clustering, input data are assigned to k clusters, with the center of each cluster taken to be the receptive field center of a hidden-layer neuron [14, 16–18]. Unfortunately, this approach does not provide any guidance as to how many clusters should be used; the number of clusters (and so, the number of receptive field centers) must be chosen arbitrarily. Another disadvantage is that the k-means approach is very sensitive to the initial starting values. Its performance will significantly depend on the arbitrarily selected initial receptive field centers.

To overcome these problems, an algorithm is proposed (as shown in Algorithm 6.1) to simultaneously estimate the number of hidden neurons and their receptive field centers. The inputs to this algorithm are the coverage vectors $\mathbf{c}_{t_1}, \mathbf{c}_{t_2}, \ldots, \mathbf{c}_{t_n}$, and a parameter β $(0 \leq \beta < 1)$ for controlling the number of field centers. The output is a sequence of receptive field centers $\boldsymbol{\mu}_1, \boldsymbol{\mu}_2, \ldots, \boldsymbol{\mu}_h$, which is a subsequence of the input vectors such that $\|\boldsymbol{\mu}_i - \boldsymbol{\mu}_j\|_{\mathrm{WBC}} \geq \beta$ for any i and j, $i \neq j$, where $\| \|_{\mathrm{WBC}}$ is the weighted bit comparison-based dissimilarity defined in Section 6.3.2.3. The algorithm not only assigns values to each receptive field center, but also decides the number of hidden neurons because each hidden neuron contains exactly one center. The larger the value of β is, the smaller the number of neurons to be used in the hidden layer, which makes the training at the second stage much faster (as explained at the end of this section). However, if the number of hidden-layer neurons is too small, then the mapping between the input and the output defined by the neural network loses its accuracy.

Once the receptive field centers have been found, we can use different heuristics to determine their widths to obtain a smooth interpolation. Park and Sandberg [20, 21] showed that an RBF neural network using a single global fixed value σ for all σ_j has the capability of universal approximation. Moody and Darken [22] suggested that a good estimate of σ is the average over all distances between the center of each neuron and that of its nearest neighbor. Here, we use a similar heuristic to define the global width σ as:

$$\sigma = \frac{1}{h}\sum_{j=1}^{h} \left\| \boldsymbol{\mu}_j - \boldsymbol{\mu}_j^* \right\|_{\text{WBC}} \tag{6.6}$$

where $\boldsymbol{\mu}_j^*$ is the nearest neighbor of $\boldsymbol{\mu}_j$. After the centers and widths of the receptive fields of the RBFs in the hidden layer are determined, the remaining parameters that need to be trained are the hidden-to-output layer weights ($w_1, w_2, ..., w_h$). To do so, first select a training set composed of input coverage vectors $\mathbf{c}_{t_1}, \mathbf{c}_{t_2}, ..., \mathbf{c}_{t_n}$, and the corresponding expected outputs $\hat{r}_{t_1}, \hat{r}_{t_2}, ..., \hat{r}_{t_n}$. For an input coverage vector $\mathbf{c}_{t_i}$, its actual output from the network is computed as

$$\hat{r}_{t_i} = \sum_{j=1}^{h} w_j R_j(\mathbf{c}_{t_i}) \tag{6.7}$$

where

$$R_j(\mathbf{x}) = \exp\left(-\frac{\left\|\mathbf{x} - \boldsymbol{\mu}_j\right\|_{\text{WBC}}^2}{2\sigma_j^2} \right) \text{ for } j = 1, 2, ..., h$$

The output of the network is:

$$\hat{\mathbf{r}} = \mathbf{A}\mathbf{w} \tag{6.8}$$

where

$$\mathbf{A} = \begin{bmatrix} R_1(\mathbf{c}_{t_1}) & R_2(\mathbf{c}_{t_1}) & \cdots & R_h(\mathbf{c}_{t_1}) \\ R_1(\mathbf{c}_{t_2}) & R_2(\mathbf{c}_{t_2}) & \cdots & R_h(\mathbf{c}_{t_2}) \\ \vdots & \vdots & \ddots & \vdots \\ R_1(\mathbf{c}_{t_n}) & R_2(\mathbf{c}_{t_n}) & \cdots & R_h(\mathbf{c}_{t_n}) \end{bmatrix},$$

$\mathbf{w} = [w_1\ w_2, ..., w_h]^T$, and $\hat{\mathbf{r}} = [\hat{r}_{t_1}, \hat{r}_{t_2}, ..., \hat{r}_{t_n}]^T$.

Also, let the expected output $\mathbf{r} = [r_{t_1}, r_{t_2}, ..., r_{t_n}]^T$ and the prediction error across the entire set of training data be defined as $\|\hat{\mathbf{r}} - \mathbf{r}\|^2$ (the sum of squared error between $\hat{\mathbf{r}}$ and $\mathbf{r}$). To find the optimal weights $\mathbf{w}^*$, we have to compute:

$$\mathbf{w}^* = \arg\min_{\mathbf{w}} \|\hat{\mathbf{r}} - \mathbf{r}\|^2 = \arg\min_{\mathbf{w}} \|\mathbf{A}\mathbf{w} - \mathbf{r}\|^2$$

For this calculation, we use the generalized inverse (Moore–Penrose pseudo-inverse) of $\mathbf{A}$ [23]:

$$\mathbf{w}^* = \left(\mathbf{A}^T\mathbf{A}\right)^{-1}\mathbf{A}^T\mathbf{r} \tag{6.9}$$

6.3.2.3 Definition of a Weighted Bit-Comparison-Based Dissimilarity

From Eq. (6.7), for a given test case t_i and its input coverage vector $\mathbf{c}_{t_i}$, the actual output $\hat{\mathbf{r}}_{t_i}$ is a linear combination of the activation functions of all hidden-layer neurons. Each R_j depends on the distance $\|\mathbf{x} - \boldsymbol{\mu}_j\|$ (referring to Eq. (6.3)). In our case, $\mathbf{x}$ is the input coverage vector $\mathbf{c}_{t_i}$, and $\boldsymbol{\mu}_j$ is the receptive field center of the jth hidden-layer neuron. So, we have $\|\mathbf{x} - \boldsymbol{\mu}_j\| = \|\mathbf{c}_{t_i} - \boldsymbol{\mu}_j\|$. From Algorithm 6.1, we observe that the set of receptive centers is a subset of the coverage vectors. This observation implies each $\boldsymbol{\mu}_j$ by itself is also the coverage vector of a certain test case. As a result, the distance $\|\mathbf{x} - \boldsymbol{\mu}_j\|$ can also be viewed as the distance between two coverage vectors.

6.4 C4.5 Decision Tree-Based Fault Localization[3]

In [19], the authors proposed a way to identify suspicious statements during debugging using a machine learning technique, the C4.5 decision tree. The technique is based on principles similar to Tarantula but addresses its main flaw: its difficulty to deal with the presence of multiple faults as it assumes that failed test cases execute the same fault(s). The improvement results from the use of C4.5 decision trees to identify various failure conditions based on information regarding the test cases' inputs and outputs. Failed test cases executing under similar conditions are then assumed to fail due to the same fault(s). Statements are then considered suspicious if they are covered by a large proportion of failed test cases that execute under similar conditions.

6.4.1 Category-Partition for Rule Induction

In order to obtain meaningful and accurate machine learning rules, it is not possible to simply use the test case input and output values. A common intuition is that it typically leads to meaningless and inaccurate rules because the machine learning algorithm cannot learn what input or output properties are potentially of interest, but can only find properties similar to those already identified manually. In other words, without some additional guidance, the learning algorithm is unlikely to find the precise conditions under which test cases fail. This guidance comes in the form of categories and choices, as required by CP [23].

The CP method seeks to generate test cases that cover the various execution conditions of a function. To apply the CP method, one identifies the parameters of each function, the characteristics (categories) of each parameter, and the choices of each category. Categories are properties of parameters that can have an influence on the behavior of the software under test (e.g. the size of an array in a sorting algorithm). Choices (e.g. whether an array is empty) are the potential values of a category that represent a certain character of the category. Test frames and test data are generated according to the categories and choices defined.

The reason for using CP here is that it is more general and encompassing than equivalence class partitioning (which only partitions input value domains), and it is one of the most well-known black-box techniques. Though applying CP clearly represents an overhead, in many environments one would be expected to use a systematic functional testing approach, and reverse engineering a test specification (i.e. categories and choices) is, in any case, a useful investment in the context of legacy systems with existing test suites.

6.4.2 Rule Induction Algorithms

A specific category of machine learning techniques focuses on generating classification rules [24]. Examples of such techniques include the C4.5 decision tree algorithm [25] or the Ripper rule induction algorithm [26]. In the current context, the rules would look like conditions on test inputs and outputs being associated with probabilities of failures. The main advantage of these techniques is the interpretability of their models: certain conditions imply a certain probability of failure.

Some techniques, like C4.5, partition the data set (e.g. the set of test cases) in a stepwise manner, using complex algorithms and heuristics to avoid overfitting the data with the goal of generating models that are as simple as possible. Others, like Ripper, are so-called covering algorithms that generate rules in a stepwise manner, removing observations that are "covered" by the rule at each step so that the next step works on a reduced set of observations. With coverage algorithms, rules are interdependent in the sense that they form a "decision list," where rules are supposed to be applicable in the order they were generated. Because this makes their interpretation more difficult, a classification tree algorithm, namely C4.5, is used in the approach. WEKA tool [24] is also applied to build and assess the trees.

6.4.3 Statement Ranking Strategies

In this section, we first revisit statement coloring according to Tarantula. We then describe how to adjust Tarantula's ranking based on a C4.5 decision tree, which is built on an abstract test suite or test specification (Section 6.4.3.2), in order to account for the diversity of execution conditions under which statements are involved in failed test cases.

6.4.3.1 Revisiting Tarantula

Suppose S is the set of executable statements of the program P being debugged and repaired, and T is a test suite (or set of test cases) for the program. Let T_F ($\subseteq T$) be the set of failed test cases and T_P ($\subseteq T$) be the set of passed test cases, such that $T_F \cup$

$T_P = T$ and $T_F \cap T_P = \emptyset$. Let $S(t)$ ($\subseteq S$) denote the set of statements executed (or covered) by a test case $t \in T$.

R_i denotes a specific rule learned by the C4.5 algorithm. The set of rules is denoted by R. Thus, $R_i \in R$. We define R_F (respectively, R_P) as the subset of rules that classifies test cases to result in failures (respectively, successes). Obviously, $R_F \cup R_P = R$ and $R_F \cap R_P = \emptyset$.

The subset of test cases in T covered by rule R_i is referred to as $T(R_i)$. If $i \neq j$, we have $T(R_i) \cap T(R_j) = \emptyset$. This latter constraint is due to the partitioning nature of the C4.5 algorithm. Test cases in $T(R_i)$ may either pass or fail. It follows that $T(R_i) = T_F(R_i) \cup T_P(R_i)$, where $T_F(R_i)$ and $T_P(R_i)$ are the failed and successful test cases covered by rule R_i, respectively. The set of statements covered by a rule R_i, that is, executed by the test cases covered by R_i, is referred to as $S(R_i)$. Obviously, $S(R_i) = \cup_{t \in T(R_i)} S(t)$.

Following the above formalism, the Tarantula color *Color*(*s*) ($\in[0, 1]$) of any statement *s* in the code is given by $Color(s) = passed(s)/(passed(s) + failed(s))$, where *passed*(*s*) and *failed*(*s*) are the percentages of successful and failed test cases, respectively, that execute statement *s*.

$$passed(s) = \|\{t \in T_P,\ s \in S(t)\}\| / \|T_P\|$$
$$failed(s) = \|\{t \in T_F,\ s \in S(t)\}\| / \|T_F\|$$

A small value for *Color*(*s*) suggests that *s* is a suspicious statement. When statements are not covered by any test case, a value of zero should be assigned to *Color*(*s*) [27, 28]. (Note that this is what the description of *Tarantula* suggests [27, 28], although the running example used by the authors shows that uncovered statements are not ranked.) However, this is questionable, as there is no information to indicate that the statement is likely to be fault-prone. In fact, no fault causing the observed failures can possibly be located in uncovered statements. This situation is of practical importance, as the presence of multiple faults often prevents certain statements from being executed.

The original *Color*(*s*) formula presented above can be re-expressed to demonstrate that the statement ranking only depends on the ratio $\|T_F(s)\| \ / \ \|T_P(s)\|$, where $T_P(s)$ and $T_F(s)$ are the set of successful and failed test cases, respectively, that execute statement *s*.

$$\frac{1}{Color(s)} = 1 + \frac{\|T_F(s)\|}{\|T_F\|} \times \frac{\|T_P\|}{\|T_P(s)\|} = 1 + \frac{\|T_P\|}{\|T_F\|} \times \frac{\|T_F(s)\|}{\|T_P(s)\|} \tag{6.10}$$

Since $\|T_P\| \ / \ \|T_F\|$ is constant for a given test set and program version, the ranking of statements, which is ultimately used to focus debugging, exclusively depends on the proportion of test cases that fail and pass when executing a specific statement *s*. Though this makes intuitive sense, there are two problems with this formula: (i) test cases may fail due to different faults, and therefore whether a statement *s* is covered by several failed test cases is not relevant, and (ii) redundant test cases that execute the system in identical or similar conditions may artificially affect the ranking.

6.4.3.2 Ranking Statements Based on C4.5 Rules

6.4.3.2.1 Heuristic

Assuming we have a large abstract test suite, we should be able to generate a C4.5 decision tree where each leaf corresponds to a rule predicting either a success or a failure. The data set on which to build the tree would then be a set of instances, each corresponding to a test case that is known to pass or fail. The attributes to be selected for the tree construction are pairs (category, choice) characterizing the specification of each test case. Each path from the root of the tree to a leaf represents a rule characterized by conditions on (category, choice) pairs. Each leaf in the tree corresponds to a partition of the data set of test case instances. A rule leads to a failure prediction when the instances in its leaf represent a majority of failure-revealing test cases, and a success prediction otherwise. Therefore, a C4.5 rule classifies a set of test cases with similar input conditions and same test results.

To understand the heuristic we are going to follow, let us first focus on Fail rules and take the example of a particular rule $Ri \in RF$. If we assume the probability of failure associated with *Ri*is very high, then what this means is that (nearly) all the test cases in *T*(*Ri*) fail under the same or similar conditions. What this suggests is that (nearly) all of the test cases fail due to similar reasons (faults). This in turn can be used to safely rank statements using a strategy similar to *Tarantula* as all test cases failing within a rule can be safely assumed, in most cases, to fail due to the same fault(s). We thus obtain a ranking per Fail rule that must then somehow be combined with the ranking of other rules to obtain a final ranking.

Within a rule, the higher the number of failed test cases covering a statement, the more suspicious the statement. Assuming that $T_F(Ri) = \{t1, t2, t3\}$, the statements executed by these three test cases are depicted in Figure 6.5. According

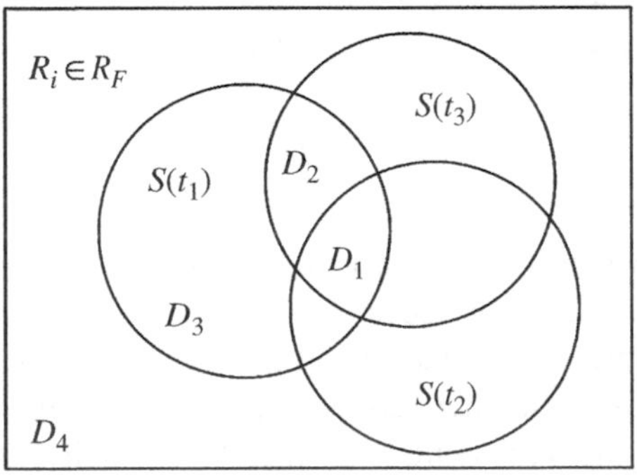

Figure 6.5 Statement divisions by test cases. *Source:* Briand et al. [19]/IEEE.

to the above hypothesis, the statements in D_1 (i.e. covered by all three test cases t_1, t_2, and t_3) should be more suspicious than those in D_2, D_3, or D_4. On the contrary, the statements in D_4 should be the safest of all. If rule*Ri* led to success predictions, we would obtain the opposite result: the statements in D_1 would be the safest, and those in D_4 would be the most suspicious. This example illustrates how for each rule we can obtain a partial ordering of statements.

6.4.3.2.2 Computing a Statement Ranking

To implement the above heuristic, we must define a mechanism to combine the ranking of all rules for a given statement. Proceeding with this goal in mind, a statement will be assigned a negative (respectively, positive) weight if it is covered by a rule that has failure (respectively, success) predictions. A high absolute value in the weight implies that a statement is executed by most of the test cases in the rule. The absolute values in the weights are normalized within [0, 1] in order to give equivalent weights to all perfect rules, i.e. rules covering test cases that lead to only failure results or only success results. However, if a rule covers test cases with mixed failure and success results, the maximum absolute weight a rule can contribute will be below 1, as determined by the distribution of the mixed results.

The fact that rules should contribute to the extent of the consistency of their test cases' behavior should be intuitive: less consistent rules have less influence on the final ranking. We have also considered weighting the rules' contributions according to their number of test cases, but this would make the results sensitive to redundant test cases, as discussed above in the case of Tarantula, and would make rarely executed faults difficult to find. Assuming that *Weight*(s) denote the overall weight of statement s, and *Weight* (R_i, s) denotes the weight of statement s for rule R_i, we obtain:

$$Weight(s) = \sum_{R_i \in R} Weight(R_i, s) \tag{6.11}$$

where

$$Weight(R_i, s) = \begin{cases} -\|T(s) \cap T_F(R_i)\| / \|T(R_i)\| & \text{if } R_i \in R_F \\ \|T(s) \cap T_F(R_i)\| / \|T(R_i)\| & \text{if } R_i \in R_P \end{cases}$$

This can be visualized as a matrix, as in Table 6.3, where columns are statements and rows are rules. The matrix contains all the weights of each statement for each rule, all within [−1, 1] as defined above. The last row represents the sum of all rule weights for a given statement, which can then be used to rank statements: statements with lower weight are ranked first, to follow Tarantula's convention for *Color*(s).

Table 6.3 Matrix of statement weight.

	s_1	s_2	s_3	...	s_o
R_{P1}	1	0.01	1	...	0.5
...	...	...	...	...	...
R_{Pm}	1	1	0.8	...	0.1
R_{F1}	−1	−1	−1	...	−1
...	...	...	...	...	...
R_{Fn}	−1	−1	−0.8	...	0
sum	−22.1	−18.7	0.06	...	−3.36

Source: Briand et al. [19]/IEEE.

6.4.3.2.3 Rule Selection

A last practical issue is to determine which rules to consider among all the ones identified in a C4.5 decision tree. In order to only account for accurate rules, it seems logical to select rules that are above a certain probability of correct (Fail/Pass) classification. We should also consider rules that are based on a large enough number of instances (abstract test cases) in order to avoid classifications that are due to chance. Deciding such selection thresholds is of course subjective, but it can be done so as to obtain a reasonable number of rules to base the ranking on and will be dependent on how accurate the rules are overall for the specific test suite under consideration. In the case study performed in [19], rules are selected with a probability of correct classification above 0.8 and a number of instances above 10, resulting in the selection of 35 Fail rules and 57 Pass rules.

6.5 Applying Simulated Annealing with Statement Pruning for an SBFL Formula[4]

Neelofar [29] proposed a parametrized hyperbolic metric (as shown below) and then applied simulated annealing to learn the parameter values, so that the resulting formula is tailored for the chosen data set when conducting SBFL.

$$\frac{1}{K_1 + \frac{nf}{F}} + \frac{K_3}{K_2 + \frac{ep}{E}} \tag{6.12}$$

The proposed metric has four adjustments: (i) to scale both *nf* and *es* values to the range 0 to 1. The aim of this is to help limit the range of values for the parameters introduced for later use. (ii) To add a parameter K_1 to the scaled *nf* value. A positive K_1 makes contours steeper, and a large enough value results in a deterministic bug optimal metric if other things remain unchanged. (iii) To add a parameter K_2 to the scaled *es* value. A positive K_2 makes contours flatter, and a large enough value results in a single bug optimal metric if other things remain unchanged (that is, K_1 is relatively small). If K_1 and K_2 are small, contour gradients change abruptly, whereas if they are both large, the gradients change slowly. (iv) To multiply the *es* term by parameter K_3. This allows us to effectively stretch or compress the contours in a horizontal direction. With large identical K_1 and K_2 values, the contours are close to straight lines, but their gradient can be adjusted using K_3. In short, the first adjustment is for scaling, while the second, third, and fourth are for making contours flatter or steeper like single bug optimal or deterministic bug optimal, respectively.

According to Neelofar, fault localization metrics rank statements on the basis of higher *ef* and lower *es*. These statements correspond to the top of the ranking and are thus the most important for performance of a metric. Statements having very low *ef* or very high *es* are ranked at the bottom and thus play a minimum role in localizing faults. There is a large number of such statements, and they contribute a substantial amount of time in training. By removing these statements from training data, training can be done more efficiently. Therefore, a statement pruning technique that removes a particular percentage of low ranked statements having minimum or no impact on fault localization during the learning phase decreases the size of training data. The technique is explained in Algorithm 6.2, where low ranked statements are pruned in different iterations of simulated annealing. The algorithm is standard simulated annealing with an addition of the statement pruning method called at line 14. No pruning is performed in the initial phases of learning to allow for initial burn-in of the algorithm. Once the algorithm achieves stability in terms of finding better values for parameters and lowering the rank percentage, bottom ranked statements are pruned. The pruning is performed in lines 20–24. It removes the bottom $n\%$ statements and replaces current training data with pruned data. The process continues until the pruning percentage is less than the maximum pruning percentage allowed. Thus, only in the first few iterations of simulated annealing would the algorithm use the whole data set for training. Later, every time pruning is performed, the size of training data decreases for further iterations.

Algorithm 6.2 Finding hyperbolic metrics using simulated annealing with statement pruning [29].

```
Input: Training
Output: best parameter values for hyperbolic metrics (k1, k2, k3)
procedure ANNEAL (training_data)
    initial_data_size ← init_size                       ▷ number of statements in training data
    initial_temperature ← init_t                        ▷ starting annealing temperature
    minimum_temperature ← min_t                         ▷ minimum annealing temperature
    maximam_pruning_allowed ← max_pruning               ▷ percentage of statements allowed to be prunced
    initial_burnin_iterations ← init_burnin             ▷ minimum number of annealing iterations only after which pruning is
                                                          allowed
    while initial_temperature ≥ minimum_temperature do
        compute k1, k2, k3 values using optimization method
        if temperature_iteration > initial_burnin_iterations then
            current_data_size ← count total number of statements in training_data
            statements_pruned ← initial_data_size − current_data_size
            pruning_percentage_applied ← 100 − ((statement_pruned / initial_data_size) × 100)
            if pruning_percentage_applied < pruning_percentage_allowed then
                PRUNEBOTTOMSTMTS(traning_data)          ▷ calling of statement pruning method
            end if
        end if
    end while
    decrease initial_temperature by a fixed value
end procedure
  ▷ Prune bottom ranked statements if pruning percentage is less than the maximum pruning percentage allowed
procedure PRUNEBOTTOMSTMTS (statements_list)
    Get list of statements and sort in descending order of their scores
    Remove bottom n% statements
    Replace training data with pruned data
end procedure
```

6.6 Conclusion

In this chapter, we introduced three unique machine learning-based fault localization techniques. Serving as pioneers in applying the concepts of machine learning to the area of debugging and fault localization, these techniques may seem simple; however, they inspire researchers to devote more efforts in applying the concepts into debugging and fault localization, and utilize the unlimited abilities provided by increasingly powerful computation systems. In the past few years, other machine learning algorithms, such as convolutional neural networks (ConvNet), support vector machines (SVM), and stochastic gradient decent (SGD), are attracting the attention of researchers from various areas and showing advantages under different disciplines. It is promising and interesting to see if these most advanced machine learning techniques can be applied to the area of debugging and fault localization, and further broaden our insights into more accurate and efficient fault localization approaches.

Notes

1 Part of Section 6.2 is from Ref. [2].
2 Part of Section 6.3 is from Refs. [10, 11].
3 Part of Section 6.4 is from Ref. [19].
4 Part of Section 6.5 is from Ref. [29].

References

1 Samuel, A.L. (1959). Some studies in machine learning using the game of checkers. *IBM Journal of Research and Development* 44: 206–226.

2 Wong, W.E. and Qi, Y. (2009). BP neural network-based effective fault localization. *International Journal of Software Engineering and Knowledge Engineering* 19 (04): 573–597. https://doi.org/10.1142/S021819400900426X.

3 Fausett, L. (1957). *Fundamentals of Neural Networks: Architectures, Algorithms, and Applications.* Prentice Hall.

4 Hecht-Nielsen, R. (1989). Theory of the backpropagation neural network. *Proceedings of the International 1989 Joint Conference on Neural Networks*, Washington, DC, USA (6 August 2002), vol. 1, 593–605. IEEE. https://doi.org/10.1109/IJCNN.1989.118638.

5 Neumann, D.E. (2002). An enhanced neural network technique for software risk analysis. *IEEE Transactions on Software Engineering* 28 (9): 904–912. ISSN 0098-5589. https://doi.org/10.1109/TSE.2002.1033229.

6 Tadayon, N. (2005). Neural network approach for software cost estimation. *Proceedings of the International Conference on Information Technology: Coding and Computing* (*ITCC '05*), Las Vegas, NV, USA (4–6 April 2005), vol. 2, 815–818. IEEE. https://doi.org/10.1109/ITCC.2005.210.

7 Su, Y. and Huang, C. (2007). Neural-network-based approaches for soft-ware reliability estimation using dynamic weighted combinational models. *Journal of Systems and Software* 80 (4): 606–615. ISSN 0164-1212. http://www.sciencedirect.com/science/article/pii/S0164121206001737.

8 Anderson, C., Von Mayrhauser, A., and Mraz, R. (1995). On the use of neural networks to guide software testing activities. *Proceedings of the 1995 IEEE International Test Conference (ITC '95)*, Washington, DC, USA (21–25 October 1995), 720–729. IEEE. https://doi.org/10.1109/TEST.1995.529902

9 Bellcore (1998). *χSuds Software Understanding System User's Manual*. Bridgewater, NJ, USA: Telcordia Technologies (formerly Bellcore). https://www.cs.purdue.edu/homes/apm/foundationsBook/Labs/coverage/xsuds.pdf.

10 Wong, W.E., Debroy, V., Golden, R. et al. (2012). Effective software fault localization using an RBF neural network. *IEEE Transactions on Reliability* 61 (1): 149–169. ISSN 0018-9529. https://doi.org/10.1109/TR.2011.2172031.

11 Wong, W.E., Shi, Y., Qi, Y., and Golden, R. (2008). Using an RBF neural network to locate program bugs. *Proceedings of the 2008 19th International Symposium on Software Reliability Engineering (ISSRE '08)*, Seattle/Redmond, WA, USA (10–14 November 2008), 27–36. IEEE. https://doi.org/10.1109/ISSRE.2008.15.

12 Lee, C.-C., Chung, P.-C., Tsai, J.-R., and Chang, C.-I. (1999). Robust radial basis function neural networks. *IEEE Transactions on Systems, Man, and Cybernetics, Part B* 29 (6): 674–685. ISSN 1083-4419. https://doi.org/10.1109/3477.809023.

13 Wasserman, P.D. (1993). *Advanced Methods in Neural Computing*, 1e. New York, NY, USA: Wiley. ISBN 0442004613.

14 Hassoun, M.H. (1995). *Fundamentals of Artificial Neural Networks*. Cambridge, MA, USA: MIT Press.

15 Singla, P., Subbarao, K., and Junkins, J.L. (2007). Direction-dependent learning approach for radial basis function networks. *IEEE Transactions on Neural Networks* 18 (1): 203–222. ISSN 1045-9227. https://doi.org/10.1109/TNN.2006.881805.

16 Dang, J., Wang, Y., and Zhao, S. (2006). Face recognition based on radial basis function neural networks using subtractive clustering algorithm. *Proceedings of the 6th World Congress on Intelligent Control and Automation*, Dalian, China (21–23 June 2006), 10294–10297. IEEE. https://doi.org/10.1109/WCICA.2006.1714017.

17 Lin, G.-F. and Chen, L.-H. Time series forecasting by combining the radial basis function network and the self-organizing map. *Hydrological Processes* 19 (10): 1925–1937. https://onlinelibrary.wiley.com/doi/abs/10.1002/hyp.5637.

18 Wan, C. and de Harrington, P.B. (1999). Self-configuring radial basis function neural networks for chemical pattern recognition. *Journal of Chemical Information and Computer Sciences* 39 (6): 1049–1056. https://doi.org/10.1021/ci990306t.

19 Briand, L.C., Labiche, Y., and Liu, X. (2007). Using Machine Learning to Support Debugging with Tarantula. *Proceedings of the 18th IEEE International Symposium on Software Reliability (ISSRE '07)*, 137–146. IEEE. https://doi.org/10.1109/ISSRE.2007.31.

20 Park, J. and Sandberg, I.W. (1991). Universal approximation using radial-basis-function networks. *Neural Computation* 3 (2): 246–257. ISSN 0899-7667. https://doi.org/10.1162/neco.1991.3.2.246.

21 Park, J. and Sandberg, I.W. (1993). Approximation and radial-basis-function networks. *Neural Computation* 5 (2): 305–316. https://doi.org/10.1162/neco.1993.5.2.305.

22 Moody, J. and Darken, C. (1988). *Learning with Localized Receptive Fields*, 133–143. Research Report YALEU/DCS/RR-649. Department of Computer Science, Yale University.

23 Ostrand, T.J. and Balcer, M.J. (1988). The Category-partition method for specifying and generating functional tests. *Communications of the ACM* 31 (6): 676–686. ISSN 0001-0782. http://doi.acm.org/10.1145/62959.62964.

24 Witten, I.H. and Frank, E. (2005). *Data Mining: Practical Machine Learning Tools and Techniques*. Morgan Kaufman.

25 Quinlan, J.R. (1993). *C4.5: Programs for Machine Learning*. San Francisco, CA, USA: Morgan Kaufmann. ISBN 1-55860-238-0.

26 Cohen, W.W. and Singer, Y. (1999). A simple, fast, and effective rule learner. *Proceedings of the Sixteenth National Conference on Artificial Intelligence and the Eleventh Innovative Applications of Artificial Intelligence Conference Innovative Applications of Artificial Intelligence (AAAI '99/IAAI '99)*, Menlo Park, CA, USA, 335–342. American Association for Artificial Intelligence. http://dl.acm.org/citation.cfm?id=315149.315320. ISBN 0-262-51106-1.

27 Jones, J.A. and Harrold, M.J. (2005). Empirical evaluation of the tarantula automatic fault-localization technique. *Proceedings of the 20th IEEE/ACM International Conference on Automated Software Engineering (ASE '05)*, Long Beach, CA, USA (7–11 November 2005), 273–282. ACM. http://doi.acm.org/10.1145/1101908.1101949. ISBN 1-58113-993-4.

28 Jones, J.A., Harrold, M.J., and Stasko, J. (2002). Visualization of test information to assist fault localization. *Proceedings of the 24th International Conference on Software Engineering (ICSE '02)*, Orlando, FL, USA (25–25 May 2002), 467–477. IEEE. 10.1145/581396.581397.

29 Neelofar, N., Naish, L., and Ramamohanarao, K. (2018). Spectral-based fault localization using hyperbolic function. *Software: Practice and Experience* 48 (3): 641–664.

7

Data Mining-Based Techniques for Software Fault Localization

Peggy Cellier[1], Mireille Ducassé[1], Sébastien Ferré[2], Olivier Ridoux[2], and W. Eric Wong[3]

[1] *INSA, CNRS, IRISA, Universite de Rennes, Rennes, France*
[2] *CNRS, IRISA, Universite de Rennes, Rennes, France*
[3] *Department of Computer Science, University of Texas at Dallas, Richardson, TX, USA*

7.1 Introduction[1]

Software engineering processes generate a large amount of data, and several authors have advocated the use of data mining methods to conduct fault localization. Many data mining methods with different merits exist, but the very first step is often to simply consider as data what was previously considered merely as a by-product of a process. One of the first historical examples of uncovering new knowledge from pre-existing data was the demonstration by Florence Nightingale (1820–1910) that soldiers died more often from bad sanitary conditions in military hospitals than from battle wounds. For her demonstration, she gathered previously ignored data and presented it in revealing graphics. This example shows that data mining is itself a process with important questions, from the selection and gathering of data to the presentation of the results. In the fault localization context, the following questions emerge: Which existing data can be leveraged to improve the localization? Which presentation of the results is best suited for the debugging process? We will illustrate the basic concepts of fault localization using a data mining technique and present three approaches to locate the faulty statements of a program. We will also address how data mining can be further applied to fault localization for GUI components.

Handbook of Software Fault Localization: Foundations and Advances, First Edition.
Edited by W. Eric Wong and T.H. Tse.

Published 2023 by John Wiley & Sons, Inc.

As software engineering data are symbolic by nature, in this chapter, we will present fault localization using symbolic methods. Symbolic methods tend to lend themselves naturally to give explanations, and this is exactly what we are looking for in fault localization. Indeed, we prefer a system with the capacity of saying "the failure has to do with the initialization of variable *x*" to a system limited to saying, "the fault is in these million lines with probability 0.527." Therefore, we will illustrate how to use two data mining techniques: association rules (ARs) [2] and formal concept analysis (FCA) [3] in fault localization.

FCA and AR deal with collections of objects and their features. The former extracts contextual truth, such as "in this assembly, all white-haired female wear glasses," while the latter extracts relativized truth, such as "in this assembly, carrying a briefcase increases the chance of wearing a tie." In a fault localization context, the former could say that "all failed tests call method *m*," and the latter could discover that "most failed tests call method *m*, which is very seldom called in successful tests."

Throughout this chapter, we use the Trityp program (partially shown in Figure 7.1) to illustrate the general method. It is a classical benchmark for test generation methods. Its specification is to classify sets of three segment lengths into four categories: scalene, isosceles, equilateral, and not a triangle, according to whether a given kind of triangle can be formed with these dimensions, or no triangle at all.

```
public int Trityp() {
int trityp;
if ((i == 0) || (j == 0) || (k == 0))
   trityp = 4;
else
{
 trityp = 0;
 if (i == j)
  trityp = trityp+1;
 if (i == k)
  trityp = trityp+2;
 if (j == k)
  trityp = trityp+3;
 if (trityp == 0)
 {
  if ((i+j <= k) || (j+k <= i) || (i+k <= j))
   trityp = 4;
  else
    trityp = 1;
 }
 else
 {
  if (trityp > 3)
    trityp = 3;
 else
     if ((trityp == 1) && (i+j > k))
       trityp = 2;
     else
       if ((trityp == 2) && (i+k > j))
          trityp = 2;
       else
          if ((trityp == 3) && (j+k > j))
            trityp = 2;
          else
            trityp = 4;
     }
   }
   return(trityp);
 }

static string conversiontrityp (int trityp) {
  switch (trityp) {
    case 1:
     return "scalene";
    case 2:
     return "isosceles";
    case 3:
     return "equilateral";
    default:
     return "not a triangle";}}
```

Figure 7.1 Source code of the Trityp program. *Source:* Cellier et al. [1]/University of Rennes.

Table 7.1 Mutants of the Trityp program.

Mutant	Faulty line
1	84 `if ((trityp == 3) && (i+k > j))`
2	79 `trityp = 0;`
3	64 `trityp = i+1;`
4	87 `if ((trityp != 3) && (j+k > i))`
5	65 `if (i >= k)`
6	74 `trityp = 0;`
7	90 `trityp == 3;`
8	66 `trityp = trityp+20;`

Source: Cellier et al. [1]/University of Rennes.

We use this benchmark to explain the ability of data mining process for localizing faults. We do so by introducing faults in the program in order to form slight variants, called mutants, and by testing them through a test suite [4]. The data mining process starts with the output of the tests, i.e. execution traces and pass/fail verdicts. The mutants can be found on the web,[2] and we use them to illustrate the general localization method.

Table 7.1 presents the eight mutants of the Trityp program. The first mutant is used to explain in detail the method. For mutant 1, one fault has been introduced in Line 84. The condition `(trityp == 2)` is replaced by `(trityp == 3)`. That fault causes a failure in two cases:

1) The first case is when `trityp` is equal to `2`; the execution does not enter this branch and goes to the default case in lines 89 and 90.
2) The second case is when `trityp` is equal to `3`; the execution should go to Line 87, but due to the fault, it goes to Line 84. Indeed, if the condition `(i+k > j)` holds, `trityp` is assigned to `2`. However, `(i+k > j)` does not always imply `(j+k > i)`, which is the real condition to test when `trityp` is equal to `3`. Therefore, `trityp` is assigned to `2`, whereas `4` is expected.

The faults of mutants 2, 3, 6, and 8 are on assignments. The faults of mutants 4, 5, and 7 are on conditions. We will present more details about multiple fault situations in Section 7.4. In this case, we simply combine several mutations to form new mutants.

7.2 Formal Concept Analysis and Association Rules[3]

FCA and AR are two well-known methods for symbolic data mining. In their original inception, they both consider data in the form of an object-attribute table. In the FCA world, the table is called a formal context. In the AR world, objects are called transactions, and attributes are called items, so that a line represents the items present in a given transaction. This comes from one of the first applications of AR, namely the basket analysis of retail sales. We will use both vocabularies interchangeably according to context.

Definition 7.1 (Formal Context and Transactions)
A formal context, $\mathcal{K}$, is a triple $(\mathcal{O}, \mathcal{A}, d)$ where $\mathcal{O}$ is a set of objects, $\mathcal{A}$ is a set of attributes, and d is a relation in $\mathcal{O} \times \mathcal{A}$. We write $(o, a) \in d$, or oDa equivalently. In the AR world, $\mathcal{A}$ is called a set of items, or itemset, and each $\{i \in A \mid oDi\}$ is the o-th transaction.

For visualization, we will consider objects as labeling lines and attributes as labeling columns of a table. A cross sign at the intersection of line o and column a indicates that object o has attribute a.

Table 7.2 is an example of context. The objects are the planets of the solar system, and the attributes are discretized properties of these planets: size, distance to the sun, and presence of moons. One can observe that all planets without moons are small, but that all planets with moons except two are far from sun. The difficulty is making similar observations in large data sets.

Table 7.2 The solar system context.

	Size			Sun distance		Moons	
	small	medium	large	near	far	with	without
Mercury	×			×			×
Venus	×			×			×
Earth	×			×		×	
Mars	×			×		×	
Jupiter			×		×	×	
Saturn			×		×	×	
Uranus		×			×	×	
Neptune		×			×	×	

Source: Cellier et al. [1]/University of Rennes.

Both FCA and AR try to answer questions such as "which attributes entail these attributes?" or "which attributes are entailed by these attributes?". The main difference between FCA and AR is that FCA answers these questions to the letter, i.e. the mere exception to a candidate rule kills the rule, though AR is accompanied by statistical indicators. In short, AR can be almost true. As a consequence, rare events as well as frequent events are represented in FCA, whereas in AR, frequent events are distinguished.

7.2.1 Formal Concept Analysis

FCA searches for sets of objects and sets of attributes with equal significance, like {`Mercury, Venus`} and {`without moons`} and then orders the significances by their specificity.

Definition 7.2 (Extent/Intent/Formal Concept)
Let $\mathcal{K} = (\mathcal{O}, \mathcal{A}, d)$ be a formal context. The collection $\{o \in \mathcal{O} \mid \forall a \in A.\ oDa\}$ is the extent of a set of attributes $A \subseteq \mathcal{A}$. It is written as extent (A). The collection $\{a \in \mathcal{A} \mid \forall o \in O.\ oDa\}$ is the intent of a collection of objects $O \subseteq \mathcal{O}$. It is written as intent(O).

A formal concept is a pair (O, A) such that $A \subseteq \mathcal{A}$, $O \subseteq \mathcal{O}$, intent(O) = A, and extent(A) = O. A is called the intent of the formal concept, and O is called its extent.

Formal concepts are partially ordered by set inclusion of their intent or extent. $(O_1, A_1) < (O_2, A_2)$ iff $O_1 \subset O_2$. We say that (O_2, A_2) contains (O_1, A_1).

In other words, (O, A) forms a formal concept iff O and A are mutually optimal for describing each other, that is, they have the same significance.

Lemma 7.1 (Basic FCA Results)
It is worth remembering the following results:

extent$(\emptyset) = \mathcal{O}$ *and intent*$(\emptyset) = \mathcal{A}$

extent(intent(extent(A))) = extent(A) and intent(extent(intent(O))) = intent(O). Hence, extent ∘ intent and intent ∘ extent are closure operators.

$(O_1, A_1) < (O_2, A_2)$ *iff* $A_1 \supset A_2$

(extent(intent(O)), intent(O)) is always a formal concept, and is written as concept(O). In the same way, (extent(A), intent(extent(A))) is always a formal concept as well, and is written as concept(A). All formal concepts can be constructed this way.

Theorem 7.1 (Fundamental Theorem of FCA [3])
Given a formal context, the set of all its partially ordered formal concepts forms a lattice called a concept lattice. Given a concept lattice, the original formal context can be reconstructed.

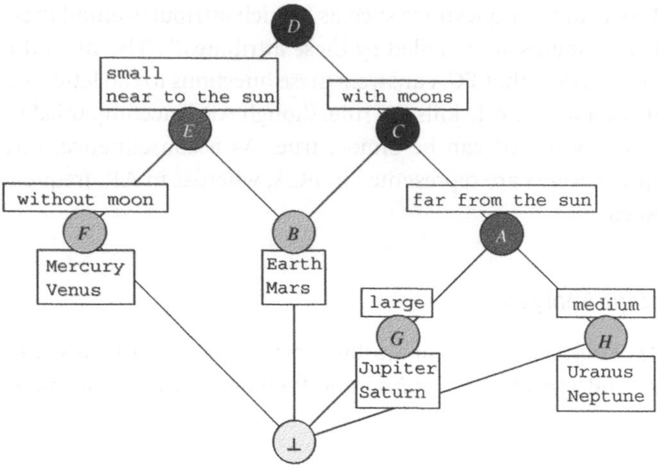

Figure 7.2 Concept lattice of the solar system context (see Figure 7.1). *Source:* Cellier et al. [1]/University of Rennes.

Figure 7.2 shows the concept lattice deduced from the solar system context. It is an example of the *standard representation* of a concept lattice. In this representation, concepts are drawn as colored circles with an optional inner label that serves as a concept identifier and 0, 1, or 2 outer labels in square boxes. Lines represent non-transitive containment; therefore, the standard representation displays a *Hasse diagram* of the lattice [5]. The figure is oriented such that higher concepts (higher in the diagram) contain lower concepts.

The upper outer label of a concept (such as large for concept *G*), when present, represents the attributes that are new to this concept intent compared with higher concepts; we call it an *attribute label*. It can be proven that if *A* is the attribute label of concept c, then *A* is the smallest set of attributes such that *c* = *concept*(*A*). Symmetrically, the lower outer label of a concept (such as Jupiter, Saturn for concept *G*), when present, represents the objects that are new to this concept extent compared with lower concepts; we call it an object label. It can be proven that if *O* is the object label of concept *c*, then *O* is the smallest set of objects such that *c* = *concept*(*O*). As a consequence, the intent of a concept is the set of all attribute labels of this concept and higher concepts, and the extent of a concept is the set of all object labels of this concept and lower concepts.

For example, the extent of concept *A* is {`Jupiter, Saturn, Uranus, Neptune`}, and its intent is {`far from sun, with moons`}. In other words, an attribute labels the highest concept to which intent it belongs, and an object labels the lowest concept to which extent it belongs.

It has been proven [3] that such a labeling, where all attributes and objects are used exactly once, is always possible. As a consequence, some formal concepts can be named by an attribute and/or an object; for example, concept G can be called `large`, `Jupiter`, or `Saturn`. But others like concept D have no such names. They are merely unions or intersections of other concepts.

In the standard representation of concept lattice, "a_1 entails a_2" reads as an upward path from $concept(a_1)$ to $concept(a_2)$. Attributes that do not entail each other, such as attributes `small` and `with moons`, indicate incomparable concepts. Note that there is no purely graphical way to detect that "a_1 nearly entails a_2".

The bottom concept, $\bot$, has all attributes and usually zero objects, unless some objects have all attributes. The top concept, $\top$, has all objects and usually zero attributes, unless some attributes are shared by all objects.

The worst-case time complexity of the construction of a concept lattice is exponential, but we have shown that if the size of the problem can only grow with the number of objects, i.e. the number of attributes per object is bounded, then the complexity is linear [6]. Moreover, though the mainstream interpretation of FCA is to compute the concept lattice at once and use it as a means for presenting graphically the structure of a data set, we have shown [6, 7] that the concept lattice can be built and explored gradually and efficiently.

7.2.2 Association Rules

FCA is a crisp methodology that is sensitive to every detail of the data set. Sometimes, one may wish for a method that is more tolerant to exceptions.

Definition 7.3 (Association Rules)
Let $\mathcal{K}$ be a set of transactions, i.e. a formal context seen as a set of lines seen as itemsets. An association rule is a pair (P, C) of itemsets. It is usually written as $P \rightarrow C$.

The P part is called the premise, and the C part is the conclusion.

Note that any $P \rightarrow C$ forms an AR. It does not mean it is a relevant one. Statistical indicators give hints at the relevance of a rule.

Given any set X, let $||X||$ denote its cardinal, or the number of elements it contains.

Definition 7.4 (Support/Confidence/Lift)
*The **support** of a rule $P \rightarrow C$, written as $sup(P \rightarrow C)$, is defined as*

$$||extent(P \cup C)||.$$

*The **normalized support** of a rule $P \rightarrow C$ is defined as*

$$\frac{||extent(P \cup C)||}{||extent(\emptyset)||}.$$

*The **confidence** of rule $P \rightarrow C$, written as $conf(P \rightarrow C)$, is defined as*

$$\frac{\|sup(P \rightarrow C)\|}{\|sup(P \rightarrow \emptyset)\|} = \frac{\|extent(P \cup C)\|}{\|extent(P)\|}.$$

*The **lift** of a rule $P \rightarrow C$, written $lift(P \rightarrow C)$, is defined as*

$$\frac{\|conf(P \rightarrow C)\|}{\|conf(\emptyset \rightarrow C)\|} = \frac{\|sup(P \rightarrow C)\|}{\|sup(P \rightarrow \emptyset)\|} / \frac{\|sup(\emptyset \rightarrow C)\|}{\|sup(\emptyset \rightarrow \emptyset)\|}$$

$$= \frac{\|extent(P \cup C)\| \times \|extent(\emptyset)\|}{\|extent(P)\| \times \|extent(C)\|}.$$

Support measures the prevalence of an AR in a data set. For example, the support of `near sun` → `with moons` is 2. Normalized support measures its prevalence as a value in [0, 1], i.e. as a probability of occurrence. For example, the normalized support of `near sun` → `with moons` is 2/8 = 0.25. It can be read as the probability of observing the rule in a random transaction of the context. It would seem that the greater the support, the better it is, but very often one must be satisfied with a very small support. This is because in large contexts, with many transactions and items, any given co-occurrence of several items is a rare event. Efficient algorithms exist for computing all ARs whose support satisfies a user-defined threshold [8–11].

Confidence measures the "truthfulness" of an AR as the ratio of the prevalence of its premise and conclusion together on the prevalence of its premise alone. Its value is in [0, 1], and for a given premise the bigger is the better; in other words, it is better to have fewer exceptions to the rule considered as a logical implication. For example, the confidence of `near sun` → `with moons` is 2/4 = 0.5. This can be read as the conditional probability of observing the conclusion knowing that the premise holds. However, there is no way to tell whether a confidence value is good in itself. In other words, there is no absolute threshold above which a confidence value is good.

Lift also measures "truthfulness" of an AR, but it does so as the increase in the probability of observing the conclusion when the premise holds with respect to when it does not hold. In other words, it measures how the premise of a rule increases the chance of observing the conclusion. A lift value of 1 indicates that the premise and conclusion are independent. A lower value indicates that the premise repels the conclusion, and a higher value indicates that the premise attracts the conclusion. For example, the lift of `near sun` → `with moons` is

0.5/0.75, which shows that the attribute `near sun` repels the attribute `with moons`; to be near the sun diminishes the probability of having a moon. The rule `near sun` → `without moons` has a support value of 0.25, confidence value of 0.5, and lift value of 0.5/0.25, which indicates an attraction; to be near the sun augments the probability of not having a moon. The two rules have identical supports and confidences but opposite lifts. In the sequel, we will use support as an indicator of the prevalence of a rule and lift as an indicator of its "truthfulness."

7.3 Data Mining for Fault Localization[4]

We consider a debugging process in which a program is tested against different test cases. Each test case yields a transaction in the AR sense, in which attributes correspond to properties observed during the execution of the test case. Two attributes, *PASS* and *FAIL*, represent the verdict of the test case. Thus, the set of all test cases yields a set of transactions that form a formal context, which we call a trace context. The main idea of the data mining approach is to look for a formal explanation of the failures.

7.3.1 Failure Rules

Formally, we are looking for AR following pattern $P \rightarrow FAIL$. We call these rules *failure rules*. A failure rule proposes an explanation to a failure, and this explanation can be evaluated according to its support and lift.

Note that failure rules have a variable premise P and a constant conclusion *FAIL*. This slightly simplifies the management of rules. For instance, relevance indicators can be specialized as follows:

Definition 7.5 (Relevance Indicators for Failure Rules)

$$\text{sup}(P \rightarrow FAIL) = \|\text{extent}(P \cup \{FAIL\})\|,$$

$$conf(P \rightarrow FAIL) = \frac{\|extent(P \cup \{FAIL\}\|}{\|extent(P)\|},$$

$$lift(P \rightarrow FAIL) = \frac{\|extent(P \cup \{FAIL\})\| \times \|extent(\emptyset)\|}{\|extent(P)\| \times \|extent(\{FAIL\})\|}.$$

Observe that $\|extent(\emptyset)\|$ and $\|extent(\{FAIL\})\|$ are constant for a given test suite. Only $\|extent(P)\|$ and $\|extent(P \cup \{FAIL\})\|$ depend on the failure rule.

It is interesting to understand the dynamics of these indicators when new test cases are added to the trace context.

Lemma 7.2 (Dynamics of Relevance Indicators with Respect to Test Suite)
Consider a failure rule $P \longrightarrow FAIL$:

A new successful test case that executes P will leave its support unchanged (normalized support will decrease slightly[5]), will decrease its confidence, and will decrease its lift slightly if P is not executed by all test cases.

A new successful test case that does not execute P will leave its support and confidence unchanged (normalized support will decrease slightly) and will increase its lift.

A new failed test case that executes P will increase its support and confidence (normalized support will increase slightly) and will increase its lift slightly if P is not executed by all test cases.

A new failed test case that does not execute P will leave its support and confidence unchanged (normalized support will decrease slightly) and will decrease its lift.

In summary, support and confidence grow with new failed test cases that execute *P*, and *lift* grows with failed test cases that execute *P* or successful test cases that do not execute *P*. Failed test cases that execute *P* increase all the indicators but successful test cases that do not execute *P* only increase *lift*.[6]

Another interesting dynamic is what happens when *P* increases.

Lemma 7.3 (Dynamics of Relevance Indicators with Respect to Premise)
Consider a failure rule $P \longrightarrow FAIL$ and replacing P with P' such that $P' \supsetneq P$:

Support will decrease (except if all test cases fail, which should not persist). One says $P' \longrightarrow FAIL$ is more specific than $P \longrightarrow FAIL$.

Confidence and lift can go either way, but both in the same way because $\frac{\|extent(\emptyset)\|}{\|extent(\{FAIL\})\|}$ is a constant.

For the sequel of the description, we assume that the attributes recorded in the trace context are line numbers of executed statements. Since the order of the attributes in a formal context does not matter, this forms an abstraction of a standard trace (see a fragment of such a trace context in Table 7.3). Thus, explanations for failures will consist in line numbers, lines that increase the risk of failure when executed. Had other trace observations been used, the explanations would have been different. For faults that materialize in faulty instructions, it is expected that they will show up as explanations to failed test cases. For other faults that materialize in missing instructions, they will still be visible in actual lines that would have been correct if the missing lines where present. For instance, a missing initialization will be seen as the faulty consultation of a non-initialized variable. It is up to a competent debugger to conclude from faulty consultations that an

Table 7.3 A trace context.

	Executed lines				Verdict	
Test case	**57**	**58**	**...**	**105**	***PASS***	***FAIL***
t_1	×	×		×	×	
t_2	×	×		×		×
...	...	...	...	...	...	...

Source: Cellier et al. [1]/University of Rennes.

initialization is missing. Note finally that the relationships between faults and failures are complex:

- Executing a faulty line does not necessarily cause a failure. For example, a fault in a line may not be stressed by a case test (e.g. faulty condition $i > 1$ instead of the expected $i > 0$, tested with i equals to 10) or a faulty line that is "corrected" by another one.
- Absolutely correct lines can apparently cause failure, such as lines of the same basic block [12] as a faulty line (they will have exactly the same distribution as the faulty line) or lines whose preconditions cannot be established by a distant faulty part.

Given any sets X and Y, let $X \setminus Y$ denote the set difference, or the set of elements in X that are not in Y.

Failure rules are selected according to a threshold support criterion. However, there are too many such rules, and it would be inconvenient to list them all. We have observed in Lemma 7.3 that more specific rules have less support. However, this does not mean that less specific rules must be preferred. For instance, if the program has a mandatory initialization part, which always executes a set of lines I, rule $I \rightarrow FAIL$ is a failure rule with maximal support, but it is also less informative. If all failures are caused by executing a set of lines $F \supset I$, rule $F \setminus I \rightarrow FAIL$ will have the same support as $F \rightarrow FAIL$ but will be the most informative. In summary, maximizing support is good, but it is not the definitive criterion for selecting informative rules.

Another idea is to use the lift indicator instead of support. However, lift does not grow monotonically with premise inclusion. Therefore, finding rules with a threshold lift cannot be done more efficiently than by enumerating all rules and then filtering them.

7.3.2 Failure Lattice

Here, we describe how to use FCA to help navigate in the set of explanations.

Definition 7.6 (Failure Lattice)
Form a formal context with the premises of failure rules. The rules identifiers are the objects, and their premises are the attributes (in our example, line numbers) (see an example in Table 7.4*). It is called the failure context.*

Observe that the failure context is special in that all premises of failure rules are different from each other.[7] *Thus, they are uniquely determined by their premises (or itemsets). Thus, it is not necessary to identify them by objects identifiers.*

Apply FCA on this formal context to form the corresponding concept lattice. It is called the failure lattice. Its concepts and labeling display the most specific explanations to groups of failed tests.

Since object identifiers are useless, replace object labels by the support and lift of the unique rule that labels each concept. This forms the failure lattice (see Figure 7.3). The overall trace mining process is summarized in Figure 7.4.

Lemma 7.4 (Properties of the Failure Lattice)
The most specific explanations (i.e. the largest premises) are at the bottom of the lattice. On the contrary, the least specific failure rules are near the top. For instance, the line numbers of a prelude sequence executed by every test case will label the topmost concepts.

The explanations with the smallest support are at the bottom of the lattice. For example, line numbers executed only by specific failed test cases will label concepts near the bottom.

Support increases when going upstream, from bottom to top. We call this the global monotony of support ordering [13]. Lift does not follow any global monotony behavior.

Table 7.4 Failure context for mutant 1 of the Trityp program with *threshold_lift* = 1.25 and *threshold_sup* = 1. (For mutant 1, the fault is in line 84. See Figure 7.1.)

	Executed lines										
Rule ID	**17**	**58**	**66**	**81**	**84**	**87**	**90**	**105**	**93**	**...**	**113**
r_1	×	×	×	×	×	×	×	×	×	...	×
r_2	×	×		×	×	×	×		×	...	×
⋮	⋮	⋮	⋮	⋮	⋮	⋮	⋮	⋮	⋮	⋮	⋮
r_8	×	×		×					×	...	×
r_9	×	×							×	...	×

Source: Cellier et al. [1]/University of Rennes.

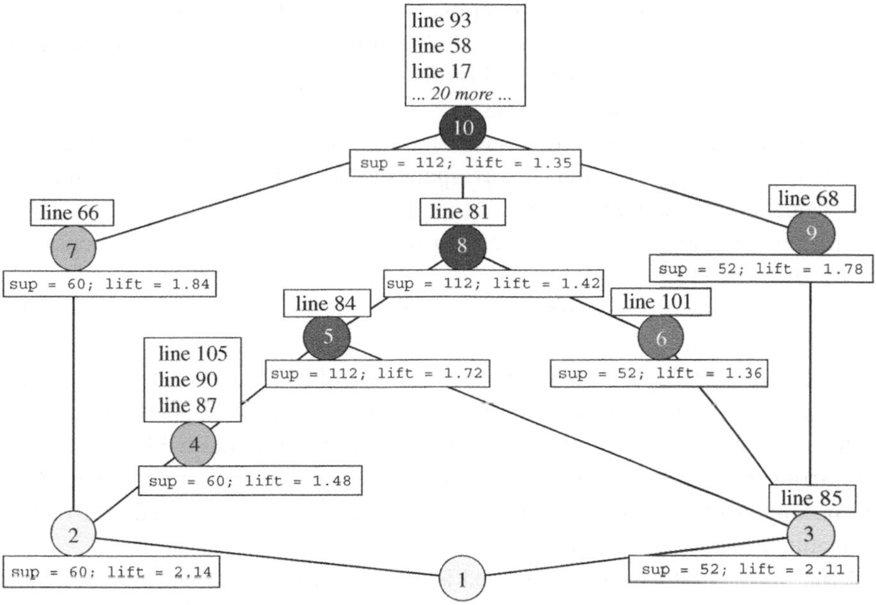

Figure 7.3 Failure lattice associated with the failure context of Table 7.4 (for mutant 1, the fault is in line 84). *Source:* Cellier et al. [1]/University of Rennes.

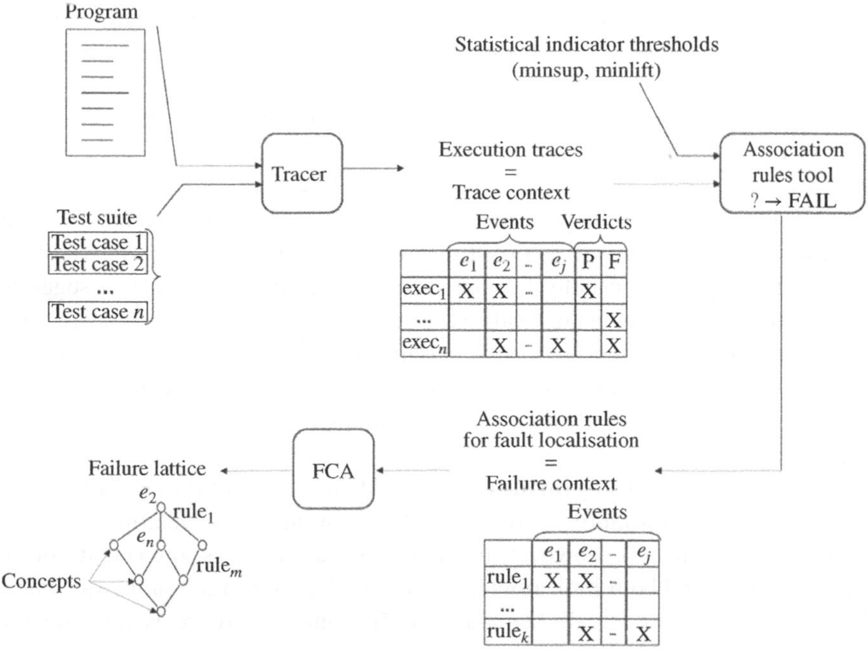

Figure 7.4 The trace mining process. *Source:* Cellier et al. [1]/University of Rennes.

Concepts form clusters of comparable concepts with the same support. For example, concepts 2, 4, and 7 in Figure 7.3 form a cluster of rules with support 60. We call them support clusters. This means that explanations of increasing size represent the same group of failures.

In a support cluster, a unique concept has the largest extent. We call it the head concept of the support cluster. It corresponds to the explanation with the highest lift value in the support cluster. More generally, lift decreases when going bottom-up in a support cluster. We refer to this behavior as the local monotony of lift ordering [13].

It is useless to investigate explanations other than the head concepts. This can be done by a bottom-up exploration of the failure lattice.

In the lattice of Figure 7.3, only concepts 2 (head of support cluster with value 60), 3 (head of support cluster with value 52), and 5 (head of support cluster with value 112) need to be presented to the debugging oracle. Concept 5 has Line 84 in its attribute label, which is the location of the fault in this mutant. The local monotony of lift ordering shows that the lift indicator can be used as a metric but only inside support clusters.

The process that we have presented is dominated by the choice of a threshold value for the support indicator. Recall that the support of an explanation is simply the number of simultaneous realizations of its items in the failure context, and the normalized support is the ratio of this number to the total number of realizations. In this application of ARs, it is more meaningful to use the non-normalized variant because it directly represents the number of failed test cases covered by an explanation. What is a good value for the threshold support? First, it cannot be larger than the number of failed test cases ($= \|extent(FAIL)\|$); otherwise, no $P \rightarrow FAIL$ rule will show up. Second, it cannot be less than 1. The choice between 1 and $\|extent(FAIL)\|$ depends on the nature of the fault, but in any case, experiments show that acceptable threshold support is quite low (a few percent of the total number of test cases). A high threshold support will filter out all faults that are the causes of less failures than this threshold. Very singular faults will require a very small support, eventually 1, to be visible in the failure lattice. This suggests starting with a high support to localize the most visible faults, and then decreasing the support to localize less frequently executed faults. The threshold support acts as a resolution cursor. A coarse resolution will show the largest features at a low cost, and a finer resolution will be required to zoom in on smaller features at a higher cost.

We have insisted on using lift instead of confidence as a "truthfulness" indicator, because it lends itself more easily to an interpretation (recall Definition 7.4 and subsequent comments). However, in the case of failure rules, the conclusion is fixed ($= FAIL$), and both indicators increase and decrease in the same way when the premise changes (recall Lemma 7.3). The only difference is that the lift indicator yields a normalized value (1 is independence, below 1 is repulsion, and over 1 is attraction). What is the effect of a minimum lift value? First, if it is chosen to be larger than or equal to 1, it will eliminate all failure rules that show a repulsion between the premise and conclusion. Second, if it is chosen to be strictly greater than 1, it will eliminate failure rules that have a lower lift, thus compressing the representation of support clusters and eventually eliminating some support clusters. Thus, the threshold lift also acts as a zoom.

This suggests a global debugging process in which the results of an increasingly large test suite are examined with increasing acuity (see Figure 7.5). Given a test suite, an inner loop computes failure rules, i.e. explanations with decreasing

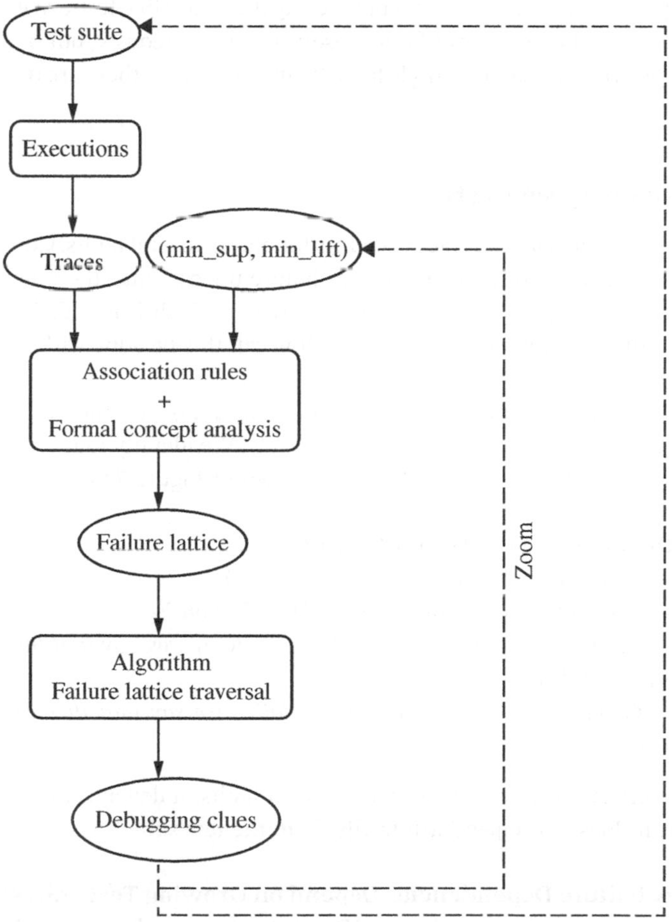

Figure 7.5 The global debugging process. *Source:* Cellier et al. [1]/University of Rennes.

support, from a fraction of ||*extent(FAIL)*|| to 1 and builds the corresponding failure lattice. In the outer loop, test cases are added progressively to cope with added functionality (such as test-driven development) or new failure reports. Thus, the global debugging process zooms into the failed test cases to find explanations for more and more specific failures.

7.4 The Failure Lattice for Multiple Faults[8]

This section extends the analysis of data mining for fault localization for the multiple fault situation. From the debugging process point of view, there is nothing special about multiple faults. Some software engineering life cycles like test-driven development tend to limit the number of faults observed simultaneously, but one can never assume a priori that there is a single fault. Thus, we assume there are one or several faults.

7.4.1 Dependencies Between Faults

In the multiple fault case, each failure trace accounts for one or several faults. Conversely, faulty lines are suspected in one or several failure traces. Thus, the inner loop of the global debugging process cannot just stop when a fault is found. The process must go on until all failures are explained. How can this be done without exploring the entire failure lattice?

Consider any pair of faults F_1 and F_2. Suppose $Fail_{F_1}$ and $Fail_{F_2}$ are the sets of failure-causing test cases that detect F_1 and F_2, respectively. We identify four types of possible dependencies between the two faults as shown in Figure 7.6.

Definition 7.7 (Dependencies Between Faults)
If $Fail_{F_1} \cap Fail_{F_2} = \emptyset$, *we say that they are independent (ID).*

If $Fail_{F_1} \subseteq Fail_{F_2}$, *we say that* F_1 *is strongly dependent (SD) on* F_2.

If $Fail_{F_1} \subseteq Fail_{F_2}$ *and* $Fail_{F_2} \subseteq Fail_{F_1}$, *that is, if* $Fail_{F_1} = Fail_{F_2}$, *we say that they are mutually strongly dependent (MSD).*

If $Fail_{F_1} \cap Fail_{F_2} \neq \emptyset$, $Fail_{F_1} \not\subset Fail_{F_2}$, *and* $Fail_{F_2} \not\subset Fail_{F_1}$, *we say that they are loosely dependent (LD).*

Note that this classification is not intrinsic to a pair of faults; it depends on the test suite. However, it does not depend arbitrarily from the test suite.

Lemma 7.5 (How Failure Dependencies Depend on Growing Test Suites)
Assume that the test suite can only grow, then an ID or SD pair can only become LD, and an MSD pair can only become SD or LD.

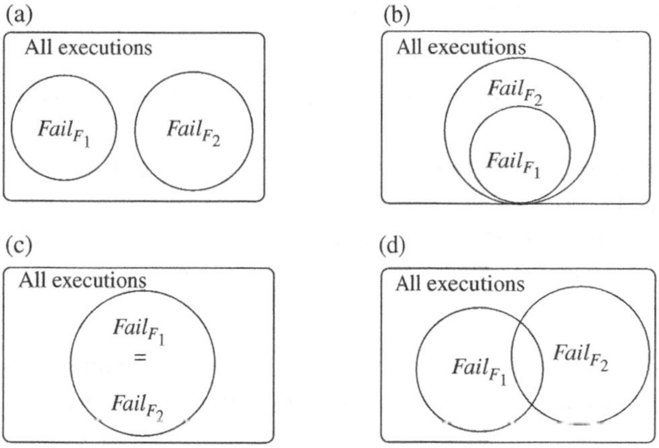

Figure 7.6 The four Venn diagrams of two-fault dependency. (a) Independent faults; (b) strongly dependent faults; (c) mutually strongly dependent faults; and (d) loosely dependent faults. *Source:* Cellier et al. [1]/University of Rennes.

This can be summarized as follows:

$$\text{ID} \rightarrow \text{LD} \leftarrow \text{SD} \leftarrow \text{MSD}$$

Note also that this knowledge, with respect to several faults and the dependencies between them, is what the debugging person is looking for, whereas the trace context only gives hints at this knowledge. The question is: how does it give hints at this knowledge?

The main idea is to distinguish special concepts in the failure lattice that we call *failure concepts.*

Definition 7.8 (Failure Concept)
A failure concept is a maximally specific concept of the failure lattice whose intent (a set of lines) is contained in a failed execution.

Recall that the failure rules are an abstraction of the failed execution. For instance, choosing threshold support and lift values eliminates lines that are seldom executed or that do not attract failure. Thus, the failure lattice describes exactly the selected failure rules but only approximately the failed executions. That is why it is interesting; it compresses information, though with loss. The failure concepts in the failure lattice are those concepts that best approximate failed executions. All other concepts contain less precise information. For the same reasons, there are much fewer failure concepts than failed executions; each failure concept accounts for a group of failures that detects some fault.

The main use for failure concepts is to give a criterion for stopping the exploration of the failure lattice. In a few words,

- the bottom-up exploration of the failure lattice goes from support clusters to support clusters as above;
- the line labels of the traversed concepts are accumulated in a fault context sent to the competent debugger;
- any time a competent debugger finds a hint at an actual fault, all the failure concepts under the concept that gave the hint are deemed explained; and
- the process continues until all failure concepts are explained.

The fault context is the part of the program that the debugging person is supposed to check. We consider its size as a measure of the effort imposed on the debugging person.

Dependencies between faults have an impact on the way failure concepts are presented in the failure lattice.

Lemma 7.6 (ID Faults with Respect to Failure Concepts)
If two faults are ID, their lines can never occur in the same failed trace, so that no rule contains the two faults, and no concept in the failure lattice contains the two faults. Thus, the two faults will label failure concepts in two different support clusters that have no subconcepts in common except $\perp$. (See Figure 7.7 for an example.)

Concretely, when exploring the failure lattice bottom-up, finding a fault in the label of a concept explains both the concept and the concepts underneath, but the faults in the other upper branches remain to be explained. Moreover, the order with which the different branches are explored does not matter.

Lemma 7.7 (LD Faults with Respect to Failure Concepts)
If two faults are LD, some failed traces contain both faults, while other failed traces contain one of the faults. They may label concepts in two different support clusters that share common subconcepts.

Concretely, when exploring the failure lattice bottom-up, finding a fault for a failure concept does not explain the other LD failure concept. Once a fault is found, shared concepts must be re-explored in the direction of other superconcepts.

Lemma 7.8 (SD Faults with Respect to Failure Concepts)
If two faults are SD, say F_1 *depends on* F_2*, a failure concept whose intent contains* $Line_{F_1}$ *will appear as a subconcept of another failure concept whose intent contains* $Line_{F_2}$ *in a different support cluster* (see Figure 7.8 for an example).

Therefore, fault F_1 will be found before F_2, but the debugging process must continue because there is a failure concept above.

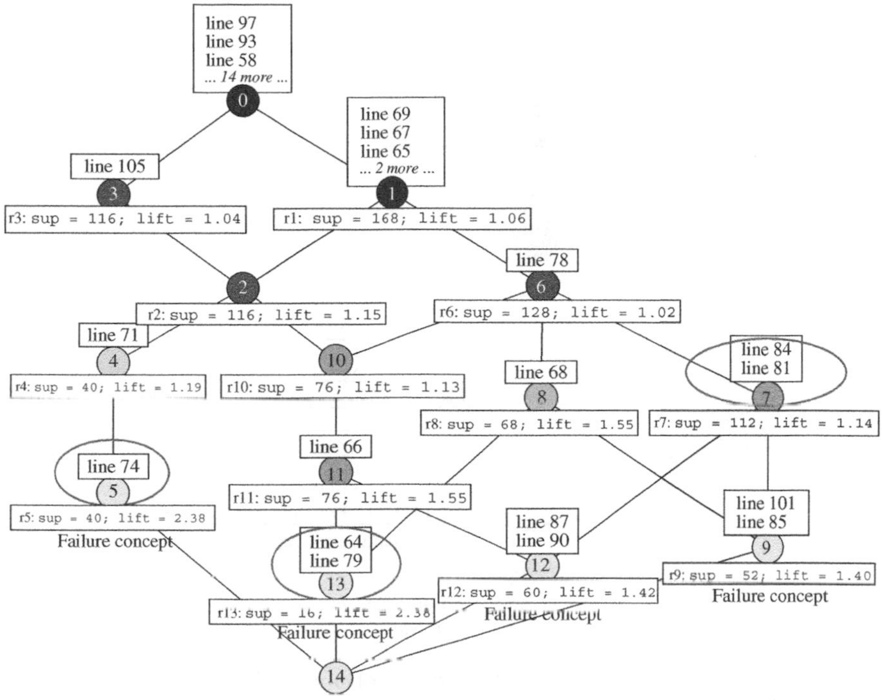

Figure 7.7 Failure lattice associated to program Trityp with ID faults of mutants 1, 2, and 6. *Source:* Cellier et al. [1]/University of Rennes.

Lemma 7.9 (MSD Faults with Respect to Failure Concepts)
Finally, if two faults are MSD, they cannot be distinguished by failed executions, and their failure concepts belong to the same support cluster. However, they can sometimes be distinguished by successful executions (such as one having more successful executions than the other), and this can be seen in the failure lattice through the lift value.

All this can be formalized in an algorithm that searches for multiple faults in an efficient traversal of the failure lattice (see Algorithm 7.1). The failure lattice is traversed bottom-up, starting with the failure concepts (step 1). At the end of the failure lattice traversal, $C_{failure\_toExplain}$, the set of failure concepts not explained by a fault (step 2) must be empty, or all concepts must be already explored (step 3). When a concept, c (step 4), is chosen among the concepts to explore, $C_{toExplore}$, the events that label the concept are explored. Note that the selection of that concept is not determinist. If no fault is located, then the upper neighbors of c are added to the set of concepts to explore (step 7). If, thanks to the new clues, the debugging oracle understands mistakes and locates one or several faults, then

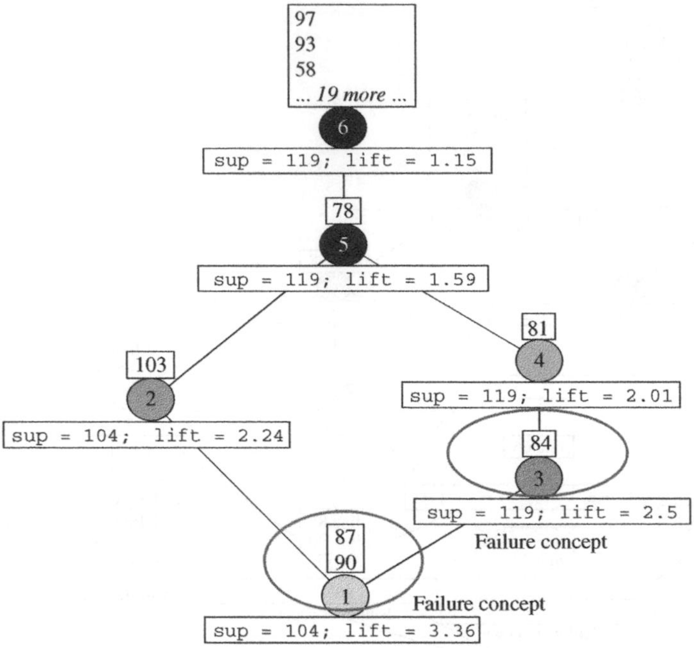

Figure 7.8 Failure lattice associated to program Trityp with SD faults 1 and 7. *Source:* Cellier et al. [1]/University of Rennes.

$C_{toExplore} :=$ *FAILURE CONCEPTS*
$C_{failure\_toExplain} :=$ *FAILURE CONCEPTS*
while $C_{failure\_to\ Explain} \neq \emptyset \wedge C_{toExplore} \neq \emptyset$ **do**
  let $c \in C_{toExplore}$
  $C_{toExplore} := C_{to\ Explore} \setminus \{c\}$
  if the debugging_oracle(*label*(c), *fault_context*(c)) locates no fault **then**
    $C_{toExplore} := C_{to\ Explore} \cup$ {upper neighbors of c}
  else
    let *Explained* = subconcepts(c) $\cup$ cluster(c)
    $C_{toExplore} := C_{toExplore} \setminus Explained$
    $C_{failure\_toExplain} := C_{failure\_to\ Explain} \setminus Explained$
  end if
end while

Algorithm 7.1 Failure lattice traversal. *Source:* Cellier et al. [1]/University of Rennes.

all subconcepts of c and all concepts that are in the same support cluster are "explained." Those concepts do not have to be explored again (step 10). This means that the failure concepts that are subconcepts of c are explained (step 11). The exploration goes on until all failed executions in the failure lattice are explained by at least one fault, or all concepts have been explored.

Note that at each iteration, $C_{failure\_toExplain}$ can only decrease or remain untouched. The competent debugger hypothesis ensures that $C_{failure\_toExplain}$ ends at empty when threshold sup = 1. In the case of an ineffective debugging oracle or a too high the threshold sup, the process would end when $C_{toExplore}$ becomes empty, namely when all concepts have been explored.

7.4.2 Example

For the example of Figure 7.7, the value of the *threshold_sup* is equal to four failed executions (out of 400 executions, of which 168 are failed executions), and the *threshold_lift* value is 1. There are four failure concepts: 5, 13, 12, and 9. Table 7.5 presents the values of $C_{toExplore}$ and $C_{failure\_toExplain}$ at each iteration of the exploration. We choose to explore the lattice with a queue strategy; it means first in $C_{toExplore}$, first out of $C_{toExplore}$. However, the algorithm does not specify one strategy.

At the beginning, $C_{toExplore}$ and $C_{failure\_toExplain}$ are initialized as the set of all failure concepts (iteration 0 in Table 7.5). At the first iteration of the `while` loop, concept 5 is selected ($c = c_5$). That concept is labeled by line 74. Line 74 actually corresponds to fault 6. Thanks to the competent debugging hypothesis, fault 6 is located. Concepts 5, 4, and 14 are thus tagged as explained. The new values of $C_{toExplore}$ and $C_{failure\_toExplain}$ are presented at iteration 1 in Table 7.5.

Table 7.5 Exploration of the failure lattice of Figure 7.7.

Iteration	$C_{toExplore}$	$C_{failure\_toExplain}$
0	$\{c_5, c_{13}, c_{12}, c_9\}$	$\{c_5, c_{13}, c_{12}, c_9\}$
1	$\{c_{13}, c_{12}, c_9\}$	$\{c_{13}, c_{12}, c_9\}$
2	$\{c_{12}, c_9\}$	$\{c_{12}, c_9\}$
3	$\{c_9, c_7, c_{11}\}$	$\{c_{12}, c_9\}$
4	$\{c_7, c_{11}, c_8\}$	$\{c_{12}, c_9\}$
5	$\{c_{11}, c_8\}$	$\{\}$

Source: Cellier et al. [1]/University of Rennes.

At the second iteration, concept 13 is selected ($c = c_{13}$). That concept is labeled by lines 64 and 79. Line 79 actually corresponds to fault 2; the competent debugging oracle locates fault 2. Concept 13 is tagged as explained.

At the third iteration, concept 12 is selected. That concept is labeled by lines 87 and 90. No fault is found. The upper neighbors, concepts 7 and 11, are added to $C_{toExplore}$, and $C_{failure\_toExplain}$ is unchanged.

At the next iteration, concept 9 is selected. As in the previous iteration, no fault is found. The upper neighbor, concept 8, is added to $C_{toExplore}$.

Finally, concept 7 is selected. That concept is labeled by lines 81 and 84. By exploring those lines (new clues) in addition with the fault context, i.e. lines that have already been explored: 87, 90, 101, and 85, the competent debugging oracle locates fault 1 in line 84. The fault is the substitution of the test of `trityp = 2` by `trityp = 3`. Concepts 12 and 9 exhibit two concrete realizations (failures) of the fault in line 84 (Concept 7). Concepts 7, 12, and 9 are tagged as explained. The set of failure concepts to explain is empty; thus, the exploration stops. All four faults (for failures above the support and lift thresholds) are found after the debugging oracle has inspected nine lines.

7.5 Discussion[9]

The contexts and lattices introduced in the previous sections allow programmers to see all the differences between execution traces as well as all the differences between AR. There exist other methods that compute differences between execution traces. We first show that the information about trace differences provided by the failure context (and the corresponding lattice) is already more relevant than the information provided by four other methods proposed by Renieris and Reiss [14] and Cleve and Zeller [15]. Then, we show that explicitly using AR with several lines in the premise alleviates some limitations of Jones et al.'s method [16]. Finally, we show that reasoning on the partial ordering given by the proposed failure lattice is more relevant than reasoning on total order rankings [16–20].

7.5.1 The Structure of the Execution Traces

The trace context contains the whole information about execution traces. In particular, the associated lattice, the trace lattice, allows programmers to see in one pass all differences between traces.

There exist several fault localization methods based on the differences between execution traces. They all assume a single failed execution and several successful executions. We rephrase them in terms of search in a lattice to highlight their advantages, their hidden hypothesis, and limitations.

7.5.2 Union Model

The union model, proposed by Renieris and Reiss [14], aims at finding features that are specific to the failed execution. The method is based on the trace difference between the failed execution f and a set S of successful executions: $f \setminus \cup_{s \in S} s$. The underlying intuition is that the failure is caused by lines that are executed only in the failed execution. Formalized in FCA terms, the concepts of interest are the subconcepts whose label contains *FAIL*, and the computed information is the lines contained in the labels of the subconcepts. The trace lattice presented in the figure is slightly different from the lattice that would be computed for the union model, because it represents more than one failed execution. Nevertheless, the union model often computes empty information, namely each time the faulty line belongs to failed and successful execution traces. For example, a fault in a condition has a very slight chance to be localized. The approach we presented is based on the same intuition. However, the lattices that we propose do not lose information and help navigate in order to localize the faults, even when the faulty line belongs to both failed and successful execution traces.

The union model helps localize a bug when executing the faulty statement always implies an error, such as the bad assignment of a variable that is the result of the program. In that case, the lattice also helps, and the faulty statement labels the same concept as *FAIL*.

7.5.3 Intersection Model

The intersection model [14] is the complementary of the previous model. It computes the features whose absence is the discriminant of the failed execution: $\cap_{s \in S} s \setminus f$. Replacing *FAIL* by *PASS* in the above discussion is relevant to discussing the intersection model and leads to the same conclusions.

7.5.4 Nearest Neighbor

The nearest neighbor approach [14] computes a distance metric between the failed execution trace and a set of successful execution traces. The computed trace difference $f \setminus p$ involves the failed execution trace f and only the nearest successful execution trace p. The difference is meant to be the part of the code to explore. The approach can be formalized in FCA. Given a concept C_f whose intent contains *FAIL*, the nearest neighbor method searches for a concept C_p whose intent contains *PASS*, such that the intent of C_p shares as many lines as possible with the intent of C_f.

As for the previous methods, it is a good approach when the execution of the faulty statement always involves an error. However, when the faulty statement can lead to both a successful and a failed execution, the nearest neighbor method is not sufficient. In addition, we remark that there are possibly many concepts of interest, namely all the nearest neighbors of the concept that is labeled by *FAIL*. With a lattice, that kind of behavior can be observed directly.

Note that in the trace lattice, the executions that execute the same lines are clustered in the label of a single concept. Executions that are nearby share a large part of their executed lines and label concepts that are neighbors in the lattice. There is therefore no reason to restrict the comparison to a single pass execution. Furthermore, all the nearest neighbors are naturally in the lattice.

7.5.5 Delta Debugging

Delta debugging, proposed by Zeller et al. [15], reasons on the values of variables during executions rather than on executed lines. The trace spectrum, and therefore the trace context, contains different types of attributes. Note that the data mining approach we have presented does not depend on the type of attributes and would apply more to spectra containing other attributes than executed lines.

Delta debugging computes the differences between the failed execution trace and a single successful execution trace using a memory graph. By injecting the values of variables of the failed execution into variables of the successful execution, the method tries to determine a small set of suspicious variables. One of the purposes of the method is to find a successful execution relatively similar to the failed execution. It has the same drawbacks as the nearest neighbor method.

7.5.6 From the Trace Context to the Failure Context

Tarantula by Jones et al. [16] computed AR with only one line in the premise. Denmat et al. [21] showed the limitations of this method through three implicit hypotheses. The first hypothesis is that a failure has a single faulty statement origin. The second hypothesis is that lines are independent. The third hypothesis is that executing the faulty statement often causes a failure. That last hypothesis is a common assumption of fault localization methods, including the data mining method that we have presented. Indeed, when the fault is executed in both successful and failed executions (such as in a prelude), it cannot be found so easily using these hypotheses. In addition, Denmat et al. demonstrated that the ad hoc indicator, which was used by Jones et al., is equivalent to the lift indicator.

By using AR with more expressive premises than in Jones et al.'s method (namely with several lines), the limitations mentioned above are alleviated. First, the fault need not be a single line but can contain several lines together. Second, the dependency between lines is taken into account. Indeed, dependent lines are clustered or ordered together.

The part of the trace context that is important to search in order to localize a fault is the set of concepts that are related to the concept labeled by *FAIL*, i.e. those that have a non-empty intersection with the concept labeled by *FAIL*. Computing AR with *FAIL* as a conclusion computes exactly those concepts, except for the *threshold_sup* and *threshold_lift* filtering. In other words, the focus is done on the part of the lattice related to the concept labeled by *FAIL*.

7.5.7 The Structure of Association Rules

Jones et al.'s method presents the result of the analysis to the user as a coloring of the source code. A red-green gradient indicates the correlation with failure. Lines that are highly correlated with failure are colored in red, whereas lines that are not highly correlated are colored in green. Red lines typically represent more than 10% of the lines of the program, without identified links between them. Other statistical methods [17–20] also try to rank lines in a total ordering. It can be seen as ordering the concepts of the failure lattice by the lift value of the rule in their label. However, as we have highlighted in Section 7.2, the monotonicity of lift is only relevant locally to a support cluster.

For example, on the failure lattice of Figure 7.3, the obtained ranking would be lines 85, 66, 68, 84, and so on. No link, for instance, would be established between the execution of lines 85 and 68.

The user who wants to localize a fault in a program has background knowledge about the program and can use it to explore the failure lattice. Reading the lattice provides the context about the fault and not just a sequence of independent lines to be examined, and it reduces the number of lines to be examined at each step (concept) by structuring them.

7.5.8 Multiple Faults

We have compared the failure lattice with existing single fault localization methods. In this section, we compare our navigation method into the failure lattice with other strategies to detect several faults.

Our approach has a flavor of algorithmic debugging [22]. The difference lays in the traversed data structure. While Shapiro's algorithm helps traverse a proof tree, our algorithm helps traverse the failure lattice, starting from the most suspicious places.

For multiple faults, Jiang et al. [23] criticized the ranking of statistical methods. They proposed a method based on traces whose events are predicates. The predicates are clustered, and the path in the control flow graph associated to each cluster is computed. In the failure lattice, events are also clustered in concepts. The relations between concepts give information about the path in the control flow graph and highlight some parts of that path as relevant to debug without computing the control flow graph.

Zheng et al. [20] proposed a method based on bi-clustering in order to group failed executions and identify one feature (bug predictor) that characterizes each cluster. They proposed to look at one bug predictor at a time. Several bug predictors can be in relation with the same fault, but no link is drawn between them. Our approach gives context to the fault, in order to help understand the mistakes of the programmer that have produced the fault.

Jones et al. [24] proposed a method that first clusters executions and then finds a fault in each cluster in parallel. The method has the same aim as our method. Indeed, in both cases, the target is to separate the effects of the different faults in order to treat the maximum of faults in one execution of the test suite, but in our approach, the clusters are partially ordered to take into account dependencies between faults.

Finally, statistical bug isolation (SBI) [18] introduces a stop criterion as we did in our algorithm. SBI tries to take advantage of one execution of the test suite. The events are predicates, and SBI ranks them. When a fault is found through ranking, all execution traces that contain the predicates used to find the fault are deleted, and a new ranking of predicates with the reduced set of execution traces is computed. Deleting execution traces can be seen as equivalent to tagging concepts, as well as the events of their labeling, as explained in debugging and fault localization with a logical information system (DeLLIS). The difference between SBI and DeLLIS is that the latter does not need to compute the failure lattice several times.

7.6 Fault Localization Using *N*-gram Analysis[10]

In the previous sections, we described the background of data mining and how it can be applied to fault localization in general. In this section, we will describe how to use data mining along with *N*-gram analysis for software fault localization.

In software fault localization, test cases are usually sets of inputs with known expected outputs. If the actual output does not match the expected output, the test case has failed. Various information can be collected during the execution of the test cases for later analysis. This information may include statement coverage (the set of statements that were executed at least once during the execution) and exact execution sequence (the actual order in which the statements were executed during the test case executions). Since we will be working only with the exact execution sequence in this paper, we refer to it as trace. Usually, the usefulness of trace data is limited by the sheer volume. Data mining traditionally deals with large volumes of data, and in this research, we apply data mining techniques to process this trace data for fault localization.

From trace data, we generate *N*-grams, i.e. subsequences of length *N*. From these, we choose *N*-grams that appear more than a certain number of times in the failed traces. For these *N*-grams, we calculate the confidence – the conditional probability that a test case fails given that the *N*-gram appears in that test case's trace. We sort the *N*-grams in descending order of confidence and report the statements in the program in the order of their first occurrence in the sorted list.

7.6.1 Background

In this section, we discuss the concepts, ideas, and definitions related to our method of solving the problem, namely execution sequences, *N*-gram analysis, linear execution blocks, and AR mining.

7.6.1.1 Execution Sequence

Let P be a program with n lines of source code, labeled by $L = \{l_1, l_2, ..., l_n\}$. For example, in the sample program *mid* from [16] in Figure 7.9, $L = \{4, 5, 6, 10, 11, 12, 13, 14, 15, 17, 18, 19, 20, 21, 24\}$ after excluding comments, blank lines, and structural constructs like "}". A test case is a set of input with known outputs. Let $T = \{t_1, t_2, ..., t_m\}$ be the m test cases for program P. Each test case $t_i = \langle I_i, X_i \rangle$ has an input I_i and an expected output X_i. When program P is executed with input I_i, it produces an actual output A_i. If $A_i = X_i$, we say that t_i is a successful test case, and if $A_i \neq X_i$, we say that t_i is a failed test case. For example, the 6 test cases for the program *mid* in [16], $T = (t_1, t_2, ..., t_6)$, are shown in Table 7.6. Let $Y = \langle y_1, y_2, ..., y_k \rangle$ be the trace of program P when running test case t. For *mid*, the trace with respect to the test case t_1 is $Y = \langle 4, 4, 5, 10, 11, 12, 14, 15, 24, 6 \rangle$. We define two sets based on the outcomes of the test cases—successful traces $Y^P = \{Y_i \mid t_i \text{ is a successful test case}\}$ and failed traces $Y^F = \{Y_i \mid t_i \text{ is a failed test case}\}$.

We define the problem as follows: *Given program P with executable statements L, test cases T, and actual outputs A, the problem is to rank the statements in L according to their probability of containing the fault.* To compare this method with other methods like [16], we report the results in terms of statements, but it can also work at function level.

7.6.1.2 *N*-gram Analysis

Given an ordered list, an *N*-gram is any sub-list of *N* consecutive elements in the list. The elements of the *N*-gram must be in the same order as they were in the original list, and they must be consecutive. Given an execution trace Y, an *N*-gram $G_{Y,N,\alpha}$ is a contiguous subsequence $\langle y_\alpha, y_{\alpha+1}, ..., y_{\alpha+N-1} \rangle$ of length N starting at position α. The set of line *N*-grams with respect to Y is $G_{Y,N} = \{G_{Y,N,1}, G_{Y,N,2}, ..., G_{Y,N,K-N+1}\}$.

```
1    #include <stdio.h>
2    int main() {
3        int x, y, z, m;
4        scanf("%d %d %d", &x, &y, &x);
5        m = mid(x, y, z);
6        printf("%d", m);
7    }
8    int mid (int x, int y, int z) {
9        int m;
10       m = z ;
11       if (y < z) {
12          if (x < y) {
13             m = y ;
14          } else if (x < z) {
15             m = y;
16          }
17       } else {
18          if (x > y) {
19             m = y ;
20          } else if (x > z) {
21             m = x;
22          }
23       }
24       return m;
25   }
```

Figure 7.9 Sample source code: *mid.c*. *Source:* Nessa et al. [25]/Springer.

Table 7.6 Test cases for program *mid*.

Test case t_i	Input I_i	Expected output X_i	Actual output A_i	Test result	Trace
t_1	3,3,5	3	3	Successful	4, 4, 5, 10, 11, 12, 14, 15, 24, 6
t_2	1,2,3	2	2	Successful	4, 4, 5, 10, 11, 12, 13, 24, 6
t_3	3,2,1	2	2	Successful	4, 4, 5, 10, 11, 18, 19, 24, 6
t_4	5,5,5	5	5	Successful	4, 4, 5, 10, 11, 18, 20, 24, 6
t_5	5,3,4,	4	4	Successful	4, 4, 5, 10, 11, 12, 14, 24, 6
t_6	2,1,3	2	1	Failed	4, 4, 5, 10, 11, 12, 14, 15, 24, 6

Source: Nessa et al. [25]/Springer.

7.6.1.3 Linear Execution Blocks

From the set of all traces, we identify the execution blocks, i.e. the code segments with a single point of entry and a single point of exit. For this, we construct the *execution sequence graph* XSG(P) = (V, E), where $V \subseteq L$ is the set of vertices such that for each $v_i \in V$, we have $v_i \in Y_k$ for some k; and E is the set of edges such that for each edge $\langle v_i, v_j \rangle \in E$, we have $v_i, v_j \in Y_k$ for some k, and v_i and v_j are consecutive in Y_k. This is similar to a control flow graph, but the vertices in an XSG represent statements rather than blocks. In this graph, there is an edge between two vertices only if they were executed in succession in at least one of the execution traces. The XSG for *mid* is given in Figure 7.10, where we can see that the blocks of *mid* are $\{b_1, b_2, ..., b_{10}\} = \{\langle 4 \rangle, \langle 5, 10, 11 \rangle, \langle 12 \rangle, \langle 18 \rangle, \langle 20 \rangle, \langle 24, 6 \rangle, \langle 14 \rangle, \langle 13 \rangle, \langle 15 \rangle\}$. Thus, the traces of test case t_1 can be converted into a block level trace $\langle b_1, b_2, b_3, b_8, b_{10}, b_7 \rangle$.

It should be noted that the definition of blocks here is different than the traditional blocks [26]. Since we identify blocks from traces, the blocks here may include function or procedure entry points. For example, $\langle 5, 10, 11 \rangle$ will not be a single block by the traditional definition since it has a function started in line 10. Due to this difference, we name the blocks as linear execution blocks, defined as follows: A *linear execution block* $B\langle v_i, v_{i+1}, ..., v_j \rangle$ is a directed path in XSG such that the indegree of each vertex $V_k \in B$ is 0 or 1. Advantages of using block traces are: (i) it reduces the size of the traces, and (ii) in a block trace, each sequence of two blocks indicates one possible branch. Therefore, in N-gram analysis of block traces, each block N-gram represents $N-1$ branches. This helps the choice of N for N-gram analysis.

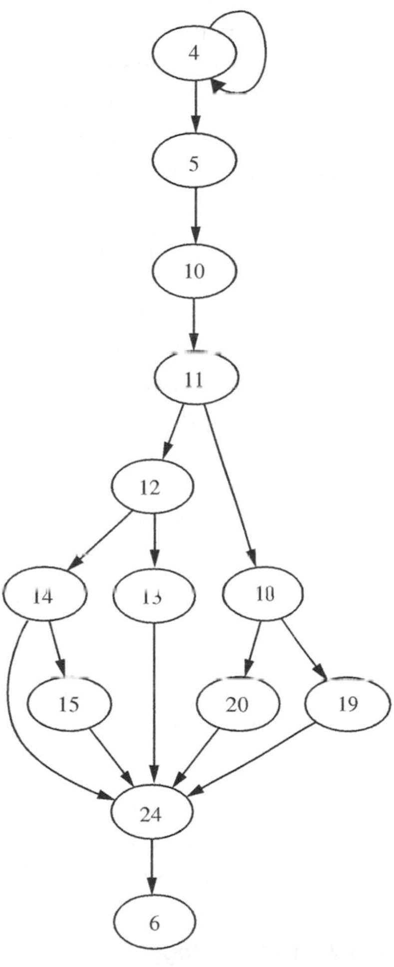

Figure 7.10 Execution sequence graph for program *mid*. *Source:* Nessa et al. [25]/Springer.

7.6.1.4 Association Rule Mining

Association rule mining searches for interesting relationships among items in a given data set [27]. It has the following two parts:

Frequent Itemset Generation. Search for sets of items occurring together frequently, called a *frequent itemset*, whose frequency in the data set, called *support*, exceeds a predefined threshold, called *threshold support*.

Association Rule Generation. Look for AR like $A \rightarrow B$ among the elements of the frequent itemsets, meaning that the appearance of A in a set implies the appearance of B in the same set. The conditional probability *Prob(B | A)* is called *confidence*, which must be greater than a predefined *minimum confidence* for a rule to be considered. More details can be found in [27].

We model the blocks as items and the block traces as transactions. For example, $Y_1 = \langle b_1, b_2, b_3, b_8, b_{10}, b_7\rangle$ is a transaction for *mid* corresponding to the first test case t_1. We generate frequent itemsets from the transactions with the additional constraint that the items in an itemset must be consecutive in the original transaction. To do this, we generate *N*-grams from the block traces, and from them, we choose the ones with at least the threshold support. For a block *N*-gram $G^P_{Y_i,N}$, *Support* is the number of failed traces containing $G^P_{Y_i,N}$:

$$Support\left(G^P_{Y_i,N}\right) = \; \| \; \{Y_j \mid G^P_{Y_i,N} \subseteq Y_j \text{ and } Y_j \in Y^F\} \; \|$$

For example, for *mid*, the support for $\langle b_2, b_3, b_8\rangle$ is 1 since it occurs in one failed trace. We add the test case type to the itemset. For example, after adding the test case type to the itemset $\langle b_2, b_3, b_8\rangle$, the itemset becomes $\langle b_2, b_3, b_8, \text{successful}\rangle$. From these itemsets, we then try to discover AR of the form "$A \rightarrow$ failed," where the antecedent is a block *N*-gram and the consequence is "failed." Therefore, the block *N*-grams that appear as antecedents in the AR are most likely to have caused the failure of the test case. We sort these block *N*-grams in descending order of confidence. For a block *N*-gram $G^P_{Y_i,N}$, *Confidence* is the conditional probability that the test case outcome is a failure given that $G^P_{Y_i,N}$ appears in the trace of that test case. That is,

$$\text{Confidence}\left(G^P_{Y_i,N}\right) = \frac{\text{Prob}\left(G^P_{Y_i,N} \subseteq Y_j \text{ and } t_j \text{ is a failed test case}\right)}{\text{Prob}\left(G^P_{Y_i,N} \subseteq Y_j\right)}$$

For example, the confidence the rule $\langle b_2, b_3, b_8\rangle \rightarrow$ failed has a confidence value of 0.33. After sorting the block *N*-grams, we convert the blocks back to line numbers and report this sequence of lines to investigate to find the fault location.

7.6.2 Methodology

As input, we use the source code, the test case types, and the traces for all the test cases, and we produce as output an ordered list of statements, sorted in order of probability of containing the fault. We first convert the traces to block traces and then apply *N*-gram analysis on these block traces to generate all possible unique *N*-grams for a given range of *N*. For each *N*-gram, we count its frequency in successful and failed traces.

The execution of the faulty statement may not always cause failure of the test case. There may be quite a number of test cases in which the faulty statement was executed but did not cause a failure. In most cases, the failure is dependent on the sequence of execution. A specific sequence or path of execution will cause the program to fail, and this sequence will be very common in the failed traces but not so common in the successful traces. Therefore, we can find the subsequences that are most likely to contain the fault by analyzing the traces during successful and failed test cases.

There are two major parameters in the algorithm. The first one is *ThresholdSup*, the threshold support for selecting the *N*-grams, and the second is N_{MAX}, the maximum value of *N* for generating the *N*-grams. Taking a low value of threshold support will result in the inclusion of irrelevant *N*-grams in consideration. Therefore, we should take threshold support at a high value. Our experience suggests that 90% is a good choice. However, the choice of an appropriate N_{MAX} is more difficult. Two execution paths can differ because of conditional branches. Such differences can be detected by 2-grams. Again, the same function can be called from different functions, which can also be detected with 2-grams. Since we are using execution blocks, an *N*-gram can capture $(N-1)$ branches, and a choice of 2 or 3 for N_{MAX} should give good results in most cases. If we use higher *N*-grams, the algorithm will still be able to find the fault, but due to larger *N*-grams, we will have to examine more lines to find the fault.

L2B (Convert Exact Execution Sequences to Block Traces): From the line level traces, we create the execution sequence graph (XSG). From the XSG, we find the Linear Execution Blocks (as described in Section 7.6.1.3). Then, we convert the traces into block traces in lines 2–4 of Algorithm 7.2.

GNG (Generate *N*-grams): In this step, we first generate all possible *N*-grams of lengths 1 to N_{MAX} from the block traces. The generation of all *N*-grams from a set of block traces for a given *N* is done in lines 1–7 of Algorithm 7.3, and the combination of all generated *N*-grams is done in lines 5–8 of Algorithm 7.2. Then, we find out how many successful and failed traces each *N*-gram occurs in.

FRB (Find Relevant Blocks): For any 1-gram, we construct a set of relevant blocks, B_{rel}, that contains only the blocks that have appeared in each of the failed traces in lines 10–14.

EIN (Eliminate Irrelevant *N*-grams): In lines 15–16, we discard the *N*-grams that do not contain any block from the relevant block set, B_{rel}.

```
procedure LocalizeFaults(Y, Y_F, K, minsup)
    for all Y_i ∈ Y do
        Convert Y_i to block trace
    end for
    NG ← Ø
    for N = 1 to NMAX do
        NG ← NG ∪ GenerateNgrams(Y, N)
    end for
    L_rel ← {n ∈ NG | ||n|| = 1}
    for all n ∈ L_rel do
      if Support(n) = ||Y_F|| then
        Remove n from NG and L_rel
      end if
    end for
    NG_1 ← {n ∈ NG | s ∉ n for all s ∈ L_rel}
    NG ← NG − NG_1
    for all n ∈ NG do
      if Support(n) < minsup then
        Remove n from NG
      end if
    end for
    for all n ∈ NG do
      NF ← ||{Y_k ∈ Y_F | n ∈ Y_k}||
      NF ← ||{Y_k ∈ Y | n ∈ Y_k}||
      n.confidence ← NF ÷ NT
    end for
    Sort NG in descending order of confidence
    Convert the block numbers in the N-grams in NG to line numbers
    Report the line numbers in the order of their first appearance in NG
end procedure
```

Algorithm 7.2 Fault localization using *N*-gram analysis. *Source:* Nessa et al. [25]/Springer.

```
function GenerateNgrams(Y, N)
    G ← Ø
    for Y_i ∈ Y do
        G ← G ∪ G_{Y_i, N}
    end for
    return G
end function
```

Algorithm 7.3 *N*-gram generation. *Source:* Nessa et al. [25]/Springer.

FFN (Find Frequent *N*-grams): In lines 17–21, we eliminate *N*-grams with support less than the threshold support.

RNC (Rank *N*-grams by Confidence): For each surviving *N*-gram, we compute its confidence using Algorithm 7.2. This is done in lines 22–26. In line 27, we then report the *N*-grams in order of confidence.

B2L (Convert Blocks in *N*-grams to Line Numbers): We convert each block in the *N*-grams back to line numbers using the XSG in line 28.

RLS (Rank Lines According to Suspicion): We traverse the ordered list of *N*-grams and report the line numbers in the order of their first appearance in the list. This is done in line 29.

If there are multiple *N*-grams with the same confidence as the *N*-gram containing the faulty statement, the best case will be the ordering in which the faulty statement appears in the earliest possible position in the group, and the worst case will be the ordering in which the faulty statement appears in the latest possible position.

7.6.3 Conclusion

In this section, we presented an approach to locate the suspiciousness statement using *N*-gram analysis. Augmenting the execution traces with data flows in order to pinpoint data-driven faults is worth investigating. Different than other fault localization techniques, such as spectrum based, the amount of data that *N*-gram requires is relatively small; this gives it an advantage in the fault localization world, where the complexity and size of software are growing dramatically. Research using exact execution sequences, as well as applying data mining to fault localization, is still in an early phase, and there are many avenues to explore and improve the effectiveness.

7.7 Fault Localization for GUI Software Using *N*-gram Analysis[11]

After describing how to use *N*-gram analysis to conduct fault localization for programs, let us see how *N*-gram analysis is used to localize the faults of GUI modules.

Unlike traditional software, test cases for testing GUI programs are event sequences instead of individual input data or files [29]. For each event, there must be a piece of source code that addresses the event; we call it the event's corresponding event handler [30]. By ranking these event handlers by their level of suspicion accounting for faults encountered during the testing, we can help programmers pinpoint the failure causing event handlers in the source code. Due to the large volume of GUI event sequences, usually infinite, we apply data mining techniques to the test data to extract the most relevant sequences.

From each test case, we generate *N*-grams, i.e. subsequences of length *N*. From these, we choose *N*-grams that appear more than a certain number of times in the event sequence of failed test cases. For these *N*-grams, we calculate the confidence: the conditional probability that a test case fails given that the *N*-gram appears in that test case's event sequence. We sort the *N*-grams in descending order of confidence and report the events of the program in the order of their first occurrence in the sorted list.

7.7.1 Background

7.7.1.1 Representation of the GUI and Its Operations

GUI Components: Objects of a GUI include some windows and all kinds of GUI widgets (such as buttons and menus) in the windows [29]. In a broad, the window itself can also be viewed as a kind of GUI widget. Each window or GUI widget has a fixed set of properties, such as the size and position of the GUI widget. At any specific point in time, the GUI can be described in terms of the specific GUI widgets that it contains and the values of their properties.

Event: The basic inputs for GUI software are events. When a GUI application is running, users' operations trigger events, and the application responds to these events. Since events may be performed on different types of GUI widgets in different contexts, yielding different behavior, they are parameterized with objects and property values. Commonly, we can use a 3-tuple $\langle a, o, v\rangle$ to represent an event, where a is the action of the event (such as clicking the mouse), o stands for the GUI widget the event deals with (such as a button), and v is the set of parameters of this action [30].

GUI test cases: Unlike traditional software, GUI test cases are usually defined as event sequences [29]. A formal representation of a GUI test case is a legal event sequence $\langle e_1, e_2, ..., e_n\rangle$ consisting of n events. "Legal" refers to the fact that for $i = 1, 2, ..., n$, the event e_{i+1} can be immediately accepted by GUI software and executed after the execution of e_i. Cai et al. extended this definition by defining GUI test cases using a hierarchical language [31]. People can first generate simple test cases as low order test cases. Then, more test cases can be generated by combining these low order test cases.

EFG and EIG: Owing to the hierarchical relationship among GUI widgets, some events can only be accepted by the GUI software after the execution of some other events. If event e_j can be immediately accepted and executed after the execution of event e_i, we say that e_j *follows* e_i, and refer to (e_i, e_j) as an event interaction. In model-based GUI testing, event flow graph (EFG) is used to model all possible event interactions of GUI software [29]. EFG is a directed

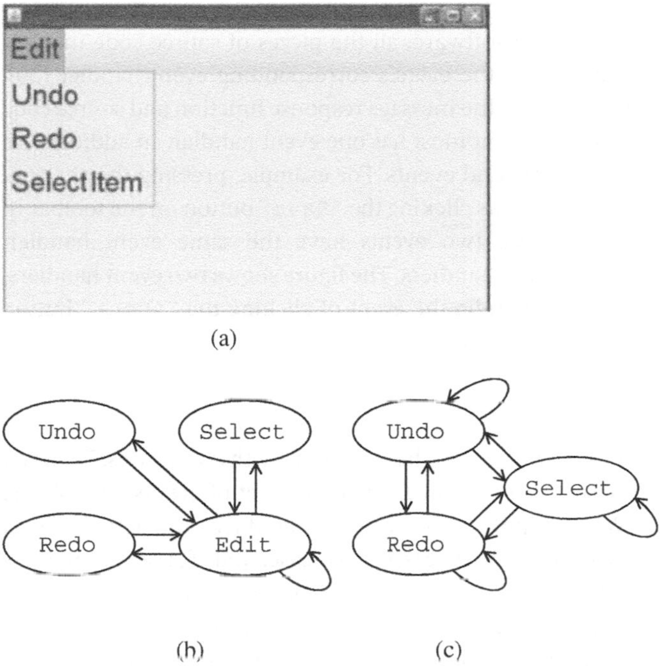

Figure 7.11 (a) A simple GUI; (b) its EFG; and (c) its EIG. *Source:* Yu et al. [28]/IEEE.

graph that contains nodes (which represent events) and edges (which represent a relationship between two events).

Event-interaction graph (EIG) is an improvement of EFG [32]. EIG nodes, on the other hand, do not represent events to open or close menus or open windows. These events are only structural events and usually do not interact with the underlying software. The result is a more compact and hence a more efficient GUI model.

Figure 7.11 presents a GUI that consists of four events: `Undo`, `Redo`, `Select`, and `Edit`. Figure 7.11b shows the GUI's EFG; the four nodes represent the four events, while each directed edge represents a "follows" relationship between two events such that the event at the tail follows the event at the head. For example, in this EFG, the event `Undo` follows `Edit`, represented by a directed edge from the node labeled `Edit` to `Undo`. Figure 7.11c shows the GUI's EIG. The `Edit` event is a menu open event, and we only use it to get the availability of the three other events, so the EIG model does not contain it. Following the deletion of event `Edit`, each edge (e_x, `Edit`) in the original EFG is replaced with edge (e_x, e_y) for each occurrence of edge (`Edit`, e_y).

7.7.1.2 Event Handler

When one event executes on the software, all the pieces of source code that are possible to be executed are called the event's corresponding event handler [30]. The event handler usually includes the message response function and source code called by this function. Each event at most has one event handler. In addition, an event handler may respond to several events. For example, pressing the shortcut key "`Ctrl+S`" has the same effect as clicking the "`Save`" button on the toolbar in Microsoft Word; therefore, these two events have the same event handler. Figure 7.12 gives examples of event handlers. The figure shows two event handlers, h_1 and h_2, which, respectively, handle the event of clicking the "`About`" button and the event of typing into the textbox.

7.7.1.3 *N*-gram

For a GUI application, let $T = \langle t_1, t_2, ..., t_n \rangle$ be the test set with n test cases. Each test case $t_i = \langle I_i, X_i \rangle$ is composed of the input I_i, which is a set of events, and X_i, the expected output of I_i. When input I_i is executed, it produces the actual output A_i. If $A_i = X_i$, then we regard t_i as a successful test case, and if $A_i \neq X_i$; then t_i is regarded as a failed test case. Let $E_i = \langle e_1, e_2, ..., e_k \rangle$ be the event sequence corresponding to test case t_i. Then, the total event sequence of the entire test set is $E = \langle E_1, E_2, ..., E_n \rangle$. We define two sets based on the outcome of the test cases: successful event sequences that is $E_p = \{E_i \mid t_i \text{ is a successful test case}\}$ and failed event sequences that is $E_f = \{E_i \mid t_i \text{ is a failed test case}\}$.

Given an ordered list, an *N*-gram is any sub-list of *N* consecutive elements in the list. The elements of the *N*-gram must be in the same order as they were in the original list, and they must be consecutive. Given an event sequence E_i, an *N*-gram $G_{E_i,N,\alpha}$ is a contiguous subsequence $E_i = \langle e_\alpha, e_{\alpha+1}, ..., e_{\alpha+N-1} \rangle$ of length *N* starting at position α. Taking all possible values of α into account, the set of *N*-grams with respect to E_i is $G_{E_i,N} = \{G_{E_i,N,1}, G_{E_i,N,2}, ..., G_{E_i,N,k-N+1}\}$. Then,

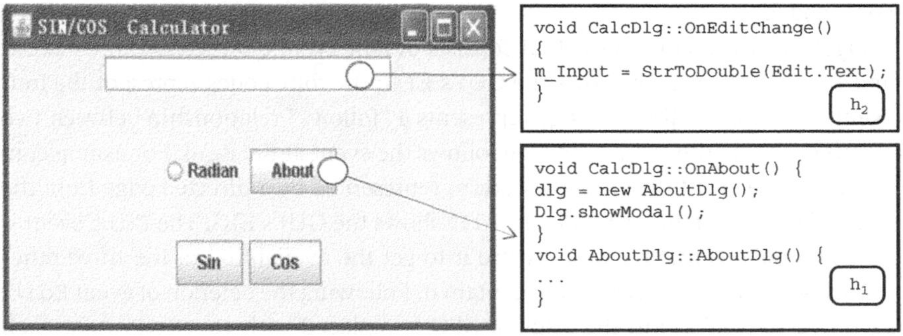

Figure 7.12 Examples of event handler. *Source:* Yu et al. [28]/IEEE.

$G_{E,N} = G_{E_1,N} \cup G_{E_2,N} \cup \cdots \cup G_{E_n,N}$ is the set of N-grams corresponding to the total event sequences E.

7.7.2 Association Rule Mining

Association rule mining searches for interesting relationships among items in a given data set [27], which involves the following two procedures:

1) ***Frequent Itemset Generation***: Search for sets of items occurring together frequently, called a *frequent itemset*, whose frequency in the data set, called *Support*, exceeds a predefined threshold (known as the *Threshold Support*). For an N-gram $G^P_{E_i,N}$, Support is the number of failed test case containing $G^P_{E_i,N}$:

$$Support\left(G^P_{E_i,N}\right) = \| \left\{E_j | G^P_{E_i,N} \subseteq E_j \text{ and } E_j \in E^F\right\} \|$$

2) ***Association Rule Generation***: Look for AR like $A \rightarrow B$ among the elements of the frequent itemsets, meaning that the appearance of A in a set implies the appearance of B in the same set. The conditional probability $Prob(B \mid A)$ is called *Confidence*, which must be greater than a predefined *Minimum Confidence* for a rule to be considered. For an N-gram $G^P_{E_i,N}$, Confidence is the conditional probability that the test case outcome is failure given that $G^P_{E_i,N}$ appears in the event sequence of that test case. That is:

$$Confidence\left(G^P_{E_i,N}\right) = \frac{\| \left\{E_j \mid G^P_{E_i,N} \subseteq E_j \text{ and } E_j \in E^F\right\} \|}{\| \left\{E_j \mid G^P_{E_i,N} \subseteq E_j\right\} \|}$$

7.7.3 Methodology

In this section, we present the methodology for GUI software fault localization [28]. As input, we use the source code, the test case types, and the event sequences of all the test cases, and we produce as output an ordered list of events, sorted in order of probability of their corresponding event handler containing the fault. We apply N-gram analysis to these event sequences to generate all possible unique N-grams for a given range of N. For each N-gram, we calculate its frequency in successful and failed event sequences. The set of N-grams and their frequencies are analyzed using the AR mining technique described earlier.

The execution of the faulty event handler may not always cause failure of the test case. There may be quite a number of test cases in which the faulty event handler is executed, but do not reveal a failure. In most cases, the failure is dependent on the execution of other events. A specific event sequence of execution will cause the program to fail, and this event sequence will be very common in the failed event sequences but not so common in the successful event sequences. Therefore, we can find the subsequences that are most likely to contain the fault by analyzing the event sequences of successful and failed test cases.

7.7.3.1 General Approach

We model the events as items and the event sequence corresponding to a test case as the transaction. For example, $E_i = \langle e_1, e_2, ..., e_k \rangle$ is a transaction corresponding to the test case t_i. We generate frequent itemsets from the transactions with the additional constraint that the items in an itemset must be consecutive in the original transaction. To do this, we generate $G_{E, N}$, and from them, we choose the ones with at least the *threshold support*. From these itemsets, we then try to discover AR of the form "$A \rightarrow$ *failed*," where the antecedent is an N-gram, and the consequence is "failed." Therefore, the N-grams that appear as antecedents in the AR are most likely to have caused the failure of the test case. We sort these N-grams in descending order of *confidence*. After sorting the N-grams, we convert the N-grams back to event orders.

7.7.3.2 *N*-gram Fault Localization Algorithm

Parameters: There are two major parameters in the algorithm: the first is *ThresholdSup*, the threshold support for selecting the N-grams, and the second is N_{MAX}, the maximum value of N for generating the N-grams. Taking a low value of threshold support will result in the inclusion of irrelevant N-grams in consideration. Giving a high value of threshold support may cause us to discard some very important N-grams. Thus, we should give *ThresholdSup* a medium value. For GUI software, the execution of event e_1 may vary because of the execution of the previous event e_2. If event sequence $\langle e_1, e_2 \rangle$ can be executed without inserting another intermediate event (say, an event to open menu), such differences can be detected by 2-grams; otherwise, such differences can be commonly detected by 3-grams. Consequently, we believe a choice of 3 for N_{MAX} should give good results in most cases. If we give N_{MAX} a higher value, the algorithm will still be able to find the fault, but due to larger N-grams, we will have to examine more event handlers to find the fault.

Algorithm Pseudocode: The main procedure **LocalizeFaults** is presented in Algorithm 7.4. It calls the function **GenerateNgrams** presented in Algorithm 7.5. Further details are explained as follows:

a) ***Generate N-grams***: In this step, we first generate all possible N-grams of length 1 to N_{MAX} from the event sequences of all test cases and then delete the duplicate ones. The generation of all N_0-grams from a set of event sequences for a

```
procedure LocalizeFaults(E, E_f, minsup)
  NG ← Ø
  for N = 1 to N_MAX do
    NG ← NG ∪ GenerateNgrams(E, N)
  end for
   E_Rel ←{n | n ∈ NG and ||n|| = 1}
   for all n ∈ E_Rel do
   if n does not exist in any event sequence of E_f then
     Remove n from NG and E_Rel
   end if
 end for
 NG_1 ← {n | n ∈ NG and for all s ∈ E_Rel, s ∉ n}
 NG ← NG − NG_1
 for all n ∈ NG do
   if Support(n) < minsup then
     Remove n from NG
   end if
end for
for all n ∈ NG do
   NF ← ||{E_k ∈ E_f | n ∈ E_k}||
   NT ← ||{E_k ∈ E | n ∈ E_k}||
  n.confidence ← NF ÷ NT
end for
Sort NG in descending order of confidence
Report the event numbers in the order of their first
appearance in NG
end proceduret
```

Algorithm 7.4 GUI fault localization using *N*-gram analysis. *Source:* Yu et al. [28]/IEEE.

```
function GenerateNgrams(E, N_0)
G ← Ø
for E_i ∈ E do
G ← G ∪ G_{E_i, N_0}
end for
for all n ∈ G do
  if n exists more than once in G then
   Remove duplicate n from G
  end if
end for
Return G
end function
```

Algorithm 7.5 N_0-gram generation. *Source:* Yu et al. [28]/IEEE.

given length N_0 is carried out in lines 2–5 of Algorithm 7.5, the deletion of duplicated N_0-grams is performed in lines 6–10 of Algorithm 7.5, and the generation and combination of all the *N*-grams, for *N* from 1 to N_{MAX} are done in lines 2–5 of Algorithm 7.4.

b) ***Find relevant events***: For any 1-gram, where the length of the sub-list is 1, we construct a set of relevant events, denoted by E_{Rel}. It contains only the events that have appeared at least in one of the failed event sequences in lines 6–11 of Algorithm 7.4.

c) ***Eliminate irrelevant N-grams***: In lines 12–13 of Algorithm 7.4, we discard the *N*-grams that do not contain any event from the relevant event set E_{Rel}.

d) ***Find frequent N-grams***: In lines 14–18 of Algorithm 7.4, we eliminate *N*-grams with support less than *ThresholdSup*.

e) ***Rank N-grams by confidence***: For each surviving *N*-gram, we compute its confidence. This is done in lines 19–23 of Algorithm 7.4. Then, we rank the *N*-grams in order of *confidence* in line 24 of the algorithm.

f) ***Convert N-grams to event numbers and rank events***: We traverse the ordered list of *N*-grams and report the event numbers in the order of their first appearance in the list. This is done in lines 25–26 of Algorithm 7.4. We define "new events" as those that do not exist in *N*-grams with a higher confidence and define "new faults" as those that do not exist in the handlers of higher ranking events. Suppose there are multiple *N*-grams with the same confidence. Given any "new event," the best situation involves the ordering in which the more "new faults" that an event handler contains, the earlier will be the position that the corresponding event appears in the event group. The worst situation involves the ordering in which the more "new faults" that an event handler contains, the later will be the position that the corresponding event appears. If two event handlers contain the same number of "new faults," we break the tie by random selection. For example, if we finally have two 2-grams $\langle e_1, e_2 \rangle$ and $\langle e_3, e_4 \rangle$ of the same confidence 0.8, suppose e_1, e_2, e_3, and e_4 are "new events" and the event handler individually contains 1, 0, 0, and 2 "new faults." Then, we obtain event orders "e_4, e_1, e_2, e_3" or "e_4, e_1, e_3, e_2" under the *best situation* and "e_2, e_3, e_1, e_4" or "e_3, e_2, e_1, e_4" under the *worst situation*.

7.8 Conclusion

Unlike traditional software, GUI test cases are usually event sequences, and each individual event has a unique corresponding event handler. Our approach applies data mining techniques to the event sequences and their output data in terms of failure detections collected in the testing phase to rank the fault proneness of the event handlers for fault localization. Our approach only focuses on how to prioritize the event handlers of the program under test. To further improve the efficiency, other fault localization techniques can be integrated with our approach so that code-level suggestions can be generated by analyzing the runtime execution data.

Notes

1 Part of Section 7.1 is from Ref. [1].
2 http://www.irisa.fr/lis/cellier/Trityp/Trityp.zip.
3 Part of Section 7.2 is from Ref. [1].
4 Part of Section 7.3 is from Ref. [1].
5 Slightly: if most test cases pass, which they should do eventually.
6 Observing more white swans increases the belief that swans are white, but observing non-white non-swans increases the interest of the white swan observations. Observing a non-white swan does not change the support of the white swan observations, but it decreases its confidence and interest. Still, the interest can be great if there are more white swans and non-white non-swans than non-white swans.
7 This is a novel property with respect to standard FCA, where nothing prevents two different objects to have the same attributes.
8 Part of Section 7.4 is from Ref. [1].
9 Part of Section 7.5 is from Ref. [1].
10 Part of Section 7.6 is from Ref. [25].
11 Part of Section 7.7 is from Ref. [28].

References

1 Cellier, P., Ducassé, M., Ferré, S., and Ridoux, O. (2018). Data Mining for Fault Localization: towards a Global Debugging Process. Research Report hal-02003069, INSA RENNES, Univ Rennes, CNRS, IRISA, France.
2 Agrawal, R., Imieliński, T., and Swami, A. (1993). Mining association rules between sets of items in large databases. *Proceedings of the 1993 ACM SIGMOD International Conference on Management of Data (SIGMOD '93)*, Washington, DC, USA (25–28 May 1993), 207–216. ACM. ISBN 0-89791-592-5. https://doi.org/10.1145/170035.170072.
3 Ganter, B. and Wille, R. (1999). *Formal Concept Analysis: Mathematical Foundations*. Springer-Verlag.

4 DeMillo, R.A., Lipton, R.J., and Sayward, F.G. (1978). Hints on test data selection: help for the practicing programmer. *Computer* 11 (4): 34–41. ISSN 0018-9162. https://doi.org/10.1109/C-M.1978.218136.

5 Ross, K.A. and Wright, C.R.B. (1992). *Discrete Mathematics*, 3e. Prentice Hall.

6 Ferré, S. and Ridoux, O. (2004). Introduction to logical information systems. *Information Processing & Management* 40 (3): 383–419. ISSN 0306-4573. https://doi.org/10.1016/S0306-4573(03)00018-9.

7 Padioleau, Y. and Ridoux, O. (2003). A logic file system. *Proceedings of the 2003 USENIX Annual Technical Conference*, San Antonio, TX, USA (9–14 June 2003). USENIX.

8 Agrawal, R. and Srikant, R. (1994). Fast algorithms for mining association rules in large databases. *Proceedings of the 20th International Conference on Very Large Data Bases* (*VLDB '94*), Santiago, Chile (12–15 September 1994), 487–499. Morgan Kaufmann. ISBN 1-55860-153-8. http://dl.acm.org/citation.cfm?id=645920.672836.

9 Brin, S., Motwani, R., Ullman, J.D., and Tsur, S. (1997). Dynamic itemset counting and implication rules for market basket data. *Proceedings of the 1997 ACM SIGMOD International Conference on Management of Data* (*SIGMOD '97*), Tucson, AZ, USA (11–15 May 1997), 255–264. ACM. ISBN 0-89791-911-4. https://doi.org/10.1145/253260.253325.

10 Pasquier, N., Bastide, Y., Taouil, R., and Lakhal, L. (1999). Discovering frequent closed itemsets for association rules. *Proceedings of the International Conference on Database Theory (ICDT '99)* Jerusalem, Israel (10–12 January 1999), 398–416. Springer, Berlin, Heidelberg. ISBN 978-3-540-49257-3.

11 Szathmary, L. and Napoli, A. (2005). CORON: a framework for levelwise itemset mining algorithms. *Proceedings of the Third International Conference on Formal Concept Analysis (ICFCA '05)*, Lens, France (14–18 February 2005), 110–113. Springer. https://hal.inria.fr/inria-00001201.

12 Wilhelm, R. and Maurer, D. (1995). *Compiler Design*. Redwood City, CA, USA: Addison Wesley Longman. ISBN 0201422905.

13 Cellier, P., Ducassé, M., Ferré, S., and Ridoux, O. (2011). Multiple fault localization with data mining. *Proceedings of the International Conference on Software Engineering and Knowledge Engineering (SEKE '11)*, Miami, FL, USA (7–9 July 2011), 238–243. Knowledge Systems Institute Graduate School.

14 Renieris, M. and Reiss, S.P. (2003). Fault localization with nearest neighbor queries. *Proceedings of the 18th IEEE International Conference on Automated Software Engineering, 2003*, Montreal, QC, Canada (6–10 October 2003), 30–39. IEEE. https://doi.org/10.1109/ASE.2003.1240292.

15 Cleve, H. and Zeller, A. (2005). Locating causes of program failures. *Proceedings of the 27th International Conference on Software Engineering* (*ICSE '05*), St. Louis, MO, USA (15–21 May 2005), 342–351. ACM. ISBN 1-58113-963-2. https://doi.org/10.1145/1062455.1062522.

16 Jones, J.A., Harrold, M.J., and Stasko, J. (2002). Visualization of test information to assist fault localization. *Proceedings of the 24th International Conference on Software Engineering (ICSE '02)*, Orlando, FL, USA (19–25 May 2002), 467–477. IEEE. https://doi.org/10.1145/581396.581397.

17 Dallmeier, V., Lindig, C., and Zeller, A. (2005). Lightweight defect localization for Java. In: *ECOOP 2005 – Object-Oriented Programming* (ed. A.P. Black), 528–550. Berlin, Heidelberg: Springer Berlin Heidelberg. ISBN 978-3-540-31725-8.

18 Liblit, B., Naik, M., Zheng, A.X. et al. (2005). Scalable statistical bug isolation. *Proceedings of the 2005 ACM SIGPLAN Conference on Programming Language Design and Implementation* (*PLDI '05*), Chicago, IL, USA (12–15 June 2005), 15–26. ACM. ISBN 1-59593-056-6. https://doi.org/10.1145/1065010.1065014.

19 Liu, C., Fei, L., Yan, X. et al. (2006). Statistical debugging: a hypothesis testing-based approach. *IEEE Transactions on Software Engineering* 32 (10): 831–848. ISSN 0098-5589. https://doi.org/10.1109/TSE.2006.105.

20 Zheng, A.X., Jordan, M.I., Liblit, B. et al. (2006). Statistical debugging: simultaneous identification of multiple bugs. *Proceedings of the 23rd International Conference on Machine Learning* (*ICML '06*), Pittsburgh, PA, USA (25–29 June 2006), 1105–1112. ACM. ISBN 1-59593-383-2. https://doi.org/10.1145/1143844.1143983.

21 Denmat, T., Ducassé, M., and Ridoux, O. (2005). Data mining and cross-checking of execution traces: a re-interpretation of Jones, Harrold and Stasko test information. *Proceedings of the 20th IEEE/ACM International Conference on Automated Software Engineering* (*ASE '05*), Long Beach, CA, USA (7–11 November 2005), 396–399. ACM. ISBN 1-58113-993-4. https://doi.org/10.1145/1101908.1101979.

22 Shapiro, E.Y. (1982). Algorithmic program debugging. PhD thesis. Yale University. New Haven, CT, USA.

23 Jiang, L. and Su, Z. Context-aware statistical debugging: from bug predictors to faulty control flow paths. *Proceedings of the Twenty-second IEEE/ACM International Conference on Automated Software Engineering* (*ASE '07*), Atlanta, GE, USA (5–9 November 2007), 184–193. ACM. ISBN 978-1-59593-882-4. https://doi.org/10.1145/1321631.1321660.

24 Jones, J.A., Bowring, J.F., and Harrold, M.J. (2007). Debugging in parallel. *Proceedings of the 2007 International Symposium on Software Testing and Analysis* (*ISSTA '07*), London, UK (9–12 July 2007), 16–26. ACM. ISBN 978-1-59593-734-6. https://doi.org/10.1145/1273463.1273468.

25 Nessa, S., Abedin, M., Wong, W.E. et al. (2008). Software fault localization using *N*-gram analysis. *Proceedings of the International Conference on Wireless Algorithms, Systems, and Applications (WASA '15)*, Dallas, TX, USA (26–28 October 2008), 548–559. Springer. https://personal.utdallas.edu/~lkhan/papers/Nessa2008.pdf

26 Agrawal, H. (1994). Dominators, super blocks, and program coverage. *Proceedings of the 21st ACM SIGPLAN-SIGACT Symposium on Principles of Programming Languages* (*POPL '94*), Portland, OR, USA (16–19 January 1994), 25–34. ACM. ISBN 0-89791-636-0. https://doi.org/10.1145/174675.175935.

27 Han, J., Kamber, M., and Pei, J. (2011). *Data Mining: Concepts and Techniques*, 3e. San Francisco, CA, USA: Morgan Kaufmann. ISBN 0123814790, 9780123814791.

28 Yu, Z., Hu, H., Bai, C. et al. (2011). GUI software fault localization using *N*-gram analysis. *Proceedings of the 2011 IEEE 13th International Symposium on High-Assurance Systems Engineering*, Boca Raton, FL, USA (10–12 November 2011), 325–332. IEEE. https://doi.org/10.1109/HASE.2011.29.

29 Memon, A.M. (2001). A comprehensive framework for testing graphical user interface. PhD thesis. University of Pittsburgh.

30 Zhao, L. and Cai, K. (2010). Event handler-based coverage for GUI testing. *Proceedings of the 2010 10th International Conference on Quality Software (QSIC '10)*, Zhangjiajie, Hunan, China (14–15 July 2010), 326–331. IEEE. https://doi.org/10.1109/QSIC.2010.11.

31 Cai, K.-Y., Zhao, L., Hu, H., and Jiang, C.-H. (2005). On the test case definition for GUI testing. *Proceedings of the Fifth International Conference on Quality Software (QSIC '05)*, Melbourne, Victoria, Australia (19–20 September 2005), 19–26. IEEE. https://doi.org/10.1109/QSIC.2005.45.

32 Memon, A.M. and Xie, Q. (2005). Studying the fault-detection effectiveness of GUI test cases for rapidly evolving software. *IEEE Transactions on Software Engineering* 31 (10): 884–896. ISSN 0098-5589. https://doi.org/10.1109/TSE.2005.117.

8

Information Retrieval-Based Techniques for Software Fault Localization

Xin Xia[1] *and David Lo*[2]

[1] *Software Engineering Application Technology Lab, Huawei, China*
[2] *School of Computing and Information Systems, Singapore Management University, Singapore*

8.1 Introduction

This chapter introduces information retrieval (IR)-based fault[1] localization techniques. To effectively manage observed failures, most open-source communities and commercial companies use bug tracking systems such as Bugzilla and Jira to create, manage, and track observed bugs during both the development and release phases. One of the challenges of using bug tracking systems is that they often contain too many bugs reports for developers to handle. This necessitates an automated tool that can help developers identify relevant files given a bug report. Due to the textual nature of bug reports, IR techniques, which refer to the activity of obtaining information resources relevant to an information need from a collection of information resources, are often employed to solve this problem, and many IR-based fault localization techniques have been proposed in literature. This chapter summarizes and categorizes research papers published from 2007 to 2016 in more than ten relevant research venues, such as International Conference on Software Engineering (ICSE), Symposium on the Foundations of Software Engineering (FSE), Automated Software Engineering Conference (ASE), International Symposium on Software Testing and Analysis (ISSTA), and International Conference on Software Quality, Reliability, and Security (QRS), to help readers get insight into the different kinds of research conducted in this area. To collect relevant papers on IR-based fault localization, we perform a systematic literature review.

To present these techniques in a systematic way, we group the papers into several categories and subcategories. We identify several categories, including

Handbook of Software Fault Localization: Foundations and Advances, First Edition.
Edited by W. Eric Wong and T.H. Tse.

Published 2023 by John Wiley & Sons, Inc.

techniques, *empirical study*, and *miscellaneous*. The techniques category contains papers that describe new IR-based fault localization techniques. In this category, we identify a number of subcategories based on the nature of the information used in the fault localization process and the IR techniques used to perform fault localization. The empirical study category contains papers that do not propose new techniques but rather investigate the effectiveness of existing IR-based fault localization techniques on various settings or IR techniques applied to fault localization. The miscellaneous category contains several papers that do not fit in the first two categories. It includes papers that propose IR-based fault localization tools and several other papers that consider unique angles to IR-based fault localization.

To improve the quality of software systems, developers often open bug tracking systems where users and testers can log issues that they have found. These issues, a majority of which are bug reports, would then be queued for developers' inspection. When a developer is assigned to a bug report, they would need to read the report, find the source code files that are responsible for the issue described in the report, and then fix the bug. The step prior to the bug fixing process is referred to as fault localization. Considering that hundreds of bug reports are received daily [1] and a software project often has thousands of source code files, the fault localization process is not trivial, and many efforts must be expended by developers.

To aid developers in performing fault localization tasks (i.e. the identification of buggy source code files given a textual bug report), many studies have proposed IR-based fault localization techniques. IR-based techniques are built on the idea that there exists a correlation between bug reports and source code. Therefore, fault localization using bug reports can be nicely mapped to an IR problem. IR [2] can be defined as the process of finding relevant documents from a document collection given an information need expressed as a query. For fault localization, the query is a bug report, the document collection is the set of source code files belonging to a software project, and the relevant documents (the result of the query) are the buggy files that are responsible for the issue described in the bug report. Since using IR-based techniques to locate the bugs can be viewed as a process of constructing a mapping between the bug reports and source code file, the quality of the bug reports can have a significant impact on the fault localization result. Therefore, it is important to use high-quality bug reports in IR-based fault localization.

Notice that the efficiency and effectiveness of IR-based techniques are noticeably affected by the quality of the bug description; therefore, it is important to use high-quality bug reports to construct the query.

Figure 8.1 shows a real bug report[2] for Eclipse 3.1 [3]. Once this report is received, the developer needs to locate relevant files among more than tens of thousands of Eclipse source files in order to fix this bug. We find that the bug report

Bug ID: 80720
Summary: **Pinned console** does not remain on top
Description: Open two **console views**, ... **Pin** one **console**. Launch another program that produces output. Both **consoles display** the last launch. The **pinned console** should remain **pinned**

```
public class ConsoleView extends PageBookView
        implements IConsoleView, IConsoleListener {...
    public void display(IConsole console) {
            if (fPinned && fActiveConsole != null) {return;}
    } ...
    public void pin(IConsole console) {
        if (console == null) {setPinned(false);
        } else {
        if (isPinned()) {setPinned(false);}
        display(console);
        setPinned(true);
        }
    }
}
```

Figure 8.1 A bug report (ID: 80720) and its relevant source code file in Eclipse. *Source:* Zhou et al. [3]/IEEE.

(including the bug summary and description) contains many words such as pin (pinned), console, view, and display. Therefore, this bug is related to features about console view. In Eclipse 3.1, there is a source code file called ConsoleView.java, which also contains many occurrences of similar words. Figure 8.1 shows a good match between the bug report and the source code.

However, in practice, developers may use different languages in the bug reports and source code, i.e. language mismatch. For example, Figure 8.2 presents another bug report[3] and its relevant source code file in Eclipse [4]. This bug report contains several keywords such as view, icon, and minimized. After checking the version control system, we found that this bug was fixed by changing the source file PartServiceImpl.java. However, PartServiceImpl.java did not contain any keywords as shown in the bug reports. Instead, the code contains keywords such as stack and placeholder. Moreover, the keywords in the bug report and its relevant source code file are semantically related through the use of the distributional hypothesis [5].

From these two examples, we notice that to accurately locate the relevant source code files by a given bug report, we should not only leverage the textual similarity between them but also consider the semantic similarity. Some techniques such as topic modeling [6] and word embedding [7] can be used to measure the semantic similarity.

Bug ID: 384108
Summary: JUnit **view icon** no longer shows progress while executing tests
Description: Before I upgraded to Juno this morning I used to happily run tests with the JUnit **view minimized**, and enjoy seeing the progress of the tests on it. Now I don't see any change on the **icon** until it passes (where a green check appears) or fails (where a red X appears) ...

```
public class PartServicelmpl implements EPartService {
    ....
    private void recordStackActivation(Mpart part) {...
      MPlaceholder placeholder = part.getCurSharedRef();
    ... }
    ...
    private void adjustPlaceholder(MPart part) {...
      MPlaceholder placeholder = part.getCurSharedRef();
    ...}
....}
```

Figure 8.2 A bug report (ID: 384108) and its relevant source code file in Eclipse. *Source:* Adapted from Ye et al. [4]/ACM.

8.2 General IR-Based Fault Localization Process[4]

In IR-based fault localization, we treat the bug report and the source code files as text documents and compute the textual similarity between them. For a corpus of files, we can rank the files based on each file's textual similarity to the bug report. Developers can then investigate the files one by one from the beginning of the ranked list until relevant buggy files are found. In this way, files relevant to the bug report can be quickly located. Clearly, the goal of fault localization is to rank the buggy files as high as possible in the list. A common fault localization process consists of four steps, i.e. corpus creation, indexing, query construction, and retrieval and ranking.

Corpus creation and refinement: The first step is to build the corpus using the source code as input. Based on the scale of the source code, corpus creation can be conducted on different granularities (such as statements, functions, or classes). Once corpus creation is finished, the refinement is needed to improve the effectiveness of IR-based fault localization. For example, some tokens, such as keywords (`int`, `double`, `char`, etc.), separators (hyphen, period, comma, etc.), and operators (such as +, −, ≥, and ≤), are too common and do not contain much information. Therefore, these tokens are removed. Some other kinds of tokens, such as English stop words ("`he`", "`she`", "`the`", and so on), are not common in the source code and do not provide much information, so they can be removed as well. Many variables defined in a program are actually a concatenation of words. For example, the variable typeDeclaration contains two words: "`type`" and "`Declaration`". The variable is Committable is composed of two words: "`is`" and "`Committable`". These composite tokens are split into individual tokens. Many tokens have the same root form. For example, "`reads`", "`reading`", and "`read`" share the same root "`read`". The Porter Stemming algorithm [8] is applied to reduce a word to its root form.

After finishing the lexical analysis for each source code file, a vector of the extracted lexical tokens is constructed using a modeling technique, such as term frequency (*tf*), inverse document frequency (*tf-idf*), latent Dirichlet allocation (LDA), latent semantic indexing (LSI), and Word2vec.

Index: After the corpus is created, all the files in the corpus are indexed. By using these indexes, one can locate files containing the words in a given query and then rank these files by their relevance.

Query construction: Fault localization considers a bug report as a query and uses it to search for relevant files in the indexed source code corpus. It extracts tokens from the bug title and description, removes stop words, stems each word, and forms the query.

Retrieval and ranking: The retrieval and ranking of relevant buggy files is based on the textual similarity between the query and each of the files in the corpus. Various approaches can be used to compute a relevance score for each file in the corpus given an input bug report.

8.3 Fundamental Information Retrieval Techniques for Software Fault Localization

8.3.1 Vector Space Model[5]

In the vector space model (VSM), each document is represented as a vector of values. Each value in the vector represents the weight of a term in the document. The order and syntactic structure of the terms in the document is not considered using this approach. One popular way to assign weights is to use the concepts *term frequency* (*tf*) and *inverse document frequency* (*tf-idf*). The standard *tf-idf* scheme assigns a weight to a term t in a document d according to Eq. 8.1.

$$\text{weight}(t, d) = tf(t, d) \times idf(t, D) \tag{8.1}$$

where t, d, D, $tf(t, d)$, and $idf(t, D)$ correspond to a term, a document, a corpus (i.e. a set of documents), the frequency of t in d, and the inverse document frequency of t in D, respectively. Term frequency is the number of times a term appears in a document; it measures how important the term is to the document. Inverse document frequency captures the rarity of a term. A rare term is more useful to differentiate one document from another. To give more weight to rare terms, inverse document frequency is calculated as the logarithm of the reciprocal of the *document frequency* (*df*). The document frequency of a term t in corpus D is the number of documents in D that contains t.

Given a query and a corpus, VSM first converts the query and each document in the corpus to bags of words. It then converts each bag of words into a vector of values by calculating the *tf-idf* weight of each term. Then, the cosine similarity between a query and all documents in the corpus is computed based on their representative vectors.

$$\cos(q, d) = \frac{\sum_{t \in (q \cup d)} \text{weight}(t, q) \times \text{weight}(t, d)}{\sqrt{\sum_{t \in q} \text{weight}(t, q)} \times \sqrt{\sum_{t \in q} \text{weight}(t, d)}} \tag{8.2}$$

where q and d are a query and a document, respectively. After computing the above scores for all documents in the corpus, we sort the documents based on their similarity scores. Finally, the top k documents are output.

8.3.2 Topic Modeling[6]

A textual document of a particular topic is likely to contain a particular set of terms (i.e. words). For example, a document about a user interface bug is likely to contain terms such as window and button. A document can be a mixture of several topics. Topic modeling models this phenomenon. A document is a bug report or a source code file, and a topic is a higher-level concept corresponding to a distribution of terms. With topic modeling, given a new bug report or a source code file, we extract a set of topics along with the probabilities that they appear in them. LDA is a well-known topic modeling technique [6].

LDA is a generative probabilistic model of a textual corpus (i.e. a set of textual documents) that takes the following as inputs: a training textual corpus and a number of parameters including the number of topics (K) considered. In the training phase, for each document s, we would get a topic proportion vector θ_s, which is a vector with K elements, and each element corresponds to a topic. The value of each element in θ_s is a real number from 0 to 1, which represents the proportion of the words in s belonging to the corresponding topic in s. After training, the LDA is used to predict the topic proportion vector θ_m for a new document m. We map the terms in the document m into a topic proportion vector θ_m, which contains the probabilities of each topic to be present in the document. After training, the LDA can be used to predict the topic for every term in a new document. For a new document m, considering K topics, we compute its topic vector z_m based on the topics assigned to its constituent terms as:

$$z_m = \langle t_1, t_2, \ldots, t_k \rangle \tag{8.3}$$

where

$$t_i = \frac{\text{Number of words assigned in the } i\text{th topic in } m}{\text{Number of words in } m}$$

By this way, we map the terms in the document m into a topic vector that contains the probabilities of each topic to be present in the document.

8.3.3 Word Embedding[7]

Distributed word representations assume that words appearing in a similar context tend to have similar meanings [5]. Therefore, individual words are no longer treated as unique symbols, but mapped to a dense real-valued low-dimensional vector space. Each dimension represents a latent semantic or syntactic feature of the word. Semantically similar words are close in the embedding space. Figure 8.3 shows some examples of word embeddings learned from posts of Stack Overflow, which are visualized in a two-dimensional space using the t-distributed stochastic neighbor embedding (t-SNE) dimensionality reduction technique [13]. Semantically close words, such as *JPanel*, *JButton*, *JFrame*, and *JLabel*, are GUI components that are close in the vector space.

Word embeddings are typically learned using neural language models. The continuous skip-gram model, a popular word to vector (Word2vec) model proposed by Mikolov et al. [14, 15], learns the word embedding of a center word (i.e. w_i) and is good at predicting surrounding words in a context window of $2k + 1$ words. The

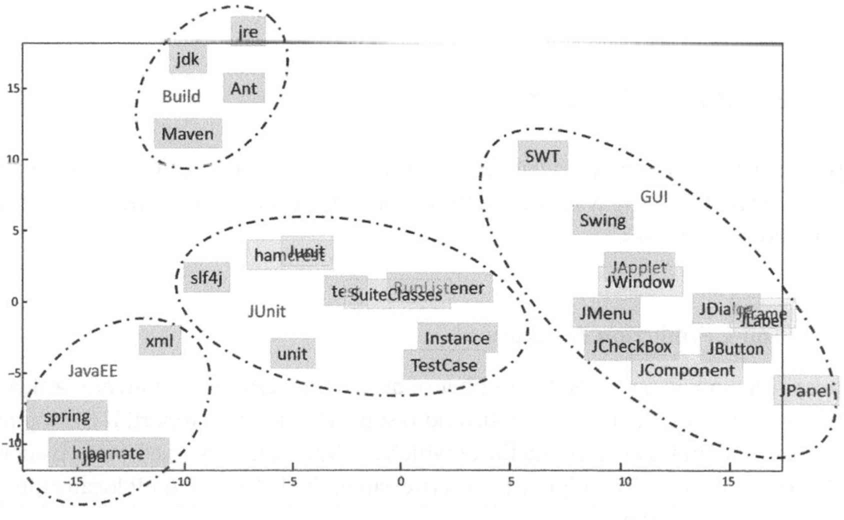

Figure 8.3 Example of word embedding. *Source:* Xu et al. [12]/IEEE.

objective function of the skip-gram model is to maximize the sum of log probabilities of the surrounding context words conditioned on the center word.

$$\sum_{i=1}^{n} \sum_{-k \le j \le k, j \ne 0} \log p(w_{i+j} | w_i) \tag{8.4}$$

where w_i and w_{i+j} denote the center word and the context word in a context window of length $2k + 1$. n denotes the length of the word sequence.

The expression $\log p(w_{i+j}|w_i)$ is the conditional probability defined using the softmax function:

$$p(w_{i+j}|w_i) = \frac{\exp\left(v'^{T}_{w_{i+j}} v_{w_i}\right)}{\sum_{w \in W} \exp\left(v'^{T}_{w} v_{w_i}\right)} \tag{8.5}$$

where v_w and v'_w are, respectively, the input and output vectors of a word w in the underlying neural model, and W is the vocabulary of all words. Intuitively, log $p(w_{i+j}|w_i)$ estimates the normalized probability of word w_{i+j} appearing in the context of a center word w_i over all words in the vocabulary. Mikolov et al. [15] propose an efficient negative sampling method to compute this probability.

The output of the model is a dictionary of words, each of which is associated with a vector representation. Given a document (such as a bug report or a source code file), its textual content will be converted into a vector by looking up the dictionary of word embeddings and concatenating the word embeddings of words comprising the textual content.

8.4 Evaluation Metrics[8]

Top-k prediction accuracy, mean reciprocal rank (MRR) [17], and mean average precision (MAP) [17] are widely used to evaluate the performance of IR-based fault localization techniques.

8.4.1 Top-*k* Prediction Accuracy

Top-k prediction accuracy is the number of bugs whose associated files are ranked in the top K ($K = 1, 5, 10$) of the returned results. Given a bug report, if the top K query results contain at least one file at which the bug should be fixed, we consider the bug to be located. The higher the metric value, the better the fault localization technique will perform.

8.4.2 Mean Reciprocal Rank (MRR)

MRR is a popular metric used to evaluate an IR technique [17]. Given a query (say a bug report *b*), its reciprocal rank is the multiplicative inverse of the rank of the first correct document (say a source code file) in a rank list produced by a ranking technique (in our case, an IR-based fault localization technique). MRR is the average of the reciprocal ranks of all bugs in a set of bug report BR, which is computed as:

$$\mathrm{MRR}(R) = \frac{1}{|\,\mathrm{BR}\,|}\sum_{b\in \mathrm{BR}} \frac{1}{rank(b)} \tag{8.6}$$

In the above equation, *rank(b)* refers to the position of the first correctly recommended source code file in the ranked list returned by an IR based fault localization technique for bug report *b*.

8.4.3 Mean Average Precision (MAP)

MAP is a single-figure measure of quality, and it has been shown to have especially good discrimination and stability to evaluate ranking techniques [17]. Different from top-*k* accuracy and MRR, which only consider the first correct result, MAP considers all correct results. For a single query (say a bug report *b*), its *average precision* is defined as the mean of the precision values obtained for different sets of top *k* documents (say source code files) that are retrieved before each relevant document is retrieved, which is computed as:

$$AvgP(b) = \frac{\sum_{j=1}^{M} P(j) \times \mathrm{Rel}(j)}{\text{Number of relevant source code files}} \tag{8.7}$$

In the above equation, *M* is the number of candidate source code files in a ranked list, Rel(*j*) indicates whether the source code file at position *j* is relevant or not (in our case, a ground truth source code file or not), and *P*(*j*) is the precision at the given cut-off position *j* and is computed as:

$$P(j) = \frac{\text{Number of relevant source code files in top}\, j \text{ positions}}{j} \tag{8.8}$$

Then, the MAP for a set of bug reports BR is the mean of the average precision scores for all bug reports in BR.

$$\mathrm{MAP} = \frac{\sum_{b\in \mathrm{BR}} AvgP(b)}{|\,\mathrm{BR}\,|} \tag{8.9}$$

In IR-based fault localization, to fix a bug, a number of source code files are required to be changed. We use MAP to measure the average performance of an IR-based fault localization technique to locate all the relevant source code files. The higher the MAP value, the better the performance of the IR-based fault localization technique.

8.5 Techniques for Different Scenarios

In this section, we categorize studies on IR-based fault localization into three groups:

Text of current bug report only: A number of IR-based fault localization techniques only measure the textual similarity between bug reports and source code files, and they do not consider additional information such as commit log, bug report history, or stack trace. Most of these techniques are proposed in the initial stage of this area.

Text and history: In this category, to recommend the relevant source code files, IR-based fault localization techniques measure not only the textual similarity between bug reports and source code files but also the source code files fixed by similar bug reports in the bug repository or commit logs in version control systems.

Text and stack/execution traces: In this category, IR-based fault localization techniques also use the stack trace or execution traces to enhance the results outputted by the IR-based fault localization techniques, which measure the textual similarity between bug reports and source code files.

We introduce these techniques in the following sections. For each category, some techniques may use a variant of the VSM model, some may use topic modeling, and others may use deep learning. We also further categorize them according to the IR techniques they use.

8.5.1 Text of Current Bug Report Only

8.5.1.1 VSM Variants

Rao et al. proposed a set of IR-based techniques to solve the fault localization problem. These techniques include the smoothed unigram model (SUM), VSM, latent semantic analysis (LSA) model, LDA model, and cluster-based document model (CBDM) [18]. They performed experiments on iBUGS [19], a benchmarked fault localization data set with 75 KLOC and a large number of bugs (291), and the comparative study found that simple text models such as SUM and VSM are more effective at correctly retrieving the relevant files from a library compared with more sophisticated models such as LDA.

In a later work, considering that most IR-based fault localization techniques focus on improving the retrieval effectiveness of these techniques and rarely consider the efficiency of such techniques for software repositories that are constantly evolving, Rao et al. proposed an incremental update framework that continuously updates the index and the model using the changes made at each commit [20]. They applied SUM and VSM on AspectJ and Joda-Time, and they found that query latency is reduced from several minutes to a fraction of a second.

Sisman and Kak proposed a query reformulation (QR) framework to improve the performance of fault localization [21]. In the QR framework, a user's search query is enriched with certain specific additional terms drawn from the highest-ranked artifacts retrieved in response to the initial query. They reformulated a query with additional terms that are deemed to be close to the original query terms in the source code on the basis of positional proximity. Experiments on more than 4000 bug reports in Eclipse and Chrome showed that the proposed QR framework leads to significant improvements in fault localization and outperforms the well-known QR methods in the literature.

Saha et al. proposed BLUiR, which leverages structure information in source code to improve fault localization accuracy [22]. In their approach, they built the abstract syntax tree (AST) of each source code file using Eclipse Java Development Tools (JDT) and traversed the AST to extract different program constructs such as class names, method names, variable names, and comments. Given a new bug report, they extracted two alternative query representations from different fields of the bug report, i.e. the summary and the description. Next, they measured the similarity between the two fields of bug reports and the structure in the source code (i.e. class, method, variable, and comments) by leveraging the Indri built-in *tf-idf* formulation.

In a later work, Saha et al. evaluated the effectiveness of BLUiR with projects using C programming language [23]. To adapt BLUiR, they used the Coccinelle C parser [24] to extract the structure information from C source code. They found that although the IR-relevant properties of C and Java programs are different, IR-based fault localization in C projects at the file level is overall as effective as in Java projects.

8.5.1.2 Topic Modeling

Lukins et al. used an LDA-based static technique for automating fault localization [25]. In their approach, they first generated an LDA model based on the corpus built on source code files. The outputs of the LDA model were a word-topic probability distribution and a topic-document distribution. Next, they used the bug reports as the query to measure the similarity between the bug reports and the generated LDA model. They performed case studies on bug reports in Rhino, Eclipse, and Mozilla, and they found that the LDA-based model achieves a much better performance than the LSI-based model.

Bread et al. combined both the LDA model and structure information in source code for fault localization [26]. In the LDA model, they used the same technique as that proposed by Lukins et al. [25]. They performed both call graph analysis and local class/inheritance analysis to determine whether other methods or classes are affected by a bug.

8.5.2 Text and History

8.5.2.1 VSM Variants

Davies et al. utilized the similarity of bug reports to enhance IR-based bug localization techniques and identify buggy methods [27]. Their approach consisted of two components: a bug description component and a source code component. For the bug description component, in the training bug reports, they first identified buggy methods related to these bug reports by mining version control systems. Next, they arranged each bug report and relevant buggy method into a pair with a label of relevant, and they also arranged each bug report and non-relevant buggy method into a pair with a label of non-relevant. Then, a classifier was built on the pairs. Given a new bug report, they inputted it and each of the methods in the source code into the classifier, and the classifier outputted the relevance of the method to the bug reports.

In the source code approach, they used *tf-idf* to measure the similarity of a new bug report to a method in the source code and ranked the methods according to their similarity score. To combine these two components, given a new bug report, they first sorted the methods according to the results (i.e. relevant or non-relevant) from the classifier built in the bug description component, and then they ranked the methods according to the similarity scores computed by the source code component.

Sisman and Kak mined the version control systems to compute a prior probability distribution for defect proneness associated with the files in a given version of the project [28]. Given a new bug report and for each source code file, they integrated the prior probability with IR techniques to compute the posterior probability that a file is relevant to the bug. The two proposed decay models, MHbPd and DHbPd, were based on the assumption that changed files are prone to be buggy in the future [29, 30]. Next, they applied several IR techniques, such as language models [2] and divergence from randomness [31].

Zhou, Zhang, and Lo proposed BugLocator, which ranks all files based on the textual similarity between the initial bug report and the source code using a revised vector space model (rVSM) and information about similar bugs that had been fixed before [3]. The assumption for rVSM is that classical VSM prefers small documents during ranking, and long documents are often poorly represented because they have poor similarity values. In fault localization, larger source code files tend to have a higher probability of containing a bug, and thus rVSM was proposed to rank larger files higher in the case of fault localization. The assumption for the similarity bug ranking component is that similar bugs tend to fix similar files.

Ye et al. proposed using learning to rank techniques to recommend relevant buggy source code files [32]. In their approach, various similarity measurements were used, i.e. surface lexical similarity, application programming interface (API)-enriched lexical similarity, collaborative filtering similarity, class name similarity, bug-fixing recency similarity, and bug-fixing frequency similarity. Next, they used the linear combination to combine these six types of similarity scores. To tune the weights for each similarity component, they applied SVMrank, a state-of-the-art learning to rank technique [33]. In particular, their approach made correct recommendations within the top ten ranked source files for over 70% of the bug reports in the Eclipse Platform and Tomcat projects.

Wang et al. proposed AmaLgam, which integrates three components (i.e. version history component, similar bug component, and structure component) to locate buggy source code files [34]. In the version history component, they assumed that a source code file that changed recently would have a high chance to be buggy in the future, and thus they assigned a score to each source code file according to the time elapsed between the change of the file and the submission of a bug report. In the similar bug component, given a new bug report, they recommended relevant source code files based on the similarity of the bug reports to the historical bug reports. In the structure component, they applied BLUiR, which was proposed by Saha et al. [22], to measure the similarities between a bug report and the structure information such as class names, method names, variable names, and comments. They combined the four types of structure information to comprise this component.

Considering that there are various variants of *tf-idf* models and yet no model can outperform the others, Wang et al. proposed a genetic algorithm (GA)-based approach to explore the space of possible compositions and output a heuristically near-optimal composite model [9]. The experiments on AspectJ, Eclipse, and SWT showed that the composite model improves the average top five prediction accuracy, MAP, and MRR by 18%, 21%, and 11%, respectively. Wang et al. also integrated the composite model into AmaLgam, and the results showed that it improves the top five prediction accuracy, MAP, and MRR scores of AmaLgam by 8%, 14%, and 7% on average, respectively.

Almhana et al. proposed a multi-objective optimization algorithm to find a balance between maximizing lexical and history-based similarity and minimizing the number of recommended classes [35]. To model a candidate solution (individual), they used a vector representation, and each dimension of the vector represented a class (source code file) to recommend for a specific bug report. Moreover, they chose lexical-based similarity (LS) and history-based similarity (HS) as two fitness functions. Experiment results showed that their proposed approach achieves a top 10 prediction accuracy score of 0.87.

Unlike the above studies, which focused on recommending buggy source code files, Wen et al. proposed LOCUS, which can not only recommend the buggy source code files but also locate the bug-introducing changes [36]. LOCUS retrieves information from software changes instead of source files, and it creates two corpora, the NL (natural language) corpus and CE (code entity) corpus, from the bug reports, commit logs, and source code files. Moreover, LOCUS performs recommendation based on three models built on these two corpora: an NL model, a CE model, and a boosting model. The NL model uses cosine similarity to measure the similarity between bug reports and source code. The CE model extracts the code-like terms from bug reports and compares each code-like term with the tokens in the CE. The boosting model is based on the assumption that changes committed recently contribute the most to fault potential. Finally, LOCUS integrates these three models to achieve a better performance.

8.5.2.2 Topic Modeling

Nguyen et al. proposed a specific topic modeling named BugScout to locate buggy source code files [37]. The assumption for BugScout is that the textual contents of a bug report and those of its corresponding source code share some technical aspects of the system, and these similar technical aspects can be used to recommend relevant source code files for a new bug report. BugScout captures these common technical aspects by two components: the S-component, which models the source files from the developers' point of view, and the B-component, which models the bug reports written from the point of view of bug reporters.

8.5.2.3 Deep Learning

Lam et al. proposed HyLoc, which combines features built from deep neural networks (DNNs), rVSM, and a project's bug-fixing history to achieve higher accuracy [38]. In HyLoc, DNN was used to bridge the lexical gap where developers may use different terms in the bug reports and in the source code. In total, they built two DNNs; one was used to learn the relations between bug reports texts and the textual tokens in code (i.e. comments), while the other was used to learn between bug reports texts and code tokens (i.e. identifiers and APIs).

Ye et al. studied work embedding from software artifacts to bridge the lexical gap by projecting natural language statements and code snippets as word embedding vectors in a shared representation space [4]. A word embedding model was first trained on API documents, tutorials, and reference documents, and then this model was aggregated to estimate semantic similarities between documents. They integrated their word embedding model into their learning to rank (LR) approach [32], and they found that using word embeddings to create additional semantic similarity features can help improve the ranking performance of their LR approach.

Uneno et al. proposed DrewBL, which uses a distributed representation of words to model the terms and code tokens appearing in the bug report and source code files [39]. Next, DrewBL was combined with other state-of-the-art fault localization techniques, such as BugLocator [3], which is based on textual similarity, and Bugspots, which is based on bug-fixing history.

8.5.3 Text and Stack/Execution Traces

Wang et al. proposed three heuristics to identify correlated crash groups automatically and then used crash correlation groups to locate and rank buggy files [40]. The three heuristics are the following: (i) Crash signature comparison. Two crashes A and B with signatures S_A and S_B are correlated if $S_A \subset S_B$ or $S_B \subset S_A$. (ii) Top frame comparison. If two crashes have the same file name in their top frame (i.e. first method signature and fully qualified file name pair in the stack trace), the two crashes are correlated. (iii) Frequent closed ordered subsets of stack trace frames (FCSF) comparison. Two crashes are correlated if they have a common FCSF. By applying these three heuristics, they identified crash correlation groups, extracted frequently failing files, and constructed characteristic vectors for these files. Each file appearing in a failing stack trace was mapped into a feature vector containing (i) the number of times that a file appeared in an FCSF, (ii) the number of times that a file appeared in an FCSF common to all stack traces in a crash correlation group, (iii) the number of times that a file appeared in lists of frequent failing files, and (iv) the number of times that a file appeared in the top ten frames of a stack trace. Next, they trained a Bayesian belief network classifier based on the characteristic vectors of these files and used it to predict buggy files for a new bug report.

Moreno et al. proposed Lobster, which locates relevant buggy source code files using stack traces and text retrieval [41]. In Lobster, stack traces submitted in a bug report are used to compute the similarity between their code elements and the source code files. Moreover, Lobster combines the stack trace-based similarity model with a textual similarity model to further improve the prediction accuracy. They evaluated their approach in 155 bugs across 14 projects, and the results showed that Lobster achieves a substantial improvement over the Lucene-based fault localization techniques.

Wong et al. used segmentation and stack-trace analysis to improve the performance of fault localization [42]. Given a bug report, their approach divided each source code file into a series of segments, and they used the segment that is the most similar to the bug report to represent the file. Next, they analyzed the bug report to identify possible faulty files in a stack trace and favor these files. Experiments on three projects (Eclipse, AspectJ, and SWT) showed that their approach significantly improved BugLocator. Moreover, segmentation and stack-trace analysis are complementary to each other for boosting the performance of bug-report-oriented fault localization.

Considering that IR-based and spectrum-based techniques both aim to identify buggy code (in the source code file level or method/block/statement level), Le et al. proposed a new multi-modal technique that combines these two types of techniques together to localize bugs [43]. IR-based techniques process textual information in bug reports, while spectrum-based techniques process execution trace (i.e. a record of which program elements are executed for each test case). Le et al.'s approach leveraged the information from the textual content in bug reports and execution traces. Specifically, they adaptively created a bug-specific model to map a particular bug to its possible location and introduced a novel idea of suspicious words that are highly associated with a bug. Experiments on 157 real bugs showed that their approach can outperform the baseline by at least 48%, 31%, 28%, and 29% in terms of the number of bugs successfully localized when a developer inspects 1, 5, and 10 program elements (i.e. top 1, top 5, and top 10) and the MAP, respectively.

8.6 Empirical Studies

There exist some empirical studies that investigate the usefulness of IR-based fault localization tools in a number of settings [23, 44–46] or the effectiveness of various techniques for IR-based fault localization [18]. We highlight them below.

Kochhar, Le, and Lo investigated a potential bias in the evaluation of IR-based fault localization studies [44]. Many studies take all issues marked as bugs in bug tracking systems to validate the effectiveness of the proposed approaches. However, Herzig et al. reported that a substantial number of issue reports marked as bugs are not bugs but rather refactorings, requests for enhancement, documentation changes, and so on [47]. These misclassifications have been shown by Herzig et al. to impact studies on defect prediction (i.e. the task of predicting which files are likely to be buggy in the future). Motivated by Herzig et al.'s study, Kochhar, Le, and Lo investigated whether the same misclassifications impact IR-based fault localization studies.

They analyzed issue reports that were manually categorized by Herzig et al. and applied a simple IR-based fault localization technique based on VSM on those issue reports. They compared the MAP of the simple IR-based fault localization techniques on issues reported as bugs (Reported) and real bug reports as classified by Herzig et al. (Actual). Using the Mann–Whitney U test, they found that there is a statistically significant difference in the MAP. The most impactful misclassifications were TEST to BUG (i.e. test case-related issues were marked as bugs) and IMPROVEMENT to BUG (i.e. perfective maintenance task-related issues were marked as bugs). The authors recommended future studies to omit bug reports in which no source code files are modified (which often corresponds to TEST to BUG) and bug reports whose summary or description fields explicitly specify the buggy files (which often corresponds to IMPROVEMENT to BUG).

Kochhar, Tian, and Lo extended Kochhar, Le, and Lo's work by considering additional biases in fault localization beyond the misclassification of issue reports [45]. They investigated three potential biases by answering three research questions: (i) What are the effects of wrongly classified issue reports on fault localization? (ii) What are the effects of localized bug reports on fault localization? (iii) What are the effects of wrongly identified ground truth files on fault localization?

The first research question was studied by Kochhar, Le, and Lo. However, the previous study performed an all-project analysis rather than a per-project analysis, which is more accurate. The second research question investigates localized bug reports whose buggy files have already been localized by developers and explicitly mentioned in the reports. Fixing such localized bug reports does not require the use of a fault localization tool. The third research question investigates wrong ground truth files. Existing fault localization studies treat all files that are fixed in a bug fixing commit corresponding to a bug report as ground truth. However, due to tangled changes and non-essential changes, not all such files may be buggy. Only cosmetic changes may have been made to some files (such as the addition of comments), which may not be relevant to the issue described in the bug report.

The authors used the data set that was manually annotated by Herzig et al. [47] to answer the three questions. Herzig et al.'s data set was input into a simple IR-based fault localization technique based on the VSM. The MAP was used as a yardstick, and the effectiveness of the simple IR-based fault localization technique for clean and dirty data sets was compared to answer the research questions. The Mann–Whitney U test was performed, and Cohen's d was calculated to check whether any difference in effectiveness was statistically significant and substantial. The study highlighted the following findings, which answer the research questions:

1) For two out of the three projects in Herzig et al.'s data set, wrongly classified issue reports do not statistically significantly impact fault localization results. They also do not substantially impact fault localization results; the effect size is less than 0.2.
2) Across all projects, localized bug reports both statistically significantly and substantially affect fault localization results. The *p*-values are less than 0.05, and the effect size is more than 0.8.
3) Across all projects, the number of clean ground truth files does not statistically, significantly, or substantially affect fault localization results. The *p*-values are less than 0.05, and the effect size is less than 0.2.

These findings highlight the need for future fault localization studies to clean up evaluation data sets and remove localized bug reports, since they skew fault localization results. Cleaning up misclassified bug reports may also remove some bias for some data sets.

Wang et al. investigated the usefulness of an IR-based fault localization tool [46]. They performed an analytical study and a user study to investigate the effectiveness of BugLocator [3], which is one of the popular IR-based fault localization techniques. They investigated three research questions: (i) What information in a bug report tends to produce good fault localization results? (ii) How do developers take advantage of existing information in the bug reports? (iii) Will developers behave and perform differently if they use an IR-based debugging tool?

To answer the first research question, the authors applied BugLocator to bug reports from four programs: SWT, Joda-Time, ZXing, and AspectJ. They compared the effectiveness of BugLocator (measured in terms of the average ranking of buggy files) when bug reports contained different pieces of information (i.e. program entity names, stack traces, and test cases). They found that there is a statistically significant difference in BugLocator's effectiveness when program entity names are present. This finding supports an earlier finding by Kochhar, Tian, and Lo [45].

To answer the second and third research questions, the authors conducted a user study with students from Georgia Institute of Technology. Overall, they had a total of 70 participants. They selected eight bugs that involve only one buggy method in one file for the user study. The user study participants were tasked to locate the methods that contain the bugs given bug reports. The authors found that without any fault localization tool, participants used names of program entities that appeared in bug reports as keywords to search for buggy files. The authors also found that, using the lists generated by BugLocator, the median time needed by participants to find and focus on the faulty file was shorter than when BugLocator was not used. However, BugLocator does not help participants find buggy methods in faulty files.

Saha et al. investigated whether fault localization techniques work well for C projects [23]. Their empirical study nicely complemented existing studies; most IR-based bug localization techniques are evaluations of Java projects, and it is unclear if they still work equally well for programs written in other commonly used languages, including C. The authors created a benchmark data set containing a total of 7500 bug reports from five popular C projects (Python, GDB, WineHQ, GCC, and Linux Kernel), and they reused an existing data set containing bug reports from three popular Java projects (SWT, AspectJ, and Eclipse). They then compared the effectiveness of an IR-based fault localization technique named BLUiR [22] applied on the C and Java projects. Their empirical study concluded with several findings, including the following: (i) the main challenge of applying

IR-based fault localization to C projects is the need to handle preprocessor directives and macros, and (ii) IR-based fault localization is comparably as effective for C projects as it is for Java projects.

Rao et al. investigated different generic text mining techniques and their effectiveness for IR-based fault localization [18]. In particular, they experimented with five techniques, namely the unigram model (UM), VSM, LSA, LDA, and CBDM. They evaluated the effectiveness of these techniques on 291 bugs from the AspectJ project, which was collected as part of the iBUGS data set [19]. Their study concluded that sophisticated text mining techniques (such as LDA, LSA, and CBDM) do not outperform simpler techniques (such as UM and VSM).

8.7 Miscellaneous

Thung et al. integrated a fault localization technique into the popular Bugzilla bug tracking system [48]. There have been many fault localization techniques proposed in literature, and some of them have been released as publicly downloadable prototypes. Unfortunately, these existing techniques and prototypes are not integrated into bug tracking systems. This makes it more difficult for practitioners to incorporate fault localization techniques into their day-to-day software development and debugging activities. Motivated by this problem, Thung et al. developed BugLocalizer, which implements BugLocator [3] as a Bugzilla extension. Developers can plug BugLocalizer into their Bugzilla instance and use BugLocator capabilities. Given a new bug report, BugLocalizer will return a ranked list of files that are most likely to be buggy. BugLocalizer can be downloaded from its GitHub site at: https://github.com/smagsmu/buglocalizer.

Wang et al. proposed an experimental platform that allows researchers to comparatively and reproducibly evaluate fault localization techniques [49].

They released the bug localization experimental platform (BOAT), which is an extensible web application that includes thousands of bug reports with known ground truth buggy source code files. Using BOAT, researchers can upload executables of their own fault localization techniques and investigate the effectiveness of their proposed technique with respect to the thousands of bug reports in BOAT. They can also compare and contrast the effectiveness of their fault localization techniques against other fault localization techniques uploaded by other researchers. BOAT is preloaded with several fault localization techniques, including a simple VSM-based technique and BugLocator [3].

Le et al. proposed a technique that can predict the effectiveness of an IR-based fault localization technique for a particular bug report [50]. Their work was motivated by the fact that an IR-based fault localization technique can perform very badly for many bug reports; for these reports, the actual buggy files can appear very low in the returned ranked list. It would then be better for developers to perform traditional debugging rather than follow the recommendation of an IR-based fault localization technique. If such cases happen frequently, the confidence of developers in using such automated debugging tools would substantially decrease, and this may lead to developers abandoning such tools [51, 52]. To mitigate this issue with the reliability of existing IR-based fault localization techniques, Le et al. built an oracle that can predict if a ranked list produced by an IR-based fault localization technique for a particular bug report is likely to be promising. Such oracles are produced by their proposed approach, APRILE, which stands for automated prediction of IR-based fault localization's effectiveness.

APRILE models a fault localization instance (i.e. the application of a bug localization technique to a bug report) as a set of features. A total of four sets of features are used: features extracted from the suspiciousness scores of files returned by an IR-based fault localization tool, features extracted from words that appear in the textual contents of a bug report, features extracted from a topic model learned from the textual contents of a bug report, and features extracted from the metadata of a bug report (such as the priority and severity of the bug report). These features are then used to build a model that can differentiate between effective fault localization instances and ineffective ones. The model was built by running support vector machine (SVM), a popular classification algorithm. In their experiments, the authors used APRILE to predict the effectiveness of BugLocator [3], BLUiR [22], and AmaLgam [34] when they are applied to more than 3000 bug reports from three popular Java projects: AspectJ, Eclipse, and SWT. The experiment results demonstrated that APRILE can accurately identify effective and ineffective fault localization instances with an F-measure of close to 70.

Xia et al. proposed a technique that can predict the location of buggy files with identifiers and comments written in a particular language (such as English), given a bug report written in another language (such as Chinese) [53]. Their study was motivated by the fact that a software can be written by developers who are familiar with a particular language but used by users who are familiar with another language. This often happens in the era of globalization, where a software product created in a particular country can be made available worldwide (such as apps in Google Play). These global users may submit bug reports in a language that the developers are not familiar with. Existing fault localization techniques would not be able to work well for such cases, since the intersection of common words between bug reports and source code files would be close to zero.

To address this challenge, Xia et al. proposed CrosLocator. It composes multiple online translators to convert bug reports written in one language to a target language, in which identifiers and comments of source code files are written in.

Multiple translators are used because each translator may not be perfect, especially considering the low quality text that often appears in bug reports. After the translation process, each bug report has multiple translated versions. For each version, CrosLocator applies BugLocator [3] to rank source code files. At the end of this process, we will have multiple ranked lists of source code files. These lists are then merged together to create a single list using a learning to rank algorithm. In experiments, CrosLocator was used to find buggy files of 50 bug reports from Ruby China with promising results. The bug reports were written in Chinese, while the identifiers and comments in source code files were written in English.

8.8 Conclusion

In the last decade, many papers on IR-based fault localization have been published in various research venues. These papers describe either new IR-based fault localization techniques, empirical studies on IR-based fault localization, IR-based fault localization tools, or supporting technologies that can help widen the adoption of IR-based fault localization. Existing IR-based fault localization techniques can be categorized based on data used in the fault localization process (i.e. text-only, text + traces, and text + history) or IR techniques used (such as VSM, topic model, learning to rank, and deep learning). In addition to papers publishing new techniques, several existing works have investigated the effectiveness of IR-based fault localization techniques on various settings or the effectiveness of various IR techniques for fault localization. Several tools have been released; Bugzilla, for example, integrates a popular fault localization technique into a popular bug tracking system, while another introduces an extensible web platform for researchers to reproducibly compare different IR-based fault localization solutions. To widen the adoption of IR-based fault localization, one work proposed a solution that can help developers deal with the unreliability of existing fault localization techniques, while another proposed a solution that enables existing IR-based fault localization techniques to still work when bug reports and comments and identifiers in source code files are written in different languages.

Notes

1 In this chapter, we use "bug" and "fault" interchangeably. We also use "programs" and "software" interchangeably.
2 https://bugs.eclipse.org/bugs/show_bug.cgi?id=80720
3 https://bugs.eclipse.org/bugs/show_bug.cgi?id=384108

4 Part of Section 8.2 is from Ref. [3].
5 Part of Section 8.3.1 is from Ref. [9].
6 Part of Section 8.3.2 is from Ref. [10].
7 Part of Section 8.3.3 is from Ref. [11].
8 Part of Section 8.4 is from Refs. [3, 16].

References

1 Anvik, J., Hiew, L., and Murphy, G.C. (2005). Coping with an open bug repository. *Proceedings of the 2005 OOPSLA Workshop on Eclipse Technology eXchange (ETX '05)*, San Diego, CA, USA (16–17 October 2005), 35–39. ACM. ISBN 1-59593-342-5. https://doi.org/10.1145/1117696.1117704.

2 Manning, C.D., Raghavan, P., and Schütze, H. (2008). *Introduction to Information Retrieval*. Cambridge University Press. ISBN 0521865719.

3 Zhou, J., Zhang, H., and Lo, D. (2012). Where should the bugs be fixed? More accurate information retrieval-based bug localization based on bug reports. *Proceedings of the 2012 34th International Conference on Software Engineering (ICSE '08)*, Zurich, Switzerland (2–9 June 2012), 14–24. IEEE. https://doi.org/10.1109/ICSE.2012.6227210.

4 Ye, X., Shen, H., Ma, X. et al. (2016). From word embeddings to document similarities for improved information retrieval in software engineering. *Proceedings of the 2016 IEEE/ACM 38th International Conference on Software Engineering (ICSE '16)*, Austin, TX, USA (14–22 May 2016), 404–415. ACM. https://doi.org/10.1145/2884781.2884862.

5 Harris, Z.S. (1954). Distributional structure. *Word* 10 (2–3): 146–162. https://doi.org/10.1080/00437956.1954.11659520.

6 Blei, D.M., Ng, A.Y., and Jordan, M.I. (2003). Latent Dirichlet allocation. *Journal of Machine Learning Research* 3: 993–1022. ISSN 1532-4435.

7 Levy, O. and Goldberg, Y. (2014). Neural word embedding as implicit matrix factorization. *Proceedings of the 27th International Conference on Neural Information Processing Systems – Volume 2* (*NIPS '14*), Montreal, QC, Canada (8–13 December 2014), 2177–2185. MIT Press.

8 Porter, M.F. (1997). An algorithm for suffix stripping. In: *Readings in Information Retrieval* (ed. K.S. Jones and P. Willett), 313–316. Morgan Kaufmann. ISBN 1-55860-454-5. http://dl.acm.org/citation.cfm?id=275537.275705.

9 Wang, S., Lo, D., and Lawall, J. (2014). Compositional vector space models for improved bug localization. *Proceedings of the 30th IEEE International Conference on Software Maintenance and Evolution*, Victoria, BC, Canada (29 September–3 October 2014), 171–180. https://doi.org/10.1109/ICSME.2014.39.

10 Xia, X., Lo, D., Wang, X., and Zhou, B. (2015). Dual analysis for recommending developers to resolve bugs. *Journal of Software: Evolution and Process* 27 (3): 195–220.

11 Xu, B., Xing, Z., Xia, X. et al. (2018). Domain-specific cross-language relevant question retrieval. *Empirical Software Engineering* 23 (2): 1084–1122.

12 Xu, B., Ye, D., Xing, Z. et al. (2016). Predicting semantically linkable knowledge in developer online forums via convolutional neural network. *Proceedings of the 2016 31st IEEE/ACM International Conference on Automated Software Engineering (ASE)*, Singapore (3–7 September 2016), 51–62. IEEE.

13 van der Maaten, L. and Hinton, G. (2008). Visualizing data using t-SNE. *Journal of Machine Learning Research* 9: 2579–2605.

14 Mikolov, T., Chen, K., Corrado, G., and Dean, J. (2013). Efficient estimation of word representations in vector space. *Proceedings of the First International Conference on Learning Representations (ICLR '13), Workshop Track Proceedings,* Scottsdale, AZ, USA (2–4 May 2013). http://arxiv.org/abs/1301.3781.

15 Mikolov, T., Sutskever, I., Chen, K. et al. (2013). Distributed representations of words and phrases and their compositionality. *Proceedings of the 26th International Conference on Neural Information Processing Systems – Volume 2* (*NIPS '13*), Lake Tahoe, NV, USA (5–10 December 2013), 3111–3119. Curran Associates.

16 Xia, X. and Lo, D. (2017). An effective change recommendation approach for supplementary bug fixes. *Automated Software Engineering* 24 (2): 455–498.

17 Baeza-Yates, R.A. and Ribeiro-Neto, B. (1999). *Modern Information Retrieval.* Addison-Wesley Longman. ISBN 020139829X.

18 Rao, S. and Kak, A. (2011). Retrieval from software libraries for bug localization: a comparative study of generic and composite text models. *Proceedings of the 8th Working Conference on Mining Software Repositories* (*MSR '11*), Waikiki, Honolulu, HI, USA (21–28 May 2011), 43–52. ACM. ISBN 978-1-4503-0574-7. https://doi.org/10.1145/1985441.1985451.

19 Dallmeier, V. and Zimmermann, T. (2007). Extraction of bug localization benchmarks from history. *Proceedings of the Twenty-second IEEE/ACM International Conference on Automated Software Engineering* (*ASE '07*), Atlanta, GA, USA (5–9 November 2007), 433–436. ACM. ISBN 978-1-59593-882-4. https://doi.org/10.1145/1321631.1321702.

20 Rao, S., Medeiros, H., and Kak, A.C. (2013). An incremental update framework for efficient retrieval from software libraries for bug localization. *Proceedings of the 20th Working Conference on Reverse Engineering* (*WCRE '13*), Koblenz, Germany (14–17 October 2013), 62–71. IEEE.

21 Sisman, B. and Kak, A.C. (2013). Assisting code search with automatic query reformulation for bug localization. *Proceedings of the 10th Working Conference on Mining Software Repositories* (*MSR '13*), San Francisco, CA, USA (18–19 May 2013), 309–318. IEEE. ISBN 978-1-4673-2936-1. https://doi.org/10.1109/MSR.2013.6624044.

22 Saha, R.K., Lease, M., Khurshid, S., and Perry, D.E. (2013). Improving bug localization using structured information retrieval. *Proceedings of the 2013 28th IEEE/ACM International Conference on Automated Software Engineering (ASE '13)*, Silicon Valley, CA, USA (11–15 November 2013), 345–355. IEEE. https://doi.org/10.1109/ASE.2013.6693093.

23 Saha, R.K., Lawall, J., Khurshid, S., and Perry, D.E. (2014). On the effectiveness of information retrieval based bug localization for C programs. *Proceedings of the 2014 IEEE International Conference on Software Maintenance and Evolution* (*ICSME '14*), Victoria, BC, Canada (29 September–3 October 2014), 161–170. IEEE. ISBN 978-1-4799-6146-7. https://doi.org/10.1109/ICSME.2014.38.

24 Padioleau, Y., Lawall, J., Hansen, R.R., and Muller, G. (2008). Documenting and automating collateral evolutions in linux device drivers. *Proceedings of the 3rd ACM SIGOPS/EuroSys European Conference on Computer Systems 2008* (*EuroSys '08*), Glasgow, Scotland, UK (1–5 April 2008), 247–260. ACM. ISBN 978-1-60558-013-5. https://doi.org/10.1145/1352592.1352618.

25 Lukins, S.K., Kraft, N.A., and Etzkorn, L.H. (2008). Source code retrieval for bug localization using latent Dirichlet allocation. *Proceedings of the 2008 15th Working Conference on Reverse Engineering* (*WCRE '08*), Antwerp, Belgium (15–18 October 2008), 155–164. IEEE. ISBN 978-0-7695-3429-9. https://doi.org/10.1109/WCRE.2008.33.

26 Beard, M.D., Kraft, N.A., Etzkorn, L.H., and Lukins, S.K. (2011). Measuring the accuracy of information retrieval based bug localization Techniques. *Proceedings of the 18th Working Conference on Reverse Engineering (WCRE '11)*, Limerick, Ireland (17–20 October 2011), 124–128. IEEE. https://doi.org/10.1109/WCRE.2011.23.

27 Davies, S., Roper, M., and Wood, M. (2012). Using bug report similarity to enhance bug localization. *Proceedings of the 2012 19th Working Conference on Reverse Engineering*, Kingston, ON, Canada (15–18 October 2012), 125–134. IEEE. https://doi.org/10.1109/WCRE.2012.22.

28 Sisman, B. and Kak, A.C. (2012). Incorporating version histories in information retrieval based bug localization. *Proceedings of the 9th IEEE Working Conference on Mining Software Repositories* (*MSR '12)*, Zurich, Switzerland (2–3 June 2012), 50–59. IEEE. ISBN 978-1-4673-1761-0.

29 Hassan, A. E. (2009). Predicting faults using the complexity of code changes. *Proceedings of the 2009 IEEE 31st International Conference on Software Engineering (ICSE '09)*, Vancouver, BC, Canada (16–24 May 2009), 78–88. IEEE. https://doi.org/10.1109/ ICSE.2009.5070510.

30 Nagappan, N., Zeller, A., Zimmermann, T. et al. (2010). Change bursts as defect predictors. *Proceedings of the 2010 IEEE 21st International Symposium on Software Reliability Engineering (ISSRE '10)*, San Jose, CA, USA (1–4 November 2010), 309–318. IEEE. https://doi.org/10.1109/ISSRE.2010.25.

31 Amati, G. and Van Rijsbergen, C.J. (2002). Probabilistic models of information retrieval based on measuring the divergence from randomness. *ACM Transactions on Information Systems* 20 (4): 357–389. ISSN 1046-8188. https://doi.org/10.1145/582415.582416.

32 Ye, X., Bunescu, R., and Liu, C. (2014). Learning to rank relevant files for bug reports using domain knowledge. *Proceedings of the 22nd ACM SIGSOFT International Symposium on Foundations of Software Engineering (FSE '14)*, Hong Kong (16–22 November 2014), 689–699. ACM. ISBN 978-1-4503-3056-5. https://doi.org/10.1145/2635868.2635874.

33 Joachims, T. (2006). Training linear SVMs in linear time. *Proceedings of the 12th ACM SIGKDD International Conference on Knowledge Discovery and Data Mining (KDD '06)*, Philadelphia, PA, USA (20–23 August 2006), 217–226. ACM. ISBN 1-59593-339-5. https://doi.org/10.1145/1150402.1150429.

34 Wang, S. and Lo, D. (2014). Version history, similar report, and structure: putting them together for improved bug localization. *Proceedings of the 22nd International Conference on Program Comprehension (ICPC '14)*, Hyderabad, India (2–3 June 2014), 53–63. ACM. ISBN 978-1-4503-2879-1. https://doi.org/10.1145/2597008.2597148.

35 Almhana, R., Mkaouer, W., Kessentini, M., and Ouni, A. (2016). Recommending relevant classes for bug reports using multi-objective search. *2016 31st IEEE/ACM International Conference on Automated Software Engineering (ASE)*, Singapore (3–7 September 2016), 286–295. ACM.

36 Wen, M., Wu, R., and Cheung, S.-C. (2016). Locus: locating bugs from software changes. *Proceedings of the 31st IEEE/ACM International Conference on Automated Software Engineering (ASE '16)*, Singapore (3–7 September 2016), 262–273. ACM. ISBN 978-1-4503-3845-5. https://doi.org/10.1145/2970276.2970359.

37 Nguyen, A.T., Nguyen, T.T., Al-Kofahi, J. (2011). A topic-based approach for narrowing the search space of buggy files from a bug report. *Proceedings of the 2011 26th IEEE/ACM International Conference on Automated Software Engineering (ASE '11)*, Lawrence, KS, USA (6–10 November 2011), 263–272. IEEE. https://doi.org/10.1109/ASE.2011.6100062.

38 Lam, A.N., Nguyen, A.T., Nguyen, H.A., and Nguyen, T. N. (2015). Combining deep learning with information retrieval to localize buggy files for bug reports. *Proceedings of the 2015 30th IEEE/ACM International Conference on Automated Software Engineering (ASE '15)*, Lincoln, NE, USA (9–13 November 2015), 476–481. IEEE. https://doi.org/10.1109/ASE.2015.73.

39 Uneno, Y., Mizuno, O., and Choi, E. (2016). Using a distributed representation of words in localizing relevant files for bug reports. *Proceedings of the 2016 IEEE International Conference on Software Quality, Reliability and Security (QRS '16)*, Vienna, Austria (1–3 August 2016), 183–190. IEEE. https://doi.org/10.1109/QRS.2016.30.

40 Wang, S., Khomh, F., and Zou, Y. (2016). Improving bug management using correlations in crash reports. *Empirical Software Engineering* 21 (2): 337–367. ISSN 1573–7616. https://doi.org/10.1007/s10664-014-9333-9.

41 Moreno, L., Treadway, J.J., Marcus, A., and Shen, W. (2014). On the use of stack traces to improve text retrieval-based bug localization. *Proceedings of the 30th IEEE International Conference on Software Maintenance and Evolution,* Victoria, BC, Canada (29 September–3 October 2014), 151–160. IEEE. https://doi.org/10.1109/ICSME.2014.37.

42 Wong, C., Xiong, Y., Zhang, H. et al. (2014). Boosting bug-report-oriented fault localization with segmentation and stack-trace analysis. *Proceedings of the 2014 IEEE International Conference on Software Maintenance and Evolution*, Victoria, BC, Canada (29 September–3 October 2014), 181–190. IEEE. https://doi.org/10.1109/ ICSME.2014.40.

43 Le, T.B., Oentaryo, R.J., and Lo, D. (2015). Information retrieval and spectrum based bug localization: better together. *Proceedings of the 2015 10th Joint Meeting on Foundations of Software Engineering (ESEC/FSE '15)*, Bergamo, Italy (30 August–4 September 2015), 579–590. ACM. ISBN 978-1-4503-3675-8. https://doi.org/10.1145/2786805.2786880.

44 Kochhar, P.S., Le, T.-D.B., and Lo, D. (2014). It's not a bug, it's a feature: does misclassification affect bug localization? *Proceedings of the 11th Working Conference on Mining Software Repositories* (*MSR '14*), Hyderabad, India (31 May–1 June 2014), 296–299. ACM. ISBN 978-1-4503-2863-0. https://doi.org/10.1145/2597073.2597105.

45 Kochhar, P.S., Tian, Y., and Lo, D. (2014). Potential biases in bug localization: do they matter? *Proceedings of the 29th ACM/IEEE International Conference on Automated Software Engineering* (*ASE '14*), Vasteras, Sweden (15–19 September 2014), 803–814. ACM. ISBN 978-1-4503-3013-8. https://doi.org/10.1145/2642937.2642997.

46 Wang, Q., Parnin, C., and Orso, A. (2015). Evaluating the usefulness of IR-based fault localization techniques. *Proceedings of the 2015 International Symposium on Software Testing and Analysis* (*ISSTA '15*), Baltimore, MD, USA (12–17 July 2015), 1–11. ACM. ISBN 978-1-4503-3620-8. https://doi.org/10.1145/2771783.2771797.

47 Herzig, K., Just, S., and Zeller, A. (2013). It's not a bug, it's a feature: how misclassification impacts bug prediction. *Proceedings of the 2013 International Conference on Software Engineering* (*ICSE '13*), San Francisco, CA, USA (18–26 May 2013), 392–401. IEEE. ISBN 978-1-4673-3076-3. http://dl.acm.org/citation.cfm?id=2486788.2486840.

48 Thung, F., Le, T.-D.B., Kochhar, P.S., and Lo, D. (2014). BugLocalizer: integrated tool support for bug localization. *Proceedings of the 22nd ACM SIGSOFT International Symposium on Foundations of Software Engineering* (*FSE '14*), Hong Kong (16–22 November 2014), 767–770. ACM. ISBN 978-1-4503-3056-5. https://doi.org/10.1145/2635868.2661678.

49 Wang, X., Lo, D., Xia, X. et al. (2014). BOAT: an experimental platform for researchers to comparatively and reproducibly evaluate bug localization techniques. *Companion Proceedings of the 36th International Conference on Software Engineering* (*ICSE Companion '14*), Hyderabad, India (31 May–7 June 2014), 572–575. ACM. ISBN 978-1-4503-2768-8. https://doi.org/10.1145/2591062.2591066.

50 Le, T.-D.B., Thung, F., and Lo, D. (2014). Predicting effectiveness of IR-based bug localization techniques. *Proceedings of the 2014 IEEE 25th International Symposium* *on Software Reliability Engineering* (*ISSRE '14*), Naples, Italy (3–6 November 2014), 335–345. IEEE. ISBN 978-1-4799-6032-3. https://doi.org/10.1109/ISSRE.2014.39.

51 Kochhar, P.S., Xia, X., Lo, D., and Li, S. (2016). Practitioners' expectations on automated fault localization. *Proceedings of the 25th International Symposium on Software Testing and Analysis* (*ISSTA '16*), Saarbrücken, Germany (18–20 July 2016), 165–176. ACM. ISBN 978-1-4503-4390-9. https://doi.org/10.1145/2931037.2931051.

52 Parnin, C. and Orso, A. (2011). Are automated debugging techniques actually helping programmers? *Proceedings of the 2011 International Symposium on Software Testing and Analysis* (*ISSTA '11*), Toronto, ON, Canada (17–21 July 2011), 199–209. ACM. ISBN 978-1-4503-0562-4. https://doi.org/10.1145/2001420.2001445.

53 Xia, X., Lo, D., Wang, X. et al. (2014). Cross-language bug localization. *Proceedings of the 22nd International Conference on Program Comprehension* (*ICPC '14*), Hyderabad, India (2–3 July 2014), 275–278. ACM. ISBN 978-1-4503-2879-1. https://doi.org/10.1145/2597008.2597788.

9

Model-Based Techniques for Software Fault Localization

Birgit Hofer[1], Franz Wotawa[1], Wolfgang Mayer[2], and Markus Stumptner[2]

[1] *Institute of Software Technology, Graz University of Technology, Graz, Austria*
[2] *Advanced Computing Research Centre, University of South Australia, Adelaide, SA, Australia*

9.1 Introduction

Since the early 1980s, artificial intelligence researchers have aimed to provide a diagnosis methodology that identifies the cause of an observed misbehavior using models of the underlying systems together with sophisticated reasoning techniques. The driving force was the notion of compositionality: to use system models capturing the behavior of components and their interconnections directly for diagnosis without the need to provide specific diagnosis-related models, which are hard to obtain and also hard to maintain in the case of system changes. Davis et al. [1, 2] dealt with root cause identification using models based on the structure of a system and the behavior of the system's components. This approach makes assumptions about the correctness of components explicit such that a reasoning mechanism can determine the potentially incorrect components that cause an inconsistency between the observed and the expected behavior. Apart from formalizing the concepts of model-based diagnosis [3–5] and providing algorithms and modeling paradigms, the model-based diagnosis research originally emphasized the diagnosis of physical systems rather than program debugging. Hence, in the early 1990s, the question arose whether model-based diagnosis could also be used for debugging purposes. In this chapter, we address this question and outline the basic principles and underlying techniques behind model-based debugging (MBD), including an in-depth analysis of the state of the art and future research directions.

Before discussing the underlying methods for modeling and algorithms behind MBD, we first introduce the basic concepts using the small program d74, which we

Handbook of Software Fault Localization: Foundations and Advances, First Edition.
Edited by W. Eric Wong and T.H. Tse.

Published 2023 by John Wiley & Sons, Inc.

```
{a=3,b=2,c=2,d=3,e=3}
s1. x = a * c;
s2. y = b * d;
s3. z = c * e;
s4. f = x + y - 2;
s5. g = y + z;

{f = 12, g = 12}
```

Figure 9.1 Program d74 for illustrating the concepts behind model-based debugging and a test case.

adopt from the d74 circuit (see [5]) that is commonly used to explain model-based diagnosis. In Figure 9.1, we depict the source code of d74, comprising five assignment statements and no control flow statements. In order to start diagnosis, we need information about the expected behavior. This may be given using a formal (and maybe partial) specification or at least one test case. Let us assume that we have the following test case that specifies the values `a = 3, b = 2, c = 2, d = 3, e = 3, f = 12,` and `g = 12` for the input variables a, b, c, d, and e as well as for the outputs f and g. When executing d74, we see that the program computes the correct value 12 for variable `g` but the incorrect value 10 for `f`. Hence, we know that d74 is not working as expected, and we are interested in identifying the cause of this inconsistency. When using spectrum-based fault[1] localization directly, we would not gain any advantage because of the missing control flow in d74; hence, each statement is equally likely to be faulty. When using program slicing, we would be able to reduce the possible causes of the misbehavior to statements s1, s2, and s4, because those statements are connected using the underlying dataflow. Variable `x` is defined in statement s1 and used in statement s4. Variable `y` is defined in statement s2 and also used in s4, and in statement s4, `f` is defined, which we know holds the unexpected (incorrect) value 10 after program execution.

So how does MBD work? As said previously, model-based diagnosis makes assumptions about the correctness or incorrectness of components explicitly. Components can be chosen at different granularity, but could be, for example, statements. For the d74 example, assume statement s2 includes the bug and all other statements behave as expected. When using this assumption, we are no longer able to obtain a value for `y` using statement s2. However, from statement s1, which is assumed to be correct, we know that `x` has to be 6, and when executing statement s3 we are able to assign the value 6 to variable `z`. Because of the missing value for `y`, we are unable to determine a value for `f` and `g` using the assignment statements s4 and s5. However, this is only true when interpreting statements s4 and s5 as assignments mapping the value obtained from the right side to the variable defined on the left side. Interpreting assignments as equations and using the information coming from the test case gets us further. Knowing that `f` has to be 12 and `x` has to be 6, `y` has to be 8 if statement s4 is correct. Unfortunately, when using this value together with the computed value for `z` and statement s5, we obtain 14 as the new value for variable `g`, which contradicts the expected value coming from the test case. Hence, we know that the assumption that statement s2 is faulty can no longer hold.

Note that when assuming either statement s1 or s4 to be faulty and the other statements to be correct, we are unable to derive a contradiction. Therefore, we have only two possible root causes for the given test case, i.e. either the bug is in line s1 or in line s4.

From this small example, we not only see the basic idea behind MBD but also that MBD makes use of the structure of programs as well as the semantics of the statements but interpreted in a slightly different way. We also see that MBD potentially improves other debugging approaches like program slicing or spectrum-based fault localization (SFL) in terms of diagnosis accuracy, i.e. in implicating fewer statements to be considered as being faulty. In the following, we discuss how to formalize MBD. We introduce algorithms for computing diagnoses using models and show how such models can be automatically extracted from programs without human intervention. We will see that this works also in the case of conditional statements, loops, and recursive function calls. In addition, we summarize empirical results obtained when using MBD, combined approaches, and open research questions and directions.

9.2 Basic Definitions and Algorithms

Let us start with the definition of MBD and discuss the underlying debugging problem. We begin with the source code of a program $\prod$, written in a programming language L, and a failed test case T_f. For simplicity of presentation, we assume the following: (i) L is an imperative sequential language and (ii) the test case T_f specifies all necessary input values for $\prod$ and at least one expected output value. For this purpose, we assume that IN and OUT are the sets of input and output variables of $\prod$, respectively. Moreover, we introduce the concept of variable environments $\sum_V$ that are functions mapping each variable in set V to its value. The semantics of $\prod$, i.e. its behavior, can be expressed in terms of a function $[\![\ ]\!]$ taking the program and its input environment Σ_{IN} and computing $\prod(\sum_{IN}) = \sum_{OUT}$. We now are able to define a test case formally as Table 9.1.

Table 9.1 Example 9.1.

Variable	Σ_{INd74}	Variable	Σ_{Od74}
a	3	f	12
b	2	g	12
c	2		
d	3		
e	3		

Definition 9.1 (Test Case)
A test case for a program $\prod$ *is a tuple* (Σ_{IN}, Σ_O) *specifying the expected output* Σ_O *for a subset of output variables* $(O \subseteq OUT)$ *in case the program* $\prod$ *is executed on the given input environment* Σ_{IN}.

Note that in the above definition, we do not require at least one output variable where we specify an expected value. If there is no output variable used in a test case, the corresponding program can never fail, and such a test case is always a successful one. Conceptually, a test case (Σ_{IN}, Σ_O) is a successful test case if the execution of the program $\prod$ leads to an environment $(O \subseteq OUT)$ equivalent to Σ_O with respect to the variables of O when using Σ_{IN} as input, where the equivalence of variable environments Σ_{V_1} and Σ_{V_2} with $V_1 \subseteq V_2$ is defined as $\Sigma_{V_1} = \Sigma_{V_2} \leftrightarrow \forall v \in V_1 : \Sigma_{V_1}(v) = \Sigma_{V_2}(v)$. Otherwise, we say that (Σ_{IN}, Σ_O) is a failed test case. The characterization of success and failure can be defined as follows:

$$\text{successful}(\Sigma_{IN}, \Sigma_O) \leftrightarrow [\![\textstyle\prod]\!](\Sigma_{IN}) = \Sigma_O$$

$$\text{failed}(\Sigma_{IN}, \Sigma_O) \leftrightarrow \neg\,\text{successful}(\Sigma_{IN}, \Sigma_O)$$

Example 9.1 *Let us consider program* d74 *given in Figure 9.1. The set of inputs* IN_{d74} *is* {`a, b, c, d, e`}, *and the set of outputs* OUT_{d74} *is* {`f, g`}. *The test case given in Figure 9.1 is* $(\Sigma_{INd74}, \Sigma_{Od74})$.

When executing d74 using the input environment Σ_{INd74}, we easily see that the computed value for variable *f* is 10 and not 12 as expected. Hence, the provided test case is a failed test case, i.e. failed for $(\Sigma_{INd74}, \Sigma_{Od74})$.

The debugging problem from an MBD perspective can now be formally characterized using the definition of failed test cases.

Definition 9.2 (Debugging Problem)
Given a program $\prod$ *and one failed test case* (Σ_{IN}, Σ_O), *the debugging problem consists of finding parts of program* $\prod$ *that are explanations for the given failed test case.*

In the following, we will further refine this definition of the debugging problem using the concepts of model-based diagnosis according to [5]. However, before that, we need a formal language for describing the models used for MBD. Without restricting generality, we make use of constraint representation of models in this chapter. Constraints and constraint solving are general concepts that allow us to formally specify a huge range of problems like satisfiability but also general equation solving. For more information regarding constraints and constraint solving, we refer the interested reader to Dechter's book [6]. In this chapter, we only consider the basic concepts of constraints and constraint solving necessary for specifying models and MBD. A constraint system is a triple (V, D, C), where V is a set of variables, D is a function mapping variables to their domain, i.e. a set of values that can be assigned to the given variable, and C is a set of constraints. A constraint $c \in C$ is itself a tuple (S, R), where $S = (v_1, \ldots, v_n)$ is the scope of c, i.e. a tuple of variables v_i from V, and R is a set of tuples $(p_1, \ldots, p_n)$, where for each $i \in 1, \ldots, n$, the value p_i is an element of $D(v_i)$. For simplicity, we assume a function scope returning the scope for a given constraint, and $R(v_1, \ldots, v_k) \subseteq 2^{D(v_1) \times \cdots \times D(v_n)}$ to refer to all tuples.

Example 9.2 *The first line of program d74 can be written as a constraint system as follows: V is the set of variables* $\{a, c, x\}$. *The domains of all variables are from the set of integers INT, i.e.* $D(a) = D(c) = D(x) = INT$. *Finally, the constraint* $L1(x, a, c) = \{(p_1, p_2, p_3) \mid p_1, p_2, p_3 \in INT \wedge p_1 = p_2 \cdot p_3\}$. *In this case, we might also write* $L1 = (x = a \cdot c)$.

In the above example, we expressed constraints using mathematical equations. From here on, we assume such a representation as equivalent to its relational representation and may use both of them interchangeably. That is, we will use $v_1 = v_2 \odot_2 \cdots \odot_{n-1} v_n$ as an alternative representation of a constraint $R(v_1, \ldots, v_n) = \{(p_1, \ldots, p_n) \mid p_1 = p_2 \odot_2 \cdots \odot_{n-1} p_n\}$ with operators $\odot_i$. In addition, we assume that we are also able to negate a constraint and build the disjunction of constraints for forming a new constraint, e.g. $x = 0 \vee y = a + b$ or $\neg (x = 0)$. We will use this representation for formalizing models. The underlying semantics of constraints are said to be equivalent to their mathematical or logical explanation.

A solution of a constraint system is a mapping of variables to values such that all constraints are fulfilled. A constraint is said to be fulfilled for a given mapping if there exists a tuple in the constraint relation that takes the same values as given in the variable mapping. If there is no such tuple, the constraint is not fulfilled. Formally, we define a solution as follows:

Definition 9.3 (Solution of a Constraint System)

Given a constraint system (V, D, C), *a function* σ *mapping all* $v \in V$ *to a value of their domain* $D(v)$ *is a solution of the given constraint system if* σ *fulfills all constraints, i.e.* $\forall (S, R) \in C : (\sigma(v_1), \ldots, \sigma(v_n)) \in R(v_1, \ldots, v_n)$.

Example 9.3 *Let us consider the constraint system given in Example 9.2. The mapping* $\sigma(a) = 2, \sigma(c) = 3, \sigma(x) = 6$ *is a solution, whereas* $\sigma(a) = 2, \sigma(c) = 3, \sigma(x) = 5$ *is not.*

For finite domains, finding a solution requires us to search for a variable mapping that fulfills all constraints. Basically, this requires us to generate an exponential number of mappings and to check each of them. However, in practice, there are much faster algorithms. Currently, fast constraint solvers and satisfiability modulo theories (SMT) solvers based on various underlying technologies are available, such as Z3 [7] and MINION [8]. Hence, we do not further elaborate on the algorithms behind constraint solving but assume a function **SOLVE** that takes a constraint system (V, D, C) and returns a set of solutions if there are any, or $\perp$ otherwise. If $\perp$ is returned, we know that the given constraint system cannot be solved and that there must be contradicting constraints.

To use constraint solving for debugging, we convert programs into an appropriate constraint representation. From the examples given in this section, we see how such a conversion, i.e. from assignments to constraints, can be achieved. For debugging, however, we need to make assumptions about the correctness or incorrectness of parts of the program explicit. We do this by introducing special Boolean variables ab_i that are `true` in case a certain part i of the program behaves not as expected, and `false` otherwise. Under this interpretation, ab_i stands for part i being abnormal. Program parts can be statements, expressions, or any other part of a given program that might represent a root cause for a detected misbehavior. For simplicity, we assume that we are interested only in labeling statements as correct or incorrect for a given failing test case. We further assume that these interesting parts are stored in a set *COMP*.[2] The selection of representative parts *COMP* fixes the granularity of diagnosis for MBD.

To come up with a constraint representation for diagnosis, we make use of ab_i for every statement i in *COMP*. If C_i is the constraint representation of statement i, then the diagnosis constraint representation can be formulated as A new constraint $ab_i \vee C_i$. This constraint formally states that if statement i is incorrect, the behavior of i is no longer determined by C_i. Otherwise, if ab_i is set to `false`, then C_i defines the component's behavior of the corresponding program part.

Example 9.4 *In Example 9.2, we discussed the constraint representation of the first line of program d74 to be:* $x = a \cdot c$. *For debugging purposes, we reformulate this line as:* $ab_1 \vee x = a \cdot c$.

Note that this constraint representation is not the only one possible. In Section 9.3, we discuss modeling for debugging in more detail and also introduce different modeling paradigms that have been used in the MBD literature. To define MBD formally, we assume a function $\boldsymbol{M}$ that maps a program into its constraint representation. Moreover, we also assume another function $\boldsymbol{M}_T$ for mapping the failed test case into a corresponding set of constraints. With these assumptions, we are now able to define the MBD problem formally.

Definition 9.4 (Model-Based Debugging Problem)
Let $\prod$ be a program, T be a failed test case for $\prod$, and COMP a set of program parts (e.g. statements). The MBD problem is to identify a subset Δ of COMP that, when the actual behavior is different from the expected behavior, explains the failed test case.

Refer to Definition 9.5 for more details about "explanations for a given failed test case."

From this problem definition, we obtain that we have to search for a suitable set Δ. In the following definition of explanation (or diagnosis), we formally define the notion of explanation in the case of debugging. This definition is basically an adaptation of the definition of model-based diagnosis according to Reiter [5].

Definition 9.5 (Diagnosis)
Given a MBD problem, a set $\Delta \subseteq COMP$ is a diagnosis if **SOLVE** $(\mathbf{M}((\prod) \cup \mathbf{M}_T(T) \cup \{\mathtt{ab}_i = \mathtt{true} \mid i \in \Delta\} \cup \{\mathtt{ab}_i = \mathtt{false} \mid i \in COMP\Delta\})$ *does not return* $\perp$.

In this definition, we assume that all elements of an explanation (i.e. a diagnosis) are abnormal (i.e. incorrect), whereas all other parts of the program work as expected. We rely on a constraint solver implementing the **SOLVE** function. The ∪ operator is assumed to combine constraint representations, i.e. the variables, domains, and constraint sets, which can easily be defined by building the union of these sets.

Example 9.5 *When mapping all statements of program d74 from Figure 9.1 to the constraint representation, we obtain the following set of constraints C:*

$$\left\{\begin{array}{l} \mathtt{ab_1} \vee \mathtt{x} = \mathtt{a} \cdot \mathtt{c} \\ \mathtt{ab_2} \vee \mathtt{y} = \mathtt{b} \cdot \mathtt{d} \\ \mathtt{ab_3} \vee \mathtt{z} = \mathtt{c} \cdot \mathtt{e} \\ \mathtt{ab_4} \vee \mathtt{f} = \mathtt{x} + \mathtt{y} - 2 \\ \mathtt{ab_5} \vee \mathtt{g} = \mathtt{y} + \mathtt{z} \end{array}\right\}$$

From these constraints together with the constraint representation of the failed test case, we are able to compute the following minimal diagnoses using **SOLVE**: {s1}, {s4}, {s2, s3}, {s2, s5}.

For practical applications, we are interested in finding parsimonious explanations. In case of diagnosis, we define a minimal diagnosis Δ as a diagnosis, where none of its proper subsets $\Delta' \subset \Delta$ is a diagnosis. To compute diagnoses, we must check all subsets of *COMP*. This is, of course, impractical because of the exponential number of subsets. Hence, to apply this method in practice, we need a more sophisticated approach. In the following, we introduce two algorithms for solving the debugging and also the diagnosis problem efficiently. One algorithm is based on the definition of diagnosis and the other on the alternative characterization of diagnosis using conflicts. A conflict used in diagnosis is a set of elements of *COMP* that lead to an inconsistency if they work as expected.

Definition 9.6 (Conflict)
Given a MBD problem, a set $\Gamma \subseteq COMP$ *is a conflict if* **SOLVE**$(\mathbf{M}(\prod) \cup \mathbf{M}_T(T) \cup \{\texttt{ab}_i = \texttt{false} \mid i \in \Gamma\})$ *returns* $\perp$.

Similar to minimal diagnoses, we define a set Γ to be a minimal conflict if Γ is a conflict for a given MBD problem and there is no proper subset $\Gamma' \subset \Gamma$ that is itself a conflict.

Example 9.6 *Let us consider the constraints used in Example 9.5 for obtaining diagnoses. The conflicts for this example are: {s1, s2, s4}, {s1, s3, s4, s5}.*

Obviously, there is a relationship between conflicts and diagnoses. Conflicts comprise all parts of the program that, when assumed to behave correctly, lead to a contradiction with the given test case. A diagnosis has to resolve all those conflicts. Hence, when taking out a (not necessarily different) element from every conflict, we obtain a diagnosis. This can be easily represented using the concept of hitting sets.

Definition 9.7 (Hitting Set)
Given a set of sets M, a set $h \subseteq \bigcup_{x \in M} x$ *is a hitting set if the intersection between h and every set of M is not empty, i.e.* $\forall x \in M : h \cap x \neq \emptyset$.

Diagnoses are characterized using hitting sets as follows: a (minimal) diagnosis is a hitting set of the set of all (minimal) conflicts. Reiter [5] proved this relationship and others. From the relationship, we can derive an algorithm for debugging that is based on conflicts and the hitting set computation as an alternative to computing diagnoses directly using a constraint solver.

Example 9.7 *Examine the two conflicts from Example 9.6: {s1, s2, s4}, {s1, s3, s4, s5}. Obviously, {s1} is a hitting set because 1 is an element of both conflicts. Another one is {4}, and there are also the hitting sets {s2, s3} and {s2, s5}, which originate from combining 2 from the first conflict with 3 and 5 from the second conflict set. All of these hitting sets are minimal, and they are all minimal diagnoses mentioned in Example 9.5.*

In the following subsection, we introduce both algorithms and also summarize empirical results about the runtime performance of both variants.

9.2.1 Algorithms for MBD

As discussed in the previous part of this chapter, there are two ways for computing diagnoses when using MBD, i.e. the direct method using the definition of MBD and the indirect one that is based on the definition of conflicts and hitting sets. For both algorithms, we assume that we have a set of conflicts M comprising the model of the program and the model of the failed test case. We assume further that we are only interested in diagnoses up to a certain given cardinality and not all of them. This is a reasonable assumption in practice because there are often too many diagnoses rather than none at all.

We first present an algorithm that makes use of a direct computation of diagnoses from an available constraint model. Nica and Wotawa [9] introduced **ConDiag**. Algorithm 9.1 shows the source code of **ConDiag**, which takes a constraint model M and the maximum cardinality of computed diagnoses n as inputs. The algorithm computes the diagnoses starting with cardinality 0 up to n. A diagnosis of cardinality 0 would be the empty diagnosis, which means that the model M comprising the behavior of the program and the given test case would work as expected. Note that this case should never be reached because of our initial assumption that the test case is a failed one. Within the loop, starting at line 2, diagnoses are computed. In line 3, an additional constraint specifying the cardinality of diagnoses to be searched for is introduced. This constraint is added in each iteration stating that the number of ab variables should be equivalent to the iteration variable i ranging from 0 to n.

Input: A constraint model M and the desired diagnosis cardinality n
Output: All minimal diagnoses up to the predefined cardinality n

1 Let DS be $\{\}$
2 **for** $i = 0$ to n **do**
3     $CM = M \cup \{\sum_{j=0}^{|COMP|}(ab_j = true) = i\}$
4     $S = p(\mathbf{SOLVE}(CM))$
5   **if** i is 0 **and** S is $\{\{\}\}$ **then**
6   **return** S
7   **end**
8     $DS = DS \cup S$; $M = M \cup \{\neg(C(S))\}$
9 **end**
10 **return** DS

Algorithm 9.1 **ConDiag**(M, n). *Source:* Nica and Wotawa [9]/Elsevier.

The computation of diagnoses of cardinality i occurs in line 4, where the constraint solver is called using the function **SOLVE**. This function returns all assignments of values for the ab variables of size i that satisfy the constraints, i.e. the diagnoses. These diagnoses are stored in a variable *DS*. Before starting the next iteration, we must ensure that no supersets of the previously generated diagnoses will be reported. For example, when using *ConDiag* on the constraints from Example 9.5, we would compute diagnoses {s1} and {s4} in iteration $i = 1$. When going to the next iteration, the constraint solver would also return diagnoses {s1, s2}, {s1, s3}, $\cdots$ because these supersets of {s1} would also explain the failed test case. To avoid computing supersets as diagnoses in successor iterations, we must introduce blocking clauses. A blocking clause is a constraint stating that we do not want to have assignments to corresponding `ab` variables anymore. For example, when {1} is a diagnosis, we do not want ab_1 to be set to `true` anymore. This can be expressed by stating the constraint $\neg(ab_1 = true)$ and adding this constraint to the model. In general, a blocking clause for a diagnosis $\{c_1, ..., c_k\}$ is a constraint $\neg(ab_{c_1} = true \wedge \cdots \wedge ab_{c_k} = true)$. In Algorithm 9.1, the function *C(S)* in line 9 returns the corresponding conjunction of `ab` literals for a given diagnosis and adds the blocking clause to model *M*.

The second Algorithm 9.2 for computing diagnoses is based on the computation of conflicts. Reiter [5] presented this algorithm in his seminal paper on model-based diagnosis, which Greiner et al. [10] improved later. Reiter's algorithm implements the hitting set computation and combines it with a theorem prover that returns conflicts whenever needed during execution. The algorithm can be seen as a conflict-driven search algorithm using a directed graph structure. Algorithm 2 implements the debugging algorithm **HSDiag**, which calls a hitting set algorithm. The hitting set algorithm **HittingSets** constructs a directed acyclic graph having nodes with an assigned label and a set h comprising a set that is currently checked for being a hitting set. A node label might be a conflict, or ✓, stating that h of the node is a minimal hitting set, or × indicating that the node will no longer be considered for computing minimal hitting sets. The set of all $h(v)$ where $label(v) =$ ✓ in the resulting graph constitutes the set of all minimal diagnoses.

Input: A constraint model M and the desired diagnosis cardinality n
Output: All minimal diagnoses up to the predefined cardinality n

```
Let G = HittingSets (M, n);
Let DS = { };
foreach v in nodes of G do
    if v = ✓ then
        DS = DS ∪ {h(v)}
    end
end
return DS
```

Algorithm 9.2 **HSDiag**(*M*, *n*). *Source:* Adapted from Greiner et al. [10]/Morgan Kaufmann.

In the following, we outline the underlying idea behind **HittingSets**, where we assume that we know all conflicts in advance. First, **HittingSets** starts with creating a root node with h set to the empty set and the label set to the first conflict. For each of the elements of a label of a node v, we introduce a new node v' with an edge from v to v'. The h for v' is formed by the union of h from its predecessor v and the chosen element of the label. Moreover, for each new node v', we search for the first conflict where the intersection with $h(v')$ is empty. This conflict is the new label of v'. If there is no such conflict, the label is ✓. If, during construction, we have a node with an h value that is a superset of an h value of another node labeled with ✓, we close this node and set the label to ×. Such nodes are never considered again. There are other rules for improving the construction like node reuse and pruning, where we refer the interested reader to Greiner et al. [10] for more details. To illustrate the principles of **HittingSets**, we give one example:

Example 9.8 *Let us consider the conflicts obtained from Example 9.6, i.e. {s1, s2, s4}, {s1, s3, s4, s5}. In Figure 9.2, we depict the growing acyclic directed graph for this example. In part (a), we see the initial state, where only the root node n_0 is constructed. The label of this node as well as h are empty. Note that in the figure, a node v is represented as v (label, h). When checking for the first conflict that has no intersection with $h(n_0)$, we obtain {s1, s2, s4}, which becomes the new label of n_0. In addition, we construct a new edge from n_0 to new nodes n_1 to n_1 for each element of {s1, s2, s4}. See subfigure (b) for the resulting graph, that also includes the new labels for each node. We see that h for n_1 and n_3 is also covered in the remaining conflict {s1, s3, s4, s5}. Consequently, the nodes are labeled with ✓. The label of node n_2 is not covered by the conflict; thus, it is labeled {s1, s3, s4, s5}. In subfigure (c), we see the final state of the graph. The h values for nodes labeled with ✓. are all minimal hitting sets, which are the diagnoses.*

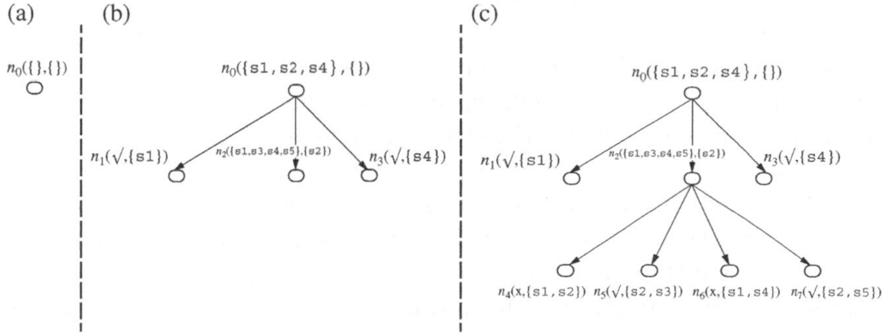

Figure 9.2 The growing acyclic directed graph for conflicts {s1, s2, s4} and {s1, s3, s4, s5}. (a) Initial state; (b) A resulting graph including the new labels for each node; and (c) Final state.

In practice, whenever we want to obtain a conflict, we must call the constraint solver. If the constraint solver returns a variable assignment, the constraint system is satisfiable, and we know that there is no conflict. Otherwise, we can extract more conflicts. In addition, it is worth mentioning that the algorithm constructs the graph in a breadth first manner. Hence, we are able to stop the computation at any level we want, thus only computing diagnoses up to a certain cardinality. The root note stands for cardinality 0, its successors for 1, and so forth.

Nica et al. [11] compared various implementations of the direct algorithm based on constraint and SAT solving with the hitting set-based algorithm for computing diagnoses. Both variants seem to be applicable for diagnosis and also for larger systems comprising up to several thousand components. Their experiments rely on circuits using only Boolean values; therefore, the results are not directly comparable to the case of MBD. From [11], we conclude that current constraint solvers are equally as fast as SAT solvers for computing diagnoses.

9.3 Modeling for MBD

In Section 9.2, we introduced functions **M** and $\mathbf{M}_T$ for mapping programs and test cases to their corresponding constraint representation that are subsequently used to derive diagnoses according to *Definition 9.5*. In general, we might not restrict the underlying model representation to constraints. It may be possible to use other formal representations such as first-order logic and propositional logic. There is only one thing that must be fulfilled, i.e. the model language has to support a reasoning mechanism that allows us to derive whether the model of the program together with the model of the failed test case and the underlying assumptions about the correctness of certain program parts are consistent. However, for simplicity and providing a unifying view on MBD, we rely on constraint representation and constraint solvers as the underlying reasoning mechanism.

In the following, we discuss modeling for MBD in more detail. In particular, we present two models of programs. The first is similar to the one we used in the introduction, capturing the behavior of programs in terms of associating values to variables. Here, we clarify questions of how to handle conditional statements, loops, and other control structures occurring in ordinary imperative programming languages. The second type of model represents the structure and the behavior of a program in a very abstract sense. Here, we only consider values of variables to be correct or not correct and allow for propagating only correct values through a program. Why are there two representations? A more abstract representation allows the computing diagnosis to be much faster than a representation that is close to the program's behavior. Hence, we are able to debug much larger programs using the abstract model. However, the diagnosis accuracy in terms of the number of computed diagnosis candidates is not that good for abstract models. Hence, for smaller programs, we may be interested in using the sophisticated model for debugging.

For both models, we will restrict our efforts to debugging at the statement level. Hence, the outcome of diagnosis are statements that are potentially leading to a faulty behavior. Note that this is not a limitation of MBD in general. In principle, the ab variables used to state incorrectness can also be assigned to expressions and other parts of a program.

9.3.1 The Value-Based Model

Since the beginning of research in MBD, value-based models, i.e. models representing the program's behavior as close as possible, have been the focus of attention. Object-oriented languages like Java various models have been suggested [12, 13] and mainly rely on a logical representation. In this subsection, we follow a more recent approach discussed in [14–16]. In the following discussion, we restrict ourselves to imperative programs comprising assignment statements, `while` statements, and `if-then-else` statements. Other statements like `do-while` statements, case statements, and recursive functions or methods can be similarly modeled. For the handling of arrays, we refer to other work such as [16] and [17].

The following modeling approach relies on the approach discussed in [16] and defines the modeling function **M**. The modeling process comprises three parts. First, the program is converted to a loop-free version. This conversion relies on unrolling loops up to a predefined depth, which is not really a restriction because for debugging we usually know the number of necessary iterations for a given test case. For simplicity, we ignore infinite loops as causes of a failure. Second, the loop-free program is converted into its static single assignment form (SSA) [18], where every variable is only defined once. Finally, the resulting SSA form is converted into a constraint representation. We now discuss these three steps in detail.

Step 1. Loop Elimination [16]

For eliminate all loops, we need a parameter that captures the maximum number of iterations to be considered. Let $n_I > 0$ be this parameter. We define loop-elimination recursively as follows:

$$\mathit{LoopFree}(\texttt{while}\ C\{B\}, n_I) = \begin{cases} \texttt{if}\ C\{B\ \mathit{LoopFree}(\texttt{while}\ C\{B\}, n_I - 1)\} & \text{if } n_I > 0 \\ \texttt{if}\ C\{\texttt{too\_many\_its} = \texttt{true};\} & \text{otherwise} \end{cases}$$

In this recursive function, each loop is converted to nested `if`-statements. In addition, we introduce a fresh variable, `too_many_its`, which is set to `true` if the considered number of iterations n_I is not large enough. For this purpose, we would add `too_many_its = false` to the input and the expected output of the program to be debugged. If we did not select enough iterations to be considered for debugging, the diagnosis will find `too_many_its` to be `true`, indicating that n_I has to be increased.

Let us illustrate the loop-unrolling using the following example:

Example 9.9 [16].

Consider the following program:

```
s1  x = in + 3;
s2  while (x > 5) {
s3          x = x - 1;
s4  }
```

When unrolling this program using $n_I = 2$*, we obtain the following loop-free program:*

```
s1  x=in+3;
s2  if(x>5){
s3      x=x-1;
s4      if(x>5){
s5          x=x-1;
s6            if(x>5){
s7                too_many_its=true;
s8          }
s9      }
s10 }
```

In this example, we see that the variable x is defined three times, i.e. in lines s1, s3, and s5. Thus, the SSA property does not hold.

Step 2. SSA Conversion

The SSA form is an intermediate representation of a program where the property that no two variable definitions assign to the same variable holds. This property of the SSA form facilitates direct conversion into its constraint representation. We briefly discuss the different steps of the SSA conversion, where we only need to consider `if-then-else` statements and assignments.

- For convert assignments, we add an index to each program variable. This index value is set to 0 at the beginning of the program. Whenever a variable is redefined in the program, i.e. it occurs at the left side of an assignment, the index value is increased by 1. This ensures that the SSA property holds. What we must do during the conversion is to store the current index value of variables, and in the case of an `if-then-else` statement, we use different index values in both branches. For more details, we refer to [14].
- For convert conditional statements, we split conversion into three sub-steps: (i) the entry condition is saved in an auxiliary variable, (ii) each assignment statement is converted following the previously stated rule, and (iii) for each conditional statement and defined variable v in its body (i.e. either *then* or *else*), we introduce the following evaluation function [16]:

$$\Phi(v_{then}, v_{else}, cond) = \begin{cases} v_{then}, & \text{if } cond = true \\ v_{else}, & \text{otherwise} \end{cases}$$

which returns the statement conditional-exit value, e.g. $v_{after} = \Phi(v_{then}, v_{else}, cond)$. Note that in this definition, the indices *then* and *else* are the largest indices for variable v occurring in the `then` and `else` block, respectively. The *after* index is the maximum value of `then` and `else` plus 1. This is also the index used for v after converting the conditional statement. It is also worth noting that in case of a nested `if-then-else` statement, the *cond* conditions must be adapted to respect the paths. We explain this using the next example.

Example 9.10 *Let us convert the loop-free program from Example 9.9 into its SSA form, as follows:*

s1 $x\_1 = in\_0 + 3;$

s2 $x\_2 = x\_1 - 1;$

s3 $x\_3 = x\_2 - 1;$

s4 $too\_many\_its\_1 = true;$

s5 $cond\_1 = x\_1 > 5;$

s6 $cond\_2 = cond\_1 \ AND \ x\_2 > 5;$

s7 $cond\_3 = cond\_2 \ AND \ x\_3 > 5;$

s8 $x\_4 = PHI(x\_2, x\_1, cond\_1);$

s9 $x\_5 = PHI(x\_3, x\_4, cond\_2);$

s10 $too\_many\_its\_2 = PHI(too\_many\_its\_1, too\_many\_its\_0, cond\_3)$

In this example, we see that the conditions used in the Φ function, which we represent as a function called `PHI` *in the program, must be adapted according to the path of the nested* `if-then-else` *statements.*

The SSA program comprises only assignment statements and a special function `PHI`, which can be easily represented using constraints. Hence, a conversion of SSA programs into their constraint representation is straightforward.

Step 3. Constraint Conversion

The final step in the conversion process takes SSA programs and converts them into an equivalent constraint representation. To encode the constraint representation as a debugging problem, we introduce the special Boolean variable ab_S for a statement with line number S, assuming that each assignment has a uniquely assigned number. Note that we do not introduce such a variable ab for assignments comprising the PHI function, because we assume that the function itself cannot be faulty. The conversion itself uses the following *conv* function, which is applied to all statements [16]:

$$conv(C_S) = \begin{cases} ab_S \vee C_S, & \text{if } C_S \text{ does not contain PHI} \\ C_S, & \text{otherwise} \end{cases}$$

For simplicity, we assume that the statements C_S can be directly represented as a constraint. Note that in the constraint representation, the assignment operator = is interpreted as an equality operator. For example, the behavior of statement s3 in Example 9.10 is represented in equational form as "$x_3 = x_2 - 1$" instead of "x_3 = x_2 – 1".

Example 9.11 *Let us continue Example 9.10. The constraint representation of the SSA program comprises the following constraints:*

$$ab_1 \vee (x_1 = in_0 + 3)$$
$$ab_2 \vee (x_2 = x_1 - 1)$$
$$ab_3 \vee (x_3 = x_2 - 1)$$
$$ab_4 \vee (too\_many\_its_1 = true)$$
$$ab_5 \vee (cond_1 = x_1 > 5)$$
$$ab_6 \vee (cond_2 = cond_1 \wedge x_2 > 5)$$
$$ab_7 \vee (cond_3 = cond_2 \wedge x_3 > 5)$$
$$x_4 = PHI(x_2,\ x_1,\ cond_1);$$
$$x_5 = PHI(x_3,\ x_4,\ cond_2);$$
$$too\_many\_its_2 = PHI(too\_many\_its_1,\ too\_many\_its_0,\ cond_3)$$

From the last example, we see that there is an ab_i for every statement i in the *SSA* form of the program ignoring the *PHI* statements. The ab_i variables have to be mapped to the statements of the original program after diagnosis, which can be done by keeping track of this mapping during conversion. Moreover, the number of ab_i variables can be reduced by using only one variable ab^O_i per statement in the original program. The ab_i in Example 9.11 can be mapped as follows: $\{ab_1\} \mapsto ab^O_1$,$\{ab_2, ab_3\} \mapsto ab^O_3$,$\{ab_5, ab_6, ab_7\} \mapsto ab^O_2$. Only for the variable `too_many_its`, there is no such mapping possible, because this variable is not used in the original program.

Steps 1–3 implement the function **M**. What is missing is a definition of the function $\mathbf{M}_T$ that maps a test case to its constraint representation. Given a test case $T = (\sum_{IN}, \sum_{O})$. all values of input variables are assigned to zero-indexed variables in the SSA representation before executing the program. All input variables in the constraint representation include the equation $\mathtt{in}_0 = \sum_{IN}(\mathtt{in})$. In the case of outputs, the conversion has to consider the maximum index of a certain variable. This index can be obtained from the conversion to SSA form. We assume there is a function μ mapping variables to their largest index. Hence, the converted expected output includes the equation $\mathtt{out}_{\mu(\mathtt{out})} = \sum_{O}(\mathtt{out})$ for output variables $\mathtt{out}$ used in O.

9.3.2 The Dependency-Based Model

In contrast to the value-based model, where concrete variable values and their constraints derived from statements are used, the dependency-based model only considers the propagation of information about the correctness of variable values through the program. The underlying idea is best described using a program. Let us consider the program given in Figure 9.1. The statement in line s1, $\mathtt{x = a * c}$, states how to assign a new value for variable $\mathtt{x}$ using the values of variables $\mathtt{a}$ and $\mathtt{c}$. If either $\mathtt{a}$ or $\mathtt{c}$ have incorrect values, then the value of $\mathtt{x}$ may also be incorrect. The same would happen if assuming statement s1 to be incorrect, i.e. comprising the bug. Hence, from this perspective, we can define a simplified model in which the value of an assigned variable can only be considered to be correct if the statement is correct, and all of its input values are correct too. Formally, we can express this representation of a statement S in logic as follows: $ab_S \vee (ok(in_1^S) \wedge \ldots \wedge ok(in_K^S) \rightarrow ok(out^S))$ and, where out^S is the output variable of statement S, and the predicate ok denotes correctness of the variable values.

Friedrich et al. [19] introduced this idea for debugging large VHDL programs. Later on, Wotawa [20] discussed the relationship with static program slicing [21] in detail. In this section, we summarize the conversion of programs and failed test cases into their dependency-based model. The main questions to be answered are the definitions of inputs and outputs for statements and how to deal with loops and conditional statements. For the conversion into dependency-based models, we consider data and control dependencies. Two statements are said to be data dependent if there is a variable defined in one statement that is referenced in a subsequent statement in the program. A statement that is in a sub-block of another statement, such as in the then-branch of a conditional statement or in the block of a `while` statement, is control dependent on the condition of the statement. Data and control dependencies are used, for example, to derive static program slices [21].

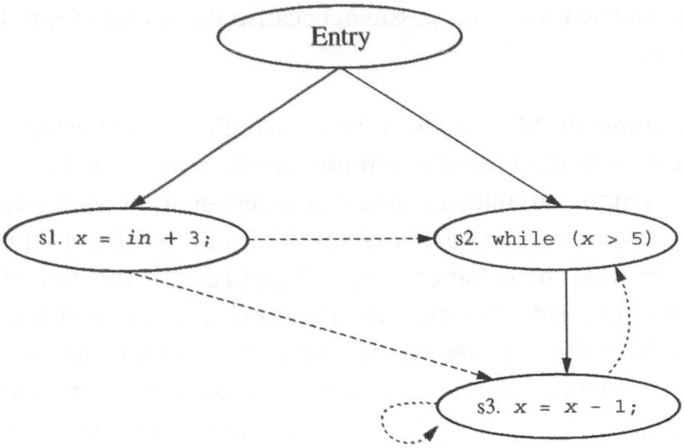

Figure 9.3 The program dependence graph for the program given in Example 9.9.

In the conversion function **M**, we follow the underlying concept described in [20]. There, the dependency information as well as information about input and outputs of statements are extracted from the program dependence graph [22]. A program dependence graph for a program represents the blocks and sub-blocks occurring in a program as well as the data dependence.

Blocks and sub-blocks are arranged hierarchically starting with a special root node ENTRY. Nodes are connected by a directed edge if one node is in a sub-block of another block, or if there is a data dependence. Let us look at an example.

Example 9.12 *In Figure 9.3, we depict the program dependence graph for the program given in Example 9.9. There are block–sub-block relations (solid edges) and data dependencies (dotted edges). The program dependence graph in this case is cyclic because the variable x is defined in statement s3 and also referenced in statement s2.*

Using this example, we can now easily define the concept of inputs and outputs. All variables that are referenced in a statement are considered inputs for that statement. Every variable that is defined in a statement is an output of that statement. If there is an edge between node *a* (other than ENTRY) and node *b* representing a block–sub-block relation, node *a* is said to be an input for node *b*. The latter rule captures the control dependencies in the program.

Example 9.13 *Let us continue Example 9.12. Node 2 is an input of node 3 because its evaluation has an influence on the computation of statement s3. If we applied the initial idea behind the dependency-based model directly, we would obtain the following rules:*

$$ab_1 \vee (ok(in) \rightarrow ok(x))$$
$$ab_2 \vee (ok(x) \rightarrow ok(2))$$
$$ab_3 \vee (ok(x) \wedge ok(2) \rightarrow ok(x))$$

When assuming that the input in is correct, i.e. ok(in), *and that the output* x *is wrong, i.e.* ¬ok(x), *we are only able to derive that statement s1 must be faulty (if we consider only faults manifesting in a single statement). However, statements s2 and s3 can be responsible as well. The reason for our inability to attribute fault to statements s2 and s3 is that there are some cycles in the graph and also as a consequence of the rules. Hence, we must remove these cycles before deriving the model from the program dependence graph.*

To solve the mentioned challenges in the last example, we make use of two ideas. The first considers cycles in the program dependence graph and their consequences. For example, if two nodes are in a cycle, the output of one node influences the input of the other node, and vice versa. Hence, we cannot distinguish those nodes for diagnosis anymore without breaking the cycle. If we only know the inputs and the expected outputs of a program, this is not possible. Hence, we can treat them as one node. The graph-theoretic concept behind coming up with a super node comprising all nodes depending on each other is strongly connected components (SCCs), which can be computed in polynomial time. Hence, the first step is to compute a graph comprising only SCCs, which is necessarily acyclic. The second idea is that we must distinguish a definition of a variable from its redefinition later on in the program. This is similar to the SSA conversion, which allows us to distinguish between different "versions" of a variable. Hence, we again will make use of the concept and add an index to all variables where the value reflects the number of redefinitions in the source code. For further details and formal definitions, we refer to [20]. Instead, we show the conversion into a dependency-based model using our example.

Example 9.14 *After applying the SCC computation on the original graph from Figure 9.3, we obtain a new program dependence graph depicted in Figure 9.4. This graph is acyclic and comprises two nodes. Again, we can use the same definition of inputs and outputs as before. Hence, the input of the first component SCC_1 comprising only statement s1 is the variable* in. *The output is* x *for SCC_1. After adding indices for variables, we are able to derive the following dependency-based model [20]:*

$$ab_{SCC_1} \wedge (ok(in_0) \rightarrow ok(x_1))$$
$$ab_{SCC_2} \wedge (ok(x_1) \rightarrow ok(x_2))$$

For a test case stating in *to be correct and* x *incorrect after executing the program, we add the constraints* $ok(in_0)$ *and* $\neg ok(x_2)$. *The model together with these*

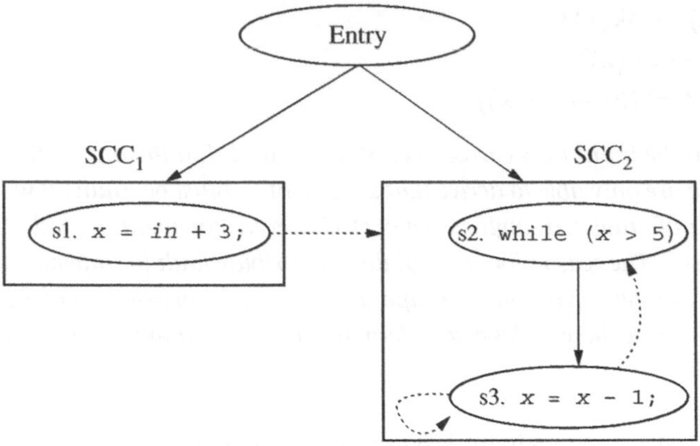

Figure 9.4 The SCC of the program dependence graph from Figure 9.3.

constraints allows us to derive either SCC_1 or SCC_2 to be the reason for the fault. Because of the fact that SCC_1 has the corresponding statement s1 and SCC_2 the two statements s2 and s3, we can conclude — in this case — that all statements might cause the misbehavior.

Let us now summarize the findings and the overall modeling process for a program Π and a test case T, which comprises three steps:

Construct a program dependence graph *PDG* for the program Π and apply the SCC algorithm to obtain an acyclic graph PDG_{SCC}.

For each node i in PDG_{SCC}, add the constraint $\mathtt{ab}_i \vee (\bigwedge_{in \in inputs(i)} \mathtt{ok(in)} \wedge \bigwedge_{out \in outputs(i)} \mathtt{ok(out)})$ to the model M.

For the test case $T = (\Sigma_{IN}, \Sigma_O)$, we will do the following:

a) For all input variables `in`, add the constraint $\mathtt{ok(in)} = \mathtt{true}$ to the test case model $\mathbf{M}_T$.
b) For all output variables `out`, check whether the program execution leads to a different value than $\Sigma_{OUT}(\mathtt{out})$. If yes, add $\mathtt{ok(out)} = \mathtt{false}$ to $\mathbf{M}_T$. Otherwise, add $\mathtt{ok(out)} = \mathtt{true}$ to $\mathbf{M}_T$.

Note that in the above model extraction algorithm, we obtain a model that is capable of locating faults at the level of SCCs. If we want to map the SCCs to statements, we must use a function returning all statements stored in an SCC. The dependency-based model as described in this subsection only propagates correct values from inputs to outputs. However, in some cases, it is also possible to derive the correctness of inputs if we know the output to be correct. When using such a model, the diagnosis accuracy can be improved. Unfortunately, such models are not generally applicable. More information about improved dependency-based models can be obtained from [23].

9.3.3 Approximation Models for Debugging

The value- and dependency-based approaches to creating models for debugging can be regarded as two approaches on opposite ends of a spectrum of possible models. While the value-based model captures the exact effects of each element in a program, the dependency-based model abstracts away the details of the actual calculation and reasons about the correctness of inputs and outputs of each component. Other debugging models can be created based on abstractions and approximations of the actual program behavior at runtime by incorporating elements of program analysis and assumptions about potential deficiencies in the program into the model construction process. We can obtain diagnostic models that can diagnose errors in programs more precisely, that is, the resulting set of possible explanations can be reduced and the user's attention can be focused on a smaller set of potential root causes of the failed tests. Moreover, abstractions can help construct efficient debugging models for large programs.

To see how abstraction can improve diagnostic outcomes, let us revisit the example given in Figure 9.3 and consider test cases where $\Sigma_{IN}(\mathtt{in}) = 3$ and $\Sigma_O(x) = 6$. For this test case, the program terminates with $x = 5$; hence, the test fails. The value-based model and the dependency-based model identify $\{ab_1\}$, $\{ab_2\}$, and $\{ab_3\}$ as possible explanations (after mapping from diagnostic components to statements). However, statement s1 cannot actually explain this failure: if variable x were assigned a different (higher) value in statement s1, the subsequent `while` loop would decrement its value such that $x \leq 5$. However, this outcome is incompatible with Σ_O as no value of x can satisfy both environments. Therefore, $\{ab_1\}$ is not an explanation. The reason that the value-based and the dependency-based model cannot rule out this spurious explanation is that these models cannot infer assertions about intermediate and final program states, such as the inequality for output x in our example. The debugging models cannot derive a conflict between the program's behavior and the test case, and the explanation is retained as a candidate. Many spurious explanations may be obtained for programs where the control and data flow within the program at runtime cannot be determined with sufficient precision in advance, for example in programs that allocate dynamic data structures, manipulate arrays, or use polymorphism.

Fortunately, the framework of MBD can accommodate a variety of different modeling methods that can address the difficult aspects of a program. Stumptner and Mayer [17, 24] introduced the use of program abstraction for handling loops and recursive functions instead of loop unrolling. In the following, we will briefly illustrate the method that is based on abstract interpretation [25], a technique commonly used in formal program analysis to infer abstract properties of programs.

The general approach of abstract interpretation is to define the effects of each statement in the program using an abstract mathematical space that enables us to retain selected properties if the precise effect cannot be inferred. By using an abstraction, information about the possible executions of a program can be calculated automatically and efficiently. These techniques are commonly employed in compilers and static analysis tools for bug finding. Moreover, calculation can be performed in a forward direction (in the same way as the program executes) and in a backward direction from the anticipated correct result environment Σ_O given in the test case toward the start of the program. This allows us to use the technique as an abstract consistency checker, akin to the constraint satisfaction procedure underlying the value- and dependency-based models.

To see how abstract interpretation can be employed for MBD, let us consider the interval abstract domain as an example. In this domain, the value of each variable is modeled as an interval `[u, v]`. The bounds u and v for this interval are calculated based on the program structure and the initial and final environments given by a test case. Any value in this interval is a possible value of the associated variable. The effects of each program statement are expressed using equations over intervals that relate the variables (interval-) values at the point before the statement to the values after the statement has executed [17, 25]. Variables defined at different statements in the program (or equations representing statements) are distinguished by a unique index.

Example 9.15 *The effects of the assignment statement s1.* `x = in + 3` *can be expressed in SSA form as* x_1 = `in + [3, 3]`*, where the latter* `in` *represents the interval value of the former variable* `in` *before executing the assignment statement, and* x_1 represents *the value of* `x` *after the assignment. The* `while` *loop statement requires multiple equations, as we shall distinguish the two possible outcomes of the expression and account for the fact that the loop head can be reached via two control flow paths: one from statement s1 and one from statement s3. This merging of control flow paths can be expressed as an equation* $x_2 = x_1 \nabla x_4$*, where* x_1 *and* x_4 *denote the versions of the variable* `x` *after statement s1 and s4, respectively, and the* ∇ *operator represents the "widening" operator that merges the two interval values and may discard some information to ensure that our analysis terminates. The equations* $x_3 = [\![x_2 > 5]\!]$ *and* $x_5 = [\![x_2 \leq 5]\!]$ *capture the two outcomes of the loop's conditional expression. The former equation corresponds to the case where the loop body is entered and the value of* `x` *is known to exceed 5. The latter equation corresponds to the case when the loop terminates and the value of* `x` *is known to be 5 or less. In each case, the interval is restricted to the values that satisfy the conditional expression* *associated with the control flow path. The equation for statement s3 is* $x_4 = x_3 - [1, 1]$. *The overall equation system representing the program is:*

$$s_1\ x_1 = in + [3, 3]$$
$$s_{2a}\ x_2 = x_1 \nabla x_4$$
$$s_{2b}\ x_3 = [x_2 > 5]$$
$$s_3\ x_4 = x_3 - [1, 1]$$
$$s_{2c}\ x_5 = [x_2 \leq 5]$$

The value of x_5 *represents the final value of x, which is compared with* Σ_O.

If cycles in the control flow occur, a fixed-point calculation is carried out to infer the environment before and after the cyclic construct. Abstract interpretation theory ensures that this calculation can be carried out efficiently while retaining precision as much as possible [25]. For example, the `while` loop in Figure 9.3 may perform any number of iterations. Although we may not know the exact value of the x_5 after the loop, we can infer that $x_5 \in [-2^{63}, 5]$ (assuming that x is a 64-bit integer). We can derive this result even if the value of x before the loop is unknown. As we already know, this result conflicts with the desired output Σ_O.

To obtain a complete diagnostic model, fault assumptions are introduced and associated with the equations. As before, we use literals ab_i and $\neg ab_i$ to denote that component i in the program is and is not assumed faulty, respectively. If $\neg ab_i$ is assumed, the equations corresponding to the program expressions associated with component i are constructed as above. Otherwise, if ab_i is assumed, a different set of equations is used that reflects the effects of the faulty component.

Different equations can be used to distinguish different faults that may arise in the program. Here, we will consider a simple case where the variables that are assigned are the same as in the given program, and the assigned values may differ from the ones calculated in the given program. Mayer [17] discusses equations for other statements under different fault assumptions, and methods to extract conflicts from the equation systems.

Example 9.16 *If statement s1 was assumed to be faulty, that is,* $ab_1 = \texttt{true}$, *then the constraint equation for* x_1 *above would be replaced with a more general one*

$$1'.\ x_1 = [-2^{63}, -2^{63} - 1]$$

which allows any value for variable x_1 (again assuming that x is a 64-bit integer).

From the above, we can conclude that even if statement s1 is assumed to assign a different value to x, the program is unable to pass the test case, as $x_5 \leq 5$ due to constraint statement s_{2c}. We can conclude that some statement in the loop must be incorrect, and statement s1 (the initialization of x) cannot alone explain the failed test.

Moreover, we can deduce that a fault in statement s3 (the decrement of `x` in the loop) cannot be the sole cause of the failure either. This leaves us with the `while` loop itself as the only (single-fault) candidate for investigation.

The construction of a debugging model using the abstract interpretation method deviates slightly from the other models discussed in this chapter, as no complete model of the program is constructed a priori. Instead, a model tailored to the test case and *fault assumptions* under consideration is created such that abstract interpretation is applied only to those program parts where some values are abstract or statements are assumed to be faulty, whereas the assumed-correct program sections where all values are known precisely are executed directly. Hence, approximations are used only when necessary. Moreover, iterating forward and backward inferences over the approximations can yield increased precision [17].

The interval-based model is only an example of an abstraction-based model. Many abstractions developed for program analysis can be employed for debugging purposes to create a model that can diagnose relevant bugs efficiently. Mayer et al. [26] compared a selection of abstraction-based models with those introduced earlier in this chapter and found that the abstract-interpretation-based method can rule out some of the spurious explanations that the value- and the dependency-based models cannot eliminate. Moreover, it was shown empirically that the abstraction-based model is more efficient for complex programs, where arrays and polymorphic programming constructs are used. The dependency-based model remains the fastest, but it was found to be less precise than the other models. Automated methods for selecting an appropriate model and for tuning the debugging and inference mechanisms to the program and test case(s) under consideration remain the subject of future research.

9.3.4 Other Modeling Approaches

The modeling approaches described previously are for extracting models automatically from the source code using techniques from program analysis. In contrast, Liver [27] discussed the use of manually generated models for diagnosing software systems. There, the argumentation was that the models should represent the correct and expected behavior, which is not the case when using automated model extraction because the latter uses a model of the faulty program. However, in practice, it seems that automated model extraction is more appropriate because it does not require additional input from the user apart from the source code and the failed test case.

Ceballos et al. [28] combined pre- and post-conditions of function with value-based models to show that such information can substantially improve diagnosis. In particular, recursive functions may be handled much more easily as unrolling or recursion is not required. This holds also for loops if loop invariants are available.

Wotawa [29] combined MBD with program mutations to not only specify the behavior of a program but also faults, thus enabling the correction of programs.

Wotawa [30] discussed the use of abstract models considering deviations of values. For example, during debugging, one may not be able to say that the value of a variable should be exactly 10 000, but one may be able to state that the calculated value is too high. Such deviations can be used for diagnosis. As shown in [30], deviation models may have a similar diagnosis accuracy as value-based models but require only a fraction of the time. The empirical results presented in Wotawa's paper are not from program debugging. However, this method has potential for application in program debugging as well. Future research is needed to evaluate the usefulness of deviation models for MBD.

9.4 Application Areas

This section gives an overview of MBD application areas and highlights some of the characteristics of the individual languages that must be considered. MBD can be used to debug programs written in all types of programming languages, ranging from logic over functional [31] to imperative and object-oriented languages. Even programs written in Verilog, VHDL, or other hardware description languages can be debugged using MBD [19, 32–34]. Some of the presented solutions are based on dependency models, while others are based on value-based models as described in this chapter.

Console et al. [35] introduced MBD for logic programs. There, the authors argued that MBD improves the more traditional algorithmic debugging approach of Shapiro [36]. Bond et al. [37, 38] identified a problem in Console et al.'s work and proposed an improved algorithm for MBD for logic programs. More recent research of MBD in declarative languages includes Felfernig et al.'s work on configuration knowledge bases [39] and Shchekotykhin et al.'s work on ontologies [40].

Mateis et al. [41, 42] and Mayer et al. [12, 13] proposed MBD for debugging Java programs. MBD for imperative and object-oriented programming languages has two peculiarities when building the model: (i) loops must be unrolled and (ii) variables need unique names for each value they are assigned. Loops can be unrolled by using the execution trace of the failed test case as a basis for the model instead of the source code. In imperative languages, a variable usually is assigned different values during the execution of the program. In a constraint system, a variable can only have one value. This issue can be solved by using the SSA form: each variable has a unique index counter. Whenever the variable is referenced, it is referenced using its current index; whenever the variable is assigned a new value, its index counter is increased.

More recent research has been focused on applying MBD to workflow processes [43] and, in particular, to service-oriented architectures (SOAs) [44]. The particularity of this application area is that the behavior of the individual services must be integrated into the model. However, services are often black boxes: the indented behavior of the service is known, but its source code is not available. This issue can be solved by modeling the individual services as look-up tables: for a certain input, the service returns a certain output. The interaction of the different services can be modeled similar to programs written in imperative languages.

9.5 Hybrid Approaches

While MBD techniques are very appealing because of their diagnostic accuracy, their computational complexity remains a major limitation. For this reason, several researchers have proposed to combine MBD with other debugging techniques, e.g. with SFL. Abreu [36, 37] and Hofer [45] are three of these techniques combining MBD and SFL.

Abreu [46] refines the spectrum-based ranking by means of MBD. In the first step, the spectrum-based ranking is computed. In the second step, MBD is used to filter out those statements that cannot explain the observed misbehavior. The remaining statements are presented to the user according to their SFL rank. If the fault is not found, a best-first search is employed in the third step that traverses the program dependency graph.

Abreu [47] makes use of Bayesian statistics: in this approach, the diagnoses are derived from the spectra information of the failed test cases by using the Staccato algorithm. Afterward, a fault probability for each diagnosis is computed by means of Bayes' rule. Finally, the diagnoses are ranked according to their fault probabilities and presented to the user.

Hofer [45] is short for spectrum-enhanced dynamic slicing and works as follows: first, the slices of the failed test cases are computed, and the diagnoses are derived from these slices by means of Reiter's hitting set algorithm [5]. Similar to Abreu, a fault probability for each diagnosis is computed afterward so that the diagnoses can be ranked. However, Hofer computes these fault probabilities using the normalized similarity coefficients of the statements contained in the diagnoses.

An empirical study [48] has shown that Abreu and Hofer outperform their basic approaches most of the time. Abreu has the best fault localization capabilities, but it is limited to small programs because of its computational complexity. For larger spreadsheets, Abreu and Hofer are good alternatives.

In addition to combining MBD with SFL, other hybrid approaches are possible, including using program slicing [21] together with MBD. Slicing would be used to reduce the search space for diagnosis, which is very similar to SFL. Because of the fact that dependency models have equal capabilities for identifying root causes than static program slices [29], we are able to use static slices directly for MBD. In particular, it can be proven that a static program slice for a faulty output variable is equivalent to a conflict when using the dependency-based model. Hence, when using slices together with the hitting set algorithm, we are able to compute diagnosis very efficiently. Wotawa [49] outlined the basic idea. Some experimental results can be obtained from Jehan [50]. Another idea would be to combine MBD with program mutations, aiming first at identifying diagnosis candidates and then searching for potential replacements. This would improve the overall diagnosis process and also allow for the repair programs. Further research is needed in order to demonstrate the usefulness of such hybrid approaches in practice.

9.6 Conclusion

MBD requires the source code and a failed test case for computing the root causes for the failures. The underlying technique makes use of a model of the program and can be automatically compiled from the source code. There are many different types of models. Some are based on concrete values and represent programs as set of constraints. Others make use of abstraction, such as only considering the correctness or incorrectness of variable values. In this chapter, we discuss the underlying foundations and algorithms and also some of the used models. More details can be obtained from the related literature.

MBD is a general technique with good diagnostic accuracy, but it requires more runtime than other approaches. When combining MBD with other techniques or using models of different abstraction, efficient debugging procedures can be obtained that combine the advantages of scalable lightweight models with precise inferences with respect to defined fault assumptions delivered by detailed models. MBD approaches are attractive particularly in semi-interactive scenarios, where the set of diagnoses can be refined incrementally by posing questions to the user. Moreover, explanations of the test case failures can be obtained.

MBD procedures offer a sound and principled reasoning framework in which domain-specific knowledge, such as focusing heuristics, fault modes, and fault probabilities, can be integrated and exploited. The techniques presented in this chapter can readily be employed for debugging of programs, computation systems such as spreadsheets (see Chapter 11 in this book), inferences in knowledge-based systems, and partially observed workflow processes.

Notes

1 In this chapter, we use "bug" and "fault" interchangeably. We also use "program" and "software" interchangeably.

2 In the original definition of model-based diagnosis (see [5]), *COMP* is used as a set of components relevant for diagnosis. We decided to use the same name to maintain a close correspondence between the original diagnosis definition and its use in debugging.

References

1 Davis, R., Shrobe, H., Hamscher, W. et al. (1995). Diagnosis based on description of structure and function. In: *Computation & Intelligence: Collected Readings*, (ed. G. F. Luger), 623–634. Menlo Park, CA, USA: American Association for Artificial Intelligence ISBN 0-262-62101-0. http://dl.acm.org/citation.cfm?id=216000.216039.

2 Davis, R. (1984). Diagnostic reasoning based on structure and behavior. *Artificial Intelligence* 24 (1): 347–410. ISSN 0004-3702. http://www.sciencedirect.com/science/article/pii/0004370284900420.

3 De Kleer, J., Mackworth, A.K., and Reiter, R. (1992). Characterizing diagnoses and systems. *Artificial Intelligence* 56 (2–3): 197–222. ISSN 0004-3702. http://www.sciencedirect.com/science/article/pii/000437029290027U.

4 De Kleer, J. and Williams, B.C. (1987). Diagnosing multiple faults. *Artificial Intelligence*, 32 (1): 97–130. ISSN 0004-3702. http://www.sciencedirect.com/science/article/pii/0004370287900634.

5 Reiter, R. (1987). A theory of diagnosis from first principles. *Artificial Intelligence* 32 (1): 57–95. ISSN 0004-3702. http://www.sciencedirect.com/science/article/pii/0004370287900622.

6 Dechter, R. (2003). *Constraint Processing*. Morgan Kaufmann. ISBN 1558608907.

7 de Moura, L. and Bjørner, N. (2008). Z3: an efficient SMT solver. In: *Proceedings of the International Conference on Tools and Algorithms for the Construction and Analysis of Systems*. Budapest, Hungary (29 March to 6 April 2008), 337–340. Springer. https://link.springer.com/content/pdf/10.1007/978-3-540-78800-3.pdf.

8 Gent, I.P., Jefferson, C., and Miguel, I. (2006). MINION: a fast, scalable, constraint solver. *Proceedings of the 17th European Conference on Artificial Intelligence (ECAI '06)*, Riva Del Garda, Italy (29 August to 1 September 2006), 98–102. IOS Press. ISBN 1-58603-642-4. http://dl.acm.org/citation.cfm?id=1567016.1567043.

9 Nica, I. and Wotawa, F. (2012). ConDiag computing minimal diagnoses using a constraint solver. *Proceedings of the International Workshop on Principles of Model-based Techniques for Software Fault Localization Diagnosis*, Great Malvern, UK (31 July to 3 August 2012), 185–191.

10 Greiner, R., Smith, B.A. and Wilkerson, R.W. (1989). A correction to the algorithm in Reiter's theory of diagnosis. *Artificial Intelligence*, 41 (1): 79–88.

11 Nica, I., Pill, I., Quaritsch, T., and Wotawa, F. (2013). The route to success - a performance comparison of diagnosis algorithms. *Proceedings of the 23rd International Joint Conference on Artificial Intelligence (IJCAI '13)*, Beijing, China (3–9 August 2013), 1039–1045. AAAI Press. http://www.aaai.org/ocs/index.php/IJCAI/IJCAI13/paper/view/6597.

12 Mayer, W., Stumptner, M., Wieland, D., and Wotawa, F. (2002). Can AI help to improve debugging substantially? Debugging experiences with value-based models. *Proceedings of the 15th European Conference on Artificial Intelligence (ECAI '02)*, Lyon, France (21–26 July 2002), 417–421. IOS Press. ISBN 978-1-58603-257-9. http://dl.acm.org/citation.cfm?id=3000905.3000994.

13 Mayer, W., Stumptner, M., Wieland, D., and Wotawa, F. (2002). Towards an integrated debugging environment. *Proceedings of the 15th European Conference on Artificial Intelligence (ECAI '02)*, Lyon, France (21–26 July 2002), 422–426. IOS Press.

14 Wotawa, F. and Nica, M. (2008). On the compilation of programs into their equivalent constraint representation. *Informatica* 32 (4): 359–371.

15 Wotawa, F., Nica, M., and Moraru, I. (2012). Automated debugging based on a constraint model of the program and a test case. *The Journal of Logic and Algebraic Programming* 81 (4): 390–407. ISSN 1567-8326. http://www.sciencedirect.com/science/article/pii/S1567832612000185.

16 Nica, M., Nica, S., and Wotawa, F. (2012). On the use of mutations and testing for debugging. *Software: Practice and Experience* 43 (9): 1121–1142. https://onlinelibrary.wiley.com/doi/abs/10.1002/spe.1142.

17 Mayer, W. (2007). Static and hybrid analysis in model-based debugging. PhD thesis. University of South Australia.

18 Cytron, R., Ferrante, J., Rosen, B.K. et al. (1991). Efficiently computing static single assignment form and the control dependence graph. *ACM Transactions on Programming Languages and Systems* 13 (4): 451–490. ISSN 0164-0925. http://doi.acm.org/10.1145/115372.115320.

19 Friedrich, G., Stumptner, M., and Wotawa, F. (1999). Model-based diagnosis of hardware designs. *Artificial Intelligence*. 111 (1–2): 3–39. ISSN 0004-3702. http://www.sciencedirect.com/science/article/pii/S000437029900034X.

20 Wotawa, F. (2002). On the relationship between model-based debugging and program slicing. *Artificial Intelligence* 135 (1–2): 125–143. ISSN 0004-3702. http://www.sciencedirect.com/science/article/pii/S0004370201001618.

21 Weiser, M. (1982). Programmers use slices when debugging. *Communications of the ACM* 25 (7): 446–452. ISSN 0001-0782. https://doi.org/10.1145/358557.358577.

22 Ferrante, J., Ottenstein, K.J., and Warren, J.D. (1987). The Program Dependence Graph and Its Use in Optimization. *ACM Transactions on Programming Languages and Systems* 9 (3): 319–349. ISSN 0164-0925. http://doi.acm.org/10.1145/24039.24041.

23 Hofer, B., Höfler, A., and Wotawa, F. (2017). Combining Models for Improved Fault Localization in Spreadsheets. *IEEE Transactions on Reliability* 66 (1): 38–53. ISSN 0018-9529. https://doi.org/10.1109/TR.2016.2632151.

24 Mayer, W. and Stumptner, M. (2004). Debugging program loops using approximate modeling. *Proceedings of the 16th European Conference on Artificial Intelligence (ECAI '04)*, Valencia, Spain (22–27 August 2004), 843–847. IOS Press. ISBN 978-1-58603-452-8. http://dl.acm.org/citation.cfm?id=3000001.3000178.

25 Cousot, P. and Cousot, R. (1977). Abstract interpretation: a unified lattice model for static analysis of programs by construction or approximation of fixpoints. *Proceedings of the 4th ACM SIGACT-SIGPLAN Symposium on Principles of Programming Languages*, Los Angeles, CA, USA (17–19 January 1977), 238–252. ACM. https://dl.acm.org/doi/pdf/10.1145/512950.512973.

26 Mayer, W. and Stumptner, M. (2008). Evaluating models for model-based debugging. *Proceedings of the 2008 23rd IEEE/ACM International Conference on Automated Software Engineering*, L'Aquila, Italy (15–19 September 2008), 128–137. IEEE. https://doi.org/10.1109/ASE.2008.23.

27 Liver, B. (1994). Modeling software systems for diagnosis. *Proceedings of the Fifth International Workshop on Principles of Diagnosis*, New Paltz, NY, USA (17–19 October 1994), 179–184.

28 Ceballos, R., Gasca, R.M., Del Valle, C., and Borrego, D. (2006). Diagnosing errors in DbC programs using constraint programming. *Proceedings of the 2005 Conference of the Spanish Association for Artificial Intelligence*, Santiago de Compostela, Spain (16–18 November 2002), 200–210. Springer. https://core.ac.uk/download/pdf/299806306.pdf.

29 Wotawa, F. (2001). On the relationship between model-based debugging and program mutation. *Proceedings of the Twelfth International Workshop on Principles of Diagnosis*, Sansicario, Italy (7–9 March 2001).

30 Wotawa, F. (2016). On the use of qualitative deviation models for diagnosis. *Proceedings of the International Workshop on Qualitative Reasoning (QR '16)*, New York, NY, USA (11 July 2016). https://spreadsheets.ist.tugraz.at/wp-content/uploads/sites/3/2016/08/qr_models_for_diagnosis.pdf.

31 Stumptner, M. and Wotawa, F. (1999). Debugging functional programs. *Proceedings of the Sixteenth International Joint Conference on Artificial Intelligence (IJCAI '99)*, Stockholm, Sweden (31 July to 6 August 1999), 1074–1079. Morgan Kaufmann. https://citeseerx.ist.psu.edu/viewdoc/download?doi=10.1.1.48.5054&rep=rep1&type=pdf.

32 Peischl, B. and Wotawa, F. (2006). Automated source-level error localization in hardware designs. *IEEE Design and Test of Computers* 23 (1): 8–19. ISSN 0740-7475. https://doi.org/10.1109/MDT.2006.5.

33 Wotawa, F. (2002). Debugging hardware designs using a value-based model. *Applied Intelligence* 16 (1): 71–92. ISSN 1573-7497. https://doi.org/10.1023/A:1012821511498.

34 Wotawa, F. (2000). Debugging VHDL designs using model-based reasoning. *Artificial Intelligence in Engineering* 14 (4): 331–351. ISSN 0954-1810. http://www.sciencedirect.com/science/article/pii/S0954181000000212.

35 Console, L., Friedrich, G., and Dupré, D.T. (1993). Model-based diagnosis meets error diagnosis in logic programs. In: *Automated and Algorithmic Debugging* (ed. P. A. Fritzson), 85–87. Berlin, Germany: Springer. ISBN 978-3-540-48141-6.

36 Shapiro, E.Y. (1982). Algorithmic program debugging. PhD thesis. New Haven, CT, USA: Yale University. https://cpsc.yale.edu/sites/default/files/files/tr237.pdf.

37 Bond, G.W. and Pagurek, B. (1994). A critical analysis of model-based diagnosis meets error diagnosis in logic programs. In: *Technical Report, Department of Systems and Computer Engineering*. Ottawa, Canada: Carleton University.

38 Bond, G.W. (1994). Logic programs for consistency-based diagnosis. PhD thesis. Carleton University. Ottawa, Ontario, Canada.

39 Felfernig, A., Friedrich, G., Jannach, D., and Stumptner, M. (2004). Consistency-based diagnosis of configuration knowledge bases. *Artificial Intelligence* 152 (2): 213–234. ISSN 0004-3702. http://www.sciencedirect.com/science/article/pii/S0004370203001176.

40 Shchekotykhin, K., Friedrich, G., Fleiss, P., and Rodler, P. (2012). Interactive ontology debugging: two query strategies for efficient fault localization. *Journal of Web Semantics* 12–13: 88–103. ISSN 1570-8268.

41 Mateis, C., Stumptner, M., and Wotawa, F. (2000). Modeling java programs for diagnosis. *Proceedings of the European Conference on Artificial Intelligence (ECAI '00)*, Berlin, Germany (20–25 August 2000), 171–175. IOS Press.

42 Mateis, C., Stumptner, M., Wieland, D., and Wotawa, F. (2000). Model-based debugging of Java programs. *arXiv preprint cs/0011027*.

43 Friedrich, G., Mayer, W., and Stumptner, M. (2010). Diagnosing process trajectories under partially known behavior. *Proceedings of the 2010 Conference on ECAI 2010: 19th European Conference on Artificial Intelligence (ECAI '10)*, Lisbon, Portugal (16–20 August 2010), 111–116. IOS Press. ISBN 978-1-60750-605-8. http://dl.acm.org/citation.cfm?id=1860967.1860990.

44 Hofer, B., Jehan, S., Pill, I., and Wotawa, F. (2015). Focused diagnosis for failing software tests. In: *Current Approaches in Applied Artificial Intelligence* (ed. M. Ali, Y. S. Kwon, C.-H. Lee, et al.), 712–721. Cham, Switzerland: Springer. ISBN 978-3-319-19066-2.

45 Hofer, B. and Wotawa, F. (2012). Spectrum enhanced dynamic slicing for better fault localization. *Proceedings of the European Conference on Artificial Intelligence (ECAI '12)*, Montpellier, France (27–31 August 2012), 420–425. IOS Press.

46 Abreu, R., Mayer, W., Stumptner, M., and van Gemund, A.J.C. (2009). Refining spectrum-based fault localization rankings. *Proceedings of the 2009 ACM Symposium on Applied Computing (SAC '09)*, Honolulu, HI, USA (8–12 March 2009), 409–414. ACM. ISBN 978-1-60558-166-8. http://doi.acm.org/10.1145/1529282.1529374.

47 Abreu, R., Zoeteweij, P., and van Gemund, A. J. C. (2009). Spectrum-based multiple fault localization. *Proceedings of the 2009 IEEE/ACM International Conference on Automated Software Engineering (ASE '09)*, Auckland, New Zealand (16–20 November 2009), 88–99. IEEE. https://doi.org/10.1109/ASE.2009.25.

48 Hofer, B., Wotawa, F., and Abreu, R. (2012). AI for the win: improving spectrum-based fault localization. *ACM SIGSOFT Software Engineering Notes* 37 (6): 1–8.

49 Wotawa, F. (2008). Bridging the gap between slicing and model-based diagnosis. *Proceedings of the 20th International Conference on Software Engineering and Knowledge Engineering*, San Francisco, CA, USA (1–3 July 2008), 836–841. Knowledge Systems Institute. https://ecommons.luc.edu/cgi/viewcontent.cgi?article=1036&context=cs_facpubs#page=865.

50 Jehan, S. (2009). Jsdiagnosis: dynamic program slicing with hitting set calculation. Master's thesis. Technische Universitat Graz.

10

Software Fault Localization in Spreadsheets

Birgit Hofer and Franz Wotawa

Institute of Software Technology, Graz University of Technology, Graz, Austria

10.1 Motivation

Spreadsheets are well known and used in many companies, such as for financial reporting, price calculations, and forecasting. Given that important decisions are often based on spreadsheets, one might expect that such spreadsheets are free from faults, but this is not the case: the list of spreadsheet errors that become publicly known is long, and the number of unreported cases may even be significantly higher. Here are some prominent examples:

- An error in the London 2012 Olympics ticketing spreadsheet was responsible for a £0.5 million damage. The synchronized swimming events were overbooked by 10 000 tickets, and ticket owners had to be upgraded to more expensive events for free as compensation [1].
- In December 2011, the US village West Baraboo discovered a simple calculating error in one of its financial spreadsheets. However, the correction of the error revealed that West Baraboo had to pay more than $400 000 in additional interests [2].
- In 2013, the Canadian power generator TransAlta bought too many US power transmission certificates at a higher price than necessary because of a copy-and-paste fault in a spreadsheet. This resulted in a damage of $24 million [3, 4].

Several institutions and companies have collected these and other examples to arouse public awareness of the risks that come with spreadsheets. The British financial model building company F1F9 published the e-book *The Dirty Dozen*, which lists 12 of the most prominent spreadsheet errors [5]. The European

Handbook of Software Fault Localization: Foundations and Advances, First Edition.
Edited by W. Eric Wong and T.H. Tse.

Published 2023 by John Wiley & Sons, Inc.

Spreadsheet Risks Interest Group (EuSpRIG) has collected additional spreadsheet horror stories.[1] In an article in the American business magazine *Forbes*, Tim Worstall considers spreadsheet environments like Microsoft's Excel as "the most dangerous software on the planet" [6].

Why are so many spreadsheets faulty? To err is human. Panko identifies the creation of spreadsheets as a complex cognitive task and estimates the human error rate when writing formulas to be 3–5% [7]. This implies that a spreadsheet with 100 formulas contains at least one fault with a probability of 95.2–99.4%. The fault probability for a spreadsheet with 1000 formulas is even greater than 99.9%. Different audits on business spreadsheets reveal that between 86 and 100% of the investigated spreadsheets contain faults [8].

In view of these examples and alarming numbers, why do so many people still use spreadsheets for finance? The answer is quite simple: spreadsheets are very flexible and easy to use. Changes can be made immediately by domain experts without a programmer's help. Therefore, it is to be assumed that spreadsheets will remain popular within the next decades.

Several researchers have proposed techniques to detect, locate, and fix faults in order to increase the quality of spreadsheets (see Jannach et al.'s overview paper [9]). In this chapter, we particularly focus on the available techniques for locating faulty cells. We demonstrate that the basic concepts introduced in the previous chapters can be easily applied to spreadsheets. In Section 10.3, we introduce the spreadsheet correspondence of slicing, namely cones. In Section 10.4, we explain how to apply spectrum-based fault localization (SFL) on spreadsheets. Section 10.5 shows how to convert a spreadsheet into a set of constraints so that model-based debugging (MBD) can be used for localizing faulty cells. Section 10.6 explains how faults can be automatically fixed. All these techniques require as input a previously observed misbehavior. A misbehavior can be detected using checking and testing approaches. We discuss such approaches in Sections 10.7 and 10.8. Finally, Section 10.9 briefly compares the different approaches.

We explain all of the presented spreadsheet fault localization techniques by means of the running example illustrated in Figure 10.1. This simple spreadsheet computes the operating income for a product for January and February absolute and in percentage of the sales revenue as well as the total operating income and the taxes. The taxes are computed as follows: if the operating income is below $3000, the taxes are a fixed amount of $100; otherwise, the taxes are 10% of the operating income. When manually investigating the values of this spreadsheet, we notice that the operating income in percentage of sales for the total column (cell D7) is higher than the value for the individual months (cells B7 and C7). From common sense, we know that the value should be between the values of B7 and C7. Therefore, we know that there must obviously be a fault in the spreadsheet. When

(a)

	A	B	C	D
1	**Item**	**Jan**	**Feb**	**Total**
2	**Units sold**	100	100	200
3	**ASP/unit**	$10	$20	**$15**
4	**Sales revenue**	$1000	$2000	$3000
5	**Expenses**	$500	$300	$300
6	**Operating income**	$500	$1700	$2700
7	**Op income in %-sales**	**50%**	**85%**	**90%**
8	**Taxes**			**100**

(b)

	A	B	C	D
1	**Item**	**Jan**	**Feb**	**Total**
2	**Units sold**	100	100	=SUM(B2:C2)
3	**ASP/unit**	$10	$20	**=D4/D2**
4	**Sales revenue**	=C4*C3	=D4*D3	=SUM(B4:C4)
5	**Expenses**	$500	$300	=SUM(C5:C5)
6	**Operating income**	=C5-C6	=D5-D6	=D4-D5
7	**Op income in %-sales**	**=C7/C5**	**=D7/D5**	**=D6/D4**
8	**Taxes**			**=IF(D6>3000,D6*0.1,100)**

Figure 10.1 Running example: (a) value view and (b) formula view. This spreadsheet is a slightly modified version of the "homework/budgetone" spreadsheet from the EUSES spreadsheet corpus. The cell D5 contains a fault.

manually investigating the cells, we will identify cell D5 as a root source for the observed misbehavior. While the manual investigation of such a small spreadsheet is easy, analyzing a large spreadsheet with several hundreds or even thousands of cells is very time-consuming and frustrating.

Therefore, we use the automated fault localization techniques to locate the root cause of the observed misbehavior.

10.2 Definition of the Spreadsheet Language

Since all approaches are built upon the same common ground, we explain the basic definitions in this section. First, we focus on the syntax of spreadsheets. Afterward, we define test cases for spreadsheets and formulate the spreadsheet debugging problem.

A spreadsheet Π consists of a set of cells *CELLS*. Each cell *c* is associated with an expression $\ell(c)$, a value $\nu(c)$, and a unique position $\varphi(c)$ within the spreadsheet. The cell's value can be directly derived from the cell expression. It may be a numeric, Boolean, string, blank, or error value. The position of a cell *c* is determined by its row index $\varphi_x(c)$ and its column index $\varphi_y(c)$. In the A1-notation, cells are indicated by their absolute positions within the worksheet with A1 representing the top left-most cell. Another possibility to denote a cell's position is the R1C1-notation, where cells are indicated relative to the position of the referencing cell. A cell expression $\ell(c)$ must meet the following syntax:

Definition 10.1 (Syntax of Cell Expressions)
The language L for cell expressions is defined recursively as follows. Note that the equal signs, the quotation marks, and the brackets are part of the cell expressions.

- Any constant $\boldsymbol{k}$ representing a numeric, Boolean, string, blank, or error value is an expression in L, known as a constant expression.
- Given any constant expression $\boldsymbol{k}$ in L, the string ="$\boldsymbol{k}$" is an expression in L.
- Given any constant expression $\boldsymbol{k}$ in L with a numeric or Boolean value, the string $=\boldsymbol{k}$ is an expression in L.
- Given any cell name c, the string $=\mathbf{c}$ is an expression in L.
- Let $\boldsymbol{\xi}$ be any expression in L. If $\boldsymbol{\xi}$ is in the format $=\boldsymbol{e}$, we define $\boldsymbol{e}$ to be a core expression. Otherwise, we define $\boldsymbol{\xi}$ itself as a core expression and denote it by $\boldsymbol{e}$.
- Given any core expression $\boldsymbol{e}$, the string $=(\boldsymbol{e})$ is an expression in L.
- Given any core expressions $\boldsymbol{e}_1$ and $\boldsymbol{e}_2$, and given any operator $\circ$ in $\{+, -, *, /, <, =, >\}$, the string $=\boldsymbol{e}_1 \circ \boldsymbol{e}_2$ is an expression in L.
- Given any core expressions $\boldsymbol{e}_1$, $\boldsymbol{e}_2$, $\boldsymbol{e}_3$, and $\boldsymbol{e}_4$, and given any operator $\circ$ in $\{<, =, >\}$, the string $=\mathbf{IF}(\boldsymbol{e}_1 \circ \boldsymbol{e}_2, \boldsymbol{e}_3, \boldsymbol{e}_4)$ is an expression in L.
- Given any cell names c_1 and c_2, the string $=\mathbf{SUM}(\mathbf{c}_1 : \mathbf{c}_2)$ is an expression in L.

Fault localization techniques rely on information about which cell names were referenced in a cell expression. Therefore, we define a function ρ that maps any given cell name to the set of referenced cell names.

Definition 10.2 (Referenced Cell Names)
We recursively define a function $\rho : CELLS \rightarrow 2^{CELLS}$ *that accepts a cell name c and returns the set of cell names referenced by* $\ell(c)$*. Note that the equal signs and the brackets are part of the cell expressions.*

- For any $c \in CELLS$, if the cell expression $\ell(c)$ is a constant $\boldsymbol{k}$, then $\rho(c)$ will be $\{\}$.
- For any $c \in CELLS$, if the cell expression $\ell(c)$ is $=\boldsymbol{k}$ for some constant $\boldsymbol{k}$, then $\rho(c)$ will be $\{\}$.

- For any $c_0 \in CELLS$, if the cell expression $\ell(c_0)$ is $=\mathbf{c_1}$ for some cell name c_1, then $\rho(c_0)$ will be $\{c_1\}$.
- For any $c_0 \in CELLS$, if the cell expression $\ell(c_0)$ is $=(\boldsymbol{e})$, then $\rho(c_0)$ will be equivalent to $\rho(c_1)$ for some $c_1 \in CELLS$ whose cell expression $\ell(c_1)$ is $=\boldsymbol{e}$.
- For any $c_0 \in CELLS$, suppose that the cell expression $\ell(c_0)$ is $=\boldsymbol{e_1} \circ \boldsymbol{e_2}$ for some operator $\circ$ in $\{+, -, *, /, <, =, >\}$. Then, $\rho(c_0)$ will be equivalent to $\rho(c_1) \cup \rho(c_2)$ for some $c_1 \in CELLS$ whose cell expression $\ell(c_1)$ is $=\boldsymbol{e_1}$ and for some $c_2 \in CELLS$ whose cell expression $\ell(c_2)$ is $=\boldsymbol{e_2}$.
- For any $c_0 \in CELLS$, suppose that the cell expression $\ell(c_0)$ is $=\mathbf{IF}(\boldsymbol{e_1} \circ \boldsymbol{e_2}, \boldsymbol{e_3}, \boldsymbol{e_4})$. Then, $\rho(c_0)$ will be equivalent to $\rho(c_1) \cup \rho(c_2) \cup \rho(c_3) \cup \rho(c_4)$ for some $c_1 \in CELLS$ whose cell expression $\ell(c_1)$ is $=\boldsymbol{e_1}$, for some $c_2 \in CELLS$ whose cell expression $\ell(c_2)$ is $=\boldsymbol{e_2}$, for some $c_3 \in CELLS$ whose cell expression $\ell(c_3)$ is $=\boldsymbol{e_3}$, and for some $c_4 \in CELLS$ whose cell expression $\ell(c_4)$ is $=\boldsymbol{e_4}$.
- For any $c_0 \in CELLS$, suppose that the cell expression $\ell(c_0)$ is $=\mathbf{SUM}(\mathbf{c_1} : \mathbf{c_2})$. Let C be the set of cells bounded by the rectangle having c_1 and c_2 at the top left and bottom right corners. Then, $\rho(c_0)$ will be C.

Example 10.1 *For our running example from Figure 10.1, the referenced cells for cells* B2*,* B4*, and* D2 *are as follows:* $\rho(\text{B7}) = \{\}$, $\rho(\text{B7}) = \{\text{B2, B3}\}$, *and* $\rho(\text{D2}) = \{\text{B2, C2}\}$.

All fault localization approaches need at least one failed test case as input. A test case must specify values for all input cells of the spreadsheet and at least the expected value of one other cell.

Definition 10.3 (Test Case)[2]

Let Input (Π) *be a function that returns the set of all cells that do not refer to any cells but are referenced in some other cells. Formally,* $Input(\Pi) = \{c \in CELLS \mid \rho(c) = \{\} \wedge c \in \rho(c') \text{ for some } c' \in CELLS\}$. *A tuple* (I, O) *is a test case for a spreadsheet* Π *if for each cell name* $c \in Input(\Pi)$*, there exists a tuple* $(c, v) \in I$ *specifying a value* v *for cell* c*,* O *is a non-empty set of tuples* (c, D) *with* $c \in (\Pi \setminus Input(\Pi))$*, and* D *is a testing predicate over the value of the cell* $v(c)$*. A test case* (I, O) *is a failed test case if there is at least one testing predicate that evaluates to false, i.e.* $\exists (c, D) \in O$ *such that* $D(v(c))$ *is contradictory. Otherwise, the test case is a successful test case.*

Example 10.2 *A test case for our running example from Figure 10.1 is the tuple* (I, O) *with* $I = \{(\text{B2}, 100), (\text{B3}, 10), (\text{B5}, 500), (\text{C2}, 100), (\text{C3}, 20), (\text{C5}, 300)\}$ *and* $O = \{(\text{B7}, v(\text{B7}) = 0.5), (\text{C7}, v(\text{C7}) = 0.85), (\text{D3}, v(\text{D3}) = 15), (\text{D7}, v(\text{D7}) > 0.5) \wedge v(\text{D7}) < 0.85)\}$. *This test case is a failed test case because the computed value of* D7 *contradicts one of its testing predicates* $(v(\text{D7}) < 0.85)$.

With the formal definition of the spreadsheet and (*failed*) test cases, we are now able to formulate the spreadsheet debugging problem.

Definition 10.4 (Spreadsheet Debugging Problem [12])
Let $\Pi \in L$ be a spreadsheet and (I, O) be a failed test case of Π. Then, (Π, I, O)) is a debugging problem.

A solution to the spreadsheet debugging problem is a set of cells that should be changed so that the computed values of the cells indicated in *O* correspond to their testing predicates, i.e. that the *failed* test case turns into a *successful* test case.

10.3 Cones

Cones in spreadsheets are the equivalent of slices in programs. Slices are computed by considering several different types of dependencies, such as data and control dependencies. However, spreadsheets do not have global control structures; all control functions (such as IF) are applied as part of a cell expression. Therefore, we only have to consider cells that are referenced in a cell expression.

Definition 10.5 (Cone [11])
The function Cone(c) returns the set of cells that directly or indirectly influence the value of cell c:

$$Cone(c) = c \cup \bigcup_{c' \in \rho(\ell(c)) \text{ such that } \ell(c') = Q} Cone(c') \tag{10.1}$$

Example 10.3 *We compute the following cones for our running example from Figure 10.1 and the test case from Example 10.2: Cone*(B7) = {B4, B6, B7}, *Cone*(C7) = {C4, C6, C7}, *Cone*(D3) = {B3, C4, D2, D3, D4}, *and Cone* (D7) = {B4, C4, D4, D5, D6, D7}.

When using cones for fault localization, we are only interested in the cones of those cells, where the testing predicate and the computed value are contradictory. For our running example, we have to inspect the five cells listed in *Cone*(D7). Given the small size of our running example, five cells is a large number that remains for manual inspection.

The size of cones can be reduced by using the concept of dicing: instead of manually investigating all five cells, we only investigate the cells that do not appear in the cones of cells where the computed values satisfy their testing predicates (positive cones). For our running example, the cells D5, D6, and D7 would remain for manual analysis, because the other cells are also contained in positive cones. While the number of cells can be significantly reduced, dicing also comes with its risks: the true fault may be absent in the reduced set of cells when (i) the output of a cell is correct even though it used an erroneous value in its computations, or (ii) the testing predicate is too weak.

Example 10.4 *Assume for our running example that O contains an additional tuple* (D8, v(D8) = 100). *The computed value of cell* D8 *satisfies this testing predicate. The cone for* D8 *is* {B4, C4, D4, D5, D6, D8}. *If we build the dice* $Cone$(D7) \ $Cone$(D8), *the result would be* D7. *The faulty cell* D5 *is absent in this dice, because the fault does not propagate to the result of cell* D8. *An example for a weak testing predicate would be* v(D5) > 0. *While this testing predicate is obviously correct, it fails to identify that the computed value is actually wrong.*

Another possibility to reduce the size of a computed cone is to use the intersection of the cones of two cells with contradictory testing predicates. In case of a single fault, this may lead to a reduction of the cone. Unfortunately, in the case of two or more independent faults, the intersection may not contain any of the faulty cells or may even be empty. Therefore, the intersection method is not well suited for fault localization purposes.

To summarize, cones as a stand-alone approach are not well suited for fault localization because (i) cones can still be large, and (ii) dice and intersections of cones may not contain the true fault. However, cones serve as input to other fault localization techniques, as we will demonstrate below.

10.4 Spectrum-Based Fault Localization

As explained in Chapter 4, similarity coefficients numerically express the correlation of an observed misbehavior and the executed statements. In the spreadsheet domain, the similarity coefficient expresses the correlation of erroneous values and the cells that contribute to the computation of these values.

To compute the similarity coefficients, we make use of an observation matrix. The spreadsheet observation matrix differs from the observation matrix from Chapter 4 in the following aspect: instead of using the execution traces of several test cases, we use a single test case (I, O) and the cones of the cells specified in O instead. The error vector indicates whether a testing predicate and the actually computed value are contradictory. These modifications are necessary because spreadsheets lack a control flow, and therefore the execution pattern would be identical for different test cases.

In principle, an arbitrary similarity coefficient can be used for computing the ranking of suspicious cells. A comprehensive list of coefficients can be found in Hofer et al.'s work [13]. As an example, we indicate Ochiai [14] below, since studies have shown that this is one of the best performing similarity coefficients [13].

Definition 10.6 (Ochiai Similarity Coefficient for Spreadsheets [13]) *The Ochiai similarity coefficient for a cell c is defined as:*

$$SC_O(c) = \frac{a_{11}(c)}{\sqrt{((a_{11}(c) + a_{10}(c))(a_{11}(c) + a_{01}(c))}} \tag{10.2}$$

where

- $a_{11}(c)$ *is the number of erroneous cells that c has contributed to:*

$$a_{11}(c) = |\{(c', D) \in O \mid c \in Cone(c') \wedge D(v(c')) \text{ is contradictory}\}|.$$

- a_{10} *c is the number of cells with correct values that c has contributed to:*

$$a_{10}(c) = |\{(c', D) \in O \mid c \in Cone(c') \wedge D(v(c')) \text{ is satisfiable}\}|, \text{ and}$$

- a_{01} *c is the number of erroneous cells that c has not contributed to:*

$$a_{01}(c) = |\{(c', D) \in O \mid c \in Cone(c') \wedge D(v(c')) \text{ is contradictory}\}|.$$

For all cells c where $a_{11}(c) + a_{10}(c) = 0$ *or* $a_{11}(c) + a_{01}(c) = 0$*, the Ochiai similarity coefficient is zero* ($SC_O(c) = 0$).

The computed similarity coefficients are used to rank the individual cells. The higher a cell's similarity coefficient is, the higher the cell is ranked. The computed Ochiai similarity coefficient is a number between 0 and 1, with 0 for the least suspicious cells and 1 for the most suspicious cells.

Example 10.5 *For our running example from Figure 10.1 and the test case from Example 10.2, we compute the observation matrix, the Ochiai coefficients, and the subsequent ranking as shown in Table 10.1.*

The faulty cell D5 *is ranked highest together with the cells* D6 *and* D7*. Having this ranking, the spreadsheet user checks the faulty cell first in the best case or the third cell in the worst case.*

SFL has several advantages over cones: (i) instead of only providing a set of suspicious cells, SFL provides a ranking of these cells. (ii) SFL is tolerant toward (a) positive cones that also include the faulty cell; (b) weak testing predicates; and (c) some wrong user input. Example 10.6 demonstrates SFL's tolerance against positive cones.

Table 10.1 Example 10.5.

Cell	Cone B7	Cone C7	Cone D3	Cone D7	a_{11}	a_{01}	a_{10}	Ochiai	Rank
B4	•		•	•	1	0	2	0.577	4
B6	•				0	1	1	0	—
B7	•				0	1	1	0	—
C4		•	•	•	1	0	2	0.577	4
C6		•			0	1	1	0	—
C7		•			0	1	1	0	—
D2			•		0	1	1	0	—
D3			•		0	1	1	0	—
D4			•	•	1	0	1	0.707	6
D5				•	1	0	0	1.000	1
D6				•	1	0	0	1.000	1
D7				•	1	0	0	1.000	1

Example 10.6 *If we add the cone of D8 again, we obtain the following observation matrix, the Ochiai coefficients, and the subsequent ranking as shown in Table 10.2.*

Now, the faulty cell is ranked only at the second position, but in contrast to the dicing version of the cones, the faulty cell is still in the set of suspicious cells.

Wrong user input is created when a user makes a mistake in one of the testing predicates. Ruthruff et al. [15] performed an empirical evaluation in which participants had to decide for two small spreadsheets (both n 30 cells) whether the computed values are correct or wrong. For the first spreadsheet, 9% of the values classified as correct had a wrong value, and 6% of the values classified as wrong were actually correct; for the second spreadsheet, 20% of the values classified as correct actually had a wrong value, and 3% of the values classified as wrong were actually correct. These numbers imply that wrong user input is indeed a common problem.

Fortunately, SFL is less sensitive against wrong input than cones. An empirical evaluation on 218 faulty spreadsheets showed that for 60% of the spreadsheets, the ranking of the faulty cells only doubles in the worst case when the user indicates one wrong testing decision [16]. However, the programmer's proverb "garbage in, garbage out" also applies to SFL: if a user indicates too many wrong testing decisions, SFL is unable to rank the actual faulty cell high.

Table 10.2 Example 10.6.

Cell	Cone: B7	C7	D3	D7	D8	a_{11}	a_{01}	a_{10}	Ochiai	Rank
B4	•		•	•	•	1	0	3	0.500	4
B6	•					0	1	1	0	—
B7	•					0	1	1	0	—
C4		•	•	•	•	1	0	3	0.500	4
C6		•				0	1	1	0	—
C7		•				0	1	1	0	—
D2			•			0	1	1	0	—
D3			•			0	1	1	0	—
D4			•	•	•	1	0	2	0.577	6
D5				•	•	1	0	1	0.707	2
D6				•	•	1	0	1	0.707	2
D7				•		1	0	0	1.000	1
D8					•	0	1	1	0	—

Spreadsheets have a peculiarity compared to other software: Copy-&-Paste is not considered a bad programming practice but rather a standard procedure. The copying of formulas is supported by the majority of spreadsheet environments via Drag-&-Drop. Cells with identical formulas in R1C1 notation and the same similarity coefficient can be aggregated in the ranking of suspicious cells to provide a better overview to the user.

Example 10.7 *The results presented in Example 10.6 can be aggregated as shown in Table 10.3.*

In this tiny example, the aggregation does not have any impact on the final result. For larger spreadsheets, a list helps the user gain a better overview and reduce the number of the presented suspicious cells.

SFL is particularly effective when there is only one faulty cell. In the case of several faulty cells, SFL may rank the faulty cells low. To overcome this weakness, researchers have proposed techniques for traditional programming languages. The adaptation of these techniques to the spreadsheet domain is an ongoing research topic.

To summarize, SFL is more powerful than cones since it computes a ranking of the cells instead of only a set of suspicious cells. Furthermore, it is more reliable than the dicing and intersection of cones in the case of several faults, weak testing

Table 10.3 Example 10.7

Cell	Ochiai	Rank
B4, C4	0.500	4
B6, C6	0	—
B7, C7	0	—
D2	0	—
D3	0	—
D4	0.577	5
D5	0.707	2
D6	0.707	2
D7	1.000	1
D8	0	—

predicates, and wrong user input. In such cases, SFL does not exclude the faulty cell(s) from the set of suspicious cells but assigns a lower similarity coefficient and subsequently a lower ranking position to them. However, in case of multiple faults, SFL as a stand-alone approach is not suitable.

10.5 Model-Based Spreadsheet Debugging

This section builds upon this chapter. As mentioned there, a diagnosis problem consists of a system description SD, a set of components COMP, and a set of observations OBS. In model-based spreadsheet debugging, the faulty spreadsheet and its formulas build the system description SD. The set of cells *CELLS* forms the set of components COMP. The failed test case $T = (I, O)$ builds the set of observations OBS. We can use different models as system description SD, such as the value-based model [17, 18] or the dependency-based model [19].

In the value-based model, the values of the spreadsheet's formulas are propagated. In such a model, SD consists of the input cells and their values, the testing decisions, and all formulas converted into constraints. Algorithm 10.1 creates a value-based constraint model from a spreadsheet Π and a test case T. While the test case can be converted straightforward (see lines 2 to 7), the conversion of formulas is more complex. First, the formulas' expressions are converted into constraints (line 9). Then, they are concatenated with auxiliary variables expressing their "health" state: either a formula is abnormal (AB) or it behaves as expected (line 10).

Algorithm 10.2 recursively converts an expression into a set of constraints: constants and references to cell names do not result in any constraints. They can be directly used by the constraints of the higher expressions (line 2). Expressions with

Inputs: A spreadsheet Π and a failed test case $T = (I, O)$

Output: A value-based constraint model M

let M be $\{\}$

foreach $(c, v) \in I$ **do**

$\quad M = M \cup \{c = v\}$

end

foreach $(c, D) \in O$ **do**

$\quad M = M \cup \{D\}$

end

foreach $c \in \Pi$ such that $\ell(c) = \rho$ **do**

$\quad (aux, M_c) =$ **ConvertExpression**$(\ell(c))$

$\quad M = M \cup M_c \cup \{AB_C \vee c = aux\}$

end

return M

Algorithm 10.1 Convert2ValueBasedModel(Π, T). *Source:* Adapted from Hofer and Wotawa [19]/Wiley.

Input: An expression e according to the syntax given in Definition 10.1

Outputs: Output variable a, and set of constraints M representing e

if e is a constant or cell name **then**

$\quad$ return $(e, \{\})$

end

if e is of the form (e_1) **then**

$\quad$ return **ConvertExpression**(e_1)

end

if e is of the form $e_1 \circ e_2$ **then**

$\quad$ let a be a new auxiliary variable

$\quad (a_1, M_1) =$ **ConvertExpression**(e_1)

$\quad (a_2, M_2) =$ **ConvertExpression**(e_2)

$\quad M = \{a = a_1 \circ^* a_2\}$, where $\circ^*$ is the constraint representing $\circ$

$\quad$ return $(a, M \cup M_1 \cup M_2)$

end

if e is of the form $f(e_1, ..., e_n)$ **then**

$\quad$ let a be a new auxiliary variable

$\quad$ **for** $i = 1$ to n **do**

$\qquad (a_i, M_i) =$ **ConvertExpression**(e_i)

$\quad$ **end**

$\quad M = \{a = f^*(a_1, ..., a_n)\}$, where f^* is the constraint representing f

$\quad$ return $(a, M \cup \bigcup_{i=1}^{n} M_i)$

end

Algorithm 10.2 ConvertExpression(e). *Source:* Adapted from Hofer and Wotawa [19]/Wiley.

parentheses can be converted into constraints by converting the underlying expression (line 5). If an expression consists of one or more sub-expressions, the sub-expressions are first converted into their constraints (lines 9, 10, and 17). Afterward, the result of the sub-expressions (represented by auxiliary variables a_i) are connected by an appropriate constraint (lines 11 and 19).

We assume that the used constraint solver supports all required operators and functions. For example, there must exist the constraint $\phi(e_1, e_2, e_3)$ implementing the function "IF": if e_1 is true, then e_2 is satisfied; otherwise, e_3 is satisfied. Some standard spreadsheet functions can be realized by combining several basic constraints: the function "SUM" can be achieved as a constraint by using the "+" operator several times. The function "AVG" can be realized by splitting it into a "SUM"-function, a "COUNT"-function, and a division.

The constraint model obtained from Algorithm 10.1 is the input to Algorithm 9.1 from this chapter, which returns the minimal diagnoses up to the indicated cardinality. Since we are interested in small diagnoses (single and double faults), we indicate as cardinality one or two. If the algorithm is not able to identify the faulty cells, we increase the cardinality.

Example 10.8 *For our running example from Figure 10.1 and the test case from Example 10.2, we obtain the value-based constraint model as shown in Table 10.4. For the sake of simplicity and readability, we removed all unnecessary auxiliary variables.*

If we call a constraint solver using Algorithm 9.1 with these constraints and $n = 1$, *we obtain* B4, C4, D4, D5, D6, *and* D7 *as single-fault explanations, i.e. three diagnoses more than when using the value-based model.*

In the dependency-based model, only the correctness information of the values is propagated. If the input values are correct and the formula is correct, then the

Table 10.4 Example 10.8.

Input	Output	Formula constraints	
B2 = true	D2 = true	$AB_{D2} \vee (B2 \wedge C2 \rightarrow D2)$	$AB_{B6} \vee (B4 \wedge B5 \rightarrow B6)$
C2 = true	B7 = true	$AB_{D3} \vee (D2 \wedge D4 \rightarrow D3)$	$AB_{C6} \vee (C4 \wedge C5 \rightarrow C6)$
B3 = true	C7 = true	$AB_{B4} \vee (B2 \wedge B3 \rightarrow B4)$	$AB_{D6} \vee (D4 \wedge D5 \rightarrow D6)$
C3 = true	D7 = false	$AB_{C4} \vee (C2 \wedge C3 \rightarrow C4)$	$AB_{B7} \vee (B4 \wedge B6 \rightarrow B7)$
B5 = true		$AB_{D4} \vee (B4 \wedge C4 \rightarrow D4)$	$AB_{C7} \vee (C4 \wedge C6 \rightarrow C7)$
C5 = true		$AB_{D5} \vee (C5 \rightarrow D5)$	$AB_{D7} \vee (D4 \wedge D6 \rightarrow D7)$
		$AB_{B6} \vee (B4 \wedge B5 \rightarrow B6)$	$AB_{D8} \vee (D6 \rightarrow D8)$

```
Input: A spreadsheet Π and a failed test case T = (I, O)
Output: A dependency-based constraint model M
1   Let M be {}
2   for (c, v) ∈ I do
3       M = M ∪ {c = true}
4   end
5   foreach (c, D) ∈ O do
6       if D and v(c) are contradictory then
7           M = M ∪ {c = false}
8       else
9           M = M ∪ {c = true}
10      end
11  end
12  foreach c ∈ Π where ℓ(c) = ρ do
13      M = M ∪ {AB_c ∨ ∧_{c_i∈ρ(c)} → c}
14  end
15  return M
```

Algorithm 10.3 Convert2DependencyBasedModel(Π, *T*). *Source:* Adapted from Hofer and Wotawa [19]/Wiley.

output value must be correct [19]. Algorithm 10.3 creates a dependency-based model for a spreadsheet Π and a test case *T*: all input values are assumed to be correct (line 2). Output cells whose computed values contradict the testing predicate are set to false (line 7); output cells whose computed values satisfy the testing predicate are set to true (line 9). For each formula cell, we add the following constraint: either the formula is incorrect (AB_c) or the "correctness: of the referenced cells implies the correctness of computed value (line 13).

The dependency-based model is more abstract than the value-based model. Thus, information gets lost, which could result in more diagnoses than when using the value-based model. However, there are two major benefits of the dependency-based model: (i) the dependency-based constraint model can be faster solved than the value-based constraint model for the same spreadsheet and test case because of a reduction of the domain. Instead of integers and reals, only Booleans are used in the dependency-based models. (ii) Because of the abstraction, the operators and functions do not need to be converted into constraints. Therefore, the implementation is easier, and changes in the spreadsheet environment (such as additional functions and renaming of functions) do not require changes in the debugging tool.

Table 10.5 Example 10.9.

Input	Output	Formula constraints	
B2 = true	D3 = true	$AB_{D2} \vee (B2 \wedge C2 \rightarrow D2)$	$AB_{B6} \vee (B4 \wedge B5 \rightarrow B6)$
C2 = true	B7 = true	$AB_{D3} \vee (D2 \wedge D4 \rightarrow D3)$	$AB_{C6} \vee (C4 \wedge C5 \rightarrow C6)$
B3 = true	C7 = true	$AB_{B4} \vee (B2 \wedge B3 \rightarrow B4)$	$AB_{D6} \vee (D4 \wedge D5 \rightarrow D6)$
C3 = true	D7 = false	$AB_{C4} \vee (C2 \wedge C3 \rightarrow C4)$	$AB_{B7} \vee (B4 \wedge B6 \rightarrow B7)$
B5 = true		$AB_{D4} \vee (B4 \wedge C4 \rightarrow D4)$	$AB_{C7} \vee (C4 \wedge C6 \rightarrow C7)$
C5 = true		$AB_{D5} \vee (C5 \rightarrow D5)$	$AB_{D7} \vee (D4 \wedge D6 \rightarrow D7)$
		$AB_{B6} \vee (B4 \wedge B5 \rightarrow B6)$	$AB_{D8} \vee (D6 \rightarrow D8)$

Example 10.9 *For our running example from Figure 10.1 and the test case from Example 10.2, we obtain the value-based constraint model as shown in Table 10.5.*

If we call a constraint solver using Algorithm 9.1 with these constraints and $n = 1$*, we obtain* B4, C4, D4, D5, D6, *and* D7 *as single-fault explanations, i.e. three diagnoses more than when using the value-based model.*

Weak testing conditions and coincidental correct output do not negatively influence the diagnosis result of MBD (see Example 10.10). However, wrong user input could result in completely wrong diagnoses. A major advantage of MBD is its ability to identify higher order faults (such as double and triple faults).

Example 10.10 *Let us examine what happens when we add the coincidental correct cell* D8 *and its testing decision* (v(D8) = 100) *to the models. To the value-based model from Example 10.8, we add the constraint* D8 = *100. To the dependency-based model from Example 10.9, we add the constraint* D8 = *true. For both models, a constraint solver would compute the same diagnoses as reported in Example 10.8 and Example 10.9, respectively.*

MBD returns a set of diagnoses, not a ranking. Several approaches combine SFL with MBD to eliminate the individual limitations (MBD: diagnoses without prioritization, SFL: single faults only). BARINEL [20], DEPUTO [21], and SENDYS [22] are some of these approaches. Even though these methods are designed for other programming languages, they can be adapted to spreadsheets.

To summarize, MBD is well suited for debugging spreadsheets containing multiple faults. It is insensitive against coincidental correctness and weak testing decisions, but it is sensitive against wrong user input. While the basic MDB approach returns a set of diagnoses as the result, approaches combining MDB with SFL additionally prioritize the computed results.

10.6 Repair Approaches

While the previously mentioned techniques locate faults, repair approaches identify the changes that need to be made in order to correct the fault. In this section, we discuss two repair techniques, namely goal-directed debugging [23–25] and mutation-based spreadsheet debugging [26]. Both techniques require the user to indicate the exact value or at least a range of the expected output value of an erroneous cell.

The goal-directed debugging approach converts the user input (the testing decisions) into constraints and propagates the constraints backward in the formulas. For each reached formula, it applies inference rules, i.e. it changes the parameters, formulas, and operators so that the constraint is satisfied. All changes that satisfy the constraints are valid repair suggestions. The inference rules are predefined. This means that the spreadsheet could only be changed in those ways that were previously specified. When the spreadsheet requires different changes, no repair suggestion is generated.

Since usually too many repair suggestions are generated, they are ranked by the approach by means of heuristics. For example, reference changes are ranked by their Manhattan distance to the original reference. Repair candidates turning a reference into a constant are ranked lower than those changing a reference to another reference. For more details, refer to Abraham and Erwig's papers [23, 24].

Example 10.11 *We restrict this demonstration to changes replacing references with other references or constants, since there would be too many possibilities for changes of the formulas to list them here. The search for a solution starts in* D7*'s formula by adding the constraints of its testing decision:* $0.5 < (\mathrm{D6}/\mathrm{D4}) < 0.85$. *We now look for repair candidates that replace either the reference to* D4 *or* D6 *by some other reference or by a constant: (i) assuming that* B4*'s value is correct, then we can try to replace* D6 *by a constant or another reference* x *with* $1500 < x < 2550$ $(0.5^*\mathrm{D4} < \mathrm{D6} < 0.85^*\mathrm{D4})$. *Therefore, any constant between 1500 and 2550 would be a repair candidate. Furthermore, changing the reference of* D6 *to any other cell containing a value between 1500 and 2550 is a solution, i.e.* C4 *and* C6. *(ii) Assuming that* B6*'s value is correct, we replace* D4 *with a constant or another reference* y *with* $3176.47 < y < 5400$. *Here, only a constant would be a valid repair candidate since there exists no cell with a value in that range. The ranking of the repair candidates for cell* D7 *is as follows:*

1) $\ell(\mathrm{D7}) = \mathrm{C6}/\mathrm{D4}$
2) $\ell(\mathrm{D7}) = \mathrm{C4}/\mathrm{D4}$
3) $\ell(\mathrm{D7}) = 2000/\mathrm{D4}$
4) $\ell(\mathrm{D7}) = \mathrm{D6}/4000$

C6's Manhattan distance to D6 is 1; therefore, this repair candidate is ranked higher than the repair candidate with C4, which has a Manhattan distance of 3. The solutions with constants are ranked lowest.

In the next step, the constraint is propagated to the referenced cells, i.e. we try to find repair candidates that fulfill either the constraint 1500 < D6 < 2550 *or* 3176.47 < D6 < 5400. D6*'s formula is* "D4-D5." *Assuming* D4 *is correct, then we must replace* D5 *with a constant or a reference between 500 and 1500. Assuming that* D5 *is correct, then we must replace* D4 *with a constant between 1800 and 2500, and so on.*

The mutation-based spreadsheet debugging approach uses genetic programming to generate repair candidates. Genetic programming adapts the concepts of evolution (mutation and natural selection) to the computer science domain. Weimer et al. [27, 28] and Arcuri [29] showed how to use genetic programming to find repair candidates for Java programs. Hofer and Wotawa [26] adapted these concepts to spreadsheets.

There are two evolution steps that must be considered when using genetic programming for spreadsheets: mutation and natural selection. A mutation is any change in the spreadsheet, such as a change of an operator. The resulting new spreadsheet is called a mutant. In contrast to the goal-directed approach, the changes in the mutation-based approach are randomly made within two dimensions: (i) the cell that is mutated is randomly picked from the cone of the cell with the contradicting testing decision.[3] (ii) The mutation operator is randomly picked from a predefined set of mutation operators. Similar to nature, many mutants are generated. The set of generated mutants is called a population. Only the fittest mutants will survive from one generation to the next (*natural selection*). We determine a mutant's fitness by the number of contradictory testing decisions. If the number of contradictory testing decisions for the mutant is higher than for the initial spreadsheet, we eliminate this mutant; otherwise, we keep the mutant in the new population. If a mutant satisfies all testing decisions, we additionally add it to the set of repair candidates. In order to keep the size of the population constant, we add copies of the initial spreadsheet to the population.

The spreadsheets contained in the new population are again mutated and evaluated. This process is repeated up to a predefined number of generations. Finally, the set of repair candidates is presented to the user.

Example 10.12 *The spreadsheet from Figure 10.1 has one contradictory testing decision. For demonstration purposes, we generate three mutants per generation and two generations in total. Changes can be made on the cells* B4, C4, D4, D6, *and* D7. *In the first round, we randomly select* B4 *to be mutated to* ℓ(B4) = B3*B3. *This results in three negative testing decisions; therefore, we eliminate this mutant. Next, we select* D4 *to mutate its formula to* ℓ(D4) = *SUM*(B4 : B4). *This mutant has only one negative testing decision; therefore, it will be added to the new* *population (mutant m_{11}). Next, we select* D7 *for mutation and change its formula to* ℓ(D7) = C6/D4. *This mutant satisfies all testing decisions and is therefore added to the new population (mutant m_{12}) and the set of repair candidates. In the end of the first round, we add one copy of the initial spreadsheet to the population to have a population size of three (mutant m_{13}). In the second round, we take mutant m_{11}, randomly choose a cell, e.g.* B4, *and change its formula to* ℓ(B4) = C3*B2. *This new mutant results in three cells with contradictory testing decisions; therefore, it is eliminated. Mutant m_{12} is mutated as follows:* ℓ(D5) = *SUM*(B5 : C3). *This mutant is added to the new population (mutant m_{21}) and to the set of repair candidates. Mutant m_{13} has the following change:* ℓ(D5) = *SUM*(C2 : C5). *This mutant is added to the new population (mutant m_{22}) but not to the set of repair candidates. Finally, the set of repair candidates is presented to the user.*

Usually, the population size and the number of generations exceed the amount of the example. While the mutation-based approach is not as efficient as the goal-directed one (because it performs many changes that worsen the result), it has one advantage over the goal-directed approach: it allows us to find repair candidates where several changes are necessary.

It often occurs that many mutants satisfy the testing decisions, yet too many repair candidates would overwhelm the user. The number of repair candidates can be reduced by computing distinguishing test cases [12, 30, 31]. A distinguishing test case I for two spreadsheets Π_1, Π_2 is a set of input values (c, v) for Π_1, Π_2 so that the values of at least one output cell[4] differ for Π_1 and Π_2.

Algorithm 10.4 explains how distinguishing test cases can be automatically computed. First, all expressions are converted into constraints (line 4) by using Algorithm 10.3 (described in Section 11.5). In order to differentiate between the constraints for the two mutants, we add a postfix to all variable names: "m_1" for all variables used in the constraints representing Π_1, and "m_2" for those representing Π_2. The constraint added in line 8 ensures that the input values are the same for Π_1 and Π_2; the constraint added in line 9 ensures that at least one value of the output cells is different. Finally, a constraint or SMT solver is called in line 10. The solver either returns a distinguishing test case, "UNSAT" (when the spreadsheets are equivalent) or "UNKNOWN" (in case of undecidability).

The user must indicate for a distinguishing test case the expected output. Having the expected output, we automatically eliminate one (or even more) of the generated repair candidates. If there are still too many repair candidates left, we generate more of the distinguishing test cases before presenting the remaining repair candidates to the user.

Repair approaches come with many limitations. The complexity of such techniques is very high because of the infinite search space. Therefore, these approaches are only suited for small spreadsheets. Furthermore, there is no guarantee that the

Inputs: Spreadsheets Π_1, Π_2 with $Input(\Pi_1) = Input(\Pi_2)$ and $Output(\Pi_1) = Output(\Pi_2)$
Outputs: Values for the input variables of a test case I

Let M be $\{\}$
foreach $\Pi_i \in \{\Pi_1, \Pi_2\}$ **do**
    foreach $c \in CELLS(\Pi_i)$ **do**
        $(a, M_c) =$ **ConvertExpression**$(\ell(c), m_i)$
        $M = M \cup M_c \cup \{a = c_{m_i}\}$
    end
end
$M = M \cup \{\wedge_{c \in Input(\Pi_1)} c_{m_1} = c_{m_2}\}$
$M = M \cup \{\vee_{c \in Output(\Pi_1)} c_{m_1} = c_{m_2}\}$
return Solve(M)

Algorithm 10.4 GetDistinguishingTestCase(Π_1, Π_2). *Source:* Adapted from Hofer et al. [30]/Wiley.

fault can be corrected: repair approaches can only correct faults by means of the predefined changes rules. If changes to the spreadsheets are needed that cannot be done by the predefined rules, no repair candidate can be generated. Further, the majority of the repair candidates does not suggest useful corrections, and still too many solutions are generated. Distinguishing test cases try to minimize the number of repair candidates, but the user has some additional effort because they have to compute the expected values for the test cases. If the user makes mistakes in doing so, repair candidates could be eliminated, which would actually correspond to the desired solution. Another problem is the risk that users take the first proposed repair candidate without verifying it [23].

10.7 Checking Approaches

Checking approaches are used to identify anomalies in spreadsheets via static analysis. The reported anomalies are not necessarily real faults: for example, correct, but complex formulas are reported to the user because they may cause problems in the future. Furthermore, false positives are often reported. Prominent examples of checking approaches are spreadsheet smells and type checking.

Spreadsheet smells are the spreadsheet counterpart to code smells, which were developed by Fowler in the 1990s [32]. Code smells are no faults per se, but they indicate that certain parts of a program's source code are difficult to understand and that these parts should be refactored. Similarly, spreadsheet smells draw the user's attention to the parts of a spreadsheet that are difficult to understand, maintain, and change.

Fowler [32] distinguished between interclass and intra-class code smells. Inter-class smells uncover problems that arise from the interaction of classes, such as classes that interact too much with each other (inappropriate intimacy smell), classes that expose their internal structure (indecent exposure smell), and methods that extensively use the methods of another class (feature envy smell). Intra-class smells uncover problems within the individual classes, including neglecting the coding standard, long methods, methods with long parameter lists, large classes (god class), large conditional blocks (conditional complexity smell), and duplicated code.

Hermans et al. [33] adapted inter-worksheet smells to the spreadsheet domain. For example, they adapted smells like the inappropriate intimacy to the spreadsheet domain and reformulated the problem that arises with this smell as follows: a strong semantic connection of two worksheets negatively influences the understandability and therefore the maintainability of a spreadsheet; making changes to one worksheet also requires knowledge of another worksheet.

Formula smells are the spreadsheet counterpart to intra-class code smells. For example, the long method smell is translated to the *multiple operations* smell, which counts the number of operations used within a single formula. The *conditional complexity* smell counts the number of nested conditionals within a single formula [34, 35].

Cunha et al. [36, 37] developed additional smells for detecting abnormalities that are unique in the spreadsheet domain, such as the reference to empty cells or the deviation of some parts of the input data. They provided a tool called the Smell-Sheet Detective,[5] which implements Hermans et al.'s inter- and intra-worksheet smells in addition to their smells.

AmCheck [38] is a tool that identifies a certain type of intra-worksheet smells: deviations within cell arrays. This approach groups cells row- and/or column-wise and checks if the cells share the same semantics. Outliers are reported as smelly cells.

Type checking techniques for spreadsheets differ from traditional type checking techniques in one important aspect: they do not report basic type checking errors such as adding an integer and a string; instead, they report more sophisticated errors like the mismatch of units. UCheck and Dimensions are well-known examples of such type checkers.

UCheck [39, 40] uses the labels as unit information and propagates this information from formula to formula. A unit can be a simple unit like "Month" or a dependent unit like "Month[Jan]." A cell can have more than one unit. Units can be combined using the AND-operator (in case of unrelated units, such as "Month[Jan]&UnitsSold") or the OR-operator (in case of related units, where units depend on the same base unit, such as "Month[Jan–Feb]." Formula cells inherit their units from the cells they reference. If a cell inherits references from several cells, the resulting combined unit must be well formed. For example, a combined unit is not well formed if units with the same dependent header are combined using the AND-operator (such as "Month[Jan]&Month[Feb]"). Computations with only partly matching dependent units also lead to violations of the well-formedness. All such violations are reported to the user as errors.

Example 10.13 *Cell C5 from Figure 10.1 has as unit Month[Feb]&Expenses. Therefore, cell* D5*'s unit is also Month[Feb]&Expenses. Cell* D4*'s unit is Month [Jan–Feb]&SalesRevenue. In cell* D6, D5 *is subtracted from* D4. *Since the month part of the units is not the same, an error is reported.*

Dimensions [41] uses the dimension information and its units to perform type checking. Frequently used dimensions in spreadsheets include length, time, and speed. The corresponding units are meter (cm, km, ft, ...), second (min, h, ...), and meter/second (km/h, ...). Dimensions analyzes labels for known dimensions and assigns the corresponding units to the input cells. These units are then propagated within the spreadsheet's formulas. Invalid operations, including adding meter and centimeter or meter and meter/second, are reported as errors.

10.8 Testing

Spreadsheet debugging is closely related to the testing of spreadsheets. In this section, we present some of the existing test approaches and concepts for spreadsheets, namely "what you see is what you test" (WYSIWYT), spreadsheet behavior-driven development (SS-BDD), and fragment-based testing.

WYSIWYT [42] is a manual testing approach. It allows users to mark cell values as correct or incorrect. WYSIWYT provides a visual overview of the testedness of a spreadsheet so that the user knows which parts of the spreadsheet need more attention.

SS-BDD [43] is a testing framework for spreadsheets that supports the implementation and automatic execution of test cases. The user has to write test scenarios in the Gherkin language, which requires for each test scenario the input (the initialization is called "Given"), the occurrence of an event (called "When"), and the outcome of the event (called "Then"). Several scenarios build a user story. The user stories are translated into executable scripts. These scripts are then executed on the spreadsheet under test. Finally, an execution report is generated with details on the successful and failed test cases.

Fragment-based testing [44] is a semiautomated testing approach. The idea behind this approach is that it is easier to build test cases for small pieces of a spreadsheet than for the whole spreadsheet. The approach automatically decomposes a spreadsheet into smaller parts, so-called fragments. The user then manually generates test cases for these fragments.

10.9 Conclusion

Checking and testing perform preparatory work for the actual debugging approaches. They are used to identify that there must be a problem in the spreadsheet. Once a misbehavior in a spreadsheet has been identified, one of the debugging techniques can be used to determine the root source of the observed misbehavior, i.e. the fault. There exists no silver-bullet for debugging spreadsheets. Each debugging technique has its own advantages and disadvantages. For different situations, different debugging techniques are better suited. Table 10.6 gives a short overview of the suitability of the different debugging techniques: the result of the goal-directed and mutation-based repair approaches seems to be the most practical for a user. However, these approaches can only be applied to small spreadsheets, and there is no guarantee that the fault can be corrected, while cones and SFL are well suited for large spreadsheets. Cones (and the deviated approaches dicing and union of cones) are not applicable in the case of coincidental correct input, several faults, and multiple faults, whereas SFL is suited for these circumstances. However, if the spreadsheet is of medium size and contains several faults, MBD is the best approach.

Table 10.6 Debugging techniques.

	Cones	SFL	MBD	Repair
Result	Set of cells	Ranking	Diagnoses	Repair candidates
Spreadsheet size	Large	Large	Medium	Small
Coincidental correctness	Not suited	Tolerant	Well suited	Suited
Wrong user input	Not suited	Tolerant	Not suited	Not suited
Multiple faults	Not suited	Limited	Well suited	Limited

Notes

1 See http://www.eusprig.org/horror-stories.html
2 Slightly modified version of Hofer et al's definition [11].
3 When several cells have contradicting testing decisions, the union of the cones is built. Another possibility would be to favor cells with a high similarity coefficient over cells with a lower similarity coefficient (i.e. using SFL as a

preprocessing step) or to compute the set of diagnoses by means of MBD and allow mutations only on cells that are contained in any diagnosis.

4 $Output(\Pi) = \{c \in CELLS(\Pi) \mid \nexists c' \text{ with } c \in \rho(c')\}$.

5 Download via http://ssaapp.di.uminho.pt/software.html

References

1 Kelso, P. (2012). Olympics: lucky few to get 100 m final tickets after synchronized swimming was overbooked by 10 000. https://www.telegraph.co.uk/sport/olympics/8992490/London-2012-Olympics-lucky-few-to-get-100m-final-tickets-after-synchronised-swimming-was-overbooked-by-10000.html (accessed January 2022).

2 Bridgeford, B.D. W. Baraboo to pay more for borrowed money than believed. https://www.wiscnews.com/baraboonewsrepublic/news/local/w-baraboo-to-pay-more-for-borrowed-money-than-believed/article_7672b6c6-22d5-11e1-8398-001871e3ce6c.html (accessed January 2022).

3 Brethour, P. Human error costs TransAlta $24-million on contract bids. https://www.theglobeandmail.com/report-on-business/human-error-costs-transalta-24-million-on-contract-bids/article18285651 (accessed January 2022).

4 Lee, J. Spreadsheet horror stories that will make you re-think your receivables management strategy. http://blog.anytimecollect.com/5-receivables-management-spreadsheet-horror-stories (accessed January 2022).

5 F1F9. The dirty dozen–12 modelling horror stories & spreadsheet disasters. https://www.f1f9.com/resources/dirty-dozen-12-modelling-horror-stories (accessed January 2022).

6 Worstall, T. (2013). Microsoft's excel might be the most dangerous software on the Planet. http://www.forbes.com/sites/timworstall/2013/02/13/microsofts-excel-might-be-the-most-dangerous-software-on-the-planet/#765cdbb572ae (accessed March 2019).

7 Panko, R.R. (2008). Thinking is bad: implications of human error research for spreadsheet research and practice. arXiv preprint arXiv:0801.3114, 21 January 2008.

8 Panko, R.R. (2008). Spreadsheet errors: what we know. What we think we can do. arXiv preprint arXiv:0802.3457. 23 February 2008.

9 Jannach, D., Schmitz, T., Hofer, B., and Wotawa, F. (2014). Avoiding, finding and fixing spreadsheet errors – a survey of automated approaches for spreadsheet QA. *Journal of Systems and Software* 94: 129–150.

10 Fisher, M. and Rothermel, G. (2005). The EUSES spreadsheet corpus: a shared resource for supporting experimentation with spreadsheet dependability mechanisms. *ACM SIGSOFT Software Engineering Notes* 30: 1–5. ACM.

11 Hofer, B., Riboira, A., Wotawa, F. et al. (2013). On the empirical evaluation of fault localization techniques for spreadsheets. In: *Fundamental Approaches to Software Engineering* (ed. V. Cortellessa and D. Varró), 68–82. Berlin, Germany: Springer.

12 Abreu, R., Außerlechner, S., Hofer, B., and Wotawa, F. (2015). Testing for distinguishing repair candidates in spreadsheets – the mussco approach. *Proceedings of the IFIP International Conference on Testing Software and Systems*, Sharjah and Dubai, United Arab Emirates (23–25 November 2015), 124–140. Springer.

13 Hofer, B., Perez, A., Abreu, R., and Wotawa, F. (2015). On the empirical evaluation of similarity coefficients for spreadsheets fault localization. *Automated Software Engineering* 22 (1): 47–74. ISSN 1573-7535. https://doi.org/10.1007/s10515-014-0145-3.

14 Ochiai, A. (1957). Zoogeographical studies on the soleoid fishes found Japan and its neighboring regions. *Bulletin of the Japanese Society of Scientific Fischeries* 22 (9): 526–530.

15 Ruthruff, J.R., Burnett, M., and Rothermel, G. (2005). An empirical study of fault localization for end-user programmers. *Proceedings of the 27th International Conference on Software Engineering (ICSE '05)*, St. Louis, MO, USA (15–21 May 2005), 352–361. IEEE. https://dl.acm.org/doi/pdf/10.1145/1062455.1062523.

16 Hofer, B. and Wotawa, F. (2015). Fault localization in the light of faulty user input. *Proceedings of the 2015 IEEE International Conference on Software Quality, Reliability and Security (QRS '15)*, Vancouver, BC, Canada (3–5 August 2015), 282–291. IEEE. https://doi.org/10.1109/QRS.2015.47.

17 Abreu, R., Hofer, B., Perez, A., and Wotawa, F. (2015). Using constraints to diagnose faulty spreadsheets. *Software Quality Journal* 23 (2): 297–322. ISSN 1573-1367. https://doi.org/10.1007/s11219-014-9236-4.

18 Jannach, D. and Schmitz, T. (2016). Model-based diagnosis of spreadsheet programs: a constraint-based debugging approach. *Automated Software Engineering* 23 (1): 105–144.

19 Hofer, B. and Wotawa, F. (2014). Why does my spreadsheet compute wrong values? *Proceedings of the 2014 IEEE 25th* International *Symposium on Software Reliability Engineering (ISSRE '14)*, Naples, Italy (3–6 November 2014), 112–121. IEEE. https://doi.org/10.1109/ISSRE.2014.23.

20 Abreu, R. and Van Gemund, A.J.C. (2010). Diagnosing multiple intermittent failures using maximum likelihood estimation. *Artificial Intelligence* 174 (18): 1481–1497.

21 Abreu, R., Mayer, W., Stumptner, M., and van Gemund A.J.C. (2009). Refining spectrum-based fault localization rankings. *Proceedings of the 2009 ACM Symposium on Applied Computing (SAC '09)*, Honolulu, HI, USA (8–12 March 2009), 409–414. ACM. https://doi.org/10.1145/1529282.1529374.

22 Hofer, B. and Wotawa, F. (2012). Spectrum enhanced dynamic slicing for better fault localization. *Proceedings of the European Conference on Artificial Intelligence*, Montpellier, France (27–31 August 2012), 420–425. IOS Press.

23 Abraham, R. and Erwig, M. (2007). GoalDebug: a spreadsheet debugger for end users. *Proceedings of the 29th International Conference on Software Engineering*

(*ICSE '07*), Minneapolis, MN, USA (20–26 May 2007), 251–260. IEEE. https://doi.org/10.1109/ICSE.2007.39.

24 Abraham, R. and Erwig, M. (2005). Goal-directed debugging of spreadsheets. *Proceedings of the 2005 IEEE Symposium on Visual Languages and Human-Centric Computing* (*VL/HCC '05*), Dallas, TX, USA (20–24 September 2005), 37–44. IEEE. https://doi.org/10.1109/VLHCC.2005.42.

25 Abraham, R. and Erwig, M. (2008). Test-driven goal-directed debugging in spreadsheets. *Proceedings of the 2008 IEEE Symposium on Visual Languages and Human-Centric Computing*, Herrsching, Germany (15–19 September 2008), 131–138. IEEE. https://doi.org/10.1109/VLHCC.2008.4639073.

26 Hofer, B. and Wotawa, F. (2013). Mutation-based spreadsheet debugging. *Proceedings of the 2013 IEEE International Symposium on Software Reliability Engineering Workshops* (*ISSREW '13*), Pasadena, CA, USA (4–7 November 2013), 132–137. IEEE. https://doi.org/10.1109/ISSREW.2013.6688892.

27 Forrest, S., Nguyen, T.V., Weimer, W., and Le Goues, C. (2009). A genetic programming approach to automated software repair. *Proceedings of the 11th Annual conference on Genetic and evolutionary computation*, Montreal, QC, Canada (8–12 July 2009), 947–954. ACM.

28 Weimer, W., Forrest, S., Le Goues, C., and Nguyen, T.V. (2010). Automatic program repair with evolutionary computation. *Communications of the ACM* 53 (5): 109–116.

29 Arcuri, A. and Yao, X. (2008). A novel co-evolutionary approach to automatic software bug fixing. *Proceedings of the 2008 IEEE Congress on Evolutionary Computation (IEEE World Congress on Computational Intelligence)*, Hong Kong (1–6 June 2008), 162–168. IEEE. https://doi.org/10.1109/CEC.2008.4630793.

30 Hofer, B., Maranhão, R., Perez, A.C., and Wotawa, F. (2014). Generation of relevant spreadsheet repair candidates. *Frontiers in Artificial Intelligence and Applications* 263: 1027–1028.

31 Wotawa, F., Nica, M., and Aichernig, B.K. (2010). Generating distinguishing tests using the minion constraint solver. *Proceedings of the 2010 Third International Conference on Software Testing, Verification, and Validation Workshops*, Paris, France (6–10 April 2010), 325–330. IEEE. https://doi.org/10.1109/ICSTW.2010.11.

32 Fowler, M. (2018). *Refactoring: Improving the Design of Existing Code*. Addison-Wesley.

33 Hermans, F., Pinzger, M., and van Deursen, A. (2012). Detecting and visualizing inter-worksheet smells in spreadsheets. *Proceedings of the 34th International Conference on Software Engineering (ICSE '12)*, Zurich, Switzerland (2–9 June 2012), 441–451. IEEE. https://doi.org/10.1109/ICSE.2012.6227171.

34 Hermans, F., Pinzger, M., and van Deursen, A. (2012). Detecting and visualizing inter-worksheet smells in spreadsheets. *Proceedings of the 34th International Conference on Software Engineering (ICSE '12)*, Zurich, Switzerland (2–9 June 2012), 441–451. IEEE. https://doi.org/10.1109/ICSE.2012.6227171.

35 Hermans, F., Pinzger, M., and van Deursen, A. (2015). Detecting and refactoring code smells in spreadsheet formulas. *Empirical Software Engineering* 20 (2): 549–575.

36 Cunha, J., Fernandes, J.P, Ribeiro, H., and Saraiva, J. (2012). Towards a catalog of spreadsheet smells. *Proceedings of the International Conference on Computational Science and Its Applications*, Salvador de Bahia, Brazil (18–21 June 2012), 202–216. Springer. http://repositorium.uminho.pt/bitstream/1822/36070/1/132.pdf

37 Cunha, J., Fernandes, J.P., Martins, P. et al. (2012). Smellsheet detective: a tool for detecting bad smells in spreadsheets. *Proceedings of the 2012 IEEE Symposium on Visual Languages and Human-Centric Computing (VL/HCC '12)*, Innsbruck, Austria (30 September to 4 October 2012), 243–244. IEEE. https://doi.org/10.1109/VLHCC.2012.6344535.

38 Dou, W., Cheung, S-C., and Wei, J. (2014). Is spreadsheet ambiguity harmful? Detecting and repairing spreadsheet smells due to ambiguous computation. *Proceedings of the 36th International Conference on Software Engineering (ICSE '14)*, Hyderabad, India (31 May to 7 June 2014), 848–858. ACM. https://dl.acm.org/doi/pdf/10.1145/2568225.2568316.

39 Abraham, R. and Erwig, M. (2004). Header and unit inference for spreadsheets through spatial analyses. *Proceedings of the 2004 IEEE Symposium on Visual Languages-Human Centric Computing*, Rome, Italy (26–29 September 2004), 165–172. IEEE. https://doi.org/10.1109/VLHCC.2004.29.

40 Abraham, R. and Erwig, M. (2007). UCheck: a spreadsheet type checker for end users. *Journal of Visual Languages and Computing* 18 (1): 71–95. 1045-926X. https://doi.org/10.1016/j.jvlc.2006.06.001.

41 Chambers, C. and Erwig, M. (2009). Automatic detection of dimension errors in spreadsheets. *Journal of Visual Languages and Computing* 20 (4): 269–283.

42 Rothermel, G., Li, L., DuPuis, C., and Burnett, M. (1998). What you see is what you test: a methodology for testing form-based visual programs. *Proceedings of the 20th International Conference on Software Engineering (ICSE '20)*, Kyoto, Japan (19–25 April 1998), 198–207. IEEE. https://doi.org/10.1109/ICSE.1998.671118.

43 Almeida, L., Cirilo, E., and Barbosa, E.A. (2016). SS-BDD: automated acceptance testing for spreadsheets. *Proceedings of the 1st Brazilian Symposium on Systematic and Automated Software Testing*, Maringa, Parana, Brazil (19–20 September 2016), 5. ACM. https://dl.acm.org/doi/pdf/10.1145/2993288.2993296.

44 Schmitz, T., Hofer, B., Jannach, D., and Wotawa, F (2016). Fragment-based diagnosis of spreadsheets. *Proceedings of the Federation of International Conferences on Software Technologies: Applications and Foundations*, Vienna, Austria (4–8 July 2016), 372–387. Springer. https://web-ainf.aau.at/pub/jannach/files/Workshop_SEMS_2016.pdf.

11

Theoretical Aspects of Software Fault Localization

Xiaoyuan Xie[1] *and W. Eric Wong*[2]

[1] *School of Computer Science, Wuhan University, Wuhan, China*
[2] *Department of Computer Science, University of Texas at Dallas, Richardson, TX, USA*

11.1 Introduction

As more and more debugging techniques are proposed, people have become interested in comparing the performance among different techniques. The most broadly adopted approach is empirical analysis [1–4]. Interestingly, though different experimental configurations are utilized, there are still many comparisons presenting consistent results.

For example, in spectrum-based fault[1] localization (SBFL), one core research direction is to propose new similarity coefficients (also known as risk evaluation formulas) in order to improve the fault localization accuracy. Some empirical studies have compared commonly used formulas [1–3, 5–7], and their results consistently indicate that Ochiai performs better than Jaccard, while Jaccard performs better than Tarantula. These consistent results cross-validate each other and imply some intrinsic relations among these formulas. Therefore, theoretical analyses are conducted to systematically mine these relations and provide definite answers. Though there are very few such studies, they play an important role to complement empirical approach in fault localization.

In this chapter, we will focus on the theoretical studies on SBFL. Let us first briefly state the problem and define notations. Given a program $PG = \langle s_1, s_2, ..., s_n \rangle$ with n statements that is executed by a test suite[2] of m test cases $TS = \{t_1, t_2, ..., t_m\}$, assume that there are P successful test cases and F failed test cases, and the coverage information is recorded accordingly. Then, we can formulate vector $A_i = \langle e_f^i, e_s^i, n_f^i, n_s^i \rangle$

Handbook of Software Fault Localization: Foundations and Advances, First Edition.
Edited by W. Eric Wong and T.H. Tse.

Published 2023 by John Wiley & Sons, Inc.

for each s_i, where e_f^i and e_s^i represent the number of test cases in *TS* that execute statement s_i and return the testing result of *fail* or *success*, respectively; n_f^i *and* n_s^i denote the number of test cases that do not execute s_i and return the testing result of *fail* or *success*, respectively [8].

A risk evaluation formula *R* is defined formally as follows [9]:

Definition 11.1 *Let I denote the set of nonnegative integers and Real denote the set of real numbers. A risk evaluation formula R is a member of the set* $F = \{R \mid R: I \times I \times I \times I \rightarrow Real\}$ *that maps the* A_i *of each statement* s_i *to its risk value. R is expected to rank the faulty statement as high as possible.*

In this chapter, we will introduce three methods for theoretically comparing different risk evaluation formulas. With these methods, we want to answer two questions among all possible risk evaluation formulas: "Which one can be maximal?" and "Does global greatest formula exist?" At the end of the chapter, we discuss how the assumptions in theoretical methods should be relaxed.

11.2 A Model-Based Hybrid Analysis

Naish et al. [6] conducted a hybrid study that was partially theoretical and partially empirical. This was the first comprehensive analysis on over 30 risk evaluation formulas. Different from previous studies that used real software, this analysis was built on a model program segment.

11.2.1 The Model Program Segment

The analysis in Naish et al. was based on the model program segment "If-Then-Else-2" (*ITE*$_2$), shown in Figure 11.1.

It can be seen that *ITE*$_2$ is a very simple program segment with a single fault on S_4. It expects to assign "`True`" to *x*. Obviously, if the buggy statement S_4 is not executed, no failure will be revealed. To model real-life coincidental correctness,

```
if (t1())
    s1();           //s1
else
    s2();           //s2
if (t2())
    x = True;       //s4
else
    x = t3();       //s4-buggy
```

Figure 11.1 Model program segment If-Then-Else-2 (*ITE*$_2$). *Source:* Naish et al. [6]/ACM.

ITE_2 assumes that S_4 returns either "`True`" or "`False`". In other words, by executing the fault S_4, there is only a possible assignment of "`False`" to x, where a failure is revealed. In [6], these two cases are treated as two separate execution paths. As a consequence, ITE_2 has eight distinct program paths, each of which leads to a definite testing result of success (seven paths) or failure (one path). This model program segment abstracts away detailed functionality and keeps important aspects for SBFL. For example, it models scenarios where a fault may or may not be executed and scenarios where an executed bug does or does not trigger a failure.

Naish et al.'s comparison is based on the performance of all possible multisets of these executions, under the following measures defined particularly for the model program segment ITE_2 [6].

Definition 11.2 ***(Score for Formula R with Paths X).***
Given a test suite TS with m test cases executed on ITE_2, let X denote a multiset of execution paths. Then, the testing results can also be determined. A formula R is used to assign rankings to S_1, S_2, S_3, and S_4 based on the coverage and testing information from X. Then, the score for R with X is 0 if S_4 is ranked after any of the other statement. Otherwise, assume that there are k statements equally top-ranked (including S_4); then, the score is 1/k.

In other words, only when S_4 is ranked at top is R scored for X.

Definition 11.3 ***(Total Score for Formula R with TS).***
The total score for R with TS is the sum of the scores for R with paths X, over all possible multisets X of m execution paths that contain at least one failed path.

In [6], the measure used to compare R is this total score. However, it is sometimes intractable to calculate this value for R. Consider a test suite TS with m test cases. It is the same as the problem of "placing m balls into p ($p = 8$) numbered bags, where seven are white bags and one is black." By executing all the m test cases on ITE_2, the number of all possible combinations (i.e. distinct multisets) of the m path executions can be determined recursively as follows:

$$f(m, p) = \sum_{i=0}^{m} f(i, p-1)$$

where for each distinct multiset, there are several equivalent recurrences. According to the binomial theorem, $f(m, p) = C(m+p-1, m) = \dfrac{(m+p-1)!}{m!(p-1)!}$.

Total score requires summing up the score with all multisets X. However, with the increase in m, the numbers of distinct multisets and possible ways to "place the balls" for each multiset will grow exponentially. To deal with this problem, Naish et al. chose to generate each distinct multiset once to evaluate the overall performance for small m; meanwhile, for larger m, they approximated the performance by randomly sampling multisets from a uniform distribution. More specifically, they repeatedly generated a random number within $[1, f(m, p)]$ and then mapped it to the corresponding multiset.

11.2.2 Important Findings

Based on the above model and measures, Naish et al. [6] presented two ranking metrics: O and O^p, and proved two optimal formulas adapted by Xie et al. [9] as follows:

$$O_{s_i} = O(A_i) = \begin{cases} -1 & \text{if } e_f^i < F \\ P - e_s^i & \text{if } e_f^i = F \end{cases} \tag{11.1}$$

and

$$O_{s_i}^p = O^p(A_i) = e_f^i - \frac{e_s^i}{P+1} \tag{11.2}$$

where P is the number of successful test cases.

Naish et al. [6] proved that both O and O^p are optimal with respect to the model program segment and the total score for all test set sizes. They gave the same rankings to all statements with $n_f^i = 0$, which includes the bug if there is a single bug. We skip their proofs here because these two formulas will be further investigated under more general cases in the following sections.

Apart from the above conclusions, Naish et al. [6] investigated the equivalence among more formulas, based on a finding that a formula $R(A_i)$ produces the same rankings as formula $f(R(A_i))$ if f is a monotonically increasing function. They found six equivalent groups (including O and O^p) among their investigated formulas. Later studies with other theoretical frameworks double confirmed these conclusions, which will be covered in later sections.

After presenting the above theoretical analysis, Naish et al. [6] then conducted a very comprehensive empirical study, including the impacts from "error detection accuracy," "the number of failures," and "buggy code execution frequency." Performance of different formulas was also compared. Since this chapter is exclusively for theoretically analysis, we skip the empirical results. Readers can refer to [6] for more detailed findings.

11.2.3 Discussion

In fact, before giving the study of [6], the authors gave preliminary proofs that formulas Tarantula and q_e are equivalent [10]. The method of proving is the same as the one in [6].

This study is not a pure theoretical method. It still involves empirical data to verify the analysis. The model cannot represent all possible faulty scenarios. For large m, random sampling is used to estimate the performance, rather than always provide definite answer. Besides, the measure is not a widely adopted one. It is defined strictly for the model, and the optimality is proven based on the measure, which is not generally applicable. Thus, it does not address the two questions in Section 11.1.

However, as the first trial, this model-based idea strongly convinces the conjecture in Section 11.1 that formulas have intrinsic relations with one another. This motivates other researchers to further seek for a more general theoretical framework.

11.3 A Set-Based Pure Theoretical Framework[3]

After the model-based method, there was a more general theoretical framework proposed by Xie et al. [9], which does not rely on any model programs or test suites. Comparisons among different formulas are based on the most commonly adopted measure, namely:

$$EXAM = \frac{Ranking\ of\ the\ faulty\ statement}{Number\ of\ statements\ in\ the\ program} \tag{11.3}$$

According to the definition, the higher the faulty statement s_f can be ranked according to the formula R, the lower *EXAM* score R can be obtained. A lower *EXAM* score indicates a better performance.

11.3.1 Definitions and Theorems

Xie et al. [9] pointed out that in SBFL, the relative risk values, rather than the absolute risk values of all statements, are the key factor determining the performance for a formula R. This is because the relative risk values determine the ranking of program statements, which is strongly related to the *EXAM* score. This leads to the core idea of this framework, namely set-division and subset relationship analysis.

Definition 11.4 ***(Subset Division).***
Given a ranking list in descending order of the risk values evaluated by a formula R, all statements (denoted as S) can be divided into three mutually exclusive subsets S_B^R, S_F^R, and S_A^R with respect to an arbitrary s_f, as follows:

1) *S_B^R consists of all statements with risk values higher than the risk value of the faulty statement s_f, that is, $S_B^R = \{s_i \in S \mid R_{s_i} > R_{s_f},\ 1 \leq i \leq n\}$.*

2) S_F^R *consists of all statements with the risk values equal to the risk value of the faulty statement* s_f, *that is,* $S_F^R = \{s_i \in S \mid R_{s_i} = R_{s_f},\ 1 \le i \le n\}$.
3) S_A^R *consists of all statements with the risk values lower than the risk value of the faulty statement* s_f, *that is,* $S_A^R = \{s_i \in S \mid R_{s_i} < R_{s_f},\ 1 \le i \le n\}$.

In the practice of SBFL, a tie-breaking scheme is required to determine the order of the statements with identical risk values, and such a scheme is also required in our theoretical analysis. This framework is not bound to any particular tie-breaking scheme. Instead, it requires that a tie-breaking scheme returns consistent rankings for all formulas, which is independent of the risk evaluation formulas. All tie-breaking schemes complying with this requirement are referred to as consistent tie-breaking schemes, which are formally defined as follows:

Definition 11.5 *Given any two statement sets* S_1 *and* S_2 *that contain elements with the same risk values, a tie-breaking scheme returns the ordered statement lists* O_1 *and* O_2 *for* S_1 *and* S_2, *respectively. The tie-breaking scheme is said to be consistent if all elements common to* S_1 *and* S_2 *have the same relative order in* O_1 *and* O_2.

To compare different formulas, some relations are defined. Let E_1 and E_2 denote the *EXAM* scores for risk evaluation formulas R_1 and R_2, respectively.

Definition 11.6 ***(Better).***
R_1 *is said to be better than* R_2 *(denoted as* $R_1 \rightarrow R_2$*) if, for any program, faulty statement* s_f, *test suite, and consistent tie-breaking scheme, we have* $E_1 \le E_2$.

Definition 11.7 ***(Equivalent).***
R_1 *and* R_2 *are said to be equivalent (denoted as* $R_1 \leftrightarrow R_2$*), if, for any program, faulty statement* s_f, *test suite, and consistent tie-breaking scheme, we have* $E_1 = E_2$.

As a reminder, relation "$\rightarrow$" is reflexive and transitive, that is, we have $R_1 \rightarrow R_1$; and if $R_1 \rightarrow R_2$ and $R_2 \rightarrow R_3$, we have $R_1 \rightarrow R_3$. Relation "$\leftrightarrow$" is reflexive, symmetric, and transitive, that is, $R_1 \leftrightarrow R_1$; if $R_1 \leftrightarrow R_2$, then $R_2 \leftrightarrow R_1$; and if $R_1 \leftrightarrow R_2$ and $R_2 \leftrightarrow R_3$, then $R_1 \leftrightarrow R_3$. R_1 is said to be *strictly better* than R_2 if we can prove that $R_1 \rightarrow R_2$ but $R_2 \nrightarrow R_1$.

Immediately from Definitions 11.6 and 11.7, we have the following property:

Theorem 11.1 *For any two risk evaluation formulas* R_1 *and* R_2, $R_1 \leftrightarrow R_2$ *if and only if* $R_1 \rightarrow R_2$ *and* $R_2 \rightarrow R_1$.

Moreover, the following sufficient condition for $R_1 \rightarrow R_2$ involving the notion of subset can be proven.

Theorem 11.2 *Given any two risk evaluation formulas R_1 and R_2, if, for any program, faulty statement s_f, and test suite, we have $S_B^{R_1} \subseteq S_B^{R_2}$ and $S_A^{R_2} \subseteq S_A^{R_1}$, then $R_1 \rightarrow R_2$.*

Proof. Consider a formula R_3 such that for any program, faulty statement s_f, and test suite, we have, $S_B^{R_3} = S_B^{R_1}$ and $S_A^{R_3} = S_A^{R_2}$. Let E_3 denote the *EXAM* score of R_3, and let L_1, L_2, and L_3 denote the ranking lists returned by R_1, R_2, and R_3, respectively. For R_1 and R_3, we have $S_B^{R_3} = S_B^{R_1}$, $S_F^{R_1} \subseteq S_F^{R_3}$ and $S_A^{R_3} \subseteq S_A^{R_1}$. If the tie-breaking scheme is consistent, s_f can never have a lower ranking in L_1 than in L_3. Therefore, we have $E_1 \leq E_3$. Now, considering R_2 and R_3, we have $S_B^{R_3} \subseteq S_B^{R_2}$, $S_F^{R_2} \subseteq S_F^{R_3}$, and $S_A^{R_2} = S_A^{R_3}$ If the tie-breaking scheme is consistent, s_f always has the same relative order with any element of $S_F^{R_2}$, in both L_2 and L_3. However, all elements in $S_F^{R_3} \setminus S_F^{R_2}$ will definitely be ranked higher than s_f in L_2, but they will not necessarily be ranked higher than s_f in L_3. As a consequence, $E_3 \leq E_2$.

Therefore, we have $E_1 \leq E_2$. Following immediately from Definition 13.6, we have $R_1 \rightarrow R_2$.

With Theorems 11.1 and 11.2, a sufficient condition for $R_1 \leftrightarrow R_2$ can be established.

Theorem 11.3 *Given any two risk evaluation formulas R_1 and R_2, if, for any program, faulty statement s_f, and test suite, we have $S_B^{R_1} = S_B^{R_2}$, $S_F^{R_1} = S_F^{R_2}$, and $S_A^{R_1} = S_A^{R_2}$, then $R_1 \leftrightarrow R_2$.*

Proof. Suppose that for any program s_f and any test suite, we have $S_B^{R_1} = S_B^{R_2}$ and $S_A^{R_1} = S_A^{R_2}$. In other words, we have $S_B^{R_1} \subseteq S_B^{R_2}$ and $S_A^{R_1} \subseteq S_A^{R_2}$ as well as $S_B^{R_2} \subseteq S_B^{R_1}$ and $S_A^{R_1} \subseteq S_A^{R_2}$. It follows immediately from Theorem 11.2 that $R_1 \rightarrow R_2$ and $R_2 \rightarrow R_1$. Therefore, we have $R_1 \leftrightarrow R_2$ after Theorem 11.1.

11.3.2 Evaluation

In principle, with all the above definitions and theorems, it becomes possible to compare two formulas regardless of program, fault, or test suite. In this section, some sample theoretical comparisons are provided for single-fault scenario, under the following assumptions:

1) The programs under debugging have a testing oracle, and the faults are deterministic ones. That is, for any test case, the testing result of either *fail* or *success* can be decided.
2) "Perfect bug detection" is assumed in SBFL, which means the fault can always be identified once the faulty statement is examined. It is generally understood

that "perfect bug detection" is usually not held in reality. However, for the formula comparison in SBFL, how programmers comprehend the given SBFL results and how well they detect the fault are generally not considered by the community.

3) Omission faults that SBFL is not designed for are not considered. It is assumed that for all observed failures, the execution of a faulty statement s_f is the cause. In other words, a statement cannot cause a failure by not being executed.
4) The test suite has 100% statement coverage and contains at least one *failed* test case and one *successful* test case.

   It is true that this constraint is not easily satisfied in practice. However, whether a test suite actually achieves 100% statement coverage does not really affect the applicability of the theoretical framework. If a statement is never covered by any test case in the given test suite, it cannot be the faulty statement that triggers the observed failures. Therefore, in practice, if a test suite does not achieve 100% statement coverage, people should first exclude the uncovered statements and only focus on the covered portion of program for the debugging purpose, in which the 100% statement coverage is then satisfied. For the uncovered statements, it is reasonable to rank them at the bottom of the ranking list [12].

   Besides, at least one *failed* test case is required for debugging. At least one *successful* test case avoids some formulas being totally undefined (such as Tarantula) or partially undefined (such as Scott).

From the definitions and the above assumptions, it follows that $1 \leq F < |TS|$, $1 \leq P < |TS|$, and $P + F = |TS|$, as well as the following lemmas.

Lemma 11.1 *For any* $A_i = \langle e_f^i, e_s^i, n_f^i, n_s^i \rangle$, *it holds that* $e_f^i + e_s^i > 0 \wedge e_f^i + n_f^i = F \wedge e_s^i + n_s^i = P \wedge e_f^i \leq F \wedge e_s^i \leq P$.

Lemma 11.2 *For any faulty statement* s_f *with* $A_f = \langle e_f^i, e_s^i, n_f^i, n_s^i \rangle$, *if* s_f *is the only faulty statement in the program, it follows that* $e_f^f = F \wedge n_f^f = 0$.

Different formulas can be proven as equivalent ones if they have the same set-division. Let us consider O and O^P as examples [13].

Proposition 11.1 $O \leftrightarrow O^P$

Proof. As shown in Section 11.2.1, we have

$$O_{s_i} = O(A_i) = \begin{cases} -1 & \text{if } e_f^i < F \\ P - e_s^i & \text{if } e_f^i = F \end{cases}$$

After Definition 11.4, we have

$$S_B^O = \left\{ s_i \mid \left(e_f^i < F \text{ and} -1 > P - e_s^f\right) \text{ or } \left(e_f^i = F \text{ and} P - e_s^i > P - e_s^f\right), 1 \le i \le n \right\} \tag{11.4}$$

$$S_F^O = \left\{ s_i \mid \left(e_f^i < F \text{ and} -1 = P - e_s^f\right) \text{ or } \left(e_f^i = F \text{ and} P - e_s^i = P - e_s^f\right), 1 \le i \le n \right\} \tag{11.5}$$

$$S_A^O = \left\{ s_i \mid \left(e_f^i < F \text{ and} -1 < P - e_s^f\right) \text{ or } \left(e_f^i = F \text{ and} P - e_s^i < P - e_s^f\right), 1 \le i \le n \right\} \tag{11.6}$$

It is not difficult to prove that the above sets S_B^O, S_F^O, and S_A^O are equal to the following sets X, Y and Z, respectively.

$$X = \left\{ s_i \mid e_f^i = F \text{ and } e_s^f - e_s^i > 0, 1 \le i \le n \right\} \tag{11.7}$$

$$Y = \left\{ s_i \mid e_f^i = F \text{ and } e_s^f - e_s^i = 0, 1 \le i \le n \right\} \tag{11.8}$$

$$Z = \left\{ s_i \mid \left(e_f^i < F\right) \text{ or } \left(e_f^i = F \text{ and } e_s^f - e_s^i < 0\right), 1 \le i \le n \right\} \tag{11.9}$$

Similarly, for $O^p = e_f^i - \frac{e_s^i}{P+1}$, we can prove that $S_B^{O^p}$, $S_F^{O^p}$, and $S_A^{O^p}$ are also equal to the above sets X in (11.7), Y in (11.8), and Z in (11.9), respectively. As a consequence, we have $S_B^O = S_B^{O^p}$, $S_F^O = S_F^{O^p}$, and $S_A^O = S_A^{O^p}$. Immediately after Theorem 11.3, $O \leftrightarrow O^p$.

By following this proof, Xie et al. further identified six equivalent groups among formulas under investigation [9, 14], namely ER1 ER6, as follows. These results incorporate the ones in [6].

Proposition 11.2 Six equivalent groups of formulas are identified among all investigated formulas.

- ER1 consists of O, O^P, and GP13.
- ER2 consists of Jaccard, Anderberg, Sørensen-Dice, Dice, and Goodman.
- ER3 consists of Tarantula, q_e, and CBI Inc.
- ER4 consists of Wong2, Hamann, Simple Matching, Sokal, Rogers and Tanimoto, Hamming etc., and Euclid.
- ER5 consists of Wong1, Russell and Rao, and Binary.
- ER6 consists of Scott and Rogot1.

This proposition can be similarly proven by showing that all formulas within each group share the same S_B, S_F, and S_A. For all formula definitions and detailed proofs, please refer to [9, 13].

Apart from equivalence, the framework is more useful in identifying *nonequivalence* by analyzing the subset relation between two formulas. Let us consider ER1 and M2 as illustrations [13].

Proposition 11.3 ER1 $\leftrightarrow$ M2, where $\text{M2} = \dfrac{e_f^i}{e_f^i + n_s^i + 2\left(n_f^i + e_s^i\right)}$.

Proof. In order to prove ER1 $\rightarrow$ M2, it is sufficient to prove $O \rightarrow$ M2. As proven in Proposition 11.1, S_B^O and S_A^O are equal to the sets defined in (11.7) and (11.9), respectively. By similar mathematical deduction, we can obtain the following:

$$S_A^{\text{M2}} = \left\{ s_i \mid e_f^i > 0 \text{ and } \frac{P + e_s^f}{F} - \frac{2F + P}{e_f^i} + 2 - \frac{e_s^i}{e_f^i} > 0, 1 \le i \le n \right\} \tag{11.10}$$

$$S_A^{\text{M2}} = \left\{ s_i \mid e_f^i = 0 \text{ or } \left(e_f^i > 0 \text{ and } \frac{P + e_s^f}{F} - \frac{2F + P}{e_f^i} + 2 - \frac{e_s^i}{e_f^i} < 0 \right), 1 \le i \le n \right\} \tag{11.11}$$

First, we will prove $S_B^O \subseteq S_B^{\text{M2}}$. Assume $s_i \in S_B^O$. Then, we have $e_f^i = F > 0$ and $(e_s^f - e_s^i) > 0$ after (11.7). As a consequence, we have

$$\frac{P + e_s^f}{F} - \frac{2F + P}{e_f^i} + 2 - \frac{e_s^i}{e_f^i} = \frac{P + e_s^f - 2F - P + 2F - e_s^i}{F} = \frac{e_s^f - e_s^i}{F} > 0$$

Therefore, $s_i \in S_B^{\text{M2}}$ after (11.10). Thus, $S_B^O \subseteq S_B^{\text{M2}}$.

Secondly, we are going to prove $S_A^{\text{M2}} \subseteq S_A^O$. Suppose $s_i \in S_A^{\text{M2}}$. Then, we have either $(e_f^i = 0)$ or $\left(e_f^i > 0 \text{ and } \frac{P + e_s^f}{F} - \frac{2F + P}{e_f^i} + 2 - \frac{e_s^i}{e_f^i} < 0\right)$ after (11.11).

- Consider the case that $e_f^i = 0$. Obviously, $e_f^i < F$. Immediately after Theorem 11.3, $s_i \in S_A^O$.
- Consider the case that $e_f^i > 0$ and $\frac{P + e_s^f}{F} - \frac{2F + P}{e_f^i} + 2 - \frac{e_s^i}{e_f^i} < 0$. Assume further that $0 < e_f^i < F$. After (11.9), we have $s_i \in S_A^O$. Next, consider the subcase that $e_f^i = F$. Then, we have $\frac{P + e_s^f}{F} - \frac{2F + P}{e_f^i} + 2 - \frac{e_s^i}{e_f^i} = \frac{e_s^f - e_s^i}{F}$. Since $\frac{P + e_s^f}{F} - \frac{2F + P}{e_f^i} + 2 - \frac{e_s^i}{e_f^i}$ and $F > 0$, we have $(e_s^f - e_s^i)$. Thus, $s_i \in S_A^O$ after (11.9).

In summary, we have proven that $S_A^{\text{M2}} \subseteq S_A^O$.

In conclusion, we have $S_B^O \subseteq S_B^{M2}$ and $S_A^{M2} \subseteq S_A^O$. Immediately after Theorem 11.2, $O \rightarrow$ M2. After Proposition 11.1, ER1 $\rightarrow$ M2.

As a reminder, this is a strictly "better" relation, that is, the reverse M2 $\rightarrow O$ does not hold. This can be easily proven by finding a counterexample. For details, readers may refer to [13].

11.3.3 The Maximality Among All Investigated Formulas

By analyzing the set division of all investigated formulas and gradually inferring their relations, Xie et al. identified two maximal groups of formulas among them, namely, ER1 and ER5 [9, 14]. Here, a risk evaluation formula R_1 is said to be maximal of a set of formulas, S, if, for any element $R_2 \in S$, $R_2 \rightarrow R_1$ implies $R_2 \leftrightarrow R_1$. In other words, there does not exist formula $R_2 \in S$ such that $R_2 \rightarrow R_1$ and $R_1 \nrightarrow R_2$. Figure 11.2 reveals part of the relations in hierarchy, where ER1 and ER5 are at the top.

In Figure 11.2, each node represents a formula or a group of formulas that are equivalent, that is, for any two formulas R_1 and R_2 in a node, we have $R_1 \leftrightarrow R_2$. The arrow from node N_1 to node N_2 means that for any formulas R_1 and R_2 in N_1 and N_2, respectively, $R_1 \rightarrow R_2$ and $R_2 \nrightarrow R_1$. Since the relation "$\rightarrow$" is transitive, for any formulas R_i and R_j in N_i and N_j, respectively, we have $R_i \rightarrow R_j$, as long as N_j is a direct or indirect descendant node of N_i in the figure. If there is no directed path from N_i to N_j, then neither $R_i \nrightarrow R_j$ nor $R_j \nrightarrow R_i$. For example, it is not difficult to prove that neither ER1 $\rightarrow$ ER5 nor ER5 $\rightarrow$ ER1 holds by giving a counterexample.

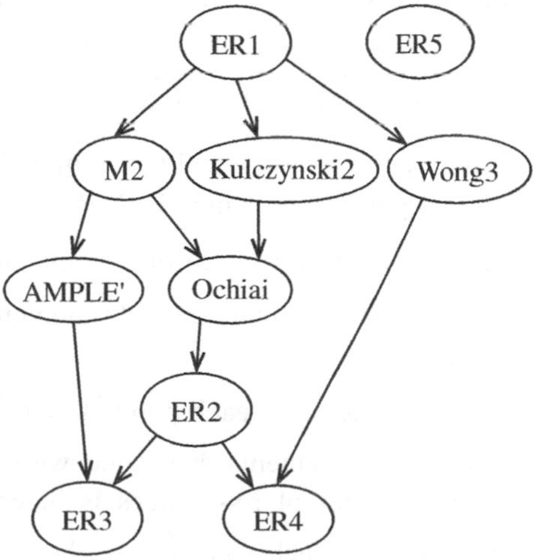

Figure 11.2 A sample performance hierarchy.

The relation between these two maximal groups shows that there is no greatest formula in the investigated ones. For more details, readers may refer to [13].

So far, we have proven "the existence of maximal formula and non-existence of the greatest formula among the investigated ones." However, these still do not address the questions in Section 11.1 completely.

11.4 A Generalized Study[4]

To answer the two questions in Section 11.1, proofs for both the greatest and maximal formulas must be generalized to all possible formulas. Yoo et al. [15] extended the framework in Section 11.3 by visualizing the SBFL space. This generalized analysis follows the assumptions in [9] and is also under single-fault scenario.

11.4.1 Spectral Coordinate for SBFL

To construct the spectral coordinate, we first need to reduce the number of dimensions in Definition 11.1 (five in total, four members of program spectrum, and one risk score). In fact, for a given pair of program and test suite, the values of F and P are constants. Thus, for each statement s_i, it follows that $A_i = \left\langle e_f^i, P - n_s^i, F - e_f^i, n_s^i \right\rangle$ after Lemma 11.1, which is denoted as $\overline{A}_i = \left\langle e_f^i, e_s^i \right\rangle$. In this way, the five dimensions in the original definition are reduced to three. Consequently, the definition of formula is rephrased as follows:

Definition 11.8 $\overline{F} = \left\{ \overline{R} \mid \overline{R} : I_f \times I_s \rightarrow Real \right\}$, *where* I_f *denotes the set of integers within [0, F] and* I_s *denotes the set of integers within [0, P], such that* $\overline{R}\left(e_f^i, n_s^i\right) = R\left(e_f^i, e_s^i, n_f^i, n_s^i\right)$.[5]

Given any values of P and F, the input domain of any formula $\overline{R}$ is shown as the grid in Figure 11.3a, where both e_f^i and e_s^i are non-negative integers $0 \le e_f^i \le F$, and $0 \le e_s^i \le P$. Given a pair of test suite and program, each point $\left(e_f^i, e_s^i\right)$ on this grid is associated with a group of statements that have the corresponding e_f^i and e_s^i values.[6]

A formula $\overline{R}$ maps each point $\overline{A}_i = \left(e_f^i, e_s^i\right)$ to a real number that is the risk value of all statements associated with this point, as shown in Figure 11.3b. Any assignment of risk values is independent of the number of statements associated with each point $\left(e_f^i, e_s^i\right)$ but solely decided by the definition of $\overline{R}$.

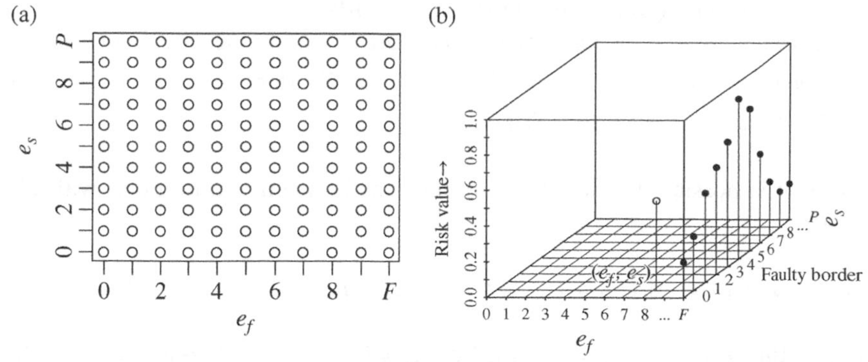

Figure 11.3 Visualizing the SBFL space: (a) spectral coordinate $\overline{A}_i$ and (b) mapping from $\overline{A}_i$ to risk values by formula $\overline{R}$. *Source:* Yoo et al. [15]/University College London.

Two components in Figure 11.3b are critical for the analysis, namely Faulty Border and Overstepping Points, which are, respectively, defined in the following Definitions 11.9 and 11.11:

Definition 11.9 (*Faulty Border*).
We call the sequential points $\langle (F, 0), (F, 1), \ldots, (F, e_s), \ldots, (F, P) \rangle$ $(0 \le e_s \le P)$ *the Faulty Border, which is denoted as E.*

It can be found that for any R, the risk values of all points on E are solely decided by their e_s. In single-fault scenario, the faulty statement s_f can only be associated with a point (F, e_s^f) on E. However, this point may also be associated with other correct statements s having $(F, e_s^i) = (F, e_s^f)$. These statements always share the same risk values as that of s_f, regardless of the selection of the formula. Points (F, e_s^i) other than (F, e_s^f) must be associated with correct statements. Depending on the adopted formula, the risk values of such points can be either greater than, equal to, or smaller than that of s_f. We use the following definition to depict the distribution of risk values on E for R.

Definition 11.10 (*Distribution on E*).
Given a formula R, we define the distribution of risk values (referred to as P_R) on E as a set of O_s^{ij}, where $O_s^{ij} = \left\langle n_s^i, n_s^j, op \right\rangle$ indicates the relation between the risk scores of two distinct points (F, n_s^i) and (F, n_s^j) on E. Given that $n_s^i < n_s^j$, op can be either ">" (i.e. $R(F, n_s^i) > R(F, n_s^j)$), "<" (i.e. $R(F, n_s^i) < R(F, n_s^j)$), or "=" (i.e. $R(F, n_s^i) = R(F, n_s^j)$).

Definition 11.11 ***(Overstepping Points Outside E).***
Let U_R denote the set of points outside E that have risk scores higher than or equal to those of some points (F, e_s^i) on E, for formula R. More formally, $U_R = \{\overline{A} \in I_f \times I_s - E \mid \exists \overline{A}' \in E \text{ such that } R(\overline{A}) \geq R(\overline{A}')\}$.

Now, it is possible to identify some relations between two formulas with U_R and P_R.

Proposition 11.4 If $U_{R1} = U_{R2} = \emptyset$ and $P_{R1} = P_{R2}$, it follows that $R_1 \rightarrow R_2$.

Proposition 11.5 If $U_{R1} = U_{R2} = \emptyset$ but $P_{R1} \neq P_{R2}$, we have $R_1 \nrightarrow R_2$ and $R_2 \nrightarrow R_1$.

11.4.2 Generalized Maximal and Greatest Formula in *F*

With the above preliminaries, Yoo et al. [15] provided answers for the identification of general maximal and greatest formulas.

Definition 11.12 ***(Generalized Maximality).***
A risk evaluation formula R is said to be a maximal formula in F if, for any formula $R' \in F$ such that $R' \neq R \wedge R' \rightarrow R$, it also holds that $R' \leftrightarrow R$.

Definition 11.13 ***(Generalized Greatest Formula).***
A risk evaluation formula R is said to be a greatest formula in F if, for any formula $R' \in F \wedge R' \neq R$, it holds that $R' \leftrightarrow R$.

Proposition 11.6 A formula R is a maximal element of F if and only if U_R is empty.

Proposition 11.6 provides a necessary and sufficient condition for a maximal formula of F. It also shows that, given any non-maximal formula R that has a non-empty U_R, we can always convert R into its maximal version R', where R' assigns identical risk values to points on E as R. However, it also assigns, to all points in U_R, a constant C whose value is smaller than the risk value of any point on E. With Proposition 11.6, we can prove that both ER1 and ER5 are maximal with respect to the generalized Definition 11.12 by showing that for any formula R in ER1 or ER5, $U_R = \emptyset$.

Proposition 11.7 There is no greatest formula in F.

Proof. Assume that there exists a greatest formula R_g. According to Proposition 11.6, $U_{R_g} = \emptyset$, and R_g is a maximal element of F. Consider the two maximal groups of formulas ER1 and ER5, which have been proven to be nonequivalent to each other [9]. It is not difficult to prove that $U_{\text{ER1}} = U_{\text{ER5}} = \emptyset$ and $P_{\text{ER1}} \neq P_{\text{ER5}}$. Thus, there are three possible cases for $P_{Rg,}$ as follows:

Case: $P_{R_g} = P_{\text{ER1}}$. It follows that, for ER5, $U_{\text{ER5}} = U_{R_g} = \emptyset \wedge P_{\text{ER5}} \neq P_{R_g}$.
Case: $P_{R_g} = P_{\text{ER5}}$. It follows that, for ER1, $U_{\text{ER1}} = U_{R_g} = \emptyset \wedge P_{\text{ER1}} \neq P_{R_g}$.
Case: $P_{R_g} \neq P_{\text{ER1}}$ and $P_{R_g} \neq P_{\text{ER5}}$. It follows that, for both ER1 and ER5, $U_{\text{ER1}} = U_{R_g} = \emptyset \wedge P_{\text{ER1}} \neq P_{R_g} \wedge U_{\text{ER5}} = U_{R_g} = \emptyset \wedge P_{\text{ER5}} \neq P_{R_g}$.

For any of the above cases, it is possible to construct another formula R' such that $U_{R'} = U_{R_g} = \emptyset \wedge P_{R'} \neq P_{R_g}$. After Proposition 11.5, we have $R' \nrightarrow \text{R}_\text{g}$ and $R_g \nrightarrow \text{R}'$. After Definition 11.13, R_g cannot be the greatest formula.

We skip the proofs for Propositions 11.4–11.6. For details, readers can refer to [15].

11.5 About the Assumptions[7]

With the above theoretical methods, we can now easily identify the maximal in F and know we can lesson our efforts to search for the "greatest." Similar to having threats to validity in empirical studies, people also have concerns about adopting assumptions in the theoretical analysis. In particular, people are interested to know whether these assumptions are feasible in practice and how they may affect the applicability of the theories. In this section, we will discuss some major concerns.

11.5.1 Omission Fault and 100% Coverage

As a coverage based debugging technique, SBFL utilizes coverage profiles and testing results to perform a risk assessment, with the intuition that a higher e_f^i or a lower e_s^i should lead to a higher risk value. In other words, SBFL is actually designed for locating non-omission faults. In other words, its responsibility is to find the root faulty statement, of which the execution will trigger failure. This is also explicitly indicated in "the assumptions of SBFL" by Steimann et al. [17]: "every failed test case executes at least one fault whose execution causes the failure." Obviously, this implies that only the risk assessment on the covered statements is meaningful, because statements that are not covered by any test case can never be the root non-omission fault of the observed failures. As a consequence, it is unreasonable to investigate statements that are not covered by any test case. This is supported by Steimann et al. [17]: "However, searching the explanation for failed test cases in code that is not covered by any test case, or even not covered by any failed test case, not only makes little sense per se."

Secondly, it is true that the constraint of 100% coverage is not easily satisfied in practice. However, whether a test suite achieves 100% statement coverage does not really affect the applicability of the theoretical framework. Let us revisit the two commonly adopted methods in dealing with non-100% coverage in empirical studies:

- Method A: Exclude the uncovered statements, and focus on the covered ones for SBFL.
- Method B: Calculate the risk values for uncovered statements in the same way as we do for covered statements, by ignoring the coverage level.

It is obvious that Method A complies with the SBFL's nature and should be adopted in reasonable studies. This is consistent with the above theoretical assumption and has been suggested by Steimann et al. [17]. On the other hand, Method B may introduce noise [17]. It may not affect some formulas with which the risk values of uncovered statements are no higher than those of the covered statements, especially lower than those of the statements with $e_f^i = F$, such as Jaccard. However, for some formulas, it is possible that the risk values of uncovered statements are higher than those of the covered statements, for example, Wong2 ($e_f^i - e_s^i$). In the latter formulas, noise from the uncovered statements may affect the performance. Things may be even more complicated in some formulas, such as Ochiai and Tarantula, and uncovered statements become undefined due to the zero-denominator. Then, defining these statements will affect the performance of the formula. Two extreme cases can be: (i) rank these statements at the top of the lists or (ii) rank them at the bottom. Obviously, these two strategies may give completely different results. The latter one gives a better performance and is essentially the same as the above Method A. (Note that it provides the same absolute ranking for the faulty statement as Method A but a lower *EXAM* score because more statements are considered, and hence there is a larger denominator. However, the comparison results between formulas are the same as the ones with Method A.)

Unfortunately, we usually cannot tell which method an experiment has taken, since it is unnecessary to report such low-level technical details in a paper. For those who use Method B, we have no way to know how they define the uncovered statements for formulas like Ochiai or Tarantula. By adding additional definitions to these formulas, they are no longer the original versions, and the comparison is actually done on the newly defined formulas Ochiai' and Tarantula' rather than their original versions. Moreover, since no details have been reported, how can we guarantee that different people use the same new definition? If different new definitions are used, they are actually investigating different formulas, and hence the results cannot be put together for cross-validation. As mentioned above, some empirical studies have suggested to use Method A to avoid the potential noise [17]. Steimann et al. also suggested to further exclude the statements with e_f 0, which was actually suggested earlier by Xie et al. [9, 12].

To summarize, the assumptions about the coverage and omission faults are far more than reasonable and should actually be adopted in both empirical and theoretical analysis. Relevant discussion has usually been omitted in empirical studies. However, as a theoretical analysis, we must list them out to provide precise proofs and definite answers.

11.5.2 Tie-Breaking Scheme

Another concern of the theoretical analysis is about the "consistent tie-breaking scheme." It is known that given a program and a test suite, the *EXAM* is codetermined by formula *R* and the adopted tie-breaking scheme. Therefore, to provide a fair comparison among formulas, the tie-breaking scheme as the fixed factor should be independent of the risk formulas. The "consistent tie-breaking scheme" can serve this purpose. In fact, this is not one particular single scheme. Instead, the consistent tie-breaking scheme covers a large family of schemes.

As a reminder, choosing the consistent tie-breaking scheme in the theoretical framework does not mean that the framework is inapplicable with other tie-breaking schemes. In fact, theorems in Section 11.3 still hold with other commonly adopted tie-breaking schemes, such as "Best," "Worst," and "Average" [16].

11.5.3 Multiple Faults

As discussed above, SBFL formulas are designed based on the intuition that "a higher e_f^i and a lower e_s^i should lead to." It is not difficult to find out that such an intuition is only meaningful for single (non-omission) fault scenarios [18]. Fortunately, DiGiuseppe and Jones [18] also have demonstrated that "in terms of localizing at least one, most prominent, fault, the performance of SBFL is not adversely affected by the increasing number of faults, even in the presence of fault localization interference." Such evidence implies that the conclusions of our theoretical analysis are equally useful for multiple faults.

On the other hand, an attractive idea was proposed to assist the application of SBFL in multiple-fault scenarios, namely parallel debugging approaches [19–21]. In these studies, test cases are first clustered into several specialized test suites based on various execution information, and each of the test suites targets an individual single fault. In practice, each specialized test suite is dispatched to a particular debugger, who is supposed to focus on the corresponding single fault. In other words, by properly clustering the test suite, the multiple-fault scenario can be transformed into a single-fault scenario, in which our theoretical framework can be applied. Further discussions on multiple faults are given in Chapter 12 titled "Software Fault Localization for Programs with Multiple Bugs."

11.5.4 Some Plausible Causes for the Inconsistence Between Empirical and Theoretical Analyses

Most of the experimental studies have shown consistent results with the theoretical analysis [1–3, 5–7]. However, there exist some studies that show inconsistence with the theoretical analysis [22–24]. Some plausible causes for the inconsistence are as follows:

The experimental setup varies in different formula investigations. For example, Yu et al. [24] and Jiang et al. [22] used different tie-breaking schemes for Tarantula and CBI.

For the existence of noise of $e_f^f < F$ for faulty statement s_f, based on the nature of SBFL and for single non-omission faults, we should have $e_f^f = F$. However, such a situation may not be observed in experiments. Note that for some crash failures, the coverage information may not be properly collected. In such cases, the program crashes when the execution reaches the faulty statement, and the coverage collector also stops working at the same time and fails to properly record the coverage of the faulty statement. Therefore, it is possible to have $e_f^f < F$, which violates the nature of SBFL. Thus, this should be considered as a type of noise, and it is actually a very common reason why the empirical results violate the theoretical analysis. Yoo et al. [15] proved that "assigning higher risk values to statements with $e_f^i = F$ than to those with $e_f^i < F$" is the necessary and sufficient condition for formulas of being maximal (intuitively speaking, these formulas are good because they assign highest risk values to the single non-omission faulty statement that always has $e_f^f = F$). In other words, maximal formulas are only interested in the "possible faulty statements whose $e_f^i = F$." Some maximal formulas even ignore the statements with $e_f^i < F$, such as Naish1 that assigns −1 to all statements with $e_f^i < F$. However, if the noise of $e_f^f < F$ is introduced, the faulty statement will not be the focus of the maximal formula, and then the performance of the formula decreases. For example, Naish1 is very sensitive to this type of noise, with which the performance of Naish1 significantly decreases.

For the existence of noise from omission faults, some people use Siemens Suite, which contains omission faults, while others use various strategies to handle this case by considering the preceding or succeeding statement of the missing statement as the "faulty statement." Furthermore, the "preceding or succeeding" statement may have different interpretations, such as "the line order of source code" or "the order according to the control-flow graph." There is no consensus on the interpretation. Such an omission fault may result in $e_f^f < F$.

Moreover, it is possible to have inconsistence between different empirical results, due to the above reasons (internal threats to validities in experimental studies), as well as the non-exhaustiveness of experimental analysis. For example, Le et al. [23] observed that Ochiai outperforms Naish2 and Naish1, which was contradictory to the experimental results in [6]. Without any theoretical analysis, it is impossible to identify whether the inconsistency is because there is actually no relation between these formulas (i.e. $R_1 \not\leftrightarrow R_2$) or because there is noise in either experiment. However, from theoretical analysis, we can have the answer. We have precisely defined the assumptions and the scope of our theoretical framework. Since all proofs of the theoretical analysis are explicitly stated, an independent verification for the results of the theoretical analysis can be easily conducted. However, it is a common practice to not provide these technical details in empirical studies, and hence it is extremely difficult, if not impossible, to verify whether an experimental analysis has been conducted without any mistake.

Notes

1 In this chapter, we use "bug" and "fault" interchangeably. We also use "programs" and "software" interchangeably.
2 The phrase "*executed* by a test suite" is used interchangeably with the phrase "*covered* by a test suite".
3 Part of Section 11.3 is from Refs. [9, 11].
4 Part of Section 11.4 is from Refs. [8, 11].
5 In our discussion, when two formulas from F are compared, it is assumed that they are being applied to the same program and test suite. Thus, in the context of such comparisons, the symbols R and $\overline{R}$ can and will be used interchangeably, as are symbols F and $\overline{F}$.
6 Note that the number of statements associated with each point $\left(e_f^i, e_s^i\right)$ is independent of the formula but solely decided by the pair of program and test suite.
7 Part of Section 11.5 is from Refs. [11, 16].

References

1 Abreu, R., Zoeteweij, P., and van Gemund, A.J.C. (2006). An evaluation of similarity coefficients for software fault localization. *Proceedings of the 12th Pacific Rim International Symposium on Dependable Computing*, Riverside, CA, USA (18–20 December 2006), 39–46. IEEE.

2 Abreu, R., Zoeteweij, P., and van Gemund, A.J.C. (2007). On the accuracy of spectrum-based fault localization. *Proceedings of the Testing: Academic and Industrial Conference Practice and Research Techniques – MUTATION*, Windsor, UK (10–14 September 2007), 89–98. IEEE.

3 Abreu, R., Zoeteweij, P., Golsteijn, R., and van Gemund, A.J.C. (2009). A practical evaluation of spectrum-based fault localization. *Journal of Systems and Software* 82 (11): 1780–1792.

4 Jones, J.A. and Harrold, M.J. (2005). Empirical evaluation of the tarantula automatic fault-localization technique. *Proceedings of the 20th IEEE/ACM International Conference on Automated Software Engineering*, Long Beach, CA, USA (7–11 November 2005), 273–282. ACM.

5 Lee, H.J., Naish, L., and Ramamohanarao, K. (2009). The effectiveness of using non redundant test cases with program spectra for bug localization. *Proceedings of the 2nd IEEE International Conference on Computer Science and Information Technology*, Beijing, China (8–11 August 2009), 127–134. IEEE.

6 Naish, L., Lee, H.J., and Ramamohanarao, K. (2011). A model for spectra-based software diagnosis. *ACM Transactions on Software Engineering and Methodology* 20 (3): 11:1–11:32.

7 Santelices, R., Jones, J.A., Yanbing, Y., and Harrold, M.J. (2009). Lightweight fault-localization using multiple coverage types. *Proceedings of the 31st International Conference on Software Engineering*, Vancouver, BC, Canada (16–24 May 2009), 56–66. IEEE. ISBN 978-1-4244-3453-4.

8 Yoo, S., Xie, X., Kuo, F.C. et al. (2017). Human competitiveness of genetic programming in spectrum-based fault localisation: theoretical and empirical analysis. *ACM Transactions on Software Engineering and Methodology (TOSEM)* 26 (1): 1–30.

9 Xie, X., Chen, T.Y., Kuo, F.-C., and Xu, B. (2013). A theoretical analysis of the risk evaluation formulas for spectrum-based fault localization. *ACM Transactions on Software Engineering and Methodology* 22 (4): 31:1–31:40.

10 Lee, H.J., Naish, L., and Ramamohanarao, K. (2009). Study of the relationship of bug consistency with respect to performance of spectra metrics. *Proceedings of the 2nd IEEE International Conference on Computer Science and Information Technology*, Beijing, China (8–11 August 2009), 501–508. IEEE.

11 Xie, X. and Xu, B. (2021). *Essential Spectrum-Based Fault Localization*. Springer.

12 Xie, X., Chen, T.Y., and Xu, B.W. (2010). Isolating suspiciousness from spectrum-based fault localization techniques. *Proceedings of the 10th International Conference on Quality Software*, Zhangjiajie, Hunan, China (14–15 July 2010), 385–392. IEEE.

13 Xie, X. (2012). On the analysis of spectrum-based fault localization. PhD thesis. Swinburne University of Technology.

14 Xie, X., Kuo, F.-C., Chen, T.Y. et al. (2013). Provably optimal and human-competitive results in SBSE for spectrum based fault localisation. *Proceedings of the 5th Symposium on Search Based Software Engineering (SSBSE '13)*, Saint Petersburg, Russia (24–26 August 2013), 224–238. Springer.

15 Yoo, S., Xie, X., Kuo, F-C. et al. (2014). No Pot of Gold at the End of Program Spectrum Rainbow: Greatest Risk Evaluation Formula Does Not Exist. Technical Report RN/14/14, Department of Computer Science, University College London (3 November 2014).

16 Chen, T.Y., Xie, X., Kuo, F.C., and Xu, B. (2015). A revisit of a theoretical analysis on spectrum-based fault localization. *Proceedings of the 39th Annual Computer Software and Applications Conference*, Taichung, Taiwan (1–5 July 2015), vol. 1, 17–22. IEEE.

17 Steimann, F., Frenkel, M., and Abreu, R. (2013). Threats to the validity and value of empirical assessments of the accuracy of coverage-based fault locators. *Proceedings of the 2013 International Symposium on Software Testing and Analysis*, Lugano, Switzerland (15–20 July 2013), 314–324. ACM. ISBN 978-1-4503-2159-4.

18 DiGiuseppe, N. and Jones, J.A. (2011). On the influence of multiple faults on coverage-based fault localization. *Proceedings of the International Symposium on Software Testing and Analysis*, Toronto, ON, Canada (17–21 July 2011), 199–209. ACM.

19 Jones, J.A., Bowring, J.F., and Harrold, M.J. (2007). Debugging in parallel. *Proceedings of the International Symposium on Software Testing and Analysis*, London, UK (9–12 July 2007), 16–26. ACM. ISBN 978-1-59593-734-6.

20 Liu, C. and Han, J. (2006). Failure proximity: a fault localization-based approach. *Proceedings of the 14th ACM SIGSOFT International Symposium on Foundations of Software Engineering*, Portland, OR, USA (5–11 November 2006), 46–56. ACM. ISBN 1-59593-468-5.

21 Zheng, A.X., Jordan, M.I., Liblit, B. et al. (2006). Statistical debugging: simultaneous identification of multiple bugs. *Proceedings of the 23rd International Conference on Machine Learning*, Pittsburgh, PA, USA (25–29 June 2006), 1105–1112. ACM. ISBN 1-59593-383-2.

22 Jiang, B., Zhang, Z., Tse, T.H., and Chen, T.Y. (2009). How well do test case prioritization techniques support statistical fault localization. *Proceedings of the 33rd Annual International Conference on Computer Software and Applications*, Seattle, WA, USA (20–24 July 2009), vol. 1, 99–106. IEEE.

23 Le, T.-D.B., Thung, F., and Lo, D. (2013). Theory and practice, do they match? A case with spectrum-based fault localization. *Proceedings of the 29th IEEE International Conference on Software Maintenance*, Eindhoven, Netherlands (22–28 September 2013), 380–383. IEEE.

24 Yanbing, Y., Jones, J.A., and Harrold, M.J. (2008). An empirical study of the effects of test-suite reduction on fault localization. *Proceedings of the 30th International Conference on Software Engineering*, Leipzig, Germany (10–18 May 2008), 201–210. ACM. ISBN 978-1-60558-079-1.

12

Software Fault Localization for Programs with Multiple Bugs

Ruizhi Gao[1], *W. Eric Wong*[2], *and Rui Abreu*[3]

[1] *Sonos Inc., Boston, MA, USA*
[2] *Department of Computer Science, University of Texas at Dallas, Richardson, TX, USA*
[3] *Department of Informatics Engineering, Faculty of Engineering, University of Porto, Porto, Portugal*

12.1 Introduction[1]

Regardless of the effort spent developing a computer program, it may still contain bugs[2] In fact, the larger and more complex a program is, the higher the likelihood that it contains bugs. When the execution of a test case on a program fails, it suggests that the program has one or more bugs. However, the burden of locating and fixing these bugs is on the programmers. To do so, they must first be able to identify exactly where these bugs are. Known as fault localization, this step can be very time-consuming and expensive [2]. Many fault localization techniques use all failed and successful test cases to prioritize code and generate a *ranking* of statements[3] in descending order of their suspiciousness values. Statements with higher suspiciousness values are pushed toward the top of the ranking, as they are more likely to contain bugs than those at the bottom with lower suspiciousness values. Programmers then examine statements from the top of the ranking to locate the first statement that contains bug(s). Fault localization techniques using this approach have been well reported in the literature [1, 3–15]. Many of these studies assume there is exactly one bug in the program. Since a single-bug assumption may not hold in practice and mixed failed test cases associated with different causative bugs can reduce the effectiveness of a fault localization technique, in this chapter, we will introduce existing techniques for debugging programs with multiple bugs.

The major difference between fault localization on programs with multiple bugs and fault localization on programs with exactly one bug is that, for programs with multiple bugs, programmers have to determine the due-to relationship [16] between a failure (and the failed test) and its corresponding bug(s), while, for

Handbook of Software Fault Localization: Foundations and Advances, First Edition.
Edited by W. Eric Wong and T.H. Tse.

Published 2023 by John Wiley & Sons, Inc.

programs with a single bug, the programmers are not required to do such a determination because there is only one bug in the program.

For programs with exactly one bug, the execution trace collected at runtime can provide information such as whether a statement is covered by a test case.[4] This trace and the corresponding execution result (success or failure) are used by various spectrum-based fault localization techniques to generate a suspiciousness ranking and help programmers locate the bug.

However, it is not appropriate to apply the same process directly to programs with multiple bugs. The major challenge lies in identifying the due-to relationship between failed test cases and the underlying causative bugs. One solution is to produce fault-focused clusters [17] by grouping failed test cases caused by the same bug into the same clusters. That is, failed test cases in the same cluster are related to the same bug, whereas failed test cases in different clusters are related to different bugs. A fault-focused suspiciousness ranking is then generated using failed test cases of a given cluster and some or all of the successful test cases. Examining code along this ranking can help programmers locate the corresponding causative bug linked to this ranking. The key component of this process is obtaining a good clustering on failed test cases. A major challenge is that we do not know the number of bugs in a program in advance. Hence, we are not able to properly determine the number of clusters or assign initial medoids (centers) to these clusters, which are required in order to use many advanced clustering techniques [16, 18, 19]. Other challenges during clustering include how to properly represent a failed test case, how to measure the difference between two failed test cases (i.e. which distance metric should be used), and how to perform the clustering based on an appropriate clustering algorithm. Different solutions to these challenges have different impacts on the clustering results, which will accordingly affect the fault localization effectiveness.

In this chapter, we will introduce fault localization techniques for programs with multiple bugs. The traditional one-bug-at-a-time technique is explained in Section 12.2, followed by two techniques proposed by Jones et al. [17] in Section 12.3. The localization of multiple bugs using algorithms from integer linear programming is presented in Section 12.4. An advanced fault localization technique for locating multiple bugs in parallel is given in Section 12.5. Other techniques are introduced in Section 12.6.

12.2 One-Bug-at-a-Time[5]

For the one-bug-at-a-time (OBA) technique, in each debugging iteration, all failed test cases (even though they are associated with different causative bugs) and all successful test cases are used in conjunction with a fault localization technique (such as crosstab [20], DStar [15], or RBF [21]) to generate a suspiciousness

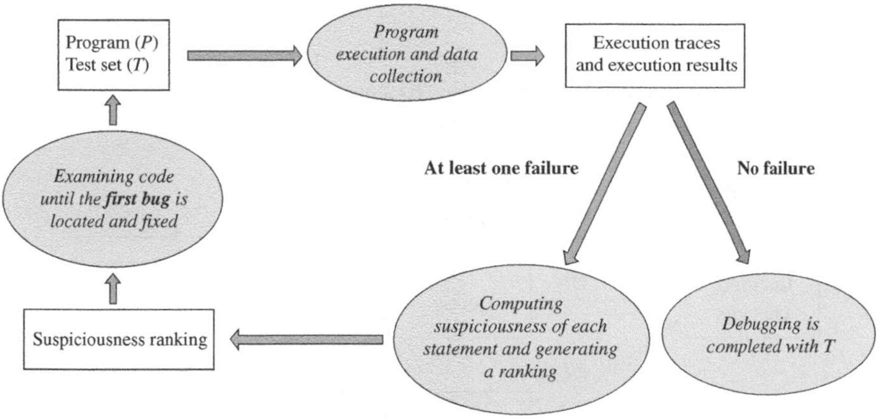

Figure 12.1 Debugging process of OBA.

ranking. Programmers fix the first bug located by the ranking and then execute the modified program against all test cases before moving on to the next iteration. The debugging process terminates when all test cases are executed successfully. Only one bug is fixed in each iteration. The process of OBA is shown in Figure 12.1.

12.3 Two Techniques Proposed by Jones et al.[6]

To achieve the goal of enabling developers to simultaneously debug multiple faults in parallel, Jones et al. [17] proposed a parallel-debugging process, which is shown by the data-flow diagram in Figure 12.2.

The program under test, P, is instrumented to produce $\hat{P}$. When $\hat{P}$ is executed with test suite T, it produces a set of successful test cases T_P and a set of failed test cases T_F, along with execution information, such as branch or method profiles. T_F and the execution information are input to the clustering technique, *Cluster*, to produce a set of fault-focused clusters C_1, C_2, ..., C_n that are disjoint subsets of T_F. Each C_i is combined with T_P to produce a specialized test suite that assists in locating a fault. Using these test suites, developers can debug the program in parallel – shown as $Debug_i$ in the figure.

The resulting changes, ch_1, ch_2, ..., ch_n, are integrated into the program. This process can be repeated until all test cases pass.

The component of this parallel-debugging process, *Cluster*, is shown in more detail in Figure 12.3. Jones et al. developed two techniques (J1 and J2) to cluster failed test cases.

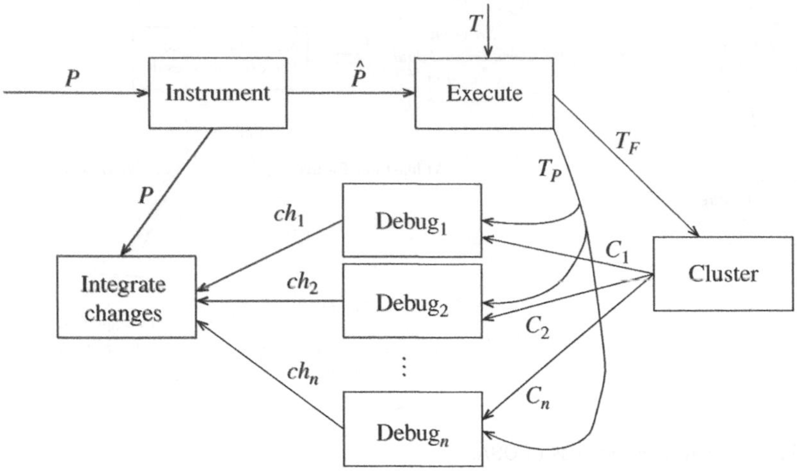

Figure 12.2 Parallel-debugging process proposed. *Source:* Jones et al. [17]/ACM.

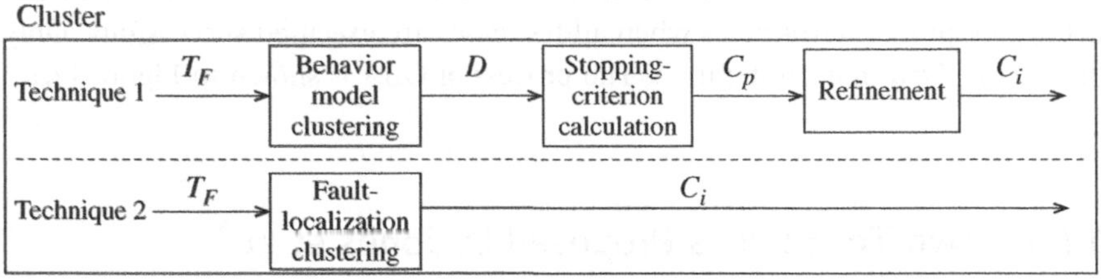

Figure 12.3 Two clustering techniques proposed. *Source:* Jones et al. [17]/ACM.

12.3.1 J1: Clustering Based on Profiles and Fault Localization Results

J1 first clusters behavior models of executions of failed test cases T_F to produce a complete clustering history (or dendrogram) D (described in Section 12.3.1). The technique then uses fault localization information to identify a stopping criterion for D and produces a preliminary set of clusters C_p (described in Section 12.4). The technique finally refines C_p by merging the clusters that appear to be focused on the same faults and outputs the final set of clusters C_i (described in Section 12.3.1.3). The first step is based on instrumentation profiles, and the second and third steps are based on fault localization results.

12.3.1.1 Clustering Profile-Based Behavior Models

To group the failed test cases according to the likely faults that caused them, Jones et al. used a technique to cluster executions based on agglomerative hierarchical clustering [22, 23]. For each test case, J1 creates a behavior model that is a

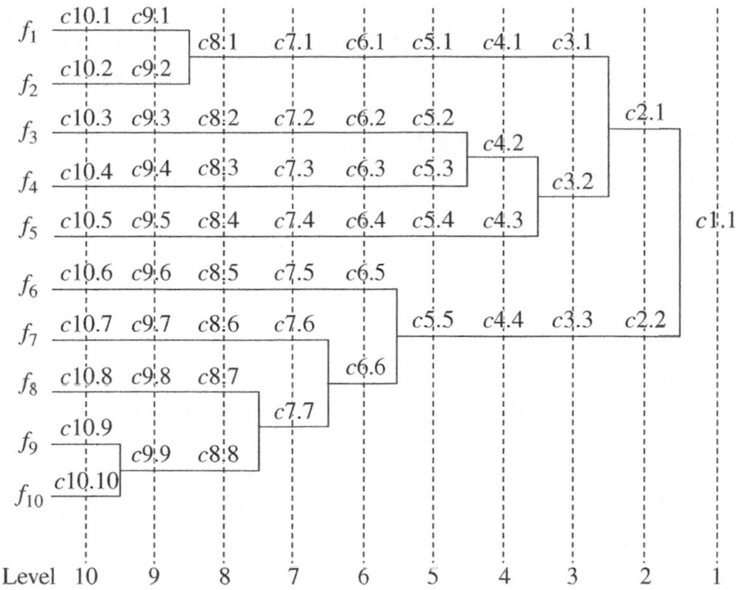

Figure 12.4 Dendrogram for 10 failed test cases. *Source:* Jones et al. [17]/ACM.

statistical summary of data collected during program execution. The specific models are discrete-time Markov chains (DTMCs), and clustering occurs iteratively with the two most similar models merged at each iteration. Every execution is represented by its branching behavior. The branching profile of an execution is represented by the percentage of times that each branch of a predicate statement was taken. Similarity is measured with a similarity metric; in this research, that metric is the sum of the absolute difference between matching transition entries in the two DTMCs being compared. Each pair of executions is assigned a similarity value that is computed by taking the sum of the differences of the branch percentage profile. J1 initially sets the stopping criterion for the clustering to one cluster, so that the clustering proceeds until one cluster remains. To illustrate the clustering, consider Figure 12.4, which shows a dendrogram that depicts an example clustering of 10 execution models.

The left side of the figure shows the 10 individual failed test cases represented as $f_1, \ldots, f_{10}$. At each "level" of the dendrogram, the process of clustering the two most similar test cases is shown. Initially, at level 10, failed test cases $f_1, \ldots, f_{10}$ are placed in clusters $c10.1$ through $c10.10$, respectively. Then, the clustering algorithm finds that $c10.9$ and $c10.10$ have the most similar behavior models and groups these two clusters to obtain a new cluster, labeled as $c9.9$, which results in nine clusters at level 9. This clustering continues until there is one cluster, $c1.1$. Conventionally, a good stopping criterion for the clustering, which is difficult to determine, is based on the practitioners' domain knowledge. Jones et al. have developed a technique that inputs the dendrogram and computes the stopping criterion based on fault localization information. This stopping criterion is described in the next section.

12.3.1.2 Using Fault Localization to Stop Clustering

A fault localization technique, Tarantula [24], is used for this secondary assessment of the clustering.

Figure 12.4 shows the process of grouping clusters until one cluster remains. Unless there is only one behavior represented by the test cases, at some point during this clustering, two clusters are merged that are not similar. In the context of fault localization, unless there is only one fault, at some point in the clustering process, the failed test cases due to one fault are merged with the failed test cases due to another fault. The technique should stop the clustering process just before this type of clustering occurs.

J1 identifies the clustering-stopping criterion by leveraging the fault localization results. It computes the fault localization ranks (the ranking of all statements in the program from most suspicious to least suspicious based on the Tarantula) for each individual failed test case (shown on the left side of Figure 12.4) using a test suite of all successful test cases with that one failed test case. Then, every time a merge is made in the clustering process, J1 calculates the fault localization ranks using the members of that cluster and the passed test cases. Thus, regarding a dendrogram, such as Figure 12.4, J1 computes fault localization ranks at every merge point of two clusters. Using these fault localization ranks at all merge points in the dendrogram, J1 uses a similarity measure to identify when the clustering process appears to lose the ability to find a fault – that is, it clusters two items that contribute to find a different suspicious region of the program. To measure the similarity of two fault localization results, the suspicious area of the program as the set of statements of the program that are deemed "most suspicious" for each of the results is defined. This process is depicted in Figure 12.5.

To decide whether two fault localization results identify the same suspicious region of the program, the threshold that differentiates the *most suspicious* statements from the statements that are *not of interest* must be established. This threshold is called *MostSusp*. For example, we may assign the value of 20% to *MostSusp*; this means that the top 20% of the suspicious statements in the rank are in the most suspiciousness set, and that the lower 80% are not of interest. To compare the two sets of statements, a set-similarity metric, *Jaccard similarity*, is used. The Jaccard metric computes a real value between 0 (completely dissimilar) and 1 (completely similar) by evaluating the ratio of the cardinality of the intersection of these sets and the cardinality of the union of these sets. The similarity of two sets, A and B, is computed by the following equation: to determine whether the two sets are *similar* or *dissimilar*, the threshold for the similarity metric must be established, which is

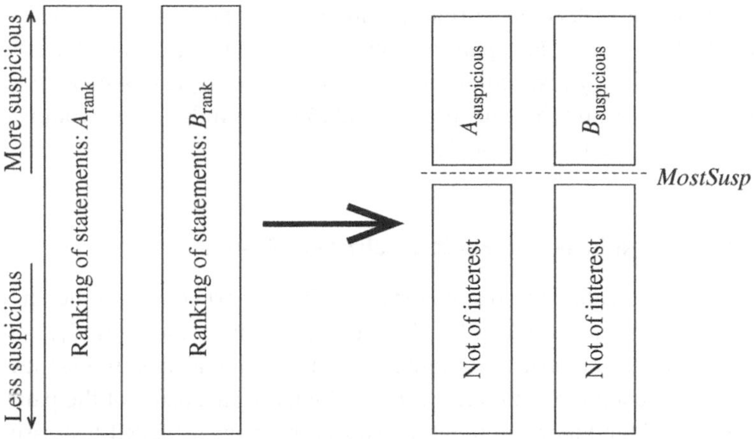

Figure 12.5 Computing the similarity of fault localization results. *Source:* Jones et al. [17]/ACM.

called *Sim*. For example, we may assign the value of 0.7 to *Sim* – this means that two sets of suspicious statements will be in the same cluster if their similarity value is at or above 0.7. In practice, these thresholds, *MostSusp* and *Sim*, are determined during a training phase that shadows the debugging process.

To determine where to stop the clustering, J1 traverses the dendrogram in reverse, starting at the final cluster. At each step, the technique examines the merged clusters at that level and computes the Jaccard similarity of the fault localization ranks of the merged cluster with its constituent clusters. When at least one of the constituent clusters is dissimilar to the merged cluster, the traversal has found new information, and thus the traversal continues (i.e. this is not the stopping point for the clustering). For example, in Figure 12.4, the fault localization result of *c*1.1 is compared with the fault localization result of *c*2.1 and *c*2.2. If *c*1.1 is dissimilar to either *c*2.1 or *c*2.2, the traversal continues.

12.3.1.3 Using Fault Localization Clustering to Refine Clusters

After the clusters have been identified using the profiles and fault localization results, J1 performs one additional refinement. Occasionally, similar fault localization results are obtained on multiple "branches" of a dendrogram. To merge these similar clusters, J1 groups clusters that produce similar fault localization results.

To identify the places where this refinement of the clustering can be applied, a pairwise comparison of the fault localization results of the clusters at the stopping-point level of the dendrogram is performed. For this comparison, the Jaccard similarity parameterized is used for this task. Then, the similar clusters are merged.

For example, in Figure 12.4, consider that the stopping point of the clustering was determined to be best at level 5. A pairwise similarity would be calculated for the five clusters at this level by inspecting the similarity of the suspicious statements that each target. If it is found that clusters $c5.4$ and $c5.5$ are similar, these would be combined to produce the final set of clusters.

12.3.2 J2: Clustering Based on Fault Localization Results

J2 uses only the fault localization results for clustering. It first computes the fault localization suspiciousness rankings for the individual failed test cases, T_F, and uses the Jaccard similarity metric to compute the pairwise similarities among these rankings. Then, J2 clusters are marked as similar by taking a closure of the pairs.

For example, consider Figure 12.6, which shows the same 10 failed test cases depicted in Figure 12.4. Each failed test case is depicted as a node in the figure. The technique combines each failed test case with the successful test cases to produce a test suite. J2 uses Tarantula to produce a ranking of suspiciousness for each test suite, and these rankings are compared using the Jaccard metric in the same way described in Sections 12.3.1.2 and 12.3.1.3. J2 records the pairs of rankings that are deemed similar (above the similarity threshold). In Figure 12.6, a pairwise similarity between failed test cases is depicted as an edge. Clusters of failed test cases are produced by taking a closure of the failed test cases that were marked similar. Using the example in Figure 12.6, test case nodes that are reachable over the similarity edges are clustered together. In this example, failed test cases f_1 and f_2 are combined to a cluster; f_6, f_7, f_8, f_9, and f_{10} are combined to a cluster; and f_3, f_4, and f_5 are each single clusters.

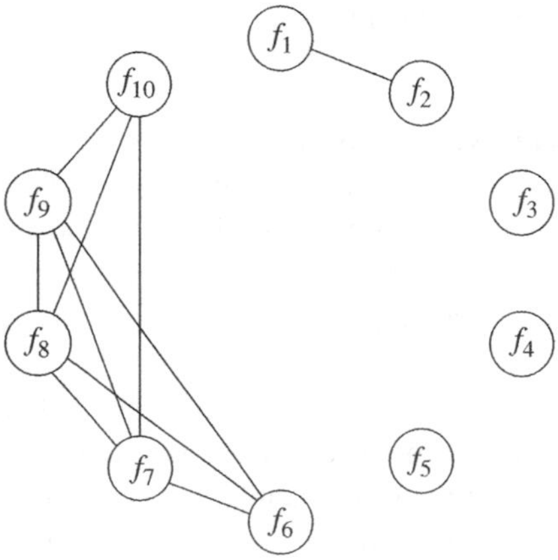

Figure 12.6 The pairwise similarity of suspiciousness computed using each failed test case is shown by a connecting line. Clusters are formed by taking a closure of the similar test cases. *Source:* Jones et al. [17]/ACM.

12.4 Localization of Multiple Bugs Using Algorithms from Integer Linear Programming[7]

Steimann and Frenkel [25, 26] used the Weil–Kettler algorithm, an integer linear programming technique, to cluster failed test cases. They claimed that computing a single ranking in the presence of multiple faults may lead to poor localization accuracy for all but the first (i.e. the most highly ranked) fault. If we were able to partition fault localization problems, we may be able to not only parallelize the search for faults, but also localize faults quicker sequentially, since the remainder of each partition (i.e. the units under test (UUTs) in it that are ranked after a localized fault) need not be inspected even if these UUTs have a higher score than the next fault. Intuitively, the performance of fault locators can be improved if the test coverage matrix (TCM) can be divided into different partitions each containing its own faults, so that fault localization in one partition can be performed independently from that in all others. One such partitioning is achieved by transforming each failed test coverage matrix (FCM) into a so-called *block diagonal matrix* (BDM), each block of which presents its own, independent fault localization problem. Note that, to compute the BDM, the passed test cases must be ignored (since they provide no evidence for the presence of faults, they do not contribute to partitioning; hence, FCM is used for the computation rather than TCM). However, for ranking within partitions, each UUT keeps its coverage by passed test cases, so that the scores calculated by the fault locators are not changed by the partitioning.

While the rearrangement of an FCM into a BDM is simple, it may not always be possible or may lead to imbalanced (e.g. one large and several small) partitions and thus remain largely ineffective. As illustrated by the example of Figure 12.7, further partitioning of FCMs is prevented by rows or columns that span what would otherwise be partitions. If these preventing rows or columns could be removed, further partitioning would be possible. For instance, in the example of Figure 12.7a, removing the third column leads to two partitions (Figure 12.7b), as does removing either the second or the third row (Figure 12.7c and d). This raises two questions:

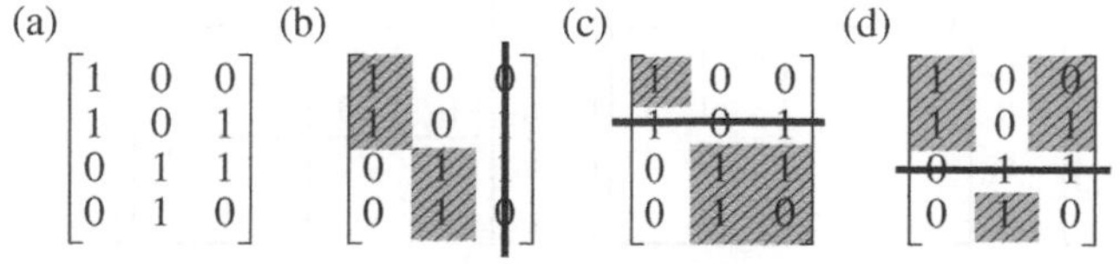

Figure 12.7 Simple FCM resisting further partitioning, and partitions made possible by removing rows or columns. *Source:* Steimann and Frenkel [25]/IEEE.

1) How are the columns or rows to be removed determined?
2) What are the prerequisites and ramifications of removing a column (corresponding to a failed test case) or a row (corresponding to a UUT) for the fault localization problem represented by the FCM?

While identifying preventing rows or columns is simple for the example of Figure 12.7, it is not if FCMs are large. Fortunately, integer linear programming has developed algorithms that allow one to derive a BDM by identifying and removing a sufficient number of disturbing rows (or columns), in the following informally referred to as "dirt." To compute BDMs with dirt, Steimann and Frenkel used the algorithm of Weil and Kettler [25], modified to minimize the size of the dirt. The modified algorithm consists of three steps. The working of the complete algorithm is illustrated in Figure 12.8, as described as follows:

1) First, the maximum transversal of the FCM is computed using the Dulmage–Mendelsohn decomposition, and the FCM is rearranged so that all rows and columns of the transversal are in the upper left of the matrix. The result is a permutation of the FCM, with a contiguous sequence of 1s in its diagonal starting in the upper left corner and an empty submatrix in the lower right, as shown in Figure 12.8b.
2) Next, the upper left submatrix is brought into block triangular form, meaning that except for some 1s below the diagonal, it has a block diagonal form (Figure 12.8c).

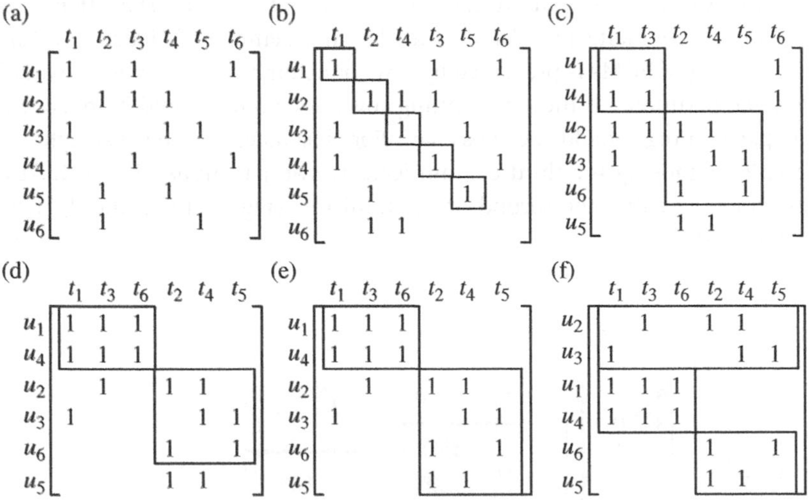

Figure 12.8 Working of the modified Weil–Kettler algorithm. The variable t_i represents a failed test case, and u_i represents a test unit. *Source:* Steimann and Frenkel [25]/IEEE.

3) Based on this permutation of the FCM, the dirt is computed as follows:

   a) For each column to the right of the block triangular part of the FCM, we divide the sum of all rows of all blocks connected by 1s in that column by the vertical dimension of the matrix. (Figure 12.8c in our example shows that the 1s in t_6 connect only the first block, which has two rows. As a result, we obtain the fraction 2/6.) In general, if this fraction is smaller than a parameter X, the blocks are merged with the column. If not, the rows containing a 1 in that column are moved to the dirt. (For our example, let us assume that X is set to 0.5. Hence, the (sole) column is merged with the upper left block, leading to Figure 12.8d.)
   b) The same is repeated for rows below the block triangular part, counting columns and using a parameter Y. As a result, the complete FCM is in block triangular form (Figure 12.8e).
   c) Next, for each block in the diagonal of the FCM, if the number of off-diagonal 1s in any column of the block connecting that block with another block divided by the vertical size of the other block is greater than Z, the two blocks, and all others connected through at least one 1 in the same column, are merged. (In the example, block 1 is connected to block 2 by at most one 1 in the same column, giving us 1/4, which is greater than $Z = 0.5$, so that the two blocks will not need to be merged.)
   d) Finally, all remaining rows with off-diagonal 1s are moved to the dirt, resulting in the FCM shown in Figure 12.8f.

After such a partitioning process, the FCM is transferred into BDM, each block of which presents its own independent fault localization problem. Then, a fault localization technique can be used on the BDM with all (or selected) test cases to generate suspiciousness rankings for locating faults.

12.5 MSeer: an Advanced Fault Localization Technique for Locating Multiple Bugs in Parallel[8]

MSeer [1] is proposed as a fault localization technique for locating multiple bugs in parallel. There are four novel aspects of MSeer.

First, in MSeer, a failed test case is represented by a suspiciousness ranking of statements generated by a given fault localization technique using the corresponding failed test and all successful tests. The ranking is in descending order of each statement's likelihood of containing bugs. The advantage of using statements rather than predicates/decisions (as in [16]) and suspiciousness rankings instead of execution traces is explained in Section 12.5.1.1.

Second, MSeer uses a revised Kendall tau distance to measure the distance between two failed test cases (i.e. two suspiciousness rankings). Although Kendall tau has been used successfully in other studies such as information retrieval [27] and bioengineering [28], it cannot be applied directly to software fault localization because it assigns the same weight to each statement no matter how suspicious. This is inappropriate and must be modified as suggested by [16]. To correct this problem, Gao and Wong [1] propose giving greater weight to more suspicious statements and smaller weight to less suspicious statements. The rationale behind this modification is explained in Section 12.5.1.2.

Third, MSeer applies an innovative approach to estimate the number of clusters and, at the same time, assign initial medoids[9] to these clusters (Section 12.5.1.3.1). A similar approach was discussed by Yager and Filev [29] and modified by Chiu [30], and it has been used in studies such as the one by Lin et al. for color image segmentation [31]. However, this approach has never been used to help programmers locate software bugs. To do so, Gao and Wong make two important changes. First, Refs. [30, 32] only mentioned that the distance between two data points needs to be measured, but they did not specify how to do it. In the MSeer study [1], such distance is measured using the revised Kendall tau in Eq. (12.2) for the reasons provided in Section 12.5.1.2. Moreover, instead of using a fixed value for a parameter that is critical in estimating the number of clusters, Gao and Wong propose to use data winsorization to help determine its value. This is necessary as different values should be used in different scenarios to improve the performance.

Fourth, MSeer performs clustering using an improved *K*-medoids algorithm (Section 12.5.1.3.2). Although *K*-medoids is a popular clustering algorithm and has been used in studies such as graph classification [33], it is too expensive for large data sets because it examines all possible combinations of *K* data points in order to find appropriate initial medoids. To address this problem, Gao and Wong propose the improved *K*-medoids using an innovative approach as described in Section 12.5.1.3.1 to help determine appropriate initial medoids without using all possible combinations. In this way, the performance of the original *K*-medoids can be significantly improved.

The major contribution of MSeer is to propose a technique that can effectively locate multiple bugs in parallel. This technique simultaneously uses the following:

- A revised Kendall tau with a greater weight for more suspicious statements to measure the distance between two failed test cases.
- An innovative approach for estimating the number of clusters and determining their initial medoids, with appropriate parameter values decided by data winsorization.
- An improved *K*-medoids algorithm for clustering without examining all possible combinations of *K* data points.

These help solve a very important problem in software engineering: how to effectively perform fault localization on a program with multiple bugs.

Case studies on seven medium-to large-sized programs (*gzip*, *grep*, *make*, *flex*, *ant*, *socat*, and *xmail*) written in different languages (C, C++, and Java) with various functionality were conducted to evaluate the effectiveness and efficiency of MSeer based on several metrics (Section 12.5.3.2). In total, 840 multiple-bug faulty versions (two-bug, three-bug, four-bug, and five-bug) of the seven programs were used. A cross-comparison between MSeer and two other techniques (one bug at a time and the second technique proposed by Jones et al. [17]) is reported in Section 12.5.3.3. The results strongly suggest that MSeer performs better in terms of both effectiveness and efficiency.

12.5.1 MSeer

We now present how MSeer effectively locates multiple bugs in a program. We first describe in Section 12.5.1.1 how failed test cases are represented and then explain in Section 12.5.1.2 a revised Kendall tau distance and the advantage of using it to measure the distances between two suspiciousness rankings. A discussion of how to estimate the number of clusters and their initial medoids appears in Section 12.5.1.3.1, followed by a description of the improved *K*-medoids clustering algorithm in Section 12.5.1.3.2. The detailed procedure for MSeer is in Section 12.5.1.4.

12.5.1.1 Representation of Failed Test Cases

To find the *due-to* relationship mentioned in Section 12.1, we propose using a clustering algorithm, *K*-medoids, to determine which failed test cases should be used, along with successful test cases to locate the corresponding causative bug. For a given failed test case, the corresponding representation can be, but is not limited to, one of the following:

a) A statement coverage vector such that an entry 1 at the ith position implies that the corresponding statement s_i is covered by the failed test, and an entry 0 implies it is not.
b) A suspiciousness ranking of statements[10] based on a given fault localization technique using the corresponding failed test and all successful tests.

Representation (a) is similar to the representation used to compute T-proximity (*trace-proximity*) [16], in which failed tests are grouped based on the similarity of their execution traces. Such a representation is also used in other multiple-bug fault localization studies [8, 25, 26]. However, as suggested by Liu et al. [16], this representation is problematic because a fault can be triggered in many different ways. As a result, execution traces of failed test cases due to the same bug can be very different. Excluding some failed test cases only because their statement coverage vectors differ from others and ignoring the fact that the failures caused by all these failed test cases are due to the same bug will reduce the effectiveness of fault localization.

Representation (b) is similar to the representation used to compute the R-proximity (rank-proximity), which has been shown to be a better representation than (a) in clustering failed tests due to the same bug [16]. Gao and Wong use representation (b) in their study. They also generate suspiciousness rankings in terms of *statements* rather than *predicates*. A potential disadvantage of the latter (as explained in [16]) is that if a bug is not in the initial set of predicates selected for examination, additional predicates need to be included via a breadth-first search on the dependence graph of the program being debugged. If too few predicates are selected, enough information for fault localization may not be conveyed, while too many predicates are in themselves a burden for developers to examine. Thus, neither leads to the best result.

12.5.1.2 Revised Kendall tau Distance

The performance of many clustering algorithms depends critically on a good distance metric over the input space [37]. To better measure the distance between suspiciousness rankings, Gao and Wong propose a revised Kendall tau distance metric. They first introduce the original Kendall tau distance and then describe how they improve it by giving greater weight to statements at the top of a suspiciousness ranking. Additional discussions can be found in Section 12.5.4.3.

The Kendall tau distance is a metric that counts the number of pairwise disagreements between two rankings of the same size [38]. The larger the distance, the more dissimilar the two rankings. Given two suspiciousness rankings ω and σ, each with m statements, their Kendall tau distance $D(\omega, \sigma)$ is defined as:

$$D(\omega, \sigma) = \sum_{1 \le i \le j \le m} K(s_i, s_j) \tag{12.1}$$

where $K(s_i, s_j) = \begin{cases} 1 & \text{if} \left(\omega(s_i) - \omega(s_j)\right) \times \left(\sigma(s_i) - \sigma(s_j)\right) < 0 \\ 0 & \text{otherwise} \end{cases}$, $\omega(s_i)$ is the position of statement s_i in ranking ω, and s_i and s_j constitute a discordant pair of statements if their relative orders in ω and σ disagree. Note that the Kendall tau distance can be normalized by dividing by $m(m-1)/2$.

To continue the discussion, let us consider the following three rankings (r_1, r_2, and r_3) with four statements (s_1 to s_4) in Table 12.1. The value of each cell gives the

Table 12.1 Three rankings r_1, r_2, and r_3, each with four statements.

Statements	s_1	s_2	s_3	s_4
Position in ranking r_1	3	1	2	4
Position in ranking r_2	4	1	2	3
Position in ranking r_3	4	2	1	3

Source: Gao and Wong [1]/IEEE.

position of the statement in the corresponding ranking. The third column shows that statement s_2 is at the top (position 1) of rankings r_1 and r_2 but at position 2 of ranking r_3.

To calculate the Kendall tau distance between r_1 and r_2, we need to count the number of discordant pairs between statements. For s_1 and s_2, $K(s_1, s_2) = 0$ because $(r_1(s_1) - r_1(s_2)) \times (r_2(s_1) - r_2(s_2)) = (3 - 1) \times (4 - 1) > 0$. Similarly, we have $K(s_1, s_3) = 0$, $K(s_1, s_4) = 1$, $K(s_2, s_3) = 0$, $K(s_2, s_4) = 0$, and $K(s_3, s_4) = 0$. Hence, $D(r_1, r_2) = \sum_{1 \le i \le j \le m} K(s_i, s_j) = 1$. Likewise, $D(r_2, r_3)$ is also 1.

However, it is not appropriate to give the same weight to all discordant pairs. More precisely, discordant pairs of more suspicious statements (those toward the top of the rankings) contribute more to the distance between two rankings than discordant pairs of less suspicious statements (those at lower positions in the rankings).

Referring to Table 12.1, the only discordant pair between r_1 and r_2 is (s_1, s_4) with corresponding statements at the third and fourth positions, while the discordant pair between r_2 and r_3 is (s_2, s_3) with corresponding statements at the first and second positions. Stated differently, the discordance between r_2 and r_3 is due to more suspicious statements, whereas the discordance between r_1 and r_2 is due to less suspicious statements. Therefore, it is reasonable to emphasize that the distance between r_2 and r_3 should be larger than the distance between r_1 and r_2. This cannot be accomplished by using the original Kendall tau distance defined in Eq. (12.2), in which $K(s_i, s_j)$ is always 1 provided that s_i and s_j constitute a discordant pair of statements regardless of their positions in the rankings. In other words, even though s_i and s_j are at very low positions in the rankings, the contribution due to their discordance to the distance is the same as that of two discordant statements at higher positions. To resolve this problem, Gao and Wong propose to assign a greater weight to $K(s_2, s_3)$ while computing $D(r_2, r_3)$, and a smaller weight to $K(s_1, s_4)$ while computing $D(r_1, r_2)$, so that $D(r_2, r_3)$ is larger than $D(r_1, r_2)$. Thus, Gao and Wong modify the Kendall tau distance[11] by taking into account the position of each statement as follows:

$$D'(\omega, \sigma) = \sum_{1 \le i \le j \le N} K'(s_i, s_j) \tag{12.2}$$

where

$$K'(s_i, s_j) = \begin{cases} \omega(s_i)^{-1} + \omega(s_j)^{-1} + \sigma(s_i)^{-1} + \sigma(s_j)^{-1} & \text{if } (\omega(s_i) - \omega(s_j)) \times (\sigma(s_i) - \sigma(s_j)) < 0 \\ 0 & \text{otherwise} \end{cases}$$

and $\omega(s_i)$, $\omega(s_j)$, $\sigma(s_i)$, and $\sigma(s_j)$ are the positions of s_i and s_j in ranking ω and ranking σ, respectively. With this modification, the lower the positions of s_i and s_j (which means they are less suspicious), the smaller the $K'(s_i, s_j)$. Referring to the above example, $D'(r_1, r_2) = \omega(s_1)^{-1} + \omega(s_4)^{-1} + \sigma(s_1)^{-1} + \sigma(s_4)^{-1} = 1.17$ and $D'(r_2, r_3) = 3$. Hence, $D'(r_2, r_3) > D'(r_1, r_2)$, which is consistent with the discussion that the discordance between r_2 and r_3 should be larger than that between r_1 and r_2.

12.5.1.3 Clustering

In data mining, the *K*-medoids clustering algorithm (hereafter, simply referred to as *K*-medoids) [19] divides data points into clusters such that members of the same cluster are as similar as possible, and those in different clusters are as dissimilar as possible. It chooses *k* data points to be the "medoids" and minimizes the distance between data points in a cluster and the medoid of the corresponding cluster. In comparison to the *K*-means clustering algorithm [39, 40] used in other fault localization studies such as [8], *K*-medoids has been shown to be very robust to the existence of noise or outliers and generally produces clusters of high quality [19]. Furthermore, the use of *K*-medoids is more applicable to situations in which the mean of the objects is not defined [41]. This is especially critical in the MSeer study, as it is difficult to define the mean of the suspiciousness rankings generated by the failed and the successful test cases.

Density-based spatial clustering of applications with noise (DBSCAN) is a clustering algorithm proposed by Ester et al. [42]. Given a set of data points, it groups points that are closely packed together (i.e. points with many nearby neighbors) and discards points that lie alone in low-density regions. Users have to define two important parameters: (i) the radius of a cluster and (ii) the minimum number of points required to form a high-density region to help DBSCAN identify whether a point is in low-density regions. If these two parameters are not set properly, some useful data points will be excluded by DBSCAN. Although this clustering algorithm has been applied to areas such as image processing [7], it is not appropriate for fault localization. This is because failed test cases for some bugs may fall in low-density regions and be excluded during clustering. As a result, critical data points that are essential to helping us locate bugs are rejected. Hence, Gao and Wong choose not to use DBSCAN in their study.

One challenge of using either K-medoids or K-means is that the number of clusters and assignments of the initial medoids (called "centers" in K-means) have to be decided first. The process of estimating the number of clusters and assignments of the initial medoids is discussed in Section 12.5.1.3.1. Then, an improved K-medoids is presented in Section 12.5.1.3.2 to divide suspiciousness rankings into K clusters so that the program failures caused by executing failed test cases in the same cluster are due to the same bug.

12.5.1.3.1 Estimation of the Number of Clusters and Assignment of Initial Medoids

The number of clusters in the MSeer study corresponds to the possible number of bugs in a program and also indicates how many *fault-focused* suspiciousness rankings (generated by failed tests in the same cluster and all the successful tests) we should have for a given debugging iteration. Since, in practice, we do not know how many bugs exist in a program, the biggest challenge to using a clustering-based multiple-bug fault localization technique is how to properly estimate the number of clusters at the beginning. This problem was also reviewed by Hogerle et al. [26].

Overestimating the cluster number will result in the generation of redundant *fault-focused* rankings and require additional effort to locate the same bug, which is counterproductive. Underestimating the cluster number means we do not have an adequate number of *fault-focused* suspiciousness rankings, which also implies that failed tests in the same cluster may not be due to the same bug. Furthermore, even if the number of clusters is correct, if the initial medoids are assigned improperly, the clustering result may only converge to a local optimum [43]. Therefore, estimating the number of clusters and assigning appropriate initial medoids are essential to MSeer. One approach is to set the cluster number to $\sqrt{M_F/2}$ for N_F failed test cases based on the work of Mardia et al. [10]. Another approach is to set the number of clusters to a small percentage of N_F (e.g. if there are 100 failed test cases, the number of clusters can be 5, which is 5% of N_F) [8, 44]. Both approaches are based on the number of failed test cases. However, neither can be used in their studies because there is no clear correlation between the number of failed tests and the number of bugs in a program. For example, using the approach by Mardia et al., if a program has 200 failed test cases, we should have 10 (namely, $\sqrt{200/2}$) clusters. However, there is no justification to argue that there are 10 bugs in the program.

Gao and Wong use an innovative approach to simultaneously estimate the number of clusters and assign initial medoids to these clusters. A similar approach was discussed by Yager and Filev [32]. They made a grid of virtual data points and computed a *potential value* for each virtual point based on its distances to the actual data points. A virtual point with many actual points nearby will have a high potential value. Then, the virtual point with the highest potential value is chosen as the first cluster center. The key idea of this algorithm is that once the first cluster center is chosen, the potential of all virtual points is reduced according to their distance from the latest selected cluster center. Virtual points near the first cluster center will have greatly reduced potential. The next cluster center is then placed at the virtual point with the highest remaining potential value. The procedure of acquiring new cluster centers and reducing the potential of surrounding virtual points repeats until the potential values of all virtual points fall below a threshold. This approach was revised by Chiu [30] to further improve its efficiency when used on large-sized data sets. It was used to solve a color image segmentation problem in a study reported by Lin et al. [31]. However, it has never been applied to the software fault localization domain. To do so, Gao and Wong make two critical changes.

- Determine how to compute the distance between two data points (namely, two suspiciousness rankings).

  The approaches reported in [32] and [30] only suggest that such a distance should be measured. However, they did not explain how exactly it should be done. Since there are so many metrics that can be used to compute the distance, their results may be very different and can have critical impacts on the performance of clustering. For example, the Euclidean distance is used in [31]. Although it can be applied to color image segmentation, it is not appropriate for software fault localization. Other metrics like the Hamming distance and the Jaccard distance are not good choices either. Refer to Section 12.5.4.3 for more discussion. To solve this problem, Gao and Wong use a revised Kendall tau distance defined in Eq. (12.2) for the reasons explained in Section 12.5.1.2.

- Assign an appropriate value to the parameter in Step 2 for a better estimation of the number of clusters.

  Instead of using a fixed value for Ψ as Chiu did in his study [30], Gao and Wong propose to use data winsorization to help determine its value. This is necessary as different values should be used in different cases to improve the accuracy of estimation.

What follows describes this approach in detail. For a set of n suspiciousness rankings $\{r_1, r_2, r_3, ..., r_n\}$, each generated by one failed test case and all successful tests, the number of clusters can be estimated as follows:

Step 1: Measure $D'(r_i, r_j)$ (the revised Kendall tau distance) between rankings r_i and r_j $(1 \le i, j \le n)$.

Step 2: Assign a potential value P_i^0 for each ranking r_i $(1 \le i \le n)$ as follows:

$$P_i^0 = \sum_{j=1}^{n} e^{-\alpha D'\left(r_i,\, r_j\right)^2} \tag{12.3}$$

where $\alpha = 4/\Psi^2$. Chiu [30] claims that Ψ is sensitive to the actual input space. Gao and Wong notice that when Ψ is set to half of the 5% winsorized mean of the distance between two distinct rankings, the number of clusters can be better estimated. A winsorized mean [45] is a winsorized statistical measure of central tendency, similar to the mean and median. It involves the calculation of the mean after replacing given parts of a probability distribution or samples at the high and low ends with the most extreme remaining values [45]. For example, given 10 numbers (from x_1, the smallest, to x_{10}, the largest), the 10% winsorized mean of these numbers is calculated as $(x_2+x_2+x_3+x_4+x_5+x_6+x_7+x_8+x_9+x_9)/10$. The 10% at the low end (x_1) and 10% at the high end (x_{10}) are replaced by the second smallest x_2 and the second largest x_{10}, respectively. The objective of winsorization is to reduce the effect of possible outliers, which has been shown to be more effective than data trimming [45]. More details about data winsorization can be found in [45, 46].

Step 3: After P_i^0 has been computed,[12] Gao and Wong choose the ranking with the highest potential value as R^θ and set its potential value as M^θ. If there are multiple rankings with the same highest potential value, they randomly choose one ranking to break the tie. If $\theta = 0$, they set R^θ as the medoid of the first cluster and proceed to Step 4. Algorithm 12.1 is used to determine whether they should add a new cluster with R^θ as its medoid, or end the procedure.

if $M^\theta > \overline{\varepsilon} M^0$ ($\overline{\varepsilon} = 0.5$ *and* $\underline{\varepsilon} = 0.15$ [8]) **then**
  | Accept R^θ as a cluster medoid and go to Step 4
else if $M^\theta < \underline{\varepsilon} M^0$ **then**
  | Reject R^θ and stop
else
  | Let D'_{min} = [shortest of the revised Kendall tau distance between R^θ and all previously found cluster medoids]
  | **if** $\frac{D'_{min}}{\Psi} + \frac{M^\theta}{M^0} \geq 1$ **then**
    | Accept R^θ as a cluster medoid and go to Step 4
  | **else**
    | Reject R^θ and set the potential value M^θ to 0
    | Select the ranking with the next highest potential value as R^θ and assign its potential value to the new M^θ
    | Repeat the stopping criterion from the beginning
  | **end**
end

Algorithm 12.1 Stopping criterion. *Source:* Gao and Wong [1]/IEEE.

Table 12.2 An example of five rankings, each with seven statements.

Statements	s_1	s_2	s_3	s_4	s_5	s_6	s_7
Position in ranking r_1	1	2	3	4	5	6	7
Position in ranking r_2	1	2	4	3	7	5	6
Position in ranking r_3	6	7	5	3	4	2	1
Position in ranking r_4	5	7	6	4	3	2	1
Position in ranking r_5	1	3	5	4	7	2	6

Source: Gao and Wong [1]/IEEE.

Step 4: Use Eq. (12.4) to update the potential value of each ranking r_i $(1 \leq i \leq n)$ and then go back to Step 3.

$$P_i^{\theta+1} \Leftarrow P_i^{\theta} - M^{\theta} \times e^{-\beta D'(r_i,\, R\theta)^2} \tag{12.4}$$

where $\beta = 4/\zeta^2$ and $\zeta = 1.5\Psi$. Note that the algorithm guarantees that no ranking will be selected as the medoid for more than one cluster.

Let us use an example of five rankings, each with seven statements as shown in Table 12.2, to demonstrate how to estimate the number of clusters and assign the initial medoid to each cluster.

First, Gao and Wong compute the potential value of each ranking (Steps 1 and 2) for iteration 0. We have $P_1^0 = 1.731$, $P_2^0 = 2.035$, $P_3^0 = 1.796$, $P_4^0 = 1.795$, and $P_5^0 = 1.433$. Based on Step 3, r_2 is set as R^0, and $M^0 = 2.035$. Since $\theta = 0$, r_2 is selected as the first medoid, and the procedure proceeds to Step 4.

We set r_3 as R^1, and $M^1 = 1.796$. Since $\underline{\varepsilon}M^0 = 0.305$ and $\bar{\varepsilon}M^0 = 1.018$, M^1 is larger than $\bar{\varepsilon}M^0$. Hence, r_3 is selected as the second medoid, and the procedure proceeds to Step 4. The updated potential values after the second iteration are $P_1^2 = 0.032$, $P_2^2 = 8.186$, $P_3^2 = 0.0$, $P_4^2 = 0.174$, and $P_5^2 = 0.128$. After comparing these values, r_4 is set as R^2, and $M^2 = 0.174$. M^2 is now less than $\underline{\varepsilon}M^0$, so r_4 is rejected as a medoid and the whole procedure ends. In summary, there are two clusters with r_2 and r_3 as the initial medoids.

12.5.1.3.2 Improved K-medoids Clustering Algorithm

K-medoids can be used to divide suspiciousness rankings into *K* clusters by minimizing the following objective function:

$$J_m = \sum_{j=1}^{K} \sum_{i=1}^{Q} D'(r_i, c_j) \tag{12.5}$$

where r_i is a suspiciousness ranking (namely, a data point) in the jth cluster, c_j is the corresponding medoid, Q is the number of rankings in the jth cluster, and K is the total number of clusters.

Referring to Section 12.5.1.2, the performance of many clustering algorithms (including K-medoids) depends on which distance metric is used. From the example therein, it is clear that the distance between two suspiciousness rankings should be computed using the revised Kendall tau defined in Eq. (12.2) instead of the original in Eq. (12.1). Problems of using other distance metrics such as Euclidean or Jaccard are discussed in Section 12.5.4.3. Hence, in the MSeer study, the distance is measured using the revised Kendall tau.[13]

Another significant problem of K-medoids is that during the optimization of Eq. (12.5), we must examine all possible combinations of K rankings as initial medoids. This can be very expensive because the number of combinations is huge for a large data set.

A variant of K-medoids, CLARA [19], has been proposed to deal with large data sets. It draws a small sample from the data set and generates an optimal set of medoids for the sample instead of the entire data set. A problem of this approach is that the quality of the clustering results depends significantly on the sample. As a result, it is not appropriate for the MSeer study.

Gao and Wong propose using the approach described in Section 12.5.1.3.1, which can help us determine appropriate initial medoids without examining all the combinations (as described above). Below, we explain the details of the improved K-medoids clustering algorithm.

Let r_i $(1 \leq i \leq n)$ be the suspiciousness ranking, c_j^θ $(1 \leq j \leq K)$ be the medoid of the jth cluster, and θ be the number of iterations with an initial value 0 before any iteration. The improved K-medoids for clustering suspiciousness rankings includes the following steps:

Step 1: Follow the steps described in Section 12.5.1.3.1 to estimate the number of clusters, K, and assign an initial medoid c_i^θ (where θ equals 0) for each cluster.

Step 2: Group rankings into clusters so that the revised Kendall tau distance between a ranking and the medoid of the cluster where it resides is less than or equal to the distance between this ranking and the medoids of other clusters of which it is not a member. If a ranking has the same distance to the medoids of multiple clusters, they randomly assign the ranking to one of these clusters.

Step 3: Use Eq. (12.6) to compute the sum of the distance between every ranking and its medoid in each cluster.

$$Sum_j^\theta = \sum_i^Q D'\left(r_i, c_j^\theta\right) \tag{12.6}$$

where Q is the number of rankings in the jth cluster.

Step 4: For the jth cluster, choose a ranking different from c_j^θ as $c_j^{\theta+1}$, and compute $Sum_j^{\theta+1}$. If there exists at least one ranking that satisfies $Sum_j^{\theta+1} < Sum_j^\theta$, then select $c_j^{\theta+1}$ as the new medoid of the jth cluster for the next iteration and go back to Step 2. Otherwise, the clustering terminates.

Let us use the same example as shown in Table 12.2 to demonstrate how rankings are clustered using the improved K-medoids. From the example in Section 12.5.1.3.1, we conclude that there are two clusters (i.e. $K = 2$) with r_2 as c_1^0 (the medoid of the first cluster during iteration 0) and r_3 as c_2^0 (the medoid of the second cluster during iteration 0). This implies that Step 1 is already complete. We now move on to Step 2. The distance between a ranking and its corresponding medoid is shown in Table 12.3.

We observe that the distance between r_1 and c_1^0 is less than that between r_1 and c_2^0 (namely, $2.529 < 28.271$). The same applies to r_2 and r_5. Hence, r_1, r_2, and r_5 are grouped together as the first cluster. On the other hand, the distance between r_3 (and r_4) and c_1^0 is larger than that between r_3 (and r_4) and c_2^0 (namely, $24.476>0$ for r_3 and $23.836 > 1.9$ for r_4). Hence, r_3 and r_4 are in the second cluster. At Step 3, we compute $Sum_1^0 = \sum_{i=1}^{3} D'\left(r_i, c_1^0\right) = 6.495$. If we choose r_1 as c_1^1, the corresponding $Sum_1^1 = 9.090$ is greater than Sum_1^0. If we choose r_5 as c_1^1, the corresponding $Sum_1^1 = 10.528$ is also greater than Sum_1^0. Similarly, if we choose r_4 as c_2^1, we have Sum_2^1 equal to Sum_2^0. Therefore, the entire clustering process is complete.

12.5.1.4 MSeer: a Technique for Locating Multiple Bugs in Parallel

We now present the details of MSeer, an advanced technique for parallel debugging of multiple bugs in the same program. Figure 12.9 gives an overview with an explanation of major steps.

Table 12.3 The distance between a ranking and its corresponding medoid.

$D'\left(r_i, c_j^0\right)$	r_1	r_2	r_3	r_4	r_5
c_1^0	2.529	0.0	24.476	23.836	3.967
c_2^0	28.271	24.476	0.0	1.9	20.1

Source: Gao and Wong [1]/IEEE.

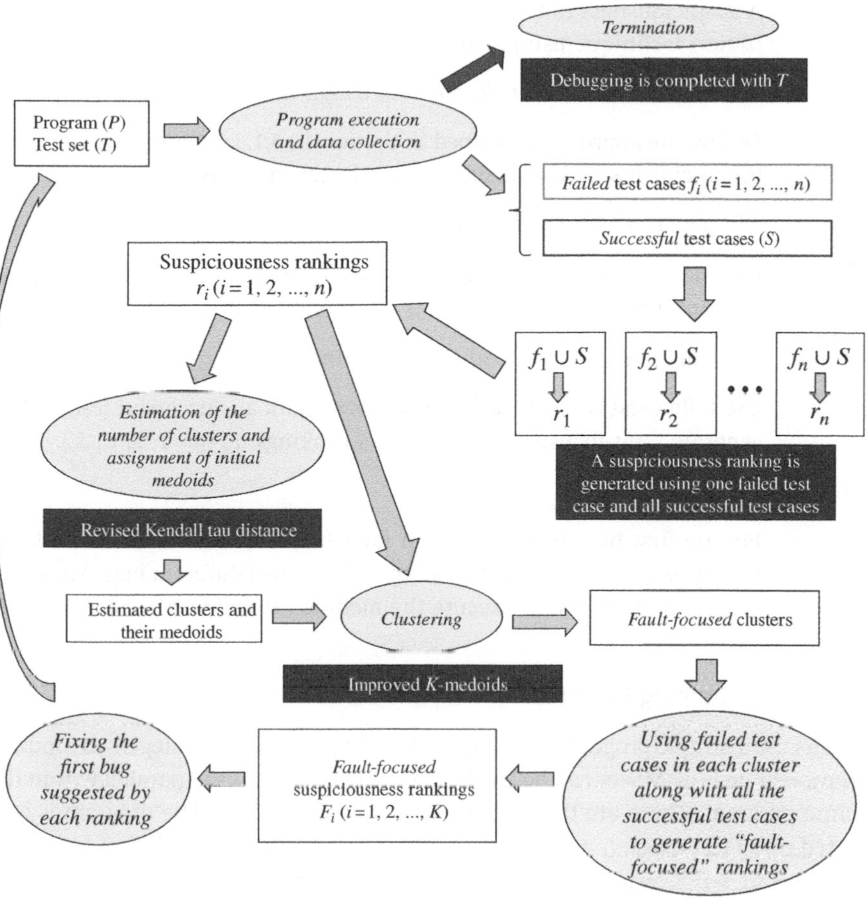

Figure 12.9 An overview of MSeer. *Source:* Gao and Wong [1]/IEEE.

Step 1: *Execute the program and collect data.*

Execute the program being debugged (P) against a set of test cases (T). Collect the statement coverage[14] with respect to each test case. We use f_i ($i = 1, 2, ..., n$) to denote n failed test cases and S as the set of all successful test cases. If there are no failed test cases, then the debugging is terminated. At this point, we can only conclude that no bugs can be revealed by the execution of test cases in T, which does not guarantee that P contains no bugs.

Step 2: *Generate suspiciousness rankings using each failed test case and all successful test cases.*

A suspiciousness ranking, r_i ($i = 1, 2, ..., n$), is generated by a fault localization technique using f_i and S.

Step 3: *Estimate the number of clusters and assign initial medoids.*

Follow the approach described in Section 12.5.1.3.1 to estimate the number of clusters, K, and assign initial cluster medoids.

Step 4: *Cluster suspiciousness rankings.*

Use the improved K-medoids described in Section 12.5.1.3.2 to cluster all the rankings generated in Step 2 into K fault-focused clusters.

Step 5: *Generate fault-focused suspiciousness rankings.*

Use failed test cases in each cluster along with all successful tests in S to generate fault-focused suspiciousness rankings, F_i ($i = 1, 2, ..., K$).

Step 6: *Fix bugs.*

Fix the first bug located by each fault-focused suspiciousness ranking. Ideally, each fault-focused ranking will lead to a different bug. After this, go back to Step 1 to re-execute the modified P against all test cases in T.

12.5.2 A Running Example

Let us use a sample program in Figure 12.10, which takes three integers as input, to demonstrate how MSeer can be used to locate multiple bugs in parallel within the same program. There are three bugs in lines s_4, s_{11}, and s_{14}. The program is executed on 13 test cases: $t_1 = \langle s_1, s_2, s_3\rangle$; $t_2 = \langle s_2, s_3, s_4\rangle$; $t_3 = \langle s_2, s_4, s_3\rangle$; $t_4 = \langle s_3, s_5, s_4\rangle$; $t_5 = \langle s_4, s_6, s_5\rangle$; $t_6 = \langle s_3, s_4, s_2\rangle$; $t_7 = \langle s_3, s_4, s_1\rangle$; $t_8 = \langle s_4, s_3, s_2\rangle$; $t_9 = \langle s_5, s_4, s_3\rangle$; $t_{10} = \langle s_6, s_5, s_4\rangle$; $t_{11} = \langle s_4, s_3, s_6\rangle$; $t_{12} = \langle s_4, s_3, s_5\rangle$; and $t_{13} = \langle s_4, s_3, s_8\rangle$. Five of these ($t_1$, t_2, t_6, t_7, and t_{11}) cause failures. In Step 2, we use the crosstab fault localization technique [20] to generate suspiciousness rankings using each failed test case and all successful test cases. Five rankings so generated are shown in Table 12.4, where the notation $r_1(t_1)$ indicates that ranking r_1 is generated using the failed test case t_1. Similarly, $r_3(t_6)$ shows that ranking r_3 is generated using the failed test case t_6, and so on. We then estimate the number of clusters in Step 3. There are three clusters with r_2, r_3, and r_5 as the initial medoids. An improved K-medoids is used in Step 4 to cluster the five rankings in Table 12.4 into three clusters: $\{r_1, r_2\}$, $\{r_3, r_4\}$, and $\{r_5\}$. At Step 5, once again, we use the crosstab fault localization technique and the failed test cases in each cluster along with all successful test cases to generate three fault-focused suspiciousness rankings, as shown in Table 12.5. Multiple statements may have the same suspiciousness value. As a result, they are tied for the same position in the ranking (see Table 12.5) at the final stage (Step 6) of locating faulty statements that contain program bugs. This is further explained as follows:

```
s1:  input a, b, c; mid = c
s2:  if (b < c)
s3:     if (a < b)
s4:         mid = c //Bug 1  mid = b
s5:     else if (a < c)
s6:       mid = a
s7:  else
s8:     if (a > b)
s9:         mid = b
s10:    else if (a < c)
s11:      mid = b //Bug 2  mid = a
s12: case mid of
s13:        a: if (b >= 2*c || c >= 2*b)
s14:               temp = (a + b + c)/2; //Bug 3  (a + b + c)/3
s15:               print temp;
s16:           else print ("a");
s17:        b: if (c >= 2*a || a >= 2*c)
s18:               temp = a + b + c;
s19:               print temp;
s20:           else print ("b");
s21:        c: if (a >= 2*b || b >= 2*a)
s22:               temp = b*c;
s23:               print temp;
s24:           else print ("c");
```

Figure 12.10 A sample program. *Source:* Gao and Wong [1]/IEEE.

Table 12.4 Five suspiciousness rankings[a].

	s_1	s_2	s_3	s_4	s_5	s_6	s_7	s_8	s_9	s_{10}	s_{11}	s_{12}
$r_1(t_1)$	6	7	4	1	15	16	21	24	22	9	10	8
$r_2(t_2)$	5	6	3	1	16	17	21	24	22	8	9	7
$r_3(t_6)$	7	8	22	10	17	18	4	6	23	1	2	9
$r_4(t_7)$	8	9	22	11	16	17	5	7	23	1	2	10
$r_5(t_{11})$	6	7	19	9	3	4	20	24	21	10	11	8

	s_{13}	s_{14}	s_{15}	s_{16}	s_{17}	s_{18}	s_{19}	s_{20}	s_{21}	s_{22}	s_{23}	s_{24}
$r_1(t_1)$	17	11	12	18	23	13	14	19	5	2	3	20
$r_2(t_2)$	18	10	11	19	23	12	13	20	4	14	15	2
$r_3(t_6)$	19	11	12	20	5	13	14	3	24	15	16	21
$r_4(t_7)$	18	12	13	19	6	3	4	20	24	14	15	21
$r_5(t_{11})$	5	1	2	16	22	12	13	17	23	14	15	18

[a] The number in each cell represents the position of the statement in the corresponding ranking.
Source: Gao and Wong [1]/IEEE.

Table 12.5 Three fault-focused rankings[a].

	s_1	s_2	s_3	s_4	s_5	s_6	s_7	s_8	s_9	s_{10}	s_{11}	s_{12}
F_1	7	7	4	1	16	16	21	24	21	10	10	7
F_2	9	9	22	12	17	17	5	8	22	1	1	9
F_3	6	6	19	9	3	3	19	24	19	9	9	6
	s_{13}	s_{14}	s_{15}	s_{16}	s_{17}	s_{18}	s_{19}	s_{20}	s_{21}	s_{22}	s_{23}	s_{24}
F_1	16	10	10	16	21	14	14	16	3	2	2	6
F_2	17	12	12	17	5	3	3	7	22	15	15	17
F_3	3	1	1	16	19	12	12	16	19	12	12	16

[a] The number in each cell represents the position of the statement in the corresponding ranking.
Source: Gao and Wong [1]/IEEE.

Assume that a number of correct statements have the same suspiciousness as a faulty statement. In the *best* case, we examine the faulty statement first. In the *worst* case, we examine it last and must examine all the correct statements with the same suspiciousness. In the *average* case, we examine some correct statements but not as many as in the *worst* case. This results in three different levels of effectiveness: *best*, *average*, and *worst*.

Some researchers may claim that instead of using both the *best* and the *worst*, we only need to report the *average*. Although it is straightforward to compute the average from the best and worst effectiveness, the converse is not true. Providing the average effectiveness offers no insight on where the best and worst effectiveness may lie and, more importantly, can be ambiguous and misleading. For example, two techniques can have the same average effectiveness, but one has a smaller range between the best and the worse cases while the other has a much wider range. As a result, these two techniques should not be viewed as equally effective as suggested by their average effectiveness.

Other researchers may argue that it is only necessary to report the worst case. However, programmers will generally not experience the worst-case scenario in practice. It is more likely that they will see something between the best and the worst scenarios. Thus, it is better to report the fault localization effectiveness for the *best*, the *average*, and the *worst* cases, and perform the cross evaluation under each scenario.

In this example, the *best* case only has to examine three statements, because F_1 has s4 ranked at the first position, F_2 has s_{11} ranked at the first position, and F_3 has s_{14} ranked at the first position. On the other hand, the *worst* case needs to examine five statements. Two extra statements need to be examined because (i) both s_{10} and s_{11} are tied in F_2, and a correct statement s_{10} will be examined before the faulty statement s_{11} is examined; (ii) both s_{14} and s_{15} are tied in F_3, and a correct statement s_{15} will be examined before the faulty statement s_{14} is examined. The *average* case needs to examine 4((3+5)/2) statements. A significant point worth noting is that all three bugs can be located in parallel by using the proposed MSeer technique in only one iteration.

12.5.3 Case Studies

Section 12.5.3.1 provides an overview of the subject programs used in case studies and data collection. Evaluation metrics are explained in Section 12.5.3.2. Results of case studies are given in Section 12.5.3.3.

12.5.3.1 Subject Programs and Data Collections

Seven subject programs are used. Five were downloaded from [47]: version 1.1.2 of *gzip* (which reduces the size of named files), version 2.2 of *grep* (which searches for a pattern in a file), version 3.76.1 of *make* (which manages the construction of executables and other products from source code), version 1.1 of the *flex* program (which generates scanners that perform lexical pattern-matching on text), and version 1.6 of *ant* (which builds Java executable files). A set of test cases and faulty versions of each program were also downloaded. Version 1.4.0.2 of the *socat* program (which establishes two bidirectional byte streams and transfers data between them) and the faulty version CVE-2004-1484 reported in [48] were downloaded from [49], whereas version 1.2.1 of *xmail* (which serves as a mail server) and the faulty version CVE-2005-2943 reported in [50] were downloaded from [51]. A set of test cases of *socat* and *xmail* were also downloaded from [49] and [51], respectively.

In addition to the faulty versions downloaded from the aforementioned websites, additional faulty versions were created using mutation-based fault injection to enlarge data sets. Studies such as [52–54] have shown that mutation-based faults can be used to simulate realistic faults and provide reliable and trustworthy results for testing and debugging experiments. Two classes of mutant operators are used:

- Replacement of an arithmetic, relational, logical, increment and decrement, or assignment operator by another operator from the same class.
- Decision negation in an *if* or *while* statement.

Studies such as [12, 13, 55] have reported that test cases that kill mutants generated by *relational* operator replacement and *logical* operator replacement are also likely to kill other mutants.

Table 12.6 gives the size (lines of code), the number of faulty versions, and the number of test cases of each subject program. These programs are either medium or large-sized, written in different languages (*gzip*, *grep*, *make*, *flex*, and *socat* in C,

Table 12.6 Subject programs.

Program	LOC	No. of faulty versions	No. of test cases
gzip	6573	23	211
grep	12 653	18	470
make	20 014	29	793
flex	13 892	22	525
ant	75 333	23	871
socat	16 576	15	213
xmail	50 366	22	314

Source: Gao and Wong [1]/IEEE.

ant in Java, and *xmail* in C++) with various functionality. Such diversity makes the results more convincing.

Faulty versions with multiple bugs were created for each program by injecting bugs from multiple single-bug versions into the same multiple-bug version. For example, a five-bug version of a program can be created by seeding bugs from five single-bug versions into the program simultaneously. Since there is more than one way to create a five-bug version, using only one may lead to a biased conclusion. To avoid this bias, 30 distinct faulty versions with two, three, four, and five bugs for *gzip*, *grep*, *make*, *flex*, *ant*, *socat*, and *xmail* were randomly created. Altogether, there were 840 multiple-bug programs in the case studies. This approach (creating multiple-bug fault versions by injecting bugs from multiple single-bug versions) has been used in many published studies [4, 8, 56, 57].

Different tools were used to collect coverage information for each test execution: a revised version of χSuds [36] for C programs, *gcov* [58] for C++ programs, and *Clover* [59] for Java programs.

Gao and Wong compare MSeer to the OBA technique and the second technique proposed by Jones et al. [17]. For each iteration in OBA, all failed test cases (even though they are associated with different causative bugs) and all successful test cases are used in conjunction with a fault localization technique to generate a suspiciousness ranking. Programmers fix the first bug located by the ranking and then execute the modified program against all test cases before moving on to the next iteration. The debugging process terminates when all test cases are executed successfully. Only one bug is fixed in each iteration.

Jones et al. [17] proposed two techniques for parallel debugging of a program with multiple bugs. It is difficult to conduct an experiment using their first technique because J1 did not provide enough detail on how user behavior models were clustered. This point has also been confirmed by Gao and Wong of [4, 26]. As a result, only the second technique (hereafter referred to as J2) is used for cross-comparison. J2 first uses Tarantula to generate suspiciousness rankings with respect to each failed test case and all successful test cases. It then measures the Jaccard distance between each pair of rankings and marks two of them as *similar* if their distance is less than 0.5 (further discussion on why the Jaccard distance is not a good candidate for measuring the distance between two rankings can be found in Section 12.5.4.3). J2 clusters these rankings by taking a closure of the pairs of rankings that are marked as similar. Fault-focused rankings are generated using all failed test cases in each cluster and all successful test cases. The major differences between MSeer and J2 are:

- J2 uses a simple distance metric (Jaccard), which cannot precisely measure the distance between two suspiciousness rankings (see Section 12.5.4.3), and they treat every statement equally without considering the fact that more suspicious statements should contribute more to the distance between two rankings than less suspicious statements (see Section 12.5.1.2). A revised Kendall tau distance is proposed in MSeer to overcome these deficiencies.
- J2 applies a hierarchical clustering algorithm, which may not be as effective and efficient as *K*-medoids [22, 23]. Instead, MSeer uses an innovative approach to estimate the number of clusters and assign initial medoids simultaneously. It then uses an improved *K*-medoids clustering algorithm to perform the clustering.

For MSeer, the last step of each debugging iteration (Step 6 in Section 12.5.1.4) involves fixing the first bug located by each fault-focused suspiciousness ranking. The same applies to J2.

In [17], suspiciousness rankings are generated using Tarantula, a fault localization technique that has been shown to be less effective than crosstab [20]. For a fair comparison, crosstab is used as the fault localization technique in all experiments to compare the effectiveness of MSeer, OBA, and J2. The possible impact of different fault localization techniques (D* [15], RBF [21], Ochiai [3], and Tarantula [24]) on results is discussed in Section 12.5.4.1.

12.5.3.2 Evaluation of Effectiveness and Efficiency

The effectiveness of multiple-bug fault localization techniques can be measured using one the following metrics:

- *Average number of statements examined*

  This metric gives the average number of statements that need to be examined to find all the bugs in a multiple-bug version of a subject program. For discussion purposes, let us assume a program *P* has *n* multiple-bug versions. Technique *X* is more effective in fault localization than technique *Y* for *P*, if

$\frac{\sum_{i=1}^{n} X(i)}{n} < \frac{\sum_{i=1}^{n} Y(i)}{n}$, where $X(i)$ and $Y(i)$ are the number of statements that need to be examined to locate all bugs in the ith multiple-bug version of P by X and Y, respectively.

- T-EXAM *score*

  The EXAM score used in previous studies [20, 21] gives the percentage of statements that need to be examined until the first bug is located. Gao and Wong extend the original EXAM and define a new metric T-EXAM for evaluating the effectiveness of multiple-bug fault localization techniques. For OBA, if there are μ debugging iterations, the T-EXAM score is defined as:

$$\text{T-EXAM} = \sum_{i=1}^{\mu} EXAM_i$$

where $EXAM_i$ is the percentage of statements that need to be examined to locate the first bug at the ith iteration. Let us use a three-bug faulty program with 200 statements as an example. Assume that a programmer has to examine 15, 20, and 18 statements in order to find the first bug in the first, second, and third iterations. $EXAM_1$ equals $100 \times (15/200) = 7.5$, and $EXAM_2$ and $EXAM_3$ equal 10 and 9, respectively. Hence, the T-EXAM score for locating all three bugs in this program is $7.5 + 10 + 9 = 26.5$.

For MSeer and J2, let μ be the number of debugging iterations and τ be the number of fault-focused suspiciousness rankings generated for each iteration. The T-EXAM is defined as:

$$\text{T-EXAM} = \sum_{i=1}^{\mu}\sum_{j=1}^{\tau} EXAM_{i,j}$$

where $EXAM_{i,j}$ is the percentage of statements that need to be examined to locate the bug referred to by the jth fault-focused suspiciousness ranking in the ith iteration. For discussion purposes, let us use a three-bug faulty program with 200 statements as an example. Assume that MSeer needs two iterations to locate all three bugs. In the first iteration, two fault-focused rankings are generated. Following the first ranking, five statements need to be examined to locate the bug, whereas ten statements in the second ranking must be examined to locate a different bug. In the second iteration, there is one fault-focused ranking that requires an examination of seven statements to locate the remaining bug. We have $EXAM_{1,1} = 2.5$ (which is 5/200), $EXAM_{1,2} = 5.0$, and $EXAM_{2,1} = 3.5$. Together, the T-EXAM for locating all three bugs is $2.5 + 5.0 + 3.5 + 11.0$. One significant difference between EXAM and T-EXAM is that EXAM gives the percentage of code that needs to be examined to locate the bug in a single-bug program or the first bug of a multiple-bug program [15], whereas

T-EXAM is a score that can be used to measure the effectiveness of different techniques to locate all the bugs in a multiple-bug program. The effectiveness of two techniques, *X* and *Y*, for debugging multiple-bug programs can be compared based on their T-EXAM scores. If *X* has a smaller T-EXAM score than *Y*, then *X* is considered to be more effective than *Y*.

- *Wilcoxon signed-rank test*

  The Wilcoxon signed-rank test (also known as the Mann–Whitney U test, which is an alternative to other hypothesis tests such as the paired Student's *t*-test and *z*-test when a normal distribution of the population cannot be assumed) [60] is also used to provide a comparison with a solid statistical basis between the effectiveness of different techniques. Since Gao and Wong aim to show that MSeer is more effective than other techniques, the difference between the number of statements that need to be examined using MSeer and another technique is computed. Gao and Wong evaluate the one-tailed alternative hypothesis that the other techniques require an examination of a greater number of statements than MSeer. All Wilcoxon signed-rank tests are run with Benjamini–Hochberg correction. The null hypothesis is:

  > H_0: The number of statements examined by other techniques to locate all bugs in a multiple-bug program $\leq$ the number of statements examined by MSeer.

  If H_0 is rejected (i.e. the alternative hypothesis is accepted), then it implies that MSeer will require an examination of fewer statements than other techniques. This also implies that MSeer is more effective than other techniques. Debugging a program using MSeer is independent of debugging the same program using other techniques (J2 or OBA). Gao and Wong assume that the differences in effectiveness using MSeer and the other techniques with respect to a reasonable number of samples (30) comply with a continuous distribution symmetric about its median.

  One way to measure the efficiency of techniques that locate multiple bugs in parallel is to use the *number of debugging iterations* needed to locate all the bugs in a faulty program. For two techniques *X* and *Y*, if the number of iterations required by *X* is smaller than that required by *Y*, then *X* is more efficient than *Y*. Note that, based on the data, even for programs with more than 50 KLOC and almost 900 test cases, the clustering can still be completed within a few minutes. This suggests that clustering will not be a factor that imposes a significant impact on the efficiency of the proposed technique.

12.5.3.3 Results

Tables 12.7–12.9 give the average number of statements that need to be examined by MSeer, OBA, and J2 with respect to 30 versions of a given program each containing α bugs ($\alpha = 2$, 3, 4, and 5). For example, the average number of statements

Table 12.7 Average number of statements examined (*best* case).

		gzip	*grep*	*make*	*flex*	*ant*	*socat*	*xmail*
Two-bug	MSeer	12.8	345.77	261.53	11.37	16.73	8.63	215.77
	OBA	28.4	361.57	592.27	33.57	18.93	22.27	473.83
	J2	53.57	368.67	364.5	27.83	23.03	27.83	436.77
Three-bug	MSeer	41.77	492.93	640.7	23.3	35.13	18.4	524.6
	OBA	85.4	525.93	888.43	72.43	37.87	37.1	621.9
	J2	113.93	547.4	722.13	63.03	43.43	81.17	570.03
Four-bug	MSeer	70.27	560.03	685.57	67.7	44.77	42.07	601.27
	OBA	162.57	589.43	1163.77	111.93	69.57	62.37	930.97
	J2	194.8	614.6	732.6	99	75.47	274.97	893.93
Five-bug	MSeer	80	598.8	1142.97	104.67	53.4	63.33	750.07
	OBA	243.7	649.23	1540.93	170.67	77.17	135.93	1232.73
	J2	275.17	672.63	1212.43	152.37	81.63	340	1184.6

Source: Gao and Wong [1]/IEEE.

Table 12.8 Average number of statements examined (*average* case).

		gzip	*grep*	*make*	*flex*	*ant*	*socat*	*xmail*
Two-bug	MSeer	45.07	498.22	536.95	43.62	39.43	23.37	448.15
	OBA	67.09	805.62	768.07	116.22	89	39.3	614.45
	J2	109.12	814.52	641.42	110.02	93.83	43.55	579.27
Three-bug	MSeer	108.17	720.7	885.59	67.35	73.5	49.04	732.77
	OBA	155.45	1171.83	1152.12	179.6	177.99	65.47	806.49
	J2	186.55	1194.04	979.15	137.93	183.55	150.65	756.48
Four-bug	MSeer	158.65	1024.55	956.62	104.6	98.24	87.07	858.75
	OBA	287.29	1339.73	1361.97	218.03	246.9	102.07	1089.55
	J2	317.67	1362.69	1033.04	192.9	252.07	362.45	1046.95
Five-bug	MSeer	199.14	1121.79	1551.17	150.23	115.94	125.45	1035.82
	OBA	414.22	1587.88	1801.7	276.8	177.22	182.35	1441.35
	J2	444.59	1610.88	1627.45	247.2	182.6	486.99	1398.77

Source: Gao and Wong [1]/IEEE.

Table 12.9 Average number of statements examined (*worst* case).

		gzip	*grep*	*make*	*flex*	*ant*	*socat*	*xmail*
Two-bug	MSeer	45.07	498.22	536.95	43.62	39.43	23.37	448.15
	OBA	67.09	805.62	768.07	116.22	89	39.3	614.45
	J2	109.12	814.52	641.42	110.02	93.83	43.55	579.27
Three-bug	MSeer	108.17	720.7	885.59	67.35	73.5	49.04	732.77
	OBA	155.45	1171.83	1152.12	179.6	177.99	65.47	806.49
	J2	186.55	1194.04	979.15	137.93	183.55	150.65	756.48
Four-bug	MSeer	158.65	1024.55	956.62	104.6	98.24	87.07	858.75
	OBA	287.29	1339.73	1361.97	218.03	246.9	102.07	1089.55
	J2	317.67	1362.69	1033.04	192.9	252.07	362.45	1046.95
Five-bug	MSeer	199.14	1121.79	1551.17	150.23	115.94	125.45	1035.82
	OBA	414.22	1587.88	1801.7	276.8	177.22	182.35	1441.35
	J2	444.59	1610.88	1627.45	247.2	182.6	486.99	1398.77

Source: Gao and Wong [1]/IEEE.

examined by MSeer with respect to the three-bug faulty versions of *gzip* is 41.77 in the *best* case, 108.17 in the *average*, and 174.57 in the *worst*. For OBA, the *best* is 85.40, the *average* is 155.45, and the *worst* is 225.50. For J2, the *best* is 113.93, the *average* is 186.55, and the *worst* is 259.17.

With respect to the 84 scenarios (seven programs with two, three, four, and five bugs, respectively, and with *best*, *average*, and *worst* cases), Gao and Wong observe that:

- MSeer outperforms OBA and J2 in all 84 scenarios. The improvement is very significant in some scenarios, for instance in the *average* and *worst* cases of *flex*, *ant*, and *grep*.
- Although the effectiveness of J2 and OBA are comparable in most scenarios, J2 is less effective than OBA in some scenarios (such as the *best*, *average*, and *worst* cases of *socat* and *gzip*).
- A close examination shows that using the J2 technique may generate redundant fault-focused rankings associated with the same bug. As a result, effort is wasted by locating the same bug more than once, which reduces J2's effectiveness. Such redundancy rarely happens when the MSeer technique is used.

Next, the evaluation using the T-EXAM score is presented. The three-bug versions of *gzip*, *grep*, and *make* in the *best*, *average*, and *worst* cases are presented in Figures 12.11–12.13. The x-axis is the T-EXAM score, while the y-axis is the corresponding percentage of faulty versions with all bugs located. For example,

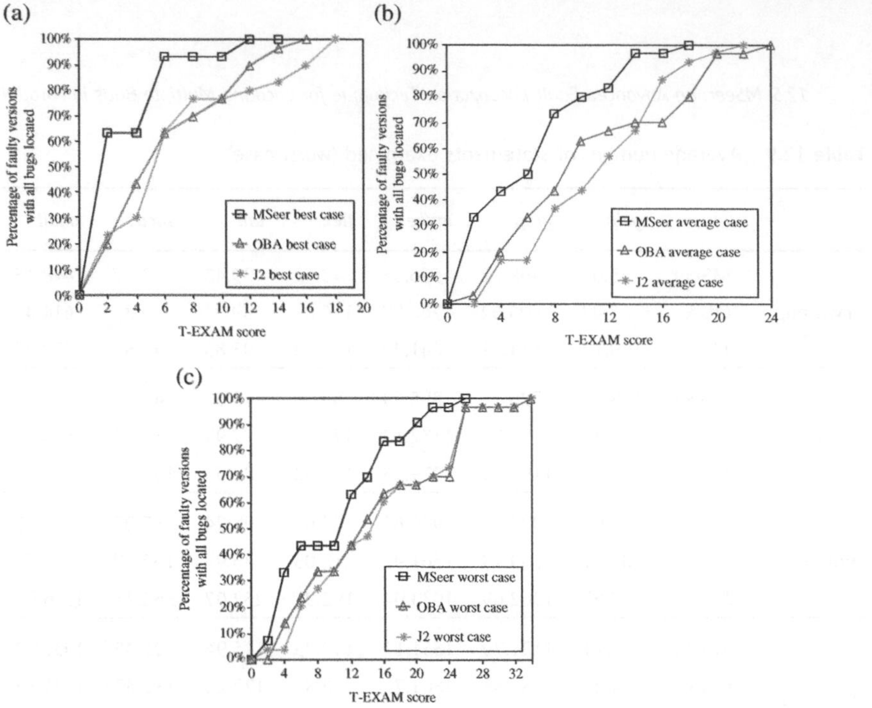

Figure 12.11 *gzip* three-bug versions: (a) best case; (b) average case; and (c) worst case. *Source:* Gao and Wong [1]/IEEE.

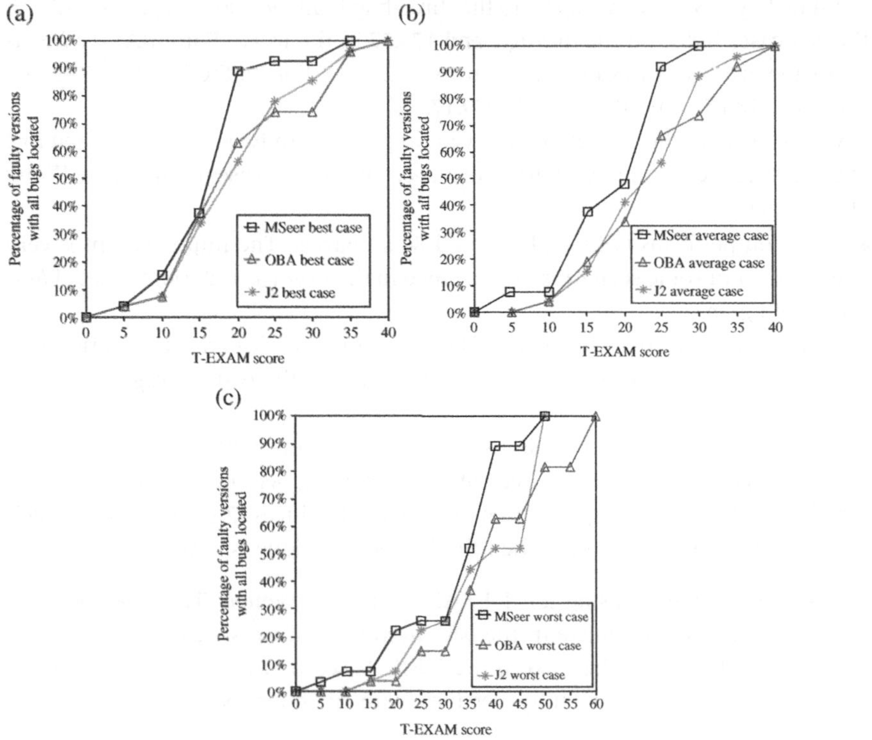

Figure 12.12 *grep* three-bug versions: (a) best case; (b) average case; and (c) worst case. *Source:* Gao and Wong [1]/IEEE.

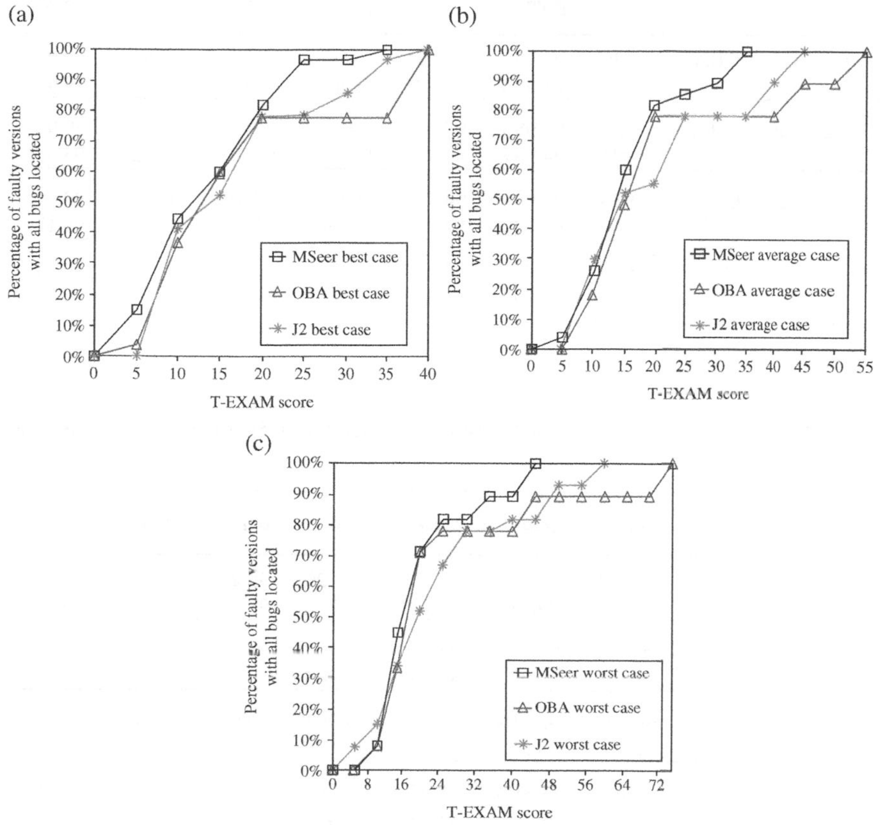

Figure 12.13 *make* three-bug versions. (a) best case; (b) average case; and (c) worst case. *Source:* Gao and Wong [1]/IEEE

referring to Figure 12.11a, when the T-EXAM score equals 4, 63.33% of the three-bug versions of *gzip* have all their bugs located by MSeer in the *best* case, 43.33% in the *average* case, and 33.33% in the *worst* case. For OBA and J2, respectively, these percentages are 43.33 and 30.00% (best), 20.00 and 16.67% (average), and 13.33 and 3.33% (worst). The T-EXAM scores in Figures 12.11–12.13 suggest that in most scenarios, MSeer is more effective than OBA and J2, whereas the latter two are comparable in effectiveness to each other. The same observation applies to other programs and faulty versions (two-bug, three-bug, four-bug, or five-bug) even though their curves are not included here due to space limitation.

Tables 12.10–12.12 give effectiveness comparisons for the *best*, *average*, and *worst* cases using the Wilcoxon signed-rank test. Each entry in these tables is the *confidence* (namely, 1−*p*-value) with which the alternative hypothesis

Table 12.10 Confidence with which it can be claimed that MSeer is more effective than other techniques (best cases).

		gzip	*grep*	*make*	*flex*	*ant*	*socat*	*xmail*
Two-bug	OBA	99.93%	93.90%	99.99%	99.99%	91.36%	99.95%	99.95%
	J2	99.40%	91.31%	91.29%	99.90%	96.66%	99.91%	99.91%
Three-bug	OBA	99.98%	97.98%	95.39%	99.99%	92.85%	99.92%	99.92%
	J2	99.99%	94.93%	89.93%	99.99%	99.91%	99.92%	95.92%
Four-bug	OBA	99.98%	92.98%	94.79%	99.99%	97.91%	99.99%	99.99%
	J2	99.94%	98.42%	87.97%	99.99%	92.96%	99.02%	99.17%
Five-bug	OBA	99.99%	99.99%	94.89%	99.99%	93.64%	99.95%	99.94%
	J2	99.99%	99.99%	86.37%	99.92%	94.43%	99.92%	99.91%

Source: Gao and Wong [1]/IEEE.

Table 12.11 Confidence with which it can be claimed that MSeer is more effective than other techniques (average cases).

		gzip	*grep*	*make*	*flex*	*ant*	*socat*	*xmail*
Two-bug	OBA	99.64%	96.96%	96.96%	99.99%	95.21%	99.96%	99.95%
	J2	99.23%	99.67%	86.72%	99.77%	98.91%	99.94%	99.80%
Three-bug	OBA	99.99%	99.99%	95.14%	99.99%	97.25%	99.94%	99.92%
	J2	99.99%	99.99%	88.15%	99.90%	99.67%	99.92%	93.33%
Four-bug	OBA	99.99%	95.35%	97.39%	99.99%	99.95%	99.99%	99.99%
	J2	99.67%	98.30%	88.12%	99.99%	93.43%	99.60%	98.39%
Five-bug	OBA	99.70%	99.90%	94.57%	99.99%	94.68%	99.94%	99.94%
	J2	99.72%	99.67%	85.15%	99.45%	94.24%	99.94%	99.42%

Source: Gao and Wong [1]/IEEE.

Table 12.12 Confidence with which it can be claimed that MSeer is more effective than other techniques (worst cases).

		gzip	*grep*	*make*	*flex*	*ant*	*socat*	*xmail*
Two-bug	OBA	99.41%	99.99%	93.93%	99.99%	99.05%	99.96%	99.39%
	J2	99.01%	99.99%	81.15%	99.61%	99.16%	99.96%	99.06%
Three-bug	OBA	99.99%	99.99%	94.89%	99.99%	99.64%	99.95%	89.99%
	J2	99.99%	99.99%	83.37%	99.81%	99.43%	99.92%	86.99%
Four-bug	OBA	99.99%	97.71%	99.99%	99.99%	99.99%	99.99%	98.99%
	J2	99.60%	98.18%	88.26%	99.99%	93.90%	99.90%	97.60%
Five-bug	OBA	99.40%	99.81%	94.24%	99.99%	95.71%	99.90%	99.40%
	J2	99.42%	99.32%	82.93%	98.93%	94.05%	99.96%	99.42%

Source: Gao and Wong [1]/IEEE.

(MSeer is more effective than other techniques)[15] can be accepted. Based on these results, Gao and Wong make the following observations:

- For *gzip*, *flex*, and *socat*, the confidence to accept the alternative hypothesis is higher than 99%.
- For *grep* and *ant*, the confidence to accept the alternative hypothesis is at least 90% and much higher in many scenarios.
- 157 of the 168 scenarios accept the alternative hypothesis with a confidence level higher than 90%, and the few exceptions still have a confidence in the 80s.

Overall, results from the Wilcoxon signed-rank test also suggest that MSeer is more effective than both OBA and J2. This is consistent with the effectiveness comparison using the average number of statements examined and the T-EXAM score.

Gao and Wong compare the efficiency of MSeer, J2, and OBA in terms of the number of iterations. For OBA, the number of iterations is the same as the number of bugs in the program. Hence, a two-bug program requires two iterations to locate both bugs, a three-bug program needs three iterations to locate all three bugs, and so on. For MSeer and J2, this number is actually an *average* number. For example, the value 1.17 in the third column and second row in Table 12.13 (which has been listed in bold) gives the *average* number of iterations required to locate both bugs over 30 distinct two-bug versions of the *gzip* program. Referring to the explanation at the end of Section 12.5.3.1, it is important to use 30 distinct versions instead of just one version to avoid possible bias.

Table 12.13 Average number of debugging iterations.

		gzip	*grep*	*make*	*flex*	*ant*	*socat*	*xmail*
Two-bug	MSeer	**1.17**	1.23	1.47	1.13	1.1	1.27	1.13
	J2	1.57	1.63	1.63	1.53	1.47	1.43	1.6
	OBA	2	2	2	2	2	2	2
Three-bug	MSeer	1.43	1.53	1.83	1.53	1.27	1.57	1.5
	J2	1.9	2.07	1.93	1.86	1.7	2	2.1
	OBA	3	3	3	3	3	3	3
Four-bug	MSeer	1.93	1.8	2.27	1.93	1.73	1.77	1.97
	J2	2.47	2.4	2.4	2.33	2.07	2.2	2.37
	OBA	4	4	4	4	4	4	4
Five-bug	MSeer	2.4	2.27	2.57	2.37	2.03	2.1	2.3
	J2	2.97	2.93	2.4	2.8	2.47	2.57	2.67
	OBA	5	5	5	5	5	5	5

Source: Gao and Wong [1]/IEEE.

Referring to the data in Table 12.13, the average number of debugging iterations required by MSeer is smaller than that required by J2, which is smaller than the number of iterations required by OBA in 27 out of 28 scenarios.

The only exception is for the *make* program, where the average number of iterations over 30 distinct five-bug versions required by MSeer and J2 is 2.57 and 2.40, respectively. Nevertheless, the difference between the two numbers is very small (only 0.17). On the other hand, each of them is only about half of the number of iterations required by OBA. A very interesting point worth noting is that even though MSeer has an average number of iterations slightly larger than J2 in this case, the average number of statements examined to locate all five bugs using MSeer is still smaller than that using J2 (referring to Tables 12.7 and 12.9, it gives 1142.97 for MSeer versus 1212.43 for J2 in the *best* case, 1551.17 for MSeer versus 1627.45 for J2 in the *average* case, and 1959.37 for MSeer versus 2042.47 for J2 in the *worst* case). With respect to the number of debugging iterations, Gao and Wong also run the Wilcoxon signed-rank test with Benjamini–Hochberg correction by setting the null hypothesis as

> H_0: The number of debugging iterations required by other techniques to locate all bugs in a multiple-bug program $\leq$ the number of debugging iterations required by MSeer.

The confidence to reject the null hypothesis is 100% for all scenarios except for one.

In sum, the data strongly suggest that MSeer is not only more effective (in terms of the number of statements examined) but also more efficient (in terms of the number of debugging iterations) than both J2 and OBA.

12.5.4 Discussions

Some interesting topics related to MSeer are discussed in this section.

12.5.4.1 Using Different Fault Localization Techniques

MSeer, OBA, and J2 all require the use of a fault localization technique to generate suspiciousness rankings. We now discuss the possible impact of using different fault localization techniques on their effectiveness. In addition to crosstab [20], Gao and Wong also use D^* (also known as DStar, where * equals 3) [15], RBF [21], Ochiai [3], and Tarantula [24]. The average number of statements examined over 30 distinct four-bug versions of *gzip*, *grep*, and *make* is shown in Table 12.14.

12.5.4.2 Apply MSeer to Programs with a Single Bug

As a multiple-bug fault localization technique, MSeer should also be effective on programs with a single bug. Gao and Wong compare the effectiveness of MSeer

Table 12.14 An example showing the differences among static, dynamic, and execution slicing.

	gzip	*grep*	*make*	*gzip*	*grep*	*make*	*gzip*	*grep*	*make*
	Best case			Average case			Worst case		
MSeer-crosstab	70.27	560.03	685.57	158.65	1024.55	956.62	247.03	1489.07	1227.67
OBA-crosstab	162.57	589.43	1163.77	287.29	1339.73	1361.97	412	2090.03	1560.17
J2-crosstab	194.8	614.6	732.6	317.67	1362.69	1033.04	440.53	2110.77	1333.47
MSeer-D*	67.27	591.47	677.03	153.17	1084.85	934.78	239.07	1578.23	1192.53
OBA-D*	154.43	665.83	1105.57	272.92	1336.13	1293.87	391.4	2006.43	1482.17
J2-D*	185.07	690.03	695.97	301.79	1347.63	981.39	418.5	2005.23	1266.8
MSeer-RBF	92.07	553.27	704.87	182.05	1020.44	997.3	272.03	1487.6	1289.73
OBA-RBF	178.83	648.37	1280.13	326.32	1525.95	1537.17	473.8	2403.53	1794.2
J2-RBF	214.27	676.07	805.87	360.44	1551.72	1169.67	506.6	2427.37	1533.47
MSeer-Ochiai	102.63	608.33	912.67	196.83	1075.2	1220.29	291.03	1542.07	1527.9
OBA-Ochiai	195.07	707.33	1396.53	344.74	1607.68	1634.37	494.4	2508.03	1872.2
J2-Ochiai	233.77	737.53	879.13	381.2	1635.23	1239.65	528.63	2532.93	1600.16
MSeer-Tarantula	115.63	702.07	996.67	212.48	1195.65	1299.67	309.33	1689.23	1602.67
OBA-Tarantula	211.33	766.27	1512.9	373.47	1741.65	1770.57	535.6	2717.03	2028.23
J2-Tarantula	253.23	798.97	952.37	412.95	1771.49	1342.94	572.67	2744	1733.5

Source: Gao and Wong [1]/IEEE.

Table 12.15 Average number of statements examined using MSeer and crosstab on programs with a single bug.

	Best	MSeer average	Worst	Best	Crosstab average	Worst
gzip	14.51	18.04	21.57	14.51	18.04	21.57
grep	117.79	128.14	138.48	117.79	128.14	138.48
make	213.75	312.32	410.89	211.52	306.83	402.13
flex	10.51	12.28	10.05	10.51	12.28	14.05
ant	16.78	27.7	38.61	14.16	20.58	37.01
socat	10.25	15.64	21.03	10.25	15.64	21.03
xmail	136	225.47	314.93	136	225.47	314.93

Source: Gao and Wong [1]/IEEE.

with that of crosstab using all seven programs (*gzip*, *grep*, *make*, *flex*, *ant*, *socat*, and *xmail*) and their faulty versions in Table 12.6. Table 12.15 gives the average number of statements examined over all faulty versions of each program.

With respect to the 21 scenarios (seven subject programs for the *best*, *average*, and *worst* cases), Gao and Wong observe that MSeer has the same effectiveness as crosstab in 15 scenarios and is only *slightly* less effective than crosstab in 6 scenarios by examining a few more statements. They choose crosstab for comparison because studies such as [15, 20] have shown that it is a very effective fault localization technique for programs with a single bug. Therefore, if MSeer is as effective as crosstab, it clearly suggests that MSeer can also be applied to single-bug programs.

12.5.4.3 Distance Metrics

Using a good distance metric is critical to the performance of clustering. To investigate whether the revised Kendall tau distance performs better than the original Kendall tau distance, Gao and Wong compare the effectiveness of MSeer using these two metrics. Table 12.16 shows the average number of statements examined

Table 12.16 Average number of statements examined using MSeer-RK and MSeer-OK.

	MSeer-RK			MSeer-OK		
	Best	Average	Worst	Best	Average	Worst
gzip	70.27	158.65	247.03	90.57	193.60	296.63
grep	560.03	1024.55	1489.07	593.33	1053.00	1512.67
make	685.57	956.62	1227.67	725.63	1019.33	1313.03

Source: Gao and Wong [1]/IEEE.

over 30 distinct four-bug versions of *gzip*, *grep*, and *make*, where MSeer-RK employs the revised Kendall tau distance and MSeer-OK uses the original Kendall tau distance.

Gao and Wong observe that the average number of statements examined in the *best* case for *gzip* is 70.27 for MSeer-RK and 90.57 for MSeer-OK. The increase in effectiveness is 28.89%, which is very significant. A similar observation also applies to another eight scenarios. These results clearly indicate that the revised Kendall tau distance should be used.

In [1], Gao and Wong used the Jaccard distance metric to measure the distance between two rankings. This is inappropriate for the reasons explained below. Given two rankings r_i and r_j, the Jaccard distance between them is defined as:

$$\text{Jaccard}(r_i, r_j) = 1 - \frac{|r_i \cap r_j|}{|r_i \cup r_j|} \tag{12.7}$$

where $|r_i \cap r_j|$ is the size of the intersection of r_i and r_j, and $|r_i \cup r_j|$ is the size of the union of r_i and r_j. First of all, the Jaccard distance metric only works on part of a ranking instead of the entire ranking. Otherwise, set r_i is the same as set r_j (except that statements may be ranked at different positions), and the Jaccard distance between any two rankings in this studies will always be zero. Second, if only statements at the top α% of two rankings are considered, the Jaccard distance may not represent the true distance between these two rankings. For example, let ranking $r_1 = \langle s_1, s_2, s_3, s_4, s_5, s_6, s_7, s_8 \rangle$ and ranking $r_2 = \langle s_4, s_3, s_2, s_1, s_8, s_7, s_6, s_5 \rangle$, and use only the top 50% of statements in each ranking to compute the Jaccard distance between r_1 and r_2. As a result, the intersection and the union of the top 50% statements of r_1 and r_2 are identical to each other. Hence, the Jaccard distance so computed is zero, which implies that there is no distance between r_1 and r_2. This conclusion is clearly very questionable. The fundamental problem is that the discordance between statements is not considered while computing the distance between two suspiciousness rankings.

Other metrics such as the Hamming distance and the Euclidean distance more strongly emphasize the difference between the same positions of two data vectors. However, with respect to a suspiciousness ranking used for fault localization, the relative order between statements is the most important attribute. Hence, while clustering suspiciousness rankings to determine the failed tests that are due to the causative bug (Step 4 in Section 12.5.1.4), it is more appropriate to use a revised Kendall tau distance as described by Eq. (12.2) in Section 12.5.1.2.

Spearman distance [57] is another metric that can be used to measure the distance between two rankings. However, Kendall and Gibbons [38] pointed out that Spearman is much more sensitive to errors and discrepancies in data and is less reliable and less interpretable than Kendall tau. Hence, the revised Kendall tau distance was used in the Gao and Wong study.

Table 12.17 Average number of statements examined using MSeer-Gao and MSeer-Mardia.

	MSeer-Gao			MSeer-Mardia		
	Best	**Average**	**Worst**	**Best**	**Average**	**Worst**
gzip	70.27	158.65	247.03	316.23	713.93	1111.63
grep	560.03	1024.55	1489.07	2520.13	4610.48	6700.83
make	685.57	956.62	1227.67	3085.07	4304.79	5524.53

Source: Gao and Wong [1]/IEEE.

12.5.4.4 The Importance of Estimating the Number of Clusters and Assigning Initial Medoids

Overestimating the number of clusters will result in the generation of redundant fault-focused rankings and expending unnecessary efforts to locate the same bug more than once. On the other hand, underestimating the number of clusters gives us fewer fault-focused suspiciousness rankings with an adverse consequence that failed tests in the same cluster may not be due to the same bug.

Gao and Wong's approach can estimate the number of clusters and assign the initial medoids simultaneously. A possible alternative is to set the number of clusters to $\sqrt{N_F/2}$ for N_F failed test cases and randomly select initial medoids as suggested by Mardia et al. [10]. Gao and Wong compare the effectiveness of MSeer using these two approaches over 30 distinct four-bug versions of *gzip*, *grep*, and *make*. The results are presented in Table 12.17, where MSeer-Gao uses Gao and Wong's approach and MSeer-Mardia follows the suggestion in [10].

Gao and Wong observe that the average number of statements examined in the *best* case for *gzip* is 70.27 for MSeer-Gao and 316.22 for MSeer-Mardia. The increase in effectiveness is 350.01%, which is very significant. A similar observation also applies to the other eight scenarios. These results clearly indicate that it is critical that MSeer should use Gao and Wong's approach to estimate the number of clusters and assign the initial medoids.

12.6 Spectrum-Based Reasoning for Fault Localization[16]

As mentioned before, spectrum-based fault localization is among the best performing techniques for fault localization [63]. The technique is particularly interesting because it is very lightweight, hence scaling to large, real systems: takes as input the so-called hit-spectra – which is an abstraction of program traces that reveal whether a component was executed or not in a given test case. Spectrum-based fault localization is mostly evaluated in the context of single faults; albeit most cases are indeed single fault ones [64], the need to handle multiple faults is also needed. Next, we discuss an approach, Barinel, by means of an example, that is capable of handling multiple faults using program spectrum only [61, 64]. Barinel is offered as part of the GZoltar tool suite [65].

12.6.1 Barinel

Consider the following hit-spectra matrix (containing a set of component[17] observations *obs* and transaction outcomes *e*), with 4 transactions[18] and 3 components:

Spectrum-based reasoning [4, 66, 67] consists of the following:

- Generate sets of components (candidates) that would explain the observed erroneous behavior.
- Rank the candidates according to their probability of being the true fault explanation.

Candidate Generation A diagnosis candidate *d* is a set of components that is said to be valid if every failed transaction involved a component from *d*. We would like to concentrate only on minimal candidates[19] because they subsume other candidates with more components [3]. Unfortunately, the minimal candidate problem is NP-hard. A minimal hitting set search (MHS[2]) algorithm [61, 68] has been proposed[20] as a heuristic-based approach to tackle the problem. The minimal hitting set problem can be formulated as follows: Given a set of elements $U = \{c_1, c_2, ..., c_M\}$ (called the universe) and a collection *S* non-empty sets whose union is equal to the universe, we define a minimal hitting set *d* as a set such that:

- The intersection of *d* with any element of *S* is not empty.
- The intersection of any proper subset of *d* with any element of *S* is empty.

Consider the example in Table 12.18. Let *S* be the set of failed transactions, that is, transactions such that $e_i = 1$. Thus, *S* has three elements $t_1 = \{c_1, c_2\}$, $t_2 = \{c_2, c_3\}$,

Table 12.18 The hit-spectra matrix.

	obs			
	c_1	c_2	c_3	e
t_1	1	1	0	1
t_2	0	1	1	1
t_3	1	0	0	1
t_4	1	0	1	0

and $t_3 = \{c_1\}$. The two minimal sets of diagnostic candidates that can explain the erroneous behavior are:

- $d_1 = \{c_1, c_2\}$
- $d_2 = \{c_1, c_3\}$

They are minimal sets because the intersection of any of their proper subsets with any element t_1, t_2, or t_3 of S is empty. Interested readers may refer to [61, 68] for more details.

Candidate Ranking For each candidate d, the posterior probability is calculated using the naïve Bayes rule (probabilities are calculated assuming conditional independence throughout the process):

$$\Pr(d \mid obs, e) = \Pr(d) \cdot \prod_{i=1}^{M} \frac{\Pr(obs_i, e_i \mid d)}{\Pr(obs_i)} \tag{12.8}$$

The denominator $\Pr(obs_i)$ is a normalizing term that is identical for all candidates and is not considered for ranking purposes. In order to define $\Pr(d)$, let p_j denote the prior probability that a component c_j is at fault. In the context of development-time fault localization, we often approximate p_j as $1/1000$, i.e. one fault for each 1000 lines of code [4, 67]. The prior probability for a candidate d is given by

$$\Pr(d) = \prod_{j \in d} p_j \cdot \prod_{j \in U \setminus d} \left(1 - p_j\right) \tag{12.9}$$

$\Pr(d)$ estimates the probability that a candidate, without further evidence, is responsible for erroneous behavior. It is also used to make larger candidates (in terms of cardinality) less probable. In order to bias the prior probability taking observations into account, $\Pr(obs_i, e_i \mid d)$ is used. Let g_j (referred to as component goodness) denote the probability that a component c_j performs normally:

$$\Pr(obs_i, e_i \mid d) = \begin{cases} \prod_{j \in (d \cap obs_i)} g_j & \text{if } e_i = 0 \\ 1 - \prod_{j \in (d \cap obs_i)} g_j & \text{otherwise} \end{cases} \tag{12.10}$$

In cases where values for *gj* are not available, they can be estimated by maximizing $\Pr(obs, e \mid d)$ (maximum likelihood estimation (MLE) for the naïve Bayes classifier [4] or a kernel density estimation [4]) under parameters $\{g_j \mid j \in d\}$.

To better illustrate this step, let us go back to our example. The probabilities for both candidates are

$$\Pr(d_1 \mid obs, e) = \overbrace{\left(\frac{1}{1000} \cdot \frac{1}{1000} \cdot \left(1 - \frac{1}{1000}\right)\right)}^{\Pr(d)} \times \overbrace{\underbrace{(1 - g_1 \cdot g_2)}_{t_1} \times \underbrace{(1 - g_2)}_{t_2} \times \underbrace{(1 - g_1)}_{t_3} \times \underbrace{(g_1)}_{t_4}}^{\Pr(obs, e \mid d)} \tag{12.11}$$

$$\Pr(d_2 \mid obs, e) = \overbrace{\left(\frac{1}{1000} \cdot \frac{1}{1000} \cdot \left(1 - \frac{1}{1000}\right)\right)}^{\Pr(d)} \times \\ \overbrace{\underbrace{(1-g_1)}_{t_1} \times \underbrace{(1-g_3)}_{t_2} \times \underbrace{(1-g_1)}_{t_3} \times \underbrace{(g_1 \cdot g_3)}_{t_4}}^{\Pr(obs,\, e \mid d)} \tag{12.12}$$

By performing MLE for both functions, it follows that $\Pr(d_1 \mid obs, e)$ is maximized for $g_1 = 0.47$ and $g_2 = 0.19$. $\Pr(d_2 \mid obs, e)$ is maximized for $g_1 = 0.41$ and $g_3 = 0.50$. Applying the goodness values to both expressions, it follows that $\Pr(d_1 \mid obs, e) = 1.9 \times 10^{-9}$ and $\Pr(d_2 \mid obs, e) = 4.0 \times 10^{-10}$, entailing the ranking $\langle d_1, d_2 \rangle$. This means that the diagnostic candidate d_1 is more probable to be the explanation for the observed failures.

12.6.2 Results

Contrary to most previous approaches, Barinel does not fall into the common category of OBA debugging approach, but rather a multiple-bug-at-a-time debugging approach (MBA) [69]. Compared to previous approaches, Barinel fares well in terms of diagnostic accuracy for both single and multiple fault programs [4]. In particular, Abreu et al. concluded that, for single fault cases, Barinel is consistently the best performing technique, finding 60% of the faults by examining less than 10% of the source code. For the same effort, using Ochiai would lead a developer to find 52% of the faulty versions, and with Tarantula only 46% would be found. For an effort of less than 1%, PPDG performs equally well as Barinel. The Barinel approach outperforms Ochiai, which is consistently better than Sober and Tarantula, as shown in Figure 12.14.

As a side effect of their study, Abreu et al. have also demonstrated that the diagnostic ranking produced by Barinel is theoretically optimal. This has then been also demonstrated in further studies [70].

Next to the formal proof of Barinel's optimality in the single-fault case, synthetic experiments with multiple injected faults have confirmed that the Barinel approach by Abreu et al. [4] consistently outperforms statistical spectrum-based approaches, as well as the previous Bayesian reasoning approach by Abreu et al. [71]. Application to a set of software programs also indicates Barinel's advantage (27 wins out of 30 trials, despite the significant variance), while the exceptions can be pointed to particular program properties in combination with sampling noise [4].

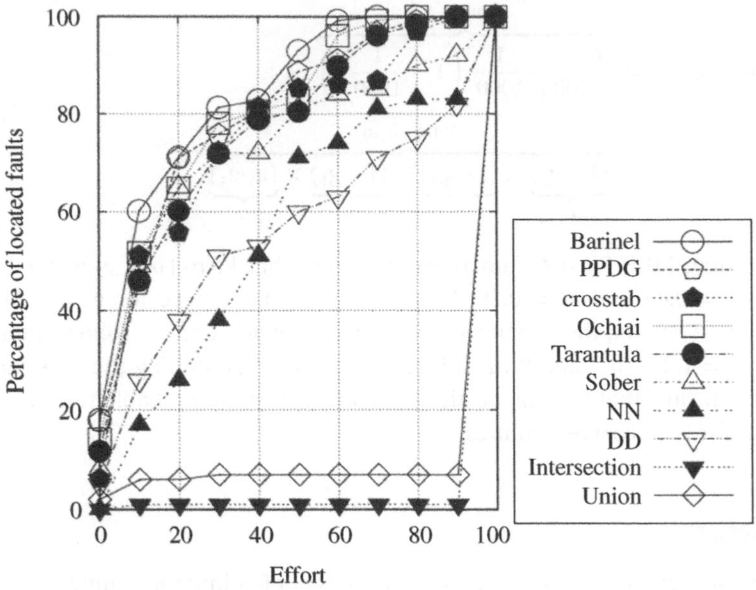

Figure 12.14 Effectiveness comparison.

12.7 Other Studies[21]

In this section, we provide an overview of related studies in addition to those discussed in the preceding sections, directing readers interested in further details to the accompanying references.

Fault localization techniques based on suspicious rankings [3–6, 12, 14, 15, 17, 18, 20, 21, 24, 73, 74] have been well reported in the literature. A survey on software fault localization [75] presents a comprehensive review of the current fault localization state-of-art. More recently, a literature review on multiple fault localization of programs has also been presented [69].

Researchers have reported studies on combining multiple fault localization techniques for better effectiveness. For example, Lucia et al. [76] leveraged the diversity of multiple existing spectrum-based fault localization techniques to better localize bugs using data fusion methods. Xuan and Monperrus [77] proposed Multric, a learning-based approach to combining multiple fault localization techniques. Debroy and Wong used a consensus-based strategy to improve the quality of fault localization [78].

Program invariants are also used in fault localization studies. Le et al. [79] proposed a fault localization technique that employs a learning-to-rank strategy, using likely program invariants and suspiciousness scores as features, to rank program methods based on their likelihood of being a root cause of a failure.

A popular but unrealistic assumption is that multiple bugs in the same program behave independently. Debroy and Wong [80] examined interferences that may take place between bugs, and they found that such interferences may manifest themselves to either trigger or mask execution failures. Results based on their experiments indicate that destructive interference (when an execution fails due to a bug but no longer fails when another bug is added to the same program) is more common than constructive interference (when an execution fails in the presence of two bugs in the same program but does not in the presence of either bug alone) because failures are masked more often than triggered by additional bugs. It is possible that a program with multiple bugs suffers from both destructive and constructive interferences. DiGiuseppe and Jones [72] also reported that multiple bugs have an adverse impact on the effectiveness of spectrum-based techniques. Similar observations have also been found in [57]. The existence of different types of interferences between multiple bugs may result in imperfect clustering such that some failed tests associated with a given bug are incorrectly grouped with failed tests responsible for another bug. However, based on their data, MSeer is sufficiently robust to absorb such noise yet still be effective in locating multiple bugs in parallel.

OBA has been adopted in studies using the DStar technique [15] and a fault localization technique based on a Bayesian reasoning framework [4]. A potential weakness of most techniques based on Bayesian reasoning [67, 81], including the technique in [4], is that they all assume program components fail independently; in other words, interferences between multiple bugs as described in [57, 72, 80] are ignored. This assumption in general does not hold in practice. In addition, although the technique described in [4] may be helpful for localizing individual bugs, it is less suitable for parallel debugging.

Other studies have also used the approach of clustering failed test cases. Podgurski et al. [82] applied supervised and unsupervised pattern classifications as well as multivariate visualization to execution profiles of failed test cases with an approach for estimating the number of clusters in order to group them into fault-focusing clusters. Steimann and Frenkel [25, 26] used the Weil–Kettler algorithm, an integer linear programming technique, to cluster failed test cases. However, both studies performed clustering of failed tests based on their execution profiles and suffered from the weakness discussed in Section 12.5.1.1 (representation (a)). A better approach is to use suspiciousness rankings to cluster failed test cases (representation (b)).

Yu et al. [57] proposed a technique to separate failed tests that only executed a single bug from failed tests that executed multiple bugs by comparing the *Ulam distance* between each pair of the rankings generated using a failed test and all successful tests. No case studies were conducted to show how their technique could improve the fault localization effectiveness.

Lamraoui and Nakajima [56] proposed a fault localization technique based on a new program encoding, *full flow-sensitive trace formula*. The proposed technique was evaluated on single-bug and multiple-bug faulty versions of a small-sized program *tcas* with 173 lines of code. This technique still follows the OBA technique.

As Open-source communities accumulate many real bug fixes, locating multiple bugs using knowledge mined from bug fixes is also feasible. Zhong and Hong [83] proposed an information retrieval-based approach called ClaFa that combines graph analysis and classification to locate multiple faults in source files. ClaFa involves two stages: model training and fault localization. In the model training stage, ClaFa builds program dependency graphs from the bug fixes and compares the graph from the buggy code with the graph from the fixed code, locates the buggy nodes, and extracts the various graph features of the buggy and clean nodes. A classification model is then trained on the extraction result. In the fault localization stage, the trained model can be used to predict whether a node of a program dependency graph is buggy or clean.

Most studies in software fault localization focus on proposing new techniques to identify suspicious locations that may contain bugs and examining their effectiveness. However, results from these studies are only approximate, and their correctness is not guaranteed. Locations so identified still need to be verified while bugs are actually fixed. Parnin and Orso [84] conducted a study to compare the actual performance of developers in debugging with and without a fault localization technique. They claimed that several assumptions made by existing fault localization techniques do not hold in practice because programmers will only examine the first few statements in a suspicious ranking. Xie et al. [85] reported that fault localization techniques may even slightly weaken programmers' abilities in identifying the root faults. On the other hand, Xia et al. [70] suggested that the studies in [84] and [86] suffered from the following drawbacks: (i) only using small-sized programs, (ii) only involving students, and (iii) only using dated fault localization techniques. In response, Xia et al. conducted a study based on four large-sized open-source projects with professional software programmers. They found that fault localization techniques could help professionals reduce their debugging time, and the improvements were statistically significant and substantial. To investigate how fault localization should be improved to better benefit practitioners, Kochhar et al. [87] highlighted some directions by conducting a literature review.

12.8 Conclusion

In this chapter, we present an overview of state-of-the-art study on software fault localization for programs with multiple bugs. Not surprisingly, most of the current research on fault localization still focuses on programs with a single bug. The challenges involved in fault localization for programs with multiple bugs appear quite daunting and do not seem easy to overcome. First, when encountering an execution failure on a program with multiple bugs, it must be ascertained whether the failure was due to just one fault or due to a combination of faults. This "due-to" relationship is not an easy one to reveal by current fault localization techniques alone. Second, even after determining such facts, the execution failure must then be linked to its corresponding causative fault(s). In the case of multiple failed executions, such failures must somehow be grouped together such that failures in the same group have the same root cause(s). Third, the task would then be to effectively and efficiently localize these multiple faults. Even given these challenges, studies explained in this section have addressed them from different directions and made some progress. In the future, studies that target a wider range of industrial programs with real bugs should be involved to further validate the effectiveness and efficiency of these techniques. Moreover, studies comparing all approaches in the same environment (i.e. same programs and same data sets), as in [88], would be a plus.

Notes

1 Part of Section 12.1 is from Ref. [1].
2 In this chapter, we use "bug" and "fault" interchangeably. We also use "programs" and "software" interchangeably.
3 The suspiciousness ranking can also be in terms of predicates, decision, function, etc.
4 In this chapter, the phrase "covered by a test case" is used interchangeably with "test cases are executed" when necessary.
5 Part of Section 12.2 is from Ref. [1].
6 Part of Section 12.3 is from Ref. [17].
7 Part of Section 12.4 is from Ref. [25].
8 Part of Section 12.5 is from Ref. [1].
9 A medoid refers to a cluster center that belongs to the corresponding cluster.
10 During the clustering phase, statements with the same suspiciousness value are sorted according to their statement number. Other techniques such as those reported in [34–36] can also be used to break the ties.
11 Instead of being used as a generic distance metric, $D(\omega, \sigma)$ is specifically designed in the MSeer study to emphasize that discordant pairs of more suspicious statements are more important than discordant pairs of less suspicious statements.
12 In the first iteration, θ is 0, and P^0 is assigned by Step 2. For subsequent iterations, P^0 is computed using Eq. (12.4).

13 Hereafter, unless otherwise specified, we use "distance" and "revised Kendall tau distance" interchangeably.
14 The execution trace of each test case in terms of other coverage criteria such as predicate can also be collected in this step.
15 If we change the alternative hypothesis to "MSeer is more effective than or as effective as other techniques," the confidence is 100% for most scenarios.
16 Part of Section 12.6 is from Refs. [4, 61, 62].
17 By component, we mean the unit by which we gather coverage. Basically, components are the columns in the hit-spectra matrix and can represent, e.g. every statement in the source code.
18 Transactions and test cases are used interchangeably.
19 A candidate d is said to be minimal if no valid candidate d' is contained in d.
20 https://github.com/npcardoso/MHS2
21 Part of Section 12.7 is from Ref. [72].

References

1 Gao, R. and Wong, W.E. (2017). MSeer: an advanced technique for locating multiple bugs in parallel. *IEEE Transactions on Software Engineering* 45 (3): 301–318. https://doi.org/10.1109/TSE.2017.2776912.
2 Vessy, I. (1985). Expertise in debugging computer programs: a process analysis. *International Journal of Man-Machine Studies* 23 (5): 459–494.
3 Abreu, R. and van Gemund, A.J.C. (2009). A low-cost approximate minimal hitting set algorithm and its application to model-based diagnosis. *Symposium on Abstraction, Reformulation, and Approximation*, Lake Arrowhead, CA, USA (8–10 August 2009). AAAI.
4 Abreu, R., Zoeteweij, P., and van Gemund A.J. (2009). Spectrum-based multiple fault localization. *Proceedings of the 24th IEEE/ACM International Conference on Automated Software Engineering (ASE '09)*, Auckland, New Zealand (16–20 November 2009), 88–99. IEEE.
5 Baah, G.K., Podgurski, A., and Harrold, M.J. (2010). Causal inference for statistical fault localization. *Proceedings of the International Symposium on Software Testing and Analysis (ISSTA '10)*, Trento, Italy (12–16 July 2010), 73–83. ACM.
6 Baah, G.K., Podgurski, A., and Harrold, M.J. (2011). Mitigating the confounding effects of program dependences for effective fault localization. *Proceedings of the Joint Meeting of the European Software Engineering Conference and the ACM SIGSOFT Symposium on the Foundations of Software Engineering (ESEC/FSE '11)*, Szeged, Hungary (5–9 September 2011), 146–156. ACM. https://doi.org/10.1145/2025113.2025136.
7 Hou, J., Gao, H., and Li, X. (2016). DSets-DBSCAN: a parameter-free clustering algorithm. *IEEE Transactions on Image Processing* 25 (7): 3182–3193.

8 Huang, Y., Wu, J., Feng, Y. et al. (2013). An empirical study on clustering for isolating bugs in fault localization. *Supplemental Proceedings of the International Symposium on Software Reliability Engineering (ISSREW '13)*, Pasadena, CA, USA (4–7 November 2013), 138–143. IEEE.

9 Li, X., Wong, W.E., Gao, R. et al. (2016). Genetic algorithm-based test generation for software product line with the integration of fault localization techniques. *Empirical Software Engineering* 23: 1–51. https://doi.org/10.1007/s10664-016-9494-9.

10 Mardia, K.V., Kent, J.T., and Bibby, J.M. (1979). *Multivariate Analysis.* Academic Press.

11 Wong, W.E., Gao, R., Li, Y. et al. (2016). A survey on software fault localization. *IEEE Transactions on Software Engineering* 42 (8): 707–740.

12 Wong, W.E. and Mathur, A.P. (1995). Reducing the cost of mutation testing: an empirical study. *Journal of Systems and Software* 31 (3): 185–196.

13 Wong, W.E., Debroy, V., and Choi, B. (2010). A family of code coverage-based Heuristics for effective fault localization. *Journal of Systems and Software* 83 (2): 188–208.

14 Wong, W.E., Debroy, V., Gao, R., and Li, Y. (2014). The DStar method for effective software fault localization. *IEEE Transactions on Reliability* 63 (1): 290–308.

15 Wong, W.E., Debroy, V., Golden, R. et al. (2012). Effective software fault localization using an RBF neural network. *IEEE Transactions on Reliability* 61 (1): 149–169.

16 Liu, C., Zhang, X., and Han, J. (2008). A systematic study of failure proximity. *IEEE Transactions on Software Engineering* 34 (6): 826–843.

17 Jones, J.A., Bowring, J.F., and Harrold, M.J. et al. (2007). Debugging in parallel. *Proceedings of the International Symposium on Software Testing and Analysis (ISSTA '07)*, London, UK (9–12 July 2007), 16–26. ACM.

18 Gore, R. and Reynolds, P.F. (2012). Reducing confounding bias in predicate- level statistical debugging metrics. *Proceedings of the International Conference on Software Engineering (ICSE '12)*, Zurich, Switzerland (2–9 June 2012), 463–473. IEEE.

19 Kaufman, L. and Rousseeuw, P.J. (1990). *Finding Groups in Data: an Introduction to Cluster Analysis*. New York NY, USA: Wiley.

20 Xia, X., Bao, L., Lo, D., and Li, S. (2017). Automated debugging considered harmful considered harmful: a user study revisiting the usefulness of spectra-based fault localization techniques with professionals using real bugs from large systems. *Proceedings of the International Conference on Software Maintenance and Evolution (ICSME '17)*, Raleigh, NC, USA (02–07 October 2016), 267–278. IEEE.

21 Wong, W.E., Debroy, V., and Xu, D. (2012). Towards better fault localization: a crosstab-based statistical approach. *IEEE Transactions on Systems, Man, and Cybernetics, Part C* 42 (3): 378–396.

22 Chen, G., Jaradat, S.A., and Banerjee, N. (2002). Evaluation and comparison of clustering algorithms in analysing ES cell gene expression data. *Statistica Sinica* 12 (1): 241–262.

23 Kaur, M. and Kaur, U. (2013). Comparison between K-mean and hierarchical algorithm using query redirection. *International Journal of Advanced Research in Computer Science and Software Engineering* 3 (7): 1454–1459.

24 Jones, J.A. and Harrold, M.J. (2005). Empirical evaluation of the Tarantula automatic fault-localization technique. *Proceedings of the 20th IEEE/ACM Conference on Automated Software Engineering (ASE '05)*, Long Beach, CA, USA (7–11 November 2005), 273–282. ACM.

25 Steimann, F. and Frenkel, M. (2012). Improving coverage-based localization of multiple faults using algorithms from integer linear programming. *Proceedings of the International Symposium on Software Reliability Engineering (ISSRE '12)*, Dallas, TX, USA (27–30 November 2012), 121–130. IEEE.

26 Hogerle, W., Steimann, F., and Frenkel, M. (2014). More debugging in parallel. *Proceedings of the International Symposium on Software Reliability Engineering (ISSRE '12)*, Naples, Italy (3–6 November 2014), 133–143. IEEE.

27 Teevan, J., Dumais, S.T., and Horvitz, E., (2007). Characterizing the value of personalizing search. *Proceedings of the International ACM SIGIR Conference on Research and Development in Information Retrieval (SIGIR '07)*, Amsterdam, Netherlands (23–27 July 2007), 757–758. ACM.

28 Sengupta, D., Bandyopahyay, S., and Maulik, U. (2010). A novel measure for evaluating and oradeed list: application in MicroRNA target prediction. *Proceedings of the International Symposium on Biocomputing (ISB '10)*, Calicut, Kerala, India (15–17 February 2010), 1–7. ACM.

29 Yager, R. and Filev, D.P. (1994). Approximate clustering via the mountain method. *IEEE Transactions on Systems, Man, and Cybernetics* 24 (8): 1279–1284.

30 Chiu, S.L. (1994). Fuzzy model identification based on cluster estimation. *Journal of Intelligent Fuzzy Systems* 2: 267–278.

31 Lin, K.Y., Xu, L., and Wu, J. (2004). A fast fuzzy C-means clustering for color image segmentation. *Journal of Image and Graphics* 9 (2): 159–163.

32 Yu, Z., Bai, C., and Cai, K. (July 2015). Does the failing test execute a single or multiple faults? an approach to classifying failing tests. *Proceedings of the International Conference on Software Engineering (ICSE '15)*, Florence, Italy (16–24 May 2015), 924–935. IEEE.

33 Riesen, K. and Bunke, H. (2009). Graph classification by means of lipschitz embedding. *IEEE Transactions on Systems, Man, and Cybernetics, Part B (Cybernetics)* 39 (6): 1472–1483.

34 Pearson, S. (2016). Evaluation of fault localization techniques. *Proceedings of the ACM SIGSOFT International Symposium on Foundations of Software Engineering (FSE '16)*, Seattle, WA, USA (13–18 November 2016), 1115–1117. ACM.

35 Sun, S. and Podgurski, A. (2016). Properties of effective metrics for coverage-based statistical fault localization. *Proceedings of the IEEE International Conference on*

Software Testing, Verification and Validation (ICST '16), Chicago, IL, USA (11–15 April 2016), 124–134. IEEE.

36 Xu, X., Debroy, V., Wong, W.E., and Guo, D. (2011). Ties within fault localization rankings: exposing and addressing the problem. *International Journal of Software Engineering and Knowledge Engineering* 21 (6): 803–827.

37 Libenzi, D. XMail Home Page. http://www.xmailserver.org (accessed January 2022).

38 Kendall, M. and Gibbons, J.D. (1990). *Rank Correlation Methods.* Edward Arnold.

39 Hartigan, J.A. and Wong, M.A. (1979). Algorithm AS 136: a *K*-means clustering algorithm. *Applied Statistics* 28 (1): 100–108.

40 MacQueen, J. (1967). Some methods for classification and analysis of multivariate observations. *Proceedings of the 5th Berkeley Symposium on Mathematical Statistics and Probability*, Berkeley, CA, USA (27 December 1965 to 7 January 1966), vol. 1, 281–297. University of California Press.

41 Sheng, W. and Liu, X. (2006). A genetic K-medoids clustering algorithm. *Journal of Heuristics* 12 (6): 447–466.

42 Ester, M., Kriegel, H.-P., Sander, J., and Xu, X. (1996). A density-based algorithm for discovering clusters in large spatial databases with noise. *Proceedings of the Second International Conference on Knowledge Discovery and Data Mining (KDD '96)*, Portland, OR, USA (2–4 August 1996), 226–231. AAAI Press.

43 Steinley, D. (2003). Local optima in *K*-means clustering: what you don't know may hurt you. *Psychological Methods* 8 (3): 294–304.

44 Dickinson, W., Leon, D., and Podgurski, A. (2001). Finding failures by cluster analysis of execution profiles. *Proceedings of the 23rd International Conference on Software Engineering (ICSE '01)*, Toronto, ON, Canada (12–19 May 2001), 339–348. IEEE.

45 Tukey, J.W. and McLaughin, D.H. (1963). Less vulnerable confidence and significance procedures for location based on a single sample: trimming/winsorization 1. *Journal of Statistics* 25 (3): 331–352.

46 Dixon, W.J. and Yuen, K.K. (1974). Trimming and winsorization: a review. *Statistiche Hefte* 15 (2–3): 157–170.

47 Software-artifact Infrastructure Repository. National Science Foundation. https://sir.csc.ncsu.edu/portal/index.php (accessed January 2022).

48 CVE-2004-1484 Detail. National Vulnerability Database, NIST Information Technology Laboratory. http://web.nvd.nist.gov/view/vuln/detail?vulnId=CVE-2004-1484 (accessed January 2022).

49 socat (2013). http://www.dest-unreach.org/socat/doc/socat.html (accessed January 2022).

50 CVE-2005-2943 Detail. National Vulnerability Database, NIST Information Technology Laboratory. http://web.nvd.nist.gov/view/vuln/detail?vulnId=CVE-2005-2943 (accessed January 2022).

51 Bellcore (1998). *χSuds Software Understanding System User's Manual.* Bridgewater, NJ, USA: Telcordia Technologies (formerly Bellcore). https://www.cs.purdue.edu/homes/apm/foundationsBook/Labs/coverage/xsuds.pdf.

52 Andrews, J.H., Briand, L.C., and Labiche, Y. (2005). Is mutation an appropriate tool for testing experiments? *Proceedings of the International Conference on Software Engineering (ICSE '05)*, St. Louis, MO, USA (15–21 May 2005), 402–411. ACM.

53 Do, H. and Rothermel, G. (2006). On the use of mutation faults in empirical assessments of test case Prioritization Techniques. *IEEE Transactions on Software Engineering* 32 (9): 733–752.

54 Namin, A.S., Andrews, J.H., and Labiche, Y. (2006). Using mutation analysis for assessing and comparing testing coverage criteria. *IEEE Transactions on Software Engineering* 32 (8): 608–624.

55 Offutt, A.J., Lee, A., Rothermel, G. et al. (1996). An experimental determination of sufficient mutant operators. *ACM Transactions on Software Engineering and Methodology* 5 (2): 99–118.

56 Lamraoui, S. and Nakajima, S. (2016). A Formula-based approach for automatic fault localization of multi-fault programs. *Journal of Information Processing* 24 (1): 88–98.

57 Yule, G.U. and Kendall, M.G. (1968). *An Introduction to the Theory of Statistics.* Charles Griffin.

58 gcov: a test coverage program. https://gcc.gnu.org/onlinedocs/gcc/Gcov.html (accessed January 2022).

59 Clover. https://www.atlassian.com/search?q=clover (accessed January 2022).

60 Lyman Ott, R. (1993). *An Introduction to Statistical Methods and Data Analysis*, 4e. Wadsworth Inc: Duxbury Press.

61 Cardoso, N. and Abreu, R. (2013). MHS2: a map-reduce heuristic-driven minimal hitting set search algorithm. *Multicore Software Engineering, Performance, and Tools: Proceedings of the International Conference (MUSEPAT '13)*, Saint Petersburg, Russia (19–20 August 2013), 25–36. Springer.

62 Perez, A., Abreu, R., and Deursen, A.V. (2021). A theoretical and empirical analysis of program spectra diagnosability. *IEEE Transactions on Software Engineering* 47 (2): 412–431.

63 Pearson, S., Campos, J., Just, R. et al. (2017). Evaluating and improving fault localization. *Proceedings of the 2017 IEEE/ACM 39th International Conference on Software Engineering (ICSE '17)*, Buenos Aires, Argentina (20–28 May 2017), 609–620. IEEE.

64 Perez, A., Abreu, R., and d'Amorim, M. (2017) Prevalence of single-fault fixes and its impact on fault localization. *Proceedings of the 2017 IEEE International Conference on Software Testing, Verification and Validation (ICST '17)*, Tokyo, Japan (13–17 March 2017), 12–22. IEEE.

65 Campos, J., André, R., Alexandre, P., and Abreu, R. (2012). GZoltar: an eclipse plug-in for testing and debugging. *Proceedings of the 27th IEEE/ACM International Conference on Automated Software Engineering (ASE '12)*, Essen, Germany (3–7 September 2012), 378–381. ACM.

66 Abreu, R., Zoeteweij, P., and Van Gemund, A.J.C. (2009). A new Bayesian approach to multiple intermittent fault diagnosis. *Proceedings of the 21st International Joint Conference on Artificial Intelligence (IIJCAI '09)*, Pasadena, CA, USA (11–17 July 2009), 653–658. IJCAI Organization.

67 Cardoso, N. and Abreu, R. (2013). A kernel density estimate-based approach to component goodness modeling. *Proceedings of the Twenty Seventh AAAI Conference on Artificial Intelligence (AAAI '13)*, Bellevue, WA, USA (14–18 July 2013), 152–158. AAAI Press.

68 Cardoso, N. and Abreu, R. (2013). A distributed approach to diagnosis candidate generation. *Proceedings of the Portuguese Conference on Artificial Intelligence*, Azores, Portugal (9–12 September 2013), 175–186. Springer.

69 Zakari, A., Lee, S.P., Abreu, R. et al. (2020). Multiple fault localization of software programs: a systematic literature review. *Information and Software Technology* 124: 106312.

70 Xie, X. Chen, T.Y., Kuo, F.-C., and Xu, B.W. (2013). A theoretical analysis of the risk evaluation formulas for spectrum-based fault localization. *ACM Transactions on Software Engineering and Methodology* 22 (4): 1–40.

71 Abreu, R., Zoeteweij, P., and Van Gemund, A.J. (2008). An observation-based model for fault localization. *Proceedings of the 2008 International Workshop on Dynamic Analysis (WODA '08), held in conjunction with the ACM SIGSOFT International Symposium on Software Testing and Analysis (ISSTA '08)*, Seattle, WA, USA (21 July 2008), 64–70. ACM.

72 DiGiuseppe, N. and Jones, J.A. (2011). On the influence of multiple faults on coverage-based fault localization. *Proceedings of the International Symposium on Software Testing and Analysis (ISSTA '13)*, Toronto, ON, Canada (17–21 July 2011), 210–220. ACM.

73 Liu, C., Fei, L., Yan, X. et al. (2006). Statistical debugging: a hypothesis testing-based approach. *IEEE Transactions on Software Engineering* 32 (10): 831–848.

74 Naish, L., Lee, H.J., and Ramamohanarao, K. (2011). A model for spectra-based software diagnosis. *Journal of the ACM Transactions on Software Engineering and Methodology* 20 (3): 1–32.

75 Wong, W.E. and Mathur, A.P. (1995). Fault detection effectiveness of mutation and data flow testing. *Software Quality Journal* 4 (1): 69–83.

76 Lucia, D. Lo, and Xia, X. (2014). Fusion fault localizers. *Proceedings of the ACM/IEEE International Conference on Automated Software Engineering (AEE '14)*, Vasteras, Sweden (15–19 September 2014), 127–138. ACM.

77 Xuan, J. and Monperrus, M. (2014). Learning to combine multiple ranking metrics for fault localization. *Proceedings of the IEEE International Conference on Software Maintenance and Evolution*, Victoria, BC, Canada (29 September to 3 October 2014), 191–200. IEEE.

78 Debroy, V. and Wong, W.E. (2013). A consensus-based strategy to improve the quality of fault localization. *Software: Practice and Experience* 43 (8): 989–1011.

79 Le, T.B., Lo, D., Goues, C.L., and Grunske, L. (2016). A learning-to-rank based fault localization approach using likely invariants. *Proceedings of the 25th International Symposium on Software Testing and Analysis (ISSTA '16)*, Saarbrucken, Germany (18–20 July 2016), 177–188. ACM.

80 Debroy, V. and Wong, W.E. (2009). Insights on fault interference for programs with multiple bugs. *Proceedings of the International Symposium on Software Reliability Engineering (ISSRE '09)*, Karnataka, India (16–19 November 2009), 165–174. IEEE.

81 de Kleer, J. (2009). Diagnosing multiple persistent and intermittent faults. *Proceedings of the International Joint Conference on Artificial Intelligence (JCAI '09)*, Pasadena, CA, USA (11–17 July 2009), 733–738.

82 Podgurski, A., Leon, D., Francis, P. et al. (2003). Automated support for classifying software failure reports. *Proceedings of the International Conference on Software Engineering (ICSE '03)*, Portland, OR, USA (3–10 May 2003), 465–475. IEEE.

83 Zhong, H. and Hong, M. (2020). Learning a graph-based classifier for fault localization. *Science China* 63(6): 1–22.

84 Parnin, C. and Orso, A. (2011). Are automated debugging techniques actually helping programmers? *Proceedings of the 2011 International Symposium on Software Testing and Analysis (ISSTA '11)*, Toronto, ON, Canada (17–21 July 2011), 199–209. ACM.

85 Xie, X., Liu, Z., Song, S. et al. (2016). Revisit of automatic debugging via human focus-tracking analysis. *Proceedings of the International Conference on Software Engineering (ICSE '16)*, Austin, TX, USA (14–22 May 2016). 808–819. ACM.

86 Xing, E., Ng, A., Jordan, M., and Russell, S. (2003). Distance metric learning, with application to clustering with side-information. *Advances in Neural Information Processing System 15*, Vancouver, BC, Canada (9–14 December 2002): 505–512. MIT Press.

87 Kochhar, P.S., Xia, X., Lo, D., and Li, S. (2016). Practitioners' expectations on automated fault localization. *Proceedings of the International Symposium on Software Testing and Analysis (ISSTA '16)*, Saarbrucken, Germany (18–20 July 2016), 165–176. ACM.

88 Durieux, T., Madeiral, F., Martinez, M., and Abreu, R. (2019). Empirical review of Java program repair tools: a large-scale experiment on 2,141 bugs and 23,551 repair attempts. *Proceedings of the Joint Meeting of the European Software Engineering Conference and the ACM SIGSOFT Symposium on the Foundations of Software Engineering (ESEC/FSE '19)*, Tallinn, Estonia (26–30 August 2019), 302–313. ACM.

13

Emerging Aspects of Software Fault Localization

T.H. Tse[1], David Lo[2], Alex Gorce[3], Michael Perscheid[4], Robert Hirschfeld[4], and W. Eric Wong[5]

[1] *Department of Computer Science, The University of Hong Kong, Pokfulam, Hong Kong*
[2] *School of Computing and Information Systems, Singapore Management University, Singapore*
[3] *School of Informatics, Computing, and Cyber Systems, Northern Arizona University, Flagstaff, AZ, USA*
[4] *Department of Computer Science, Universität Potsdam, Brandenburg, Germany*
[5] *Department of Computer Science, University of Texas at Dallas, Richardson, TX, USA*

13.1 Introduction

In the previous chapters, we introduced and reviewed techniques in several main fault[1] localization categories, such as traditional, slicing-based, and spectrum-based fault localization. Techniques in different categories have their own advantages, strengths, and ideal scenarios. In this chapter, we will present emerging, innovative techniques on top of these established categories. We will answer the following questions:

- How can we apply the scientific method to fault localization?
- How can we locate faults when the test oracle is not available?
- How can we automatically predict fault localization effectiveness?
- How can we integrate fault localization into automatic test generation tools?

Specifically, Section 13.2 will give an in-depth examination of common difficulties of fault localization and how to alleviate them by applying different techniques from different aspects. An introduction to a scientific, systematic hypothesis-testing methodology and how to apply them in practice will be provided in this section. Other techniques that help practitioners identify and assign appropriate

Handbook of Software Fault Localization: Foundations and Advances, First Edition.
Edited by W. Eric Wong and T.H. Tse.

Published 2023 by John Wiley & Sons, Inc.

developers to specific bug reports will be presented. We will also give a comprehensive review of different kinds of debuggers that can help practitioners better understand the behavior of the system under test and identify failure causes. Section 13.3 will present a methodology that can locate faults without a test oracle by checking metamorphic relations of the system under test using symbolic execution. Detailed running examples will be given to illustrate how to use the semi-proving approach to locate faults in different kinds of locations, such as statements, predicates, and loops. Section 13.4 will describe a machine learning approach to determine if a fault localization tool generates effective fault localization suggestions. In the final Section 13.5, we will discuss how to use the automated test case generation tool and other approaches to generate better test cases for fault localization.

13.2 Application of the Scientific Method to Fault Localization[2]

Fault localization is largely an attempt to understand what causes failures [1]. Starting with reproducing the observable failure in the form of a test case, developers follow failure causes and their effects on the infection chain back to the root cause (defect). To localize failure causes, they examine involved program entities, distinguish relevant from irrelevant behavior, and clean the infected states. After understanding all details of failure causes and their effects, developers will be able to identify and correct the root cause. However, this idealized procedure requires deep knowledge of the system and its behavior [2] because failures and defects can be far apart from each other [3]. Developers may not be familiar with the numerous program entities that are involved in long-running infection chains. This forces them to tackle unfamiliar source code to determine whether or not the behavior is correct. Localizing failure causes tends to be a tedious activity because developers are not able to investigate infection chains in a systematic way. There are two main reasons: deficiencies in standard development tools and inadequate knowledge about debugging methods [4–6]. Common debugging tools – including symbolic debuggers and test runners – do not support identification and tracking of infection chains [7]. Symbolic debuggers only provide access to the last point of execution without access to the program history or hints about suspicious behavior. Similarly, test runners only verify whether observable failures still exist. Both tools suffer from missing advice about causes and lack the capability to systematically follow failures back to their defects. Thus, developers must figure out on their own what is wrong and how to trace failure causes that occurred in the past.

Debugging with outdated but still prevalent tools leads more to a guessing game than a systematic procedure to localize failure causes. In addition, the lack of debugging knowledge also forces developers to apply disorganized trial and error approaches [4, 6]. Programming courses often pay little attention to debugging, and specific debugging courses are rare and optional. Therefore, developers must rely exclusively on their experience and intuition. Without feedback on inefficient methods, this often leads to large differences in debugging skills. Experienced developers are able to locate defects up to three times faster and add fewer new failures than novices [8, 9].

13.2.1 Scientific Debugging

To prevent debugging by disorganized trial and error, experienced developers apply the scientific method and its systematic hypothesis testing [1, 6]. With the help of the scientific method as shown in Figure 13.1, developers are able to obtain thorough explanations for failures by creating, evaluating, and refining failure-causing hypotheses. Starting with the observation of a reported failure, developers create an initial hypothesis concerning the problem. With this hypothesis, they predict program behavior and validate their expectations by experimenting with the system under observation. Depending on these experimental results, developers draw a conclusion that leads to a refined or alternative hypothesis. If the hypothesis cannot explain earlier observations or predict future ones, developers repeat the prediction, experiment, and conclusion step. In the end, a conclusive hypothesis represents a diagnosis that determines the infection chain and the root cause of the failure. As the scientific method is a general process, there are a number of concrete debugging strategies that convert a hypothesis into a diagnosis [6]. Apart from strategies such as binary search, depth-first search, and deductive analysis, breadth-first search has proven itself as the most efficient for experts [2]. In this case, developers start with

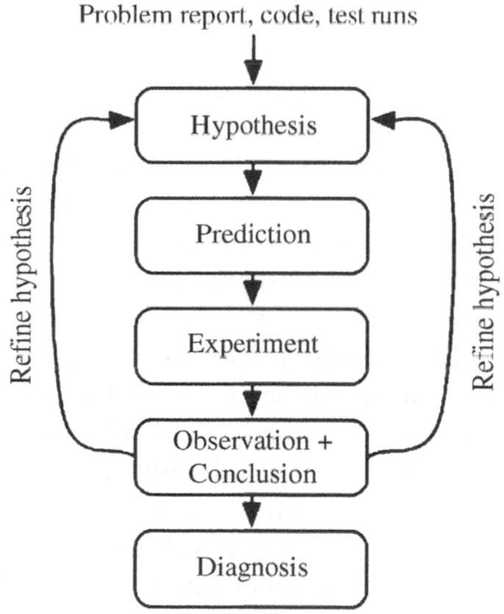

Figure 13.1 The scientific method supports a systematic procedure to reveal the infection chain. *Source:* Perscheid [10]/ Universität Potsdam.

a broad hypothesis on the infected system parts that is increasingly refined with detailed program comprehension until the root cause is found.

However, even when using the scientific method, the search for failure causes can still be a laborious task. In each iteration, developers have to choose from the countless possibilities of failure causes to create and evaluate suitable hypotheses. The efficiency of this procedure strongly depends on available expert knowledge and the abilities of debugging tools.

Different from a manual debugging session with the scientific method, algorithmic debugging is a semi-automatic approach [11] that interactively guides developers along infection chains. It systematically creates hypotheses asking developers about possible infections. Depending on their answers, it refines hypotheses and isolates failure causes step by step. There are implementations for the logic programming languages Prolog [11] and the imperative language Pascal that realize the concept with the aid of program slicing [12]. Furthermore, declarative debugging [13] generalizes algorithmic debugging for diagnosing failures in arbitrary programming languages. However, the general approach does not scale with the increasing complexity of current programs [1]. Developers have to answer either too many or too generic questions.

13.2.2 Identifying and Assigning Bug Reports to Developers

For the identification of the causes of a failure or the interpretation of suspicious entities, developers' expertise significantly influences the required effort [14]. More experienced developers create better hypotheses and predictions, require fewer iterations, and reveal failure causes faster than novices that do not know the code base [9, 15]. There are several automatic approaches that deal with the identification of proper expert knowledge with respect to a reported failure. They analyze bug and source code repositories and assign new failures to similar bug reports and their previous developers.

The expertise recommender [16] proposes a general architecture allowing for the administration of user profiles for arbitrary collaborative development activities. As an example, they instantiate their framework for the implementation activity of a real-world software company. In doing so, they figure out the fundamental "Line 10 rule"[3] that recommends expertise by considering the change history of source code. Developers who last modified a specific source code artifact have the most up-to-date knowledge. The expertise browser [17] automatically quantifies people with desired knowledge about source code by analyzing more information from change management systems and the program's history. Developers collect experience atoms for specific system parts where they have recently fixed a problem or enhanced a feature. From these expertise profiles, other stakeholders identify individuals with a broad expertise in specific system parts.

Ownership maps [18] present a compact overview for all files and their evolution with respect to corresponding expert knowledge. With the help of concurrent versions system (CVS) logs, it analyzes the commit history, identifies the file ownership, and visualizes the results. Among others, these maps help answer overall questions such as which author developed which part of the system at what time. XFinder [19] is an Eclipse extension that recommends a ranked list of developers to assist with changing a given file. A developer-code map created from version control information presents commit contributions, recent activities, and the number of active workdays per developer and file. On the supposition that people who have substantially contributed in the past are likely the best for future changes, the tool identifies experts for specific projects, packages, and files. The accuracy of the first three recommended developers is between 43 and 82%. The emergent expertise locator [20] approximates, depending on currently opened files and their histories, a ranked list of suitable team members. All of these approaches rely on the assumption that the programmer's activity indicates some knowledge of code. An empirical study [21] about the "Line 10 rule" investigated the frequency and recency of source code interactions. As a result, it confirmed the rule and presented additional factors that also indicate expertise knowledge, such as authorship or performed tasks. With these findings, subsequent approaches enhanced the results of pure history information with usage expertise [22] and considered the application of API methods and source code familiarity [23], which additionally analyzes developers' interaction with code.

There are also specific bug triage techniques that focus on the analysis of bug and source code repositories to automatically assign bug reports to the most qualified developers. A first bug triage approach [24] categorizes the textual descriptions of already solved reports and assigns developers to similar bugs. With a supervised Bayesian machine learning algorithm, this method correctly predicts 30% of all developer-to-bug report mappings. An improved semi-automated machine learning approach [14, 25] works on open bug repositories and learns the relationship between developers and bugs from a large number of already resolved reports. It classifies new incoming reports with the help of text categorization and recommends a few developers that have worked on similar problems before. The evaluation reports a high precision between 57 and 64% for two out of three large open source projects. Develect [26] applies a similar approach, but it matches the lexical similarities between the vocabulary of bug reports and the diffs of developers' source code contributions. Its evaluation achieves 33.6% precision for the most qualified developer and 71.0% recall that the perfect match is within the top ten. As an alternative to comparing and classifying bug reports, the developer selection approach [27] studies the assignment of change requests in open source projects and discovers that source code repositories also provide valuable information for assigning change requests. With information retrieval techniques, the proposed method identifies a set of best candidates that have resolved similar change requests in source code. An extension to XFinder [28] builds on the same idea; it identifies bug-related source code and then recommends proper expertise for changing these entities. A study [29] with project experts confirmed that both source code and bug repository approaches are good at finding suitable developers.

As bug reports are still reassigned to better suited developers [30], novel approaches enlarge the analysis scope. Bug tossing graphs [31] improve other bug triage methods by revealing the relationship between reassignments, developers, and bug reports. Their results present a reduction in reassignments by up to 72% and an improvement in accuracy of 76% for the first five recommendations. Another framework for automated bug triage [32] further suggests to consider not only the bug history and software repositories but also the developer's expertise, workload, and personal preferences. Finally, WhoseFault [33] and Team Navigation, as part of the test-driven fault navigation [10], consider anomalies in source code. Starting with spectrum-based fault localization to find suspicious source code entities, they mine history information for expertise and create a weighted mapping between locations and developers. With a probability of around 80%, they recommend the suitable developer in the first three recommendations. Even if both approaches have been developed independently and in parallel, there are quite similar but also different in the applied metrics (Tarantula vs. Ochiai) and the granularity (statement vs. method level).

13.2.3 Using Debuggers in Fault Localization

In general, debugging with standard tools faces several challenges with respect to localizing failure causes and defects. Nowadays, almost all development environments include test runners and symbolic debuggers as their debugging tools of choice. Unfortunately, not only are many of these tools decades old, but they are also not well-suited for the systematic following of infection chains backward to their root causes.

Test runners only execute test cases and verify if failures occur or not. There is no additional information such as differences between failed and successful tests. Hence, developers cannot restrict the search space to suspicious program entities that could help in creating initial hypotheses and making predictions. Furthermore, they can only experiment with test runners to a limited extent. For example, developers are not able to observe which parts of the program are being executed.[4] This task typically requires other tools such as symbolic debuggers. Only the test result feedback is helpful for a diagnosis because the correctness of fixes is directly reflected in successful test cases.

Symbolic debuggers suffer from missing advice on causes of failures and back-in-time capabilities. They only allow developers to stop a program and to access the run-time stack at a particular point in time. Neither do they report what is going wrong, nor do they offer capabilities to trace infection chains backward. A probable outcome of this is that developers rely primarily on their intuition for creating hypotheses and experiment with the system only in the forward direction, even though the defect is located in the past. Since it is hard to understand failure causes and how they occur, developers may prefer to follow a disorganized trial and error when debugging with these tools.

To trace infection chains from observable failures back to their root causes, omniscient debuggers (ODBs) record all executed events and present the collected data post-mortom. Therefore, they allow developers to navigate an entire program history and answer questions about the cause of a particular state. The ODB [34] records every event, object, and state change until execution is interrupted. However, the required dynamic analysis is quite time- and memory-consuming. The performance slows down up to 300 times, and the memory consumes up to 100 MB per second. Unstuck [35] is the first back-in-time debugger for Smalltalk. As the tool stores execution traces in memory like ODB, it suffers from similar performance problems and relatively small traces. WhyLine [36] allows developers to ask a set of "why did" and "why didn't" questions about the entire execution history. Combining static and dynamic slicing, call trees, and several other algorithms, the approach can answer, for example, why a line of code has not been reached. Traceglasses [37] records compact execution events of Java applications. By querying and transforming these events, developers have a comfortable navigation through large execution trees. JHyde [38] is a hybrid debugger for Java that integrates declarative with back-in-time debugging. With the help of generated hypotheses, developers can explicitly follow the infection chain backward. Moreover, there are already straightforward back-in-time debuggers in commercial development environments, such as Microsoft's IntelliTrace for Visual Studio 2010.

However, all of these ODBs do not scale well with long execution traces including intensive data. For that reason, other approaches aim to circumvent these issues by focusing on performance improvements in return for a more complicated setup. The trace-oriented debugger (TOD) [39] combines an efficient instrumentation mechanism and a specialized distributed database for capturing exhaustive traces. This approach requires considerable infrastructure and setup costs, and moreover imposes high run-time overheads and resource requirements. A novel indexing and querying technique [39] ensures scalability to arbitrarily large execution traces and offers an interactive debugging experience that outperforms existing back-in-time debuggers. Object flow analysis [40, 41], in conjunction with object aliases, also allows for a practical back-in-time debugger. The approach leverages the virtual machine and its garbage collector to remove no longer reachable objects and discard corresponding events. Tracing is fast and memory consumption is low; however, it requires an adapted virtual machine, and discarding events limit the approach because failure causes may be included in objects that are no longer in use. The Compass debugger [42] builds on top of the object flow analysis and presents an innovative user interface for back-in-time debuggers. In addition to standard tracing via call trees, this debugger allows developers to follow corrupted objects in order to find failure-inducing methods.

Instead of recording all events until the program stops, simulated back-in-time debuggers rely on reversing program execution. ZStep95 [43] for the functional programming language Lisp allows developers to step a program in both the forward and backward directions. In doing so, a call graph is visualized in real-time so that changes are directly visible. There are also reverse debuggers for stack-based imperative programming languages such as Java and C. In Java [44], new operational semantics that define reversed byte code instructions and side-effect logs that can be restored later on allow developers to execute programs backward. In C [45], a virtual machine simulates the program execution in both directions and records run-time data depending on developers' needs. Although all approaches are able to go back in time, they are limited to step by step debugging. Developers cannot directly follow cause–effect chains because the entire execution history is missing.

Another kind of simulated back-in-time debugging is to periodically record complete program checkpoints and re-execute them later. During this partial re-execution, the program can be analyzed and stopped when required. With the break at an earlier point in time, developers have the impression to debug backward. Igor [46] delegates the process of checkpointing to the operating system that then incrementally stores memory snapshots. This expensive method allows for reverse execution, selective searching of past data, and substitution of program entities. Spyder [47] combines dynamic slicing and backtracking to identify causes and effects between statements and states. While automated dynamic slicing determines affected statements [48], backtracking restores program states from re-executed checkpoints at previously defined breakpoints. A more lightweight replay debugger for Standard ML [49] creates checkpoints as first-class continuations. This allows a flexible mechanism to replace execution and provide reverse execution for the user and the interpreter. Bidirectional debugging [50] provides not only forward and backward commands by checkpointing, but also I/O-logging that ensures a deterministic re-execution. Previous approaches cannot guarantee the same execution path, which sometimes leads to wrong results. In general, so-called record and replay techniques such as DejaVu [51] prevent this problem by first recording non-deterministic program points and later replaying their results. Jockey [52] is a user-space library that combines record and replay with checkpoints. It rewrites all non-deterministic system calls and CPU instructions and takes periodic snapshots to enable time traveling in distributed Linux programs. Backstep [53] inserts an undo command into the debugging process of the Java Eclipse development environment. Each time a method is entered, a checkpoint is created that allows for restarting the method from its invocation. However, all checkpoint approaches have scalability issues because they strongly depend on the size and frequency of their checkpoints.

Apart from back-in-time debuggers, there are other debugging tools that support the search for failure causes. Coca [54] is a debugger for C that automatically adds breakpoints at control flow and data events. The analysis is done on the fly, and the program stops as soon as a specified event occurs. Query-based debugging [55] allows for an efficient search for relationships in large object spaces after a program stops. In a more dynamic version [56], similar queries continuously check objects while running and will instantly stop if a violation is found. Snapshot query-based debugging [57] further optimizes performance and proposes a more specialized query language. Pervasive debuggers [58] allow developers to inspect concurrent and distributed applications. In a virtualized environment, such debuggers have full control over every component and their interactions. At each point in time, they can stop them in a consistent state independent of network latency, different programming languages, and multiple hosts. Object-centric debugging [59] proposes to primarily consider objects and their interactions instead of stack-based run-time environments. The approach sees objects as the key abstraction and presents a new debugger that answers more object-related questions. The visual symbolic debugger [60] shows all possible execution paths without running the program. The applied symbolic execution helps developers understand behavior in small parts of the code. Moreover, there are visualization concepts that directly support debugging. The data display debugger [61] shows data structures as graphs that can be refined step by step. The debugging canvas [62] offers a two-dimensional pan-and-zoom surface for arranging code bubbles [63] that represent call paths, variable values, and source code snippets. Thus, developers can see everything regarding the current debugging task at a glance.

However, starting debugging at observable failures still compels developers to analyze a great number of failure causes and their effects until they find the root cause [3]. Back-in-time debuggers do not support direct navigation along the infection chain [38]; developers must examine an enormous amount of data manually in order to create proper hypotheses. The missing classification of suspicious and harmless behavior leads to numerous and often laborious decisions involving which execution subtree to follow [1]. Furthermore, most back-in-time debuggers often come with a performance overhead [34] or a more complicated setup [39] that does not allow for a seamless and immediate access to run-time information [64]. Unfortunately, this overhead renders these tools rather impractical for frequent use. Thus, the infection chain is hard to trace, developers require a large amount of time, and debugging the entire test case execution becomes a laborious activity.

To solve this issue, the test-driven fault navigation [10] and its PathFinder back-in-time debugger combine a lightweight recording mechanism for unit tests and various fault localization techniques. The approach quickly provides established dynamic views due to the concept of stepwise run-time analysis [65]. It does not record each event beforehand; rather, developers specify interest in particular parts, which are then refined on demand in additional test case re-executions. Furthermore, the tool classifies traces with spectrum- and state-based techniques and thereby allow developers to understand erroneous behavior directly. Without this concept, developers require more internal knowledge to isolate the infection chain and decide which path to follow.

13.2.4 Conclusion

Quickly identifying the infection chain is key for locating failure causes. An effective and efficient fault localization is not likely to be achieved by disorganized trial and attempts. We have therefore presented scientific and systematic hypothesis testing, as well as how to apply them in practice. It drives practitioners to create, evaluate, and refine failure-causing hypotheses in iterations. Besides the discussion on methodology of fault localization, assigning bug reports to the appropriate testers is another challenge in fault localization. Experiences and techniques, such as "Line 10 rule" and version control-based ownership/developer maps from the industry settings, are good practices to be applied. More advanced bug triage techniques (based on machine learning, lexical similarity, etc.) have been shown to be more effective for bug assignment. Last but not least, having a good tool can further improve the performance of fault localization. Despite the popularity of the symbolic debuggers in industry, it cannot provide advice on failure causes and back-in-time capabilities. Some advanced debuggers, such as ODBs, simulated back-in-time debuggers, and query-based debugging, are attempting to make bugging much easier, more intuitive, and more effective without introducing too much overhead.

13.3 Fault Localization in the Absence of Test Oracles by Semi-proving of Metamorphic Relations[5]

In software testing, an *oracle* is the mechanism to determine whether the output of a program agrees with the expected result. Weyuker [66] defined a program as non-testable if an oracle does not exist or requires too many resources to apply. In many real-world applications, automatic oracles do not exist, or else there would be no need to develop the software in the first place. Furthermore, in complex online applications such as pervasive computing, web services, and web search engines, the vast amount of data in continuous executions is too resource demanding for manual or automatic verification of the test outputs. This is known as the *oracle problem*. To alleviate the challenge, metamorphic testing (MT) has been proposed to verify necessary properties that may be derived from the target function or algorithm. Such properties are known as metamorphic relations (MRs).

In traditional fault localization approaches, the suspiciousness of individual program entities, such as statements or branch conditions, is evaluated according to the statistics of their successful and failed executions. This relies on the presence of a test oracle. Furthermore, such suspiciousness is probabilistic, and hence program entities with high suspiciousness may not necessarily be faulty. Cause and effect are usually not taken into account. The approach presented in this subchapter addresses these problems.

The idea of the semi-proving technique to fault localization in the absence of an oracle is inspired by MRs. In Section 13.3.1, we will provide readers with the background concepts of MT and MRs. In Section 13.3.2, we will give an overview of the semi-proving approach to fault localization using symbolic evaluation. Section 13.3.3 will discuss the need to go beyond symbolic evaluation. Section 13.3.4 will outline a successful initial empirical study, confirming that we are indeed in the right direction. Section 13.3.5 will provide readers with detailed illustrative examples. Section 13.3.6 will give a comparison with related work. Section 13.3.7 will conclude the subchapter.

To the best of our knowledge, semi-proving is (i) the first methodology to integrate proving, testing, and debugging using symbolic evaluation, and (ii) the first technique for fault localization in the absence of a test oracle. The present subchapter serves as an introduction to the semi-proving technique for fault localization in the absence of test oracles using MRs. We refer readers to Chen et al. [67] for technical details of the methodology, implementation, and empirical studies.

13.3.1 Metamorphic Testing and Metamorphic Relations

Metamorphic testing (*MT*) was first introduced in Chen et al. [68] to alleviate the oracle problem, especially in nonnumeric programs beyond simple trigonometric identities [69]. Since then, MT has grown into a full methodology with numerous areas of applications [70, 71]. Even though the sine function is usually used as the motivating example in most MT papers for ease of understanding, real-world applications are not restricted to numerical programs. For instance, a real-life Google search using the keywords

```
hotels near "Children's Hospital" Chicago
```

produced 2.77M results. There was no oracle to verify the correctness. Based on an intuitively necessary property that a more specific search should produce less results, we conducted MT using a follow-up test case

```
hotels near "Children's Hospital of Chicago"
```

which produced 5.00M results. This revealed a failure in the search engine.

In this section, we will introduce the basic concepts of MT and MRs. Consider a program without a test oracle. When we run it against a test case, there is no expected outcome for us to decide whether the execution is successful or a failure. Nevertheless, the process still provides us with useful information. Based on the original test case, a follow-up test case may be constructed according to some necessary property that may be inferred from the target function or algorithm. Such a necessary property is known as a *metamorphic relation*. It is a Boolean expression relating the inputs[6] and outputs of multiple executions of the same program, instead of a relationship between the inputs and outputs of a single execution. Consider, for example, a program `sine(x)` that calculates the value of sin x. The property $\sin(\pi - x) = \sin x$ may be identified as an MR. The corresponding MT will involve two executions, namely, running `sine(x)` and `sine(pi-x)`. Even if we have no idea whether either of these executions results in a success or a failure, we can check whether `sine(pi-x)` = `sine(x)`, which corresponds to the MR $\sin(\pi - x) = \sin x$. If the actual execution results do not satisfy the expected property within rounding limits, a failure is revealed.

In general, an MR may involve one or more source inputs and one or more follow-up inputs, and the follow-up inputs may depend not only on the source inputs but also on the source outputs. On the other hand, some program testers have expressed concern that MRs are difficult to conceive. We appreciate that the average software engineer may not prefer complex theoretical concepts even though they are applicable to more generic situations. In this subchapter, we will restrict our discussions to *basic* MRs, defined as follows:

Definition 13.1 (Basic Metamorphic Relation)

Let f be a target function or algorithm. Suppose there exist two relations ~ and ≈ such that, for any inputs x_1 and x_2 and their corresponding outputs $f(x_1)$ and $f(x_2)$, the following property is satisfied:

$$\textbf{\textit{MR}}: \textit{If } x_1 \sim x_2, \text{ then } \langle x_1, f(x_1)\rangle \approx \langle x_2, f(x_2)\rangle.$$

We say that MR is a metamorphic relation. We also say that x_1 is a source input, $f(x_1)$ is the source output, x_2 is a follow-up input, and $f(x_2)$ is the follow-up output.

For the sine example, the MR is simply

$$\textbf{\textit{MR}}: \text{If } x_2 = \pi - x_1, \text{ then } \sin x_2 = \sin x_1.$$

More generally, an MR may involve multiple source inputs or multiple follow-up inputs. Researchers interested in the formal details may refer to Section 2.2 (The Intuition and Formalization of MT) of Chen et al. [72]. Nevertheless, the basic Definition 13.1 is sufficient for most real-world situations. Some notable applications are bioinformatics [73], citation indexes [74], compilers [75], database management systems [76], and search engines [77]. In the remaining part of this subchapter, therefore, the term "metamorphic relation" will mean the *basic* concept with only two executions involving one source input and one follow-up input.

13.3.2 The Semi-proving Methodology

13.3.2.1 Semi-proving by Symbolic Evaluation

In traditional software testing, a failure-causing test case is some concrete input such as ⟨1, 2, 0⟩ that leads to an erroneous concrete output such as "2". Such concrete values do not give human debuggers much clue about the underlying cause of the failure. The semi-proving methodology [67, 78] extends the use of concrete inputs to symbolic inputs, to which we may apply symbolic evaluation [79–81] and constraint solving [82–84] techniques. For instance, the inputs are in the form of ⟨a, b, c⟩ instead of ⟨1, 2, 0⟩, the outputs are in the form of "b + c", and the failing conditions are in the form of "$(a \neq 0) \wedge (b \neq 0) \wedge (c = 0)$". The symbolic failing conditions provide detailed debugging information to human developers. For example, the constraint expression "$(a \neq 0) \wedge (b \neq 0) \wedge (c = 0)$" stipulates the precise condition of a *set* of failure-causing inputs rather than a specific concrete input like ⟨1, 2, 0⟩.

Even when an MR of a program is satisfied by all the concrete test cases in a test suite, it remains uncertain whether the MR is satisfied by untested inputs. In semi-proving, global symbolic evaluation can be used in such circumstances to prove that the MR is fulfilled by all possible inputs.

Thus, the semi-proving methodology integrates program proving, testing, and fault localization. An automated system has been developed to process C programs. Based on the concept of MRs, users may select necessary properties for the target function or algorithm and conduct semi-proving via symbolic evaluation and constraint solving as follows:

a) For programs for which global symbolic evaluation can be achieved and the relevant constraint expressions can be solved, semi-proving either *proves* that the relevant MR is satisfied, or *identifies all the inputs* that fail to satisfy the metamorphic property.
b) Even for programs that are too complex for global symbolic evaluation or constraint solving, semi-proving can still be utilized as a *testing* technique for specific symbolic test cases.

c) Constraint solvers can determine precise failing conditions from the failure-causing symbolic inputs identified in (a) or (b). Such conditions serve as diagnostic information for *fault localization*.

Symbolic evaluation has been studied extensively not only in software engineering but also in compilers [85, 86] and programming languages [87]. Advanced techniques and automated tools for optimizing constraint analysis have been developed. They support various data structures from arrays to complex dynamic data types [85, 86]. Computer algebra systems such as Mathematica [88] support symbolic computing as a standard feature.

Please refer to Chen et al. [67, 78] for technical details of the semi-proving methodology and implementation. In the remaining part of this subchapter, we will concentrate on semi-proving as a fault localization technique.

13.3.2.2 Semi-proving as a Fault Localization Technique

Most traditional fault localization techniques rank the suspiciousness of program entities, which may be a statement or a branch condition. The suspiciousness is evaluated according to the statistics of the successful and failed executions of these entities. Thus, a program entity designated as most suspicious only means that it has the highest probability of defect based on a number of test runs.

As explained in Section 13.3.1, an MR specifies a necessary property between any source test case and follow-up test case. The condition under which the two test cases satisfy the MR is called an *MR-preserving condition* (*MPC*). The condition under which the two test cases violate the MR is called an *MR-failing condition* (*MFC*). The semi-proving technique supports fault localization by identifying these two conditions. It then traces a deterministic cause-effect chain of the failure rather than a statistical probability. Like the full semi-proving methodology, the fault localization technique is based on global symbolic evaluation and constraint solving. An automatic system has been developed for the debugging of C programs.

The following is a brief summary of the semi-proving technique for fault localization. Illustrative examples will be given in Section 13.3.5.

1) Instrument the source code of the program P in question before compilation in order to allow the semi-proving system to collect execution traces.
2) Let I be a symbolic input. A typical example is a tuple of symbolic variables ⟨a, b, c⟩. Conduct global symbolic evaluation of program P against I. Let $O_1, O_2, \ldots, O_n$ be the symbolic outputs corresponding to path conditions $C_1, C_2, \ldots, C_n$ respectively.[7]
3) Let I' be a follow-up symbolic input based on some MR. Conduct global symbolic evaluation of program P against I'. Let $O'_1, O'_2, \ldots, O'_m$ be the symbolic outputs corresponding to path conditions $C'_1, C'_2, \ldots, C'_m$, respectively.

4) For every $i = 1, 2, ..., n$ and $j = 1, 2, ..., m$, if C_i and C'_j are not contradictory, check whether the MR is satisfied under the conjunction $C_i \wedge C'_j$. If the answer is yes, the condition (within $C_i \wedge C'_j$) under which the MR is satisfied is reported as an MPC. If the answer is no, the condition (within $C_i \wedge C'_j$) under which the MR is violated is reported as an MFC.
5) Compare the execution traces of the successful and failed executions related to the MPC and MFC, respectively. Report the differences as potential causes of the failure. For instance, the difference between the traces of an MPC and an MFC may be located to be the condition ($z > x$) within a predicate ($z \geq x$) in a specific program statement.

13.3.3 The Need to Go Beyond Symbolic Evaluation

Symbolic executions may not be completed for every branch, especially when complex loops, arrays, or pointers are involved. Following the techniques in *concolic* testing [72, 89, 90], which combines *conc*rete and symb*olic* executions, we explore the symbolic execution tree systematically using bounded depth-first search. An upper bound is preset for the depth of the search so that all loops (including infinite loops) will terminate at some point.

Furthermore, global symbolic evaluation may not be fully achieved because of the path explosion problem. The semi-proving fault localization tool uses heuristic approaches to pick more suspicious paths. For example, if a path is related to more MR failures than others, it will be selected for further symbolic evaluation.

Other algorithms and tools have also been developed to address the efficiency issue when the number of paths is large. For instance, the Java PathFinder model checker [91] uses a backtracking algorithm to traverse the symbolic execution tree rather than starting all the symbolic evaluations from scratch.

13.3.4 Initial Empirical Study

The Siemens suite [92] is a set of most commonly used programs in empirical studies on software testing and debugging. In particular, Chen et al. [67] selected its `replace` program as the subject for their initial empirical study. It was downloaded from http://pleuma.cc.gatech.edu/aristotle/Tools/subjects. The golden (or fault-free) version contains 563 lines of code and 20 functions. Thirty-two faulty versions have been created by the Siemens researchers [92] through manual fault injection. They cover the maximum varieties of logical faults among the Siemens programs.

The `replace` program checks whether any part of an input string matches a specified regular expression and, if so, replaces that part by a predefined string.

It has three parameters in the format "`replace` *pattern substitute input*". The *pattern* is a standard Unix regular expression such as "`Ste[vph]*[ae]n$`", where "`Ste`" is a string of characters; "`[ae]`" denotes "a" or "e"; "`[vph]*`" denotes repeated occurrences of the characters "v", "p", and "h"; and "`n$`" indicates that "`n`" is the last character of the input string. If any part of the *input* satisfies the *pattern*, it will be replaced by the *substitute*. For example, "`replace 'Ste[vph]*[ae]n$' 'Steve' 'Stephen'`" will produce the nickname "`Steve`" as output. The same nickname will be produced for input strings like "`Steven`" and "`Stephan`". However, if the input string is "`Ivan`" or "`Stephanie`", the output will be identical to the input string. No replacement will be made.

We identified four MRs for the `replace` program. One of them, for instance, made use of the equivalence of regular expressions involving square brackets. Thus, "`[vph]`" is equivalent to any of its permutations such as "`[phv]`" or "`[vhp]`". In this way, "`replace 'Ste[vph]*[ae]n$' 'Steve' 'Stephen'`" is equivalent to "`replace 'Ste[phv]*[ea]n$' 'Steve' 'Stephen'`".

Based on the four MRs, the semi-proving testing technique through global symbolic evaluation revealed failures in 31 of the 32 faulty versions. Then, the semi-proving fault localization technique detected *all* the MFCs. The initial empirical study demonstrates the effectiveness of the semi-proving approach to testing and fault localization. More details of the study are available in Chen et al. [67].

13.3.5 Detailed Illustrative Examples

In this section, we present four worked examples to illustrate different aspects of the semi-proving technique for fault localization. Only simple programs are included for ease of understanding, and hence the expected outputs are quite obvious to most programmers. However, we will not make use of the oracle and will conduct testing and fault localization through MRs.

We will present the *complete* global symbolic evaluation process for fault localization in these examples for the purpose of illustration. In real life, debuggers may stop the process for program repair when a major fault has been identified.

13.3.5.1 Fault Localization Example Related to Predicate Statement

Consider a program `triangle`(x, y, z) that accepts the lengths of the three sides ⟨x, y, z⟩ of a triangle as input to determine whether it is equilateral, isosceles, or scalene. An obvious MR is that if we permute the input from ⟨x, y, z⟩ to another sequence such as ⟨y, x, z⟩ or ⟨x, z, y⟩, the output result will remain unchanged.

A faulty version $\overline{\texttt{triangle}}_1$(x, y, z) is shown in Figure 13.2. The branch condition `(z == x)` in line `11` is erroneously coded as `(z >= x)`.

A failure is revealed when testing the program against the symbolic source input ⟨a, b, c⟩ and the symbolic follow-up input ⟨b, a, c⟩. In certain circumstances, the

```
    #include <iostream>
    #include <string>
    using namespace std;
    main() {
    float x, y, z;
    string type;
1   cin >> x >> y >> z;
2   if (x <= 0 || y <= 0 || z <= 0 || x + y <= z || y + z <= x || z + x <= y)
3     type = "error";
    else {
4     type = "scalene";
5     if (x == y && y == z)
6       type = "equilateral";
7     else if (x == y)
8       type = "isosceles";
9     else if (y == z)
10      type = "isosceles";
11    else if (z >= x)       // Should be (z == x)
12      type = "isosceles";
    }
  }
```

Figure 13.2 Faulty program $\overline{\texttt{triangle}_1}$(x, y, z) to classify a triangle as equilateral, isosceles, or scalene. The conditional statement 11 is erroneous.

result of $\overline{\texttt{triangle}_1}$(a, b, c) is "scalene" but that of $\overline{\texttt{triangle}_1}$(b, a, c) is "isosceles". This violates the MR triangle(x, y, z) = $\overline{\texttt{triangle}}$ (y, x, z) for any inputs ⟨x, y, z⟩ and ⟨y, x, z⟩.

Let us apply the semi-proving fault localization technique in Section 13.3.2 to identify the MFCs and MPCs with a view to finding the cause of the failure. We conduct global symbolic evaluation for the source input ⟨a, b, c⟩ and the follow-up input ⟨b, a, c⟩. The respective paths, path conditions, and outputs are shown in Tables 13.1 and 13.2.

We review all the conditions in the program that lead to two different results of "scalene" and "isosceles" in the source and follow-up executions. This is achieved by analyzing the conjunctions (C3 ∧ C6 ′), (C4 ∧ C6 ′), (C5 ∧ C6 ′), (C6 ∧ C3 ′), (C6 ∧ C4 ′), and (C6 ∧ C5 ′).

a) Consider (C3 ∧ C6 ′). The conditions C3 and C6 ′ do not overlap with each other, and hence they do not contribute to any failure. By the same argument, the conjunctions (C4 ∧ C6 ′), (C6 ∧ C3 ′), and (C6 ∧ C4 ′) are not related to the failure.

b) On the other hand, the expression (C5 ∧ C6 ′) can be evaluated to "¬C1 ∧ (a ≠ b) ∧ (b > c) ∧ (c > a)", which is not a contradiction. But the output under C5 is "isosceles" and that under C6 ′ is "scalene", which reveals a failure. Constraint solving shows that the MFC is "(c + a > b) ∧ (b > c) ∧ (c > a) ∧ (a > 0)".

   The execution may have failed under condition C5 or condition C6'. We will process each case in turn.

Table 13.1 Global symbolic evaluation results of $\overline{\texttt{triangle}_1}$(a, b, c).

Path	Path condition	Output
P1: (1, 2, 3)	C1: $(a \le 0) \vee (b \le 0) \vee (c \le 0) \vee (a + b \le c) \vee (b + c \le a) \vee (c + a \le b)$	error
P2: (1, 2, 4, 5, 6)	C2: $\neg C1 \wedge (a = b = c)$	equilateral
P3: (1, 2, 4, 5, 7, 8)	C3: $\neg C1 \wedge \neg(a = b = c) \wedge (a = b)$	isosceles
P4: (1, 2, 4, 5, 7, 9, 10)	C4: $\neg C1 \wedge \neg(a = b = c) \wedge (a \neq b) \wedge (b = c)$	isosceles
P5: (1, 2, 4, 5, 7, 9, 11, 12)	C5: $\neg C1 \wedge \neg(a = b = c) \wedge (a \neq b) \wedge (b \neq c) \wedge (c \ge a)$	isosceles
P6: (1, 2, 4, 5, 7, 9, 11)	C6: $\neg C1 \wedge \neg(a = b = c) \wedge (a \neq b) \wedge (b \neq c) \wedge (c < a)$	scalene

Table 13.2 Global symbolic evaluation results of $\overline{\texttt{triangle}_1}$(b, a, c).

Path	Path condition	Output
P1′: (1, 2, 3)	C1′: $(b \le 0) \vee (a \le 0) \vee (c \le 0) \vee (b + a \le c) \vee (a + c \le b) \vee (c + b \le a)$	error
P2′: (1, 2, 4, 5, 6)	C2′: $\neg C1' \wedge (b = a = c)$	equilateral
P3′: (1, 2, 4, 5, 7, 8)	C3′: $\neg C1' \wedge \neg(b = a = c) \wedge (b = a)$	isosceles
P4′: (1, 2, 4, 5, 7, 9, 10)	C4′: $\neg C1' \wedge \neg(b = a = c) \wedge (b \neq a) \wedge (a = c)$	isosceles
P5′: (1, 2, 4, 5, 7, 9, 11, 12)	C5′: $\neg C1' \wedge \neg(b = a = c) \wedge (b \neq a) \wedge (a \neq c) \wedge (c \ge b)$	isosceles
P6′: (1, 2, 4, 5, 7, 9, 11)	C6′: $\neg C1' \wedge \neg(b = a = c) \wedge (b \neq a) \wedge (a \neq c) \wedge (c < b)$	scalene

b1) Suppose that the output value of "`isosceles`" from the source execution under condition C5 is erroneous. The failure may be due to the output value or the condition (or both).

If the output value "`isosceles`" is erroneous, we can determine from the corresponding path condition P5 that a potential cause of the failure is the assignment '`type = "isosceles";`' in statement 12 of the program.

If condition C5 is erroneous, we search for all the other source execution(s) that lead to a consistent result of "`scalene`" as the follow-up execution under C6′. We find consistency only under (C6 ∧ C6′), which can be evaluated to "$\neg C1 \wedge (a \neq b) \wedge (a > c) \wedge (b > c)$". Constraint solving shows that the MPC is "$(a \neq b) \wedge (b + c > a) \wedge (a > c) \wedge (c + a > b) \wedge (b > c) \wedge (c > 0)$".

Comparing the MPC with the MFC in the first paragraph of (b), we show that the execution fails when (c > a). In this way, if condition C5 is erroneous, we can determine from the corresponding path condition P5 that a potential cause of the failure is the branch condition (z > x), which is part of the predicate in statement 11 of the program.

b2) Suppose that the output of "scalene" from the follow-up execution under condition C6′ is incorrect. The failure may be due to a missing else branch or an erroneous condition C6′.

For the former case, we can determine from the corresponding path condition P6′ that a potential cause of the failure is a missing else branch for the predicate statement 11 of the program.

For the latter case of an erroneous condition C6′, we look for all the other follow-up execution(s) that lead to a consistent result of "isosceles" as the source execution under C5. We find consistencies under (C5 ∧ C3′), (C5 ∧ C4′), and (C5 ∧ C5′). Consider (C5 ∧ C3′) first. The conditions C5 and C3′ do not overlap with each other, and hence they do not contribute to any failure. By the same argument, the conjunction (C5 ∧ C4′) is not related to the failure. On the other hand, the expression (C5 ∧ C5′) can be evaluated to "¬C1 ∧ (a ≠ b) ∧ (c > a) ∧ (c > b)", which is not a contradiction. Constraint solving shows that the MPC is "(a ≠ b) ∧ (a + b > c) ∧ (c > a) ∧ (a > 0) ∧ (c > b) ∧ (b > 0)". Comparing this MPC with the MFC in the first paragraph of (b), we find that the execution fails when (b > c). In this way, if condition C6′ is faulty, we can determine from the corresponding path condition P6′ that a potential cause of the failure is the branch condition (x > z), which is the negation of the predicate in statement 11 of the program.

c) Similarly, the expression (C6 ∧ C5′) can be evaluated to "¬C1 ∧ (a ≠ b) ∧ (a > c) ∧ (c > b)", which is not a contradiction. But the output under C6 is "scalene" and that under C5′ is "isosceles", thus unveiling another failure. Further constraint solving shows that the second MFC is "(b + c > a) ∧ (a > c) ∧ (c > b) ∧ (b > 0)".

The execution may have failed under condition C6 or condition C5′. We will again process each case in turn.

c1) Suppose the output of "scalene" from the source execution under condition C6 is erroneous. The failure may be due to a missing else branch or an erroneous condition C6.

For the former case, we can determine from the corresponding path condition P6 that a potential cause of the failure is a missing else branch for the predicate statement 11 of the program.

For the latter case of an erroneous condition C6, we look for all the other source execution(s) that lead to a consistent result of "isosceles" as the follow-up execution under C5′. We find consistencies under (C3 ∧ C5′), (C4 ∧ C5′), and (C5 ∧ C5′). Consider (C5 ∧ C3′) first. The conditions C3 and C5′ do not overlap with each other, and hence they do not contribute to any failure. On the other hand, the expression (C4 ∧ C5′) can be evaluated to "¬C1 ∧ (a ≠ b) ∧ (b = c) ∧ (c ≠ a)". Constraint solving indicates that the MPC is "(a ≠ b) ∧ (b = c) ∧ (2 * b > a) ∧ (a > 0) ∧ (b > 0)". Comparing this MPC with the MFC in the first paragraph of (c), we find that the execution fails when (c > b). In this way, if C6 is faulty, we can determine from the corresponding path condition P6 that a potential cause of the failure is (z > x), which is part of the predicate in statement 11 of the program. Similarly, the expression (C5 ∧ C5′) can be evaluated to "¬C1 ∧ (a ≠ b) ∧ (c > a) ∧ (c > b)", which is not a contradiction. Constraint solving shows that the MPC is "(a ≠ b) ∧ (a + b > c) ∧ (c > a) ∧ (a > 0) ∧ (c > b) ∧ (b > 0)". Comparing this MPC with the MFC in the first paragraph of (c), we find that the execution fails when (a > c). In this way, if C6 is faulty, we can determine from the corresponding path condition P6 that another potential cause of the failure is the branch condition (x > z), which is the negation of the predicate in statement 11 of the program.

c2) Suppose the output of "isosceles" from the follow-up execution under condition C5′ is incorrect. The failure may be due to the output value or the condition.

If the output value "isosceles" is erroneous, we can determine from the corresponding path condition P5′ that a potential cause of the failure is the assignment 'type = "isosceles";' in statement 12 of the program.

If condition C5′ is erroneous, we search for all the other follow-up execution(s) that lead to a consistent result of "scalene" as the source execution under C6. We find consistency only under (C6 ∧ C6′). As in (b1), the MPC under (C6 ∧ C6′) is "(a ≠ b) ∧ (b + c > a) ∧ (a > c) ∧ (c + a > b) ∧ (b > c) ∧ (c > 0)". Comparing this MPC with the MFC in the first paragraph of (c), we find that the execution fails when (c > b). In this way, if C5′ is faulty, we can determine from the corresponding path condition P5′ that a potential cause of the failure is the branch condition (z > x), which is part of the predicate in statement 11 of the program.

Considering the majority of the potential causes of the failure for the MR $\overline{\texttt{triangle}_1}$(a, b, c) = $\overline{\texttt{triangle}_1}$(b, a, c), we conclude that the failure is attributed to the faulty predicate in statement 11 of the program.

13.3.5.2 Fault Localization Example Related to Faulty Statement

A second faulty version $\overline{\texttt{triangle}_2}$(x, y, z) is shown in Figure 13.3. The assignment statement 'type = "isosceles";' in line 12 is erroneously coded as 'type = "scalene";'.

```
   #include <iostream>
   #include <string>
   using namespace std;
   main() {
   float x, y, z;
   string type;
1  cin >> x >> y >> z;
2  if (x <= 0 || y <= 0 || z <= 0 || x + y <= z || y + z <= x ||
   z + x <= y)
3     type = "error";
   else {
4     type = "scalene";
5     if (x == y && y == z)
6        type = "equilateral";
7     else if (x == y)
8        type = "isosceles";
9     else if (y == z)
10       type = "isosceles";
11    else if (z == x)
12       type = "scalene";    //  Should be "isosceles"
   }
   }
```

Figure 13.3 Faulty program $\overline{\texttt{triangle}_2}$(a, b, c) for classifying a triangle as equilateral, isosceles, or scalene. The assignment statement 12 is erroneous.

A failure is detected when testing the program against the symbolic source input ⟨a, b, c⟩ and the symbolic follow-up input ⟨b, a, c⟩. Under certain situations, the result of $\overline{\texttt{triangle}_2}$(a, b, c) is "scalene" but that of $\overline{\texttt{triangle}_2}$(b, a, c) is "isosceles". This violates the MR triangle(x, y, z) = triangle(y, x, z) for any inputs ⟨x, y, z⟩ and ⟨y, x, z⟩.

We apply the semi-proving fault localization technique to determine the MFCs and MPCs with a view to identifying the cause of the failure. We perform global symbolic evaluation for the source input ⟨a, b, c⟩ and the follow-up input ⟨b, a, c⟩. The respective paths, path conditions, and outputs are listed in Tables 13.3 and 13.4.

We check all the conditions in the program that lead to two different results of "isosceles" and "scalene" in the source and follow-up executions. This can be done by reviewing the conjunctions (D3 ∧ D5′), (D3 ∧ D6′), (D4 ∧ D5′), (D4 ∧ D6′), (D5 ∧ D3′), (D5 ∧ D4′), (D6 ∧ D3′), and (D6 ∧ D4′).

a) Consider (D3 ∧ D5′). The conditions D3 and D5′ do not overlap with each other, and hence they do not contribute to any failure. By the same token, the conjunctions (D3 ∧ D6′), (D4 ∧ D6′), (D5 ∧ D3′), (D6 ∧ D3′), and (D6 ∧ D4′) are not related to the failure.
b) On the other hand, the expression (D4 ∧ D5′) can be evaluated to "¬D1 ∧ (a ≠ b) ∧ (b = c) ∧ (c ≠ a)". However, the output under D4 is "isosceles" while that under D5′ is "scalene", which reveals a failure.

Table 13.3 Global symbolic evaluation results of $\overline{\texttt{triangle}}_2$(a, b, c).

Path	Path condition	Output
Q1: (1, 2, 3)	D1: $(a \le 0) \vee (b \le 0) \vee (c \le 0) \vee (a + b \le c) \vee (b + c \le a) \vee (c + a \le b)$	error
Q2: (1, 2, 4, 5, 6)	D2: $\neg$D1 $\wedge (a = b = c)$	equilateral
Q3: (1, 2, 4, 5, 7, 8)	D3: $\neg$D1 $\wedge \neg(a = b = c) \wedge (a = b)$	isosceles
Q4: (1, 2, 4, 5, 7, 9, 10)	D4: $\neg$D1 $\wedge \neg(a = b = c) \wedge (a \neq b) \wedge (b = c)$	isosceles
Q5: (1, 2, 4, 5, 7, 9, 11, 12)	D5: $\neg$D1 $\wedge \neg(a = b = c) \wedge (a \neq b) \wedge (b \neq c) \wedge (c = a)$	scalene
Q6: (1, 2, 4, 5, 7, 9, 11)	D6: $\neg$D1 $\wedge \neg(a = b = c) \wedge (a \neq b) \wedge (b \neq c) \wedge (c \neq a)$	scalene

Table 13.4 Global symbolic evaluation results of $\overline{\texttt{triangle}}_2$(b, a, c).

Path	Path condition	Output
Q1′: (1, 2, 3)	D1′: $(b \le 0) \vee (a \le 0) \vee (c \le 0) \vee (b + a \le c) \vee (a + c \le b) \vee (c + b \le a)$	error
Q2′: (1, 2, 4, 5, 6)	D2′: $\neg$D1′ $\wedge (b = a = c)$	equilateral
Q3′: (1, 2, 4, 5, 7, 8)	D3′: $\neg$D1′ $\wedge \neg(b = a = c) \wedge (b = a)$	isosceles
Q4′: (1, 2, 4, 5, 7, 9, 10)	D4′: $\neg$D1′ $\wedge \neg(b = a = c) \wedge (b \neq a) \wedge (a = c)$	isosceles
Q5′: (1, 2, 4, 5, 7, 9, 11, 12)	D5′: $\neg$D1′ $\wedge \neg(b = a = c) \wedge (b \neq a) \wedge (a \neq c) \wedge (c = b)$	scalene
Q6′: (1, 2, 4, 5, 7, 9, 11)	D6′: $\neg$D1′ $\wedge \neg(b = a = c) \wedge (b \neq a) \wedge (a \neq c) \wedge (c \neq b)$	scalene

The execution may have failed under condition D4 or condition D5′. We will process each case in turn.

b1) Suppose that the output of "`isosceles`" from the source execution under condition D4 is erroneous. The failure may be due to the output value or the condition.

Assume that the condition D4 is erroneous. We search for all the other source execution(s) that lead to a consistent result of "`scalene`" as the follow-up execution under D5′. We find consistencies under (D5 ∧ D5′) and (D6 ∧ D5′). Consider (D5 ∧ D5′) first. The conditions D5 and D5′ do not overlap with each other, and hence they do not contribute to any failure. By the same token, the conjunction (D6 ∧ D5′) is not related to the failure. Thus, no source execution leads to a consistent result of "scalene" as the follow-up execution under D5′.

We conclude, therefore, that condition D4 cannot be erroneous but that the output value "isosceles" must be incorrect. We can further determine from the corresponding path condition Q4 that a potential cause of the failure is the assignment 'type = "isosceles";' in statement 12 of the program.

b2) Suppose that the output of "scalene" from the follow-up execution under condition D5′ is incorrect. The failure may be due to a missing else branch or an erroneous condition D5′.

Assume that the condition D5′ is erroneous. We search for all the other follow-up execution(s) that lead to a consistent result of "isosceles" as the source execution under D4. We find consistencies under (D4 ∧ D3′) and (D4 ∧ D4′). Consider (D4 ∧ D3′) first. The conditions D4 and D3′ do not overlap with each other, and hence they do not contribute to any failure. By the same argument, the conjunction (D4 ∧ D4′) is not related to the failure. Thus, no source execution leads to a consistent result of "scalene" as the follow-up execution under D4.

We conclude, therefore, that condition D5′ cannot be erroneous but that there must be an else branch missing. We can further determine from the corresponding path condition Q5′ that a potential cause of the failure is a missing else branch for the predicate statement 11 of the program.

c) Similarly, the expression (D5 ∧ D4′) can be evaluated to "¬D1 ∧ (a ≠ b) ∧ (b ≠ c) ∧ (c = a)", which is not a contradiction. But the output under D5 is "scalene" and that under D4′ is "isosceles", thus unveiling another failure. Constraint solving shows that the MFC is "(a ≠ b) ∧ (c = a) ∧ (2 * a > b) ∧ (a > 0) ∧ (b > 0)".

The execution may have failed under condition D5 or condition D4′. We will process each case in turn.

c1) Suppose that the output of "scalene" from the source execution under condition D5 is erroneous. The failure may be due to the output value or the condition.

Assume that the condition D5 is erroneous. We look for all the other source execution(s) that lead to a consistent result of "isosceles" as the follow-up execution under D4′. We find consistencies under (D3 ∧ D4′) and (D4 ∧ D4′). Consider (D3 ∧ D4′) first. The conditions D3 and D4′ do not overlap with each other, and hence they do not contribute to any failure. By the same argument, the conjunction (D4 ∧ D4′) is not related to the failure. In short, no source execution leads to a consistent result of "`isosceles`" as the follow-up execution under `D4′`.

We conclude, therefore, that condition `D5` cannot be erroneous but that the output value "`scalene`" is incorrect. We can further determine from the corresponding path condition `Q5` that a potential cause of the failure is the assignment '`type = "isosceles";`' in statement `12` of the program.

c2) Suppose the output of "`isosceles`" from the follow-up execution under `D4′` is incorrect. The failure may be due to a missing `else` branch or an erroneous condition `D4′`.

Assume that the condition `D4′` is erroneous. We search for all the other follow-up execution(s) that lead to a consistent result of "`scalene`" as the source execution under `D5`. We find consistencies under (`D5` ∧ `D5′`) and (`D5` ∧ `D6′`). Consider (`D5` ∧ `D5′`) first. The conditions `D5` and `D5′` do not overlap with each other, and hence they do not contribute to any failure. By the same token, the conjunction (`D5` ∧ `D6′`) is not related to the failure. Hence, no source execution leads to a consistent result of "`scalene`" as the source execution under `D5`.

We conclude, therefore, that condition `D4′` cannot be erroneous but that there must be an `else` branch missing. We can further determine from the corresponding path condition `Q4′` that a potential cause of the failure is a missing `else` branch for the predicate statement `11` of the program.

Considering all the analyses for the potential causes of the failure for the MR $\overline{\texttt{triangle}_2}$(a, b, c) = $\overline{\texttt{triangle}_2}$(b, a, c), we conclude that the failure is due to a faulty assignment statement `12` or a missing `else` branch for the predicate statement `11`.

13.3.5.3 Fault Localization Example Related to Missing Path

A third faulty version $\overline{\texttt{triangle}_3}$(x, y, z) is shown in Figure 13.4. The conditional statement '`if (z == x) type = "isosceles";`' in lines `11` to `12` has been left out by mistake.

A failure is revealed when testing the program against the symbolic source input ⟨a, b, c⟩ and the symbolic follow-up input ⟨b, a, c⟩. In certain circumstances, the result of $\overline{\texttt{triangle}_3}$(a, b, c) is "`scalene`" but that of $\overline{\texttt{triangle}_3}$(b, a, c) is "`isosceles`". This also violates the MR `triangle(x, y, z)` = `triangle(y, x, z)` for any inputs ⟨x, y, z⟩ and ⟨y, x, z⟩.

We apply the semi-proving fault localization technique to identify the MFCs and MPCs with a view to finding the cause of the failure. We conduct global symbolic evaluation for the source input ⟨a, b, c⟩ and the follow-up input ⟨b, a, c⟩. The respective paths, path conditions, and outputs are shown in Tables 13.5 and 13.6.

```
   #include <iostream>
   #include <string>
   using namespace std;
   main() {
   float x, y, z;
   string type;
1  cin >> x >> y >> z;
2  if (x <= 0 || y <= 0 || z <= 0 || x + y <= z || y + z <= x || z + x <= y)
3     type = "error";
   else {
4     type = "scalene";
5     if (x == y && y == z)
6        type = "equilateral";
7     else if (x == y)
8        type = "isosceles";
9     else if (y == z)
10       type = "isosceles";
      // Missing path:
11    // else if (z == x)
12    //    type = "isosceles";
      }
   }
```

Figure 13.4 Faulty program $\overline{\texttt{triangle}}_3$(a, b, c) for classifying a triangle as equilateral, isosceles, or scalene. The path related to statements 11 and 12 is missing.

We review all the conditions in the program that lead to two different results of "isosceles" and "scalene" in the source and follow-up executions. This is achieved by analyzing the conjunctions (E3 ∧ E5′), (E4 ∧ E5′), (E5 ∧ E3′), and (E5 ∧ E4′).

a) Consider (E3 ∧ E5′). The conditions E3 and E5′ do not overlap with each other, and hence they do not contribute to any failure. By the same token, the conjunction (E5 ∧ E3′) is not related to the failure.

b) On the other hand, the expression (E4 ∧ E5′) can be evaluated to "¬E1 ∧ (a ≠ b) ∧ (b = c) ∧ (c ≠ a)", which is not a contradiction. But the output under E4 is

Table 13.5 Global symbolic evaluation results of $\overline{\texttt{triangle}}_3$(a, b, c).

Path	Path condition	Output
R1: (1, 2, 3)	E1: (a ≤ 0) ∨ (b ≤ 0) ∨ (c ≤ 0) ∨ (a + b ≤ c) ∨ (b + c ≤ a) ∨ (c + a ≤ b)	error
R2: (1, 2, 4, 5, 6)	E2: ¬E1 ∧ (a = b = c)	equilateral
R3: (1, 2, 4, 5, 7, 8)	E3: ¬E1 ∧ ¬(a = b = c) ∧ (a = b)	isosceles
R4: (1, 2, 4, 5, 7, 9, 10)	E4: ¬E1 ∧ ¬(a = b = c) ∧ (a ≠ b) ∧ (b = c)	isosceles
R5: (1, 2, 4, 5, 7, 9)	E5: ¬E1 ∧ ¬(a = b = c) ∧ (a ≠ b) ∧ (b ≠ c)	scalene

Table 13.6 Global symbolic evaluation results of $\overline{\texttt{triangle}_3}$(b, a, c).

Path	Path condition	Output
R1′: (1, 2, 3)	E1′: (b ≤ 0) ∨ (a ≤ 0) ∨ (c ≤ 0) ∨ (b + a ≤ c) ∨ (a + c ≤ b) ∨ (c + b ≤ a)	error
R2′: (1, 2, 4, 5, 6)	E2′: ¬E1′ ∧ (b = a = c)	equilateral
R3′: (1, 2, 4, 5, 7, 8)	E3′: ¬E1′ ∧ ¬(b = a = c) ∧ (b = a)	isosceles
R4′: (1, 2, 4, 5, 7, 9, 10)	E4′: ¬E1′ ∧ ¬(b = a = c) ∧ (b ≠ a) ∧ (a = c)	isosceles
R5′: (1, 2, 4, 5, 7, 9)	E5′: ¬E1′ ∧ ¬(b = a = c) ∧ (b ≠ a) ∧ (a ≠ c)	scalene

"isosceles" and that under E5′ is "scalene", which reveals a failure. Constraint solving shows that the MFC is "(a ≠ b) ∧ (b = c) ∧ (2 * b > a) ∧ (a > 0) ∧ (b > 0)".

The execution may have failed under condition E4 or condition E5′. We will process each case in turn.

b1) Suppose that the output value of "isosceles" from the source execution under condition E4 is erroneous. The failure may be due to the output value or the condition.

If the output value "isosceles" is erroneous, we can determine from the corresponding path condition R4 that a potential cause of the failure is the assignment 'type = "isosceles";' in statement 10 of the program. If condition E4 is erroneous, we search for all the other source execution(s) that lead to a consistent result of "scalene" as the follow-up execution under E5′. We find consistency only under (E5 ∧ E5′), which can be evaluated to "¬E1 ∧ (a ≠ b) ∧ (b ≠ c) ∧ (c ≠ a)". Constraint solving shows that the MPC is "(a ≠ b) ∧ (b ≠ c) ∧ (c ≠ a) ∧ (a + b > c) ∧ (b + c > a) ∧ (c + a > b) ∧ (a > 0) ∧ (b > 0) ∧ (c > 0)". Comparing the MPC with the MFC in the first paragraph of (b), we show that the execution fails when (b = c). In this way, if condition E5 is erroneous, we can determine from the corresponding path condition R5 that a potential cause of the failure is the branch condition (y = z), which is the predicate in statement 9 of the program.

b2) Suppose that the output of "scalene" from the follow-up execution under condition E5′ is incorrect. The failure may be due to a missing else branch or an erroneous condition E5'.

Assume that the condition E5′ is erroneous. We look for all the other follow-up execution(s) that lead to a consistent result of "isosceles" as the source execution under E4. We find consistencies under (E3 ∧ E4′) and (E4 ∧ D4′). Consider (E3 ∧ E4′) first. The conditions E3 and D4′ do not overlap with each other, and hence they do not contribute to any failure. By the same argument, the conjunction (E4 ∧ E4′) is not related to the failure. Thus, no follow-up execution leads to a consistent result of "isosceles" as the source execution under E4.

We conclude, therefore, that condition E5′ cannot be erroneous but that there must be an else branch missing. We can further determine from the corresponding path condition R5′ that a potential cause of the failure is a missing else branch for the predicate statement 9 of the program.

c) Similarly, the expression (E5 ∧ E4′) can be evaluated to "¬E1 ∧ (a ≠ b) ∧ (b ≠ c) ∧ (c = a)", which is not a contradiction. However, the output under E5 is "scalene" and that under E4′ is "isosceles", thus unveiling another failure. Further constraint solving shows that the second MFC is "(a ≠ b) ∧ (c = a) ∧ (2 * a > b) ∧ (a > 0) ∧ (b > 0)".

The execution may have failed under condition E5 or condition E4′. We will again process each case in turn.

c1) Suppose the output of "scalene" from the source execution under condition E5 is erroneous. The failure may be due to a missing else branch or an erroneous condition E5.

For the former case, we can determine from the corresponding path condition R5 that a potential cause of the failure is a missing else branch for the predicate statement 9 of the program.

For the latter case of an erroneous condition E5, we look for all the other source execution(s) that lead to a consistent result of "isosceles" as the follow-up execution under E4′. We find consistencies under (E3 ∧ E4′) and (E4 ∧ E4′). Consider (E3 ∧ E4′) first. The conditions E3 and E4′ do not overlap with each other, and hence they do not contribute to any failure. By the same argument, the conjunction (E4 ∧ E4′) is not related to the failure. Thus, no follow-up execution leads to a consistent result of "isosceles" as the follow-up execution under E4′.

We conclude, therefore, that condition E5 cannot be erroneous but that there must be an else branch missing. We can further determine from the corresponding path condition R5 that a potential cause of the failure is a missing else branch for the predicate statement 9 of the program.

c2) Suppose the output of "isosceles" from the follow-up execution under E4′ is faulty. The failure may be due to the output value or the condition.

If the output value "isosceles" is erroneous, we can determine from the corresponding path condition R4′ that a potential cause of the failure is the assignment 'type = "isosceles";' in statement 10 of the program.

If condition E4′ is erroneous, we search for all the other follow-up execution(s) that lead to a consistent result of "scalene" as the source execution under E5. We find consistency only under (E5 ∧ E5′). As in (b1), the MPC under (E5 ∧ E5′) is "$(a \neq b) \wedge (b \neq c) \wedge (c \neq a) \wedge (a + b > c) \wedge (b + c > a) \wedge (c + a > b) \wedge (a > 0) \wedge (b > 0) \wedge (c > 0)$". Comparing this MPC with the MFC in the first paragraph of (c), we find that the execution fails when $(c = a)$. In this way, if E4′ is faulty, we can determine from the corresponding path condition R4′ that a potential cause of the failure is the branch condition $(z = y)$, which is part of the predicate in statement 9 of the program.

Considering the majority of the potential causes of the failure for the MR $\overline{\mathtt{triangle}}_3(a, b, c) = \overline{\mathtt{triangle}}_3(b, a, c)$, we conclude that the failure is attributed to a missing else branch for the predicate statement 9 of the program.

13.3.5.4 Fault Localization Example Related to Loop

Consider a program $\mathrm{sum}(x_1, x_2, \ldots, x_{n-1}, x_n)$ that accepts a sequence of integers and compute their sum. The sequence is terminated by $x_n = 0$. An obvious MR is that if we permute the input subsequence from $\langle x_1, x_2, \ldots, x_{n-1} \rangle$ to another subsequence such as $\langle x_2, x_1, \ldots, x_{n-1} \rangle$ or $\langle x_{n-1}, x_2, \ldots, x_1 \rangle$, the output result will remain unchanged.

A faulty version $\overline{\mathrm{sum}}(x_1, x_2, \ldots, x_{n-1}, x_n)$ is shown in Figure 13.5. The statement "sum = sum + x;" in line 4 is miscoded as "sum = x;".

A failure is detected when testing the program against the symbolic source input $\langle a, b, c \rangle$ and the symbolic follow-up input $\langle b, a, c \rangle$. Under certain situations, the result of $\overline{\mathrm{sum}}(a, b, c)$ is a but that of $\overline{\mathrm{sum}}(b, a, c)$ is b. This violates the MR $\mathrm{sum}(x_1, x_2, \ldots, x_{n-1}, x_n) = \mathrm{sum}(x_2, x_1, \ldots, x_{n-1}, x_n)$ for any inputs $\langle x_1, x_2, \ldots, x_{n-1} \rangle$ and $\langle x_2, x_1, \ldots, x_{n-1} \rangle$.

```
    #include <iostream>
    using namespace std;
    main() {
    int x;
1   int sum = 0;
2   cin >> x;
3   while (x != 0) {
4      sum = x;    // Should be "sum = sum + x;"
5      cin >> x;
       }
6   cout << sum << "\n";
```

Figure 13.5 Faulty program $\overline{\mathrm{sum}}(x_1, x_2, \ldots, x_{n-1}, x_n)$ for computing the sum of a sequence of integers. The assignment statement 4 in the while loop is erroneous.

Table 13.7 Symbolic evaluation results of $\overline{\text{sum}}$ (a, b, c).

Path	Path condition	Output
S1: (1, 2, 3, 6)	F1: (a = 0)	0
S2: (1, 2, 3, 4, 5, 3, 6)	F2: (a ≠ 0) ∧ (b = 0)	a
S3: (1, 2, (3, 4, 5)$^+$, 3, 6)	F3: (a ≠ 0) ∧ (b ≠ 0) ∧ (c = 0)	b

Table 13.8 Symbolic evaluation results of $\overline{\text{sum}}$(b, a, c).

Path	Path condition	Output
S1′: (1, 2, 3, 6)	F1′: (b = 0)	0
S2′: (1, 2, 3, 4, 5, 3, 6)	F2′: (b ≠ 0) ∧ (a = 0)	b
S3′: (1, 2, (3, 4, 5)$^+$, 3, 6)	F3′: (b ≠ 0) ∧ (a ≠ 0) ∧ (c = 0)	a

We apply the semi-proving fault localization technique to determine the MFCs and MPCs with a view to identifying the cause of the failure. We perform global symbolic evaluation for the source input ⟨a, b, c⟩ and the follow-up input ⟨b, a, c⟩. The respective paths, path conditions, and outputs are shown in Tables 13.7 and 13.8. In particular, "(3, 4, 5)$^{+}$" represents two or more iterations of the sequence of statements 3, 4, and 5.

We check all the conditions in the program that lead to two different results of a and b in the source and follow-up executions. This can be done by reviewing the conjunctions (F2 ∧ F2′) and (F3 ∧ F3′).

a) Take (F2 ∧ F2′). The conditions F2 and F2′ do not overlap with each other, and hence they do not contribute to any failure.
b) On the other hand, the expression (F3 ∧ F3′) is not a contradiction. Constraint solving shows that the MFC is "(a ≠ 0) ∧ (b ≠ 0) ∧ (c = 0)". But the output under F3 is b while that under F3′ is a, which reveals a failure.

   The execution may have failed under condition F3 or condition F3′. We will process each case in turn.

   b1) Suppose that the output of b from the source execution under condition F3 is erroneous. The failure may be due to the output value or the condition.

   Assume that the condition F3 is erroneous. We search for all the other source execution(s) that lead to a consistent result of a as the follow-up execution under F3′. We find consistency only under (F2 ∧ F3′). But the conditions F2 and F3′ do not overlap with each other, and hence they do not contribute to any failure. Thus, no source execution leads to a consistent result of a as the follow-up execution under F3′.

We conclude, therefore, that condition F3 cannot be erroneous but that the output value b must be incorrect. We can further determine from the corresponding path condition S3 that a potential cause of the failure is the assignment "`sum = x;`" in statement 4 of the program.

b2) Suppose that the output of a from the follow-up execution under condition F3′ is faulty. The failure may be due to the output value or the condition.

Assume that the condition F3′ is erroneous. We look for all the other follow-up execution(s) that lead to a consistent result of b as the source execution under F3. We find consistency only under (F3 ∧ F2′). However, the conditions F3 and F2′ do not overlap with each other, and hence they do not contribute to any failure. Thus, no follow-up execution leads to a consistent result of b as the source execution under F3.

We conclude, therefore, that condition F3′ cannot be erroneous but that the output value a must be incorrect. We can further determine from the corresponding path condition S3′ that a potential cause of the failure is the assignment "`sum = x;`" in statement 4 of the program.

Considering all the potential causes of the failure for the MR $\overline{\texttt{sum}}(\texttt{a, b, c}) = \overline{\texttt{sum}}(\texttt{b, a, c})$, we conclude that the failure is due to a faulty assignment statement 4 of the program.

13.3.6 Comparisons with Related Work

Spectrum-based fault localization (SBFL) is one of the best-known techniques in automatic program debugging. A program spectrum is a programming entity such as a statement or a branching condition. A typical SBFL system collects the execution statistics of all the program spectra against successful and failure-causing test cases. It then ranks the program spectra using a risk evaluation formula. The most popular evaluation formula and one of the earliest is *Tarantula* developed by Jones et al. [93]:

$$\frac{a_{\rm ef}/(a_{\rm ef} + a_{\rm nf})}{a_{\rm ef}/(a_{\rm ef} + a_{\rm nf}) + a_{\rm ep}/(a_{\rm ep} + a_{\rm np})}$$

where $a_{\rm ef}$ and $a_{\rm nf}$ denote the number of failure-causing test cases that execute and do not execute the program spectrum in question, respectively, while $a_{\rm ep}$ and $a_{\rm np}$ denote the number of successful test cases that execute and do not execute the program spectrum, respectively. Many other similar formulas have been proposed, as reviewed in Naish et al. [94]. Xie et al. [95] subsequently proved that only five existing evaluation formulas are maximal but the popular Tarantula is not among them. Readers may refer to Chapters 4 and 11 of the present *Handbook* for details.

SBFL differs from the semi-proving approach in three aspects: (a) SBFL assumes the existence of a test oracle to determine whether a test result is a failure or a success. (b) SBFL is based on the statistics of successful and failure-causing test cases rather than precise conditions. (c) SBFL does not look into the cause-effect chain of a failure. To alleviate the test oracle problem, Xie et al. [96, 97] proposed the application of MRs and program slicing to SBFL. However, they do not consider the issues highlighted in (b) and (c).

To tackle the cause-effect issue, Zeller and Hildebrandt [98] propose the Delta Debugging algorithm to identify the difference between a successful test case and the corresponding failure-causing test case so as to derive a minimum test case that can replay the failure. This is achieved by tracing the state differences in variables and values between the successful and failed executions of the two inputs. After multiple evaluations, the algorithm works out a cause-effect chain [99] of the states that lead to the failure. However, Delta Debugging only handles concrete inputs. There may be numerous causes of a failure related to a variable and a value. The semi-proving approach identifies failure-causing constraint expressions, which provide more information about the nature of the fault. Furthermore, Delta Debugging requires a "testing function" to determine whether an input leads to a failure. This is different from the semi-proving approach, which does not require an oracle.

To exploit model checking, Jobstmann et al. [100] propose to specify systems in linear temporal logic (LTL) and portray fault localization and repair as an LTL game between the input environment and program fixes. Könighofer and Bloem [101] further extended the formalism through symbolic execution and constraint solving. However, the model-checking approach assumes the existence of a specification to determine the test oracle [102].

The base semi-proving fault localization technique [78] is limited by complexity problems in traditional symbolic evaluation. *Concolic* testing, which combines *conc*rete and symb*olic* executions, has been developed [72, 89] to tackle the difficulties of such evaluations. For instance, when a complex symbolic expression cannot be handled by the constraint solver, the algorithm will replace individual symbolic values with concrete values so as to accomplish the process. Chen et al. [67] have applied some of the concolic techniques to the semi-proving methodology, as illustrated in Section 13.3.5 of this chapter. Furthermore, concolic fault localization [103] and concolic metamorphic debugging [104] have recently been developed. The latter is similar to the semi-proving approach. It has been pointed out in Cadar and Sen [79] and Sen [90] that concolic approaches are sound but not complete because, as some of the symbolic evaluations are replaced by concrete executions, "they may not be able to generate test inputs for some feasible execution paths." In other words, all the revealed failures and faults are genuine, but not all the genuine failures and faults are revealed. This is, indeed, the limitation of all software testing techniques.

13.3.7 Conclusion

Traditional fault localization techniques rely on a mechanism, known as a test oracle, to determine whether an execution is successful or a failure. However, a test oracle is often missing or too difficult to apply in real-world systems. In this subchapter, we present a semi-proving methodology for fault localization without the need of a direct test oracle. The method is based on MRs and symbolic evaluation. It hinges on causes and effects instead of statistical probabilities. It unveils definite failing conditions rather than program entities that have a higher chance to cause the failure. In complex situations where symbolic evaluation cannot be applied to completion, we may apply heuristic techniques to tackle the problem.

13.4 Automated Prediction of Fault Localization Effectiveness[8]

As described in Chapter 4 of the present *Handbook*, SBFL tools have been proposed. The output of these tools is a ranked list of program elements sorted based on their likelihood to be the root cause of a set of failures (i.e. their suspiciousness scores). Unfortunately, for subtle bugs, the root causes may be low in the ranked list. This phenomenon may cause developers to distrust fault localization tools. Recently, Parnin and Orso highlighted in their user study that many participants do not find fault localization useful if they do not find the root cause early in the list [105].

To address the above issue, we present an approach, named *Predicting Effectiveness of Fault localization* (PEFA), which predicts whether the output of a fault localization tool can be trusted or not. If the output is unlikely to be trusted, developers can switch to traditional debugging approaches rather than spending time going through the list of most suspicious program elements one by one. To achieve the goal, we extract values of several features related to the effectiveness of fault localization tools and utilize a machine learning algorithm to train a model that evaluates the effectiveness of the results generated by a fault localization tool. In this approach, an output of a fault localization tool is considered to be effective if the root cause appears in the top ten most suspicious program elements.

13.4.1 Overview of PEFA

The goal of PEFA is to predict if a particular fault localization tool is effective for a particular set of execution traces. We refer to the application of a fault localization tool on a set of execution traces to return a list of suspicious program elements as a *fault localization instance*. PEFA categories a fault localization instance to be effective if the root cause is located among the top 10 most suspicious program elements. Note that ties are randomly broken. For example, if the top 20 program elements are sharing the same suspiciousness scores, we randomly select 10 out of the 20 to be the top 10. Furthermore, in case the root cause spans more than one program element (i.e. basic block), as long as one of the program elements is in the top 10, we consider the fault localization instance to be effective.

The overall framework of PEFA is shown in Figure 13.6. PEFA has two phases: training and deployment. In the training phase, PEFA takes as input a set of training fault localization instances. Each of these instances has the following information:

1) Program spectra corresponding to successful and failed execution traces.
2) A ranked list of suspiciousness scores that are assigned by the fault localization tools to the program elements.
3) An effectiveness label: effective (if the root cause is in the top 10 program elements) or ineffective (otherwise).

The training phase consists of two processes: feature extraction and model learning. During the feature extraction process, we extract from training data a number of feature values that shed light on important characteristics that potentially differentiate effective from ineffective instances. Tables 13.9 and 13.10 show descriptions of these features. In total, we extract 50 features, in which 15 features are from input execution traces (as in Table 13.9), and the remaining 35 features are from the suspiciousness scores output by the tool (as in Table 13.10). In the model learning process, the feature values of the training instances along with their effectiveness labels are then employed to build a discriminative model that can predict whether an unknown fault localization instance is effective or not. This discriminative model is then forwarded to the subsequent deployment stage.

The deployment stage consists of two processing steps: feature extraction and effectiveness prediction. Similar to the training phase, we extract feature values from unknown instances whose labels, effective or ineffective, are to be predicted. These values are then input to the discriminative model learned in the training phase. The model then outputs a prediction.

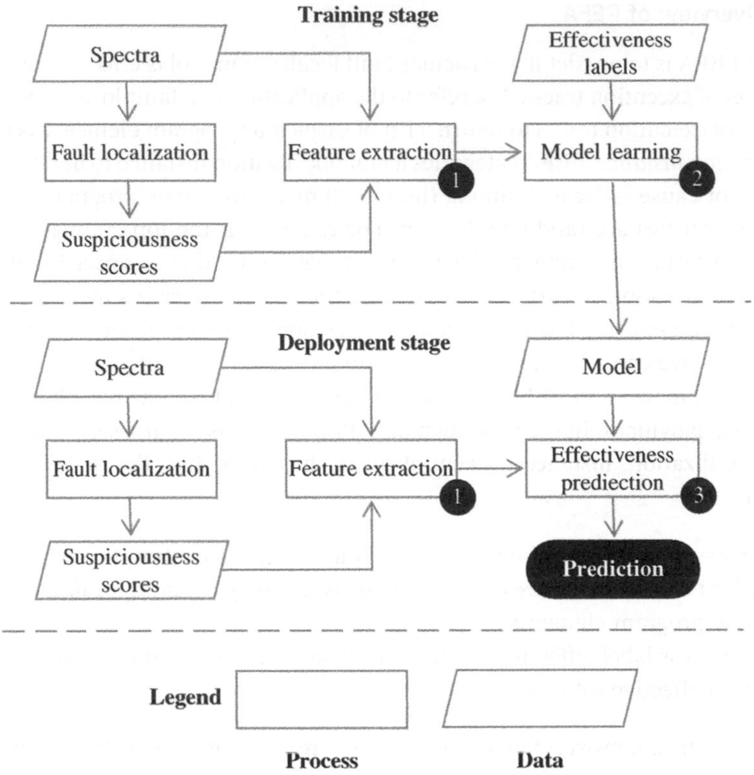

Figure 13.6 Overall framework of PEFA. *Source:* Le et al. [106]/Springer.

Table 13.9 List of features extracted from program spectra.

ID	Description
	Input: Execution Traces (5 Features)
T_1	Number of traces
T_2	Number of failed traces
T_3	Number of successful traces
T_4	$T_3 - T_2$
T_5	$\frac{T_2}{T_3}$
	Input: Program Elements (10 Features)
P_1	Number of program elements covered in the failed execution traces
P_2	Number of program elements covered in the successful execution traces
P_3	$P_2 - P_1$

Table 13.9 (Continued)

ID	Description
P_4	$\frac{P_1}{P_2}$
P_5	Number of program elements that appear only in failed execution traces
P_6	Number of program elements that appear only in successful execution traces
P_7	Highest proportion of failed execution traces that pass by one program element
P_8	Second highest proportion of failed execution traces that pass by one program element
P_9	$P_7 - P_8$
P_{10}	$\frac{P_8}{P_7}$

Source: Le et al. [106]/Springer.

Table 13.10 List of partial features extracted from suspicious scores.

ID	Description
	Output: Raw Suspiciousness Scores (10 Features)
R_1	Highest suspiciousness score
R_2	Second highest suspiciousness score
R_i	ith highest suspiciousness score, where $i = 3, 4, ..., 10$
	Output: Simple Statistics (6 Features)
SS_1	Number of distinct suspiciousness scores in $\{R_1, ..., R_{10}\}$
SS_2	Mean of $\{R_1, ..., R_{10}\}$
SS_3	Median of $\{R_1, ..., R_{10}\}$
SS_4	Mode of $\{R_1, ..., R_{10}\}$
SS_5	Variance of $\{R_1, ..., R_{10}\}$
SS_6	Standard deviation of $\{R_1, ..., R_{10}\}$
	Gaps (11 Features)
G_1	$R_1 - R_2$
G_2	$R_2 - R_3$
G_i	$R_i - R_{i+1}$, where $i = 3, 4, ..., 9$
G_{10}	$\mathrm{Max}_{i=1,2,...,9}(G_i)$
G_{11}	$\mathrm{Min}_{i=1,2,...,9}(G_i)$
	Relative Differences (8 Features)
C_1	$\frac{R_2 - R_{10}}{R_1 - R_{10}}$
C_i	$\frac{R_{i+1} - R_{10}}{R_1 - R_{10}}$ where $i = 2, 3, ..., 8$

Source: Le et al. [106]/Springer.

13.4.2 Model Learning

The model learning process takes as input a set of training instances with their effectiveness labels and extracted feature values. Note that each of the instance is represented as 50 feature values (also known as feature vectors) produced by the feature extraction process. The output of this process is a discriminative model for effectiveness prediction. To train such models, we utilize and extend the state-of-the-art support vector machine (SVM) algorithm [107] to create SVM^{PEFA}.

As a matter of fact, they are usually more ineffective than effective fault localization instances, and imbalanced training data is one of the main issues that impacts the prediction accuracy of SVM models. SVM^{PEFA} is capable of handling the imbalanced data issue. SVM^{PEFA} balances training data by duplicating effective instances that are closer to one of the ineffective ones. Since every fault localization instance has a 50-dimensional vector of extracted feature values (see Tables 13.9 and 13.10), we assign a score to every effective instance by computing the highest cosine similarity between that instance to the ineffective ones. Then, we duplicate effective instances with highest assigned scores in order to balance the data. Finally, we run the SVM algorithm on the balanced data to train a discriminative model.

13.4.3 Effectiveness Prediction

The model learning process outputs a model that is capable of predicting if a new instance (i.e. a fault localization instance whose effectiveness is unknown) is effective or not. The new instance needs to be converted to a set of feature values shown in Tables 13.9 and 13.10 via the feature extraction process. Then, the created feature vector is forwarded to the constructed SVM^{PEFA} model to predict the effectiveness label (i.e. effective or ineffective) of its corresponding instance.

13.4.4 Conclusion

In this section, we have presented an approach to predict the effectiveness of the results generated by fault localization tools using machine learning. A discriminative model, SVM^{PEFA}, is constructed by using the SVM algorithm along with 50 features values extracted from training data. Then, 50 new feature values generated by using a fault localization tool on a system under test will be taken as input by the SVM^{PEFA} to output a prediction result. This approach can alleviate the problem that a practitioner can be misguided by the fault localization tool and wastes a large amount of time. Based on the domain knowledge and prediction results generated by this approach, practitioners can make better decisions regarding whether they should follow the suggestion generated by the fault localization tool or locate the bug by themselves under their specific situation.

13.5 Integrating Fault Localization into Automated Test Generation Tools

Why has fault localization not been widely adopted in industrial practice or in most research-driven efforts to test and debug software systems? There are numerous possible reasons, many due to the limitations of current techniques [105]. However, one possibility that has been relatively less explored is that current efforts are often targeting both the wrong tests and the wrong framework for testing.

Evaluations of software fault localization techniques, whether human experiments [105] or quantitative evaluations in research papers proposing novel techniques [108–110], are usually based on a limited set of human-generated tests. These are usually either the standard test suite for an open source project or the widely used "Siemens" or SIR suite studied in the software testing literature [111]. These suites are usually essentially regression suites, containing a relatively small set of tests produced in a few similar ways:

- unit tests produced by developers,
- tests that detect a set of previously corrected defects, or
- tests added to enhance the code coverage (and thus future defect detection) of the suite.

Such suites are unlikely to be optimal for fault detection, for a number of reasons. For one thing, such suites are often constructed to minimize the overlap of tests. Developers, for example, are unlikely to produce two unit tests that perform almost the same sequence of operations, but with one small change to the parameters passed to a method; such tests will often be combined, with the two methods called in succession after the conditions for the call have been set up. In general, regression suites are ideally small and non-redundant. Tests are, for good reasons, optimized for readability and efficient execution, not automated debugging. These goals may be in tension with the ideal tests for localization, which could be expected (with a variety of approaches) to benefit from redundancy and statistical randomness.

The fact that typical test suites may be unsuitable for fault localization purposes has inspired efforts to improve fault localization by generating more tests that are optimized for localization, such as the search-based approach of Campos et al. [112] and the concolic [113] execution approach of Artzi et al. [114].

13.5.1 Localization in the Context of Automated Test Generation

There is a possible approach to mitigating this problem that requires no new techniques or methods. Fault localization methods with low overhead, in particular SBFL methods, can easily be integrated into some software test generation tools. Rather than using an existing test suite as the basis for localization, a tool could collect data on successful tests as it performs testing and then use that data to automatically provide a localization for any failed tests. Many tools collect code coverage as they run in order to guide future testing or simply provide feedback to users on the effectiveness of the tool. In such cases, collecting the information required for simple SBFL may add essentially no overhead to testing. Moreover, the tests produced during automated testing are likely to be highly redundant, statistically diverse, and very large in number. Storing the generated tests (except those exposing faults or providing new coverage) is not necessary for most SBFL algorithms. Integrating more powerful, and potentially more effective, localizations based on mutation testing [108, 110] would require storing successful tests, and certainly lose the advantages of on-the-fly instantly available localizations due to high computational costs. For this reason, the approach seems most suitable for a combination of lightweight test generation and lightweight fault localization.

In addition to providing a possibly better set of tests without the need for novel testing techniques (or the cost of additional test generation for purposes of localization only), lightweight automated testing tools may provide a better setting for automated fault localization than is considered in studies such as Parnin and Orso [105]. In the usual setting, determining what aspect of a program is involved in a fault is often not difficult: the failed test presents a focused and often comprehensible scenario, usually arising from human-directed effort. The difficult cases usually involve systems where even such scenarios execute a very large amount of code, and traditional localizations, even if correct, may not provide enough information to understand the complex behavior and debug the problem. The proposed use of localization that has not proven valuable enough to be adopted can be summarized as follows: developers debugging the software (fixing its defects) use localization to more quickly discover the code that needs to be changed to correct a fault based on human-generated tests. In automated testing, however, the scenario changes in several ways.

First, random, symbolic, or search-based techniques can all produce tests that, even when minimized by Delta Debugging, happen to make use of irrelevant method calls that a human would not include in a test case for a fault. Simply focusing attention on the core behavior that is common to failed tests may be sufficient to enable a test engineer to debug the problem, or at least choose the most suitable test to report to developers.

Second, because they rely on simple oracles such as "does not crash" or property-based specifications, automatically generated tests can often be more effectively reduced in size by Delta Debugging than human-produced tests. This makes SBFL approaches more effective – in some limited experiments, Delta Debugging a failed test improves the ranking of the fault more effectively, on average, than switching from the worst SBFL formula to the best SBFL formula.

Finally, as hinted when we noted that localization may simply help a test engineer choose the most suitable test to report to developers, automated testing is more often applied by outsiders than is debugging from regression tests or user-submitted failures. Outsiders, whether researchers, a quality assurance team, or security auditors, may be motivated to apply fault localization to choose a good failed test to report, rather than to precisely identify and correct a fault. This may reduce the need for very high accuracy in localizations that has limited their acceptance in the more traditional setting.

13.5.2 Automated Test Generation Tools Supporting Localization

Surprisingly, given that tools such as afl-fuzz [115] and EvoSuite [116] already collect coverage information (and the authors of the latter are also active in fault localization research), most of the well-known open source automated testing tools do not support even simple fault localization. With afl, tests are output as files, so running a conventional coverage tool to produce localizations would be relatively easy to add on as an external tool. Unfortunately, EvoSuite tests are JUnit tests that require the EvoSuite framework, which includes instrumentation that might conflict with other code coverage tools (https://www.evosuite.org/documentation/measuring-code-coverage), so supporting localization reliably would likely require additions to EvoSuite itself.

The template scripting testing language (TSTL) [117–120], a domain-specific language [121] tool for preparing test harnesses, includes a random test generator that supports fault localization. The tool initially supports only the simple Tarantula [92] formula. Adding fault localization using Tarantula required only about 50 lines of code and less than half an hour of development time. Given the ability to collect coverage and determine which tests fail and which tests pass, SBFL is trivial to implement. Changing the formula or adding another formula would even be easier, given that the basic data required for standard spectrum-based fault localization has already been collected and an output mechanism for results has been implemented. See [122–125], for instance.

In the absence of studies or widespread adoption, it is hard to say how useful such a feature is to users of TSTL. However, we note that for the early stages of simple data structure testing and development, localization, even using the

Tarantula formula, is perfect almost one quarter of the time, and the fault is usually in the top handful of suspicious statements.

The primary question in the initial test generation for an in-development program is how often the localization speeds up defect correction or identification. For purposes of bug reporting, the TSTL developers have found it helpful. Adding localization methods to automatic test generation tools offers considerable potential benefits at a very low cost, given the ease of implementation.

13.5.3 Antifragile Tests and Localization

The idea that automatically generated tests may be reduced via Delta Debugging better than human-generated tests is related to an unexplored hypothesis: property-based tests [126] may be more robust than human-generated tests in a more general sense. In fact, they may be antifragile in the sense of Taleb [127]. Small changes or perturbations of a human-generated test will often make the test fail for reasons that do not relate to an actual fault of the software. The test simply becomes invalid when modified, because it checks a very specific behavior of the system. A property-based test (which is much more common in automated test generation), however, often benefits from perturbations. Indeed, this benefit is part of why mutations and crossover in genetic/search-based test generation [128, 129] can be effective. This means that localization methods based on automatically generated, property-based tests can apply far more aggressive "experimental" methods than have traditionally been of interest in literature. Modifying a test to determine how it reacts, in order to determine causality, is not a novel idea in the field [130], but if automatic test generation becomes more popular, it may have a much more interesting future than in the past.

13.5.4 Conclusion

In this section, we have discussed why human-generated test cases are not ideal for the fault localization technique and explained how to mitigate this problem by combining automated test case generation and fault localization. This approach has already been adopted by several tools, such as afl-fuzz and TSTL.

However, these tools currently only support few basic fault localization techniques. More efforts are needed to integrate more advanced fault localization techniques and refine the current approaches of the way that test case generation and fault localization technique work together to achieve better performance. Finally, antifragile tests may be used to improve fault localization.

Notes

1 In this chapter, we use "bug" and "fault" interchangeably. We also use "programs" and "software" interchangeably.
2 Part of Section 13.2 is from Perscheid [10].
3 The name corresponds to the position of author credentials in change log messages.
4 The phrase "a statement is *covered* by a test case" is used interchangeably with "a statement is *executed* by a test case."
5 Part of Section 13.3 is an extension of Chen et al. [67, 78].
6 For ease of presentation, we will use the word "input" to mean an "input case," which may comprise more than one individual element. For example, if a program requires three parameters, a tuple such as ⟨1, 2, 0⟩ will be known as one input rather than three inputs.
7 In contract, given a concrete input ⟨1, 2, 0⟩, there will only be one concrete output such as "2", and the path condition is not known.
8 Part of Section 13.4 is from Le et al. [106].

References

1 Zeller, A. (2006). *Why Programs Fail: a Guide to Systematic Debugging.* Elsevier. ISBN 978-1-55860-866-5.
2 Vessey, I. (1985). Expertise in debugging computer programs: a process analysis. *International Journal of Man-Machine Studies* 23 (5): 459–494. ISSN 0020-7373. https://doi.org/10.1016/S0020-7373(85)80054-7.
3 Liblit, B., Naik, M., Zheng, A.X., Aiken, A., and Jordan, M.I. (2005). Scalable statistical bug isolation. *Proceedings of the 2005 ACM SIGPLAN Conference on Programming Language Design and Implementation* (*PLDI '05*), Chicago, IL, USA (12–15 June 2005), 15–26. ACM. ISBN 1-59593-056-6. https://doi.org/10.1145/1065010.1065014.
4 Grtker, T., Holtmann, U., Keding, H., and Wloka, M. (2008). *The Developer's Guide to Debugging*. Springer.
5 Hailpern, B. and Santhanam, P. (2002). Software debugging, testing, and verification. *IBM Systems Journal* 41 (1): 4–12.
6 Metzger, R.C. (2004). *Debugging by Thinking: a Multidisciplinary Approach.* Digital Press.
7 Lieberman, H. and Fry, C. (2001). Will software ever work? *Communications of the ACM* 44 (3): 122–124.
8 Gould, J.D. (1975). Some psychological evidence on how people debug computer programs. *International Journal of Man-Machine Studies* 7 (2): 151–182.
9 Gugerty, L. and Olson, G.M. (1986). Comprehension differences in debugging by skilled and novice programmers. *Proceedings of the First Workshop on Empirical*

Studies of Programmers, Washington, DC, USA (5–6 June 1986), 13–27. Ablex Publishing. https://dl.acm.org/doi/abs/10.5555/21842.28883.

10 Perscheid, M. (2013). Test-driven fault navigation for debugging reproducible failures. PhD dissertation. Universität Potsdam.

11 Shapiro, E.Y. (1982). *Algorithmic Program Debugging*. Yale University.

12 Fritzson, P., Shahmehri, N., Kamkar, M., and Gyimothy, T. (1992). Generalized algorithmic debugging and testing. *ACM Letters on Programming Languages and Systems (LOPLAS)* 1 (4): 303–322.

13 Naish, L. (1997). A declarative debugging scheme. *Journal of Functional and Logic Programming* 1997: Article 3. https://scholar.lib.vt.edu/ejournals/JFLP/jflp-mirror/articles/1997/A97-03/A97-03.html.

14 Anvik, J., Hiew, L., and Murphy, G.C. (2006). Who should fix this bug? *Proceedings of the 28th International Conference on Software Engineering*, Shanghai, China (20–28 May 2006), 361–370. ACM.

15 Vessey, I. (1989). Toward a theory of computer program bugs: an empirical test. *International Journal of Man-Machine Studies* 30 (1): 23–46.

16 McDonald, D.W. and Ackerman, M.S. (2000). Expertise recommender: a flexible recommendation system and architecture. *Proceedings of the 2000 ACM Conference on Computer Supported Cooperative Work*, Philadelphia, PA, USA (2–6 December 2000), 231–240. ACM. https://dl.acm.org/doi/pdf/10.1145/358916.358994.

17 Mockus, A. and Herbsleb, J.D. (2002). Expertise browser: a quantitative approach to identifying expertise. *Proceedings of the 24th International Conference on Software Engineering (ICSE '02)*, Orlando, FL, USA (19–25 May 2002), 503–512. ACM. https://dl.acm.org/doi/pdf/10.1145/581339.581401.

18 Girba, T., Kuhn, A., Seeberger, M., and Ducasse, S. (2005). How developers drive software evolution. *Proceedings of the Eighth International Workshop on Principles of Software Evolution*, Lisbon, Portugal (5–6 September 2005), 113–122. IEEE. https://doi.org/10.1109/IWPSE.2005.21.

19 Kagdi, H., Hammad, M., and Maletic, J.I. (2008). Who can help me with this source code change? *Proceedings of the 2008 IEEE International Conference on Software Maintenance*, Beijing, China (28 September to 4 October 2008), 157–166. IEEE. https://doi.org/10.1109/ICSM.2008.4658064.

20 Minto, S. and Murphy, G.C. (2007). Recommending emergent teams. *Proceedings of the Fourth International Workshop on Mining Software Repositories*, Minneapolis, MN, USA (19–20 May 2007), 5. IEEE. https://doi.org/10.1109/MSR.2007.27.

21 Fritz, T., Murphy, G.C., and Hill, E. (2007). Does a programmer's activity indicate knowledge of code? *Proceedings of the 6th Joint Meeting of the European Software Engineering Conference and the ACM SIGSOFT Symposium on The Foundations of Software Engineering*, Dubrovnik, Croatia (3–7 September 2007), 341–350. ACM. https://dl.acm.org/doi/pdf/10.1145/1287624.1287673.

22 Schuler, D. and Zimmermann, T. (2008). Mining usage expertise from version archives. *Proceedings of the 2008 International Working Conference on Mining Software Repositories*, Leipzig, Germany (10–11 May 2008), 121–124. ACM. https://dl.acm.org/doi/pdf/10.1145/1370750.1370779.

23 Fritz, T., Ou, J., Murphy, G.C., and Murphy-Hill, E. (2010). A degree of knowledge model to capture source code familiarity. *Proceedings of the 32nd ACM/IEEE International Conference on Software Engineering (ICSE '10)*, Cape Town, South Africa (1–8 May 2010), 385–394. ACM.

24 Murphy, G. and Cubranic, D. (2004). Automatic bug triage using text categorization. *Proceedings of the Sixteenth International Conference on Software Engineering & Knowledge Engineering*, Banff, AB, Canada (20–24 June 2004), 1–6. Citeseer.

25 Anvik, J. (2006). Automating bug report assignment. *Proceedings of the 28th International Conference on Software Engineering (ICSE '06)*, Shanghai, China (20–28 May 2006), 937–940. ACM. https://dl.acm.org/doi/pdf/10.1145/1134285.1134457.

26 Matter, D., Kuhn, A., and Nierstrasz, O. (2009). Assigning bug reports using a vocabulary-based expertise model of developers. *Proceedings of the 2009 6th IEEE International Working Conference on Mining Software Repositories*, Vancouver, BC, Canada (16–17 May 2009), 131–140. IEEE. https://doi.org/10.1109/MSR.2009.5069491.

27 Canfora, G. and Cerulo, L. (2006). Supporting change request assignment in open source development. *Proceedings of the 2006 ACM Symposium on Applied Computing*, Dijon, France (23–27 April 2006), 1767–1772. ACM. https://dl.acm.org/doi/pdf/10.1145/1141277.1141693.

28 Kagdi, H. and Poshyvanyk, D. (2009). Who can help me with this change request? *Proceedings of the 2009 IEEE 17th International Conference on Program Comprehension*, Vancouver, BC, Canada (17–19 May 2009), 273–277. IEEE. https://doi.org/10.1109/ICPC.2009.5090056.

29 Anvik, J. and Murphy, G.C. (2007). Determining implementation expertise from bug reports. *Proceedings of the Fourth International Workshop on Mining Software Repositories*, Minneapolis, MN, USA (19–20 May 2007), 1–8. IEEE. https://doi.org/10.1109/MSR.2007.7.

30 Guo, P.J., Zimmermann, T., Nagappan, N., and Murphy, B. (2011). Not my bug! and other reasons for software bug report reassignments. *Proceedings of the ACM 2011 Conference on Computer Supported Cooperative Work*, Hangzhou, China (19–23 March 2011), 395–404. ACM. https://dl.acm.org/doi/pdf/10.1145/1958824.1958887.

31 Jeong, G., Kim, S., and Zimmermann, T. (2009). Improving bug triage with bug tossing graphs. *Proceedings of the 7th Joint Meeting of the European Software*

Engineering Conference and the ACM SIGSOFT Symposium on The Foundations of Software Engineering, Amsterdam, Netherlands (24–28 August 2009), 111–120. ACM. https://dl.acm.org/doi/pdf/10.1145/1595696.1595715.

32 Baysal, O., Godfrey, M.W., and Cohen, R. (2009). A bug you like: a framework for automated assignment of bugs. *Proceedings of the 2009 IEEE 17th International Conference on Program Comprehension*, Vancouver, BC, Canada (17–19 May 2009), 297–298. IEEE. https://doi.org/10.1109/ICPC.2009.5090066.

33 Servant, F. and Jones, J.A. (2012). WhoseFault: automatic developer-to-fault assignment through fault localization. *Proceedings of the 2012 34th International Conference on Software Engineering (ICSE '12)*, Zurich, Switzerland (2–9 June 2012), 36–46. IEEE. https://doi.org/10.1109/ICSE.2012.6227208.

34 Lewis, B. (2003). Debugging backwards in time. *arXiv preprint cs/0310016.*

35 Hofer, C., Denker, M., and Ducasse, S. (2006). Design and implementation of a backward-in-time debugger. *Proceedings of the 7th Annual International Conference on Object-Oriented and Internet-based Technologies, Concepts, and Applications for a Networked World*, Erfurt, Germany (18–20 September 2006), 17–32. Gesellschaft fur Informatik.

36 Ko, A.J. and Myers, B.A. (2008). Debugging reinvented: asking and answering why and why not questions about program behavior. *Proceedings of the 30th International Conference on Software Engineering (ICSE '08)*, Leipzig, Germany (10–18 May 2008), 301–310. ACM.

37 Sakurai, K., Masuhara, H., and Komiya, S. (2010). Traceglasses: a trace-based debugger for realizing efficient navigation. *IPSJ Special Interest Group on Programming* 3 (3): 1–17.

38 Hermanns, C. (2010). *Entwicklung und Implementierung eines hybriden Debuggers für Java*. Verlag-Haus Monsenstein und Vannerdat.

39 Pothier, G., Tanter, É., and Piquer, J. (2007). Scalable omniscient debugging. *ACM SIGPLAN Notices* 42: 535–552. ACM.

40 Lienhard, A. (2008). *Dynamic object flow analysis*. PhD thesis. University of Bern.

41 Lienhard, A., Girba, T., and Nierstrasz, O. (2008). Practical object-oriented back-in-time debugging. *European Conference on Object-Oriented Programming*, Paphos, Cyprus (7–11 July 2008), 592–615. Springer.

42 Fierz, J. (2009). Compass–flow-centric back-in-time debugging. Master's thesis. University of Bern, Switzerland.

43 Lieberman, H. and Fry, C. (1997). ZStep95: a reversible, animated source code stepper. In: *Software Visualization: Programming as a Multimedia Experience* (ed. J. Stasko, J. Domingue, M. Brown and B. Price), 277–292. MIT Press.

44 Cook, J.J. (2002). Reverse execution of java bytecode. *The Computer Journal* 45 (6): 608–619.

45 Koju, T., Takada, S., and Doi, N. (2005). An efficient and generic reversible debugger using the virtual machine based approach. *Proceedings of the 1st ACM/USENIX International Conference on Virtual Execution Environments*, Chicago, IL, USA

(11–12 June 2005), 79–88. ACM. https://dl.acm.org/doi/pdf/10.1145/1064979.1064992.

46 Feldman, S.I. and Brown, C.B. (1988). Igor: a system for program debugging via reversible execution. *Proceedings of the 1988 ACM SIGPLAN and SIGOPS Workshop on Parallel and Distributed Debugging*, Madison, WI, USA (5–6 May 1988), 112–123. ACM.

47 Agrawal, H., DeMillo, R.A., and Spafford, E.H. (1993). Debugging with dynamic slicing and backtracking. *Software: Practice and Experience* 23 (6): 589–616. https://doi.org/10.1002/spe.4380230603.

48 Agrawal, H. and Horgan, J.R. (1990). Dynamic program slicing. *Proceedings of the ACM SIGPLAN 1990 Conference on Programming Language Design and Implementation (PLDI '90)*, White Plains, NY, USA (20–22 June 1990), 246–256. ACM. https://dl.acm.org/doi/pdf/10.1145/93548.93576.

49 Tolmach, A. and Appel, A.W. (1995). A debugger for standard ML1. *Journal of Functional Programming* 5 (2): 155–200.

50 Boothe, B. (2000). Efficient algorithms for bidirectional debugging. *Proceedings of the ACM SIGPLAN 2000 Conference on Programming Language Design and Implementation*, Vancouver, BC, Canada (18–21 June 2000), 299–310. ACM.

51 Choi, J.-D. and Srinivasan, H. (1998). Deterministic replay of Java multithreaded applications. *Proceedings of the SIGMETRICS Symposium on Parallel and Distributed Tools*, Welches, OR, USA (3–4 August 1998), 48–59. ACM.

52 Saito, Y. (2005). Jockey: a user-space library for record-replay debugging. *Proceedings of the Sixth International Symposium on Automated Analysis-Driven Debugging*, Monterey, CA, USA (19–21 September 2005), 69–76. ACM. https://dl.acm.org/doi/pdf/10.1145/1085130.1085139.

53 Chapman, D. (2008). Backstep: Incorporating Reverse-Execution into the Eclipse Java Debugger. Technical report, University of Auckland.

54 Ducassé M. (1999). Coca: an automated debugger for C. *Proceedings of the 1999 International Conference on Software Engineering (ICSE '99)*, Los Angeles, CA, USA (16 22 May 1999), 504–513. ACM. https://doi.org/10.1145/302405.302682.

55 Lencevicius, R., Hölzle, U., and Singh, A.K. (1997). Query-based debugging of object-oriented programs. *ACM SIGPLAN Notices* 32: 304–317. ACM.

56 Lencevicius, R., Hölzle, U., and Singh, A.K. (1999). Dynamic query-based debugging. *Proceedings of the European Conference on Object-Oriented Programming*, Lisbon, Portugal (14–18 June 1999), 135–160. Springer.

57 Potanin, A., Noble, J., and Biddle, R. (2004). Snapshot query-based debugging. *Proceedings of the 2004 Australian Software Engineering Conference*, Melbourne, Victoria, Australia (13–16 April 2004), 251–259. IEEE. https://doi.org/10.1109/ASWEC.2004.1290478.

58 Ho, A. and Hand, S. (2005). On the design of a pervasive debugger. *Proceedings of the Sixth International Symposium on Automated Analysis-Driven Debugging*, 117–122. ACM.

59 Ressia, J., Bergel, A., and Nierstrasz, O. (2012). Object-centric debugging. *Proceedings of the 34th International Conference on Software Engineering (ICSE '12)*, Zurich, Switzerland (2–9 June 2012), 485–495. IEEE. https://doi.org/10.1109/ICSE.2012.6227167.

60 Hähnle, R., Baum, M., Bubel, R. and Rothe, M. (2010). A visual interactive debugger based on symbolic execution. *Proceedings of the IEEE/ACM International Conference on Automated Software Engineering*, Antwerp, Belgium (20–24 September 2010), 143–146. ACM. https://dl.acm.org/doi/pdf/10.1145/1858996.1859022.

61 Zeller, A. and Lütkehaus, D. (1996). DDD: a free graphical front-end for UNIX debuggers. *ACM SIGPLAN Notices* 31 (1): 22–27.

62 DeLine, R., Bragdon, A., Rowan, K., Jacobsen, J., and Reiss, S.P. (2012). Debugger canvas: industrial experience with the code bubbles paradigm. *Proceedings of the 2012 34th International Conference on Software Engineering (ICSE '12)*, Zurich, Switzerland (2–9 June 2012), 1064–1073. IEEE. https://doi.org/10.1109/ICSE.2012.6227113.

63 Bragdon, A., Reiss, S.P., Zeleznik, R. et al. (2010). Code bubbles: rethinking the user interface paradigm of integrated development environments. *Proceedings of the 32nd ACM/IEEE International Conference on Software Engineering (ICSE '10)*, Cape Town, South Africa (1–8 May 2010), 1: 455–464. ACM.

64 Ungar, D., Lieberman, H., and Fry, C. (1997). Debugging and the experience of immediacy. *Communications of the ACM* 40 (4): 38–43.

65 Perscheid, M., Steinert, B., Hirschfeld, R., Geller, F., and Haupt, M. (2010). Immediacy through interactivity: online analysis of run-time behavior. *Proceedings of the 2010 17th Working Conference on Reverse Engineering*, Beverly, MA, USA (13–16 October 2010), 77–86. IEEE. https://doi.org/10.1109/WCRE.2010.17.

66 Weyuker, E.J. (1982). On testing non-testable programs. *The Computer Journal* 25 (4): 465–470.

67 Chen, T.Y., Tse, T.H., and Zhou, Z.Q. (2011). Semi-proving: an integrated method for program proving, testing, and debugging. *IEEE Transactions on Software Engineering* 37 (1): 109–125.

68 Chen, T.Y., Cheung, S.C., and Yiu, S.M. (1998). Metamorphic testing: a new approach for generating next test cases. Technical Report HKUST-CS98-01. Hong Kong University of Science and Technology.

69 Cody, W.J. (1980). *Software Manual for the Elementary Functions (Prentice-Hall Series in Computational Mathematics)*. Prentice-Hall, Inc.

70 Segura, S., Fraser, G., Sanchez, A.B., and Ruiz-Cortés, A. (2016). A survey on metamorphic testing. *IEEE Transactions on Software Engineering* 42 (9): 805–824.

71 Chen, T.Y., Kuo, F.-C., Liu, H. et al. (2019). Metamorphic testing: a review of challenges and opportunities. *ACM Computing Surveys* 51 (1): 4:1–4:27.

72 Dhok, M., Ramanathan, M.K., and Sinha, N. (2016). Type-aware concolic testing of JavaScript programs. *Proceedings of the 38th International Conference on*

Software Engineering (ICSE '16), Austin, TX, USA (14–22 May 2016), 168–179. ACM. https://dl.acm.org/doi/pdf/10.1145/2884781.2884859.

73 Chen, T.Y., Ho, J.W.K., Liu, H., and Xie, X. (2009). An innovative approach for testing bioinformatics programs using metamorphic testing. *BMC Bioinformatics* 10 (1): 1–12.

74 Zhou, Z.Q., Tse, T.H., and Witheridge, M. (2021). Metamorphic robustness testing: exposing hidden defects in citation statistics and journal impact factors. *IEEE Transactions on Software Engineering* 47 (6): 1164–1183.

75 Le, V., Afshari, M., and Su, Z. (2014). Compiler validation via equivalence modulo inputs. *Proceedings of the 35th ACM SIGPLAN Conference on Programming Language Design and Implementation*, Edinburgh, United Kingdom (9–11 June 2014), 216–226. ACM. https://dl.acm.org/doi/pdf/10.1145/2666356.2594334.

76 Rigger, M. and Su, Z. (2020). Detecting optimization bugs in database engines via non-optimizing reference engine construction. *Proceedings of the 28th ACM Joint Meeting on European Software Engineering Conference and Symposium on the Foundations of Software Engineering (ESEC/FSE '20)*, Virtual Event, USA (8–13 November 2020), 1140–1152. ACM.

77 Zhou, Z.Q., Xiang, S., and Chen, T.Y. (2016). Metamorphic testing for software quality assessment: a study of search engines. *IEEE Transactions on Software Engineering* 42 (3): 264–284.

78 Chen, T.Y., Tse, T.H., and Zhou, Z.Q. (2002). Semi-proving: an integrated method based on global symbolic evaluation and metamorphic testing. *Proceedings of the 2002 ACM SIGSOFT International Symposium on Software Testing and Analysis (ISSTA '02)*, Roma, Italy (22–24 July 2002), 191–195. ACM. https://dl.acm.org/doi/pdf/10.1145/566171.566202.

79 Cadar, C. and Sen, K. (2013). Symbolic execution for software testing: three decades later. *Communications of the ACM* 56 (2): 82–90.

80 Coen-Porisini, A., Denaro, G., Ghezzi, C., and Pezzé, M. (2001). Using symbolic execution for verifying safety-critical systems. *Proceedings of the Joint 8th European Software Engineering Conference and 9th ACM SIGSOFT International Symposium on Foundation of Software Engineering*, Vienna, Austria (10–14 September 2001), 142–151. ACM. https://dl.acm.org/doi/pdf/10.1145/503209.503230.

81 King, J.C. (1976). Symbolic execution and program testing. *Communications of the ACM* 19 (7): 385–394.

82 de Moura, L. and Bjørner, N. (2008). Z3: an efficient SMT solver. *Proceedings of the International Conference on Tools and Algorithms for the Construction and Analysis of Systems*, Budapest, Hungary (29 March to 6 April 2008), 337–340. Springer.

83 DeMillo, R.A. and Offutt, A.J. (1991). Constraint-based automatic test data generation. *IEEE Transactions on Software Engineering* 17 (9): 900–910.

84 Jaffar, J., Michaylov, S., Stuckey, P.J., and Yap, R.H.C. (1992). The CLP(R) language and system. *ACM Transactions on Programming Languages and Systems* 14 (3): 339–395.

85 Fahringer, T. and Scholz, B. (2000). A unified symbolic evaluation framework for parallelizing compilers. *IEEE Transactions on Parallel and Distributed Systems* 11 (11): 1105–1125.

86 Fahringer, T. and Scholz, B. (2003). *Advanced Symbolic Analysis for Compilers: new Techniques and Algorithms for Symbolic Program Analysis and Optimization*, vol. 2628. Springer.

87 Xie, Y., Chou, A., and Engler, D. (2003). ARCHER: using symbolic, path-sensitive analysis to detect memory access errors. *Proceedings of the Joint 9th European Software Engineering Conference and 11th ACM SIGSOFT International Symposium on Foundations of Software Engineering*, Helsinki, Finland (1–5 September 2003), 327–336. ACM. https://dl.acm.org/doi/pdf/10.1145/940071.940115.

88 Wolfram, S. (2003). *The Mathematica Book*, 5e. Wolfram Media.

89 Sen, K., Marinov, D., and Agha, G. (2005). CUTE: a concolic unit testing engine for C. *Proceedings of the Joint 10th European Software Engineering Conference and 13th ACM SIGSOFT International Symposium on Foundations of Software Engineering*, Lisbon, Portugal (5–9 September 2005), 263–272. ACM. https://dl.acm.org/doi/pdf/10.1145/1095430.1081750.

90 Sen, K. (2007). Concolic testing. *Proceedings of the 22nd IEEE/ACM International Conference on Automated Software Engineering*, Atlanta, GA, USA (5–9 November 2007), 571–572. ACM. https://dl.acm.org/doi/pdf/10.1145/1321631.1321746.

91 Havelund, K. and Pressburger, T. (2000). Model checking JAVA programs using JAVA PathFinder. *International Journal on Software Tools for Technology Transfer* 2 (4): 366–381.

92 Hutchins, M., Foster, H., Goradia, T., and Ostrand, T. (1994). Experiments on the effectiveness of dataflow- and controlflow-based test adequacy criteria. *Proceedings of the 16th International Conference on Software Engineering (ICSE '94)*, Sorrento, Italy (16–21 May 1994), 191–200. IEEE. https://ieeexplore.ieee.org/stamp/stamp.jsp?arnumber=296778.

93 Jones, J.A., Harrold, M.J., and Stasko, J. (2002). Visualization of test information to assist fault localization. *Proceedings of the 24th International Conference on Software Engineering (ICSE '02)*, Orlando, FL, USA (19–25 May 2002), 467–477. ACM. https://dl.acm.org/doi/10.1145/581339.581397.

94 Naish, L., Lee, H.J., and Ramamohanarao, K. (2011). A model for spectra-based software diagnosis. *ACM Transactions on Software Engineering and Methodology* 20 (3): 11:1–11:32.

95 Xie, X., Chen, T.Y., Kuo, F.-C., and Xu, B. (2013). A theoretical analysis of the risk evaluation formulas for spectrum-based fault localization. *ACM Transactions on Software Engineering and Methodology* 22 (4): 31:1–31:40.

96 Xie, X., Wong, W.E., Chen, T.Y., and Xu, B. (2013). Metamorphic slice: an application in spectrum-based fault localization. *Information and Software Technology* 55 (5): 866–879.

97 Xie, X., Wong, W.E., Chen, T.Y., and Xu, B. (2011). Spectrum-based fault localization: testing oracles are no longer mandatory. *Proceedings of the 2011 11th International Conference on Quality Software*, Xi'an, China (13–14 July 2011), 1–10. IEEE.

98 Zeller, A. and Hildebrandt, R. (2002). Simplifying and isolating failure-inducing input. *IEEE Transactions on Software Engineering* 28 (2): 183–200.

99 Zeller, A. (2002). Isolating cause-effect chains from computer programs. *Proceedings of the 10th ACM SIGSOFT International Symposium on Foundations of Software Engineering*, Charleston, SC, USA (18–22 November 2002), 1–10. ACM. https://dl.acm.org/doi/pdf/10.1145/605466.605468.

100 Jobstmann, B., Griesmayer, A., and Bloem, R. (2005). Program repair as a game. *Proceedings of the 17th International Conference on Computer Aided Verification*, Edinburgh, Scotland, UK (6–10 July 2005), 226–238. Springer.

101 Könighofer, R. and Bloem, R. (2011). Automated error localization and correction for imperative programs. *Proceedings of the International Conference on Formal Methods in Computer-Aided Design*, Austin, TX, USA (30 October to 2 November 2011), 91–100. FMCAD Inc.

102 Griesmayer, A., Staber, S., and Bloem, R. (2010). Fault localization using a model checker. *Software Testing, Verification and Reliability* 20 (2): 149–173.

103 Oh, C., Schaf, M., Schwartz-Narbonne, D., and Wies, T. (2014). Concolic fault abstraction. *Proceedings of the IEEE 14th International Working Conference on Source Code Analysis and Manipulation*, Victoria, BC, Canada (28–29 September 2014), 135–144. IEEE. https://doi.org/10.1109/SCAM.2014.22.

104 Jin, H., Jiang, Y., Liu, N. et al. (2015). Concolic metamorphic debugging. *Proceedings of the IEEE 39th Annual International Computers, Software and Applications Conference*, Taichung, Taiwan (1–5 July 2015), 232–241. IEEE. https://doi.org/10.1109/COMPSAC.2015.79.

105 Parnin, C. and Orso, A. (2011). Are automated debugging techniques actually helping programmers? *Proceedings of the 2011 International Symposium on Software Testing and Analysis*, Toronto, ON, Canada (17–21 July 2011), 199–209. ACM. ISBN 978-1-4503-0562-4. https://doi.org/10.1145/2001420.2001445.

106 Le, T.-D.B., Lo, D., and Thung, F. (2015). Should I follow this fault localization tool's output? *Empirical Software Engineering* 20 (5): 1237–1274.

107 Han, J., Pei, J., and Kamber, M. (2011). *Data Mining: Concepts and Techniques*. Morgan Kaufmann.

108 Hong, S., Lee, B., Kwak, T. (2015). Mutation-based fault localization for real-world multilingual programs. *Proceedings of the 2015 30th IEEE/ACM International*

Conference on Automated Software Engineering (ASE '15), Lincoln, Nebraska (9–13 November 2015), 464–475. IEEE. https://doi.org/10.1109/ASE.2015.14.

109 Jones, J.A. and Harrold, M.J. (2005). Empirical evaluation of the Tarantula automatic fault-localization technique. *Proceedings of the 20th IEEE/ACM International Conference on Automated Software Engineering (ASE '05)*, Long Beach, CA, USA (7–11 November 2005), 273–282. ACM. https://dl.acm.org/doi/pdf/10.1145/1101908.1101949.

110 Moon, S., Kim, Y., Kim, M., and Yoo, S. (2014). Ask the mutants: mutating faulty programs for fault localization. *Proceedings of the 2014 IEEE Seventh International Conference on Software Testing, Verification and Validation*, Cleveland, OH, USA (31 March to 4 April 2014), 153–162. IEEE. https://doi.org/10.1109/ICST.2014.28.

111 Rothermel, G. and Harrold, M.J. (1998). Empirical studies of a safe regression test selection technique. *IEEE Transactions on Software Engineering* 24 (6): 401–419.

112 Campos, J., Abreu, R., Fraser, G., and d'Amorim, M. (2013). Entropy-based test generation for improved fault localization. *Proceedings of the 2013 28th IEEE/ACM International Conference on Automated Software Engineering (ASE '13)*, Silicon Valley, CA, USA (11–15 November 2013), 257–267. IEEE. https://doi.org/10.1109/ASE.2013.6693085.

113 Godefroid, P., Klarlund, N., and Sen, K. (2005). DART: directed automated random testing. *Proceedings of the 2005 ACM SIGPLAN Conference on Programming Language Design and Implementation*, Chicago, IL, USA (12–15 June 2005), 213–223. ACM.

114 Artzi, S., Dolby, J., Tip, F., and Pistoia, M. (2010). Directed test generation for effective fault localization. *Proceedings of the 19th International Symposium on Software Testing and Analysis*, Trento, Italy (12–16 July 2010), 49–60. ACM. ISBN 978-1-60558-823-0. https://doi.org/10.1145/1831708.1831715.

115 Zalewski, M. American fuzzy lop (2.35b). https://lcamtuf.coredump.cx/afl (accessed January 2022).

116 Fraser, G. and Arcuri, A. (2011). EvoSuite: automatic test suite generation for object-oriented software. *Proceedings of the 19th ACM SIGSOFT Symposium and the 13th European Conference on Foundations of Software Engineering*, Szeged, Hungary (5–9 September 2011), 416–419. ACM. https://dl.acm.org/doi/pdf/10.1145/2025113.2025179.

117 Azimi, P. Mittal, P. Holmes, J. TSTL: the template scripting testing language. https://github.com/agroce/tstl (accessed January 2022).

118 Groce, A. and Pinto, J. (2015). A little language for testing. *NASA Formal Methods Symposium* (27–29 April 2015), 204–218. Springer.

119 Groce, A., Pinto, J., Azimi, P., and Mittal, P. (2015). TSTL: a language and tool for testing (demo). *Proceedings of the 2015 International Symposium on Software Testing and Analysis*, Baltimore, MD, USA (12–17 July 2015), 414–417. ACM. https://dl.acm.org/doi/pdf/10.1145/2771783.2784769.

120 Holmes, J., Groce, A., Pinto, J. et al. (2018). TSTL: the template scripting testing language. *International Journal on Software Tools for Technology Transfer* 20 (1): 57–78.

121 Fowler, M. (2010). *Domain-Specific Languages*. Pearson Education.

122 Agrawal, H., Horgan, J.R., London, S., and Wong, W.E. (1995). Fault localization using execution slices and dataflow tests. *Proceedings of the Sixth International Symposium on Software Reliability Engineering*, Toulouse, France (24–27 October 1995), 143–151. IEEE.

123 Wong, W.E., Debroy, V., Gao, R., and Li, Y. (2014). The DStar method for effective software fault localization. *IEEE Transactions on Reliability* 63 (1): 290–308.

124 Wong, W.E., Debroy, V., and Choi, B. (2010). A family of code coverage-based heuristics for effective fault localization, *Journal of Systems and Software* 83 (2): 188–208.

125 Wong, W.E., Debroy, V., and Xu, D. (2012). Towards better fault localization: a crosstab-based statistical approach. *IEEE Transactions on Systems, Man and Cybernetics, Part C: Applications and Reviews* 42 (3): 378–396.

126 Claessen, K. and Hughes, J. (2011). Quickcheck: a lightweight tool for random testing of Haskell programs. *ACM SIGPLAN Notices* 46 (4): 53–64.

127 Nassim Nicholas Taleb (2012). *Antifragile: Things That Gain from Disorder*, vol. 3. Random House.

128 Ali, S., Briand, L.C., Hemmati, H., and Panesar-Walawege, R.K. (2009). A systematic review of the application and empirical investigation of search-based test case generation. *IEEE Transactions on Software Engineering* 36 (6): 742–762.

129 McMinn, P. (2004). Search-based software test data generation: a survey. *Software Testing, Verification and Reliability* 14 (2): 105–156.

130 Groce, A., Chaki, S., Kroening, D., and Strichman, O. (2006). Error explanation with distance metrics. *International Journal on Software Tools for Technology Transfer* 8 (3): 229–247. ISSN 1433-2787. https://doi.org/10.1007/s10009-005-0202-0.

Index

Handbook of Software Fault Localization: Foundations and Advances, First Edition.
Edited by W. Eric Wong and T.H. Tse.

Published 2023 by John Wiley & Sons, Inc.

e

Printed and bound by CPI Group (UK) Ltd, Croydon, CR0 4YY
08/10/2024
14570379-0001